THE HISTORY OF THE PRINCE OF WALES' OWN
CIVIL SERVICE RIFLES

By the courtesy of the Governor and Company of the Bank of England, the possessors of the original print.

The uniform is similar to that worn by the Somerset House Volunteers of the period.

London : Published, August 30th, 1804, by John Wallis, Jun., 16, Ludgate Street.

Frontispiece.

THE HISTORY OF THE PRINCE OF WALES' OWN CIVIL SERVICE RIFLES

Printed and bound by Antony Rowe Ltd, Eastbourne

TO THOSE
CIVIL SERVICE RIFLEMEN
WHO LAID DOWN THEIR LIVES
IN THE GREAT WAR

NOTE BY THE EDITOR

These pages have been put together under pressure of the desirability of placing their contents without further delay in the hands of a public virtually limited to Regimental members past and present, their relatives and friends. They do not aim higher than setting on record the unvarnished chronicles of several generations of volunteers who have never yielded place to any in their pride and love of regiment.

Before the close of the last century the story of the Regiment's thirty years' existence had been written by the officer who to-day has been the right hand of the Editor in the task of bringing the record down to the year of the War. The latter has to thank Colonel Merrick for giving up much of his time to this object, and for allowing a reprint of the earlier portion.

Captain Bell was good enough to make himself responsible for the tale from the year 1909 to 1914. Major Kirkby has kindly given his supervision in preparing certain tabular statements which are found as appendices. Yet this book would never have reached the printers' hands but for the initiative shown by Captain Davenport as regards the narrative of the first Battalion in War. His achievement prompted the search for an author who could and would do the same for the widely ranging story of the movements of the second Battalion. Into this gap stepped Major Benké who, in a short space of time delivered the completed task. It will be agreed that both these officers, aided in some parts by collaborators, have produced a readable and human account of those events of which they can speak at first hand, made clearer by the excellent sketch maps which accompany the narratives of operations.

To Major Duncan Lewis, the writer of those pages in which the necessarily uneventful story of the third Battalion is found, we express our indebtedness. Captain Doubleday is best fitted to tell of the beneficent work of the Regimental Aid Fund, and thanks may be expressed here on behalf of all those who benefited by the activities of himself and his fellow-helpers. In the very difficult task of compiling the lists of all ranks who served in the Regiment during war time, we have to thank Major Ramsbotham—the Adjutant—for his energy in this and, indeed, in all matters connected with the needs of the Regiment.

Attention is directed to the statistics relating to the numbers who served in the Regiment, and who were transfers, which will be found at the end of Appendix VI.

Nine hundred and sixty-seven commissions were granted from the ranks. The Dead number 1,227.

CONTENTS

CONTENTS

xii

CONTENTS

CONTENTS

APPENDICES

PLATES*

* It might be explained that the photographs here reproduced were not selective but rather those which were at hand available for publication. A larger collection of portraits might have been secured had there been more time.

SKETCH MAPS

(1ST BATTALION)

(2ND BATTALION)

HISTORY OF
THE CIVIL SERVICE
RIFLE VOLUNTEERS

CHAPTER I

1859-1909*

FOR the purpose of tracing the first authentic record of Volunteers connected with the Civil Service, it is necessary to call attention to the raising of the Loyal Volunteers of London in 1798. About that year, when we were at war with France and Spain, were fighting in India, and almost all over the world, and the country was denuded of troops, the rich citizens of London began to get alarmed at their unprotected state, in the event of rebellion or riot at home. They petitioned the King, and a charter was granted, authorising the formation of armed associations in London and the environs.

The " Loyal Volunteers of London," as they were called, were therefore raised to uphold the cause of the King and of order. Their motto was " *Pro Rege et Patria.*"

Among the corps thus raised was that of the " Somerset House Volunteers." A picture of one of these gentlemen, as copied from a book by T. Rowlandson, in the British Museum, may now be seen in the Orderly Room at the Audit Office.

Somerset House Volunteers, 1798.

The Somerset House Volunteer Association consisted only of two companies of light infantry, under the command of Walter Sterling, Major Commandant. The Captains were J. Stewart and W. Harrison. The corps was not to go out of the district of Somerset House and St. Mary-le-Strand, but with its own consent.

---

* This history, up to the year 1891, was written and published in that year by Lieut. (now Lt.-Col.) Edward Merrick, C.S.R.V. He has brought his narrative down to 1909 for the purpose of this volume.

Bank of England Volunteers, 1798.

Among those who would have cause for anxiety at such a period would naturally be the Governor and Directors of the Bank of England, and certainly they showed great public spirit. They headed a voluntary contribution to the revenue in this year, with a subscription of £200,000. They also raised from their employés a corps of volunteers, 450 strong, to protect the Bank.

This corps was under the command of Thomas Whitmore, and Rowlandson tells us that it was presented with colours on 2nd September, 1799, by the lady of Samuel Thornton, Esq., Governor of the Bank of England, in Lord's Ground, Marylebone. A picture of this ceremonial, painted by Stoddart, is to be seen now in the Bank.

These Loyal Volunteers of London were, however, entirely swamped by the great volunteer movement, which swept throughout the country in 1802, caused by the extensive preparations then being made by Bonaparte to invade England.

Volunteers of 1802.

In this war-scare, which far exceeded in its intensity that of 1859, 420,000 Volunteers were enrolled in a few months—many more, in fact, than the Government could or ever did arm.

The Civil Service were represented in this body by two corps : the Excise Corps, which in 1804 was 576 strong, under the command of Lord George Seymour, and the Customs Corps, about 300 strong.

In the same year (1804), the Bank of England had a corps of 433, under the command of William Manning, and a supplementary corps of 122, under the command of Beeston Long.

Some of the records of the last-named corps are still in existence in the Bank. From them we gather that the parades were usually held at 7 or 8 a.m. The most notable period in their history appears to have been in 1812, at the time of the assassination of Mr. Percival in the House of Commons. In the state of public alarm that followed this event, it was considered necessary that the Bank Volunteers should be under arms to guard the Bank, night and day.

Disbandment.

At the signing of the general treaty of peace in 1814, the joy of the country at what it believed to be the conclusion of its long and exhausting wars, was shown by the haste with which the Volunteers were at once disbanded.

The Corps of the Civil Service shared with others in votes of thanks passed to them by both Houses of Parliament, and letters from the Commander-in-Chief (the Prince Regent) were received, thanking each corps for its valuable services. From the records already referred to, we find that a special " march past " before the Lord Mayor, at the Mansion House, brought the military duties of the Bank officials of that generation to an end.

We now pass over a space of 45 years, during which the military spirit of the Service may be said to have lain dormant, until we approach the event with which the true interest of our story begins, viz., the year 1859, and the birth of the Corps to which we have the honour to belong.

To the Members of the Audit Office (now the Exchequer and Audit Department), Somerset House, must, without doubt, be assigned the honour of having founded the Civil Service Volunteer Corps.

General Meeting at Audit Office.

The Volunteer Force of to-day, as everybody knows, sprang into existence in the year 1859, and was occasioned by the warlike attitude of the Emperor of the French and the blustering threats of his generals. The notable circular of the Secretary of State for War to the Lords Lieutenant, which called the Volunteers into existence, was dated 12th May, 1859, and on the 18th May a meeting, which had been formally convened " to take into consideration the formation of a Rifle Volunteer Corps from the Members of the Civil Service," was held at the Audit Office. Mr. F. A. Hawker was the prime mover in this proceeding, and he presided at the meeting.

Now, if everything had proceeded as satisfactorily as the energetic and spirited action of these early pioneers deserved, the " Civil Service " would have been one of the first Metropolitan Corps formed, and its order of precedence would therefore have been far in advance of what it ultimately became. But, unfortunately, we have here another example of the old proverb, " the more haste," &c., for, notwithstanding the circular of the Secretary of State, the War Office were by no means ready to respond with any degree of generosity to the crowds of enthusiastic civilians who at once cried out on all sides to be armed.

The utmost conceded was that Volunteers should be allowed in certain cases to *purchase* their own arms and equipment.

First Attempts at Formation.

The desire, however, of the Audit Office Meeting was that special favour should be shown to Civil Servants, so it was decided to express the views of the meeting in the following letter, which was despatched, not to the War Office, but to the Prime Minister himself, Earl Derby :

"Audit Office, 20th May, 1859.

"My Lord,—I have the honour to transmit to your Lordship a copy of the Resolutions passed at a meeting of gentlemen of the Audit Office, held on the 18th instant to take into consideration the formation of a Volunteer Rifle Corps from the members of the Civil Service and I beg leave respectfully to request that your Lordship will be pleased to cause me to be furnished with replies to the Resolutions in question for the information of the gentlemen in this office who have signified their desire to join a Civil Service Rifle Corps.

" The junior members of the Civil Service being generally in the receipt of small incomes, your Lordship will perceive that the only difficulty in obtaining volunteers from the Civil Service is the expense attending their outfit. I would therefore, venture more particularly to draw your Lordship's attention to the 3rd Resolution, in which we request that the arms and accoutrements only may be supplied to volunteers from the members of the Civil Service by Her Majesty's Government ; *and as this is a question which affects nearly the whole body of the Civil Service, who are anxious to enrol themselves into a Volunteer Rifle Corps,* I trust that your Lordship will not think us intrusive in asking you to take these Resolutions into your favourable consideration.

" We hope your Lordship will pardon us if we have taken any liberty in bringing this subject under your consideration, but as Civil Servants of the Crown we are anxious that we should not be behind others in the present movement in favour of the formation of Volunteer Rifle Corps.

" I have, &c.,

" F. A. HAWKER."

The reply to this letter came from the War Office, and affords an admirable illustration of the amount of official support, which the Volunteer movement received in its infancy.

" War Office, 31st May, 1859.

" Sir,—I am directed by Secretary Major-General Peel to acknowledge the receipt of your letter of the 20th instant, on the subject of a Civil Service Volunteer Corps, which has been forwarded to this office by Lord Derby.

" In reply, I am to inform you that the Government have decided not to supply arms to Volunteer Corps, either by sale or otherwise ; and that General Peel does not consider the case of the gentlemen on whose behalf your application has been made to be one in which he can sanction a departure from the general rule.

" I am, &c.,

" H. R. DREWRY."

Thus closed the first act in the attempt to form a Civil Service Rifle Corps, for this snub appears to have had the effect of

quenching the military ardour of the Auditors to such an extent
that several months elapsed before they recovered from it.

In October, however, roused by events going on around them,
they took heart once more, and returned to the charge. By this
time Government had partially thawed, under the influence of
the excitement throughout the country. Lord Ranelagh's
Committee had sat at the War Office, and it had been decided
to issue arms to Volunteers at the lavish rate of one rifle to
every four men enrolled.

In answer, therefore, to a letter despatched to him by Mr.
Hawker, the Secretary of State for War stated, in a reply dated
7th November, 1859, that he would be happy to recommend
Her Majesty to accept any offer of the service of a Company or
Sub-division of Volunteers, which he might receive from Mr.
Hawker through the Lord-Lieutenant of the County.

Audit Corps Formed.

Forthwith, at a general meeting held in the Audit Office on
the 10th November, it was resolved, " That it was desirable that
a Sub-division of not less than forty effectives be at once formed
in the Audit Office, and that other departments be invited to
co-operate by raising Companies or Sub-divisions with the view
of promoting the formation of a Brigade."

From this time forward enthusiasm and hard work were the
order of the day. A circular letter to other Government Departments was issued, and the nucleus of the Corps was at once
formed by the immediate election of forty-six members of the
Audit Office.

In a few days the number of effective members enlisted had
reached seventy. Affairs were pushed on with great energy,
and on the 25th November, 1859, at half-past four in the afternoon, the first drill of the Civil Service Volunteers was held in
Westminster Hall—one Sergeant Chace being the Instructor.

Other Corps Formed.

The Auditors were not to be left long in sole possession of
the military arena of the Civil Service, for Corps were being
rapidly raised in the Post Office, Inland Revenue, Customs,
Whitehall, and Admiralty.

An unsuccessful attempt was made to raise a Corps in the
British Museum.

Almost all of these Corps date their origin from the circular
issued from the Audit Office, inviting the co-operation of their
department. So rapidly were they organised, that towards the
end of December, 1859, they appear to have got into fair working
order ; and in answer to an invitation from the Audit Office,

a Provisional Council, consisting of two representatives from each Corps, assembled for the purpose of taking the necessary steps to amalgamate the whole into one Brigade.

First Council Meeting.

This first meeting of the Council was held on the 7th January, 1860.   The following members were present, as the first chosen representatives of their divisions, and to them may be justly attributed the title of ·' The Fathers of the Regiment " :—

> Captain F. A. Hawker, Audit Office Corps, in the chair.
> Lieutenant Vine, Audit Office Corps.
> Captain Harrington, Post Office Corps.
> Mr. T. Angell, Post Office Corps.
> Mr. W. Willis, Admiralty Corps.
> Mr. A. Brady, Admiralty Corps.
> Mr. F. B. Garnett, Inland Revenue Corps.
> Mr. J. H. Dwelly, Inland Revenue Corps.
> Mr. J. H. Lilley, Customs Corps.
> Mr. Wybrow, Customs Corps.
> Mr. Tom Taylor, Whitehall Corps.
> Mr. Richard Mills, Whitehall Corps.

Containing, as this list does, the names of so many men that have since become eminent in the Service, it affords ample evidence that the Regiment could have suffered from no lack of talent in the conduct of its affairs in its early days.

Title of Corps.

The first proceeding of the Council after electing Mr. Francis Taylor, of the Audit Office, its secretary, was to resolve that the amalgamated corps (now found to consist of 658 effective and 410 honorary members, and stated to be " daily increasing ") should be called the " Civil Service Rifle Brigade." The Admiralty representatives suggested the " Crown Rifle Brigade," but their amendment was not received with favour.

Uniform.

The Council next launched into the important subject of uniform, a subject of which the details occupied their attention at several successive meetings, and in regard to which some of the members displayed great energy. Apparently unmindful of the terrors of a military tailor's bill, each attended the meeting in the pattern of uniform that he individually recommended. Mr. Tom Taylor was one of these energetic members, and to him it appears that the regiment was indebted for the pattern of most of the uniform ultimately selected ; for we find that with regard to the full dress of both privates and officers, the decision of the Council was that " the uniform worn by Mr. Tom Taylor be adopted."

The uniform as then fixed was similar in all main points to that so recently discarded. It was, perhaps, a little more sombre in appearance, for the royal blue facings, silver lace, and Prince of Wales' feathers were added at a later date (1863). The cost, including chako, was £4 4s.

Affairs were not to remain for long in the semi-amalgamated corps in a state of perfect harmony. A disagreement, amounting to an open breach, even occurred on this early question of uniform ; for at the third meeting of the Council, held on the 31st January, a letter from the Customs Corps was read, stating that " *they declined to adopt the ornaments on the belts as decided upon by the Council, and that they would therefore have no participation in the arrangements of the Civil Service Regiment.*"

Customs Corps Secede.

The Customs had, from the first, shown an inclination to fall off. It appears that, being a strong corps, they considered they were entitled to be represented on the Council by more than two representatives.

With an expression of regret for their withdrawal, " more especially on a matter so trivial," the Council accepted the loss ; and when the authority for the amalgamation was ultimately received from the War Office, it referred only to the 27th Middlesex (Inland Revenue), the 31st (Whitehall), and the 34th (Admiralty), which were to be amalgamated with the 21st Middlesex (Audit Office and Post Office), the battalion to be entitled " The Civil Service Corps of Rifle Volunteers," with an authorised maximum strength of 800.

Prince of Wales.

At its second meeting, the Council had decided upon the important step of inviting the Prince of Wales to accept the Honorary Colonelcy of the Regiment. They were induced to take this step by the hopes held out to them through Mr. George Alexander Hamilton, Secretary to the Treasury, to whose influence the success of the application was mainly attributed ; for by the beginning of May an intimation was received that, with the sanction of Her Majesty and the Prince Consort, His Royal Highness had graciously consented to accept the post. And from the honour thus accorded it the Regiment has never ceased to derive the greatest benefit. To be singled out in these early days as the Regiment through whom this mark of Royal favour was to be shown to the Volunteer force, was a distinction which placed it at once in the forefront of public estimation, whilst the interest which, on many occasions, the Prince has since exhibited in its welfare has contributed largely to the prosperity of the corps.

Chaplain.

The first Staff appointment which the Council succeeded in filling was that of Chaplain, offered to, and accepted by, the Rev. Charles Kingsley, afterwards Canon Kingsley.

C.O.

The important post of Lieutenant-Colonel or Commanding Officer was not so easily filled. It was offered first to Sir E. Lugard, and afterwards to Lord West, but both were unable to undertake the duties. At length, at a meeting held on the 15th May, on a proposition of Captain Mills, the Council decided that Viscount Bury be invited to take the command of the regiment. This application proved more successful, for although Lord Bury had connected himself to a slight extent with the " Artists' " Corps, which had just been formed, the impediment was soon removed, and before the end of June his lordship attended a meeting of the Council, and a few days afterwards was gazetted Lieutenant-Colonel of the Regiment.

Lord Bury at this time occupied the official position of Treasurer to the Royal Household, and, together with Lord Ranelagh, Lord Elcho, and the Duke of Westminster, was one of the prominent leaders of the Volunteer movement.

Adjutant.

The appointment of an Adjutant also caused difficulty. A committee consisting of a few members of the Council was elected to consider the applications for the post. The choice of this committee fell upon Captain Ennis, who was a member of the Corps, and Captain-Commandant of the Inland Revenue Companies. Captain Ennis had at one time been in the " Hussars."

The War Office, however, refused to accept Captain Ennis as Adjutant, on the ground that he was over fifty, and that his service in the army had been in connection with the Cavalry. The feeling in the Regiment was very strong against this decision, and grave consequences with regard to the prosperity of the Corps were said to be likely to ensue if the War Office refused to appoint so popular an officer.

One of the first tasks which Lord Bury undertook, by desire of the Council, was to overcome the objection raised by the War Office. In this he was successful, and Captain Ennis was appointed to the post, which, however, he held for two years only, when he resigned.

Surgeon.

With the authority for the appointment of Captain Ennis to the Adjutancy came also that of Dr. Spencer Smith to the post

CIVIL SERVICE RIFLES 9

of Surgeon. This gentleman resigned only a few years ago, after a service of 24 years. In the early days his office was by no means the apparent sinecure it has since become, for it was the duty of the Surgeon, or the Assistant Surgeon, to attend at the range whenever target practice was held, and for the zealous and kind manner in which this duty was carried out, at great sacrifice of time and convenience, the Commanding Officer, in regimental orders, expressed the warmest thanks of the Regiment.

The amount of zeal with which the Surgeons entered upon their work in those days is exemplified by the following unpleasantly expressive item in the Regimental accounts of that period :

" To set of Amputating Instruments kept at the
Range - - - - - - - - £4 4 o."

Major.

The War Office, at that time, required that Majors of Volunteer Corps should have served in the Army, so that it was not until April, 1861, that the post of Major was filled by the appointment of Major Leslie (late Captain 1st Life Guards).

With this exception the formation of the Regiment may now (June, 1860) be said to have been complete. It was composed as follows :

A Company	(Audit Office)	81	Captain	Hawker.
B & C ,,	(Post Office)	133	,,	Harrington.
			,,	Du Plat Taylor.
D & E ,,	(Inld. Revenue)	102	,,	Dalbiac.
			,,	Ennis, junr.
F & G ,,	(Whitehall)	153	,,	Tom Taylor.
			,,	Mills.
H ,,	(Admiralty)	64	..	Willis.
		533		

Composition of Corps.

These numbers scarcely convey a correct impression of the hold which the corps had secured upon the Civil Service. It must be remembered that, in addition to the effective strength as given above, there were at least 500 honorary members including many who occupied leading official positions. These were individuals who were debarred by age or other reasons from drilling, but who, nevertheless, were quite as enthusiastic in advocating the new " movement " as their more active comrades in the ranks.

Of the latter it may be said that, on the whole, they were men of more advanced age and position than we are now accustomed to see in the ranks. Shouldering the rifle amongst them were many men now of note—Lord Lingen, Sir R. G. C. Hamilton, Lord Teynham, and others. The name of Mr. Tom Taylor the well known dramatic author, afterwards editor of *Punch*, has already been mentioned ; whilst other literary and scientific men the corps could then claim were Professor Huxley, Professor Tyndall, Mr. Anthony Trollope, Mr. W. S. Gilbert, and Mr. Edmund Yates.

To turn from the doings of the Council to those of the Regiment itself, we find that the first parade of the combined corps " for the purpose of drilling as a battalion " was held at Somerset House on the 28th March, 1860.

First Battalion Drill, &c.

This parade was in plain clothes and without arms, but in the following week the regiment mustered in uniform and under arms. Captain Ennis (afterwards Adjutant) took the command at these drills.

The following week the regiment was ready for its first " march out." This notable event was held at Wimbledon, amidst torrents of rain, and is commemorated by a sketch made by Captain Angell, a photograph of which hangs in the Orderly Room. The expense of this march was defrayed by a collection of ten shillings per man.

From this time, instruction in battalion drill proceeded with great vigour. The use of the West London Cricket Ground at Brompton was obtained for the purpose, and the regiment marched there weekly, whilst other battalion drills and " skeleton drills " for officers were held almost daily at Somerset House.

Matters proceeded so rapidly on the appointment of a Lieutenant-Colonel, that Lord Bury considered that the Corps might be safely exposed to the perils of a sham fight to be held by the Metropolitan Volunteers at Bromley, on the 14th July. This, however, did not appear to be the opinion of the regiment itself when the day arrived. The muster was very small. It was attributed afterwards by Lord Bury in Orders, to the fact that " many members of the regiment had resolved not to come on account of the danger to be apprehended from the inexperience of their comrades in firing drill."

The members themselves, however, seemed very anxious to remedy this minor defect on their part, and musketry instruction now became the rage. To carry this out successfully it was necessary that a staff of Volunteer Instructors should be raised, who in their turn should instruct the other members of the Regiment.

Musketry Instruction.

The arduous duties carried out by these Volunteer Musketry Instructors certainly entitle them to especial mention. At their head was Captain Du Plat Taylor, assisted by Ensign Campbell and Battalion Instructor Halliday. The first Company Instructors in the order of merit in which they passed their examination were :

Sergeant Rule.	Sergeant Plaskett.
,, Powell.	,, Trickett.
,, Bond.	Corporal Hamilton.
,, Lockhart.	Sergeant Cardin.
,, Crispin.	,, Potter.
,, Pitt.	Corporal Baker.
Corporal R. G. Hamilton.	Sergeant Pidcock.
,, Churchill.	,, Jackson.

Every available place in the neighbourhood of Somerset House was occupied nightly by squads practising " position " and " aiming " drill, and by August, Captain Du Plat Taylor was able to take his first squad to the Wimbledon range for ball practice. This was carried out in the strictest and most methodical manner, for even in those days, Captain Taylor began to earn for himself the character of the strict disciplinarian for which he has since been so noted. The following facts are gathered from the regulations laid down by him in Regimental Musketry Orders :

" All Target Practice to be performed in Uniform, in Full Marching Order.

" Members proceeding to Wimbledon for Firing Practice to fall in in Military Order at the station at Putney, and march to the range under the command of the senior present. On arrival at the range they would be delivered over to the Senior Musketry Instructor. The return to Putney to be conducted in the same manner. *Strict silence to be maintained in the ranks throughout the whole of the proceedings.*

" With the view of avoiding the heavy expenses incurred by the hire of Butt Markers, the duties to be undertaken by members of the Corps ; three non-commissioned officers and three privates being previously detailed on each occasion.

" Should any member so detailed refuse or neglect to attend, he would be disqualified from competing for Regimental Prizes."

However necessary these rules may have been at the time, it need scarcely be observed that before long they were found to be irksome. Rumour reports that on the occasion of a squad, on its return from the ranges in the dark, being marched into a ditch, open mutiny broke out with regard to the obnoxious rules, and that Captain Taylor was thereupon constrained to

relax his discipline until he could find more tractable material to
work upon than the " gentlemen of the Civil Service."

Queen's Review.

Two events of the year 1860 must not be omitted. One was
the first grand Volunteer Review before the Queen, in Hyde
Park, when the Civil Service, under Lord Bury, formed part of
a brigade under Lord Ranelagh.

In reference to this event Lord Bury states, " The behaviour
of all ranks on the ground was steady and soldierlike, and the
general appearance presented by the Regiment was all that
could be desired."

Another was the celebration of the Prince of Wales' birthday
by an inspection at Somerset House, followed by a Regimental
Dinner.

CHAPTER II

Eccentricities.

LOOKING back from the sober routine of the volunteering of to-day, to this strange period when every one was a recruit, it is only natural that eccentricities should be apparent on all sides. The enthusiasm that pervaded all ranks was, of course, immense, and the amount of drilling done, especially by the Officers and Non-Commissioned Officers was enormous. A golden age was this for the Army Drill-Instructors. Elderly recruits of a nervous temperament hesitated to exhibit themselves in the ranks until they had been privately coached in the initial mysteries of drill, in the seclusion of their own apartments. Uniform was worn on every possible occasion, at drill or on the range. It is said that after one occasion when Lord Bury had appeared at the range in plain clothes, he received a letter from an indignant private, expressing a hope that such a slight would not again be cast upon members of the regiment.

One Rule passed by the Council was that Honorary Members should be entitled to appear on parade in uniform, with a scarlet sash as a distinguishing ornament.

Another Rule strikes us as still more eccentric. Privates *when off parade* should be allowed to wear a sword similar to that worn by officers, but in a black leather scabbard. What the privates were supposed to want to do with their sword when off parade it is difficult to imagine.

With the close of the drill season the Regiment does not cease to show signs of interesting activity. Whilst in winter quarters it enlivened its repose with various festive gatherings having for their main object the support of the regimental band, which was in want of funds.

Dramatic Performance.

Perhaps the most interesting of these gatherings is an Amateur Dramatic Performance, held at the Lyceum Theatre, wherein the corps exhibited an array of talent, of which it might justly feel proud. The performance was so successful that it was repeated. The following is a copy of the programme :

14   PRINCE OF WALES' OWN

Civil Service Rifle Volunteers.

HONORARY COLONEL, H.R.H. THE PRINCE OF WALES, K.G.
LIEUTENANT-COLONEL, VISCOUNT BURY, M.P.
On WEDNESDAY, MAY 22, 1861,
WILL BE PERFORMED, FOR THE SECOND TIME, AT THE
THEATRE ROYAL LYCEUM,
By Special Desire,
The original Comedy by CAPTAIN TOM TAYLOR, C.S.R.V.,
ENTITLED :
" A LESSON FOR LIFE."

LORD GREYSTOKE - - - -		Lieutenant DEWAR
THE HON. MARMADUKE	Under-	Captain J. DU PLAT
DACRE - - - graduates		TAYLOR
REREDOSS - - - of St. Bar-		Mr. MILLS.
HORSLEY - - - nabas		Lieutenant T. ANGELL
CROUCH - - - College,		Lieutenant W. S. GILBERT
STRETCHER - - - Cambridge		Serjeant BAUKE
VIVIAN - - -		Captain HOOD

COLEPEPPER (Senior Tutor of St. Barnabas) Captain MILLS
OPPENHARDT   (A German Jew) - Captain TOM TAYLOR
BASEWITZ -   (A Swindler)   - Ensign EDMUND YATES
DR. VIVIAN   (A Country Vicar) - Private R. MORRISON
MR. GRAY - (A Country Attorney) - Mr. W. H. LONG
TOPHAM - - - - - Lieutenant GARNETT
MURCOTT - - - - - Serjeant WALSHE
LADY VALECRUCIS - - - Mrs. STIRLING
THE HON. MABEL VALECRUCIS - Miss ELLEN TERRY
MARY FORD - - - - - Miss KATE TERRY
    (By kind permission of A. Wigan, Esq., T.R. Saint James')
NANNY KETTLEWELL - - - Mrs. STEPHENS

TO BE PRECEDED BY AN ORIGINAL COMEDIETTA, IN ONE ACT,
" IF THE CAP FITS,"
WRITTEN BY
CAPTAIN HARRINGTON, C.S.R.V., and ENSIGN EDMUND YATES,
C.S.R.V.
THE PERFORMANCES TO CONCLUDE WITH
" THE HAPPY MAN,"
A FARCE,
By Private SAMUEL LOVER, of the London Irish Rifle Volunteers.
THE BAND OF THE REGIMENT WILL ATTEND.

Regimental Ball.

A Regimental Ball was also given at Willis's Rooms, in aid of
the same object. In the list of the Lady Patronesses are the
names of :
        The Duchess of Manchester.
        The Duchess of Wellington.
        The Countess Russell.

Viscountess Palmerston.
Viscountess Bury.
Lady Elcho.
Mrs. Gladstone.

Band.

The Band, on behalf of which so much energy was expended, was composed of 25 members, the greater number of whom were amateurs. It appears to have been in an excellent state of efficiency, as it gained prizes at various band contests, which it was then the fashion to hold. It was under the charge of an energetic and capable bandmaster, Mr. J. Moirato Davis ; but very valuable assistance was rendered to its efficiency by Mr. W. P. Jones, of the Audit Office. Its annual cost to the regiment appears to have been about £300.

Subscription Fund.

As there was no Government grant in those days to assist in defraying the expenses of the corps these had to be met entirely by voluntary contributions, and the subscriptions of members.

The Council issued a circular asking for assistance from the whole of the Civil Service. Subscriptions flowed in liberally. In the Inland Revenue and Whitehall Divisions alone the subscriptions in the first year exceeded £1,000.

1861. First Easter Monday Review.

The opening of the year 1861 was marked by the first Easter Monday Review. This was held at Brighton. Some difference of opinion was displayed by the various Volunteer Commanding Officers as to the advisability of holding this review. Lord Bury opposed the idea. He expressed his opinions on the point in a Regimental Order to the following effect :—

" I do not think the proposed expedition judicious in a political point of view. I think it inconsistent with the purely defensive character of the Volunteer movement to make demonstrations on the coast."

Of course, under these conditions the Civil Service Regiment refrained from demonstrating ; or, at all events, they joined with a few other like-minded corps, and so effectually concealed their demonstrations among the bushes of Wimbledon Common, that they evidently felt satisfied that not the slightest exasperation could have been felt on their account by the most bellicose of Frenchmen.

1862.

Little else of importance occurred to mark the year 1861, so we will pass at once to the second Easter Monday Review, which ushered in the drill season of 1862.

By this time it would appear that Lord Bury's views had changed, for the regiment not only attended the Review, but in a Regimental Order, in which he praises the steadiness of the battalion on that occasion, Lord Bury states—" It is an honour to have taken part in such a day."

Another event of this year was a review by the Duke of Cambridge at Wimbledon, when we are told that His Royal Highness expressed his praise on witnessing the advance of the battalion extended as skirmishers.

To show the satisfactory state of affairs at this period, I cannot do better than again to quote from Regimental Orders as follows :

" The Lieutenant-Colonel cannot but congratulate the Regiment on the fact that at the close of their third drill season, they occupy a most satisfactory position among the Volunteer Corps of the country : the organisation is complete ; the numbers are increasing ; the Officers have passed the ordeal of a searching examination ; the Drill is improved ; the Musketry Instruction, which was from the first the strongest point in the organisation of the Regiment, has even improved in efficiency ; and the number both of effectives and of marksmen is fully equal, in proportion to numbers, to any other Volunteer Corps. The Lieutenant-Colonel need not point out how much the efficiency of a Regiment depends on its Non-commissioned Officers. We are fortunate in having a body of Non-commissioned Officers who thoroughly know their duty. The Skirmishing Drill of the Regiment is better done, and much more clearly understood than in former years. *In conclusion, the Lieutenant-Colonel confidently believes that the utmost unanimity and good feeling exists throughout the Regiment.*"

The last statement appears, in the present day, a rather strange and superfluous one to put into Regimental Orders ; but it is evident that its meaning was fully understood at the time. Enthusiastic volunteer as Lord Bury was, and evidently taking a delight in his duties as Commanding Officer, he must have frequently felt that to rule a body of gentlemen volunteers, in a very elementary stage of military knowledge and discipline, was a somewhat formidable and even thankless task. Every member of the corps—officer, non-commissioned officer, and private—had an opinion to express on every point, and he expressed it freely. Plenty of evidence exists of burning questions which agitated, and sometimes even threatened the unity of the corps ; but the great tact displayed by Lord Bury, his forbearance and kindly courtesy, which disarmed all opposition, led the corps safely through all.

One incident which occurred about this period, and the explanations with regard to which occupy the greater part of three Regimental Orders, was, that a part of the Regiment had expressed unwillingness to join in a march out with the " Artists' "

Corps, owing to what Lord Bury describes as " an absurd wish attributed to him to bring about an amalgamation between the Civil Service Regiment and the Artists'."

But it is not necessary here to go into the details of these almost forgotten grievances, which, although interesting as showing what may be called the *morale* of the Corps at that period, are perhaps best buried in oblivion.

CHAPTER III

1863. Prince of Wales' Challenge Cup.

AT the commencement of the year 1863, the Prince of Wales showed his interest in the Corps by presenting it with a Challenge Cup of the value of 100 guineas. The nominal right to hold this cup for a year is still annually shot for ; but it is customary for the Commanding Officer to retain it in his own custody.

This was the year of the Prince of Wales's marriage, and on the 7th March the Regiment took part in the parade of the Metropolitan Volunteers in Hyde Park, on the arrival of the Princess Alexandra in London. The " Civil Service " were granted the post of honour on the right of the line, on this occasion.

The Regiment again attended the Easter Monday Review at Brighton, and earned golden opinions for itself, receiving, we are told, from Officers of high rank, great commendation for their steadiness at drill.

In this year (three years after their formation) the Volunteers were first thought worthy of an annual Capitation Grant by the Government. £1 was paid for every efficient member who completed three Company and six Battalion Drills.

Adjutants : Captain Adair, 1862-3.
Captain Lombard, 1864-1886.

It has not yet been mentioned that Captain Alexander W. Adair was appointed to the Corps as Adjutant, in May, 1862. Towards the close of this year (1863) he resigned, and with the opening of 1864 we form the acquaintance of one who has left an indelible mark on the history of the Civil Service Rifles. On the 17th March, 1864, Captain Graves C. Swan Lombard (late of the 16th Regiment) was appointed Acting Adjutant, and for the long period of 22 years from this date his name appears at the foot of Regimental Orders.

There is no doubt but that, from his very first appearance in the Corps, Captain (afterwards Major) Lombard ingratiated himself into the goodwill of all its members ; and it is little to say, that all who had the pleasure of serving with him will ever have pleasing recollections of his kindly manner, his admirable tact, his quiet but firm discipline. These, with many other excellent qualities, combined to make him, in the opinion of all the true model of a Volunteer Adjutant.

One of the first Orders signed by Major Lombard was, however, somewhat unfortunate, containing as it did the following paragraph :—

"The Post Office Companies will proceed to Harrow on Saturday, 24th inst., to join in a Field Day with the Harrow School and other Corps. Each member to provide himself with twenty rounds of ball cartridge."

It is never too late to acknowledge a mistake, so on the 26th inst. (only *two* days after the Review was held) the correction comes :

"In the Order of the 17th inst., the words ' BALL cartridge ' should have been ' BLANK cartridge.' "

Let us hope the Harrow boys suffered no inconvenience from the error.

1864.

The year 1864 is noted for two events of importance. The first was a Review in Hyde Park, when the " Civil Service " formed part of a brigade under the command of the Prince of Wales. The second was an Inspection of the Regiment by the Prince on the 15th June, at Somerset House. A letter from the Prince to Lord Bury was afterwards published in Orders, in which His Royal Highness stated that both he and the Princess, who accompanied him, were much gratified by the Inspection.

The events of one year are now found to be so much like those of another that it is unnecessary to follow each year in detail. We will, therefore, only refer to the prominent features which mark from this time the history of the Corps.

Shooting of Period.

A few words about the shooting of the period. " H " Company appears to have been the best shooting Company at this time, whilst " C " Company stood by far the lowest in the list of marksmen. Private E. Plasket was evidently the " crack " shot of the Regiment. Lord Bury's name also figures well in Regimental Competitions. In 1865 he headed the 3rd class scores with 72 out of a possible 80—a score which even in these days of Martinis would be treated with great respect.

Majors.

In 1865, Members of the Regiment for the first time filled the post of Major, the two senior Captains, Hawker and Du Plat Taylor, being promoted.

1866—Bank of England Company.

An important event in the history of the Corps occurred in 1866, in the formation of a new Company, composed of members of the Clerical Establishment of the Bank of England. The Bank had as yet taken no active part in the Volunteer movement; but the Directors, following the traditions of their predecessors of the last century, were very favourably inclined towards it. It was with little difficulty, therefore, that Mr. Kingsmill, to whose energy the formation of the Company was principally due, succeeded in recruiting a sufficiently large contingent to make them an acceptable acquisition to any leading Metropolitan Corps.

An attempt was made to draw them into the ranks of the London Rifle Brigade. Although not servants of the Crown, however, it was felt that there were bonds of affinity which drew them closer to the Civil Service than to any other Corps. Lord Bury's sanction was readily obtained, and in July, 1866, they joined, 140 strong, under the command of one of the Directors of the Bank—Captain J. P. Currie.

To make room for the new Company, the 1st Whitehall, or F Company, which was then in a weak state, was amalgamated with the 2nd Whitehall, or G Company, and the Bank took rank after the Admiralty as the K Company.

Camp at Wimbledon.

In the Orders of 1866 we find the first notice of a Regimental Camp, to be held at the Wimbledon Meeting. These were the days when Wimbledon was the *only* camp—a huge Volunteer " picnic," suggestive of camp bonfires and unlimited festivity. It was certainly the first experience which the Regiment appears to have had in camp life. In the Order giving details, one of the most prominent paragraphs recommends members to bring *sheets* and a *corkscrew* !

Major Du Plat Taylor.

In April, 1868, Major Du Plat Taylor resigned. Major Du Plat Taylor had from the first been one of the most prominent and energetic officers of the Corps. He had a strong desire, which he expressed in a circular issued in 1864, to raise a third Company in the Post Office, and then to form a separate battalion under his own command. Although not successful in this very questionable scheme, he now resigned in order to take command of a new corps (the 49th, now the 24th Middlesex), raised from the Sorters and Letter Carriers of the Post Office. His success at the head of this regiment is well known.

The vacancy caused by this promotion was filled by the promotion of Captain Currie, of the Bank of England, to be Major.

1871.

The next events of importance occur in the year 1871. This was a period of some military excitement, caused by the Franco-German War. The old Enfield rifle was called in, and the Snider breechloader issued to Volunteers.

School of Instruction.

Schools of Instruction for Volunteer Officers were instituted by the Army authorities. These supplied a want that had been much felt, as much by the " Civil Service " as by other Corps ; for although the more energetic Officers occasionally obtained permission to be attached to a Regiment of Regulars for a short period, the instruction thus obtained does not appear to have been very thorough.

Indeed, the blunders of Commanding Officers, eccentric words of command, and suchlike, form the staple commodity of the " Volunteer " humour of the period. It is related that on one occasion, when the " Civil Service " were marching down Fleet Street, a Field Officer, rushing to the front, delivered himself of the following : " Battalion—FOURS RIGHT. No, I mean FOURS LEFT. No—er—er—. D——n it. *Turn up Fetter Lane.*"

Lord Bury was the first Officer of the Corps to take advantage of the new institution, and in 1871 he attended the School at Chelsea Barracks, and obtained the " pass " certificate. Since that time it has been the rule for all Officers to pass the School as soon as possible after receiving a commission.

Major Hawker.

In this year (1871) Major Hawker resigned. On his resignation he was entertained by the Regiment at a dinner given in his honour at St. James's Hall ; and, in a special Regimental Order issued for the occasion, he was thanked by Lord Bury for the services which he had rendered the Corps. His vacancy was filled by the promotion of Captain Mills.

We now approach a period when a greater variety was displayed in the annual military programme of the Corps. Camps of Instruction were instituted—the first in 1873. Detachments from the Corps attended the Autumn Manœuvres of the Army and the Aldershot Summer Drills ; but to these matters we will refer more fully in a subsequent chapter.

50th Middlesex Formed.

In 1875 a new Corps (one of the last formed in Middlesex) was raised from the porters and subordinate establishment of the Bank of England. After the disbandment of the Bank Volunteers in 1814, the Directors still considered it advisable to train a certain number of their *employés* to the use of arms, to be employed, if necessary, for the defence of the Bank. Their porters and messengers were specially selected with a view to this purpose, and arms and uniform were provided by the Bank. The year 1875 found them a rather antiquated body of men, armed with the Brown Bess musket, with which weapon they made an annual excursion to the butts, and underwent their sole military exercise, at great peril to themselves and to the surrounding neighbourhood.

At this period, efforts were made to bring them within the scope of the Volunteer Regulations. The only difficulty in the way was the requirement of the Directors to employ them solely for the defence of the Bank property. After some demur, however, the Government consented to admit them, and they were enrolled as the 50th Middlesex—afterwards changed to the 25th.

The Corps consisted of one Company only, about 100 strong, under the command of Captain Gray, Chief Accountant of the Bank. They chose for their uniform the dark-green and busby of the Rifle Brigade, and were attached for drill purposes to the " Civil Service " Corps.

Dramatic Society.

In 1876 a Regimental Dramatic Society was inaugurated with great *éclat*. Although the Corps was unable to boast of such noted names as were seen on the programme of its performance of 1861, yet there was found to be an abundance of dramatic talent in its ranks. Moreover, some of the celebrities referred to gladly gave their services to their old Corps. Mr. W. S. Gilbert personally superintended the rehearsals for the production of one of his own plays, " On Guard," which was selected for the opening performance ; and the veteran Mr. Tom Taylor contributed a Prologue for the occasion.

For several years the Club continued to give excellent performances in St. George's Hall, and with the funds thus obtained gratuitous entertainments were provided at the various Camps.

Aldershot, Wimbledon, and the Camps of Instruction owe many a jovial evening to the efforts of the Dramatic Club. There came a time, however, when the support given by the general body of the Corps began to fall off, and it was necessary to discontinue the performances. Let us hope that it will not be long before the dramatic spirit again revives in the ranks.

Major Currie.

In 1879 Major Currie resigned. The Regiment had benefited much by Major Currie's services. Lord Bury having suffered from bad health about this period, Major Currie for some time carried out the duties of Commanding Officer, and earned for himself much popularity in the Corps. His post was filled by the promotion of a brother Director of the Bank, Captain A. G. Sandeman, of K Company.

Lord Bury.

Mention should not be omitted of the fact that at this period (1878–80) the Corps had the gratification of seeing its Commanding Officer (Lord Bury) occupying the post of Under Secretary of State for War. In this capacity he presided over a Committee appointed by Government to investigate and report on the requirements of the Volunteer Force. There is no doubt that the more generous treatment which the Force has received from Government of late years is owing in a great degree to the Report of this Committee.

Title Altered.

In 1880 a scheme for re-numbering the Middlesex Corps was adopted by the War Office. Many of the Corps formed in 1860 had become defunct or had been amalgamated with others. The " Civil Service," from the 21st, thus became the 12th Middlesex. A few years later, when the territorial system was arranged, they were classified as the 5th Volunteer Battalion of the King's Royal Rifle Corps, but this title has not yet been adopted.

21st Year.

In 1881 the Volunteer Force celebrated its coming of age, and Her Majesty marked the event by reviewing her " citizen soldiers." The English Volunteers mustered in Windsor Great Park, on the 9th July, 1881, and marched past their Sovereign. A few weeks later the Queen proceeded to Scotland, and reviewed the Scottish Corps at Edinburgh.

The " Civil Service " decided to celebrate their arrival at maturity by a grand dinner of past and present members. The Prince of Wales graciously consented to preside on the occasion, and this necessitated delaying the festival until the following year. The dinner was ultimately held at Willis's Rooms, on the 1st March, 1882. The demands for admission were many times in excess of the space available, and the process of balloting for tickets was resorted to in the case of past members.

A distinguished company of guests were invited to meet the Prince, who, as Chairman, made several speeches, in the course of which he warmly complimented the regiment, and expressed his wish to meet it at the Portsmouth Review the following Easter. This wish was carried out. The Prince was present at Portsmouth for some days, and appeared in public on each occasion in his uniform as Colonel of the Civil Service Corps.

At the march past, on the day of the Review, he took command of the battalion, and marched past at its head.

Her Majesty further complimented the Volunteer Force in this year, by appointing, for the first time, certain of its commanding officers Aides-de-Camp to the Queen. Lord Bury was one of the six selected for this honour.

In 1884 Major Sandeman resigned, and the Honourable Arnold Keppel, the eldest son of Lord Bury, formerly of the Scots Guards, was appointed junior Major.

Change of Rifle.

In 1885 the Snider Rifles were called in and Martinis issued to Volunteer Corps. For a few years before this, a limited number of Martinis had been lent to each corps for the use of men who shot for the Queen's Prize at Wimbledon. (The rifles of the " Civil Service " were again changed in 1890 for Martinis of a later pattern, with which the sword-bayonet was issued in lieu of the bayonet of the old type.)

Adjutants.

In 1886 Major Lombard retired from the post of Adjutant, having served to the full limit of age allowed by the War Office Regulations in force on his appointment. The Corps now came under the operation of the rule at present in force, by which an officer on the Active List of the Army is appointed for five years only, when he returns to his regiment. Under this rule Captain A. G. S. Beadnell, of the King's Own Scottish Borderers, was appointed, *vice* Major Lombard.

Jubilee Year.

The Volunteer " events " which marked the Jubilee Year of 1887 will ever make it memorable to those who took part in them. The Civil Service Corps were fully represented at each of these—The Royal Procession to the Abbey ; the March Past the Queen at Buckingham Palace, when the Corps had the honour of being led by H.R.H. the Prince of Wales ; and last, but not least, the gigantic Military Review at Aldershot. On the last-mentioned occasion, in order to parade at the early hour of four in the morning, the detachment was billeted for the previous night at Somerset House.

CHAPTER IV

Wimbledon Ranges.

No history of the Corps could be accepted as complete which omitted an account of the Wimbledon Ranges ; for it is around them that, with many of us, the pleasantest memories of volunteering life will cling—some of its sweetest triumphs, and also, perhaps, some of its keenest disappointments. *Here* we have endeavoured to learn, with more or less success, how to bear the pride of victory, as well as the sting of defeat, with that impassive demeanour which is held to become the well-bred Briton.

Then, too, are they not the more interesting because they are, in themselves, *glorious* ranges ? Not, perhaps, with regard to their adaptability to good shooting. They have a fish-tail wind that is trying, and a semaphore that is—worse. But the grand view ! Across the wide common, with its gorse, heather, and fern, its quiet dells, its shady copses, and its broad, open, wind-swept plateaux, to the beautiful glades of Richmond Park, and far, far away to the distant Surrey Hills. Then, the pure, bracing breeze, coming as it does just over the top of Leith Hill, straight from the sea, giving more health and vigour in one short afternoon than any doctor's tonic taken for a month.

Every landmark around has been familiar to us for years, and most are associated with some incident which renders them attractive. Here, for instance, is the spot where we fired our first shot as a recruit. (We have never fired at that ridiculous distance since.) How well do we remember that awful event ! How we screwed up our courage to the sticking-point, firmly resolved to " let off " that dread weapon ; but in our own mind the immediate future was full of vague uncertainty. With what feelings of utter indifference we received the sergeant's congratulations that we had hit the target. It had gone off ! We were alive and well, and the world moved on as before ! There was no room in our mind for anything else.

Well, well ! That intense feeling of respect for a loaded rifle very soon wore off. Let us return to the sober facts of history. The Wimbledon Ranges have been used by the " Civil Service " from the very commencement of the Corps. The Sub-Committee appointed by the Council in 1860 to seek for a Range were not long in discovering Wimbledon. The Ranges were then in the possession of the 11th Surrey Volunteers, who rented them from the Lord of the Manor, Earl Spencer, for the sum of one shilling yearly. They agreed to allow the " Civil Service " to share the shooting accommodation, on the understanding that the latter paid three-fourths of the cost of the erection of the Butts.

One feels compelled to remark that the Regimental authorities have never been very happy in their management of matters connected with these ranges. Affairs were commenced with a lawsuit, brought by the contractor who erected the Butts, and the Corps lost the day.

In 1861 the London Scottish, who had opened adjoining ranges, proposed to build a Shooting House. They invited the " Civil Service " to join them in the undertaking, and to become joint owners. The Council, however, did not consider it advisable to do so, but preferred to pay a yearly rent for a share in the tenancy. In 1864 the Council again refused an offer to become joint owners, and the result has been that the Corps has paid in annual rent considerably more than would have sufficed to build the house, enjoying meanwhile comparatively poor accommodation, and having no voice in its management.

Matters were considerably disturbed in 1871 by the passing of the Wimbledon Commons Act, and by the appointment of Conservators to protect the interests of the Common-holders. The Act went so far as to recognise the established privileges of the Volunteers in using the Ranges, although shooting was henceforth restricted to certain days of the week, and to certain hours of the day. But ever since then the Conservators of the Common, with their restrictions, protests, and objections, have been a thorn in the side of the Regimental Range Committee.

In 1880 a lawsuit was commenced by the tenant of the land bordering the Common near the Range, on the ground that injury was caused by bullets falling on his land. The action was brought against the " Civil Service " only, but had for its object the closing of the whole of the Ranges in this corner of the Common. After being protracted over a period of several years, the action resulted in the closing of the 1st class targets, and the substitution of wooden or canvas targets, instead of iron, at the 2nd class range.

With this concession the Corps may be said to have established its title to the use of the Ranges. The War Office have lately instituted more than one careful inspection, and have decided that they are " safe," so that it may be hoped that the Corps will continue to enjoy possession for many years to come.

The Flagstaff.

A noteworthy object on the Wimbledon Range is the flagstaff. This is 153 feet high, and has the reputation of being the tallest flagstaff in England of one piece only. It is known as the "Douglas Pine," and is the product of Vancouver's Island. It was presented to the London Scottish in 1872 by an old member of the Corps, who had settled on that island and felled it on his own land. The recruit is usually informed that it took two ships to bring it over ; the explanation that one ship brought it to Liverpool and the other to London being reserved.

It will be noticed that the little stick in question is protected by a somewhat formidable lightning-conductor, its predecessor having been destroyed by lightning one afternoon whilst shooting was going on at the Range.

We must not quit Wimbledon without a passing comment on the Wimbledon Camp.

Wimbledon Camp.

The " Civil Service " was among the earliest of the Metropolitan Corps which formed its own private camp at the great rifle meeting, and from 1864 to 1885 the dark blue flag with its Prince of Wales's Feathers was always to be seen flying in its own peculiar corner of the enclosure. This unbroken record of nearly a quarter of a century was not obtained, however, without some trouble. In the early days, when camping out was a novelty, and Wimbledon afforded the only means of enjoying that novelty, there was little difficulty in ensuring a good attendance ; but, with the rise of Camps of Instruction and the Aldershot Camps, applications for the Wimbledon tents, with their somewhat heavy fees, began to fall off. For many years it was kept up merely by the efforts of a small band of enthusiasts, to whom the Wimbledon " picnic," with its jovial round of holiday mirth, had a peculiar charm. The support of the general body of the Corps fell off to such a marked extent that in 1886, four years before the National Rifle Association removed to Bisley, the Camp was discontinued.

Shooting.

To pass from Wimbledon and to remark briefly on the shooting records of the Regiment is an easy digression.

The " Civil Service " has never yet had the good luck to provide the winner of the Queen's Prize, and this fact is sometimes thrust forward by the thoughtless to detract from its merits as a " good shooting Corps." A simple computation will show that, with 200,000 Volunteers to shoot for it, a Corps of 600 strong will have done its duty if it wins the prize once in 333 years ! But members of the Corps have on more than one occasion run the winner very hard. Lord Bury himself was second for the prize in 1861.

Others who have been within measurable distance are : Private

W. A. Impey (Audit Office) in 1869, Lieutenant J. Mitford (Post Office) in 1875, and Sergeant W. W. Akhurst (Post Office) in 1885. Wimbledon honours have also been earned for the Corps by Sergeant J. P. Wright (Bank of England), winner of the Grand Aggregate in 1874 ; Captain H. W. E. Jeston (National Debt Office), winner of the N.R.A. Challenge Cup in 1869 ; and teams who have on various occasions won the Mappin Challenge Cup for running and shooting.

Nor can we in the present year (1891) admit that the shooting of the Corps shows any sign of declining. In the War Office Returns for the last two years it stood first of the Metropolitan Corps, and second in the Home District. The Regimental Team rejoice in an almost unbroken series of victories in the numerous matches it has shot in the same period ; whilst Private Rothon, Corporal Matthews, and Corporal Clunan well maintained the credit of the Corps at the first meeting of the National Rifle Association on Bisley Common. In addition to this, in Private Rothon the Corps has the winner of the Champion Badge of Middlesex for 1890, and, having been chosen to shoot in the English " twenty," he made the highest score in the International Match of 1891.

A few words about Aldershot.

The Aldershot Drills.

The Aldershot Summer Drills appear to have been instituted when the Autumn Manœuvres, held in 1872-3, were discontinued. The " Civil Service " first sent a detachment to Aldershot in 1875, and from that date, with but few exceptions, they have annually sent a Company. This Company has been almost always attached to the Provisional Battalion commanded by Colonel Du Plat Taylor, of the Post Office Volunteers. Of all the efforts taken to instil a military training into the Volunteer none perhaps have had so great an effect as the " Aldershot Week." The complete change of life experienced by thus suddenly adopting the soldier's daily routine and hard fare, the living with and fraternising with soldiers, the feeling that you are for the time being actually paid as a soldier, that you are watched by military police lest you should desert, that the Mutiny Act has been read over you, which says that if you disobey your officer you shall be shot—all this is calculated to make the most light-hearted Volunteer feel that he is in earnest at last. He enters into the spirit of the work, enjoys the novelty of the situation—knowing that it won't last long—and generally comes home, grimy, sunburnt, and, in his own eyes at least, a soldier to the backbone. The stamp it puts on a man is never effaced. To say " he is an Aldershot-man " means that he is entitled to considerable respect as a good Volunteer.

Camps of Instruction.

Aldershot may have been instrumental in giving us a leaven of good soldiers, but nothing has had so great an effect in changing the conditions of our Volunteer life as the Camps of Instruction. As the greater part of Battalion drills are now done in Camp, it is hardly possible for a member, as was the case in old days, to make himself efficient by toddling round the quadrangle at Somerset House ; and this change has almost banished from the ranks the individual generally described as the "old-fashioned Volunteer."

The first Regimental Camp of Instruction was pitched on Wimbledon Common on the 12th May, 1873. It lasted three days only, a longer time being forbidden by the provisions of the Wimbledon Commons Act. The weather was very cold, with occasional snow. The nightly attendance averaged about 100.

In the following year, 1874, Major Currie lent a field at Esher for the purpose. This Camp lasted six days, and was memorable for being the scene of one of those foolish escapades—a night attack, delivered with great spirit by a local corps, and repulsed with equal ardour by the "Civil Service." In the present day, with increased knowledge of military tactics, Volunteer officers recognise the absurdity of such attacks.

In 1875, the Camp was pitched in a portion of Wimbledon Park known as the Leg of Mutton Field, Southfields. Here also it was located in 1876 and 1877. In the following year, 1878, a very enjoyable Camp was held in Sandown Park, Esher.

1879 will be for ever memorable, to those who took part in it, as the year of the *mud* Camp, held in a small field, or rather swamp, attached to an empty house near Putney Heath.

Finally, in 1880, was discovered that very acme of positions— a spot suited above all others for an encampment of Metropolitan Volunteers—the Old Deer Park at Richmond.

The Old Deer Park.

Here the Corps has encamped every year since,* and, indeed, it would be difficult to find a more advantageous camping-ground. Interesting in its associations as one of the oldest Royal Parks in England, originally attached to Richmond Palace, it gives for drill purposes an extensive area of slightly undulating parkland, ornamented with picturesque groups of trees, among which are some patriarchs so venerable as to make one imagine

---

* Up till 1898, but not since.

that they might have looked down upon the grand tournaments held on that spot by the Tudor Kings.

Long may it be before any over-zealous War Office official shall reform the Richmond Camp of Instruction out of existence. Let us hope that for many a future generation the Civil Service Recruit may do his lonely midnight sentry-go, in the quiet seclusion of the Old Deer Park, with no greater peril to encounter than the ghost of a Maid of Honour !

CHAPTER V

ABOUT the year 1888 a considerable decline in the recruiting power of the Regiment became apparent, owing chiefly to the reduction of the establishments of many Government Offices in consequence of the lengthening of the official day to seven hours. There were no new entrants into the Service, and consequently no material for recruiting.

By many, however, the cause was ascribed to the unattractive uniform. This idea gained ground, and Lord Bury allowed the opinion of the whole Regiment to be taken on the matter.

This was not the first time that the members of the Regiment had been canvassed with regard to a change of uniform. In 1862 a proposal was raised in favour of *scarlet* ; and again, in 1881, when Lord Bury wished his Corps to take the lead in adopting a recommendation of the War Office Committee, of which he was Chairman, and change to a uniform similar to " regulars " ; but on both of these occasions a large majority of the members were found to be thoroughly conservative. The helmet had been adopted in lieu of the Shako in 1881, but, with this exception, the uniform remained as it had been fixed in 1863.

Change of Uniform.

Other views now prevailed, and out of 300 who answered the circular addressed to them, and who expressed any opinion at all in the matter, 220 were in favour of a change. After a considerable time had been taken in arriving at a decision, it was resolved to discard the dark grey for a very light grey, retaining the Royal blue facings and the black belts of the old uniform.

The sanction of the Honorary Colonel and of the War Office having been obtained, the change was carried out at the commencement of 1890. Taking advantage of a grant from the Volunteer Equipment Fund raised by the Lord Mayor (Sir James Whitehead), the Corps at the same time furnished itself with greatcoats and the full equipment considered necessary by the War Office ; so that at the Inspection of this year the Regiment paraded in its new uniform, and, for the first time, fully equipped.

The Inspection of 1890 was also remarkable for another event of importance. For some time past Lord Bury had been announcing his intention of shortly resigning the command of the Corps, which he had now held for thirty years.

A few months before, the officers of the Corps, foreseeing the coming resignation, had presented Lady Bury with an oil painting of his Lordship, in the uniform of the C.S.R.V. The portrait, by a rising young artist of the day, had been exhibited at the Grosvenor Gallery, and had been very favourably noticed.

Resignation of Lord Bury.

At the close of the Inspection referred to (held in the Camp in the Old Deer Park, Richmond) Lord Bury, in a few earnest words, regretfully bade farewell to the Regiment in which he had spent so large a period of his life, and with which he expressed a hope that his family would henceforward be always connected. He then formally handed over the command to his successor, Major and Honorary Lieutenant-Colonel Mills ; and, with an outburst of hearty cheering in his honour, the Civil Service Corps took leave of its first Commanding Officer.

Staff Promotions.

On the resignation of Lord Bury, and the appointment of Lieutenant-Colonel Mills to the command of the Regiment, Captain and Honorary Major J. J. Cardin, of the Post Office, was promoted to the post of Major ; and it is doubtful if in the whole history of the Corps can be recorded any more popular promotions than these two.

Building of Head Quarters.

There remains now but one more event to chronicle in order to bring this brief category to a close, viz., the building of a Regimental Headquarters. Ever since its formation the only apology for a Headquarters which the Corps possessed consisted of a single room, kindly lent by the authorities of the Exchequer and Audit Department, in which the business of the Regimental Staff was conducted. It had been felt for some time that the satisfactory condition of the Corps justified an effort being made to provide its members with similar accommodation to that possessed by most of the London Corps. The chief difficulty was that of obtaining a favourable site at an outlay within reasonable limits. This difficulty was at length overcome mainly by the exertions of Colonel Mills, through whose agency the Government were induced to lend, under very favourable conditions, a piece of ground between the two west wings of Somerset House, approached from the Embankment by what was originally the West Watergate.

It was estimated that a building suitable for the purpose could be erected on this site for about £3,000. At a meeting of officers, at which Lord Bury presided, held at the Audit Office on 19th February, 1890, it was decided to attempt to raise this sum by an appeal for subscriptions addressed principally to the upper ranks of the Civil Service. H.R.H. the Prince of Wales was graciously pleased to head the list with a donation of one hundred guineas. The Governor and Directors of the Bank of England subscribed a like sum, and within a few months Colonel Mills had personally collected £1,300 from the ministerial and permanent heads of Departments and others of high rank in the Government Offices.

1892.

In 1892 the Headquarters Building was formally opened. The Prince of Wales, as Honorary Colonel, had announced his intention of performing the ceremony, but was prevented by the lamentable death of the Duke of Clarence which occurred in January, and the duty was carried out by H.R.H. the Duke of Connaught. The event was followed by a succession of " At Homes," dances, and other festivities to give the Regiment a house warming in its new home.

The home itself was much appreciated, and at once began to have a marked effect on the popularity and, consequently, upon the strength and efficiency of the corps. It had, moreover, the great merit of having been provided free of all future debt ; for it had been the firm principle of Colonel Mills, to whose efforts the building was due, that not a brick should be laid until the whole of the money required for building and furnishing had been deposited in his hands.

Many London Regiments had built themselves fine Headquarters about this time, but in doing so had left themselves with the burden of a debt which sadly crippled them for many years. It was not indeed until the buildings were handed over to the War Office on the formation of the Territorial Force that many Commanding Officers were relieved of heavy financial embarrassments on this account.

Colonel Mills having successfully carried out the final task he had set himself, now retired after thirty-three years of arduous service. He was then the only member left in the corps who had served in it from its commencement. In the following year he became Comptroller and Auditor-General, and received the honour of knighthood.

Major Viscount Bury* succeeded to the Command, and the vacant post of Field Officer was filled by the promotion of Major H. B. H. Tytheridge.

---

* In 1891 the 6th Earl of Albemarle died. He was a Waterloo veteran. By his death the first Commanding Officer succeeded to the earldom, and gave his name to the Hon. Arnold Keppel.

C

1893.

The Regiment now entered upon an era of rising strength and vigorous efficiency. Officers keen to learn found in Captain Barton an Adjutant who was as keen to teach. Parties on outpost work, road sketching, military topography, etc., were soon to be found ranging the outskirts of London and of any other place where the Civil Service were encamped, and the result was seen in after years, when the Army List recorded a far higher list of qualifications in " extra subjects " to the officers of the Corps than to any other in the country.

Recruiting flourished, until in 1896 the Corps attained its full strength of 800, and returns were only kept within authorised limits by ruthlessly striking off would-be non-efficients.

1894.

In 1894 the Earl of Albemarle, the Regiment's first Commanding Officer, died, and Colonel Viscount Bury succeeded to the title.

The Corps attended the Easter manœuvres at Windsor in this year, when its Commanding Officer secured for it the much appreciated privilege of being quartered at Eton College.

In July, 1894, Lieutenant-Colonel Cardin (Senior Major) resigned after a period of thirty-four years' service in the Corps. The vacant post was filled by the promotion of Captain and Honorary Major J. Mitford.

1895.

On the 25th May, 1895, the Prince of Wales held an inspection of the Regiment at Chelsea Barracks. The parade strength was 719 Civil Service, and 93 Bank of England (25th Middlesex). The Prince, who wore the new light grey uniform of the Corps, presented the first issue of the Long Service Medal to 40 officers and men. The Officers' Volunteer Decoration had been bestowed in 1892 on 17 officers (retired and serving) of the Corps, with the Prince's own name heading the list.

The shooting of the Regiment was much restricted this year by the closing of all but the short (300 yards) range at Wimbledon, owing to the efforts of the Conservators of the Common, who alleged danger to the public.

It was not until 1898, that by the opening of the ranges at Runemede, the Regiment was again able to fire the full musketry course, and the Wimbledon ranges were finally abandoned.

1896.

In 1896 Captain G. Lamb, Leinster Regiment, was appointed Adjutant in the place of Captain Barton, whose time having expired, returned to his regiment. It was with great regret that the Civil Service parted with this officer.

1897.

1897 was the year of the Diamond Jubilee of Queen Victoria. Unlike the Jubilee of 1887, when the Metropolitan Volunteers turned out in their full strength to line the route, battalions were now restricted to two companies of 25 file each. The Civil Service Companies were commanded by the two senior captains, Major Miall and Captain Merrick.

At the great Royal Naval Review at Spithead, the " H " (Admiralty) Company under Captain Danter had the unique experience of providing a Guard of Honour in the battleship *Empress of India ;* perhaps the only occasion on which the Volunteer Force was represented in a Naval Review.

In this year the Regimental Signalling Party, who for some time had never failed to secure a high place in the list of those presenting themselves for official examination, now passed first in the Kingdom.

1898. " Prince of Wales' Own."

In February, 1898, the Prince of Wales honoured the officers by attending a Mess Dinner held at the Whitehall Rooms. Responding to the toast of his health, the Prince complimented Lord Albemarle on the efficiency of the Regiment, and spoke warmly of the pleasure it gave him to remember how long he had been its Honorary Colonel—the oldest Colonel, he thought, in the Volunteer Force. It was announced shortly afterwards that the Regiment was to be called " The Prince of Wales's Own."

1899.

Facilities were now being given for Volunteers to do as much training as possible with regular troops, and the Civil Service took advantage of this during the Easter period. In 1898 a strong detachment were quartered at the Albuhera Barracks, Aldershot, and in 1899 the whole Battalion were accommodated at the Inkerman Barracks, Woking, with the 2nd East Surrey Regiment. In reporting on outpost operations carried out on the latter occasion, the Brigadier said : " The outpost work was good. The placing of picquets, groups and supports left nothing to be desired and reflects great credit on the Company officers."

An admirable test of the state of efficiency at which the Volunteer Force had now arrived was afforded this year by the Royal Review of Metropolitan Volunteers on the Horse Guards Parade, held to commemorate the fortieth year of the Force. Before midday hardly a uniform was to be seen in the streets ; but by four in the afternoon 30,000 Volunteers had mustered at their Headquarters, marched to St. James' Park, and formed up in Brigades. From thence in rapid succession, after a complicated and trying movement, owing to the awkwardly confined space, they marched past in column of double Companies, debouching from the Park by the gate allotted to them to their respective Headquarters, and by 8.0 p.m. this little army had vanished back to civilian life. The steadiness and precision of movement, the quiet, orderly behaviour, the neat and soldierly appearance of the men made, without doubt, a great impression on authorities and public alike.

It was well that this was so, for before the year had closed the first demand of the country for real service was to be made on the Force. The South African war was straining the powers of our small regular army to its utmost limit, and in December there was a sudden call upon the Volunteers for detachments for voluntary service in South Africa. This call would have been responded to much more readily if the military authorities had not hampered it with many apparently needless restrictions. The City Imperial Volunteers raised by the Lord Mayor was the only body allowed to retain its identity as a Volunteer unit. It was to this force, therefore, that London volunteers pressed forward, and for the small quota which the Civil Service were asked to supply, three or four times the number at once presented themselves for medical inspection.

The Regiment had the pleasure of seeing its Commanding Officer, the Earl of Albemarle, chosen for the command of the infantry battalion ; but although several other officers volunteered their services these posts were almost entirely reserved for members of the City Corps.

The history of the City Imperial Volunteers has been recounted at length elsewhere. Suffice it to say that the Regiment embarked on the 20th January, 1900, and after a period of preliminary training in South Africa, joined the 21st Brigade under General Bruce Hamilton. After continuous marching for about fifty days the Battalion reached Pretoria on the 5th June, and on the 12th June fought in the battle of Diamond Hill.

An interesting impression of the effect they produced on that occasion was furnished in a speech made at a public gathering by an officer commanding a squadron of the Royal Horse Guards present on the field :

" We were drawn up," he said, " on the flank of the line at the foot of the hill, when word came down to us that the City Imperial Volunteers were advancing to attack. With great interest we watched through our glasses to see how volunteers would act in coming into action. They came over the brow of the hill in excellent formation, pressing forward as steadily as at a review. ' Why ! ' we exclaimed, ' You can't tell them from Regulars ! ' "

So impressed was the speaker that he determined then and

Photo by J. H. Lile & Co.

Sgt.-Major P. Kenny. Q.-M. F. J. Michôd. Major R. Mills.
Capt. G. C. S. Lombard.
Major J. P. Currie. Lt.-Col. Viscount Bury.

1899. OLD DEER PARK, RICHMOND.

Photo by W. S. Stuart.

Major W. Danter. Capt. J. W. Smith-Neill, Major Lamb, Adjt.
Scots Guards.
Lt.-Col. Tytheridge, V.D. Col. Earl of Abemarle.

To face page 36.

there that if ever he had the chance he would command a battalion of Volunteers.

The officer was the Earl of Arran, afterwards commanding the Civil Service.

1900.

The City Imperial Volunteers returned home in November, and were given a tumultuous welcome as they marched through London on the afternoon of Saturday, the 21st November. The route was lined by all the Metropolitan Volunteer Battalions ; and so enthusiastic was London to welcome its " heroes " that it was with the greatest difficulty that the route could be kept clear.

Unfortunately, Lord Albemarle had been attacked with fever at Cape Town and was unable to embark, thereby missing the welcome accorded to his Battalion.

The returned warriors of the Civil Service were entertained by the rest of the Regiment at a great banquet given in their honour in the King's Hall, Holborn, on the 10th December.

In all 136 members of the Corps served in South Africa, principally in the Yeomanry. Of these five were killed or died in hospital.

Trooper A. E. Trembath (Imperial Yeomanry) earned the D.C.M., and was promoted to rank of Lieutenant for distinguished service in action.*

As the country was denuded of troops in this year the Government decided to establish Emergency Camps of Militia and Volunteers during the summer months. Brigade Camps lasting for a month were formed, and each Corps was requested to keep fifty per cent. of its strength in attendance for the whole period.

The South London Brigade consisting of
    2nd (South) Middlesex
    7th Middlesex (London Scottish)
    12th Middlesex (Civil Service)
    13th Middlesex (Queen's Westminsters)
    20th Middlesex (Artists)
went into camp on Farnborough Common from the 7th July to the 7th August. The Civil Service was by far the strongest battalion in attendance, and at its Inspection held on Saturday, the 21st July, the Battalion, including one Company of the 25th (Bank of England), stood over 1,000 on parade.

Permission was obtained this year to increase the establishment of the Battalion by two Companies and the maximum strength to 1,000. The two new Companies were " F "

* Lieutenant Trembath was killed in 1915 whilst serving with the 1st Battalion in France.

Company, recruited from the clerical staff of the London County Council, and " I " Company, formed of cyclists.

1901. Field Army Brigades.

On the 22nd January, 1901, Her Majesty Queen Victoria died. The Regiment was informed in due course that the King would honour it by continuing to retain the position of Honorary Colonel.

In April, 1901, the Regiment lost its Commanding Officer by the promotion of Lieutenant-Colonel the Earl of Albemarle to the command of the Norfolk Volunteer Infantry Brigade. Colonel Tytheridge, who had temporarily commanded during the absence of Lord Albemarle in South Africa, now succeeded to the command.

The experience of the South African war had forcibly impressed the country with the fact that in the Volunteer Force it possessed an asset deserving of greater encouragement and development than it had hitherto obtained. As a result of this feeling, the higher military authorities issued new and more stringent conditions of efficiency in an endeavour to bring the backward Corps up to the general level.

Regimental Camps of Instruction were now abolished and replaced by Brigade Camps. The Old Deer Park, Richmond, where the Battalion had encamped for nineteen years in succession (1880 to 1898) was to harbour it no more. Easter Manœuvres, Whitsuntide Marching Columns, Aldershot Provisional Battalions, Clacton Seaside Engineering Camps all dropped out ; and energies were concentrated on securing a maximum muster at the Brigade Camp, where it was necessary to maintain an attendance of half the full strength (500) for the period of fourteen days in order to earn the War Office grant.

The position in which the Regiment might find itself in the event of a national emergency had long been a subject of uncertainty and doubt.

The Treasury had firmly expressed themselves on this point in a Minute issued in 1899 and published in Regimental Orders, as follows :—

" The Volunteer Force was primarily formed for Home Defence, and there seems special objections to a regiment like the Civil Service Rifles serving abroad. The men have their public duties to perform at home, and if they were sent abroad, untried men must be temporarily employed in their places for the performance of Civil Service professional work."*

* There is no doubt that if it had not been for this attitude adopted by the Treasury and firmly maintained up to 1914, and the hampering effect it had upon Regimental authorities, the Civil Service would have been found in that fateful year among the first of the Territorial battalions on the field of war.

CIVIL SERVICE RIFLES   39

The Battalion, nevertheless, was selected as one of those to be placed in the " Field Army Brigades " which were formed under the new scheme of Home Defence. At first it was placed in the 24th (Volunteer) Brigade, consisting of 2nd (South) Middlesex, 12th Middlesex (Civil Service), 21st Middlesex, and 4th (Volunteer Battalion) Royal West Surrey Regiment.

Camp was formed this year at Jubilee Hill, Aldershot, under the Officer Commanding the District.

1903.

In 1903 Brigades were re-organised, and the Civil Service, with the Queen's Westminsters, London Irish and 2nd London formed the 23rd Brigade under Colonel Jerrard. This officer held training camps as follows :

    1903.—Shorncliffe.
    1904 and 1905.—Sway (New Forest).
    1906.—Shorncliffe.

About this time the Regiment effected certain changes in its uniform with the view of making it more suitable for work in the field. The helmet was altered to a shape which was perhaps less artistic, but gave greater comfort, and had not the disadvantage possessed by its predecessor of disabling the wearer from shooting when lying down. The tunic or jacket was made much looser and contained serviceable pockets. Puttees were adopted in lieu of gaiters, and enamelled belts were discarded in favour of dull black leather.

Altogether it now formed a very serviceable yet attractive uniform. Its invisibility at a distance was remarkable, and was the subject of trequent remark by distinguished foreign officers attending manœuvres.

1902.

Captain B. J. Majendie, King's Royal Rifles, was appointed Adjutant in November, 1902, *vice* Major Lamb, retired. Captain Majendie's experiences in the South African war had been somewhat unique and unfortunate. Whilst accompanying a troop of cavalry sent out as a patrol from Ladysmith on the day that war was declared, the party were surrounded and captured by the enemy and held prisoners in Pretoria until that place was taken by General Roberts in the following year. Captain Majendie was the first Adjutant which the Corps had secured from the regular regiment of which it formed a Volunteer battalion ; and by his efforts and instruction the Battalion became " riflemen," and adopted rifle drill and customs. But the fact that officers were always trained at the Guards' Schools of Instruction, where the drill of the rifleman is unknown, was a drawback to this arrangement.

In 1902, Major and Honorary Lieutenant-Colonel Danter, who had been appointed Major in 1897, resigned through bad health. The Battalion owed much to Colonel Danter for his hard and brilliant work for many years. To his energy and leadership in their early years may be mainly attributed the successes which the Regiment were now securing in its signalling section and in the School of Arms.

School of Arms.

To the latter institution a word is now due. Ever since the Headquarters had been opened, the athletic youth of the public offices in London had been attracted to this excellent training school in their midst. During the winter months the building was thronged to overflowing on " School " nights with perspiring youth in flannels, as class after class followed each other in unceasing relays for hours. Organising, directing and instructing this untiring energy were Danter, Brett, W. H. D. Clarke, Whitehurst,Weeks, Bell, Kirkby and others, ably supported, of course, by the most skilled instructors that the Guards and Aldershot could supply.

The result had now become apparent in the wonderful series of successes the School achieved, not only in the Home District Tournaments, but at the Royal Military Tournaments in competition with the Navy and Army.

A list of winners of Challenge cups and championship and silver medallists is given in Appendix No. V.

In addition to these successes, the School of Arms obtained 39 second and 18 third prizes at the R.M. Tournament, and an even greater number of prizes at the competitions of the Metropolitan Territorial School of Arms Association.

The most successful period for the Regimental School was during the first decade of the present century, when those fine all-round athletes Hobbins, Marsh and Chalke were in the hey-day of their prowess, and Major Brett, the oldest man in the competitions of 1907, won the Officers' Bayonet Challenge Cup.

In the previous year the Regimental Officers' Team won the Inter-Regimental Bayonet Fighting Cup, beating the R.M.A., with its large complement of officers to select from, in the final. This was the only occasion on which the Cup was wrested from the Regulars or Navy.

The Light-Weight Tug-of-War Team in 1904 became the permanent possessors of the R.M.T. Cup, which they had won three times in four years.

" Daily Telegraph " Cup.

In 1902 the Corps secured an honour for which it had striven for many years, and which, although as a rule honourably

placed in the strenuous competition, it had never yet succeeded in obtaining. This was the *Daily Telegraph* Cup for
marching and shooting, competed for at the Home District Rifle
Meeting by teams from most of the battalions of regulars and
volunteers in the district. And now, under the leadership of
Captain F. J. Brett, supported by Sergeant W. H. D. Clarke,
it was won four years in succession, a feat never performed by
any other battalion.

1904.

In 1904, Colonel Tytheridge resigned and the Earl of Arran,
late Captain, Royal Horse Guards, was appointed Commanding
Officer. Captain and Hon. Major E. Merrick and Captain R. G.
Hayes were promoted Field Officers.

At the end of 1906 the Field Army Brigades were abolished,
as preparations were then being made for a much greater call
upon volunteers than that entailed by the existing scheme of
Home Defence.

Troubled by the incessant cry for economy in military expenditure from their supporters on one side and the imminence
of a European war with insufficient military strength on the
other, the Government turned again to the Volunteer Force
for aid.

The Territorial and Reserve Forces Act, 1907.

The Territorial and Reserve Forces Act was passed in 1907,
by which the Force might at once become an integral part of
the Army on a threat of war.

The Brigade Camp of 1907 held at West Tarring, near Worthing, was therefore the last camp of the Civil Service Volunteers.
Before the summer training camps of 1908 were formed, the
Corps had been disbanded and re-enrolled, the grey uniform had
been discarded, and a new khaki-clad battalion of Territorial
soldiers of the King, 800 strong, stood ready to ask His Majesty
to be again their Honorary Colonel. The request was granted,
and the *London Gazette* announced that :

" His Majesty the King has been graciously pleased to signify
his royal pleasure that he will continue to remain Honorary Colonel
of the Corps on its transfer to the Territorial Force."

The transfer throughout the Force was not made without
difficulty or without great effort on the part of its leaders.
Much nervousness existed as to the liabilities to be incurred
under the Act, the additional claim upon a man's spare time,
the suggested penalties in case of default, etc. The efforts of
the leaders were not assisted by the singularly inept methods
of the military authorities. The Act provided that the Volunteer

should be re-attested on entering the new Force. The Attestation Form at first issued by the War Office contained a long list of questions to be answered by the recruit. Prominent across the face of the form was the statement :

" You are hereby warned that if it is found that you have given a false answer to the following questions you will be liable to imprisonment with hard labour."

In this grateful and tactful manner it was proposed to greet the patriotic citizen on taking the first step towards his additional burden. But the protests of Volunteer Commanders were loud and the obnoxious form was quickly withdrawn.

15th (Co. of London) Battalion, 4th London Brigade.

The Battalion, under the title of the " 15th (County of London) Battalion the London Regiment," was placed in the 4th London Brigade of the 2nd London Division, the brigade being constituted as before (the old " Grey Brigade "), and still under the Lieutenant-Colonel commanding the Scots Guards Regiment.

The first training camp of the Territorial Brigade was held at West Down, Salisbury Plain, from August 2nd to 16th, 1908, Colonel Inigo Jones, Scots Guards, in command. The Civil Service were by far the strongest battalion in the camp ; the London Scottish and other corps having as yet been able to raise but a few companies for the new Force. This result had been achieved in spite of the fact that Treasury Regulations had been issued, regarding leave to be granted to Territorials in Government Departments for camp training, in which the conditions were much less generous than those formerly accorded to volunteers by Heads of Departments.

Fortunately, an officer of the Corps, Lieutenant F. H. D. Acland, having been elected M.P. for Richmond (Yorks), had been given the post of Parliamentary Secretary to the War Office. By his influence the Secretary of State for War, Mr. Haldane, commenced a tour of inspection of Territorials by visiting the camp at Salisbury Plain and lunching with the " Civil Service." On his attention being drawn to the new leave conditions, Mr. Haldane was good enough to attend the Regimental Prize Distribution at the close of the year and publicly announced that more generous conditions should be issued.

1908.

In August, 1908, the Earl of Arran found himself compelled, with regret, to resign the command. Notwithstanding the fact that his former military experience had been entirely that of a cavalry officer, Lord Arran had, by his personal efforts, kept up the high standard of steadiness and efficiency in drill to which the Battalion had attained, and his popularity as a Commanding Officer had never been exceeded by any. It was with sorrow that every member of the Corps heard of his decision to resign.

The command was taken over temporarily for a few months by Major and Hon. Lieutenant-Colonel Merrick, who, then in his thirty-third year of service, declined to allow his name to be put forward for further promotion. In December, 1908, the regiment found in Major the Hon. C. S. H. D. Willoughby, late of the Scots Guards, a Commanding Officer admirably qualified to lead it through the period of preparation for more serious military work which was now before it as a battalion of the Territorial Force.

In the change from a unit of the loosely-organized mass of Infantry and Garrison Artillery which constituted the Volunteer Force, to that of a strictly regulated battalion of the new Territorial Army (with its Brigade and Divisional Staffs, its due proportion of Cavalry, Field Artillery and Transport) the Corps had been trimmed and shorn of many of its former privileged adjuncts. Its establishment of officers was considerably reduced, and with great regret it lost its Honorary Chaplain, the Rev. Canon Duckworth. Canon Duckworth had served the Corps loyally for 23 years. He took great pride in never being a "non-efficient," was always on parade at the annual inspection, and wherever the regiment was encamped its Chaplain never failed to appear on the middle Sunday to conduct the service and preach his annual sermon.

The Battalion also lost its two bands, and its company of cyclists was abolished.

The drills and camp trainings required were not as extensive as those afforded by the Corps under Volunteer conditions ; but this was amply compensated for by the benefit derived, especially by officers, from the training given by Brigade and Divisional Staffs.

Instructional tours, in which officers of Cavalry, Artillery, Infantry and Transport met, took place frequently to important military positions in the neighbourhood of London. In these the Division (*minus* the men) would move by Manœuvre Orders duly issued by Divisional, Brigade and other Commanders of units, billet or bivouac on positions previously inspected and reported upon, throw out outposts, resume column of route, move on to the battle position and engage the enemy in the neighbourhood of Dunstable, Canterbury or other place selected. In its early days the 2nd London Division on these occasions had the advantage of the admirable instruction of Colonel Stanley Maude (afterwards General Sir Stanley Maude) as chief of the taff.

1910.*

The commencement of the training year saw the duties of
Adjutant taken over by Captain Fitzclarence of the Royal
Fusiliers, an officer of wide experience and one who had had
some previous knowledge of the working of a force recruited
under the voluntary system. From his first appearance on
parade his popularity was assured, and he ably seconded the
efforts made by Colonel Willoughby to bring the regiment up
to a high state of efficiency.

Training during the year followed the usual course. The
Easter training was carried out at Windsor, and the Annual
Training Camp at Minster-on-Sea was of an exceptionally
interesting nature. In the opinion of many it represented the
ideal camp training for the Territorial Force, consisting as it
did of practical musketry and field manœuvres, winding up
with an extensive trek through the pleasant lanes of northern
Kent. A most enjoyable fortnight was spent, and the members
of the Battalion returned at the end of it to their everyday
avocations feeling satisfied that they had made some real progress towards fitting themselves to fulfil the duties for which
the Territorial Force was intended. The Brigadier gave expression to his views on the following terms :

" The Brigadier wishes to thank all ranks of the Brigade for
their loyal co-operation and unflagging zeal and keenness during
the Annual Camp this year, more especially during the week's
bivouac and hard marching, which was a severe test to untrained
troops and in which the Brigade acquitted itself to his entire satisfaction. He attributes this success in a great measure to the fine
spirit and soldierlike pride which has ever distinguished the Grey
Brigade, and has once again successfully brought it through a
trying time. He hopes and thinks that, though the work has been
hard, the results have been great, and that all ranks are more fitted
to take their part in active service should the necessity arise."

A Regimental Athletic Club was formed with the twofold
object of securing the best possible representation in the Territorial Sports and Marathon Race held annually in June and of
fostering athletics from a military standpoint throughout the
Battalion. The Committee did valuable work, and as the
result of its labours the Regimental Team was enabled to take
a high place in the Marathon Race.

This year the Regiment had to mourn the loss of its Honorary
Colonel, His Majesty King Edward VII. He had been associated with the regiment over the long period of fifty years.

Major R. B. Hughes, who had been Quartermaster to the

---

* From this point to the outbreak of war the annals are continued by
Captain Bell, late Civil Service Rifles.

Battalion since the early nineties, was compelled, much to his regret, to resign his appointment this year. The regiment felt at his departure a regret equal to his own. Quartermaster-Sergeant W. H. D. Clark succeeded him, and the ability and hard work which he put into the arrangements for the Annual Camp contributed in no small degree to the success of that outing.

The announcement that the Regiment had been honoured by the appointment of the Rev. Canon Herbert Hensley Henson, D.D., as its Chaplain was received with gratification by the Battalion. Canon Henson had been approached because his church—St. Margaret's, Westminster—is regarded as the church of Parliament and the Civil Service.

1911.

The Easter Training this year took place at the Guards' Depot at Caterham. The opportunity thus afforded to the officers and non-commissioned officers of the Battalion to see the course of instruction through which a recruit of the Regular Army had to pass was most valuable.

The Battalion was called on to furnish a number of detachments in connection with the Coronation festivities this year, and acquitted itself well throughout. The Major-General in command of the Division expressed his entire satisfaction with the way in which the various duties were performed. As the personal gift of His Majesty on the occasion of his coronation, the Coronation Medal was awarded to the Commanding Officer, the Officers Commanding the detachments, the Quartermaster, Regimental Sergeant-Major, the senior N.C.O. and senior Private.

Annual training in camp took place at Dover. The political situation at home and abroad was not all that might be desired, and amongst all ranks was the feeling that before the camp terminated the Battalion might be called on for more serious work than that usually carried out on these occasions. Not until the Battalion had entrained for return to London could it be said that the tension had relaxed. The Major-General in his remarks on the training said that he noticed with pleasure the very good work done by all units, work which showed a distinct advance on any previously performed. He referred to the satisfaction given him by the cheerful way in which hardships, which resulted from the unavoidable stoppage of railway transport, had been borne by all ranks.

The Regiment furnished a detachment consisting of 1 officer, 1 N.C.O. and 4 men to attend the investiture of H.R.H. the Prince of Wales at Carnarvon on July 13th, 1911.

The efforts put forth by the Regimental Sports Club in connection with the annual Marathon Race only just failed of success, the Battalion team finishing second.

1912.

This year saw the old pattern Slade-Wallis equipment replaced by the Mills web equipment. The change was much appreciated and every one felt that with the supply of the new pack and haversack it was no longer necessary to rely for essentials on the kit-bag, and that, as a consequence, the mobility of the Battalion was greatly increased.

A feature of the year was the Whitsuntide outing arranged at Bisley for the purpose of drill and musketry. The detachment was favoured by good weather and had the opportunity of firing under the most favourable conditions all the practices laid down for the annual course.

Colonel Willoughby, who had been in command of the Regiment since 1908, was appointed to the command of the 6th Infantry Brigade on May 14th, 1912, and was succeeded by Major R. G. Hayes. Colonel Willoughby during his period of command had endeared himself to all ranks, and the Regiment parted with him with sincere regret. He issued a Farewell Order in the following terms :

" In relinquishing his official connection with the Regiment, Colonel Willoughby desires to thank the Officers, N.C.O.'s and men for their loyal co-operation and constant support they have so freely rendered him throughout the period that it has been his privilege to command the Battalion."

A further loss to the Battalion was that of Major F. J. Brett, who resigned on April 27th, 1912. " Freddie's " honours and achievements in the world of sport would fill a book by themselves. He was the life and soul of the Regimental School of Arms and his successes in bayonet fighting, fencing, etc., will long be remembered. His success in winning, in the year 1907, at the age of forty-six, the individual Bayonet Fighting Competition at the Royal Military Tournament is one which it can safely be said will never be equalled.

The practice of having the Easter training at the Guards Depot at Caterham had now become established, and the welcome which was always given the detachment there made the outing one to be looked forward to. The annual training in camp took place this year at Frith Hill, Aldershot, and was notable for the inclement weather experienced. The incessant rain may, however, have been a blessing in disguise, inasmuch as it prevented the rations being smothered with the black sand peculiar to this locality. Despite the unpleasant conditions, the troops kept remarkably free from illness. A feature of the training was Brigade movements in close formation, and it was a matter of no little astonishment to all ranks to see how easily and without confusion large bodies of well-organised and disciplined troops could be moved over rough and uneven ground. On the return of the Battalion from camp, the following extract from a War Office letter was published in Regimental Orders :

" The Army Council have expressed their appreciation and that of the Secretary of State for War for the excellent spirit which was shown by the Territorial troops in camp this year. The weather has been most inclement and the soldierly spirit in which the troops bore their discomforts was most praiseworthy."

1913.

A review of the London District Territorial Troops by His Majesty the King took place in Hyde Park on July 5th, 1913. The Battalion was well represented.

The annual camp was held this year at Abergavenny in South Wales. The Battalion had never before been called on to proceed so far afield for its training, and the visit to Wales was looked forward to with eager anticipation. The Brigade arrived at Abergavenny on Sunday, July 27th, and soon got to work on the programme laid down. The first week was devoted to section, company and battalion training, and on the Monday in the second week all surplus canvas was struck and a week's trek commenced. The first day's march brought the Battalion via Crickhowell to Glanusk Park, where a bivouac was formed. Many members of the Battalion were glad of the opportunity thus afforded to renew acquaintance with Lord Glanusk, an acquaintance first formed while he was Adjutant of the City Imperial Volunteers and maintained during his tenure of command of the Guards Depot at Caterham. On the following day the march was resumed, and the Battalion reached " The Forest," via Tretower and Cwm-du. Wednesday saw the Battalion *en route* for Tal-y-maes, encountering on its way an opposing force at the Pass of Rhin Truman. The pass was forced and the troops eventually reached their camp at Tal-y-maes, situated amongst some of the finest scenery in Wales. There Battalion and Brigade manœuvres were carried out for a couple of days, after which the return to Abergavenny was commenced and the old quarters reached at the end of the week. The Brigade returned to London on Sunday, August 10th, well satisfied that the military authorities had succeeded in combining an enjoyable holiday with a considerable amount of military training. A tribute to the popularity of the conception can be found in the fact that out of a battalion 779 strong, 735 attended the camp.

1914.

All other events of the year 1914 were dwarfed by the outbreak of the war with the Central Powers and the embodiment of the Territorial Force. As every one recollects, the call was sudden. The Battalion was carrying out the programme laid down for its peace training, and had actually arrived at Perham Down Camp, Salisbury Plain, for its annual camp training. Its stay there was but short—in fact, only a matter of hours— and it found itself back in London within twenty-four hours of having left it. The mobilization arrangements which had not long before been tested under the supervision of the Brigadier worked well, and a time of busy preparation set in.* At the outset the Battalion received with astonishment the news that the Government had decided that members of the Civil Service called up on embodiment would not be allowed their civil pay, and would have to depend entirely on their Army pay of their rank plus the usual allowances. It was felt that a decision such as this would interfere greatly with the efforts made to fill up the gaps in the Regiment, and would make difficult the provision of the necessary reserve of men. Representations were at once made to the Prime Minister, Captain Parish, the Adjutant, even going so far as to interview him on the subject before he had breakfasted on the morning following the announcement. The Prime Minister agreed to have the matter further considered, and the result was so far satisfactory that the flow of recruits continued.

The Battalion commenced its move to its war station in the neighbourhood of Watford on August 11th, bivouacked at Edgware for the night, and continued the march the following day. The troops stood the trying march well. The Battalion took up its quarters in and around the village of Bedmond and remained there until early in November, when it moved into billets in the town of Watford. A number of changes in personnel took place. Colonel the Earl of Arran, a former Commanding Officer of the Regiment, was given command of the Battalion, Lieutenant-Colonel Hayes being appointed to the command of the second line. The news of Lord Arran's appointment was received with great gratification, and every one present on parade in the little park at Bedmond on the day on which he joined the

---

* " We went to Somerset House and dismissed, but assembled again on the Tuesday, and on Wednesday we were mobilised. The battalion of 800 odd were accommodated in the corridors of Somerset House, and we fed à la picnic in the square."—*Extract from letter dated Feb. 5th*, 1915.—ED.

Battalion will remember the stirring and inspiring words in which he addressed them, winding up his remarks by stating in a very determined way that, "We have a long way to go, but we are going to get there." To the great regret of the whole Battalion Lord Arran was obliged later on to relinquish the command to rejoin his old regiment, the Royal Horse Guards. His place was taken by Colonel Renny, late of the Indian Army, and under him the Battalion moved to France on March 17th, 1915.

PART TWO

1st Battalion Civil Service Rifles

By Captain P. Davenport, M.C.*

INTRODUCTION

A FEW words on the manner in which the story of the 1st Battalion was written will not be out of place, and may help to explain the delay in producing the book and the obvious errors of omission which have been committed.

When the Battalion went to France two diaries were kept at headquarters—the War Diary, in which were recorded all the military exploits of the Battalion, and the Regimental Diary, which contained all the " personal gossip " in the Regiment, as well as accounts of tours in the front line. This Regimental Diary was started by Capt. Parish, who was then Adjutant, with the idea that it should be printed and published at the end of the war. But owing to frequent changes in the personnel of Battalion Headquarters, the book was not kept up to date, and there are, in consequence, several big gaps in its pages. It was finally closed early in 1918, when Colonel Segrave decided that as the keeping of two diaries entailed a certain amount of duplication of work, the War Diary should, in future, be a complete record of the history of the Battalion. From that time, therefore, the War Diary contained every item of interest to the Battalion, including such details as the names of the members of football teams and the artistes at Battalion concerts.

With these two books, therefore, I began in the winter of 1919 to collect material for a history. A committee was formed, on which I tried to get a representative of each Company and Specialist Section, and here I should like to acknowledge my indebtedness to these gentlemen, each one of whom has taken an active interest in the preparation of the book :—R. H. Burden, D.C.M., R. G. Callingham, S. L. Clements, E. Cooke, D.C.M., C. Ibbett, M.M., F. A. Lewis, M.M., R. H. Maddocks, F. C. Robertson, D.C.M., G. M. Sladden and R. C. Sugars, D.C.M.

In addition C.S.M. T. P. Brett, M.C., and Sergeant C. M. A. Tucker were kind enough to place at my disposal a book of notes, letters, and extracts from private diaries which they had collected, dealing with the first year of the career of the Battalion in France. Sergeant Tucker has been most energetic

* Appointed 2nd Lieut., 11th June, 1915 ; to France, December 24th, 1915 ; acting Captain, 1917 ; Adjutant, 27th June, 1917.—EDITOR.

throughout in his efforts to collect further material and to improve the crude story which I presented to the committee.

The story was written in instalments and so read to the committee, who criticised it and amended it, and it was then typed by Sergeant Tucker. The typed copy was then circulated among different members of the committee, who suggested further amendments, and the result is now presented to the Regiment as a simple record of the outstanding features of life in the 1st Civil Service Rifles in France.

I am fully conscious that there are grave omissions, notably in respect to paragraphs of appreciation of individuals. There are many more members deserving of special mention than appear in these pages, but I have included all who were brought to my notice and who, in my opinion, played a prominent part in the success of the Battalion. At the same time there are some whom I have missed, and to avoid doing these an injustice it was at one time suggested that all references to individuals should be cut out, but there are some who played such a big part in our history that no story of the Battalion would be nearly complete without mention of them.

As to the literary style and arrangement of the book, I am told by one of my critics that it is dull and lifeless, and that the descriptions of battles are not sufficiently picturesque. My only reply is that I have aimed at an accurate description rather than at a highly coloured style, and I hope my critics will bear in mind that, prior to this effort, I have never attempted anything more ambitious in the literary line than a love letter.

In addition to members of the committee the following members of the Regiment have very kindly written contributions :— G. C. G. Andrews, C. E. Bassett, E. De Ath, C. N. Burdock, C. Manthorpe, L. C. Morris, M.C., V. Stewart, J. H. Swain, and W. G. Skillern. To these gentlemen I should like to express my grateful appreciation.

February, 1921.   PAUL DAVENPORT.

CHAPTER I

AT the annual dinner in London on St. Patrick's Day the survivors of those who constituted the original 1st Battalion of the Civil Service Rifles commemorate the historic day on which the Regiment first sent a Battalion on active service—the 17th of March, 1915.

It was hardly realised when that Battalion went to France that it would soon become the highest of distinctions in the Regiment to be described as a " 17th of March man," but this distinction is fully recognised now, and he is a much envied man who has the right to attend the Annual Commemoration Dinner.*

There were about 1,100 all ranks who, after eagerly awaiting, during seven long months of training, the summons to join the B.E.F. in France, achieved their ambition on St. Patrick's Day, 1915, and entrained at Watford in the early hours of the morning. Throughout their stay in Watford, where they had been billeted since November, 1914, they had received the warmest hospitality, and it is not surprising, therefore, that their pride in going to the front was tinged with regret at leaving such good friends.

After a roundabout journey, Southampton was reached at 11.0 a.m., and the Battalion had to confine itself for the rest of the day to a few hundred yards of quay, impatiently awaiting embarkation, which was not carried out till dusk. Four boats were used—the *Balmoral, City of Chester, Jupiter* and *Munich*— boats used in the piping times of peace for pleasure trips along the coast. There were no bands playing, no cheering crowds, but just three or four bored officials, embarkation officers, and dock policemen. Thus the 1st Civil Service Rifles,† under the command of Lieut. Colonel A. M. Renny, left England, having

---

* This dinner was instituted on the 17th March, 1916, in the Reserve Battalion Camp at Hazeley Down, Winchester, where already a number of the originals who had been wounded, had returned. To Captain G. C. Grimsdale fell the honour of taking the chair at the first of these functions, which it was decided should be held annually so long as any " 17th of March men " should live to attend them.

† See Appendix for list of officers.

on board the four boats thirty officers, 1,046 other ranks, and
78 horses.

In addition, Captain H. B. Farquhar had taken a small
advance party some days earlier.

On the whole the Civil Service Rifles weie not favourably
impressed with Havre where the battalion disembarked at
about 9.0 a.m. on the 18th of March, the chief disappointment,
perhaps, being that there were little or no signs of the Great
War. No welcoming crowds of pretty French girls were there
to meet them, and almost unnoticed they marched through the
town and up the hill which led to the camp above Harfleur.
Here the troops, perspiring after the steep climb, in what they
thought was full marching order, learnt that there were many
more things for the unfortunate Infantry soldier to carry in
France. Winter clothing was issued, and although it was very
welcome on that bitterly cold afternoon, the weight of it made
everyone look forward with more than usual keenness to the
coming of Spring.

A bitterly cold night was spent in the tents, and at 3.0 p.m.
on the following day, the Battalion made its first acquaintance
with the troop trains of the B. E. F.—the men's compartments
of which bore the now familiar legend :—

Chevaux (en long)	-	8
Hommes	- -	37–40

Lieutenant A. Roberts and fifty-nine other ranks had to be
left behind as a first reinforcement—an arrangement made by
a thoughtful G. H. Q. to ensure that the whole of the Civil
Service Rifles should not be wiped out in their first battle.

After a most wearisome journey, lasting twenty-four hours,
the Battalion detrained at the little station of Berguette.

The march from Berguette to the billets in the village of
Cauchy a la Tour was an ordeal never to be forgotten by those
who suffered it. Fifteen miles on pavè roads, in full marching
order with a blanket in addition, tested to the uttermost men
who were already fatigued by the extreme discomfort of the
cattle train. But Cauchy was reached, without loss, at midnight, and to the consternation of all ranks, no trace could be
found of the billeting party or of the billets. This was indeed
a bitter blow to the exhausted troops, who settled down in the
main street, and began to wonder whether they had to march
still further, for there were no signs of life in Cauchy. The
situation was eventually saved by waking up M. le Maire, on
whom, it is said, Lieutenant Carlisle so successfully tried his
French that billets were found after the Battalion had been
waiting in the road for two hours. Some say the straw was
clean, others say it was otherwise, but it mattered little that

night. Any place was good enough, provided the troops could be left to sleep in peace.

It is believed that after the billeting party had left Havre, the destination of the 47th Division was changed, and the Civil Service Rifles were already at St. Omer before any message reached the billeting party, who did not arrive at Cauchy until about twenty-four hours after the Battalion was billeted.

The Battalion trained, somewhat impatiently, for three whole weeks at Cauchy a la Tour. The troops, it must be admitted, were bored with it, as would appear from the following description in a letter home :—

"The village is in the middle of a flat colliery district. The northern horizon is filled with great hills of slag from the mines—like Egyptian pyramids, whence comes an eternal shrill whistle. The well in the market square from which we draw our water is 100 feet deep, and it is difficult to get near the bucket for the crush of civilians and khaki. The women are mostly fat and sans corsets. They sell French papers and herald their approach with a toot of a horn. Mud carts are drawn by dogs. Horses can be seen working treadmills. The constant stream of motor lorries bringing food stores to the front passes along the highway. We hear the distant boom of big guns—a famous part of the firing line is 18 miles away. But the preponderant thought with us all is ' Where is this bloody war ? ' "

On the 22nd of March, the Battalion was inspected by Field-Marshal Sir John French, accompanied by General Sir Douglas Haig and General Sir Chas. Munro. The Commander-in-Chief's remark " The men are splendid " was afterwards reproduced in large type on the Civil Service Recruiting Posters in London underneath a photograph of Sergeant G. L. Eager, looking very much at home in a trench.

The first Civil Service Rifles Sports Meeting in France took place in a small rough field in Cauchy a la Tour, on the afternoon of the 28th March. The following account of it is taken from the Regimental Diary :—

"The events included 500 yards—winner, Private L. P. Winter, of ' D ' Company ; 250 yards (Sergeants)—Sergeant Rathbone (a dark horse) ' thrown in ' with 20 yards start ; 250 yards (officers)—Captain and Adjutant F. W. Parish 1st, Captain W. F. K. Newson 2nd ; Second Lieutenant Benké 3rd. Inter-Company tug-of-war—' A ' Company beat ' B ' Company on the third pull. Officers three-legged race—Second Lieutenants Benké and Stevens easy winners. Lieutenants Chalmers and Carlisle next. Inter-Company team race (1 officer, 20 other ranks)—' B ' Company 1st, ' D ' Company 2nd. Inspection of Officers' chargers and also of transport horses for best turnout ; two races of 250 yards for ' visitors '—the small boys of the village who also participated in scrambles for small change. Obstacle race, where one obstacle proved too much for all

but six starters—Lance-Corporal Cocky Oliver 1st ; Lance-Corporal
H. Battersby 2nd ; Lance-Corporal W. J. Irving 3rd.   The Commanding Officer afterwards distributed prizes to the winners.
Much amusement caused by their nature.   We had broken away
from the salad bowl, tea spoon and tobacco cabinets, etc. and
substituted packets of chocolate, tinned fruit, tins of sardines,
box of candles (though Cauchy is illuminated throughout by
electricity), and, for officers, tins of dubbin and bully beef tin
openers."

It may, perhaps, be remarked that all the winners at this
Sports Meeting mentioned in the Regimental Diary have
survived the war—with the sad exception of Lieutenant R.
Chalmers.

The only other incident of note during the training at Cauchy
was the visit to the Division of the Bishop of London, who,
according to the Regimental Diary, was touring the back areas.
His Lordship preached to the 140th Brigade on the 29th of
March, but the only comment that can be found is that " We
had to wear our heavy packs and were kept waiting for some
time."

On the last day at Cauchy, the 6th of April, news was received
of the first death in the Battalion on active service.   Private W. E.
Little of " D " Company, who had left the Battalion on the 4th,
suffering from cerebro spinal meningitis, having died in hospital
at St. Omer.   Thus the 17th of March men had already lost one
man before they reached the firing line.

CHAPTER II

On the 7th of April the Battalion left for Bethune and the forward area. The villagers gave the men a very hearty send-off, for the Civil Service Rifles had thoroughly captured the hearts of all at Cauchy, who had done their best to fête their heroes overnight.

After sleepy Cauchy, Bethune was voted top hole. The shops in the old town were quite Parisian, and every one indulged in dainty but unsatisfying gâteaux and steaming bowls of hot chocolate. For the *bon viveurs* there were excellent dinners in the ancient Hotel du Nord ; for the artistic the delicate traceries in the fine old church.

Bethune already showed some scars of the war, and the building in which the Battalion was housed, Le College des Jeunes Filles, had lost most of its windows, but otherwise it made a comfortable billet. Here Lieutenant A. Roberts arrived with thirty other ranks from the Base—evidently O.C. Reinforcements thought it was high time the Civil Service Rifles suffered some casualties. On the following day the Civil Service Rifles made its first acquaintance with the trenches. " A " and " B " Companies were detailed for working parties in support trenches, while to " D " Company fell the honour of being the first Civil Service Rifle Company to go into the front line. It was the good fortune of the Battalion to be initiated in the mysteries of trench warfare by the 4th (Guards) Brigade, and the arrangement was that each Company should go in for twenty-four hours " under instruction " before the battalion held a section of the line alone. " D " Company accordingly joined the 2nd Coldstream and survived their twenty-four hours without loss, but the first battle casualties in the Battalion were suffered by " B " Company, who, with " A " Company, were returning from their working party at Cuinchy, when Privates W. Bartram and H. H. Russell were wounded by a rifle bullet, which passed through the thigh of one man and hit the calf of the other. It is said that the wounded men were deeply concerned on two accounts—they had seen no Germans either alive or dead, and it was pay day and they had not drawn their pay !

There is no doubt that this first visit to the front line was productive of a sense of disappointment. War had, till then, been regarded as a glorious thing, a thing of bugles and flashing bayonets, of courage in hand-to-hand encounters, and above all, of excitement. But this first experience showed it to be a thing of drab monotony, of dull routine, of the avoidance of being killed, of an invisible enemy. And so the letters of these days, which were to have been of enthralling interest, were, instead, just catalogues of the minor duties and details of trench life. Among them, however, is one that cannot but prove of subtle humour to the infantryman of later years—1916 and onwards. An extract is here reproduced.

" You should see the R.E. out in front mending the barbed wire— and when a flare goes up, dropping instantly and looking like sand- bags, to be up and working like mad as soon as darkness ensues again—cool beggars they are—odd bullets flying all the time."

On the other hand, R. W. Softly's account of the first journey up to the line would not make the soldier of 1918 envy the man of 1915 :—

" ' B ' Company had come provided with all kinds of supplies— firewood in abundance—and tied on to most of the packs was a ' grand pain.' Though man may live on bread alone I defy him to live solely on Army biscuit. We certainly thought we had reached the limit as beasts of burden, but as we waited at the first communication trench, some Guardsmen passed by. Instead of our modest bundles of firewood, they carried enormous tree branches. Half of them possessed frying pans or braziers, and many of them carried a pair of rubber trench boots so hung round the neck that it looked as if they were carrying on their shoulders a limp individual whose head and trunk were missing. When I add that they also carried picks and shovels, you will understand if we were inclined to regard them as a race of supermen as they filed past us in the setting sun."

An important event was the taking-over by the whole Bat- talion, on the 13th of April, of a sector of the line—the real thing at last ! Here, indeed, was an event to set the many scribes of the Battalion busy. Of all the experiences of the war, probably none made such a vivid and lasting impression on all ranks in the Regiment, and certainly none was more fully written up by the members as this first tour in the firing line of a Battalion of the Civil Service Rifles. In the light of after events in the war, it was a very quiet and peaceful tour, and probably much the same as the initial experience of many other Battalions, but it was none the less the realisation of all that these men had been training for since the outbreak of war, so it is small wonder that no detail was omitted, so far as the censorship regulations allowed, from the hundreds of descriptive letters

sent home at this time. Probably all of them described how
the Battalion paraded in Bethune (the names of places are
included here, though they were doubtless suitably disguised
in those letters home) in full marching order, wearing greatcoats, on the afternoon of April 13th, 1915, and marched via
the village of Beuvry to the La Bassée Canal, the latter part
of the march being by platoons at 100 yards distance. Here
was the old familiar " artillery formation " in real life at last !

Even the landmarks along the side of the Canal received
their share of attention, and mention is made of the two pontoon
bridges, between which at one point the stiff hind legs of a horse
stuck out of the water, of the broken telegraph wires along the
Canal bank, and of the ruined buildings just short of Windy
Corner, where the mile-long, narrow, winding, brick-paved
communication trenches were entered. These had homely
names—" Cheyne Walk," " Battersea Road," " City Road,"
and the dug-outs had such names as " St. Albans Villa," " Le
Petit Riche," " Funland," and so on.

Of the many trying journeys of an infantry battalion, none
is worse than the " hesitation march " along a communication
trench. The floor of the trench is uneven and is full of holes,
there are numerous obstructions across the top, causing the
weary soldier to go down almost on all fours ; there are numerous
momentary halts for no apparent reason, and whenever the
party does seem to get moving, sure enough the cry will come
along, " lost touch in rear." A few muttered curses as the
troops sink down on the bottom of the trench to await the
word " all up in rear " when another start is made. It is now
found that they have lost touch in front, and the leading men
are going " all out " to catch up.

The communication trench leading to the front line at Givenchy
was apparently no exception to the rule, as will be gathered
from the following account :

" It takes half an hour to trudge up to the firing line, and, if in
rear of the platoon, it is exceedingly difficult to keep in touch. No
matter how desperately you strive to catch up, the pack of the man
in front is always just on the point of disappearing round the corner.
Stray shots whizz past from time to time. . . ."

The perspiring troops, having negotiated the communication
trench, arrived at last in the front line at Givenchy, and the
Battalion relieved the 1st Herts Regiment in the sector known
officially as B1, but better known as the Duck's Bill.

The frontage held was about 400 yards, and the front line
was about half a mile in front of Battalion Headquarters and
the Battalion Reserve.

Two Companies, " B " and " D," occupied the front line,

and "A" and "C" were in reserve in the ruined houses of Givenchy on both sides of the canal. The village post office was used as Battalion Headquarters with the Signal Station in the cellar.

The tour was a distinctly peaceful and uneventful one, which later on would scarcely have been mentioned in a letter home, but the regimental diary describes it in detail and tells how, after a quiet day, things livened up at night and in the reserve billets "a curious sound is heard every few seconds—smack, smack, as bullets spend themselves on the walls around. These are probably fired by the Germans at our fellows in the trenches, and, going high, hit the houses at a height of perhaps ten feet from the ground. Others, however, are probably fired from fixed rifles at gaps where we are supposed to pass frequently— along the bridge and other places, and a lucky shot might catch one of us. At nine o'clock we are startled by a tremendous explosion. It is one of our big guns, nicknamed ' Little Willie,' on a railway mounting. It moves along the railway by the canal, and after firing four or five rounds it wisely goes home."

The Companies changed round on the second day, and in the evening of the third day the Battalion was relieved by the 1st Herts Regiment, and returned to the college at Bethune. The troops now felt they were real soldiers, though doubtless some were surprised to find that they could spend three days in the line without seeing a German. The only unpleasant feature in an otherwise very satisfactory forty-eight hours in the line was the casualty just before the relief to Private R. Pulman, of "D" Company, who was badly wounded in the head by a bullet. Private Pulman died in hospital in Bethune the following day, and his platoon attended the funeral.

The only other casualties were also in "D" Company— Sergeant G. F. Anderson and Private I. Spielman—both wounded.

The novelty of front line trenches had not yet worn off, and having had a not unpleasant taste of trench life, the troops were quite keen to go in again. So it is recorded that "We had heard a rumour that after doing our forty-eight hours in the trenches we were to return to Cauchy, so we are now pleased when we hear that we are to go again to the trenches to-day (the 19th of April)".

The second trip to the line was very much like the first one, but on the first morning the Battalion lost one who for many years had served with great distinction. Private A. E. Snell-grove, of "B" Company, who was killed outright by a bullet through the head, had been a crack shot in the Regiment as long ago as the Volunteer days. Although he had left the Regiment some time before the war, he was one of the first men

CIVIL SERVICE RIFLES 68

to rejoin in August, 1914. A quiet, modest and unassuming fellow, Private Snellgrove had many friends in the Regiment, to whom his death came as a great shock. He was buried in the Guards' Cemetery at Givenchy.

The Battalion was holding a section of the line immediately north of the previous sector, and the area now held included what was known as the " Keep " at Givenchy. This was an old farm building with a courtyard in which the Guards had made a flower bed, which they called St. James's Park. Here were regimental badges of various Guards Regiments worked in box or privet hedging. Not to be outdone, the Civil Service Rifles planted their crest in privet hedging alongside the others.

Two days in this sector, one day's respite in billets at Le Preol, and then two more days in the former sector B1, brought to a close the first experience of the 140th Infantry Brigade in holding the front line, for on the 24th of April the Brigade was relieved and the Civil Service Rifles marched via Beuvry, Bethune and Chocques to rest billets at the village of La Beuvrière—a village a little larger than Cauchy and a little more pleasantly situated.

The village lay between two well-wooded uplands. Companies were billeted in small farms by the side of main roads and the men slept warmly on straw of suspicious character. As often as not there was a pigsty next door. Battalion Headquarters was in a house in the square next the grey old monastery —then used as a hospital. The parade ground was down the hill over the railway, bounded on one side by a swift-flowing brook good for a dip after a game of football. A favourite morning's training was to steer a way by compass through the thick undergrowth of a wood, six square miles in area, to the east of the village.

The troops now felt quite familiar with the trenches, and were glad to have an opportunity of talking over their experiences in the comparative comfort of the estaminets. As there had been no further casualties there was a fairly cheerful atmosphere to greet the remainder of the first reinforcement— twenty-eight N.C.O.'s and men who joined from Havre on the 27th of April. The Battalion had, however, lost a good many men through sickness—an outbreak of measles being the chief cause. Already two officers, Lieutenants Radice and Benké, had returned to England through sickness, and, in addition, 2nd Lieutenant F. J. Smith, " A " Company, was so badly injured in a football match at La Beuvrière on the 2nd of May against the Post Office Rifles, that he had to return to England. The loss of Frank Smith was keenly felt in the Battalion, of which he had been a member since 1906. As a sergeant in " B " Company he was very popular, both with his brother N.C.O.'s and with the men.   He was a thorough sportsman in every way, and his appointment to a commission in the Regiment only about a month before was very popular with all ranks.

It was while at La Beuvriére that the Battalion received for each Company a travelling kitchen.   Hitherto cooking had been done in the camp kettle, or " dixie," and there had been very little variety in the meals.   After a long march, there was always a tedious waiting for meals, but the " Company Cooker " was to revolutionise that, for dinners could be cooked on the march—and what is more, they were.   So the infantryman salutes the inventor of the " Company Cooker."

After nearly a fortnight's rest the Division went back to war, and the Civil Service Rifles, pausing for one night in very dirty reserve billets at the village of Gorre, found themselves on the 9th of May on the fringe, as it were, of the battle of Festubert, where they were holding the intermediate line of breastworks, behind the 6th London Regiment.

Although Festubert was not a battle of such magnitude as the operations of 1916 and later, it was an event of no small importance at the time.   The first attack was delivered on the 9th of May with the object, ultimately, of gaining the Aubers Ridge—which dominates Lille and La Bassée.   The battle went on intermittently for some days and in the end was not successful.

But although the Battalion held a kind of " watching brief " during this battle, recollections of Festubert are not by any means pleasant.   The ground was so marshy that it was impossible to dig trenches, and the line hereabouts was held by a series of sandbagged barricades, approached by two roads (Willow Road and Yellow Road) devoid of any kind of cover.   Having negotiated these roads, the men of the front line of barricades were little, if any, better off than those in support at the so-called Welsh Chapel, while the Reserve Company " billets " between Welsh Chapel and Le Plantin could not be called healthy.

It was at Festubert that the Battalion first became acquainted with the realities of war, and although the men were employed practically throughout in holding the line, burying the dead, and on working and carrying parties, with a little patrol work thrown in, there were many gallant deeds done, and at the same time many gallant fellows were lost.

The most vivid impression of Festubert is associated with the enormous number of dead, who were not only lying about the ground, but in some places actually formed the barricades.   It was often necessary for the members of burying parties to wear the primitive gas masks, and it was here that " Paddy " Brett, the C.S.M. of " D " Company, a man in his forty-third year, smoked for the first time in his life.

The actual number of dead buried by the Civil Service Rifles in this area is not known, but a very reasonable estimate puts it at 350 in three days.

The survivors of " B " Company, in particular, have most unpleasant recollections of the night when they had to crawl over piles of corpses in order to go forward to occupy an advanced position.

Among other incidents of Festubert, mention should be made of the scouting and patrolling done almost nightly by 2nd Lieutenants W. E. Ind and F. F. Trembath, Sergeant B. K. Ware, Lance-Corporal G. C. G. Andrews, and Privates R. W. Kelley and T. Taylor. The work of patrolling No Man's Land was not at this time so simple and commonplace as it became later on, and the patrolling done by these men is mentioned specially, not because it was the first time it had been done in the Battalion, but because more than at any other time it was done in earnest, and was productive of really useful information.

But although the first day of the battle was uneventful so far as the Civil Service Rifles were concerned, it must not be imagined that no fighting at all was done at Festubert. For it was here that the first decorations for gallantry in the field were awarded to men of the Battalion. On the night of the 25th of May, eight bombers were sent to the assistance of the Post Office Rifles in an attempt to clear a trench. After a stubborn fight the position was captured, but of the eight bombers only four returned alive, and two of these were wounded. The excellent work of these four was recognised by the award to each of them of the D.C.M. These were thus the first members of the Regiment to receive decorations in this war :—

Private W. H. Brantom, " B " Co.   Private S. Lawrence, " C " Co.
Private H. Harris, " A " Co.   Private S. W. Mills, " A " Co.

The four who were killed were Privates W. S. Curtis, " B " Company ; A. J. F. Tracey, " D " Company ; P. A. L. Madell, " D " Company ; and A. N. Sharp, " C " Company.

On the same night Lieutenant R. Chalmers, known affectionately as " Cissie," was in charge of a working party of " B " Company digging in No Man's Land, when he had occasion to take out a small patrol. He came across a party of bombers of the Post Office Rifles who were short of bayonet men. Without a moment's hesitation, Lieutenant Chalmers picked up a rifle and bayonet from a man who had become a casualty, and joining the bombers, rallied them on the parapet to resist an enemy " rush." He was soon in the thick of the fight and, while gallantly leading this party of strangers, he received two bullet wounds which afterwards proved fatal. Like the unselfish fellow he had always been, he ordered the stretcher-

E

bearers to attend to the other wounded first. When he himself was afterwards carried back, he died in hospital at the village of Chocques.

It is difficult indeed to do justice to Lieutenant Chalmers. He had only just joined the Regiment when war broke out, but from the first he proved himself a real enthusiast, thoroughly unselfish, and ever ready to volunteer for any work—however unpleasant. He became a great favourite with the N.C.O.'s and men who served under him, and his death was keenly felt by his many friends in the Regiment. He had already been commended by the Commanding Officer for good work in the front line on three occasions, and his behaviour at the time when he was mortally wounded was typical of one of the bravest fellows any Battalion could wish for.

The 25th of May was indeed a bad day for the Battalion for, in addition to Lieutenant Chalmers and the bombers before mentioned, many of the stalwarts were killed or wounded on that day. Captain A. E. Trembath,* O.C. " C " Company, who had served with great distinction in the South African War, was killed in helping one of his wounded officers (Lieutenant F. C. Olliff). It was an unfortunate affair for " C " Company, who also lost old friends in Lance-Sergeant J. Smith (killed) and Lieutenant A. C. Bull (wounded) at the same time. " C " Company having already lost more than their share of old stagers in this area could ill afford to lose any of these, and another who had had long service in the Company was Lance-Corporal Battersby—well known for his football and long distance running—who was so severely wounded on the 17th of May that he lost an eye.

The " C " Company losses by no means exhaust the Battalion's chapter of accidents, for " B " Company lost one of the finest men in the Battalion in Lance-Corporal G. S. Scarr, who died on the 26th of May in hospital at Chocques from wounds received on the previous night. Lance Corporal Scarr was well known throughout the Battalion for many years for his pure unselfishness and nobility of character. He was a man who always played for his side and not for himself.

It was at Chocques, too, that Lieutenant H. R. E. Clark, the Battalion Machine Gun Officer, died of wounds received on the 24th of May. He had joined the Battalion soon after the outbreak of war, and had quickly won the confidence and

---

* Captain Allen Edward Trembath, born 22nd October, 1879, joined 12th Middlesex before the Boer War, transferred to Middlesex Yeomanry, 1899. South Africa mentioned in despatches, D.C.M. ; later, wounded and invalided. Granted commission Middlesex Yeomanry ; returned to South Africa till end of war. 1914 rejoined Civil Service Rifles, later taking a commission.

(*Photo by Hennigan, Watford*).

W. H. BRANTOM, D.C.M.
1st Batt.
Afterwards 2nd Lieutenant 2nd Batt.
Killed in Action at Souchez,
3rd July, 1916.

(*Photo by Coles, Watford*).

CAPT. ALLEN EDWARD
TREMBATH, D.C.M.
D.C.M., South Africa, 1900.
Commission Middlesex Yeomanry.
In 1914 rejoined Civil Service Rifles
and later took a Commission.
Killed in Action at Festubert,
25th May, 1915.

(*Copy by Pflitz*).

LIEUT. ROBERT CHALMERS.
Born April 13th, 1894;
Died 25th May, 1915, of wounds
received in Action at Festubert.

To face page 66.

respect of the men whom he led so well. The loss of Lieutenant Clark was a particularly sad blow for his father, Lieutenant and Quartermaster W. H. D. Clark, who for many years had been such an enthusiastic worker for the good of the Regiment. The hearts of all ranks went out to him in sincere sympathy in his very sad bereavement.

Amid so many bitter memories it is good to have one incident of an amusing nature, and the story of the capture by " B " Company, assisted by a platoon of " D " Company, of what became known afterwards as " Civil Service Trench," affords the one note of comic relief in the dismal story of Festubert. The gallant charge was led at dead of night by Major H. V. Warrender (who was then commanding " B " Company), ably supported by the veteran Robb, who was in charge of the Company Officer's Mess. Robb, it is said, was armed with a Primus stove, but it is not known whether this was meant for a miniature flammen-werfer attack or whether it was to ensure a hot meal for his Company Commander on arrival at the objective! Any hopes of V.C.'s in the Company were doomed to disappointment, for the trench when reached was found to be deserted, save by the few corpses that had been left behind. So at last an operation was undertaken without a casualty, and shortly after this the merry (!) month of May came to an end, and the Battalion said good-bye to Festubert—the land of mud, blood and stench!

CHAPTER III

A "BON WAR"

THE inhabitants of the little mining village of Les Brebis displayed little or no surprise when they were called from their beds in the middle of the night to greet the Civil Service Rifles on their arrival from Sailly Labourse—another mining village where a peaceful week had been spent after Festubert.

The natives of Les Brebis were now quite accustomed to being awakened at all hours of the night to receive new lodgers, for their houses were the billets of the Battalion in reserve to the front line at Grenay and Maroc, near by.

The heat during the day of the 7th of June had been of the real midsummer variety, and it was little better at night, when the march from Sailly Labourse took place. It was not a long march, but the troops were very thankful when it ended, for they found their equipment very heavy on that hot June night.

Les Brebis had had a most extraordinary experience during the war. Here was a village only about two miles from the front line, practically untouched, and fully inhabited with civilians who still went about their daily round as in pre-war times. The mines were still being worked, and an excellent bathing place was found under the water tower of the electric light works.

The men were billeted for the first time in France in close billets, six men on an average sleeping on the small attic floors of the miners' cottages. The miners and their families were very friendly disposed towards the Civil Service Rifles to judge from the scribe who says :

" Mesdames were very good to us and cooked the delicacies we purchased in the town with the utmost care. There was a barrel of beer in almost every billet, and veal cutlets, cut thin and ' done to a turn,' with pommes de terre frites, egg salad and stewed fruit made a favourite meal. Indeed, a French housewife, whose mari was having a hard time in the Vosges on a couple of sous a day expressed her conviction in a burst of confidence that ' English soldat do no work and eat too much.' "

The early months of the summer of 1915 were passed very

pleasantly in this mining district without any event of importance.

The front line was well furnished with various home comforts taken from the almost deserted village of Maroc, the enemy was some distance away, there was little shelling and there were very few casualties. Indeed it was, after Festubert, very much in the nature of a picnic. No Man's Land was a field of waving corn, with scarlet poppies and blue cornflowers to complete the rural scene. New potatoes and other fresh vegetables, red currants and gooseberries could be picked in abundance from the gardens near the trenches, and there are men who claim to have slipped away from the line to a neighbouring estaminet " to have a quick one " between their turns of sentry duty in the line.

The chief enemy was the ferocious fly, which, according to one victim, " crawled under our clothes, down our backs, between our eyelids and into our mouths and ears. Over one dug-out a wit had inscribed Itch Den (Ich Dien) below the Prince of Wales's feathers, testifying to the fact that we were now not only doing our bit but being well bitten in the process."

More than one scribbler relieved the monotony of trench routine by recording this phase of the Great War in his diary :

" ' The chief fatigues,' according to Loxdale, ' were sand-bagging, water fetching and dug-out digging, and the game in connection with them all was to dodge them. This was generally effected by never being about when fatigues were going. Other methods which still worked occasionally were preoccupation with imaginary duties, profound slumber, or serious indisposition at the psychological moment."

A night fatigue was humorously described by Beatty as follows :

" To the uninitiated who have only witnessed the carrying of a plank along the King's highway, plank-carrying may appear, at first sight, a very humdrum occupation. But when two men endeavour to negotiate the twists and turns of a tortuous trench— some alliteration, what !—bearing on their shoulders a 12 ft. plank, the possibilities are endless.

" It was a beautiful summer night : the stars were starring in the heavens as is their wont : the poppies on the parapet were gaily popping and Ebo Smith and I were lying in the trench bottom wrapped in slumber, overcoats and waterproof sheets.

" Suddenly we were rudely awakened by the raucous voice of an N.C.O. exclaiming, ' Five men wanted for fatigue.' We told him ' Yes,' and went to sleep again. But it was no use. He kept on chanting in a dismal monotone :

" ' Five men from No. 2 are wanted for fatigue,' and we had perforce to rise and follow him. After wandering for some distance, we reached a pile of planks which we had to carry, and this is where the fun started.

" The diabolical malice of things inanimate is well known. The propensity for bread-and-butter to fall face downwards on the best Brussels carpet, and the elusive gambols of the wily collar stud are everyday occurrences ; but for absolutely fiendish cunning commend me to a 12 ft. plank.

" We had not gone more than one hundred yards along the trench before my rifle got between my legs and the piling-swivel caught in my puttee. I, naturally enough, leant the plank on the parapet and bent down to unfasten my leg. This was the opportunity for which the plank, having lulled us into a false sense of security by its apparent docility, was waiting. With diabolical malice it leapt from the parapet and smote me on the back of the head. As there were no stretcher-bearers in the neighbourhood I quickly recovered, and we proceeded on our pilgrimage.

" Ere long we arrived at an exceedingly sharp turn, the projecting piece being made of sandbags. We were just thinking of sitting down to discuss the matter when one of the men in the traverse came to our aid. Poor lad ! He didn't know that plank.

" ' We'll shove it over the top,' " quoth he ! and, seizing one end, leapt lightly to the top of the pile of sandbags ere we could warn him.

" His retribution was swift. The pile of sandbags collapsed, our good Samaritan was hurled through the air, the plank swung round and hit him on the head, while the avalanche of sandbags buried Ebo Smith. I dug Ebo out, We thanked our friend, hoped we hadn't upset him, and left him seated and thinking deeply amidst the debris of this ruined traverse.

" Whether the plank had satiated its lust for blood or whether it was again a case of the triumph of mind over matter, I know not, but it gave us no more trouble, and we returned to our slumber glowing with self-satisfaction at the thought of work well done."

These long spells of trench life gave splendid opportunities for letter writing, and P. J. Tickle, in one of his letters, tells how the Battalion thus early had experience of the guide who got lost—a bitter experience which became all too common later on.

" After three days at Le Philosophe we wended our weary way to the beginning of the small French communication trench, where we picked up a guide from the battalion we were relieving. Did I say ' Guide.' By all the gods man ever swore by, but he was *no* guide. Before reaching the support line there is only one turning—newly cut by the British and perhaps the narrowest I have ever cursed about. This guide managed to get us a mile down it before discovering his mistake. We didn't half laugh. It's an hour's hard pushing to achieve such a distance through such a trench in full marching order. Not satisfied with having lost his way, he endeavoured to make up for lost time, and finished the course an easy first with the rest of us breathless and knocked, straggling at wide intervals. . . ."

So the summer wore on, the war being so quiet that it was not uncommon for the Battalion to remain sixteen days in the front line without relief. One tour was very much like another, and the following by Irving is an excellent description of a typical relief and march to billets.

"24th July, 1915.

"Hurrah! Hurrah!! Hurray!!! I'm clean! clean! clean! Also lice free! Oh, it is simply great!

"After a second stay of 16 days we left the firing line on the night of the 22nd in the usual downpour. These affairs are rather impressive in a way. Let us try to give you an idea.

"First of all, there's the packing up and the cleaning of the trench and dug-out for the new-comers. Then the long wait, each man in his firing position, for the relief. Then the crushing past the full laden crowds in the narrow trench.

"Then the long winding, never ending, communication trench with its slippery floor, treacherous holes and deep muttered oaths in the caressing whisper of the drizzle and the soft darkness. Till you emerge into the quiet deserted streets of the cemetery-like town, cross the main road, enter the twisted iron gates and pass up the dark avenue of trees—a long, black line of dirty, merry warriors. Now you're within the shadow of the ruined church, fit place for poets to weep. There it is outlined against the flying clouds, its jagged grey tower, its dead clock always pointing at ten to two— and the huge gaping black wounds in its sides. As you pass, the edifice is lit up grotesquely and ghostlike by the pale light of a distant trench flare, and you catch a fleeting glimpse of the ruined interior where now the rude winds roar over the heaps of debris and round the tottering pillars and broken altar making sport of all these sacred things long held dear by so many—the whole an eloquent and terrifying protest against the God-defying Hun!

"Then you go out into the wind-swept plain, following the line of broken telegraph poles, dodging stray wires and shell holes—the long, dark, single file—trudging, silent and sodden. Till at last you reach the warm shadows of the village with its odd lights veiled, and at the far end our farm billet with its clean straw and a dry and dreamless slumber.

"That was the night before last.

"Yesterday was a good day's work. I cleaned up everything I had, equipment and kit, and with wild glee flung myself into washing all my underclothes, socks and handkerchiefs, and drying them, for it was a washing day to gladden Mother's heart. And to crown all, a starko behind the yellow stack—free, unfettered and with an unlimited supply of water. One of God's most wonderful creations. How we worshipped it body and soul. Oh, the glory of it! To be clean again is great! Great!!!! We sang and danced and ran and jumped and shouted and flung our glad laughter to the blue skies, and were thankful withal. Oh, Earth and Sky, and Wind and Trees, and Green Grass and Strength of Man, Glory!"

"W. J. IRVING."

* * * * * *

During the whole of this time the French were making a desperate struggle in the neighbourhood of Souchez and the Lorette Heights—and occasional glimpses of this area were to be had, though it was mostly enveloped in a thick cloud of smoke from the bursting shells. The efforts of the French, however, may have diverted the attention of the Boche, for he was certainly very kind to the neighbourhood of Grenay and Maroc during this pleasant summer weather. In fact, he seems to have been more severe on the villages of Le Philosophe and Mazingarbe (where the Battalion was sometimes billeted when in reserve) than he was on the front line. At Le Philosophe on one occasion a shell hit Battalion Headquarters, wounding a number of Headquarters Company, including all the regimental police.

The event of the summer was the granting of leave to England to a small party of the Battalion. The news was first received on the 4th of July at Mazingarbe, and the C.O. (Colonel Renny), the R.S.M. (Sergeant-Major A. Toomey) and Sergeant F. S. Thurston were the first in the Regiment to enjoy the most coveted privilege of the British soldier in France. Thereafter the allotment of leave to the Battalion was at the rate of two officers and four other ranks per week, though this rate was not kept up for very long.

Colonel Renny, it should be mentioned, did not return from leave, as he was detained in hospital in England. As Commanding Officer, he was very popular with all ranks, and for his age his energy was marvellous. The Battalion was very sorry to lose its " little Indian Colonel," as he was called. The men felt they would miss him most in the front line, where it was a very familiar sight to see him wandering round, indifferent to danger or discomfort, but determined to see things for himself. Colonel Renny was succeeded by Major H. V. Warrender, who had hitherto commanded " B " Company. Major Warrender was gazetted Lieutenant-Colonel in August, and remained in command until the end of 1916. He thus holds the distinction of having commanded the Battalion in war for a longer period than any other commanding officer.

Trench life in the Grenay lines got very monotonous by July and the popular grouse in the Battalion hereabouts referred to the absence of the much-advertised Kitchener's Army. A notice chalked on a billet door in Quality Street read :

> " Lost, stolen or strayed,
> Kitchener's Army.
> Last seen in England in early spring."

and the ditty often sung about this time which ended

> " If Kitchener's Army don't come out very soon
> 'Twill be all up with this 'ere blasted platoon,"

BREVET COL. A. M. RENNY, Ret. Ind. Army.
Commanded 1st Battalion, November, 1914—July, 1915.

To face page 72.

gives evidence of the general feeling of boredom which began to threaten the Battalion.

However, a portion at least of Kitchener's Army appeared in due course in this area, and during the last two days spent in trenches to the right of the Double Crassier marked on the map as W–2, the Battalion shepherded a kilted regiment on its trial trip in the trenches. They were Scotch right enough (15th Division), both in speech and character, and one of them, after breakfast on the first day, asked in all seriousness what time the " char-rge " was. He considered there ought to be at least one every day. Another canny one, suspecting the " bona-fides " of his tutor, when asked what port he had embarked from, replied " Ah'll no tell 'e." Yet another youthful Jock when told to go on sentry immediately climbed out in front and began to march up and down at the slope.

Their commissariat went wrong and they got no food for twenty-four hours. Their hosts saw to it that they had enough to eat, and before dawn had picked sufficient mushrooms for the combined messes, and by dinner enough young new potatoes, carrots, red currants and gooseberries for a good meal.

After a few days in trenches at Le Philosophe, the 47th Division moved into Corps Reserve, the Civil Service Rifles occupying their old billets at La Beuvrière early in August.

The Battalion now lost a very old friend in Lieutenant and Quartermaster W. H. D. Clark, who was ordered to England to take up an appointment in the Ministry of Munitions. Lieutenant Clark had joined the Civil Service Rifles as a private in 1888, and had served continuously since that time, rising through the various ranks of N.C.O. to R.Q.M.S. until he was appointed Quartermaster in 1910. Mr. Clark had been at all times a most enthusiastic worker for the Regiment, and his energy knew no bounds. He took away with him the most cordial good wishes of all ranks. Another old friend in R.S.M. A. Toomey, a Scots Guardsman who for many years had been on the permanent staff of the Battalion, succeeded to the appointment of Quartermaster, and C.S.M. Jolliffe of " C " Company acted as R.S.M. Bernard Jolliffe was undoubtedly one of the most popular members of the Regiment, and it was distinctly un-fortunate that ill-health compelled him to return to England a few months after taking up his new duties.

The time at La Beuvrière was spent in Sports (Brigade and Divisional), Football and Cricket, Inspections and Training.

The Battalion distinguished itself by easily defeating both the 6th London Field Ambulance and the Post Office Rifles at cricket and the 4th London Field Ambulance at football. As these teams had previously done well, it was considered a fine performance on the part of the Civil Service Rifles to beat them

all. G. Wright, H. E. R. Warton and J. H. Hunt of " D "
Company shone as batsmen, and Wright and Second Lieutenant
Stevens were the most successful bowlers.   Lance-Corporal C.
Palser of " C " Company won the quarter mile at the Brigade
Sports, and Corporal Williams of the Transport Section was
second in the High Jump at the Divisional Sports, where Private
W. H. Domoney, an " A " Company bomber, won the open
competition for bomb throwing.

It was not all Sports and Pastimes at La Beuvrière, however,
and soon the numerous parades and inspections began to pall
even as trench life had done.   The now historic Brigade Order
ordaining that in future the brass tabs on the equipment and
the metal parts of entrenching tool handles were to be polished
caused one of the Regimental scribes to break into verse, and
his effort was a popular item at Company and Regimental
Concerts.   It was described as the turn of the evening at a
Regimental Concert held some months later, and attended by
the offending Brigadier himself and the Commanding Officer.

CHAPTER IV

LOOS AND THE SPINNEY

A RETURN was made to the trenches at Maroc on the 1st September, when it was found that the war had livened up considerably during the three weeks' absence at La Beuvriére. The aerial torpedo made its first appearance to the Battalion, and to judge from the following letter home from a member of " B " Company, caused some consternation :—

" When we first took these trenches over from the French there was hardly a shell or a bullet all day. Now Hell is let loose. The very first morning we were introduced to a novelty in the shape of a gigantic bomb. The trench trembled and the air rushing into our dug-outs almost blew us off our seats. We rushed out to see what damage had been done, and could hardly believe our eyes when we found that the bomb had exploded about 300 yards in front of the trench. The next one burst not 40 yards away, and after the blinding flash and the crash of the explosion I felt nothing. The explosion is apparently upward rather than outward. It is thought that the offending mortar works on a pair of rails and is whisked back by the force of the recoil into the side of the slag heap. Smoke rises when the bomb is fired, but a heavy shelling at this spot failed to silence it. Now an Artillery Observation Officer watches the spot all day, and immediately the smoke is observed his battery fires and tries to catch the mortar before it gets back under cover."

*　　*　　*　　*　　*

Preparations for the big attack at Loos now overshadowed everything else, and the Battalion was out every night on working or carrying parties—such light jobs as carrying gas cylinders, digging assembly trenches and bridging trenches. All who took part in them are agreed that these gas cylinder fatigues were the most strenuous they ever had to do. On the first night there were two men to each cylinder. The cylinder weighed 180 lbs., and the men in addition carried their rifles and 100 rounds of ammunition in bandoliers. The numerous turns in the trenches were almost impassable obstacles, and to realise the difficulty of lifting the cylinders round the corners one must have done the deed. Arrived at last at the front line, the cylinder had to be lifted up high and a sort of juggling feat indulged in to get it into the correct position desired by the critical Royal Engineer.

Fatigues generally in these days were much more difficult than at any other time of the war. Light railways had not yet been developed, and it was not realised at this time how great a handicap it was for a man to have two bandoliers of ammunition swinging round his neck while he worked.

Apart from the working parties, a happy time was spent at the little village of Houchin, where there was much cricket and feasting and very little drill, and it was here that the Battalion first had the use of motor buses in France.

When the battle eventually took place on the 25th September, the Civil Service Rifles, as at Festubert, held a watching brief, being in Brigade Reserve to the 6th and 7th Battalions, and it was thought that this was the origin of the title of "God's Own."

To the Civil Service Rifles the battle of Loos was chiefly a spectacle, since, with the exception of two platoons of " B " Company, the whole Battalion looked on from the reserve trenches. The fate of those two platoons, however, brought home to their friends the realities of battle.

Soon after the attack started, No. 6 Platoon went forward over the top as a bomb-carrying party. Starting out twenty-five strong the party soon suffered heavy losses, and only three men of the party survived unhurt. No. 8 Platoon went to the rescue, and although their fate was much better, they, too, had their losses.

The killed included the ever-popular Lance-Corporal Tommy Dodge, a great personality both in the Civil Service Rifles and in the Civil Service Rugby Football Club.

Of the survivors, mention must be made of Corporal F. H. Chinn, who had been sent with five men to establish a bomb store in the second German trench. As the five became casualties, he made three journeys up the side of the Double Crassier alone, carrying each time as many bombs as he could collect.

*   *   *   *   *

After Loos there was a short rest at Verquin and Nœux-les Mines, where, on the 8th October, the Battalion lost the valuable services of Captain H. H. Kemble, who became second in command of the 23rd Battalion. As officer in command of " D " Company, Captain Kemble had won the admiration and respect of all ranks who served with him, and who were genuinely sorry to lose him.

The winter campaign of 1915-1916 now set in in earnest, and from this time onwards there was a long struggle against the rain, mud, and trenches that were continually falling in.

A fleeting visit was paid to the neighbourhood of Hulluch, where the Battalion was in reserve during the struggle on the 13th October, and narrowly escaped the fate which befel a Battalion of the Black Watch who went down in attempting the impossible feat of cutting their way, under very heavy machine-gun and artillery fire, through enemy wire of incredible thickness.

On the 28th October, "A" and "C" Companies had the honour of representing the Battalion at an inspection by His Majesty the King in a field near the village of Haillicourt.

Soon after their return the weather went from bad to worse. Everywhere men were huddled on the firestep with just a ground-sheet rigged over a couple of rifles placed across the trench—the "shelter" thus formed carefully collecting and depositing the rain-water down the neck of the passer by! On every ration fatigue to the "lone tree" you floundered up to the knees in mud and water. Private Beatty, of "A" Company, soothed his feelings one night on slipping head first into a slimy shell-hole with the following impromptu :—

> " Mis-ry unspeakable,
> Horrible, shriekable,
> Groundsheets unleakable,
> I don't think.
> Rain never ending,
> On us descending,
> Simply heartrending.
> Gawd——! "

when he fell backwards into another shell-hole, and the rest is unprintable.

The effect of the incessant rain and water-logged trenches began to tell on the spirits of all ranks. The days of hot meals in trenches had not then arrived. Sheepskin coats, leather jerkins and woollen gloves had not, at any rate, been issued to the Civil Service Rifles, while gum boots, though sometimes heard of, were seldom, if ever, seen. On many occasions, too, the only implements available for the work of baling out the water and thin mud from the trench bottom were picks and shovels !

It is characteristic of the spirit of the troops that there are so many good stories told of this period of discomfort. Although it was found that the working parties increased as the strength of the Battalion decreased, it was also found that the rum ration increased, and one man of "A" Company benefited so much by the extra ration that when his next turn for sentry duty came, he faced the wrong way on the fire step and called the attention of his platoon sergeant to a wood, which he said he could swear was not in front of him during his previous turn of sentry duty !

Another story is told of the same man, who was a Scotsman, during another of his turns of sentry duty. His platoon commander suspected him of being asleep, and brought his sergeant along to confirm or allay his suspicions. The man was resting his head on the parapet and apparently gazing straight to his front. The platoon sergeant said he felt sure the man was awake, but suggested to his officer that he might test him with a franc. The officer thereupon slipped a franc note on to the parapet in front of the sentry's face. Without taking his eyes off his " front," the sentry promptly opened his mouth and took the bait. " The franc is yours," said Lieutenant Bates, whose doubts as to the alertness of his sentry were now dispersed.

By way of a diversion, the Battalion was inspected during one of the short rests in support trenches, by a civic dignitary from London, accompanied by his Press photographer. Of all the discomforts of life in France few, if any, were more irksome to the British soldier than being visited by a civilian, looking clean, and fat, and comfortable, who would return home and have it duly advertised in the Press that he had just been to the front to see things for himself.

It will always be a mystery to the troops why so many civilians were allowed to come on these " Cook's tours " to France at the nation's expense, and if the visitors had only thought for a moment what effect their " patronage " had on the weary soldier, who generally had to give up a few hours of his well earned rest for an extra parade, there would not perhaps have been so many photographs in the Press of " Mr. —— wearing his steel helmet and box respirator while visiting the troops in France." The troops would not have minded so much if only the distinguished civilian had included a visit to the front line in his " tour of the trenches " !

In addition to the physical strain due to the continuous exposure to atrocious weather, Companies in turn occupying the " Spinney " trenches towards the end of the period had their nerves sorely tried by the eccentricities of enfilade fire. Shells burst against the inside of the parapet, and there were some parts of the line in this very narrow salient which appeared to be exposed to fire from the rear as well as other directions !

There were as many as thirty casualties a day—a high average for a trench tour. At one place in front of a steep quarry— subsequently evacuated during bombardments—men were constantly employed in filling and placing sandbags on the parapet as fast as they were knocked down.

The communication trenches were impassable and consequently the wounded could not be taken down until night, when a perilous journey had to be made over the open country, the stretcher bearers picking their way between shell holes filled with water. There were no roads leading up to the line, the district seemed to be unusually difficult to explore, and parties of men were continually going astray.

The wastage in personnel due to the appalling weather and shelling had so mounted up, that when eventually relief came, the Battalion marched, or rather dragged itself out only about 300 strong.

The following extract from the diary of a bomber gives a characteristic description of the close of this extraordinarily uncomfortable period of the winter campaign of 1915-16.

" We were thankful, I can tell you, to make tracks at last for the reserve line, but it was raining hard and it damped our spirits to find our new trench waterlogged. We bombers had not been in our dug-out an hour before one earth wall collapsed and buried our equipment and belongings. We were too tired to grumble, but propping up the fallen corrugated iron roof to form a side, we slept soundly beneath the ruins. In the morning, in spite of the rain and liquid mud, we set to and made a dug-out with groundsheets and one or two pieces of corrugated. Our new abode was the envy of our comrades. It had even a covered in hall where we cleaned our boots before being permitted to enter. Then we won a brazier, collared some wet coke, charcoal and wood logs and kept up a good fire. I took off my boots every time I came in from a fatigue and dried my socks and puttees. We sat round the brazier at night, and by the light of the glowing and smoking logs—for candles we had none—told stories and sang songs and were some company. But our nerves were still strung, and when whizbangs came over our way we fell down on the floor in strategic positions. The mud was still awful, and everywhere the trench and ramshackle shanties were falling in.

" It happened, however, a fine frosty night on that 13th November, when we were relieved by the 1st Cameron Highlanders— as fine a regiment of Scotch troops as you could wish to see. The Highland accent was particularly soothing. We marched as far as Mazingarbe that night.

" Next morning was the day for Divisional Relief, and as the Battalion marched out of the village, other troops were marching in. It was a fine, dry, frosty morning, and official War Office cinema operators took pictures all along the route—we with our trench mud still on us, some wearing sleeping helmets in lieu of caps buried in fallen trenches, a be-draggled· and motley band, hardly able to put one foot before another—and the incoming troops marching on the other side of the road spotlessly clean and fit.

" As we neared the railhead at Noeux les Mines the Battalion found its old self and tried to sing with as much vigour as trench throats would allow :

' As we're marching down the Broadway side,
Doors and windows open wi—de :
We know our manners,
We spend our tanners,
We are respected wherever we may go,
We are the London Bhoys ! ' "

" It was fine to be in the train again, and to see cows once more browsing at peace in the fields.   We all fell in love with Lillers and soon forgot our troubles."

*   *   *   *   *   *

Memories of what was afterwards known as " the 1st Lillers " (for the Battalion visited Lillers again at the next Corps Reserve) are of the pleasantest.   The billets were good, there were plenty of sports and amusements, and there was an appreciable increase in the leave allotment to the Battalion.

CHAPTER V

THE last month of 1915 found the Civil Service Rifles in trenches in what was justifiably called a " hot corner." After the holiday at Lillers, the Battalion went to occupy the well-known Hairpin trench, near Loos.

Some months previously the general run of the German front trench had been along the crest of a ridge, the English line being parallel and about 100 yards below. An attempt to capture the crest had only partially succeeded, and about fifty yards of the German trench was occupied by English troops. A trench was dug from each end of this strip to the English front line, thus forming the Hairpin. On each side of the captured piece of trench a stretch of about 50 yards was left unoccupied by either side, but obstructed by the usual block guarded by bombers.

To connect up their front line again the Germans dug a trench in front of the captured piece.

It will readily be understood that this was not a healthy spot, and the advantage of holding the captured 50 yards of German trench was a very doubtful one, as the occupants came in for a very liberal bombardment.

But *the* tragedy of the Hairpin came on the night of the 20th December, when the Battalion was ordered to send all its bombers, together with some bayonet men from " B " Company, over the top on the right of the Hairpin to jump into the German trench and bomb along it, while a party from the 7th Battalion restored a barricade (in the German front line adjoining the afore-mentioned captured strip of 50 yards) which the Germans had rushed early that morning.

The attack was most gallantly led by the Battalion Bombing Officer, 2nd Lieutenant A. M. Thompson, an officer of the 14th Royal Fusiliers, attached to Civil Service Rifles, but from the outset there was not the slightest chance of success. However, 2nd Lieutenant Thompson and the N.C.O.'s and men with him went to their end unflinchingly, and though the enemy put down an impenetrable barrier of bombs, rifle grenades and machine-gun bullets, the tragic scheme went on until all officers and N.C.O.'s taking part had been put out of action.

F

There were many most valuable lives lost on that night unfortunately, as it turned out, to no purpose, for the Germans a few days later blew up the whole trench and a number of the 23rd London Regiment, who were holding it, went with it.

Although Second Lieutenant Thompson had only been with the Battalion a few months, he had speedily won the confidence and respect of all ranks, for at all times he set a fine example of courage and devotion to duty. He was buried the next evening in the right leg of the Hairpin.

Of Lance-Corporal L. H. Druett, who died a true hero's death in that disastrous enterprise, it is difficult indeed to speak sufficiently highly. His sterling qualities as a soldier, a companion, and a real white man, won for him the respect and admiration of the most careless.

Associated for a long time with Lance-Corporal Druett was Private A. B. Evans, otherwise "Taff" Evans, known to the bombers as "The Bird" (having a trick of putting his head to one side like a magpie), another of the stalwarts who lost his life in the struggle at the Hairpin while going to the assistance of another bomber ; and, among others, mention must be made of Lance-Corporal M. Roach, who was in charge of a large party of "B" Company bombers and bayonet men, and who was fatally wounded whilst working on one of the barricades, after doing splendid work that night, and of Private E. G. Crockett, who, although severely wounded in the stomach, walked unaided to the Dressing Station over 100 yards away, but it was impossible to save his life, and he died in hospital nearly a fortnight later. Both were great favourites in "B" Company, where they had been well known for their good sportsmanship and cheerfulness.

The bombers were naturally hit harder than other sections in this sad business, and another who could ill be spared was Private H. M. Nash, a modest and unassuming fellow, who had only recently become a bomber. It is said that he threw his bombs like a cricket ball some 45 yards, and, after his officers and N.C.O.'s had been hit, he performed many deeds of gallantry before he met his death.

Enough has been written to give an idea of the losses at the Hairpin. They were all men whose places it was felt could never be adequately filled, and consequently the Battalion was not in a particularly joyous mood for Christmas, which was spent in trenches and cellars near the Water Tower at Vermelles. The conditions did not lend themselves to a merry Christmas, for there was no chance at all of celebrating Christmas Day, and it was not until Boxing Day that the Christmas letters and parcels were received.

In consequence of an alarm, a sudden move had to be made

BETHUNE SQUARE.

DOUBLE CRASSIER, LOOS, 1915.

To face page 82.

on Christmas Eve to support positions at Vermelles, and the whole of that day and Christmas Day were spent in " standing to," so there was little opportunity for merry-making. But on Christmas night the alarm died down and a move was made to huts at Noyelles, where some succeeded in dining not wisely but too well on parcels from home, puddings from the *Daily News*, and Army rum. The Battalion canteen managed at this time by Ibbett, had now got into its stride, and its stock included welcome barrels of stout, in addition to champagne, port, sherry, whisky and a few other " dainties."

New Year's Eve was not even as cheerful as Christmas Eve, for the Battalion was now in the front line at the Hohenzollern Redoubt, and the artillery on both sides were busy playing the old year out—the infantry in the front line getting the full benefit of it.

But before the New Year was many hours old, the Battalion had a real stroke of good luck—a German mine blew up prematurely in front of them, thus saving them from what was easily the most unpopular frightfulness of the war !

The New Year was also marked by an act of gallantry which was afterwards recognised by the award of the Military Medal to the two men concerned—Corporal P. J. Tickle and Drummer H. Hogwood.

The Hohenzollern Redoubt was not a pleasant spot. There had been a good deal of fighting in the neighbourhood during the past three months, and khaki figures still lay stiff and grim in No Man's Land where they had fallen. There were therefore no regrets when the Division was relieved by a Cavalry Division about the middle of January, 1916, and the 47th Division relieved the 18th French Division in the Loos sector.

The Civil Service Rifles brought to a close its long association with this neighbourhood by a short spell of trench warfare in the trenches on the eastern fringe of the village of Loos, and on the famous Double Crassier. The situation on the Double Crassier was unique in a way, for both English and German trenches ran across these two big slag heaps. The troops invariably returned from these trenches looking like so many coal miners, for there was coal dust floating about everywhere.

The district lived up to its peace-time reputation as a centre of mining activity, for the hated mine warfare was pursued freely about this time with the usual accompaniment of minenwerfers. Otherwise life hereabouts was more or less uneventful, except for a big display of war-time fireworks on the Kaiser's birthday, January 27th. It was thought the great War Lord would celebrate his birthday by making a big attack, but on the front occupied by the 47th Division he was apparently satisfied with a heavy bombardment.

There have been numerous poets in the ranks of the Civil Service Rifles, and there are many creditable effusions which, perhaps through the modesty of the poet, will never see the light of print. Some, however, have been saved, including some verses on the exploits of Private Beatty, a bomber of " A " Company, an odd, scraggy little man, with a husky voice, known to his intimates as Potgut Woodbine. He is immortalised by Hanna in his

NEW SONG OF HIAWATHA.

" Came my youngling—Pip. Q. Emma,
She the youngest of my offspring,
She the peardrop of my eyelid—
Grinning, dribbling, gurgling came she.

Thus the buxom Pip. Q. Emma—
' Say, oh, Father Potgut Woodbine,
Thou who could'st outrun the lithe¦louse ;
Thou who never more wilt form fours,
What did'st thou when on the warpath
Strode the Hare–Hun–Scare–Hun–Willies ? '
Breathless paused she for an answer.

Childling, daughter of the prairies,
Born where rushing waters thunder
(Near the Elephant and Castle
Hard against the Old Kent Gas Works)—
Listen how my kinsman Potgut
Put to flight the wily Hun-bird ;
Popped it right up Hiawatha,
Fritz von Rudolph Hiawatha
And his spouse, Frau Minen Werfer.

Know you first how Hiawatha
Wooed his buxom Minen Werfer—
Learned the names of all her spare parts,
Learned her—barrel, charge and striker,
Strength of charge and detonator—
Took to parts her complex innards,
At her home, the Trench Mawt Ah Skool.
Skool am Trenchgranatenkruppe
Bureau Bomski vor Vlamingen
Mawt Ah Markwun Star How Itza
Teufel Bligh Mee Mawt Ah Oh Mi.

Took he Minnie to his bosom,
On his deer-skin wore her totem,
Wore he swankily Kross Mawt Ahs,
Token of his life's gymkhana.
Not that Fritz's life was one huge joke !
Or as ripe as Methu-Selah's—

Trained he three moons with his Minnie,
Three moons—no leave—hell's sweat—oh, hell !
Three months with the Umpteenth Na Poos.

Up the line went Hiawatha
In a truck designed for cattle
Labelled ' London via Calais,'
By a poor misguided Fun-Man,
Poor, deluded fool Hun-Fun-Man,
Reveller in Herr Wolffe's Folk-lore—
Grimm, Hans Andersen and Æsop
(Mighty joss-men in invention,
Fertile in imagination).
Westward on his way to Calais
Blithely journeys Hiawatha,
Counts the hours till on the Boulevard
He shall dance with Minen Werfer ;
Counts the hours—and in the meantime
Bully beef imbibes—and curses.

To a full stop came the puff-puff,
Is this Calais, guard, or Paris ?
Houndsditch, Croydon, Piccadilly ?
New Cross Empire or the Abbey ?
Tersely came the answer—' *Hulluch.*'

Up the trench went Hiawatha,
With his jolly old Trench Mawt Ah,
Grunting, sweating, cursing, went he,
Vanished all his former blitheness.

On his side the British Tumai,
Mustered in his front-line trenches,
Mustered.   Picked men of the Lun-duns.
From the Base Camps, o'er the Prairies,
Came the Warriors from The Village,
Little Village by The River,
Lun-Dun, homestead of the Cocquenays.
Came the Blackfoot Cee Essah Hipes,
Came the jolly old Westminsters.
Came Loo Eeza's own Shoshonies,
Came the Choctan Stepney Long-Bows.
Came the Amazon-like Scott Ish,
Sinkers of the raiding ' Emden,'
Maid-like clad, yet Mighty Warriors.

Never could one say of ' Minnie '
As of Darling Clementine—
' Light she was and like a fairy '—
For her Bore was 4·9,
Treble ply in all her braces
(Which were not the same as Fritz's)

Manners none had Minen Werfer,
Minen Werfer, Strafe-ing Mawt Ah.
Spat she openly with gusto,
Vomited great land-torpedoes—
Spat she rations of contumely
At the grim-faced, grimy Tumai.

In the trench among the Tumais,
Sore-strafed, half-drowned, tortured Tumais,
Was thy kinsman Pot-Gut Woodbine,
Bomber Pot-Gut Bee Tee Woodbine,
Crouching red-faced o'er his brazier,
Puffing, blowing at the embers,
Heeding not the rage of Minnie.
Reckless he of flying fragments
Till a piece dropped in his dixie,
Flopping, dropped right home to Dixie.
Up rose Pot-Gut in his anger,
In his hand he seized a Mills Bomb,
In a loud voice bellowed ' Pin Out '
(War-cry of the Cee Ess Bombers).

Strong of arm was Pot-Gut Woodbine,
He could throw ten Mills Bombs upward,
Throw them with such strength and swiftness,
That the tenth had left his fingers
Ere the first to earth had fallen.

In the neck, poor Minen Werfer
Got she six of Pot-Gut's Mills Bombs ;
In the neck, or rather barrel,
Other four got Hiawatha,
Got, nor thanked the Lord for sending.
Woke he in the med'cine wig-wam,
Life had ceased to be one Huge Joke,
' Where is now my Minen Werfer,'
Cried he, and from out the darkness,
Through the noise of many waters
Came the answer, ' Minnie ?   Fini !
Fini !   Na poo !   Compris.   Got me ? '
Loud his voice raised Hiawatha
In a howling lamentation—
' Farewell,' said he, ' Minen Werfer '
' Farewell, O my Strafeing Mawt Ah,'
Both my ears are buried with you,
All my hair you've taken with you !
Come not back again to labour,
Come not back again to swelter
Up the line with post and rations.
Soon your footsteps I shall follow
To the regions of the cursed.
To the Hell reserved for Hun-men.'

This did I, O Pip. Q. Emma,
In the Great War with the Hun-man,
Thus fought I, your mighty kinsman,
Bomber Bee Tee Pot-Gut Woodbine.

From my knee slid Pip. Q. Emma,
What a liar !   Pot-Gut Woodbine ! "

It was agreed by all that this gem should not be lost to the
world, and it was reproduced some months afterwards in the
Hazeley Wail, a magazine published by the 1st Battalion wounded
who had returned to the Reserve Battalion.

*   *   *   *   *   *

Hopes were now raised by rumours of another period in Corps
Reserve and a return to Lillers, but the Division was not destined
to leave without a little excitement, for in the early hours of the
15th of February, the last day at Loos was heralded by the
blowing of a big mine by the Germans under the front line
held by the 7th London Regiment on the immediate right of the
Civil Service Rifles. A diary of a bomber describes it thus :—

" This morning I had just fallen asleep, after an arduous night
fatigue, followed by a cold stand-to, when the earth walls of the
dug-out shook with so violent a tremor that I thought we should
have been buried alive. I rushed outside to find the enemy firing
like mad ! Rifle grenades, trench mortars, aerial torpedoes, and
death-dealing whiz bangs were falling in all directions. Some 50
yards to our right a new volcano now reared its ugly sides to Heaven.
The Teutons had got their own back. The mine was theirs. But
before the earth had finished falling, our Private Sugars (attached
140th Brigade Machine Gun Company) from the front line trench,
about 50 yards from the mine had turned his machine gun on to
the position, and his continuous stream of lead stopped the German
attempts to rush the crater. Indeed, a heap of slain told the losses
of their bold but fruitless attacks. Alas ! a party of the Seventh
had met the fate we so dreaded ourselves ! They had gone up with
the mine ! Truly our luck was in.

" In half an hour all firing ceased as if by consent, and we settled
down to prepare breakfast. Bulldog Harris, the C.S.M. of ' C '
Company, had been issuing rum at the time of the explosion. With
great presence of mind he had saved the precious liquid from the
falling debris with his cap. So we got our ration. Many of the new
draft needed such a pick-me-up, for we quite thought the strafe was
a prelude to a German attack. The enemy was said to have massed
his reserves on this front in readiness for an offensive.

" Thank God we are to be relieved to-night ! To-morrow we
should be on terra firma again, far away from the terrors of mines
and counter-mines. There will be no need to watch the sky for
those fatal rockets or to fall flat on the trench path to escape the
full fury of the nasty tearing Minnie.

" To good old Lillers with its ancient market place and quaint mediæval images of the saints carved in niches over the principal shops—a town now flowing with Bass, Worthington and cheap champagne—snug Auberges, too, where you can dine in luxury for 1 franc, 75 cents. To Lillers! "

* * * * * *

The troops were naturally in the best of spirits on the morning of the departure for Lillers. The transport had to go the whole way by road, and started in a perfect blizzard at about 5.0 a.m.

The rest of the Battalion went by rail as usual from Nœux-les-Mines, and, soon after arriving at Lillers, the welcome news arrived that the Division had said good-bye to the Loos sector, and on its return to the front line would try conclusions with the Boche in a new area.

There were many informal " celebrations " of the completion of the first year in France during a very pleasant fortnight spent in Lillers, where, in spite of intense cold and much snow, all ranks contrived to be merry and to forget the war, except for the various alarms, notably the two days' stand-to in billets for Verdun.

A typical Company " celebration " held at the Restaurant Picot on the 27th of February has been recorded :—

" Covers were laid for 40. Our spirits were high and our appetites huge as we tucked into two helpings each of soup, sardines, tongue, chicken and peas, fruit, blanc mange and dessert. At 6.0 p.m. we could toast each other in French beer, cheap champagne and port.

" During some of the courses, Cooper, Lawman and others warbled sweetly at the piano, and by the time the dessert course was reached, the fun had become fast and furious. Old Picot himself, a fat and jovial Frenchman of 50, danced and frolicked with the youngest.

" There were no speeches made or toasts drunk to those whose faces we so sadly missed at the festive board, but was it altogether fancy that made us feel their presence ? "

* * * * * *

The occasions on which an infantry soldier in France was able to have a bath were so few and far between in these early days, that the event was usually recorded in the official Regimental War Diary. In the mining districts advantage was generally taken of the civilian baths at the mine heads, but sometimes the Divisional baths were installed in breweries, electric light works, or, in fact, anywhere near a water main. The baths naturally could not be near the billets of all units in the Division, so that a bath was often preceded and succeeded by a long march in full marching order at a most inconvenient time of day.

These objections were ultimately overcome in the Civil Service Rifles by Lieutenant-Colonel Segrave, who brought canvas baths

MACHINE-GUN POSITION,
GIVENCHY,
April, 1915.

FESTUBERT CHURCH,
May, 1915.

LEWIS GUNNERS OF CIVIL
SERVICE RIFLES,
Vermelles, Christmas Day, 1915.

FRONT TRENCH,
OPPOSITE HULLUCH,
Held and consolidated by
Civil Service Rifles after
unsuccessful attack by 1st
Division on 13th October,
1915. A Machine-Gun
Officer and a Gun Team
in " Cubby Holes " cut in
sides of trench.

GARE ALLEY, LOOS,
November, 1915.

" THE TOWER BRIDGE," LOOS,
View from Firing Line on Hill 70,
February, 1916.

from London, won a Soyer stove or two from Ordnance, and instituted the Civil Service Rifles baths, which were open daily whenever the Battalion was out of the line.

The ceremonies at the Divisional baths generally took place during a Battalion's rest in Divisional or Corps Reserve, and a scribe of " B " Company was so impressed with the baths at Lillers as to write the following account in a letter home :—

" Platoons went in turns to the brewery for a bath. Imagine, if it is not too shocking, twelve of us at a time bathing in a mash-tub, and the unusual spectacle of 24 feet and I don't know how many toes meeting in the middle. No wonder somebody described the atmosphere as ' foetid.' You kept on losing the soap and diving for it under other fellows' legs.

At Poperinghe, later on, the baths were run by a hustler who could now get a lucrative appointment on the District Railway. After three weeks of trench life, a man was allowed exactly thirty seconds under the hot spray and was then allowed to dry himself in a strong breeze while the minions of the Divisional Laundry Officer disinfected his clothing, which in some baths had to be strung up in a bundle on a hook to protect him from pickpockets.

* * * * *

The first year in France was rapidly drawing to a close, and though many gaps had been caused in the ranks by casualties and many by members of the Regiment being appointed to commissions in other Regiments, the Battalion as a whole had undergone little change. The work of the first year could be looked upon with satisfaction, and although "God's Own" Civil Service Rifles had not taken part in any big assault, there had been many little items of " dirty work " done.

The short stay at Lillers passed all too quickly and soon the Battalion trekked out in the snow, the remainder of the time in Corps Reserve being spent in training at the villages en route to the new area.

CHAPTER VI

THE new area proved to be the northern end of the famous Vimy Ridge, which the Battalion approached by easy stages, for although the Division took over the " Carency Sector " of the line on the 13th of March, it was not until the 10th of April that the Civil Service Rifles went into the front line. The interval had been spent in reserve billets in the French huts in Bouvigny Woods, in the partially deserted village of Villers au Bois, the wholly deserted village of Carency, the fully inhabited and rather pretty (for the Pas de Calais) village of Fresnicourt, and in the support trenches on the hill known as Notre Dame de Lorette (or Lorette Spur). These trenches had looked down on the long struggle by the French in 1915 for Souchez, the famous Zouave Valley, and for a footing on Vimy Ridge.

Lorette Spur was the most popular of all trench areas with the men, for by day there was no movement allowed and they were thus left undisturbed. It was here that the first anniversary of landing in France was spent. What little shelling there was went to Battalion Headquarters in the ruined village of Ablain St. Nazaire, and by night the working parties were all in the neighbourhood of the trenches occupied by the men themselves.

The Lewis Gunners were particularly happy on Lorette Spur, for they had good dug-outs and little or no work to do. It was in these trenches where Private Roessli (a Lewis Gunner) distinguished himself as a sculptor, for he had ample opportunities and much good material in the chalk with which the dug-outs were lined.

Evidence of the popularity of Lorette Spur is found in Corporal " Paddy " Guiton's description :—

" Shortly after this we wended our weary way to the trenches lying in the valley under one of the spurs of the Lorette heights. There we relieved a battalion of the Yorkshire Regiment, ' the old tin pots.' I asked one of the outgoing N.C.O.'s what the place was like. He replied in his quaint northern dialect : ' It's like convalescent whoam, lad.'

" We lived in the so-called dug-outs, or rather surface shanties in this region, and ' C ' Company, at any rate, had quite a ' cushy ' time. There were numerous fatigues, of course, but the Hun let us alone, and we had great comfort—derived from the fact that we had fires with real coal as fuel. There was quite a good fireplace in my lair, which was inhabited by four other N.C.O.'s, and our picnics here even on rations (without parcels) were singularly delightful. These fires were only allowed during the hours of darkness as the smoke might otherwise be perceived by enemy observers.

" We renewed our coal periodically by making nocturnal visits to the old sugar refinery at Souchez, nothing of which now remains but a mass of twisted iron girders and a heap of stones mixed with coal slack. This ground is that so valiantly won back by the French during our attack at Loos, and previously in May, 1915, was the scene of the most bitter and desperate fighting. The ground in the neighbourhood is scarred with the almost obliterated remains of old trenches and we found an interesting pastime in reconstructing the scenes and locating the various trenches held by our allies and the enemy.

" Sometimes in the evening we held sports meetings, of which an organised rat hunt formed the principal feature. On these occasions, Sergeant Chick distinguished himself greatly. Even now I can see his lean figure, leading the chase, a thick stick brandished in his right hand.

" My enjoyment of the life at Notre Dame de Lorette was too full to last, and one evening quite unexpectedly, ' Bulldog ' Harris warned me to prepare for leaving with the billeting party.

" Good-bye, Loretto ! I earnestly hope that all the troops who are bearing the heat and burden of the day will find the same calm and contentment that I did under the shadow of your frowning cliffs."

*   *   *   *   *

The front line trenches on Vimy Ridge were considerably cleaner than those at Loos, and although there was an extraordinary amount of mine blowing, there were times in the early spring of 1916 when life even in the front line was not too bad.

Out at rest, excellent sport was to be had in the nightly rat hunts in Bouvigny Woods, as well as cricket and football, and the Officers' Riding School under Lieut. W. H. Craig, the new Transport Officer, who had originally come to France as Transport Sergeant.

The situation in the front line astride the Souchez River was somewhat uncommon, for there was no trench at all, the line being held by means of three breastworks, each holding about a platoon, about 100 yards apart. The remainder of the Battalion occupied a quarry and an old trench behind.

It became quite a daily practice of the enemy at this time to blow a mine at sunrise and sundown.

On the afternoon of the 29th of April, 1916, a mine was blown under the front line held by the 6th Battalion, on the immediate right of the Civil Service, who were astride the Souchez River. The 6th suffered heavy casualties and two sections of bombers and two Lewis Gun teams were sent from the Civil Service to assist them.   Sergeant E. M. Knapp in charge of the bombers, was conspicuous throughout for his fearless and untiring work on the crater.   He himself organised the bombing posts, not only of his own men, but also those of the 6th Battalion.

In recognition of his splendid work on this occasion, Sergeant Knapp was awarded the D.C.M.   This gallant conduct was typical of all the work done by Sergeant Knapp, who was a real tower of strength to the Battalion bombers.   As a leader of men he was unrivalled, and his zeal and enthusiasm were a constant inspiration to the men he loved so much and who in turn loved him.   As a parade N.C.O. Sergeant Knapp was once described as a " Ragtime " soldier, but his enthusiasm and sterling work in the face of danger endeared him to the hearts of all men in the Battalion.   All members of the 1st Civil Service Rifles were justly proud of " Knappski "—a leader whom the men would follow anywhere.

Other members of the Regiment who distinguished themselves on the 29th of April immediately the mine was blown were Corporal (afterwards Sergeant) E. M. Nottingham, attached to the 140th Brigade Trench Mortar Battery, who gained the D.C.M., and Corporal Smedling, also with the Trench Mortar Battery, who gained the M.M.

From the time of his arrival in France in March, 1915, to the time of his death at the battle of Messines in June, 1917, Sergeant Nottingham had proved himself a man who scorned danger and loved the life of the trenches.   The exploit which won him his D.C.M. was only one of many such in the life of a most capable leader, who will never be forgotten by those who served with him.

The month of May, 1916, opened with a pleasant picnic in Bouvigny Woods, followed by a restful spell in the trenches on Lorette Spur.   Here there was an excellent view one night of the explosion of six British mines in rapid succession on Vimy Ridge, accompanied by an unparalleled display of fireworks of all descriptions.   As the men watched the display from a comfortable distance at the top of Notre Dame de Lorette, not one had the least suspicion that it was very soon to be the cause of the most severe blow that fortune had so far dealt to the Civil Service Rifles.

CHAPTER VII

VIMY RIDGE, 1916

On a gloriously sunny afternoon in May, a man was dozing outside his hut in the pretty little woods at the village of Camblain L'Abbé, where the Civil Service Rifles were billeted in Brigade Reserve. The Brigade had just taken over the Berthonval sector of trenches on Vimy Ridge, and the Civil Service Rifles were to spend a week in what appeared to be the most delightful village they had visited in Northern France.

It was one of those days when it feels good to be alive. The birds sang sweetly in the trees, and the delightful natural fragrance of spring was everywhere.

The afore-mentioned man, like many of his friends, had partaken of a comfortable dinner, washed down with what was known as Royal Shandy—a mixture of stout and sweet champagne, and as he settled down to a comfortable afternoon nap he reflected that, after all, war was not too bad. Some of the more energetic of his friends had gone for a walk to the neighbouring village of Aubigny, others were busy writing letters, but he preferred to have a lazy afternoon of pleasant reflection. There would be many more opportunities for excursions to Aubigny, as the Battalion had a whole week before it in these delightful surroundings. Perhaps in the evening he would visit the local cinema, as he had not been to see " the Pictures " for some time. However, that could wait too if he did not feel energetic. How he wished the Division could stay in this sector for the rest of the war ! There had not been much front line work lately—a Battalion only seemed to get one week in four in the front line, and when there it was not too bad— a few mines to make a little excitement, but then these were very regular, as they always went up at sunrise and sunset in this district, so you knew when to expect them. Yes, he thought, as he dozed off to sleep, " It's a bon war here." He had just fallen asleep when he was roughly shaken and told that the Battalion was to " fall in " at once.

" I think they might have left us alone on a Sunday," he groused as he quickly got his equipment together. " Who is it this time, I wonder ? The Bishop of London or Horatio

Bottomley ? And why have we to march to Villers au Bois to see him ? If he wants to preach to us why can't he come here ? However, perhaps it's one of these infernal training gags. Major General wants to see how long it takes to move his reserves about on a summer Sunday evening. Wonder if we shall get back before the estaminets close ? "

Similar thoughts were expressed by other members of the Battalion, for the only order was "Battalion will parade at once and march to Villers au Bois. Dress, full marching order."

Although the order came round in the middle of tea, the Battalion was on the road in an astonishingly short space of time, and after a hot and dusty march a halt was called in a field near the battered old church of Villers au Bois. Here many of the men took the opportunity to strip to the waist and rub themselves down with towels. Speculation was still rife as to what it all meant, but the general opinion was that it was a training stunt, which was regarded as the very worst taste on the part of those in authority. Rumours of " dirty work afoot," however, began to spread through the ranks, and soon the order came to occupy what was known as the Maistre Line—a line of trenches that had been planned as a third line of defence in this sector.

Once outside the village a wonderful sight met the eye. About two or three miles away, hanging over the area of the front line trenches on Vimy Ridge, was a dense cloud of bursting shells, and to make the scene more weird, not a sound could be heard, either of guns or of the explosion of the shells, although it was a beautiful still evening. The bombardment, although confined to an area of little more than a square mile, was by far the most intense yet witnessed by the Civil Service Rifles.

The Battalion was no sooner in position in the Maistre Line— a trench about two feet deep, than orders were received to move forward by Companies.

" B " Company led off, followed by " C " Company, two Lewis guns, two sections of bombers, Battalion H.Q. and " D " Company, and the remaining Lewis guns brought up the rear. " A " Company remained behind to bring up rations and water.

The advance was along a very shallow and narrow communication trench, and the scene of slaughter was approached through a barrage of tear gas. Owing to the movement of other bodies of troops progress was very slow, with the result that the Battalion endured some hours of tear gas, but the line moved slowly but surely towards the Cabaret Rouge on the Bethune–Arras Road, the site of a ruined estaminet where the Brigade Headquarters was now situated, just on the western side of the Zouave Valley.

In the words of the Regimental Diary :—

" The enemy was indulging in the most intense bombardment we had witnessed. He must have employed guns of every possible calibre. The air was just one solid mass of bursting shells."

* * * * * *

" We had little or no information as to what was happening, and as darkness had now gathered and we were in entirely strange trenches, there did not seem much chance of finding out."

* * * * * *

The leading Company (" B "), under Captain H. B. Farquhar, reached Brigade Headquarters at Cabaret Rouge at 10.15 p.m., and was ordered to report to the Commanding Officer of the Battalion holding the left of the 140th Brigade Front. After being loaded up with bombs and an extra 100 rounds of ammunition per man, they staggered forth through the barrage of the Zouave Valley, where the bombardment raged with its most intense fury, and arrived almost exhausted at the Battalion Headquarters of the left sub sector of what was known as the Berthonval Sector shortly after 1.0 a.m., on May 22nd. The awful barrage of the valley had been negotiated almost without loss.

The Company Commander was told on arrival at Battalion Headquarters that the line of resistance and support line had been lost, and that his Company would deliver a counter attack at 2.0 a.m. It was then 1.30 a.m., and there was therefore no time to make any reconnaissance, nor was it possible to get any information at all as to the precise situation. Captain Farquhar was told that on his right the 6th and 7th Battalions would co-operate, on his left a company of the London Irish, and with him would be a party of bombers and details of the Post Office Rifles, but where any of these troops were to be found was not vouchsafed to him. He was told that one of his flanks would rest on Ersatz Trench, but as he had never heard of Ersatz Trench, nor was anyone there to show him where it was, he might just as well have been told to rest his flanks on the Unter den Linden. He was unable to find out whether there were any British troops between him and the Bosche, or how much of the line he was supposed to capture.

However, with these scant particulars, and with the information that the objective was about 600 yards up the side of the Ridge, Captain Farquhar was ordered to start his counter attack at 2.0 a.m.

He called his Platoon Sergeants and his only other officer (Lieutenant B. Scott) together, and acquainted them with the scheme, and arranged his men in two waves, 6 and 8 Platoons under Lieutenant Scott in the first wave, and 5 and 7 Platoons in the second wave.

Reports differ considerably as to what exactly happened afterwards, for it must be remembered that the operations were carried out in total darkness, save for the fitful glare of the German rockets and Verey lights, and as it is difficult to get a reliable description of any battle, even in daylight, it is even more difficult to describe this scramble in the dark, in country which was strange to the attacking forces, few, if any, of whom knew where to look for friends or foes. But there is no doubt that the attack was launched at 2.0 a.m., and that " B " Company advanced in two waves up the slopes of Vimy Ridge, with no artillery, machine guns or Lewis guns supporting them, and that very soon they came under such a murderous and intense fire from enemy artillery, trench mortars, machine guns and rifles, that very few survived unwounded. As far as can be gathered from survivors, it appears that after taking the British front line at 9.0 p.m., the enemy at once put out a barbed wire obstacle, and the survivors of " B " Company claim that a number of their men actually reached the wire, where, of course, they were helpless.

The vast majority of " B " Company having been killed or wounded, the foremost of the unwounded survivors, finding they were now in a hopeless position, appear to have decided to take cover in shell holes and await developments. Here they remained throughout the whole of the following day in scorching sunshine, looking for the best way of escape, and at nightfall they were able to make their way back.

So much, and no more, is known of the fate of " B " Company, but " C " and " D " Companies, who had followed them through the valley, were more fortunate, for the former, under Captain G. A. Gaze, arriving at the Battalion Headquarters at 1.50 a.m., were ordered to support the 18th Battalion (London Irish) at once. As he was unable to get in touch with the London Irish, Captain Gaze, assisted by a Company of the Post Office Rifles, formed a defensive flank in Granby Street, where " C " Company, dog tired as they were, set to work at once to make a decent position, and at the same time scoured the country around in search of the wounded, many of whom were rescued   It was in this work of rescue that C.S.M. R. H. Harris (Bulldog Harris) excelled himself. He went far afield in his search for his bosom friend, " Kaffir " Howett, who, as C.S.M. of " B " Company had gone down in the van of the attacking party. Harris was unable to find his friend who was so dear to him, but he succeeded in bringing in several others of the wounded, and carried on his work of rescue untiringly until daylight. It should be remembered that the whole of this rescue work was done under incessant machine gun and artillery fire.

Another who accomplished great deeds on this occasion was

Sergeant T. P. Chick, of "C" Company. It was daybreak when his attention was caught by a wounded man of the Post Office Rifles, who was lying out in front of the trench. He at once announced his intention of going out to assist him, if possible, and although it was now fully light, he persisted in going out once more, and safely reached the wounded man.

Sergeant Chick was crawling back, and was not more than ten yards from the parapet, when he was shot just over the heart, and died about ten minutes afterwards.

He died for another, and his end was typical of his life of noble self-sacrifice in the interests of others.

It became a habit at one time among some troops in the Division to estimate the amount of work done by a unit by the number of casualties suffered, but although a heavy casualty list certainly indicates a "bloody" time, it does not follow that a unit which suffers few or no losses has done nothing.

Of the three Companies involved in the fighting at Vimy (for "A" Company took no part in the operations beyond carrying rations), "C" and "D" Companies appear to have got off comparatively lightly so far as casualties are concerned, though it was due to the efforts of these two Companies that a new front line was established so soon.

Under Captain A. Roberts, "D" Company was the last to cross the Zouave Valley, and on arriving at Battalion Head-quarters the Company was ordered to support "B" Company. Captain Roberts had least time of all in which to find out any-thing about the situation, but he led his men up the slope and they eventually occupied the old Reserve Line of the Battalion originally holding the sub-sector. This line they now con-verted into the British front line, and "D" Company, with a few remnants of the Post Office Rifles, held it from Granby Street to Ersatz Trench—the intended flanks of "B" Company's counter attack.

Prominent among the "D" Company men who helped in the rescue of the "B" Company wounded was Corporal R. J. B. Beazley, described by his C.S.M. as one of the best little fellows in the Regiment. He made at least half a dozen journeys "out in front" always returning with a wounded man.

A feature of the operations so far had been the entire silence of the British Artillery—it was afterwards said that the enemy attack took place in the middle of an artillery relief. But no sooner had "D" Company dug a decent front line trench than the British Artillery began to knock it about, and Captain Roberts had to complain of shorts several times during the day.

The situation became quiet soon after daybreak and "C" and "D" Companies were able to carry on with their work in peace for a few hours, but during the day the enemy from time

G

to time put down an intense barrage, lasting generally for about half an hour, when the whole valley was filled with smoke, debris and sheets of flame. Happily, there were few further casualties on this account, and although the dose was repeated late at night when the Battalion was relieved by the 24th London Regiment, there was little further loss and the Zouave Valley was left as it had been found—in a mass of smoke and bursting shells.

The battle of Vimy Ridge, although not much more than a minor operation—it is believed to have been the sequel to the blowing of the six British mines in the vicinity on the night of the 15th of May—has been described at some length because it was the most important event so far in the life of the Civil Service Rifles in France. Hitherto the Battalion had succeeded in preserving more or less its original identity, but here, in the short space of twenty-four hours, practically all that was left of the original " B " Company had been swept away. It is perhaps because of the sudden nature of the operation that the losses came as such a shock to the surviving members of the Battalion.

Captain H. B. Farquhar had long been the idol of " B " Company, and a great favourite in other Companies in the Battalion. He had done what he could to save his men from the awful disaster, but as a soldier he had to obey orders, and, having called his platoon sergeants together and told them all he knew he bravely bade them good-bye, and, like the rest of his Company, went to his doom without flinching.

Captain Farquhar has often been described as the finest Company Commander the Battalion ever possessed.

He was keen, energetic and unselfish, a real pattern to his officers, N.C.O.'s and men. A survivor of the " B " Company of Captain Farquhar's day has written an admirable character sketch of " the skipper " and his henchman, Lieutenant Bobby Scott, who perished with the first wave at Vimy.

" CAPTAIN FARQUHAR.—The skipper was a strong man. For all his wit, sometimes sardonic, but always merry, he could be a man of beaten steel on occasion.

" ' Old ' ' B ' Company knew him ' well at Watford, but ' old ' C ' Company really made his acquaintance in France.

" In the line he ignored danger in a matter-of-fact way that inspired us as much as the theatrical bravado of a shallower man would have unsettled us. In those never-ending front line spells just before the ' first Lillers ' he heartened us through many a weary night as no other man I know could have done. To me, as a hardened and persistent night sentry, he seemed to be an almost permanent feature of the landscape of ' No man's land,' strolling serenely up and down as if taking a leisurely constitutional. He was always on the spot when anything happened, and I think we got his habit of never shirking any objectionable job which could possibly be considered ' up to us ' to do.

" LIEUTENANT SCOTT.—' An officer and a gentleman ' is probably the most overworked if not the most misapplied phrase in the military dictionary. It is too often thoughtlessly bestowed on any nice-mannered, band-box officer. But it fitted Mr. Scott. He was a real soldier and he was an instinctive gentleman."

Captain Farquhar had been ably supported by his C.S.M., F. Howett, known for many years throughout the Battalion as Kaffir Howett.

The Kaffir had made a name for himself long before the war broke out, for he was for a long time associated with " Bulldog " Harris as the life and soul of the Regimental School of Arms. These two inseparables were also prominent members of the Civil Service Rugby Football Club.

As a soldier, Kaffir Howett had many of the sterling qualities of his Company Commander. He was a stern disciplinarian and was fearless in the line, but while, he too, had a subtle sense of humour, he was more of the " strong silent man " than of the " merry and bright."

The only consoling reflection about the loss of these more than gallant fellows is that they could not have died in better company, but what magnificent deeds would have been done later in the year by such fellows as Farquhar, Scott, Howett and Chick, and to them must be added Sergeant A. J. Andrews (Long Andrews or Driver Andrews to his intimates) another old pillar of " B " Company, who before the war had made a name on the football field, and Corporal S. Crocombe, a staunch N.C.O. of " B " Company, who, although rescued on the night of the battle, succumbed to his wounds five days later.

Besides the killed, a number of the stalwarts of the Battalion were wounded. In " B " Company alone, these included Sergeants A. W. Hodgson, who had already been wounded once, and F. Tyler (known as Wat Tyler), and Corporals H. W. Rowland and F. Plaster, four N. C. O.'s who had been prominent members of the Company for many years, whilst " D " Company had to deplore the loss of Sergeant G. Wright, who in addition to his fine military record, performed great deeds on the cricket field.

The Lewis Gunners also had their losses, the outstanding one being Lance-Corporal " Cocky " Oliver (wounded) whose ready wit on all occasions was such a valuable asset to the Lewis Gun Section.

CHAPTER VIII

CALONNE RICOUART AND SOUCHEZ

It will be gathered from the foregoing that, in whatever light the operation on Vimy Ridge was regarded by the General Staff, to the Civil Service Rifles it was a battle of some importance, and the loss of so many of the leading members naturally plunged the survivors into something approaching deep depression as they trudged wearily back to Camblain l'Abbé on the morning of the 23rd of May. The Transport limbers were met at Villers au Bois, and many weary men were thankful to shed their equipment here, and some of the more exhausted managed even to secure a lift for the rest of the journey.

The Transport Section, too, had played its part in the battle, for every available horse and man had been employed during the 22nd of May carrying bombs and ammunition across the track to Cabaret Rouge in daylight. Fortunately they had escaped any loss, either of men or horses.

Camblain l'Abbé was now very different from the quiet little village that had seemed so far removed from the war two days before. The whole Brigade occupied the billets recently allotted to the Civil Service Rifles, and it was here that the news of the counter attack by the 142nd Infantry Brigade was awaited with such keen interest on the night of the 24th. The attempt, however, like that of another Division a few days later, was unsuccessful, and the crest of Vimy Ridge remained in German possession until the Canadian victory of the 1st of April, 1917.

" The feelings of men leaving the danger zone for a period of rest defy accurate portrayal. Each one has his own individual thoughts, but they may be summed up in one word ' contentment.' " Thus writes a well-known N.C.O. of " C " Company, who went so far as to say that the tension had been so great for a short period that, on knowing himself to be out of immediate danger for the time being, he felt as if he could have marched fifty miles, with full pack and blankets thrown in !

" Every force has a recoil," he continues, " and most men feel tremendously bucked on leaving the trenches for a spell out of the line.

" It was thus with feeling of great relief that the Battalion marched to Calonne Ricouart on the 25th of May, there to forget their sorrows in the work of training and reorganisation."

It is pleasing to be able to record the recognition, in the shape of honours and awards, of some of the many acts of gallantry performed in the Battalion on Vimy Ridge, and while at Calonne Ricouart it was heard that the work of C.S.M. R. H. Harris and Second Lieutenant F. Osborne was recognised by the award of the Military Cross ; and Lance-Corporal Mark W. Hall, the leading stretcher-bearer of " B " Company, Sergeant W. R. McKinley of " A " Company, Private S. H. Bressey of " D " Company and Private L. Flanagan of " B " Company were awarded the Military Medal.

Sports Meetings of various descriptions were held at Calonne Ricouart, and as the billets were good and the weather generally was fine, the troops soon began to recover their good spirits.

The Transport field was approached by a one-sided rustic bridge over a stream. On one occasion almost the entire section endeavoured to make " Onions," the mascot, mule take a bath from this bridge. The old lady, however, was proof against all efforts, and the only thing that happened was that the side of the bridge gave way. Lower down the road was a picturesque water mill, and next to this an estaminet, "Au Joli Pêcher," provided liquid refreshment. Here Mlle. Felicité always had a roomful of thirsty *soldats* who required a great deal of la bière to wash the dust out of their throats.

Large drafts of officers and men began to arrive from England, and very soon the Battalion became once more up to strength, and to complete the refitting, short rifles were now issued to all N.C.O's and men in place of the long Lee Metfords with which they had hitherto been armed.

The event of the " rest " was an original revue entitled " Spit and Polish," performed on the afternoon of the 10th of June at the Cinema, Divion. The " leading lady" has given the following account of the affair.

" The first rehearsal took place in Lieutenant Sharratt's billet. After a lot of smoking and talking, but very little rehearsing, the parts were allotted as follows :—

The Bogus Brigadier -	-	Private Teasdale.
Adjutant - - -	-	Private Graham.
Sergeant-Major -	-	Private Lloyd.
Colonel Straws, I.D. -	-	Private Chisholm.
Real Brigadier -	-	Second-Lieutenant W. H. Brantom.
Hon. Lady Lizzie -	-	Private C. Cooper.

" The plot was written round the Hon. Lady Lizzie, who, bent on war work, obtained a situation as typist in the orderly-room where two Tommies—one disguised as a Brigadier and the other as an Adjutant—had decided to run the war in their own way. Eventually the real Brigadier comes on the scene. Lady Lizzie turns out to be his daughter and marries the bogus Brigadier, Sir Charles Chaplin !

" The revue was performed four days after the first rehearsal. Fortunately little memorising was needed as we relied chiefly on gags. On the morning of the performance Captain Ind came over to Divion to censor the dress rehearsal. Needless to say he cut out some of the best things, though, even then, the show had some ' kick ' left in it. And perhaps the revue *was* a trifle crude in places. But there was no holding a man like Teasdale. With his quick wit and fertile brain it required some nimbleness of mind to keep pace with him in *everything*—especially as I was playing the girl's part !

" I don't think anybody who was there will forget the occasion. The battalion had marched from Calonne, a distance of three miles, and arrived at the Cinema three-quarters of an hour before time, thus giving the boys an opportunity for a concert to themselves.* The noise was terrific, the bombers singing their particular songs and being howled down by the Lewis Gunners with their own pet ditties, and vice versa. When ' Posh Harry' arrived he was greeted with the refrain :

" I wish I were an R. S. M.
Earning lots of dollars.
Etc., etc., etc."

" The first half of the programme consisted of single turns frantically applauded. Then came the revue.

" I won't attempt to describe it fully, but who will quite forget the beauty chorus of those thirty nice, smart soldiers, headed by Knapp, singing in harmony to the tune of ' Boiled Beef and Carrots, that opening chorus :

" Spit and Polish ! Spit and Polish !
Our fathers said in days of yore.
That Spit and Polish would win this war.
Don't walk about like dirty dogs
Or lads from Eton College,
The only way to win this war
Is—Spit and Polish ! "

" Of this chorus, Sidwell, he of the staring eyes, was great as the man who fainted on actually seeing the kidneys and best parts of the meat handed to his Company when drawing rations at the Q.M. Stores !

" The great moment, however, was Teasdale's entry as the Brigadier (on a chair with the back for the horse's head) with umpteen ribbons on his chest, wonderful top boots—his whole appearance a thing of joy ! He kept the house in a boisterous thunder of hilarious applause right through to his final inspection of the beauty chorus when he presented a tin of Brasso to poor old Knapsky ! "

---

* The pioneers (of whom the lengthy Foote and Ginger Facon were notorious members) in the meantime prepared the stage, proving themselves expert stage carpenters.

The revue was a happy conclusion to a very enjoyable stay at Calonne Ricouart, and shortly afterwards a return was made to the front line trenches known as the Souchez Sector, a little north of the village of Souchez.

The outstanding features of life in this area were the heavy trench mortars used by the Bosches in the line, and the very happy days in Noulette Woods, near the village of Aix Noulette, when out of the line.

Early in July the Battalion was ordered to raid the enemy trenches in the Bois en Hache, just north of Souchez, but although five officers and 100 other ranks were specially trained for the event, it was a dismal failure, and it has long been a forbidden topic of conversation in Civil Service Rifles circles. Fortunately the casualties were few, and the Battalion left the area shortly afterwards to return to the dreaded Berthonval sector on Vimy Ridge.

On this occasion, however, a very peaceful time was spent in the front line, and it was hard to believe that it was the scene of the big fight of two months ago.

The thoughts of every one were now turned to the big offensive in the Somme district, and for some time the distant rumble of guns, heard daily from morning till night, had given rise to discussions as to when the 47th Division would move south to join in the fray.

It was therefore no surprise when the Civil Service Rifles marched out of Camblain l'Abbé on the 26th of July, 1916, after four very happy days in that pleasant village, to start the great trek to the Somme district.

CHAPTER IX

THE TREK

DURING its career in France, the Civil Service Rifles have frequently moved over long distances by route march—a practice known as "trekking"—but the great march of 1916 seems so to have dwarfed all other performances of a similar nature, that it is always referred to simply as "the trek," and it is agreed by all who took part in it, that the trek was one of the most enjoyable experiences the Civil Service Rifles had during the war.

At the same time the period was one of the most strenuous, the daily programme of work being sometimes so crowded that it hardly seemed worth while to go to bed. The Divisional Commander was evidently a firm believer in early rising, for réveillé was often sounded at the early hour of 3.30 a.m.

The route from the mining district to the valley of the Somme was distinctly roundabout, and for the first two or three weeks of the trek the Division got farther and farther away from its destination, until eventually it came to rest near the coast in the Abbéville district.

A pleasant march on the first day brought the Civil Service Rifles to the village of Houdain, where Lieutenant G. G. Bates organised a very successful Mess Dinner for officers at the Café du Centre, and on the following day, after a short march, the village of Valhuon, near St. Pol, was reached, where four enjoyable days were spent in lovely summer weather. The weather, indeed, was a little too summer-like on the day of the march from Valhuon to Croisette. Not only was it so far the hottest day of the year, but the march took place during the hottest time of the day, and when Croisette was reached at 3.30 p.m. many had fallen by the wayside. Other units of the Division had similar experiences, and hereafter early rising was the order of the day, réveillé generally being sounded about an hour before dawn so that training could be finished before the heat of the day.

A common occurrence during the marches on the trek was the failure to observe the infantryman's most valuable charter—ten minutes' halt in every hour. The marches were usually by Brigades, and the starting point was often a mile or so away from the billeting area. For some strange reason the march to the starting point was wont to be hurried, and what should have been the first halt was omitted altogether.

Towards the end of the march, again, the leading Battalion, on approaching the village in which it was to be billeted, would often cut out the halt as the appointed time was reached, and go straight on to the billets. The succeeding Battalions on such occasions would follow like sheep, irrespective of whether they were billeted in the same village or in another one two or three miles farther on.

In these circumstances it is not surprising that marches which on paper looked nothing out of the ordinary were found to be very arduous and trying, and men were frequently guilty of the " crime " of falling out on the march.

At first early rising was voted a success by all ranks, but when an afternoon parade was introduced and later an evening parade just to fill up the day, the troops began to feel that though it was " nice to get up in the morning," it was certainly " nicer to stay in bed."

A day's rest at Croisette was followed by a march to Fortel, where, during a four days' stay, a delightful batning place was discovered in the swift-flowing, icy cold waters of the River Canche. " A " and " D " Companies and the Lewis gunners have happy recollections of this stream, for the most part of the two hours' route march by Companies which formed part of the daily programme was spent in and around the bathing place.

The 4th of August at Conteville was marred by the sudden introduction of an evening parade. The move from Fortel had taken place in the early hours of the morning, and after a very short march Conteville was reached at about 10.0 a.m. The troops were still congratulating themselves on their luck when the order came round that all units in the Division would at once start to practise an attack on a wood or village.

The wandering life was resumed on the 5th of August, when the Division moved to the training area near Abbéville, the Civil Service Rifles being billeted in the little village of Drucat. The Division now settled down to serious work, and for three weeks the troops trained strenuously every day. It is interesting to note that the Division trained for its share in the battle of the Somme near the historic battlefield of Crécy.

But although there was much hard work and the billets at Drucat were poor—so poor that in many cases both officers and men slept in gardens or fields—and the inhabitants inclined to be hostile, memories of August 1916 are among the happiest of the war.

A great drawback, however, was the scarcity of beer. The estaminets in the village had none at all, nor did they attempt to get any, for they were thus able to get rid of their stock of atrocious wines. The Regimental Canteen eventually came to the rescue by securing a supply of beer from Abbéville.

The weather at first was all that could be desired, and bathing was indulged in daily. At the end of the fields occupied by the Lewis gun section and the Transport lines ran a narrow, shallow stream. The men of the Transport section, by damming the stream with a wall of filled sandbags, managed to construct a pool just big enough for a man to plunge in, and the bathing pool was thoroughly appreciated by officers and men alike.

A number of N.C.O.'s and men were allowed to go to Abbéville each day, and a merry day in the old French town usually ended with the hiring of antiquated " voitures " for the journey home. The said " voitures " were invariably driven by members of the Civil Service Rifles, the lawful owners or drivers always being willing to hand over the reins, and many were the chariot races run on the road from Abbéville to Drucat by rival parties from the Civil Service Rifles, the winning post being the Company parade ground, where the races ended just as the Company was on parade for roll call.

Cricket was played in the Lewis gun field, where, also, an al fresco concert was given one day by a concert party sent by Miss Lena Ashwell. The weather was most unkind that day, but the spirits of the concert party, like those of the troops, were not to be squashed by the rain, and the artistes, five charming English ladies and two gentlemen, gallantly stuck it until the deluge became so terrific that the noise of it drowned the efforts of the whole party to sing " Chalk Farm to Camberwell Green."

What testimony to the attractiveness of the party could be more eloquent than the simple fact that none of the audience left the field ! The appreciation of the audience was not limited to the performance. It was a rare and refreshing feast to see those five pretty English girls, especially to those, and they were many, who had not been privileged to see an English girl for more than a year. Moreover, the Civil Service Rifles were told that they were the first real fighting troops to be entertained by these ladies, who had hitherto had to content themselves with entertaining those whose duties kept them at the Base.

Colonel Warrender thanked the artistes in his most delightful style and expressed the sentiments of all ranks when he said that it was the most enjoyable concert that had ever been given to the Battalion.

While at Drucat the Battalion received a consignment of what at first were thought to be toy bread-carts, such as are used in London suburbs. But on inquiry it was found that these were the new " Hand Carts, Lewis Gun," intended to replace the limbers.

These little carts were first " tried out " on the departure from Drucat on the 20th of August with disastrous results. The shafts broke before the first halt, and ere long each team of Lewis gunners was stripped to the waist, their clothes and equipment piled high on to the carts while they tugged and pushed at their vehicles, gallantly struggling to keep up with the Battalion. But in spite of these determined efforts they were all very badly " tailed off."

The route march concluded with an outpost scheme, and in the evening the Civil Service Rifles were billeted in Villers Sous Ailly, a pretty little village, conspicuous for the excellent spirit of hospitality shown by the inhabitants—a welcome change from recent experiences. The only regret about Villers was that the Battalion had to leave the next morning.

The farce of the Lewis gun handcarts was continued, and in spite of a great display of inventive genius by the Lewis gunners, they were quite unable to keep up with the Battalion. Perhaps the best suggestion was that of the man who said the Lewis gunners should take turns at carrying the carts on their backs !

It was said the carts had passed a severe test in the courtyard of the War Office and had been found to run smoothly when empty.

Leaving Villers Sous Ailly, two uncomfortable nights were spent at Naours and Mirvaux (considered by many to be the most dilapidated village in Europe outside the " forward area," and where one man pushed a whole wall down by simply leaning against it !), and on the 23rd of August the 140th Infantry Brigade reached Franvillers, near the Amiens-Albert road. Here there appeared to be a concentration of all the flies on the Western front, and it was thought that these were to take part in a new form of attack !

Franvillers and district was used as a kind of " finishing school " for troops in training for any particular phase of the battle of the Somme in 1916, and as it was fairly near to the battlefield, it had become an unusually busy centre. Troops from all parts of the United Kingdom seemed to have passed through and every available inch of space was used for billets. The billets, owing chiefly to overcrowding, were very uncomfortable and very dirty, and the natives were beginning to get tired of the troops.

The training was of the very strenuous type—drills before breakfast, attack practice after breakfast, musketry and digging in the afternoon, and route march in the evening. It was now known that the attack which was being practised daily over a taped course was to be on a certain wood, but the name of the wood was so far kept secret.

But in spite of this crowded programme, there were some who found time for trips to Amiens, and there were many who enjoyed the excellent bathing in a natural pool in the Ancre at Heilly, a village south of the Amiens-Albert road.

It was at Franvillers that Sergeant R. F. M. Bigby earned the gratitude of his comrades by securing an issue of rum for all. According to his story he was drinking beer in an estaminet, when the Regimental Medical Officer came in on a tour of inspection, accompanied by the A.D.M.S. A mild outbreak of enteric in the Division was causing the medical fraternity some anxiety at the time, and efforts were being made to discover the cause of it. The A.D.M.S. asked Sergeant Bigby what he was drinking, but, on being informed, instead of ordering any, as Bigby had expected, the doctor inquired about the quality of it. The gallant sergeant assured the medicos that the quality was poor, but that if followed by a ration of rum there were no ill effects. On the contrary, a ration of rum at night, especially during bad weather and in bad billets, had been found to be a pretty sure prevention against enteric, which complaint, added Bigby—as the medicos were doubtless aware—was getting rather troublesome at Franvillers. But then, there had not been an issue of rum so far in that village, so could one be surprised ?

When, very shortly after this interview, a ration of rum was issued to the troops, there were few in the Division who did not acclaim the name of Bigby !

Early in September it became known that the 47th Division was to attack the German positions in and around High Wood— positions which had already been captured by more than one Division, but afterwards retaken by the Germans, who, throughout six weeks of heavy fighting, had resisted all attempts to dislodge them permanently. To the Civil Service Rifles were allotted the first German lines in the wood itself, with the 7th Battalion on their right and the 17th Battalion on their left. Henceforth there was a state of suppressed excitement in the Battalion, and all ranks took the very keenest interest in the full dress rehearsals over a marked-out battlefield, which occupied the last days of training at Franvillers. These " shows " were attended by the whole Division, including Artillery, Trench Mortars, and the contact aeroplanes attached to the Division, and the attack was practised with zero at every possible hour of the day or night.

By the time Franvillers was left, on the 12th of September,

every man understood what he had to do and where he had to go in the battle.

A few privileged persons had been to see a demonstration of the great secret of the war—the Caterpillars, as they were called in those days, also frequently referred to at this time as the " Hush ! Hush ! " These new engines of warfare, which soon became known as Tanks, were to make their first bow to the public by assisting in the attack on High Wood, where two of them were eventually allotted to the Civil Service Rifles in place of an artillery barrage.

After leaving Franvillers, the Battalion took the fine Route Nationale to Albert, " a city of empty and ruined houses, some occupied by our troops, others barred and bolted as if a very plague had taken off the population." The Civil Service Rifles passed right under the shadow of the ruined cathedral with the gilded Madonna and Child hanging face downwards from the top of the steeple. From Albert the Battalion marched to Becourt Wood and relieved the 2nd Royal Sussex in what looked like a big rubbish tip, remaining there in reserve until the 14th.

The scene which met the eye after passing through Albert has been recorded by Corporal De Ath, who was attached to the 140th Trench Mortar Battery.

" I shall never forget the sight that met our eyes on the other side of the town," writes De Ath. " It took us some time to realise that we were looking on what was to us, an almost incredible and unheard of thing—a vast armed camp just behind the trenches and well within shell fire. As far as the eye could see there were miles of tents, bivouacs, limbers and horse lines. Huge dumps of supplies and ammunition covered the ground, and between them, in any old corner, were the big guns—huge monsters roaring incessantly and devouring the great piles of shells stacked around. Everywhere were scenes of the greatest activity, and one could only rub one's eyes and gasp at this astounding spectacle. The colossal cheek of that great camp rather shocked us, but there it was, unconcerned and undisturbed, thanks to our magnificent aircraft, constantly patrolling above with never an enemy plane daring to do likewise.

" We pitched our bivouacs on the crest of a ridge just behind the old front line, and to the left of Becourt Wood. From that high point we got a good view of the surrounding country. At our feet the usual flotsam and jetsam of abandoned trenches with their tangled heaps of barbed wire. Away behind us was the wooded country-side which came as a change after the drab monotonous scenery of the Flemish Flats. Closer at hand the ruined Cathedral caught one's eye.

" But away in front, in the wake of the advance, the picture was entirely different. It was a scene of desolation—a desert of low ridges, scarred and marked by blurred lines of chalk trenches and shell holes. Here and there a few jagged tree stumps stood out, but nearly every feature of the landscape had been swept away by the furious pounding of our shells.

" All along the sky line our heavy shells and shrapnel were bursting continually, so that the smoke never ceased. Now and again it would slacken only to break out again with double intensity. Behind and around us the ' Heavies ' boomed and roared, whilst in front in every little valley and hollow, even in the open without pretence of cover, our 18-pounders snapped and barked viciously, alternating with the deeper notes of the 4·5's and the 60-pounders. Between whiles one heard the heavy ' crump ' of the Hun shells.

" A confused blur showed where a village once stood, but only a heap of rubble and dust was left, revealed more often than not by the junction of several roads. In the dip below lay Fricourt, to the left Thiepval and Pozieres where bloody fights raged on July 1st. Further away the green mass of Mametz Wood, still providing excellent cover in spite of the thinning out it had undergone. Further on lay Contalmaison, Montauban and the Bazentins, with Delville Wood to the right, and there on the crown of the ridge a little bunch of tree stumps marked the wood that was to be our goal, the key to the desperate game that we were to play on the morrow. The country seemed surprisingly difficult. A series of low hills and ridges plentifully dotted with woods and villages and traversed by numerous sunken roads, culminated in the ridge which overlooked the plain of Bapaume. Most of that ridge was already ours, but in many places the enemy still hung out with stubborn tenacity. It looked terrible country to fight through—naturally strong and made almost impregnable by German science and skill.

It was realised that the Civil Service Rifles were about to go through the most severe test in their history, by the side of which Festubert, Loos, and even Vimy Ridge would be insignificant. The thorough training which had just been completed, however, had filled all ranks with confidence, and the great Somme trek, which ended on the 14th of September with the relief of the 1st Surrey Rifles in the front line trenches in High Wood, brought to a close a period of training which for really strenuous work has never been beaten. Some, in fact, allege that the Division was overtrained at this time, and that the " finishing school " at Franvillers had nearly finished them off. But in spite of these allegations, it is believed that the Battalion had never been better prepared for battle.

CHAPTER X

WHAT a wonderful scene it was along the New German Road on the afternoon of the 14th of September—a never-ending transport column moving along in broad daylight, conveying ammunition and R.E. material for the big fight. An object of special interest to the Civil Service Rifles was one of the tanks which was passed on the road. The men studied it critically and expressed a pious hope that it would turn up all right on the day.

Although the road was so crowded with traffic, there was little shelling, and after passing Bazentin-le-Grand the long communication trench was entered and the front line reached without loss.

High Wood was about the last vantage point that the enemy held along the ridge. Only a few jagged trees remained and the ground was littered with broken limbers and pitted with innumerable shell holes which literally intersected one another. Various trenches ran through the Wood, of which the greatest part was held by the enemy.

The relief over, it became known that zero for the attack would be at 5.50 a.m. on the morrow, and thereupon a weird silence fell over all the area of the assembly trenches, where the men were packed like sardines in a tin. Many chapters have been written in an attempt to describe the eve of a battle, but the finest description ever written falls very short of expressing the feelings and thoughts of the men as they wait in their assembly trenches for the dawn.

No attempt will be made here to describe the eve of High Wood. Suffice it to say that it was a very quiet night; that the troops, as they stood squashed up in Black Watch Trench, fervently hoped that their fate on the morrow would be better than that of the Battalion whose name the trench bore; and that the only fellows who got any sleep were those who crept out into No Man's Land to lie down in shell holes. Rum was issued at dawn, and after a sleepless night it was unusually welcome.

And now zero hour approached, and thoughts turned to the

tanks, which were due to be on the German front line five minutes before zero. The time drew nearer, but no tanks appeared, and a few minutes before zero, Company Commanders received a message telling them to send an officer to guide the tanks, if seen. Thus, the Civil Service Rifles were handicapped at the start, for the tanks were neither seen nor heard.

Owing to the irregular formation of the assembly trenches, " B," " C " and " D " Companies had been instructed to creep out before zero, so that when the attack started they would be forming a straight line with " A " Company, who were on the extreme right. These Companies accordingly began to creep up soon after 5.30 a.m. The fight, therefore, can be said to have started well before zero, for at once as these men left their trenches, German rifles opened fire, followed by machine guns, and by zero hour the three left Companies of the Civil Service Rifles, together with the Battalion on their left, were already being treated to a murderous fire from a multitude of machine guns and rifles in the German front line trenches. At the same time down came the German artillery barrage on the assembly trenches. As there was no artillery support whatever, the attack at this point was held up, but not before about four-fifths of " B," " C," and " D " Companies had been either killed or wounded.

" A " Company, on the right, fared much better. They did not leave their trenches until zero, and their course led them out of the wood almost immediately. Consequently, when they started, the German machine guns were already busily occupied with the other Companies, and " A " Company carried the first and second German trenches outside High Wood with comparatively little loss. Arrived at the objective, a certain amount of hand-to-hand fighting took place, in which Sergeant H. B. Riddell and Second Lieutenant L. L. Burtt, distinguished themselves, the former being chiefly instrumental in putting a machine gun out of action, though he was wounded in the fight.

The Battalion signallers following up " A " Company had established a station in the captured trench, and as their lines held for some time, the details of how " A " Company had fared were quickly sent down to Battalion Headquarters.

" A " Company had already taken a number of prisoners, and they now proceeded to bomb along the captured trench towards where they expected to find " B " Company, but it was soon realised that the other Companies had been held up. The situation with these Companies was very grave. The Company Commanders of " B " and " D " Companies, Captains Leslie Davies and Arthur Roberts, had been killed, while Captain Geoffrey Gaze, commanding " C " Company, was wounded, but

Photo by Coles, Watford.

CAPT. GEOFFREY A. GAZE.

Photo by Hana Studios, Ltd.

CAPT. A. ROBERTS.

Photo by Coles, Watford.

CAPT. LESLIE DAVIES.

Killed in Action 1916, and buried in one grave at High Wood, 15th Sept., 1916.

refused to go down. Captain Gaze, in fact, was the only officer in these three Companies remaining at duty. A good many of the senior N.C.O.'s had also been killed and wounded, but thanks to the timely efforts of C.S.M. Brett of " D " Company, C.S.M. Harris of " C " Company, and the surviving N.C.O.'s of all three battered Companies, the remnants were formed up again in the assembly positions, ready for another attempt.

Meanwhile the tanks had not shown up, though one of them later on, after nearly smashing up Battalion Headquarters, got stuck in a communication trench, and materially interfered with the removal of the wounded. Its pilot got out, and, going into Battalion Headquarters, asked the Commanding Officer where High Wood was. Colonel Warrender's reply is not recorded.

The other tank eventually got into action somewhere in front of " D " Company's objective, and then caught fire.

At 11.0 a.m. the 140th Infantry Brigade Stokes mortar battery came to the rescue. Captain Good, who was in command, had had his guns on the spot overnight, and had been anxious to give the attacking infantry some support. On the ground that surprise was to be the key-note of the attack, however, the authorities decided to keep the Stokes guns, like the artillery, silent. Captain Good and his men responded magnificently when they were given the permission they sought so eagerly, and for twenty minutes, " feeding their voracious little pets with bombs until they grew too hot to touch," as De Ath says, the battery put down such an accurate and intense bombardment on the German front line that " C " and " D " Companies, when they went forward again, carried their objectives without much difficulty. The trench mortars had fired close on 800 rounds in twenty minutes—a feat afterwards described by 4th Army Headquarters as the most brilliant piece of work in the history of trench mortars.

" C " Company was gallantly led for a second time by Captain Gaze, but he was killed before reaching the objective.

By noon the whole of High Wood was in British possession, together with what was known as the Switch Line beyond, and the Civil Service Rifles had taken many prisoners and machine guns. The price of victory, however, was terrible, and only 150 of the four Companies reached their objective.

The foregoing is an attempt at a description of the first phase of the battle of High Wood, as it appeared to one who was present on the spot. A well-known war correspondent seems to have had a better view of the fight, for he related in detail in a London newspaper how the tanks captured High Wood !

The first stage of the battle was over, but there was much more to follow. The remnants of the Battalion advanced a

H

little beyond the trench known as Switch Line and dug themselves in in a new trench, and the afternoon was spent in hard work in consolidating these positions, which were, however, subject to considerable shelling by heavy artillery.

During the day the 6th and 8th Battalions had pushed through to take trenches some distance beyond, known as the Flers Line (connecting the village of Flers with Eaucourt L'Abbé), and the Starfish, an intermediate line.

These operations only partially succeeded, so at 5.30 in the evening of the 15th of September, the 1st Surrey Rifles, who were in reserve, were sent out to attack the western half of the Starfish Line and the strong point known as the Cough Drop. The Civil Service Rifles were to occupy the Starfish when the 1st Surrey Rifles vacated it. The latter, however, on emerging from High Wood in artillery formation, were immediately caught by an intense enemy artillery and machine-gun barrage, and the attack failed.

A similar experiment was tried at 9.0 a.m. the next morning with the 23rd Battalion, but, although they advanced a considerable distance, they were unable to reach the Flers Line. The Boches, however, obliged by withdrawing to the Flers Line, and the 6th and 8th Battalions occupied part of the Cough Drop and the Starfish Line respectively. The 23rd Battalion included two ex-Civil Service Riflemen in Major Kemble and Second Lieutenant J. H. Hunt, who lost his life in this attack. As a sergeant in " D " Company, J. H. Hunt had been exceptionally popular, and the keenest regret was felt among his many friends when he left to take his commission.

When darkness fell on the first night of the battle, the melancholy work of the burial of the dead was begun. The special party told off for this work dug graves in High Wood itself, and all the dead who could be found were buried side by side there.

The night of the 15th September presented a very striking contrast to the previous night, when peace and quiet had reigned in High Wood. The heavy artillery, with which the enemy was so well supplied, pounded away continually at the new trenches and at the supporting field gun batteries on the edge of the wood. Amid the noise of the shells could often be heard the groans of the wounded who had not yet been brought in, the shouts of the search party of stretcher bearers, and the curses of a ration or carrying party who had got lost. But above all was the ceaseless wail of the field guns, echoing over the wilderness. Listening to them on that night one could almost imagine that they, too, were mourning for the gallant fellows who had lost their lives that day, and who were now being laid to rest. To many who were there the peculiar echo

of the field gun ever afterwards brought back vivid memories
of those terrible nights in High Wood.

There were many incidents and sights at High Wood which
left a lasting impression on the minds of the survivors. The
impressions of Corporal M. J. Guiton, of " C " Company, who
lost a leg there, are typical of many others in the Battalion :—

" That day I saw sights which were passing strange to a man of
peace. I saw men in their madness bayonet each other without
mercy, without thought. I saw the hot life's blood of German and
Englishman flow out together, and drench the fair soil of France.
I saw men torn to fragments by the near explosion of bombs, and—
worse than any sight—I heard the agonised cries and shrieks of men
in mortal pain who were giving up their souls to their Maker.

" The mental picture painted through the medium of the eye
may fade, but the cries of those poor, tortured and torn men I can
never forget : they are with me always. I would I had been deaf
at the time."

* * * * *

The day after the first attack was spent in the new trench,
where the garrison was shelled by heavy guns nearly all day.
The Adjutant, Lieutenant W. E. Ind, who had been full of
energy from the start, was a very frequent visitor, and in the
evening he brought the good news that the Battalion was to go
forward to occupy a trench which had deep dug-outs and which
wasn't shelled. Tired as they were, the troops jumped at the
idea, and were ready in less than no time. The Adjutant led
the way in a pitch black darkness to the expected comfort,
which proved in the end to be a trench two feet deep, which had
been started by the Germans as a cable trench.

It had been reported that the 6th Battalion was holding the
Flers Line, and the Civil Service Rifles were accordingly going
to occupy Drop Alley, a communication trench leading from
the strong point called the Cough Drop to the Flers Line. But
on arrival at the Cough Drop, Lieutenant Ind found that the
report was untrue, and he had perforce to squeeze his small
body of men in the western half of the Cough Drop and the
afore-mentioned cable trench which ran out of it. It had been
a long and weary journey, but the men set to work like niggers
to dig a decent trench. There were now only two officers and
about 100 other ranks, but these included a good sprinkling of
seasoned warrant officers and N.C.O.'s, and the force made up
in quality what it lacked in quantity. C.S.M. Callingham and
Sergeant Irving of " A " Company had done their comrades a
very great service by struggling along with a jar of rum, which
was practically all that turned up that night in the shape of
rations, unless mention is to be made of rations sent up by a
thoughtful Quartermaster for the two officers—a bag of candles !

The process of digging in was no sooner finished than the exhausted troops had to stand to for about an hour and a half, on information from the 6th that the enemy was " coming over in large numbers."

So the day went on with a constant succession of alarms, intense bombardments and standing to. It was indeed a trying time for all that was left of the four Companies and Lewis gun teams who, forty-eight hours ago, had been so full of hope. But they all " stuck it " very valiantly, and the excellent spirits of the men—prominent among whom were Lance-Corporal F. A. Coward and his Lewis gun team, Privates Hundleby, Lynch, and E. H. Lyons—together with the splendid example set by Paddy Brett and Bob Harris, served to sustain the excellent morale of the Civil Service Rifles. Special mention should be made of the excellent patrol work done by Sergeant D. Gooding, of " D " Company, who went out in broad daylight " to find touch on the left." The left flank of the position was exposed, and it was not known whether friend or foe occupied the country beyond. Sergeant Gooding, with two men, started off, there-fore, without any information and, although under rifle fire from shell holes and isolated posts, they carried out a complete reconnaissance of the country which separated the Civil Service Rifles from the nearest friendly troops, four or five hundred yards away. Many others of that little band distinguished themselves by their devotion to duty during a day when there was no communication of any kind from Battalion Headquarters, and the party in the line became attached to the 6th Battalion in the Cough Drop.

On the 18th, a small reinforcement arrived in the shape of three officers—Lieutenants W. L. C. Rathbone, G. M. Hoste, and B. K. Ware, and fifty other ranks, from the " Non Starters " camp in Bottom Wood, where a few officers and other ranks had been kept out of the fight in order to form a nucleus for reorganisation in case of heavy losses.

Before being relieved on the night of the 19th September by the 1st Battalion The Black Watch, the Civil Service Rifles undertook two more operations. The first was an advance into the Flers Line on the 18th, but as the enemy had by now evacuated this trench, the advance passed off without loss.

But the enemy still held the junction of the Flers Line and Drop Alley, and that portion of the Flers Line west of the junction. The New Zealanders had a party in the Flers Line between the Bosches and the Civil Service Rifles, but the Civil Service Rifles had a small force under Lieutenant B. K. Ware in Drop Alley. These two forces attempted, by joint bombing attacks, to dislodge the Bosches, but the attempt failed. The men were now thoroughly exhausted, for in addition to the

enormous amount of work of the past few days and the excitement of the fray, the last twenty-four hours had been endured
in a pitiless rain, which caused huge chunks of the trenches
to give way. There was mud and rain everywhere and, as there
was no shelter, rifles and Lewis guns eventually became choked
with mud. It was while in this state that the enemy attempted
to drive Lieutenant Ware's party out of Drop Alley. He
partially succeeded at first, but was afterwards driven back.
But at 7.0 p.m. on the 19th, he came again with renewed vigour,
and got down Drop Alley, where the defending troops, with
rifles and Lewis guns out of action, and themselves quite worn
out, were unable to dislodge him. They did not give up without
a struggle, however, and Lieutenant Ware died that night in a
plucky attempt to achieve the impossible. Thus ended the
operations of the Civil Service Rifles at High Wood, but it was
indeed a skeleton of a battalion that Lieut.-Colonel Warrender
led down the New German Road to Bottom Wood on the morning
of the 20th September. Round a huge bonfire these remnants
threw themselves down to get their first rest since leaving
Becourt Wood, and here a pause was made to count the cost
of what was so far the greatest trial of the Civil Service Rifles
and, at the same time, surely their greatest achievement.

To this day, High Wood is regarded by many as the finest
performance of the Battalion during the war. But whether
this is true or no, it is certain that this battle was the most
distinctive landmark in the history of the Civil Service Rifles,
for it was at High Wood where the first great changes took place
in the personnel of the Battalion. Some say it was the last of
the original Battalion, but such a statement is open to question.

Many old faces had gone, but the old spirit still remained,
and there were enough old hands left to train drafts in the way
they should go, and to tell them what manner of men they had
been whose places these freshmen had the honour to fill.

There fell during the fighting at High Wood, so many of the
real flower of the Battalion that it is impossible to do justice
to them by any eulogy here, and it would be invidious to single
out any in particular among so many illustrious dead. Their
names will all be found recorded elsewhere. Suffice it to say
that they died like the true Englishmen of tradition, every one
gallantly and gamely carrying on against odds. In the four
days the casualties amounted to 15 officers, 365 other ranks.

CHAPTER XI

EAUCOURT L'ABBE AND THE BUTTE DE WARLENCOURT

THE so-called camp in Bottom Wood was the essence of discomfort, but after a meal and a few hours rest, a welcome move was made in the evening of the 20th September to Albert, where one night was spent in deserted houses.

The march was continued the following day, and the Battalion arrived at a tented camp in a wood just outside the village of Henencourt, where Corps Headquarters was situated in a magnificent château, the grounds of which were a replica of those of the Palace of Versailles. There was little to suggest the luxury of Versailles, however, in the camp occupied by the Civil Service Rifles, for although the Battalion was depleted, the accommodation was scarce and every one was crowded.

The process of refitting and reorganisation was begun, and to a draft of one officer and 375 other ranks, who joined at Henencourt was added a fair sprinkling of officers, N.C.O.'s and men who had missed High Wood through leave, courses, or other causes. Thus the strength of the Battalion was restored on paper, but in actual fact it was still but a shadow of its former self.

The officers spent most of their time at Henencourt Wood in writing letters of condolence to bereaved parents, and the Company Quartermaster Sergeants and senior N.C.O.'s were busy packing up and sending off the personal effects of the killed and wounded, so that on the whole, the ten days' sojourn in this camp was not a joyous one. The Divisional Follies tried to cheer things up by giving a show one evening, but the proceedings fell flat, and those who wanted a little diversion while the Battalion was at Henencourt sought it in Amiens.

The last day of the month of September, 1916, found the Civil Service Rifles once more on the way back to war, for after spending one night in Albert, they occupied some disused trenches, entirely devoid of dug-outs, in what was known as the Quadrangle, near Mametz Wood. Here they waited eagerly for news of the attack by the 141st Brigade on the village of Eaucourt L'Abbé, for which the 140th Brigade was in reserve.

Numerous contradictory reports reached Colonel Warrender

during the few days spent in the Quadrangle, but at last it became known definitely that Eaucourt L'Abbé had been captured, and that the 140th Brigade would go there to relieve the 141st, but would only hold the line—there would not be any further attack !

The relief which took place on the night of the 4th October, when the Civil Service Rifles relieved the Poplar and Stepney Rifles in the Flers Line at Eaucourt L'Abbé, was an ordeal almost as trying as a battle.

The march from the Quadrangle began at 4.0 p.m. on the 4th, and the tail of the Battalion reached the Flers Line at dawn the next day. The event was so unique that no apology is offered for a somewhat lengthy description :—

All was going well until the corner of High Wood was reached, where, according to plan, guides would be picked up. There were, however, several corners to High Wood, and the Lewis gun limbers, mess cart and medical cart were not taken to the same corner as the one to which the Battalion went.

After a very long delay, while Lewis guns, etc., were carried through the wood from the limbers to the Battalion over many awkward obstacles such as wide trenches and barbed wire, a start was made by half the Battalion, and about two hours afterwards the remainder of the Battalion was ready. The way was along a track of sticky mud of the typical Somme variety. The night was pitch black and the men slipped about and frequently their feet stuck in the mud. It was often necessary for two men to pull at another man to get him out of the mud, and as they got their man out they found themselves stuck in in turn. At one time Colonel Warrender was heard to tell the M.O. that a man had fallen down, but he feared it was no use going back to him " as he must have been trampled in by now." The progress along the track, slow as it was, became slower still when one after another the guides announced that they were lost and had not the slightest idea in which direction to go. A touch of humour crept into the adventure when Colonel Warrender, addressing a guide who said he hadn't the remotest idea where he was, told him to go back to his Commanding Officer and report that he was of no use !

After many hours the Cough Drop was reached by the party bringing up the rear, which included Battalion Headquarters, and here one of the other Companies was met coming in the opposite direction. They, too, had a guide who was lost. The Adjutant now took up the running alone and plunged into the darkness on an exploring tour. He soon came back, and then led the whole party, now consisting of a good many more than half the Battalion, through Drop Alley to the Flers Line. The going now began to tell on the exhausted troops and several there were who collapsed unconscious in Drop Alley, weighed down by the heavy loads they were carrying, and did not finish their journey until the following day.

The Flers Line is chiefly remembered for the number of dead, both English and German, who were still lying about on the floor of the trench and on all the firesteps. There were a few hurriedly-made dug-outs, but these were in such a filthy state as to be unfit to occupy, and although much hard work was done for the next two days, the cleaning of the trench was still unfinished when the troops learnt to their astonishment, on the 7th of October, that they were to attack the Butte de Warlencourt and the Warlencourt Line—an objective some 2,800 yards distant.

Zero was at 2.0 p.m., and the Companies occupied the same relative positions as at High Wood, " A " Company again being on the right. The three Companies on the left were unfortunate once more, for they had to file through the village of Eaucourt l'Abbé soon after leaving their assembly trenches and extend into waves again after negotiating the village. They were caught by the full fury of the German artillery barrage, and those who got through the village were swept down by a most intense machine-gun fire. " A " Company on the right made some little progress, and after crossing the Eaucourt l'Abbé-Le Barque road dug a new line alongside the remnants of other units of the Division, all of whom had met a similar fate. Another attempt was made at night by the 142nd Brigade, but as these troops had not even seen the country in daylight, their attempt failed so completely that they were all withdrawn shortly after zero.

The attack on the Butte de Warlencourt failed, like many attacks subsequently delivered by other Divisions, and the famous Butte did not fall into English hands until the German retreat from the Somme battlefield during the winter of 1916–17.

The attack of the 7th of October differed in many respects from that of the 15th of September. On this occasion there had been no training, no rehearsal over a marked-out course, and in fact some of the troops did not even know there was to be an attack until an hour or so before zero. Even then there were many who were not sure what was the objective. To this day there are some in the Civil Service Rifles who talk of it as the attack on Eaucourt l'Abbé. There was an artillery creeping barrage on this occasion, it is true, but as it moved at the rate of 100 yards per minute and there were 2,800 yards between the jumping-off trenches and the objective, the advancing waves of infantry soon got badly left behind. Tanks were said to be co-operating, but nothing was seen of them.

There were only two officers per Company present on this

occasion, and the C.S.M. and one or two senior N.C.O.'s of each Company were kept out of the fight, so the experienced soldier was in a distinct minority. More than half of the Battalion had never been under fire before, and, as these had only joined a few days previously, a good many of them were not known even by name to the older members of their Platoons. Thus it came about that many men were reported missing on this occasion, and, as none of the survivors knew them, it was impossible to say with any certainty where they had last been seen.

The losses on the 7th of October amounted to five officers, 344 other ranks, and although numerically they are not quite so great as at High Wood, it should be remembered that on this occasion the Battalion was not more than 500 strong at the outset.

During the operations around Eaucourt l'Abbé there was one member of the regiment who added to his already brilliant reputation as a soldier. The work of Lieutenant W. E. Ind on this occasion was more than wonderful. Quickly grasping the situation when the attack failed, by his hard work and resourcefulness he succeeded in restoring something like order out of chaos, not only in his own unit but also in several neighbouring units.

The relief by the 7th Seaforth Highlanders on the 9th of October was a welcome contrast to the previous relief in this sector. The troops quickly found their way out and before midnight had reached the transport lines in Bottom Wood.

Three nights were spent in Albert before the Division entrained on the 13th of October for Longpré, near Abbeville, en route for the Ypres Salient.

Before leaving Albert, the Quartermaster aroused the wrathful indignation of the C.Q.M.S.'s by the issue of a quantity of clothing and equipment which had been applied for at Henencourt. Many of the men for whom it was intended had now become casualties, but that made no difference to the Quartermaster's stores of the Civil Service Rifles. The most important article of clothing was the clean shirt which was issued just before leaving Albert. The troops had not had a clean shirt for many weeks, and the one they discarded was naturally somewhat the worse for wear. One C.Q.M.S. on inquiring at the Orderly Room what should be done with the old shirts was told by an Orderly Room clerk to burn them. The clerk was trying to be funny, but the Q.M.S. missed the point of his humour, and all Companies thereupon threw their old shirts on the dust heap. When he was demobilised some years later the C.Q.M.S. was still explaining to the authorities why he had destroyed his ultra-lousy shirts.

The train journey from Albert to Longpré is surely a record even for the R.O.D. A distance of just over thirty miles was covered in the astonishingly short time of twenty-six hours, during which time many men had left the train, dined in Amiens, visited the local cinema, and still caught the train up again without being recorded as absent. Indeed, during one part of the journey there seemed to be more men walking than were riding. At the same time every one seemed conscious of the fact that he had said good-bye to the dreaded Somme battle-field, so few felt disposed to complain of the shortcomings of the R.O.D.

After detraining at Longpré, two happy days were spent in the village of Villers-sous-Ailly. The men received a hearty welcome from the natives and M. le Maire, who seemed to be the greatest French authority on the organisation of an English infantry battalion. This worthy was very popular with the billeting party, for he had his village completely mapped out, and could tell them whether a particular barn was big enough to hold a platoon, a section, or a Lewis gun team.

The Battalion returned to Longpré on the 16th of October and entrained for Caestre, which was reached in the early hours of the following morning, whence a long and uninteresting march brought the Battalion to scattered billets outside the village of Boeschepe, and after another long march on the 19th, the Civil Service Rifles relieved the 16th Battalion Australian Infantry in support to what was called the Bluff Sub-sector (or Canal Sub-sector) south of Ypres, and close to what had once been the Ypres-Comines canal.

CHAPTER XII

A REST CURE IN THE YPRES SALIENT

To those whose memories of Ypres are only associated with thoughts of mud and slaughter, and who at the mention of the word "Salient" instinctively think of the horrors of Passchendaele, the Menin Road and Hooge, it will seem incredible that there was a time during the war when the Ypres Salient was peaceful and quiet, a place where Divisions, shattered on the Somme, came for recuperation.

It was in such a state that the 47th Division found the Ypres Salient in October, 1916, and after what had been endured in the previous month, it was particularly welcome.

In the Civil Service Rifles reconstruction had only just begun. No drafts had reached the Battalion, which was very much below strength. Some Companies had only one officer, the Company Commander, and practically no N.C.O.'s above the rank of Lance-Corporal. It was well, therefore, that there was no fighting and the sound of a shell was the exception rather than the rule.

The Division had had no experience of trench warfare for some months, and when the Civil Service Rifles on the 24th of October, 1916, relieved the Post Office Rifles in the front line in what was called the Ravine, a section of the Bluff Sector, they found several features of trench warfare which were quite new to them.

In the first place, each Company had a cookhouse in the trenches, and the Company cooks came in with their Companies and cooked all the meals on the spot. Rations were pushed up almost to Company Headquarters in trucks along a light railway, and there was a dump of R.E. material actually in the Battalion area. These were all amenities of trench life hitherto unknown, and all helped to convey the idea that the Civil Service Rifles were making a new start in life. These conditions helped materially to restore the confidence and fighting spirit of troops who were rapidly approaching the "fed-up" state.

The trenches were mostly sandbagged barricades such as had been seen as Festubert, but here they were neatly revetted with expanded metal, and although there was a good deal of water, all the trench floors were boarded. There were recesses labelled for bombs and S.A.A., and although the trench shelters were not by any means shell-proof, the majority at least were weatherproof.

There were many ambitious schemes for winter comforts. A Brigade gum boot store with lots of thigh gum boots was already established, and large shelters were being erected in each Battalion area as drying rooms, where men would be able to dry their clothes. These shelters, however, never got into working order. Another novelty was the precaution taken to prevent trench feet or frost bite. It was arranged that every man should change his socks and rub his feet with whale oil every day, the old socks being sent down every night and exchanged at the Divisional Laundry for alleged clean ones which were brought up with rations the following night.

Thus it was hoped to combat some of the evils which beset the Army during the previous winter, and there is no doubt that these measures bore good fruit, for the losses through sickness during the winter of 1916–17 were less than half those of the previous winter.

But although the prospect at the beginning of winter was very bright, and the troops were looking forward confidently to a spell of quiet life, it was not long before things began to liven up, as though the Ypres Salient had begun to look to its reputation.

The change was first noticeable when, on returning to the front line after a few days in Divisional Reserve at Ottawa Camp, near the village of Ouderdom, the Battalion took over a section of the front line in what was called the Hill 60 Sector, on the 13th of November.

These trenches differed in many respects from those in the Ravine, in spite of the fact that they were practically adjacent. Mining activities were carried on here on a very elaborate scale, and there were several deep tunnels, some, it was said, running as far forward as the German front line on Hill 60 itself. These tunnels were all being worked by one of the Australian Tunnelling Companies, to whom working parties were sent day and night. The main line of the Ypres-Roulers railway ran through the sector, and the old railway cutting formed the right boundary of the Battalion front. The trenches had been in existence for many months, and owing to the continual bombardments, the ravages of weather, and the quaint ideas of sanitation of former occupants of the sector, the area could hardly claim to be a health resort. Large fat rats abounded in and around every trench, and so fat were they that they had lost their turn of speed, and fell easy victims to any who could find time to hunt them. Bully beef and Maconochie's famous meat and vegetable rations were to be found everywhere, Some men say that these were often used in place of trench boards.

Those working in the tunnels with the Australians were impressed, almost awestruck, by the magnitude of the mining operations, which they felt sure would end one day in a miniature earthquake, and they fervently hoped they would be at a safe distance when that should happen. The tunnels were lighted by electricity, the power for which was produced by a gas engine installed underground. A privileged few were allowed to explore the wonderful Berlin Sap, a long tunnel which stretched from some distance in rear of Battalion Headquarters to the German lines.

But it must not be imagined that the troops enjoyed home comforts in this area. The Companies holding the left of the Battalion front had practically no protection from either shell fire or weather, and those who have occupied the curiously-named Metropolitan Left and Metropolitan Right will be ready to swear that there was no more miserable place on the western front. They were, however, little better off than those who were stowed away in the tunnels of Marshall Walk, where the atmosphere reduced the occupants, packed in tight, to a state of coma.

The enemy had now begun to bombard the area fiercely with various kinds of shells and minenwerfer bombs, but fortunately he was kind enough, at first at all events, to limit his bombardments strictly to certain hours of the day. His special effort was always served up during the two hours after lunch, and strangely enough it was mostly bestowed on the Marshall Walk area, where the troops were able to squeeze into the tunnels. The men in other parts of the line had to sit under a ground sheet or a bit or corrugated iron and hope that nothing would come their way. In this way five somewhat anxious days were endured with comparatively few casualties before the Battalion moved into support in another of the wonders of the Ypres Salient—the Railway Dug-outs. These were dug-outs formed by tunnelling into the railway embankment between the village of Zillebeke and Ypres itself. Half the Battalion was accommodated here, the men occupying wire beds which were erected in tiers. The atmosphere was thick, to say the least, and fatigue parties were frequently told off to try to fan the foul air out with gas fans. The other two Companies were at Battersea Farm and Château Belge.

The Railway Dug-outs area had its advantages, however, for there was little shelling and there were opportunities during the day to wander out into the fresh air, to visit the Brigade canteen, and sometimes to visit the ruins of the historic city of Ypres. The working parties at night were employed in pushing trucks of R.E. material along what remained of the railway line to the ration dump of the front line Battalion, in the Hill 60 sector. On the whole the five days at Railway Dugouts were written down as not too bad, and after five more days in the front line in Hill 60 sector, the end of November saw the Battalion in Divisional Reserve in the huts at Ottawa Camp.

The Division had now settled down to a very stereotyped form of warfare, and as there seemed every likelihood that no move would take place for some months, an elaborate programme of work for improving the accommodation both in trenches and camps was embarked upon.

There were two Brigades holding the line and one in reserve occupying four hutted camps in the neighbourhood of the villages of Ouderdom and Busseboom. It was arranged that whenever a Brigade was in reserve, the various Battalions should always go to the same camp. So it came about that the Civil Service Rifles always went to Ottawa Camp. This arrangement, it was hoped, would encourage Battalions to work hard at camp improvements. Works Officers were appointed and pioneer platoons were detailed in each Company for this purpose, but every time the Civil Service Rifles returned to Ottawa Camp they swore no work had been done since they were last there.

Somebody did work in Ottawa Camp, however, for in course of time it became transformed from the sea of mud, with a collection of broken-down, draughty huts, into a tolerably comfortable camp—if any camp in Belgium could be comfortable. The Battalion Mess for sergeants was revived, and under the stewardship of Sergeant R. F. M. Bigby, a fairly successful attempt was made to restore the former glory of the Civil Service Rifles Sergeants' Mess.

In looking back on the year spent in the Ypres Salient, the average member of the Civil Service Rifles, full of the bitter memories of the Menin Road, Hooge and Château Wood, is apt to forget that there was a time when life was quite enjoyable in Ottawa Camp, with the trips to Poperinghe, where there was much gaiety.

It is quite true, however, that at first Ottawa Camp was better known for its discomfort than for anything else, and it was a curious fact that Halifax Camp, which was the home of one of the Support Battalions of a Brigade holding the front line, was much more comfortable.

The month of December 1916 is chiefly notable for the formation of what was known as the " football team "—two officers (Second Lieutenants H. S. Gosney and C. E. Groves) and fifty other ranks. This team began to train for a raid on

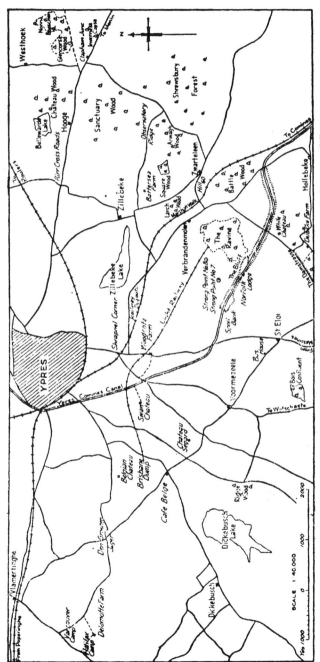

SKETCH MAP TO ILLUSTRATE THE TWELVE MONTHS IN THE YPRES SALIENT OCTOBER 1916 - SEPTEMBER 1917

the German trenches, when they hoped to atone for the ill-luck which had attended previous Civil Service Rifles' raids.

The party was housed in reserve dug-outs in the trenches about Château Ségard, one of the support positions for the Ravine sector, and in addition to training in the surrounding trenches after dark, parties went up to the front line nightly to patrol No Man's Land and inspect the enemy wire.

The scheme was entered into with enthusiasm by the whole party, which was split up into six groups, each with a definite job to do, and they were all brim full of confidence when, at 5.45 p.m. on the 23rd of December, they set out from the front line on their adventure—to the strains of music from a violin in the German lines!

The troops entered the German front line safely enough and worked their way round the appointed area. The opposition, not very strong, was quickly overcome, but no prisoners could be brought back. Two Bosches did get as far as the parapet but there they decided to stay, and as nothing would induce them to come over, " they had to be disposed of," as one of the N.C.O.'s afterwards said in his report.

The return home at the appointed time was carried out successfully and as numerous identifications were brought back, the object of the raid had been achieved. The casualties were very few, but unfortunately they included two killed—Lance-Corporal A. T. C. Geary and Private A. F. Pearson.

The success of the raid put the whole party in good spirits for Christmas, which, as in 1915, was spent in the trenches. The Christmas celebrations duly took place, however, early in January at Ottawa Camp, when each Company had a Christmas dinner and concert. The festival lacked nothing on account of the postponement, and in many sections of the Battalion it was kept up for several days. To celebrate their success the survivors of the raid were given a dinner at which the heroes of the evening were Lance-Sergeant H. J. Steele and Corporal J. H. Swain, who had both been awarded the M.M.

CHAPTER XIII

THE SALIENT IN WINTER

LIFE in the Ypres Salient could now no longer be described as a rest cure, for in addition to increased activity on both sides in the line, the weather was of the real wintry type.

The trenches, where there had been " water, water, everywhere," had become ice-bound, and remained so for many weeks. Trench stores were often taken over by a C.S.M. who could scarcely see them through the ice, but who was told that he would " find they were all right when the thaw came."

To complete the wintry scene, snow had fallen and cast a mantle of white over the ugly sights of war. The Ravine certainly looked pretty now, with the feathery snowflakes glistening on the trees, and here and there an icicle giving the genuine Christmas card impression. No Man's Land, too, has rarely looked more picturesque with the festoons of barbed wire daintily picked out in white. Yes, it was a beautiful scene on a moonlight night in January 1917, but the sentry on the firestep in the front line, with feet frozen, nose, ears and hands feeling as though they were about to drop off, had no eye for such beauty. His idea of beauty at the time was a little so-called dug-out, with a ground sheet or an old post bag (contrary to G.R.O. " XYZ ") hanging over the entrance, and inside a glorious warm " fug " with three or four of his pals stewing in the fumes given off by a tiny brazier. It was so cold on the firestep and the front line trenches were so near to each other, that he daren't stamp his feet, for fear of being heard in the German line. Not that it mattered a great deal about being heard, thought the sentry, for with his hands in such a frozen state that he did not know whether he was holding his rifle or not, he couldn't do much to stop the Bosche if he did come over to-night. Things would not be much better when the Battalion was relieved. He supposed it would be Ottawa Camp again, where it was bitterly cold and the Quartermaster would never give you any fuel. Why couldn't he have a job like " Posh Harry " at the Brigade School, he wondered ? At any rate, there would be a comfortable billet there, and a fire. He must get a stripe, that's what it came to, and then if he could not get a job at the Brigade School or at the Divisional School in Poperinghe, at any rate he might get sent there on a course. He was fed up with this life, he was sure, and when his turn of sentry duty was finished and he was promptly put on an ice-breaking fatigue, he began to think that there was some sense after all in the peace talk that one read of in the newspapers at this time. If only they would talk about it seriously ! But what could one expect when the newspaper folk described the peace talk as " an insult to Tommy in the trenches " ?

Meditations such as the foregoing were not uncommon in the early part of 1917, when the wintry weather was almost the sole topic of conversation. But what was dreaded more than the frost and snow was the thaw which would follow, and how every man prayed that his Battalion would move into Divisional Reserve the day the thaw came !

Before the thaw came, however, the Civil Service Rifles were to have a little excitement in the front line, for one night in the middle of January, the Bosche, who had evidently been reading the story of the escape of Mary Queen of Scots from Lochleven Castle, had attired his patrols in white raiment and sent them out across the snow. The trick came off, and the Bosches entered the trench known as Berry Post, inflicted casualties on the garrison, and got back to their own lines unhurt.

This feat so impressed the authorities that by the time the thaw had fairly set in, white patrol jackets were awaiting collection from ordnance.

Many Transport men have unpleasant recollections of nights on this sector, where rations were taken up to the front line in trucks drawn by mules on the light railways from Woodcote Farm. In theory, loaded trucks were picked up at the Farm and hauled to the Ravine or elsewhere, there unloaded, and taken back to be ready for use next day. In practice, the trucks were usually at the wrong end of the railway to start with ; and when obtained they invariably came off the rails at intervals on the up-journey—to a chorus of curses from the accompanying fatigue party. Drivers have bitter memories of nights when shelling occurred while trucks were off the rails. They admit that it was only human for the fatigue party to go to ground ; but they still cannot see how one man could be expected to manage a distracted mule and also unload, re-rail and re-load a truck of trenchboards.

It was here that Onions, chief Bolshevik of the Battalion mules was lost. After the line had been broken by shell-fire, she was sent up at dawn to bring back stranded trucks. Enemy observers traced her back to Brisbane Dump and sent out an S. O. S. reporting her presence there. Onions left hastily with a dislike of barrage fire and a wound in the head, and was sent forthwith to the Base to be seen no more by the Civil Service Rifles.

* * * * * *

Small drafts were continually arriving during the winter of 1916–17, and they often included several old N.C.O.'s and men of the original Battalion, who were coming out for their second trip to France. Such men were generally given a rousing send off by their companions at Hazeley Down Camp, Winchester, where the Reserve Battalion was stationed. The war cry of the returned warriors at the time was " Everybody once, before anybody twice " and the unofficial flag, known as the " Twicers " Flag, which was usually carried aloft on the march to the station, has since been framed, and now hangs in the Civil Service Rifles' Club to commemorate the once famous " F " Company of the Civil Service Rifles Reserve Battalion.

For some unknown reason the officers joining the Battalion belonged to regiments outside London. There were representatives of the various Battalions of the Manchester Regiment, the Northern Cyclists and the Hampshire Regiment. In fact, so many changes had taken place among the officers of the Battalion, that by February, 1917, not a single one remained of those who had embarked as officers in March 1915.

An interesting innovation during the early weeks of 1917, was the starting of a Regimental Drum and Fife Band. The R. S. M. called it a Corps of Drums, the troops knew it at first as those —— tin whistles, but under the leadership of Sergeant Drummer Harmon, the Regimental Band became an accomplished fact, and the Civil Service Rifles had music on the march for the first time since coming to France—except for the early spring of 1916, when " Mattie " Hull conducted a mouth organ and tin whistle band among the Lewis gunners.

A change from the eternal round of trench life came about towards the end of February, when it fell to the lot of the Civil Service Rifles to act for one month as Works Battalion in the Tenth Corps area. The Companies were scattered over a very wide area, " A " being at Chateau Belge, near Kruistraathoeke, " B " at Coppernollehoek and Poperinghe, " C " at Pacific Sidings between Busseboom and Poperinghe, and " D " at Vancouver Camp, close to Vlamertinghe. Battalion Headquarters remained at Ottawa Camp. The Companies were employed daily on working parties, chiefly under the Canadian Railway Construction Company, on work connected with the laying of a light railway from Poperinghe to the forward area. After the discomforts of trench life, the change was very welcome, particularly with " B " Company, who had rather wonderful billets, and " C " Company, who were all under one roof within easy distance of Poperinghe.

The Companies were still scattered on the 17th of March, so it was not possible for the Battalion to celebrate the day with a united gathering, but " C " Company had a very successful show at Pacific Siding which was attended by representatives from all the other Companies. The Sergeants held a belated but very hearty celebration on another day, and a party from " B " Company held a dinner in Poperinghe.

*   *   *   *   *   *

Throughout the first six months of the time spent in the Ypres Salient, the Transport Lines were established at a typical Belgian farm, and consequently no gathering of Transport men is now complete without a few tales of Delanotte Farm.

In addition to the Transport, the Quartermaster and his staff spent a good deal of their time at Delanotte Farm, where also the Civil Service Rifles' dentist, Corporal E. Pitt, was installed with all his stock in trade. The Civil Service Rifles claim to be unique among Infantry Battalions in the B. E. F. in that they alone possessed their own dentist, who, although fully qualified, was primarily an infantryman and was not one of the R. A. M. C. attached.

During his service in France, Corporal Pitt has attended to a distinguished clientele, including at least one Brigadier General, but he showed no class distinctions in his dental chair, and the humble private was always sure of just as careful treatment as was given to his Brigadier.

Pitt often had to work amid strange surroundings, but his surgery at Delanotte Farm was perhaps his best known home, and one of his patients has recorded his impressions of it :

" In the last great European War the ambitious Emperor who may be regarded as the Kaiser's prototype stated that an army marched on its stomach. But what is a stomach without its teeth ? (vide any advertisements of ' a complete set from one guinea upwards '). At any rate the British Army has come to regard the teeth of its lads as anxiously as the fond mother regards her little one's chewing organs. These few remarks will serve to introduce our hero.

" Imagine a brick farm-house in a part of Belgium where the mud is too muddy for words. The house nestles in a swamp of green viscous slime. This was for many months the locale of the C.S.R. Transport while the boys were disporting themselves in the ditches (misnamed ' trenches ') in the Ypres district. The room of the farmhouse was of fairly decent size, with a low ceiling supported by stout smoke-grimed beams. It was always well patronised by the lads of the Transport, who would discuss the inevitable eggs and chips and sip their coffee or beer all day long. At a large sink by the window the good lady of the house, assisted variously by a submissive husband, a daughter (who could by no stretch of imagination be called a coquette !) and a son, seemed eternally engaged either in preparing a salad of chickweed and groundsel (or so it seemed), or in counting the stock of dried haricots. In the other corner by the window, there was a complete dental establishment installed. This was the scene of the labours of the indefatigable Pitt, and there was nothing of the horse-doctor's methods about him. I can assure you that he wielded the cocaine-injecting needle as expertly as the one and only Sherlock himself. Did you want a tooth scraped or stopped, or filled, or coddled in any way whatever, our dentist would say ' right,' and place a fresh cigarette in his holder (would that I received a royalty on the cigarettes he smoked !) Then he would select some fearsome-looking—but really harmless— instruments from his plenteous stock, and carry on. His sideline (something like the ' making bricks in spare time ' stunt) was treating cases that would ordinarily fall to the care of the M.O. if he were available. It was surprising how the fame of Pitt spread near and far ; and many and various were his clients. The amusing part was the complete nonchalance of the people of the house. They would carry on their weird and wonderful culinary processes at the sink while the amateur doctor extracted teeth and poured away bloody water and rinsed foul dressings under their very noses. In this atmosphere of eggs and chips, steaming coffee, stale beer, tobacco smoke, flies, and sometimes washing, Pitt carried on his labours day by day, month by month, until the Battalion was sent away to happier (?) hunting grounds. . . .

" Jolly old Pitt ! How many of us had cause to bless the fact that we could go to him for healing balm in our time of bitter sorrow ! "

* * * * * *

The Battalion was reassembled after being employed for a month as Works Battalion, and on the 21st of March renewed its acquaintance with the front line trenches in the Ravine. The trenches were no longer ice-bound, but the official first day of Spring did not live up to its name, for snow and sleet fell throughout the night. Eight uneventful days in the Ravine were followed by a similar period in support in the neighbourhood of Swan Château and Château Segard. Hitherto when the Battalion had been at Swan Château the chief recreation had been sliding on the pond in the château grounds. Captain Ind, in fact, made a nightly practice of leading Headquarter Company in sliding on the ice by moonlight. On this occasion, however, boating and fishing were freely indulged in. There was an odd looking craft on the pond, which was in great demand, and the most popular bait for the fish seemed to be a Mills bomb— though this bait was not sanctioned by the B.E.F. Angling Society. It was in fact forbidden by G.R.O., so it naturally follows that no angler was ever known to use the bait.

Any man who thought the Battalion had come to the Ypres Salient for boating and fishing, however, was rudely disillusioned when a return was made to the front line in the familiar Ravine. The London Irish had just finished a big raid on the German lines when the Civil Service Rifles relieved them on the night of the 7th of April, and henceforth things livened up very considerably in this sector, where life had previously been tolerably quiet. The Bosche now bombarded furiously, and on the 9th of April (Easter Monday) he raided the Battalion on the immediate left of the Civil Service Rifles, causing pretty heavy casualties. The raid took place at 6.30 p.m. and the accompanying fireworks were kept up throughout the night. As a sample of the frightfulness that could be served up in the Salient, it was fairly complete, and the Civil Service Rifles, although not in the raided trenches, lost thirteen killed and eighteen wounded during the night.

The Division very soon afterwards had to take over a little more of the line immediately south of the Ypres—Comines Canal, known as the Spoil Bank Sector, and as it meant giving up the hated Hill 60 Sector, the change was a very popular one.

Ottawa Camp now came within the area of another Division, and the Civil Service Rifles, on being relieved on the 12th of April by the First Surrey Rifles, moved into Divisional Reserve in Devonshire Camp, near Busseboom.

Early in April rumours of a big Spring offensive began to relieve the monotony, and the story was passed from one to another in strict confidence that the Civil Service Rifles would soon attack a château in a wood just south of the canal, where the Adjutant was of opinion that " we shall have some interesting wood fighting."

The next trip to the front line was to the Spoil Bank section itself, whence rumour had it that the attack would some day be launched, and amateur tacticians were thus able to study the scheme on the spot. A preliminary reconnaissance generally ended in the observer hoping he would be away on leave or on a course when the attack should eventually take place.

An unsuccessful attempt at a raid by the enemy at 4.30 a.m. on the 25th April was the only incident of note in a somewhat uninteresting stay in the front line, where nearly every trench appeared to be open to direct observation from the Bosche. The mystery about the Spoil Bank sector, with its trenches so open and devoid of shelter, was that in five days there were only eight casualties, all of which occurred during the enemy's attempted raid. The bombardment during the raid was such as to make every man look forward with more than usual keenness to the relief on the following night by the 6th Battalion, when the Civil Service Rifles moved to Dominion Camp, adjoining Devonshire Camp.

CHAPTER XIV

THE MORINGHEM TREK

A LONG stay of eleven days in Dominion Lines ended with a return to the Support positions around Swan Château on the 8th of May, but only three days were spent here (during which time there were thirteen casualties, an unusually high number for the comparative safety of support positions) before the Battalion was relieved by the Poplar and Stepneys, and moved back to the village of Dickebusch for two days, before starting on the "Moringhem Trek," the first affair of its kind since the memorable trek to the Somme.

The trek began on the 13th of May with a march to the village of Watou, and the old soldier now knew that he would soon be taking part in an attack. "They're not taking us all this way for exercise, or simply for our amusement" he told the latest joined recruit as they marched along, "but it's worth it to get away from the Salient for a few days and to see the civvies once more without any fear of shelling. And remember, when we go over the odds are generally about four to one on a blighty, so don't worry."

The billets were good in Watou, but they were even better in the village of Sercus, where the Battalion, after marching through Hazebrouck, spent the second night. General regret was felt that only one night was spent in this village, and on the third day, after passing through Arques and St. Omer, the training area was reached and the Companies were billeted in the village of Moringhem and the neighbouring villages. On the whole the billets were poor and uncomfortable, besides being scattered. "A" and Headquarters Company were in Moringhem itself, "B" and "C" were about a mile and a half away in Petit Difques, and "D" were in the little hamlet of Cuslinghem.

It was announced that about three weeks would be spent in this district, and a somewhat ambitious programme of sports and recreation was drawn up. The training was often finished soon after mid-day. An inter-platoon football competition was started, and preliminary heats for the Battalion Sports

Meeting, to be held on the 20th of May, were run off during the early days of the " holiday."

The Brigadier having expressed a wish that officers and men should be given facilities to visit St. Omer, parties were made up each day for that purpose. The men generally went in G.S. wagons and limbers, and the officers usually returned *a voiture.*

A novelty in Regimental Sports was introduced on the 19th of May at what was reported in the *Financial Times* as the Moringhem May Meeting, when the only event was a horse race for officers' chargers.

The race took place after church parade, and was over a five furlong course behind the village church. Unfortunately, one or two of the starters were not quite sure where the course was, and consequently several horses had to wait at " the tapes" while Battalion orderlies scoured the village for missing runners and jockeys. More unfortunate still was the experience of the " bookie " who, at great trouble, had secured costumes for himself and his clerk, but who spent the morning wandering about the neighbouring hills, vainly searching for the course, and cursing his clerk for a fool.

Lieutenant Craig, the Transport Officer, acted as starter to a field of seven. The Adjutant's horse, Bunty, was first away, but his jockey lost a stirrup and could not keep the lead. Entering the straight, the Medical Officer (Captain C. M. Gozney) on the Boy, was in front, and, shaking off the challenge by Bunty and Sunshine, he rode a good race and won by a short head from the former, with Sunshine (ridden by Captain F. D. Balfour) close up third. The winner started at 5-2, Bunty at 3-1, and Sunshine at 100-3 . The favourite Polly (5-4), ridden by Captain Bowers Taylor, a heavyweight jockey, was quite unable to give the weight away to the leaders. The bookie, it should be mentioned, arrived on the course just in time to " pay out," as there had been considerable ante-post betting, and all the placed horses had been well backed.

The Battalion Sports Meeting on the following day was marred by orders to send off a digging party of 200 other ranks to dig trenches on the training ground. The whole Battalion had turned up on the Transport Field, and cookers were in attendance so that tea could be had on the ground, but after the departure of the working party, interest in the Sports died down, and the crowd, somewhat disappointed, filtered away.

Much keener interest was taken in the Inter-platoon football competition, in the final of which Numbers 5 and 15 Platoons met three times at Moringhem without being able to come to a decision. Two hours exciting play on each of the first two occasions failed to produce even a goal, but at the third meeting, play actually continued until Lights Out, when the score was two goals all. It should, perhaps, be mentioned that in these days of summer time it was not uncommon for Lights Out to be sounded while it was still daylight. The football final was not decided until after the Battalion had been in the front line. The score on that occasion, when Number 15 Platoon won by no less than nine goals to nothing, was an eloquent but sad testimony to what had happened since the three drawn games at Moringhem.

The stay at Moringhem differed in many respects from the preparation for the Somme battle in 1916. On this occasion the Division marched straight to its training ground, which was reached in three days. The marked out course quickly made its appearance, and it was made known at the outset that the 140th Brigade was training for the attack on the German positions around the White Château, just south of the Canal, near Hollebeke. Moreover, the " non-starters " were selected at the beginning of the training, and the rehearsals were carried out with the officers, N.C.O.'s and men who were going to take part in the actual attack.

The training was nothing like so strenuous as that for the High Wood battle, and the men thus finished their day's work with sufficient energy left for football and other sports in the evening. In one respect the experience of the Somme preparation was repeated. The Adjutant, Captain W. E. Ind, M.C., threw himself whole heartedly and enthusiastically into the work of training the Battalion and had very quickly mastered every detail of the scheme. It was very largely due to his efforts that the Civil Service Rifles left Moringhem thoroughly prepared for their share in the battle and so full of confidence in their success.

On the whole a very happy time had been spent at Moringhem, and there was no great anxiety to leave the place on the 31st of May, when the Battalion returned by train from St. Omer to Poperinghe, where, as they marched out of the station, the troops were greeted at once with a few shells—just as a reminder that they were back in the Salient.

The discomforts of the Ypres Salient were rarely more forcibly illustrated than on the afternoon of the arrival at the so-called tented camp in Dominion Lines. The march from Poperinghe Station took place in the afternoon, and the Battalion marched into Dominion Lines with visions of a comfortable camp and a welcome cup of tea ! The men were doomed to disappointment, for the " camp " proved to be a strip of waste ground, very dusty, and without even a blade of grass on it. There were a few bivouac sheets to be issued to each Company, and there were about three bell tents for officers. Beyond this there was not a stick of camp equipment of any kind. The disappointment was all the keener because the Area Commandant was a Civil Service Rifles officer, and it was thought he might have treated his own Regiment a little better. The other three Battalions of the Brigade were comfortably housed in huts.

The country all around presented a very different aspect from that seen in the autumn of 1916, when the Division came to Ypres for a rest. On all sides one now saw signs of the coming offensive. The roads were lined with big ammunition dumps, a few of which were blown up nightly by Bosche artillery fire, which had increased very considerably during the past month. The English artillery, too, had increased their activity, and some wonderful bombardments were witnessed both by day and night. The Bosche, in fact, could not have had much doubt of what was in store for him. The only doubt in his mind would be how much longer he would be allowed to remain in his front line trenches.

A mysterious-looking enclosure, marked " Segregated Area," attracted a good deal of attention from the curious among the troops, who, after reading the notice outside, that no horses could be admitted, discovered that many tanks were housed there. Members of the Civil Service Rifles who had been on the Somme heaved a sigh of relief when they learnt that, although tanks were co-operating in the coming attack, none were allotted a definite part in the task of their Battalion.

The 2nd of June was devoted to final preparations for the battle. Officers got their men together for a little extra talk, and all ranks eagerly studied maps and aeroplane photographs, of which there was a generous supply and which showed clearly how thoroughly the artillery had prepared the way. There was an atmosphere of suppressed excitement similar to that of the days before High Wood, but on this occasion there was greater confidence, inspired by the unmistakable evidence on all sides of the magnificent work of the artillery and the Air Force.

Company Commanders went up to reconnoitre the support positions which the Battalion was to occupy the next day, and working parties were sent out along the cross-country tracks, which had been made to ease the traffic along the roads. These parties were occupied all day in the pleasant task of filling up the shell holes which the Bosche had made overnight.

The battle surplus to be left behind when an Infantry Battalion took part in an attack had by this time been clearly defined by General Headquarters, and consequently a large party of " non-starters " joined the Divisional Reinforcement Camp before the Battalion left for the trenches on the 3rd of June. These included, in addition to two of the regular Company

Commanders, representatives of every platoon and specialist section in the Battalion—picked N.C.O.'s and men who would form a worthy nucleus on which to build a new Battalion in the event of heavy casualties being suffered. The Divisional Reinforcement Camp was commanded by Lieut.-Colonel Warrender, who had left the Civil Service Rifles the previous November to command the 47th Divisional School at Poperinghe.

CHAPTER XV

THE Regimental Diary gives a detailed description of the career of the Civil Service Rifles from the time of leaving Dominion Lines on the night of the 3rd of June to the return from the trenches after the battle :—

" Just before we started for the trenches at 10.0 p.m., the Bosche dropped a few big shells on the track near the segregated area, so it was felt that as we had to pass this point the war had started in earnest. Fortunately the whole Battalion passed this area without mishap, and the journey to the trenches was very quiet until we approached Café Belge, when we received a message that the Bosche was shelling that spot freely with gas shells. The information proved to be true, and the Battalion had its first experience of a real gas shell bombardment—happily without any casualties. We reached the support positions—trenches in the vicinity of Swan Château and Château Segard—without any further adventure, and after relieving the Poplar and Stepney Rifles, spent a quiet night in very crowded quarters.

" The Battalion spent three days in these trenches, and on the whole they were very pleasant. The weather was good, and there were practically no working parties, so the men got plenty of time for rest. The time was spent in such final preparation for the attack as issuing bombs, rifle grenades, ground flares, picks, shovels and chewing gum (one stick between two) and rations for ' the day.' The Company Commanders reconnoitred the assembly positions on the morning of the 6th, and by that afternoon everything was ready for the move up to the assembly trenches. The whole Battalion was in excellent spirit and every one was full of confidence. The men had taken a very keen interest in the orders and every man knew the part he had to play.

" We had a quiet move to the assembly trenches at night, and although the tracks and back areas were receiving their usual nightly ration of shells, there were no casualties.

" It was now known that the attack would be delivered at dawn, and the few hours before zero were spent in comparative peace. The trenches were those occupied by the Civil Service Rifles on their last visit to the front line. ' A ' Company was in the old Lock House, near the Spoil Bank by the side of the Canal. The remaining Companies were on their right in West Terrace and Grenade Trench, in the order in which they were to attack. ' D ' was on the right,

CIVIL SERVICE RIFLES 141

'B' next, 'C' next, and for the attack 'A' Company came out of the Lock House and formed the left flank.

" Zero for the great 2nd Army attack was at 3.10 a.m. on the 7th of June, but our Battalion took no part in the first phase. An hour before zero, all Company Commanders were to report to Battalion Headquarters to be on the spot if anything went wrong with the first phase. Battalion Headquarters was in a smelly, wet dug-out in West Terrace. It had walls of brick and some attempt at a concrete roof. The party assembled there consisted of the Commanding Officer, Lieutenant-Colonel H. Marshall (Hampshire Regiment), the Adjutant, Captain W. E. Ind, M.C., and the four Company Commanders—'A' Company, Captain A. Bowers Taylor (Manchester Regiment, attached) ; 'B' Company, Captain G. C. Grimsdale ; 'C' Company, Second-Lieutenant P. Davenport ; and 'D' Company, Second-Lieutenant G. Hasleham (Manchester Regiment, attached). The Signals Officer, Second-Lieutenant R. W. Illing and the Bombing Officer, Second-Lieutenant O. E. Burden, also hovered about, and there was the usual ' chorus' generally found hanging round Battalion Headquarters—servants, police, pioneers, signallers and runners. Wallis, the ' head waiter,' moved about as unconcerned as ever, with sandwiches and whisky and soda for the guests. The gathering reminded one of Bairnsfather's sketch, ' An hour before going into trenches.' Ind tried hard to keep the conversation going ; Grimsdale, who occupied one of the few seats, appeared somewhat subdued, though he had a few knotty problems to put to the assembly. Hasleham, who squatted tailor fashion on the floor, went to sleep, while Bowers Taylor and Davenport spent the time trying to follow his example—without much success.

" At 3.10 a.m. precisely, the floor, walls and ceiling began to rock furiously, and we realised that the Australian tunnellers in Marshall Walk had not boasted idly when they told us last November that their mine under Hill 60 would one day stagger humanity. A moment later, another big mine went up at St. Eloi, and at the same time the most wonderful bombardment there has every been known was let loose. Big guns, howitzers and field guns seemed to be firing from everywhere behind us, and one could not help feeling overawed by the magnificence of our artillery. The machine guns joined in the fun, and the whole thing inspired every one with great confidence. No human beings could possibly withstand such a bombardment. It was the noise of the bombardment, so often described as drumfire, which was mistaken afar off for the noise of the mines, and imaginative journalists with a keen sense of hearing afterwards wrote tales of how they had heard the mines in London. The mines actually made comparatively little noise.

" We had three hours to wait before our time came to jump off, so we tried to see what was going on in front, where the 7th and 8th Battalions were attacking the White Château and neighbouring trenches. Little could be seen, however, beyond a big cloud of dust and here and there a tank toiling over the shell holes. The Bosche, apparently, had no guns to spare for us, as he left us entirely alone, and at 5.15 a.m. we moved up to our jumping off trenches undisturbed.

" The Adjutant, who for many weeks had worked on this scheme harder than the producer of plays ever worked on a great masterpiece, came up to see us off, and as the situation was so quiet we were able to form up in waves outside our jumping-off trenches. Our new padré, too, came along to wish the ' dear lads ' the best of luck, and to distribute a large quantity of cigarettes. A staunch friend to the troops at all times, the Rev. Ernest Beattie was surely the most cheery padré a Battalion could have had. It did one good to see his genial smile whenever he came round the line.

" The first wave consisted of one platoon of each Company, ' A ' on the left under Sergeant Steele, then 'C' (Second-Lieutenant Stoneman), ' B ' (Sergeant G. T. Bachell), and ' D ' (Second-Lieutenant G. T. Mellett). An additional platoon of ' B ' under Second-Lieutenant Temple was attached to this wave which, under the command of the Officer Commanding ' C ' Company, moved off at 6.25 a.m. The Battalion scouts, who had previously gone forward to reconnoitre, had just returned and reported that all had gone well with the Post Office Rifles, who were holding all their objectives, and that the stream beyond, which we had to cross, was practically dry and offered no obstacle.

" The first wave had a good start, and in a line of sections in single file went unhindered through the three objectives held by the Post Office Rifles and across the aforesaid stream in the White Château grounds, until it opened out to two lines in extended order and halted under the barrage in a hollow in front of the first objective, Oak Crescent, a trench just south of the White Château stables. The first wave of the 6th Battalion, who were attacking the stables on our left, moved off at the same time. While waiting for the barrage to lift, we suffered a few casualties.

" The scene in the hollow while waiting for the barrage to lift was a truly remarkable one. The inevitable mixing up of waves had occurred, and the 2nd, 3rd and 4th waves, who were following the first at five minute intervals, here became merged into one mass, and the scene looked like the field for a big cross-country race. The mix-up had occurred owing to the men crossing the rough ground much more quickly than had been expected. In the background a tank was slowly making its way across the line of our advance to assist the 6th Battalion at the stables if necessary. A small crowd gathered round it and watched it with interest. What was most extraordinary was the very slight enemy fire, and men were able to sort themselves out more or less with ease.

" When the barrage lifted, the first wave went forward to assault Oak Crescent, but the difficulty was not so much to capture it as to recognise it, for our guns had done their work so well that it was hard to find the place where the trench had been—and there was no trace of a Bosche either alive or dead. The second wave, consisting of one platoon of ' C ' Company under Sergeant Glass, and one platoon of 'D' Company with Company Headquarters, arrived to ' mop up ' the trench, but as they could not find any trench to mop up, they devoted their time to trying to dig one instead. About this time the Officer Commanding ' A ' Company, Captain A. Bowers Taylor, was killed, and the Officer Commanding ' D ' Company,

Photo by The Chesterfield Studios Co., Chesterfield.

CAPTAIN W. E. IND, M.C.
Adjutant 1st Batt., 15th March, 1916, till his death in
Action, 7th June, 1917.

To face page 142.

Second-Lieutenant Hasleham, was wounded, and in addition the Battalion suffered its most serious loss since leaving England. Lieutenant Ind, who, in his eagerness to see that everything went well, had followed the Battalion up to the hollow ground before the first objective, was hit in the head by a piece of shell, and, although he was taken down immediately, he was so badly wounded that he died the same evening without recovering consciousness in No. 10 Casualty Clearing Station, near Poperinghe. So the Civil Service Rifles lost the finest Territorial soldier who ever served with them. Fortunately the news did not get round for some time, but it had a somewhat depressing effect when it became known, for needless to say, Lieutenant Ind was loved by every officer, N.C.O. and man in the Battalion. No man could have worked harder for the welfare of a Battalion than he did, nor could anyone be more fearless and unselfish than he was. He had been with the 1st Civil Service Rifles continuously since the Foreign Service Battalion was formed, and throughout he had devoted himself wholeheartedly to the Regiment, whose members he was ever ready to help in any way he possibly could. He was a magnificent soldier, a thorough gentleman, and an ideal friend, and his loss has left a gap in the Battalion which can never be adequately filled. He had been looked upon for so long as so essential a part of the Battalion that his many friends found it difficult to realise that he had been killed.

" By a strange coincidence, Lieutenant-Colonel H. H. Kemble, M.C., the Commanding Officer of the 23rd London Regiment (who, as Captain Kemble, had been Ind's Company Commander in the Civil Service Rifles during their first six months in France) was mortally wounded almost at the same time as his old friend, and died the same night in the same ward. These two old comrades were buried side by side in the Military Cemetery just south of Poperinghe between the railway and the road to Westoutre.

" Lieutenant-Colonel Kemble's death was lamented by all who knew him in the Civil Service Rifles, where he was so well known and respected as a very gallant Company Commander.

" But although, as has been stated, the loss of Lieutenant Ind had a somewhat depressing effect, it did not interfere with the attack, and the third wave, consisting of one platoon of ' A ' Company (Second-Lieutenant G. W. Ackworth), one of ' C ' Company (Second-Lieutenant T. Woods), one of ' B ' (Second-Lieutenant Samuel) and one of ' D ' (Second-Lieutenant Margrett), under the Officer Commanding ' B ' Company, moved through the line of what was once Oak Crescent, and took their objective, Oblong Trench, with little opposition. •

" The fourth wave, also consisting of a platoon from each Company ('A,' Second-Lieutenant L. C. Morris, ' B,' Second-Lieutenant C. Stevenson, ' C,' Second-Lieutenant C. V. Marchant, and ' D,' Second-Lieutenant Moran), now moved through Oak Crescent and amalgamated with the first wave. The two together then moved forward, with an additional platoon of ' A ' Company (Second-Lieutenant A. Wilson) on the left, and captured the final objective, Oblong Reserve, where a few tired and frightened Germans readily gave themselves up.

" About 200 yards beyond the final objective was a ruined building, known as Delbske Farm, surrounded by a trench. The instructions were that a patrol was to be pushed out to the farm, which, if not held strongly, was to be rushed and captured. A kind of scramble was accordingly made for the farm by a party consisting of ' C ' Company Headquarters, and Nos. 9 and 11 Platoons, with Sergeant Steele's platoon of ' A ' Company and any odd men of other Companies who happened to be handy. The farm and trench were taken with little opposition, and about thirty prisoners came pouring out of the building anxious to be shown the way ' home.'

" In every case throughout the day the objective had been captured with ease. There were very few Bosches to be found, and these immediately gave themselves up without a struggle when we entered their trenches. Indeed, the only infantry action took place after the trench at Delbske Farm had been taken, when patrols, going out to right and left, were subject to rifle fire from Bosche patrols, who later in the morning seemed to have recovered from their fright sufficiently to inflict a few casualties on the occupants of the trench outside the farm. It was here that Sergeant Steele and Corporal Freeman, of ' A ' Company, after doing sterling work on patrol, were shot through the head and killed instantly.

" Late in the afternoon the Bosche began shelling heavily, but although our aeroplanes twice reported him to be massing for counter-attack, he was effectively dispersed by our artillery and did not even leave his trenches.

" The night was fairly quiet except for some desultory shelling ; but the troops were all very tired after their efforts of the past 24 hours, and it came as a very pleasant surprise when early on the morning of the 8th, the 2nd Leinsters arrived and relieved us. The four Companies moved back to Ecluse Trench—a support trench running south from the canal about half a mile behind our original assembly positions. It was quite a comfortable place and the weather was fine and warm. The tired troops were therefore able to enjoy a solid day's sleep, undisturbed by shells. They were all very proud of their victory, and when they were not sleeping they were all talking at once, comparing souvenirs and recounting their various experiences."

*   *   *   *   *

So ended the first phase of the capture of the Messines-Wytschaete Ridge. It had been a wonderful demonstration of the power of artillery supported by a thorough aeroplane reconnaissance. From the point of view of the infantry it had been a " walk over," at least so far as the Civil Service Rifles were concerned. Tales were told of hand-to-hand struggles in the vicinity of the White Château, but the German troops opposed to the Civil Service Rifles evidently knew whom they had to deal with and they wisely refrained from indulging in any fighting. The casualties, happily, were few, and the victory, considering the number of objectives and the extent of ground covered, was undoubtedly a cheap one. It was illustrated very clearly, however, how impossible it is, when advancing over a wide area of rough ground, to arrive at the distant objective in anything like the waves laid down in the training pamphlets.

Here were conditions ideal for a model attack—excellent artillery support, well-trained 'men, every one of whom was keen and clearly understood the scheme which had been so thoroughly rehearsed, and a very weak opposition, and yet the attack became little more than a scramble after the first objective was passed. At the same time the troops had taken and held all the objectives allotted to them, and there was a feeling of satisfaction among the members of the Civil Service Rifles that the Battalion had done all that it was asked to do in what was, so far, the greatest British victory of the war.

After two days' rest in Ecluse Trench a return was made to the front line, and the 6th Battalion were relieved on the 10th of June in a trench known as Opal Reserve—on the left of Oblong Reserve, familiar to the Civil Service Rifles as one of their objectives on the 7th. Battalion Headquarters was in what was left of the White Château itself.

Although only two days were spent here it was a much more trying experience than the battle had been, and the casualties suffered were considerably more than the average for merely holding the line. The Bosche had now reorganised his artillery, and he was using it to some purpose on the White Château and its grounds. The first taste of the trouble was given to No. 9 platoon of " C " Company on their way to the front line. Starting out with about twenty men under Second Lieutenant Stoneman, only nine reached the front line in Opal Reserve, four having been killed, and seven wounded.

The front line trench, which was mostly mud, was held by " B " and " C " Companies, " A " and " D " being in reserve in a series of German " pill box " shelters. Second Lieutenant L. L. Burtt was now in command of " B " Company, and it is said he spent the time in being pulled out of the mud by his Sergeant-Major (R. H. Burden), and in turn pulling him out. There was no shelter of any kind for either of the front line Companies, but " C " Company Headquarters occupied a niche cut out of the wall of the trench, and there the Company Commander sat with an officer on each side of him, like statues in the walls of a cathedral.

The time here was spent in clearing the trench of the ever-falling debris, dodging shells, and digging a jumping-off trench for the 41st Division, who were shortly to continue the advance. For this purpose they relieved the 47th Division on the night of the 12th of June, and the Civil Service Rifles gladly handed over their strip of mud to the 18th Battalion K.R.R., and made

K

their way out to Chippewa Camp, near Reninghelst, where they arrived at about 6.0 a.m. on the 13th of June, so tired that they didn't care a fig who held the Messines-Wytschaete Ridge.

*   *   *   *   *   *

In accordance with the usual practice after a big battle, the Division went right back for rest and reorganisation, and after two days' marching the Civil Service Rifles, on the 16th of June, reached the village of Ebblinghem, between Hazebrouck and St. Omer.

The twelve days spent in this village were chiefly devoted to preparing for an inspection by the Divisional Commander, and training for the Divisional Water Carnival at Blaringhem. An al fresco concert in " D " Company's billet on the 23rd of June threatened to fall flat, but the arrival, at a gallop, of a limber with a large barrel of beer on board set things moving, and the concert finished very well.

The Divisional Water Carnival was held in the canal at Blaringhem on the 26th, and the crowd of visitors made one think of a Town Regatta on the Thames, the fair sex being well represented. The weather was gloriously fine, and the comic events were well to the fore in the programme. The Battalion carried off its fair share of the honours, the chief success being that of the R.Q.M.S., W. B. Hart, who built the winning boat in the odd craft race, cleverly rowed by R. D. Tidmarsh, who won an easy victory by a distance. A small lottery was arranged for the visitors, and Mdlle. Victoria, the fair damsel at the Civil Service Rifles Headquarters billet, won the first prize. This brought to a close the holiday at Ebblinghem, for the march back to the war was begun on the morning of the 28th, and, after staying one night at Meteren and one night at Voormezeele, the month of July found the Civil Service Rifles in support in what had been the German front line immediately south of the Canal.

The weather was bad, the trenches were in a perfectly rotten state of repair, and the men had no protection against persistent shelling. Three very unlucky days were spent here, during which time the losses from shell fire amounted to about forty all ranks, and on the night of the 3rd of July, after being relieved by Companies from the 21st, 22nd, and 23rd Battalions, a weary and somewhat fed up Battalion made its way to Murrumbidgee Camp—a hutted camp near the village of La Clytte.

The chief attraction here was a bathing pond which, although somewhat " soupy," was well patronised by the troops.

FRANCIS WOODBINE PARISH, 1915.
Captain, King's Royal Rifle Corps ; Adjutant, Prince of Wales's Own
Civil Service Rifles.
His wound, sustained in action on the Western front, was a contributory
cause of his death in 1921.

To face page 147.

CHAPTER XVI

AMONG the prominent events which may be regarded as land-marks or milestones in the career of the Civil Service Rifles in France, two have already been passed—Vimy Ridge and High Wood. The third milestone was one of a different character, but the arrival of Lieut.-Colonel F. W. Parish, M.C., to take command most certainly marked the beginning of a new phase in the life of the Battalion. As the pre-war Adjutant, Captain Parish had played a great part in the training of the Civil Service Rifles for war, and all who knew him at the time will remember his keenness. He left the Battalion at the end of October, 1915, to be G.S.O. III of the 19th Division, and afterwards took command of one of the Service Battalions of the North Staffords, with whom he was severely wounded in the Somme Battle of 1916.

It was soon found that he had lost none of his enthusiasm for the Civil Service Rifles, and although a great many changes had taken place since he left, there were still a good many who remembered him, and as he walked along the trenches in Bois Confluent, near St. Eloi, on the 9th or July, he could not mistake the welcome that was shown to him in the faces of all his old friends. The Battalion, sad to relate, had become somewhat stale and had a tired look, and the new Commanding Officer supplied just the touch of renewed vigour which had been lacking of late. He took the earliest opportunity to tell the troops that he was glad to see them all, but that they were not quite the Battalion of old, and he would not be content until they were. He said they were not as clean as they might be, and although they had fought well, they were not so smart, and their discipline was not so good as it should be. All these things, he said, must be put right, and, as there was no time like the present, he put his preaching into practice right away in the support positions in Bois Confluent.

There followed such a craze for cleaning up clothing and equipment as had not been known for many months, and all ranks entered into the new spirit with enthusiasm. Ten rough days in front line trenches around the gates of the White Château grounds on the Hollebeke Road, where the Germans shelled all day and every day, and where one side or the other carried out a raid nearly every night, ended in the Battalion being relieved on the night of the 24th of June by the 18th King's Royal Rifles, and moving to Carnarvon Camp, near Westoutre, one of the most uncomfortable camps occupied by the Civil Service Rifles during the war.

After one day's rest the work of " restoration " was resumed, and vigorous " spit and polish " was indulged in for three days before the Commanding Officer inspected the Battalion. In a breezy speech he said he could already see a distinct improvement, and he felt sure a further improvement would follow.

On the 30th of July the Civil Service Rifles became the envied of all the other units in the Division as they marched to Wippenhoek Siding near Abeele, and entrained for St. Omer, whence a short march brought them to Tatinghem. Here the Battalion was to carry out a training programme, consisting chiefly of musketry on the 2nd Army ranges near Moulle.

     *   *   *   *   *

In his work of revival, there is no doubt that Colonel Parish had everything in his favour. In the first place he had sole command of the unit and was not worried by any orders from either Brigade or Division. The training was to be done entirely under the Commanding Officer's own arrangements, the only condition laid down being that every one must have musketry practice on the range. In the second place the Battalion was sent to a pleasantly situated training area many miles from the firing line, and thirdly the billets were excellent—in many cases better than the men had ever had before in France. Practically every sergeant, at least, had a real bed in an inhabited house.

In these circumstances it would have been strange indeed if all ranks had not responded wholeheartedly to the call of their Commanding Officer, whose enthusiasm quickly spread throughout the Battalion. It is true the " spit and polish " days of General Cuthbert were put into the shade by the scrubbing and polishing which were indulged in from morning till night in the early days at Tatinghem, and all the time-honoured jokes and gags about Bluebell Metal Polish, Kiwi, etc., were literally worked to death. Men groused and joked alternately about the new craze, and one wag chalked up on a billet door a colourable imitation of the Regimental crest, beneath which he had substituted the words " Ich Posh " for the actual motto. Thanks to the inclement weather, there was no chance during the first few days to do anything but remain in billets and "clean up," and when eventually the rain ceased and Colonel Parish saw his Battalion on parade, he was so proud of the men that he spent a good deal of his spare time thereafter in persuading General Officers and others to come and inspect them. The Civil Service Rifles, in consequence, underwent inspections during this holiday by General Plumer (twice), Brigadier-General Kennedy, and Brigadier-General Bailey, in addition to numerous inspections by the Commanding Officer. The men endured these ordeals with little or no grousing—for they had now learnt to take a proper pride in their smart appearance.

The Commanding Officer's chief worry was lack of a parade ground where he could drill his battalion, and the Adjutant was ordered to find one. It was in vain that he said the local farmers objected to their pasture being ruined by the tramping of army boots, so eventually he discovered a field without a gate to it, and hoped the farmer would not turn up during battalion drill. The farmer did not appear himself, but his wife came on parade and protested so loudly to the Adjutant that the Commanding Officer exclaimed in a loud voice "Send that woman off parade. This is not a woman's battalion." This brilliant sally, however, was wasted on the woman, who continued to protest volubly—and those who have heard a French peasant woman when she is roused will realise how difficult it was to induce her to leave the field.

The great day of the training was the Regimental Rifle Meeting, run almost on Bisley lines, which was held on the ranges at Moulle, on the 6th of August. Prizes were offered for the best sergeant and the best corporal in the Battalion, for the best private in each Company, and for each member of the Platoon having the highest average. In addition, all prize winners were to have a day's leave.

The Prize Meeting was a great success, and the keenest interest was taken in the competitions, on which there were various sweepstakes, while, in addition, two members of the Battalion "made a book" on one of the competitions, their most profitable dupe being the Commanding Officer himself.

" C " Company appear to have swept the board as far as Platoon averages went, as two of their Platoons took the first two places, and one other tied with numbers eight (" B " Company) and thirteen (" D " Company) for third place. The following received silver wrist watches suitably engraved for the occasion :—

Best Sergeant in the Battalion :
  Sergeant H. Salmon - 'C' Company.

Best Corporal :
  Corporal O. L. H. Levey ' C ' Company.

Best Privates :

'A' Company	- Privates L. W. V. Wilkinson and H. A Vernham, tied.
'B' Company	- Private W. J. Tuckett.	
'C' Company	- Privates E. A. Honney and A. Strong tied.
'D' Company	- Private F. T. G. White.

The Officers' competition was won by Second-Lieutenant G. E. Tatum, 'C' Company.

Shortly after the Rifle Meeting the Battalion became attached to the 142nd Brigade, and this caused a move to Moringhem, but after two General Officers' inspections in four days the Civil Service Rifles, to their great joy, returned to their old billets, the 140th Brigade having been sent to the Tatinghem area for training.

The puzzle so far had been the absence of the marked-out or " flagged " course, and speculation was rife as to how soon the familiar signs would appear on the training ground, but beyond practising an advance (through fields of cut corn) in what the Commanding Officer called lines of " worms," no very warlike movements were undertaken, nor was there any mention of a coming operation. So the holiday at Tatinghem came to an end without any rehearsing of a set piece which had been such a conspicuous feature of former holidays of this kind.

Just before leaving Tatinghem, a mild interest was taken in the appearance on parade of a second Colonel, wearing the uniform of a Scottish regiment, who inspected the Battalion on the 23rd of August, and thereafter did not miss a parade. There were numerous speculations as to who was this unassuming-looking fellow in the Scotch cap, and what did he want, but no one guessed what a great part he was soon to play in the history of the Regiment.

A seemingly endless column of motor buses and lorries took the 140th Brigade back to the war on the 24th of August, and the Civil Service Rifles occupied Vancouver Camp, which seemed dreadfully uncomfortable after the luxury of Tatinghem. The accommodation was poor, and the day was cold with a biting wind howling and blowing the dust over everything. The troops experienced very much the same kind of feeling as on return to a City office after a month at the seaside or in the country, and before turning in for the night a rumour went round that the Division would very soon attack Polygon and Glencorse Woods, beyond Westhoek Ridge. Pleasant dreams!

CHAPTER XVII

LAST DAYS IN THE YPRES SALIENT

As a sequel to overnight rumours, all officers were taken the next day to study a ground plan of the country from Passchendele to Westhoek Ridge—an excellent model of what had now become the most famous battlefield on the western front. The parts which specially interested the Civil Service Rifles were the wood known as Nonne Boschen and Glencorse Wood. In the afternoon the N.C.O.'s were taken to see the model, and it was explained to them that they were soon to attack the positions in the two woods mentioned. These had been captured more than once during the past week or two, but in each case the captors had been pushed back by a German counter-attack.

The next step followed at a very early hour the morning after, when a party of officers boarded a bus outside camp, and long before daylight were deposited outside the Asylum at Ypres. Crossing the now world-famous city, they passed out at the Menin Gate and down the dreaded Menin Road to Hooge, whence they made a general reconnaissance of the country from Bellewarde Ridge over Westhoek Ridge. The situation in the front line seemed a trifle obscure, and those holding it did not altogether cheer their visitors up when discussing the proposed attack. It certainly surprised the said visitors to learn that one group of old gun pits, where they were supposed to assemble for their attack, was being held by the Bosches. This news, however, did not have any serious effect on the scheme, and the following day a party of N.C.O.'s accompanied the Adjutant on a similar reconnaissance. Rain poured in torrents from start to finish, and it is feared that the party, absolutely wet through to the skin, did not display very great enthusiasm for their work that day.

There followed a lecture by the Commanding Officer in the Vancouver Theatre on the coming attack. The Army School lecturer of these days still laboured under the delusion that the assaulting infantry in an attack arrived at the objective in waves, in spite of ditches, water jumps, barbed wire or other obstacles. To hear him talk of the attack it all seemed so easy, that one could only wonder why it had not been done before—preferably by the staff of an Army School.

Colonel Parish, who had been an instructor at the Senior Officers' School at Aldershot earlier in the year, contrived to instil his optimism into the troops, who entered on the flagged course rehearsals the next day with considerable enthusiasm. Even the two men of " C " Company who were detailed to wade through a marsh, said to exist in No Man's Land, were heard to joke about their " chances."

Consequently the troops, although not generally bellicose, were almost eager for the fray, as there was a distinct feeling among them that something big should be done to justify the recent holiday. Thus it came about that members of the Battalion were heard to say that they were looking forward to the battle. This attitude was certainly a novelty, for although there was never a lack of volunteers for any enterprise, however dangerous, nor was there ever any disposition to " swing it " before a battle, it had for a long time been the practice to look askance at any man who claimed to be keen on a fight. The recognised attitude in public circles, both on the part of officers and other ranks, was that of a pacifist. " Live and let live " was claimed as their motto by some of the most zealous soldiers, simply because they hated the idea of being dubbed " fire-eaters," and often a most gallant fighter would be one who asserted loudly that he was always very " windy," to use popular parlance, or that there was nothing he dreaded more than going over the top. However, on the occasion referred to, officers and men were more honest, and most, if not all, readily asserted their keenness for the difficult and somewhat complicated form of attack which they were soon to undertake in the neighbourhood of Westhoek Ridge.

The rehearsals over the marked-out course went on from day to day, sometimes in the presence of the Divisional Commander, Major-General Gorringe, and nearly always in the presence of the Brigade Commander, Brigadier-General Kennedy, with various members of the gilded staff in the offing. Still, the Civil Service Rifles, equipped with two Lieutenant-Colonels, and fired with enthusiasm, disarmed criticism, and the Generals regarded Glencorse Wood and the curiously-named Nonne Boschen (Nuns' Wood) as practically captured. They had, however, reckoned without the weather.

The big offensive which took place in the Ypres Salient from July to September, 1917, is remembered more by the atrocious weather which accompanied it throughout—and finally ruined it—than by any other feature. Hopes had run high, as details of the ambitious scheme leaked out, that this great push was going to hasten very considerably the end of the war. The

Bosche evidently feared that such might be the result, to judge from the stubborn resistance he put up, and the number of big guns he brought to bear on the district, and it was the eternal shelling during these three months, combined with what was probably a record in bad weather even for France, which caused men ever after to speak with bated breath of " Passchendaele."

To have been through Passchendaele was regarded as having endured the most severe trial of the war, but " Passchendaele " when referred to in this connection, included not only the little village of that name and the ridge adjoining it, but the whole of the devastated area in the Ypres Salient where the fighting was so keen during the last wretched months of the so-called summer of 1917. Passchendaele, therefore, can be stretched to include Glencorse and Polygon Woods and the Westhoek Ridge, for here the full fury of this terrible battle against the combined forces of the Bosche and the weather was felt, and as far as the Civil Service Rifles were concerned, they were knocked out by the weather before they reached the " starting gate."

Throughout the last few days of August the rain fell almost continuously. The marsh referred to, through which two men had to wade, had now become a pond, and the rest of the country on Westhoek Ridge had become a sea of mud. The attack, after being postponed from day to day, was finally abandoned on the 31st of August, when the advance party, under the Adjutant, was actually on parade ready to start for the trenches. A limber containing medical stores, signalling equipment, etc., had already been despatched for the Menin Road, where it was to await the advance party. The advance party was dismissed, the limber brought back, and later in the evening it became known that the attack was definitely abandoned so far as the 47th Division was concerned.

The news created something akin to consternation in the Battalion, where the men felt the keenest disappointment at the loss of such an opportunity to prove their worth, but none felt it more keenly than Colonel Parish. It transpired that he had not recovered from his head wound received on the Somme in 1916,* and he was therefore to return to England, but he had succeeded in persuading the authorities to allow him to see this battle through before going away. It thus came as a very bitter blow to him, who had devoted so much energy and zeal to improving the fighting spirit, that he should have to leave without ever having commanded his Battalion in the front line.

His grief was shared by all ranks in the Battalion, for although he had only been in command for six weeks, he had worked a

---

* This wound contributed to his untimely death on 9th Oct., 1921. He is buried at Hawarden.

wonderful change, and had inspired every one by his enthusiasm for the Civil Service Rifles.

There was not an officer, N.C.O. or man who had served under him who did not feel how very much the Regiment owed to Colonel Parish. It had been a real pleasure to serve under him in any capacity, and there was a genuine and universal regret felt at his departure. The benefit of his six weeks' command was felt in the Battalion throughout the rest of the war.

Colonel Parish said good-bye on parade on the 23rd of September, when he told the men how sorry he was to go, but assured them all that it was only for a little while, for he would be back as soon as the powers that be would allow him. He felt sure that when that time came, Colonel Segrave, to whom he was handing over his command, would be able to tell him that this was still the finest Battalion in the Division.

This, then, was the explanation of the "quiet, unobtrusive Colonel in the Scotch cap" who had been living with the Civil Service Rifles for the past fortnight. He had a difficult task before him, coming as he did, after one who had become such a hot favourite with all under his command. Colonel Segrave did not start off with the "new broom" tactics, for there was very little that he wished to alter, and it was his desire to continue on the lines of his predecessor. He told the Battalion, when he took his first parade on the 4th of September, how proud he was to be given command of the Civil Service Rifles, but it is safe to say that not even he guessed how great was to be his love for this Regiment before the end of his régime.

Very soon afterwards the Battalion relieved the 2nd South Lancashire Battalion in support trenches round about Hooge and Château Wood on the Menin Road, and here were spent the last seven days of the eleven months' sojourn in the Ypres Salient. The experience of these seven days was a fitting conclusion to all that had been endured in the past year, for they were days during which the Salient lived up to its worst reputation.

The relief of the 2nd South Lancashires was carried out in daylight on the 9th of September, and the Bosches welcomed the change by indulging in a general bombardment of the area, which caused a few casualties in "A" Company before they reached their new positions.

The Battalion was disposed round about the site of the village of Hooge. There were no trenches, although there were several marked on the map, and the sole accommodation was found in old concrete shelters which until recently had housed the Germans. "A" Company, however, occupied part of the Menin tunnel, which had once been a triumph of German field engineering. This ran underneath the Menin Road, and inside had

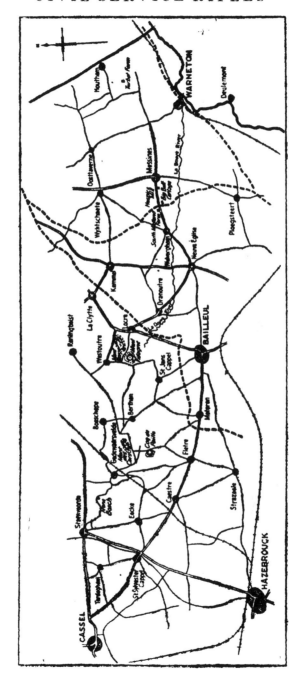

been a trench tramway, along which the enemy stores and rations had been brought up. The main signal lines also ran along, and it was noticed that these had been neatly pinned into the walls of the tunnel—in contrast to the English method of laying lines criss-cross along open trenches in such a manner as to catch the occupants across the throat. This method of fixing lines, so common throughout the British area, caused more bad language on a dark night than any other provocation in France.

The Menin tunnel may have been a safe refuge in the early days of its existence, but now it was in a deplorable condition. Daylight was admitted at very frequent intervals by the huge gaping holes caused by the heavy artillery of both sides, but in spite of these the atmosphere inside was almost overpowering, and the protection from shell fire was purely imaginary.

Gas shells were scattered freely over the area both day and night, and the casualties increased each day. During the bombardment of the night of the 11th of September, Lance-Corporal Foote, of the Headquarters Pioneers, distinguished himself by carrying a wounded man from the ruins in Château Wood occupied by Battalion Headquarters right down the Menin Road to the dressing station at the famous Birr cross roads.

The discomforts increased each day, and the bombardments of the main track to the front line—the Kanwan track, which had formerly taken place at regular times each day, now became more frequent and irregular. The whole Battalion made the perilous journey along this track nearly every day, for huge carrying parties had to be provided to carry R. E. material and ammunition up to Clapham Junction—the Headquarters of the front line Battalion. There were many signs of the recent advance to be seen on the way to Clapham Junction, the most noticeable being a mass of ruined tanks which looked as though they had all been put out of action in trying to mount the embankment along a part of the Menin Road.

On the 15th of September began a series of practice barrages, and the long-suffering infantry now had to endure the retaliation in addition to other bombardments. Following one of the practice barrages the 7th Battalion, holding the front line, sent forward a party and captured a strong point. " C " Company, under Captain L. L. Burtt, went up at night to work for them, and their journey along Kanwan Track ranks as one of the worst experiences of the Company during the war. Misfortune befell the party from the start, and the intense shelling combined with the pitch-black darkness of the night caused the journey to Clapham Junction to degenerate into a scramble. This was practically the closing incident in the eleven months spent in the Ypres Salient, for on the following afternoon the

2nd Australian Infantry Battalion arrived, and the Civil Service Rifles made their way down the Menin Road, strewn with all the débris of war, with here and there a dead horse, and so to Château Segard, where one night was spent before marching to the village of Steenvoorde and saying good-bye for ever to the hated Ypres Salient.

The departure from the Salient was not without its thrills for the Lewis Gunners, who had been left with their guns on the Menin Road near Hooge awaiting the limbers. These had to pass a corner on the Ypres side of Birr Cross Roads known as Hell Fire Corner, and it so happened on this evening that the spot was justifying its name, for it had been shelled so heavily that the dump of R.E. material and ammunition by the roadside was all ablaze—thus completely shutting off the Transport. This state of affairs lasted for some hours, but Sergeant Sladden solved the difficulty by taking his limbers round by a devious route through Zillebeke, and eventually got the limbers away without loss.

The Transport Section had had many exciting trips along the Menin Road, and they were proud of the fact that they were able to leave the Ypres Salient without having lost a horse in that area.

CHAPTER XVIII

THE long march to Steenvoorde—17 miles—was endured cheerfully by all ranks, who were overjoyed at leaving Belgium. It was felt that whatever the new area was like, it would not be worse than the experience of the past few weeks. What a tremendous change from the haven of rest of eleven months ago! There were many who would even prefer to go through the Somme experience of a year ago rather than return to the Menin Road.

Those who had been left out as " non-starters " for the battle which did not take place rejoined at Eecke, a little village near Caestre, where two days were spent before the Battalion entrained at Caestre shortly after midnight on the 22nd of September, and started in the best of spirits for the Arras front.

After resting for two nights at the delightful village of Frevin-Capelle, near the source of the Scarpe, a short march in delightful weather brought the Civil Service Rifles to Aubrey Camp—a camp of Nissen huts and tents on the Lens-Arras Road near Roclincourt. A night spent in Aubrey Camp was followed by a march to the front line at Gavrelle where old friends were found in the Drake Battalion of the 63rd (Naval) Division. This Battalion had been attached to the Civil Service Rifles for instruction in trench warfare at Souchez in June 1916.

There followed a spell of peace and quiet which compared very favourably even with the early days at Ypres. The absence of shelling was very noticeable and the trenches were clean and dry. Moreover there was an occasional deep dug-out and as the ground was chalky—it was the southern extremity of Vimy Ridge—more were to be dug by the Royal Engineers. There were never many deep dug-outs in English trenches, but whenever the ground was suitable there were always a good many either under construction or proposed.

There was a good water supply from a well in the trenches, and rations were brought to within 100 yards of Battalion Headquarters, and the Battalion held the front line for eight days without showing any sign of wear. Everyone was happy, except perhaps the energetic Commanding Officer, who wanted to get on with the war. He had little or no use for the quiet life of Gavrelle and seemed happier amid the turmoil of the Ypres salient.

It was intended that the Division should make a long stay in this sector, and elaborate plans for a winter scheme of defence were made by the Divisional Commander. As in the Ypres salient, a Battalion when out at rest was always to occupy the same camp—in order to encourage the men to work on camp improvements. The Civil Service Rifles accordingly set to work on Aubrey Camp, and Colonel Segrave claims that his men laid more trench boards per acre than could be found at any other place on the Western front. He also established the Battalion Baths, so that henceforth the Civil Service Rifles would be independent of the Divisional Baths Officer.

Football matches, trips to Arras, and the concerts given by the Divisional Follies were the chief diversions, and, at the end of October, a very successful Regimental concert was held in the Divisional Cinema, the surprise turn of the evening being the R.S.M.'s rendering of " Take me back to dear old Blighty."

The good spirits of the troops were further raised by a very welcome increase in the leave allotment, which for some time had been very poor, and all leave records were broken on the 6th of November when a party of sixty other ranks left by the light railway from Roclincourt en route for " Blighty."

The Transport and Quartermaster's Stores were housed in Roclincourt in the most comfortable billets they had had for some months. It was here that the Transport Section received a shock in the shape of a comb-out by the Commanding Officer. Colonel Segrave was a keen student of man power, and in investigating the strength of his Battalion, he found the Transport Section considerably overstaffed, with the result that eleven of them rejoined their Companies in the trenches.

The sectors of the front line held by the Civil Service Rifles were alternately the Gavrelle Sector, and the posts just south of Oppy Wood. Of these the Gavrelle sector was much the more popular, though neither could compare with the support positions in the Railway Cutting and Roundhay Camp, just by the Arras-Bailleul Road.

It was while at Roundhay Camp that the peaceful life was disturbed by startling rumours of a move to another front, and on the 15th of November, weight was given to the rumours by the sudden closing of the Brigade School. Leave, it was said, was stopped, and amid consternation groups of men gathered all over the camp to discuss the situation, those who wanted to be funny talking of ice cream and stilettos—for it was understood the Division was bound for Italy.

The " holiday " in the Arras district came to an abrupt end

on the 18th of November, when the 13th East Yorks Battalion arrived, and the Civil Service Rifles left by Light Railway, and after a merry trip in the toy train, reached a camp of French huts at Ecoivres. There, in spite of rumours, a party of thirty other ranks went on leave, but speculation was rife as to whether they would complete their full time.

A few days were spent at Ecoivres, with many football matches, which included a Rugby trial match on the 20th of November. Interest in the Rugby match was diverted by the news, which arrived during the game, of the brilliant success of the 3rd Army near Cambrai. The attack had been kept secret, and the news came as a great surprise. It was said the Hindenburg Line was broken, the cavalry and tanks were pursuing the retreating enemy, and Cambrai itself would soon fall. In fact, the war would soon be over. Orders received that night for a move on the morrow gave rise to further speculation as to the destination of the Division, and at the " calling over of the card " in the Officers' Mess, the betting was evens Cambrai, 6–4 Italy, and 100–1 England.

*   *   *   *   *   *

The movements of the Division during the last ten days of November, 1917, were such as would baffle the keenest member of the enemy Intelligence Department. Units appeared to be moving from one village to another with no particular object in view, and during the first few days of the trek from Ecoivres the Battalion Commanders themselves had no idea whether they were bound for Italy or the Cambrai front. The Civil Service Rifles started with a succession of short marches, and as a rule the billets were poor and the villages somewhat squalid. There was, however, little time to " grouse," for the order to move on was usually received before the men had time to look round. After a night in billets at Hermaville and a night of extreme discomfort in dilapidated huts at Wanquetin, the village of Gouy en Artois was reached, where it was learnt that the Division was now in the Fifth Corps (3rd Army) and it was evident therefore that the move to Italy was " off."

On the 24th of November the Battalion occupied a hutted camp in Courcelles le Comte, a ruined village won from the Bosches during their winter retreat of 1916. The roads and hamlets in this district were still clearly marked with the big signboards erected during the German occupation, and at one end of Courcelles could be seen the remains of a German cinema or theatre.

The camp itself had been built by English troops, and had at one time been a well laid out camp of Nissen huts ; but now it was the abomination of desolation. The linings of the huts had been torn off for firewood, the windows were broken, the doors torn off their hinges, and every hut was strewn with rubbish. Fortunately only one night was spent in these conditions, and the march was resumed the next afternoon.

The march to Le Transloy on the 25th of November was unique. For the first hour everything went well, but from that time onwards the column was rarely on the move for more than ten minutes every hour. The usual order of things was thus reversed, and instead of a ten minutes halt in every hour, there was a ten minutes march per hour. Every road leading into Bapaume was choked with troops, and a perspiring A.P.M. was trying to sort out those bound for the front from those coming out into reserve.

Tea was served in the twilight on the Bapaume Road, and the next halt found the Battalion in the main street of the town. There were some there who had hoped to see Bapaume in 1916, but although they had ample opportunity to admire the ruins in the bright moonlight, they had now lost all interest in their surroundings, and many passed through without even knowing the name of the place.

Thoroughly fed up, the troops reached their camp shortly before midnight, and to crown a very miserable day they were so frightfully crowded into the huts that they could scarcely find room to lie down. " Posh Harry " was almost speechless when he saw his billet. " What I want to know," he spluttered, " is where did the R.S.M. of the Guards sleep last night ? They say the Guards were here, but I'm sure their R.S.M. would not sleep in there."

The discomfort of that camp, however, was eclipsed on the night of the 27th of November, when the Battalion bivouacked in a field of rich creamy mud at Doignies, the journey from Le Transloy having been made by bus to Velu, and thence by route march, each man carrying his blanket over his arm.

L

CHAPTER XIX

Two of the most serious checks to the 3rd Army advance on Cambrai were the villages of Bourlon and Fontaine Notre Dame, respectively at the north-west and south-east corners of Bourlon Wood. The latter village, too, was almost at the entrance to Cambrai on the Bapaume-Cambrai road.

Both these villages had been captured towards the end of November, but were afterwards retaken. The Guards Division, who had preceded the 47th Division, accordingly attacked them again, and before the Civil Service Rifles left Le Transloy it was learned that the attack had succeeded, though the enemy very soon recaptured both villages once more.

It was understood, however, that the English advance was to continue, and when the Civil Service Rifles reached Doignies, the battle surplus had already been sent back to the Divisional Reinforcement Camp. As the situation in the front line underwent such frequent changes, there had been nothing in the nature of a rehearsal of the coming battle, which it was expected would be more in the nature of open warfare than had been any of the previous operations of the 47th Division.

On arriving at Doignies, Colonel Segrave received orders for his Battalion to occupy part of the Hindenburg Line on the following day (the 28th), and at a very early hour, he started with his Adjutant, Medical Officer, Signals Officer and four Company Commanders for the Headquarters of the front line brigade. The Battalion, in fighting order, moved off later in the morning and occupied a part of the Hindenburg Line nearly due west of Graincourt.

At Brigade Headquarters Colonel Segrave learnt that he was to relieve one of the Cavalry regiments holding the front line in Bourlon Wood, but the date of relief was not then settled. He therefore took his party across country, passing within a hundred yards or so of Graincourt, across sunken roads, to a sugar factory on the Bapaume-Cambrai road, where it was understood a guide would be found.

Leaving the sugar factory, many signs of the recent advance were seen, German equipment, rifles and ammunition being scattered almost everywhere. Derelict English tanks and aeroplanes were also to be seen, and the landscape generally presented a desolate picture.

The Cavalry Headquarters occupied what had been a pretty chalet in a delightful spot in the middle of the wood—an ideal place for a summer picnic. There was no suggestion of a summer picnic about it now, however, for the bitter fighting of

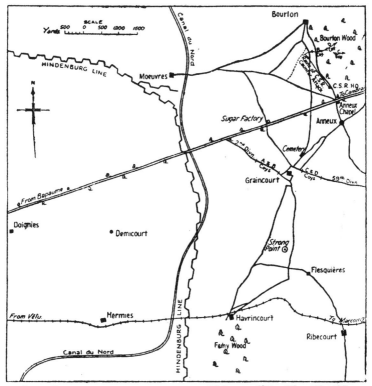

SKETCH MAP TO ILLUSTRATE THE MOVEMENTS OF THE C S R FROM 28 Nov 1917 TO 6 Dec 1917

the past few days had left its mark everywhere, and in and around the chalet were gathered weary warriors, eagerly awaiting the news of their relief.

The members of the reconnoitring party had only just thrown off their equipment for a rest when it was found that they had been brought to the wrong place, so, dispensing with the doubtful services of a guide, Colonel Segrave led his officers through the wood in search of some one willing to be relieved by his Battalion. The right place was found to be in a small

German dug-out in the road leading to the village of Bourlon along the western edge of the wood, and here the Colonel, learning that he was to take over that night the positions held by the 2nd Dismounted Cavalry Brigade and the 2nd/5th West Yorks Battalion, made his dispositions and set off with his Adjutant and Medical Officer to find his Battalion in the Hindenburg Line. The Company Commanders remained behind to look round their respective fronts.

On his way back, Colonel Segrave surprised a member of the R.A.M.C. at a dressing station by begging from him a tin of bully beef and a biscuit. The spectacle of a Colonel eating bully beef was too much for the R.A.M.C. man, who stared after the three officers as though he had seen ghosts.

A long wait for orders in the Hindenburg Line ended in the Battalion moving off without any at 9.0 p.m. There was a bright moon, and the night was perfectly quiet at the start, when there was nothing to suggest the exciting time that was in store for the troops before they were to arrive at the front line. But on reaching the Relay Post on the Cambrai road, where the guides and Company Commanders were to have been, the head of the Battalion became enveloped in a barrage of gas shells. The rest of the journey was what is known as " windy " in the extreme. Gas masks had to be worn, and in pushing through the barrage, some casualties were suffered, one platoon of " C " Company losing very heavily after passing Battalion Headquarters.

The relief was complete at about 2.0 a.m., and except for gas shelling the situation became much quieter.

" B " and " D " Companies held the front line, the former, under Lieutenant C. M. Kilner, being on the left, just outside the southern edge of the village, and with half a Company on each side of the road leading from Battalion Headquarters to the village. " D " Company, under Captain R. Middleton, connected with the right of " B " and held a position inside the wood and about 300 yards south-east of the village. " D " Company Headquarters was in a most palatial deep-dug out which had formerly been the Headquarters of a German artillery brigade. " C " Company, under Captain T. H. Sharratt, was in support near " D." Soon after taking up their positions, both " B " and " D " Companies sent out patrols towards the village, but although Lieutenant W. E. Hoste took his patrol into the village, and entered one or two houses, no Bosches were found.

The quiet night was followed by a distinctly noisy day, throughout which the enemy heavily bombarded the front line positions, the whole of the wood, and the roads all round the outside of the wood.

In the middle of the morning, the Brigadier arrived with the

BOURLON WOOD FROM SOUTH-WEST CORNER, 1917.

To face page 164.

news that there would be no further advance, and that the positions now being held were to be consolidated. " A " Company, who were in reserve, under Lieutenant L. C. Morris, M.C., round about Battalion Headquarters, accordingly spent the rest of the day in carrying barbed wire, pickets, sandbags and ammunition from a dump at the cross roads known as Anneux Chapel to a forward dump near Battalion Headquarters. The casualties during the day amounted to one officer and no less than fifty four other ranks—a pretty heavy toll for a day when no attack took place !

In the opinion of those holding the line, the decision not to advance any further was unnecessary—it was felt that the Battalion might well be engaged very soon in defensive rather than offensive operations, and some such idea was in the mind of Colonel Segrave as he went round the Battalion front that day.

Any remaining doubts as to the enemy intentions were dispersed on the morning of the 30th of November, which opened with an intense bombardment from German guns of every calibre. Smoke barrages were put down on the flanks of the intended attack, and before long the enemy infantry could be seen advancing in many waves from the country beyond Bourlon village. The Battalion was not in signal communication with anybody, either Brigade Headquarters or adjoining units, and the Commanding Officer had therefore to rely on the services of runners and four pigeons. According to the rules of the signal service, pigeons had to be despatched in pairs, so the stock was only good for two messages. When it is mentioned that it took a good runner well over an hour to reach Brigade, the state of isolation of the Battalion will be realised.

The battle raged throughout the morning without any infantry engagement on the front held by the Civil Service Rifles, though S.O.S. rockets were seen on several occasions on adjoining sections of the line.

Company Commanders reported that the attack appeared to be directed on the sectors held on each side of them, but up to midday they had not been interfered with. The waves of enemy infantry had advanced diagonally across their front, and both " B " and " D " Companies had put in some excellent work with rifles and Lewis guns. The enemy, however, was extraordinarily well served by his low-flying aeroplanes, which seemed to swarm like bees over the Battalion area, and the machine-gun fire from these caused a good many casualties during the day.

Prominent among the early incidents of the battle was the performance of Lance Corporal S. Fletcher of the Battalion scouts, and a " D " Company runner who brought the first report from the front line to Battalion Headquarters. The distance they had to cover was more than a mile over very rough country, but in their anxiety to deliver the result of their observations as quickly as possible they ran the whole way, although fully equipped, and carrying rifles. The effort proved too much for the runner, who collapsed on reaching Battalion Headquarters, and fell unconscious down the stairs of the dug-out without being able to deliver his message. The N.C.O. was little better off, but after a time he recovered sufficiently to be able to give a good account of what was going on.

Soon after midday the S.O.S. signal was seen on the Battalion front, and it was reported that a gap had been made in the Brigade front on the left of the line held by " B " Company.

The Support Company, " C," led by 2nd Lieutenant C. V. Marchant, had by this time moved up to reinforce " B " and " D " Companies, who had both suffered heavy losses. The remnants of the left platoon of " B " Company, finding the line originally held by the Battalion on their left to be unoccupied, pushed along to try to find touch. Instead of finding their friends, however, they found Bosches in large numbers, who appeared to come from all sides, with the result that about ten of the Civil Service Rifles were taken prisoners.

Lieutenant Kilner, observing the enemy in the left rear of the Battalion front, gathered the rest of his Company together and formed a defensive flank in the sunken road on the Western edge of the wood. Meanwhile, Colonel Segrave formed up the personnel of Battalion Headquarters and his reserve Company, " A," and led them in two waves across the open country outside the wood. Leaving the vicinity of Battalion Headquarters at about 4.0 p.m., they advanced through heavy fire from rifles, machine guns, and low-flying aeroplanes, and although they suffered many casualties, they succeeded before dusk in restoring the line as originally held, and later in the evening established touch on the left with the Post Office Rifles, who had come up from Brigade Reserve to reinforce the line. The example set by their Commanding Officer inspired the men of the Civil Service Rifles with such confidence and enthusiasm, that they carried out their advance as at a Salisbury Plain manœuvre, the Colonel, with a map in one hand and a whistle in the other, giving his directions by signal.

Colonel Segrave's prompt action was specially commended in a pamphlet afterwards published by General Headquarters entitled " The Story of a Great Fight," and those who were with him on that day regard it as the finest example of leadership in the history of the Battalion. There was nothing theatrical about the affair—it was just done in the calm and methodical manner in which Colonel Segrave always behaved in the front line.

Photo by Langfier, Ltd.

LT.-COL. W. H. E. SEGRAVE, D.S.O. (H.L.I.)
Commanded 1st Battalion, 3rd September, 1917, to 6th August, 1918.

To face page 166.

The effects of the continuous gas shelling during the past three days had told heavily on the Battalion—particularly the Headquarters Company and "A" Company. Of the Headquarters Officers, Colonel Segrave was the only one remaining on the night of the 30th of November, and during the day he had lost no less than four Adjutants, the last one being an Artillery Liason Officer whom he had converted into an infantryman. The other ranks of Headquarters fared no better, but the losses in the Companies holding the front line were heavier still, and when the 1st Surrey Rifles arrived on the night of the 1st of December, and the Civil Service Rifles moved back into tents at Femy Wood near Havrincourt, the losses in Bourlon Wood were found to be 12 officers, 278 other ranks. At Femy Wood it was found that the Colonel himself was badly gassed, and he too left for hospital on the 2nd of December.

Although it is not possible here to pay just tribute to those gallant fellows individually, special mention must be made of the great loss the Battalion suffered by the death of three of its members who had already done great things, and who would have risen to higher rank in the Regiment before long had they been spared.

C.S.M. Mansbridge, of "D" Company, was as gallant in the front line as he was smart and efficient on the parade ground. An old member of the Regiment who thoroughly understood his brother Warrant Officers, N.C.O.'s, and men, he would undoubtedly have made an ideal Regimental Sergeant Major for the Civil Service Rifles.

Sergeant H. L. Smith, who was acting C.S.M. of "A" Company, had a multitude of friends in all Companies. As "Inky" Smith he had been one of the shining lights of the Lewis gunners, of whom he was one of the first members. He had fought with distinction at Vimy Ridge, and on the Somme, and, like Mansbridge, he was a "17th of March man." Both were men who quickly won the respect of all who served with them.

Second Lieutenant C. V. Marchant, of "C" Company, was a comparatively young member of the Regiment. Not yet twenty years old, he had just completed a year's service with the Battalion in France, and during that time he had become very popular with the men of "C" Company, with whom he had served gallantly in the Ypres Salient, and particularly at the battle of Messines. He was cool in battle, keen and fearless. He met his death while leading his Company through the awful barrage of shells and machine gun bullets, but he faced it unflinchingly. The Battalion could ill afford to lose such an officer, who in spite of his youth would soon have made an excellent Company Commander.

"C" Company also lost two valuable members in C.S.M. F. C. Robertson, D.C.M., who was severely wounded on the 29th of November, and Sergeant O. L. H. Levey, wounded on the 30th. Both were "17th of March men," and Robertson had been a member of the Regiment for many years before the war. He was a quiet unassuming fellow, who was never found wanting, and who was never "rattled" even under the greatest provocation and in the most trying circumstances.

Sergeant Levey was a most enthusiastic member of the Regiment who had distinguished himself by his skill with the rifle. Fortunately he recovered sufficiently from his wounds to return to the Regiment some months later, when he quickly rose to the rank of C.S.M. of his Company. His prowess in the football field gained him fame not only in the Battalion, but throughout the Division.

In addition to the fighting portion of the Battalion, the Transport Section and Quartermaster's staff suffered casualties in and around Bourlon Wood, the Quartermaster himself, Lieutenant W. G. Hodge, better known as "Ben Hodge," being gassed on the night of the 29th November while at Battalion Headquarters. On the same night the Transport Column was heavily shelled on the Bapaume—Cambrai Road, with the result that several of the most experienced drivers and horses were wounded.

But in spite of the heavy casualties in Bourlon Wood, and the fact that the enemy bombardment was the most severe and prolonged that the Battalion was called upon to face during the war, the men of the Civil Service Rifles could look back with justifiable pride on their share in the battle, during which they did not yield an inch of ground, although the Bosches gained considerable success in neighbouring parts of the line.

The remnants of the Battalion numbered only about 200, all ranks, when they reached Femy Wood on the 2nd of December with scarcely a kick left in them after their exertions of the past few days, and it came as a great surprise when they had to return to the front line on the 4th of December reinforced by a handful of officers and other ranks from the "non-starters' camp."

In order to cover the withdrawal of the 142nd Infantry Brigade from Bourlon Wood, a defensive position on either side of the village of Graincourt was taken up, and there, on the 5th and 6th of December, the Battalion gave yet another exhibition of splendid fighting qualities in its second defensive battle within a week.

The officers who had come up included Major H. Marshall, who was in command of the Battalion, Major H. F. M. Warne, who acted as his second in command, and Captain L. L. Burtt, who commanded "C" and "D" Companies, now formed into one Company. " A " and " B " Companies were amalgamated under Lieutenant L. C. Morris, M.C.

The positions were taken up at dusk, " A " and " B " Companies being on the left along a sunken road running in a north-westerly direction from about the centre of the village, and " C " and " D " on the right were along a similar road which ran due east from the village. The village itself was not occupied, but posts were established near the cemetery in the sunken roads north-east of the village. These were withdrawn at dawn. The 2nd Division was on the left of " A " and " B " Companies, and the 59th Division was on the right of " C " and " D " Companies.

The troops from the front line in Bourlon Wood passed through as arranged, the evacuation of the wood having been rendered necessary owing to the forcing in by the Germans of both arms of the Cambrai salient.

The whole front was patrolled throughout the night, but until daylight nothing was seen or heard of the enemy, whose front line was about two miles away. Numerous explosions heard in the wood showed that the Royal Engineers were destroying dug-outs and anything likely to be of use to the enemy.

The garrison on the right, numbering less than 120, all ranks, after trying to dig themselves in in the frost bound ground along the side of the road, moved forward to a well-camouflaged German trench which started just outside the village and continued almost to the 59th Division on the right. Leading out of the back of the trench were four old gun pits with the dismantled 5.9's still there, and at the village end was a trench running forward at right angles.

It should be mentioned that at the outset it was understood that the garrison would be withdrawn after twenty-four hours, but, as after events show, the troops were doomed to disappointment.

The two halves of the Battalion were not in touch with each other at all, and as they fought during these few days as separate units, their experiences are dealt with separately.

At daylight on the 5th of December it was seen from the trench occupied by " C " and " D " Companies that the Germans had discovered the withdrawal from Bourlon Wood, for small parties of them were seen wandering about the deserted front line and in the wood itself, great interest being shown in a derelict tank, which was subsequently used as a signal station.

It was not, however, until the afternoon that the enemy approached to within reasonable distance of Graincourt, but his patrols now became very active, first coming on in small parties, which were easily dispersed by rifle and Lewis gun fire, and later in larger numbers, which were also dispersed in the same way. Some excellent shooting was indulged in about this time by the gallant little bands on either side of the village, but although they were able to keep the enemy off while the daylight lasted, it was obvious that the small force defending the village would not be able to prevent him from entering Graincourt during the night. With the coming of darkness it was found that a considerable number of Germans had reached the village, for patrols and even ration parties encountered them, both in front and in rear of the defending garrison. Runners were also involved in small fights, which were quite frequent during the night on the fringes of the village. In one of these a German machine gun team was overwhelmed, the gun and one man being captured, and the rest of the team being killed.

Just as the men of " C " and " D " Companies were expecting to be withdrawn, Major Warne arrived from Battalion Headquarters to take command of the garrison on the right, with orders to hold the position for another twenty-four hours, and, on withdrawal, to occupy a strong post in the rear.

One must have endured the strain of prolonged fighting in a precarious position, worn out by constant watching, with little food or water, and many other discomforts too numerous to mention, in order to realise how intense was the disappointment of these men who, thinking that Major Warne came to tell them their work was done and to take them back to rest, learnt that their job had only just begun.

At about 5.0 a.m. on the 6th, a Lewis gun was posted in the road about 300 yards south of the village with orders to deal with the enemy there as far as possible, but to withdraw if the opposition became too strong, to a strong post about a mile further down the road towards the village of Flesquieres. An enemy patrol soon tried to rush the gun, but without success, and a wounded prisoner was captured as a result.

At daylight two parties tried to rush the gun. Both were beaten off, but not before the gun team had suffered two casualties. As other parties of the enemy were on the move for a further attack, the gun team was ordered to withdraw to the aforementioned point, where the gun was soon in action again in helping to repel an attack on the strong point itself.

Meantime Major Warne's force was still holding on, and the incidents of the 6th of December are thus described by Sergeant C. Manthorp, who, with Sergeant E. Cooke, was conspicuous throughout the operation by gallantry and good leadership :—

" When dawn broke on the 6th, we were very much on the alert to see what surprises were in store for us, and directly we could see any distance we were well rewarded. The whole German army seemed to be advancing, line after line, crossing the skyline and coming directly for us. Fortunately for us their orders were obviously not to attack, for when the front line got to within 600 or 700 yards from our trench, they started digging in, or at least making a trench sufficiently deep for protection from our fire. Whilst the advancing and entrenching was proceeding, we, of course, indulged in a fair amount of rifle practice, and not without good results, though, of course, the distance was rather great for anything sensational. After digging-in, the Bosche lay quite dormant for some hours, and we, of course, were on tender-hooks to know what his next move would be, for with the little force at our disposal, it would have been hopeless to expect us to hold off what must have been thousands of Bosches, should they have chosen to attack.

" It was early afternoon before the next move came. Then all the lines of Bosches in front of us attacked, but right across our front on to the 59th Division, the movement being for them a half left movement. Then we had all the shooting we desired. The machine-gunners had a fine time, and so did our riflemen, who were mostly collected in the four gun pits, which were higher than the floor of the trench and enabled us to fire over our camouflage, which was composed of wire netting, turf, etc., and made firing from the greater part of the trench impossible.

" By about 3.0 p.m. the Bosches appeared to have gone right through the position held by the 59th Division, and it looked to us as if the latter had been compelled to retire by weight of numbers. Of course this made our position untenable with the Bosches in our right, rear, and working round us, and the village between us and the remainder of our Battalion also in enemy hands.

" About 70 yards in rear of our trench and parallel with it, ran a sunken road, connecting the village on our left. Parties of Bosches commenced to approach each way along this road, and this forced us to withdraw most of our garrison from the trench and form a semi-circle with each end resting on the road. Things soon became very exciting, and then those of us who were out at the back of the trench, received the order to retire. From the sunken road back to the permanent front line must have been about 1½ miles, and that journey proved about the most exciting that any of us had experienced. The party's strength was two officers and probably about 100 other ranks, and the retirement was done in extended order. At the start off we were received with fire from nearly every direction, and also a little shell fire which may or may not have been meant for us. After going about half a mile, we had the best part of the whole business. We came across at least 100 of the enemy in more or less close order, and did not actually discover them until they were within about 100 yards of us, owing to the folds in the ground. It is difficult to say who appeared to be the most surprised, they or us, but we did not give them long to think about it. We flopped and opened rapid fire on them, and also got our Lewis guns going. Our Lewis gunners had been cursing about their loads, but we were more than glad of the guns under the circumstances. This big party of Bosches quickly took fright and it was laughable to see them all double off back towards home like a flock of sheep. It was a marvellous target, only about 200 or 300 yards away. You simply couldn't miss, and, of course, our success gave us great help on our journey, for most of us were nearly done, owing to the bitter nights we had had with no proper hot food. Having disposed of this body, we encountered no further opposition from Fritz except occasional rifle fire, and we took four stray Germans prisoners along with us. We were then about three-quarters of a mile from our goal, and came upon a small cable trench about three feet deep running towards our lines. Just about this time, one of our own aeroplanes came upon the scene and indulged in a little machine-gun practice on us, but quickly discovered his mistake. Still, it all helped to cheer us on the way. I was about the first to get into the cable trench, and with the prisoners in front, led the way back to where the Royal Welsh Fusiliers were holding the permanent line. They also mistook us for Bosches, possibly because of the four prisoners in front, and subjected us to rather severe machine-gun fire. It was not till I had waved my shrapnel helmet for some time on top of my rifle as high as I could hold it, that they recognised us as friends. Then one of our officers, who happened to be with them, got out of the trench and led us in. It appeared that they had already beaten off one attack during the afternoon, so one could not be surprised at their mistaking us for foes.

" After some delay we eventually got the remains of the two Companies back to Rest Camp, whence we had started off on the evening of the 4th. There were about 15 of ' C ' Company who got out and 40 of ' D ' Company.

" Those of us who did get through can certainly look back upon the affair as one of the most strenuous and exciting experiences we had in France."

Sergeant Cooke has also written an excellent description of the same action, which bears out his comrade's story :—

" Daylight on the 6th found everything quiet, but during the morning large bodies of troops were observed filing into Anneux— a village between Graincourt and Bourlon Wood—and it was evident that an attack from this direction was to be expected. The arrival of a motor car, which was at first mistaken for a tank, caused some excitement, but, apart from this and visits from scouting planes, nothing of interest happened until about 3.0 p.m. when the attack from Anneux was launched.

The attack, in the form of several waves of infantry, was mainly directed against the positions right of Graincourt, leaving ' A ' and ' B ' Companies practically untouched.

The remaining Companies, leaving the gun pits and taking up positions in the open from which more effective use of the rifle could be made, opened a steady and accurate fire on the advancing waves, with the result that the attack on their immediate front crumpled up.

" Attention was now diverted to the right flank, where the enemy appeared to be meeting with more success, and it was discovered that the Battalion on the right had retired earlier in the day—their withdrawal having been hidden from the Civil Service Rifles by rising ground between the two positions.

" The situation was now serious, as the enemy had closed round the right rear of ' C ' and ' D ' Companies, whilst at the same time the left rear of the position was threatened by troops from Graincourt, and the order was given for the garrison to cut its way out and make for the strong points in front of Flesquieres.

" Many casualties from machine-gun fire were suffered in getting clear of the encircling troops, but about 50 of the two Companies were left to continue the journey back to the strong points.

" After numerous encounters with isolated machine-gun posts this party ran into some 200 or 300 of the enemy in an organised line of shell holes before the positions in front of Flesquieres, where the attack had been beaten off earlier in the afternoon, and, as the line was well supplied with light machine guns, the chances of getting through seemed decidedly slender until a Red Cross man advanced making the usual signs of surrender.

" The effect was remarkable, for no sooner had his action been seen than, with a yell, the Civil Service Rifles charged down on the enemy, who, being taken by surprise, hastily crowded off into a small valley, where they afforded excellent targets for the remaining ammunition of the riflemen and Lewis gunners.

" A few prisoners were collected, and a fresh start made for the British lines, but, owing to the gathering twilight the party was mistaken for the enemy and subjected to heavy machine-gun fire which caused further casualties.

" Eventually, by working their way down a shallow ditch originally intended for a telephone cable, the battered remnant of ' C ' and ' D ' Companies managed to get near enough to attract the attention of a machine-gun officer who guided them into the Strong Point from which the long and slippery march back to Havrincourt was commenced."

* * * * * *

When the withdrawal from Graincourt began, the right garrison had been divided into two parties, the smaller, consisting of Major Warne, Captain Burtt, Second-Lieutenants Potts and Houslop, with about 20 or 30 other ranks, being in the trench, and the larger party, under Second Lieutenants Lacy and King, being outside. Second Lieutenant Lacy was wounded during the withdrawal, and afterwards died of wounds, whilst Second Lieutenant King was last seen in the rear of the party as it withdrew, binding up a wounded N.C.O., and was afterwards taken prisoner. The officers and men in the trench found themselves surrounded by Boches, and after lying quiet for some time they decided to try to work their way back to the British lines.

Darkness had now fallen, and they had not gone far on their journey before they ran into a large body of the enemy, who took them prisoners and led them back through Graincourt and Bourlon Wood, stopping at the late " D " Company

Headquarters, thence via Cambrai to Le Cateau, where they were split up into different camps.

Much space has been given to the description of the action of " C " and " D " Companies because, of the two halves of the Battalion, their task was much the more complicated. " A " and " B " Companies, on the left of the village, were in touch with Battalion Headquarters throughout.

The big German attack on the 6th of December moved across their front, but well away from their positions. They were thus able to put in some excellent shooting with comparatively little opposition from the enemy. Their patrols, however, were frequently in contact with enemy patrols, and fought with great credit in the numerous " street corner " fights on the outskirts of the village.

The left garrison was withdrawn at 5.30 p.m. on the 6th, and reached Havrincourt without any serious interruption.

The Regimental Aid Post was withdrawn at 6.0 p.m., all the wounded who could be found having been sent down.

Battalion Headquarters reached Havrincourt shortly before midnight, and after a day in tents in Havrincourt Wood, the Battalion moved, on the 8th of December, to billets in the village of Bertincourt, where at last there was time to pause and count the cost. The stay in this village was simply a repetition of the experience in Henencourt Wood in 1916, with the melancholy writing of letters of condolence and despatching of " effects."

After a week spent at Bertincourt, where the remainder of the " battle surplus " rejoined from the Divisional Reinforcement Camp, the Battalion moved up to take over a piece of line in front of Havrincourt. The troops had been hoping to go back for a rest, and the return to the line came as a not very pleasant surprise, and the statements of Company Commanders that the Battalion would certainly be back at rest for Christmas were received with a certain amount of scepticism.

The neighbourhood of Graincourt proved to be a less exciting place on this occasion, and after six cold but uneventful days the Battalion set off by train to the back area for a rest, and for what was generally felt to be a well-deserved Christmas holiday.

Snow lay thick on the ground when the Battalion marched into the village of Morlancourt, where it was to spend the rest. If the weather was seasonable, that is more than could be said for most of the billets, and a good deal of work had to be done in some of them to obtain any degree of comfort. The Christmas spirit, however, was abroad, and the troops, after their recent experiences, were not in the mood to worry about minor discomforts. The place was hardly one " to write home about," but the estaminets were plentiful and well stocked, and as a change from Bourlon Wood or even Bertincourt, the village of Morlancourt, with all its drawbacks, was appreciated.

Parades were few, and preparations for Christmas festivities were the order of the day. These were to take the form of plenty to eat, plenty to drink, and concerts and sing-songs in some of the largest halls and barns of the village. Time was too short to permit of the production of a revue or pantomime, though a cynic suggested that the authorities had some such idea in their minds when they called on the Quartermaster's staff to provide a guard one evening.

The Christmas dinners were a great success. No building, of course, could be found in the village to accommodate the whole Battalion, but it was found possible for " A " and " B " Companies to sit down to dinner together in one place, and " C " and " D " in another. All the officers met together for dinner later in the day.

The fare was varied and plentiful, joints of pork making a welcome change from the everlasting beef and mutton of the Army menu. Concerts and other forms of merrymaking passed away the remainder of the day, and the good spirits of the troops testified to their enjoyment of the Christmas festivities.

The sergeants were planning a dinner for the New Year, and preparations were practically complete when a hard-hearted Staff ordered a move to the neighbouring villages of Ribemont and Mericourt, where the other Battalions of the Brigade were already stationed. The remainder of the holiday was spent in these villages, where the Civil Service Battalion, as last comer, was unfortunate in the allotment of billets, and the men were spread over a large area.

The postponed sergeants' dinner, attended by the Commanding Officer and acting Adjutant, was held at Ribemont.

On the 10th of January the Battalion moved back by train to work, spending one night at Bertincourt before moving up to support positions in the village of Ribecourt. Now followed two tours, to the sectors in front of Ribecourt and Flesquières, during which there is little outside the ordinary events of trench warfare to record. While in reserve, the Battalion was stationed at Bertincourt, a dilapidated village, where some of the billets were Nissen huts and others damaged houses, and where the chief feature at the time was mud. This neighbourhood was a favourite one for the operations of the Boche night bombers. The Civil Service Rifles had had previous experience of this form of annoyance in billets, and in spite of the extra duties occasioned by Lewis gun anti-aircraft posts, the troops soon regarded the nightly visits of the planes as philosophically as the most hardened Londoner.

At the beginning of February the man-power question was so

acute in the British Infantry that it was decided to reduce Infantry Brigades from four to three Battalions—" in order to make a Brigade more mobile and more easily controlled by the Brigade Commander," said the official explanation. In the 47th Division the three Battalions to be broken up in consequence of this order were the 6th, 7th, and 8th City of London Battalions, who, with the Civil Service Rifles, had till then formed the 140th Brigade. The 17th and 21st Battalions (Poplar and Stepneys and First Surrey Rifles respectively) were transferred from the other Brigades of the Division to complete the 140th. This measure came to the Battalions broken up as an unexpected and sudden shock, the force of which will be fully understood and appreciated by every soldier who knows the strength of the bonds which keep the members of a Battalion together. The men of the Civil Service Rifles, realising what their own feelings would have been if it had fallen to their lot to be split up, were full of sympathy for the fellows who had been their comrades and their rivals for nearly three years of active service.

A number of officers and other ranks of the 6th Battalion were transferred to the Civil Service, and, in spite of the soreness which they must have felt at the loss of the identity of the Battalion whose high name and fame they had helped to win, they settled down to give to their new unit the same wholehearted service that they had given to their own.

One of the results of this reorganisation was the acquisition by the Civil Service of the brass band of the 6th Battalion. Strengthened by the inclusion of some of the more expert musicians of the existing drum and fife band, this band, under the direction of Sergeant W. H. Blackmore, quickly became one of the most valuable assets of the Regiment, and remains so to this day, for Mr. Blackmore still has charge of the Regimental Band, which includes in its ranks the majority of the men who served with him in France. The Regimental Band is one of the most successful features of the post-war Civil Service Rifles.

CHAPTER XX

THE RETREAT

ALTHOUGH a big German offensive had been expected for some weeks, and elaborate preparations to meet it had been made during the winter months, there were few signs of the eve of a big battle when the Civil Service Rifles, after a two hours' train journey from Etricourt, arrived at Winchester Valley late in the evening of the 19th of March, and relieved the 1st Berkshire Regiment (2nd Division) in Lincoln Reserve, the support line on Beaucamp Ridge, near Villers Plouich. The Poplar and Stepneys and London Irish were in the front line, and the 20th of March passed off very quietly.

It was thought that the Brigade was in for another spell of peaceful trench warfare, similar to those experienced before the short and pleasant stay at Manancourt. The rumours of the coming battle, which had been so strong during the winter months, had, in fact, begun to die down. The optimistic went so far as to think that the enemy attack would not take place, whilst the " quietly confident," thinking of the days of strenuous digging on those wide trenches behind the Hindenburg Line— the " Tank traps"—with the miles of barbed wire obstacles which had been erected all around, felt that, even if the enemy did launch a big attack, he would not get beyond the Hindenburg Line. Not even the most pessimistic had imagined the great crisis through which the Allied armies were to pass before another month was over. Nor was there any indication in the daily routine that the authorities were anticipating such a titanic struggle in the near future. Leave, regarded by the soldier as the most reliable " Military Barometer," was still being granted, and the allotment was indeed very much better than at any other time during the war. Men were actually going home on leave within six months of their last arrival in France, and in such circumstances how could one take any but the rosiest view of the future ? The German attack, if it came off at all, would probably be a repetition of Bourlon Wood, and after that both sides would settle down to another long spell of trench warfare. It was folly to talk, as the newspapers were doing, of a decisive battle.

When day broke on the 21st of March, however, it was clear that there had been some truth in the " big battle " rumours, for the first day of spring was heralded by such an intense enemy bombardment that there was no longer any doubt that the Bosche was making a supreme effort, beside which all his previous attacks faded into insignificance.

The difficulty at first was to find out where the attack was being pushed home, for in spite of the bombardment, which lasted from 4.30 a.m. until 11.0 a.m., there was no infantry engagement on the 21st of March on the 140th Brigade front. It was fortunate, too, that this was so, for the gas shells fell so freely all around that box respirators had to be worn continuously for six and a half hours.

There have been many attempts to write the story of the great retreat and, generally speaking, the experience of one battalion was much the same as that of any other. But it is well-nigh impossible to describe in detail the career of any unit throughout the most strenuous days of the fighting— the 21st to the 26th of March. During these days battalions often became split up into several parties engaged in different small fights, where none knew how the battle fared with their comrades in other parts of the field. The war correspondents, it is true, saw the Allied troops fighting every inch of ground, and killing thousands of Germans as they fell back, but it was difficult indeed for those engaged in the fighting to ascertain what the situation was, and a total lack of information was one of the outstanding features of the retreat. It was only when they ultimately got back into reserve, some days after, that the troops were able to learn from the newspapers that the Germans had been badly beaten all along the line. " Still," thought the British Tommy, who had marched in six days across country covered by two ordnance maps, " I don't altogether like this new style of winning the war."

The story of the Civil Service Rifles during these critical days of their career in France is told briefly in the official War Diary, which contains just a simple record of their movements without any comment.

In that record it is told how the Battalion, which was in support in Lincoln Reserve on the morning of the 21st, became at night the front line battalion, the 17th and 18th Battalions having been withdrawn. The second day of the battle was quiet on the Civil Service Rifles' front, and the Battalion remained undisturbed in Lincoln Reserve until the early hours of the 23rd, when, orders having been received to withdraw, a position was taken up on the Dessart Ridge Switch, on the right of the Metz-Fins Road. The line was complete by dawn, the dispositions being " A " Company on the left, with their left flank on the road

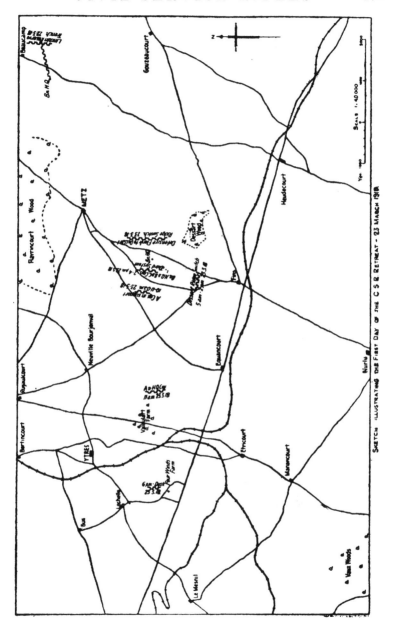

and their right in touch with " B," with " C " and " D " on the right of " B " : Battalion Headquarters was established in a bank about half a mile behind.   " A " was afterwards, owing to congestion, withdrawn to a position slightly in rear of the two companies.

The 23rd of March was the most critical day in the career of the Civil Service Rifles in France.   The official narrative disposes of it in less than a page, but a whole book could be written on the many situations which arose on that day, and the many acts of heroism, determination and devotion to duty performed by different members of the Battalion.

The story of the fighting can be followed more or less from the map on the opposite page.

Immediately the position on Dessart Ridge Switch was taken up, i.e., about 5.0 a.m., " D " Company on the right became engaged with the enemy, who attempted to rush in from the right flank, which was unprotected, and by 7.0 a.m. the Battalion was engaging the enemy all along the line.   At 8.0 a.m. the enemy made a determined bombing attack on the right of " D " Company, and established machine gun posts which enfiladed the position.   Shortly afterwards large numbers of troops were seen to be retiring, apparently from the position known as Metz Switch.   Colonel Segrave went over and rallied these, and took them forward with his Headquarters Company to the ridge between Metz and Dessart Wood (east of the Metz-Fins Road), and took up a position facing east, and at right angles to the Dessart Switch line.   This was done to form a rallying line for retiring troops and a defensive flank to Dessart Ridge Switch.

After shelling the whole area for an hour or two more, the enemy gained a little more ground and established further machine-gun posts, this time towards the left, south and south-east of Metz.   Shortly after noon, troops on the left retired, leaving the left flank of the Civil Service Rifles exposed, and the Battalion now held an isolated position with the enemy working his way round both flanks.   The Headquarters Company was accordingly withdrawn to the Vallulart Wood Line, and the remaining Companies, in the Dessart Switch Line facing South, continued the fight in the same position, forming a flank to what had been the third British system of defensive positions, now occupied by some Civil Service Rifles and other troops.

This third system and the Dessart Switch Line were abandoned at about 4.0 p.m., but " D " Company on the right had by this time been surrounded and was never extricated.   The cause of this disaster was the fact that the Company's right flank was completely " in the air " from the time it reached the position.   Indeed, this may be said of every position the

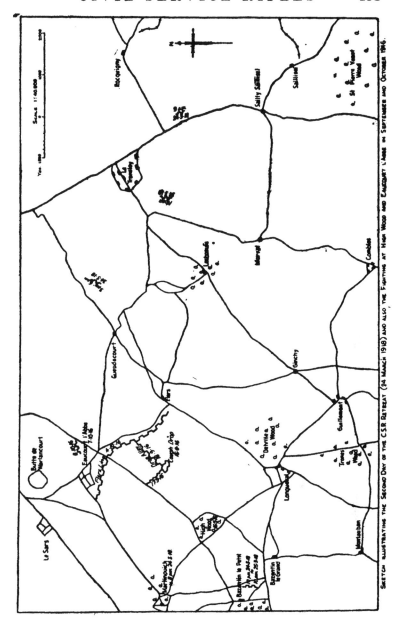

SKETCH ILLUSTRATING THE SECOND DAY OF THE CSR RETREAT (24 MARCH 1918) AND ALSO THE FIGHTING AT HIGH WOOD AND EAUCOURT L'ABBE IN SEPTEMBER AND OCTOBER 1916.

Battalion took up during the day. There was not at any time any support on the right flank, the troops of the 9th Division (5th Army) having already departed before the fighting began. Many explanations of these repeated withdrawals have since been made, both in after-dinner speeches and in statements to the Press. At least one book has been written on the subject. There was, and apparently still is, considerable difference of opinion as to the justification for the action of the troops of the 5th Army. This story is not concerned with the controversy. The statement is made simply to illustrate how the Civil Service Rifles, on the right of the 47th Division, felt the full effect of the rapid withdrawal of the troops on their right.

The movements of the various parts of the Battalion after 4.0 p.m. on the 23rd are not even now very clear. Battalion Headquarters (less Headquarters Company) left the third system at 4.0 p.m. and moved to Rocquigny, when Colonel Segrave collected a party of about fifty and put them in position along a ridge north of Four Winds Farm, about a mile and a half south-west of Ytres, where they remained until the enemy drove them out at dusk.

At this point the official narrative breaks down with the remark : " By this time the remnants of the Civil Service Rifles were split up into so many parties, whose movements are too complicated to follow." The survivors from those small parties, remembering their night of wandering in the dark over rough and strange country, and their inexplicable reunion at dawn, will bear out the truth of the last sentence.

By 9.0 a.m. on the twenty-fourth, the Battalion had been reduced to a mere handful of troops, who were worn out by their twenty-four hours' continuous fighting. The fate of the majority of the absentees was only too well known, but there were a good many missing whose fate was uncertain. The survivors, however, gallantly stuck to their task, and, numbering about 150, they took up a position under Colonel Segrave, just east of the Bapaume-Peronne road, and about a mile south-east of Le Transloy. Here they remained in support of a party of the 1st Surrey Rifles holding the higher ground to the east, until at noon they had to move back another two miles almost due west, and a position was taken up about half a mile south of Le Transloy and just off the western side of the Le Transloy-Combles road. This position was only held for three hours, when the party, now acting as a rearguard, moved round the western side of Le Transloy to a line north-east of Gueudecourt, whence they were withdrawn at 5.30 p.m. by order of the Brigade Commander through Gueudecourt and Flers to Martinpuich.

It was still light when Martinpuich was reached, and there were a few of the 150 or so survivors to whom the sight of the ruins of Eaucourt L'Abbé and the Flers Line recalled their grim struggle of October 1916. It was by no means a happy co-incidence that brought the Civil Service Rifles back to this battlefield, where, eighteen months previously, they had paid such a price for the capture of High Wood. On their previous visit to this area they had been filled with confidence and the offensive spirit. They had felt they were really doing something towards winning the war. To retreat across the same country now made it seem as though all the labours of the past eighteen months had been wasted—the lives lost in vain. It had been better if this battlefield had not been reached until darkness had fallen, and perhaps spared those men the bitter reflections on the autumn of 1916 and all they had gone through since.

There was little time, however, for reminiscences, for only a very short stay was made in Martinpuich, and 10.0 p.m. found the Battalion reforming at Bazentin-le-Petit, where further officers and other ranks rejoining brought the strength up to about 230 all ranks. An outpost position was then taken up along the eastern edge of Bazentin-le-Petit and occupied until 10.0 a.m. on the 25th, when a withdrawal was made to Con-talmaison Ridge, where the Battalion remained until 3.0 a.m. on the 26th.

After the rapid changes of position during the past two days it had seemed quite a long stay on Contalmaison Ridge, but the troops were not destined to settle there, and the next move was to Bouzincourt. The fighting had now ceased for the time being, so far, at least, as the Civil Service Rifles were concerned, but there was still no rest to be had, and it was not until after a five hours' march via Contalmaison, La Boiselle and thence across country to Aveluy and Bouzincourt, that billets were reached. The Battalion was now supposed to be resting, but after eight hours in Bouzincourt, the men were on the march again, and at 4.0 p.m. on the 26th they trudged along to billets at Louvencourt, where the night was spent.

At 9.0 a.m. on the 27th the march was resumed and after a rest for an hour or two at Clairfaye Farm, a move was made to billets at Toutencourt, where a halt was made for quite twelve hours! During these marches the Battalion had been in reserve, but now it began to move back to the front line, but before relieving the 6th Buffs (12th Division) in Aveluy Wood on the night of the 29th, a very welcome twenty-four hours' rest had been enjoyed in billets at Warloy.

While the fighting portion of the Battalion had been having such a strenuous time in the retreat, the Administrative portion had also had plenty of excitement, and the men of the transport section and Quartermaster's staff had frequently had to think about knocking the ashes out of their rifles and sharpening their bayonets during days when they were often in touch with the enemy. For a time they had to carry on as a separate unit, and the story of their travels is told in the following narrative contributed by Transport-Sergeant G. M. Sladden, to whom much credit is due for the withdrawal of the Regimental transport without the loss of a man or a horse.

" The period of the ' Great Retreat ' was an arduous one for the Battalion Transport, entailing conditions vastly different from the ordered routine incidental to trench warfare. Their lines were stationed on the 21st March in a field on the Metz–Fins road, the Quartermaster's stores being then in Metz, where the Battalion had been billeted prior to relieving the 2nd Division in the line. The stores were filled with an unusually heavy stock of material, including the blankets of the Battalion, the officers' valises and the men's packs. In fact, mobile conditions did not exist at this time.

" Early on the morning of the 22nd the hostile attack developed on our part of the front, and it rapidly became apparent that the attack was making headway, though hitherto no news had been heard of the great German success on the previous day further south. To the right was seen an aerial attack in great force on the 9th Division, of which some details soon began to pass in retreat by the transport lines. The officers' mess cart, which had gone early to Nurlu canteen, returned to report the canteen shelled out and Nurlu deserted. Soon orders arrived that the Battalion was to retire after nightfall to the Dessart Switch line, and the Transport to withdraw to Bus. Accordingly, all wagons not required to take up rations and move the Battalion that night were sent off at once with loads to Bus, and orders to return for a second load as soon as possible. Blankets were sent first, valises were left for the second journey : but the congested state of the roads and the rapidity of the enemy advance upset all calculations. The A.S.C. wagons, which were to have cleared the Quartermaster stores, were prevented by the road controls from returning to Metz. Consequently, there are certain officers who cherish regretful memories of persistent but futile efforts to induce a harsh War Office to compensate them for the loss of valuable but non-regulation articles of kit. Some of the limbered wagons—luckier or perhaps swifter than the A.S.C. motors—got back to the Transport lines late that night and picked up second loads. They were none too soon, for as they finished loading they were fired upon by machine guns from a patrol which had reached the ridge overlooking the lines from a few hundred yards away. The wagons, luckily, were standing in a sunken road and down this they were able to escape without casualty. Meanwhile, the ration wagons had gone up to the line, where they found the front line now withdrawn to the support line and preparing to evacuate the position. Ammunition dumps—notably the great dump at Trescault—were being blown up all round : indications of a big retreat abounded. Having delivered rations, the column waited to pick up Lewis guns and other equipment, and to take them back to the new position. Gradually the guns came down until all but one had arrived ; the Battalion was clear and platoons of other Battalions continued to file by—still no Lewis gun. Yet orders were definite, to wait till all the guns had come. But when the last platoon of the last Battalion had passed, it seemed certain that the missing gun must have gone some other way. The boy who stood on the burning deck was doubtless noble but certainly idiotic : moreover, it seemed possible that the fifteen guns on the wagons *might* be wanted. So orders were stoutly disobeyed and away went the wagons. They had been warned not to go back by the route by which they had come up, which had been reported occupied by the enemy ; so in the blackness of a pitch-dark night, over unreconnoitred ground, they made a bee-line for the road between Metz and Trescault.

> " Over hill, over dale,
> Through bush, through briar,
> Over park, over pale,
> Through trench, through wire—"

and hit it at last, though once nearly ingulfed in a bog. And so up the Fins road to the appointed place, where everything was safely handed over. The next stage was to the Transport lines, where the trekking loads of the wagons were waiting to be picked up ; but, at a short distance from the lines, bullets coming from that direction made it appear probable that the enemy was in possession, and this was confirmed by the Battalion Intelligence Officer who happened to meet the column at this juncture. Nothing for it then but to get away and join up with the rest of the Transport at Bus.

" At Bus the whole of the Brigade Transport was standing by waiting orders to move ; so the tired horses could not even be unharnessed. There was, however, opportunity to water and feed both for horse and man before a move was made, which was not actually until midday The line of march was by Le Mesnil and Saillisel to Le Transloy, over by roads much cut up. At one point the column had to pass over a quaking bog, of which the thin crust had to be continually reinforced, after the passage at the gallop of each vehicle, with fascines, bits of plank, and anything that came handy. The prevailing fine weather was a god send ; without it the column could not have passed this spot. Night had fallen before the column pulled off the road on to a shell-riddled stretch of the old Somme battlefield where wagons and horses could only stand higgledy-piggledy wherever a spot without a shell-hole could be found. Here the A.S.C. supply wagons were waiting, and at once rations were loaded on the limbers and sent off to find the Battalion. This was successfully done, and meanwhile the remaining horses and men were able to snatch a little sleep, though standing by to move at ten minutes' notice. Orders were hourly expected, for the front line was falling back fast, and shortly before midnight part of it— in the shape of ' A ' Company, which had lost touch—drifted into the lines in search of the rest of the Battalion. After they had pushed forward again to take up a defensive position it was found that other units of the Brigade Transport had moved off. Assuming that orders had miscarried (as afterwards was found to be the case), and knowing that if the column was to get away at all, it must be before dawn, a move was made without orders. It was found afterwards that the rest of the Brigade marched via Les Boeufs, where they had some casualties through shell fire ; so the choice of route of the 15th via Saillisel and Combles was a lucky one, for the column was unmolested on this road except by a little heavy shrapnel that did no harm. Some trouble was caused at Saillisel, where, just as dawn began to break, and with the enemy on a ridge only a short distance away, the road was found to be blocked by part of an ammunition column. After some difficulty they were passed—another stroke of luck, for it was heard afterwards that this column failed to get away. Combles, too, was found to contain the Divisional Ordnance Depot, where all stores were being destroyed. A few men were able as they passed to snatch articles of kit that they had lost : the Battalion saddler still mourns over his failure to ' scrounge ' a complete saddler's outfit. He found it too heavy to catch the last wagon and stow it there.

" It took a weary while to reach Bazentin Le Petit that day, for after Ginchy the road was congested with an enormous mass of traffic. However, it was done, and horses and men, utterly weary hoped for a little rest there. But it seemed that the march would never end, for orders came for the retreat to continue ; and at dusk all (except enough cookers and ration wagons to supply the Battalion with food that night) moved off via Albert to a new halting ground. During the afternoon a slight diversion had been caused by several enemy aeroplanes that came over and dropped a few bombs intended for the Brigade Transport ; it was, however, a very timid raid of the tip-and-run variety and did no harm. Of a very different kind was the relay raid that the column passing through Albert that night experienced. From dark to light a succession of machines dropped bombs up and down the main street of Albert and the main roads approaching the town. The street was full of moving traffic, and things were made much worse by many motor transport drivers leaving their lorries standing and taking cover in houses. It seemed at one time as if the column of the 140th Brigade would be utterly unable to go forward ; but the acting Transport Officer and Quartermaster, Lieutenant A. L. Mills, did excellent work in sorting out the disorganised mass of vehicles ahead, and the Brigade column finally got through with far fewer casualties than might have been expected, and of these the 15th incurred none. Meanwhile the ration column had set out with an escort of armoured cars to meet the Battalion at Bazentin Le Grand. The Battalion was, for the moment, not holding a position, and it was possible to give every man the good, hot meal of which he stood in need. The escort proved unnecessary, and as it was growing light when Albert was passed on the return journey, the ration column escaped the bombing that the others had undergone. But the bodies and the wreckage showed them how much Albert had suffered that night. They rejoined the rest of the transport in the small hours of the morning of the 25th, but within four hours the whole column was on the move again to just outside Millencourt. Here was another short halt, during which the 15th acquired two ' buckshee ' horses—one of them an excellent animal, who served them well until he was killed six months later, the other

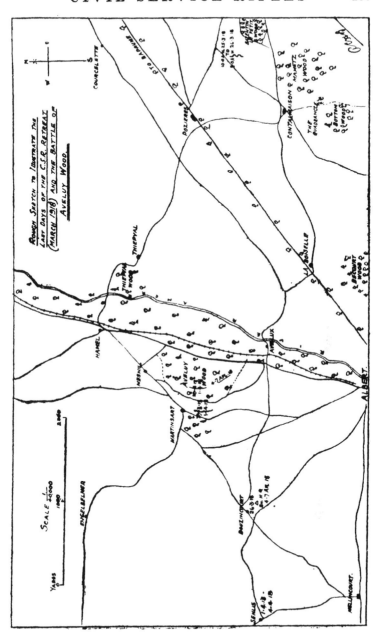

blind and vicious : it was easy to guess how he came to be roving free—and he was soon given his freedom back again. Tired though every man and beast was, it was necessary to move again that afternoon, because the unit was said to be on the wrong side of road. They were sent to a pitch which was also useless because too soft for wagon or horse lines—involving another move, unauthorised this time. Rations went up as soon as the third move had been carried out, and after a long wait at the rendezvous were sent back to the lines, for the Battalion was at last coming out of the line. The ration column got back to the lines just in time to move with the rest of the Transport to Bouzincourt, where the relieved Battalion was met early on the morning of the 26th. From which time for a while the history of the movements of the Transport merges again with that of the Battalion as a whole.

      *   *   *   *   *   *

A second phase of the fighting opened when the Battalion moved to Aveluy Wood on the night of the 29th of March.

There had been no time for a proper re-organisation, and the troops had not yet recovered from their exertions during the retreat. The casualties since the morning of the 21st of March numbered no less than 350 (all ranks) and as no reinforcements had joined, it was as well that the second phase opened quietly.

One and a half companies occupied an outpost position in Aveluy Wood, and the remainder of the Battalion was in a ravine 800 yards south of Martinsart. The 22nd Battalion was on the left, with a gap of 400 yards between the two units. For three days this position was held, and except for hostile shelling there was little enemy activity, the casualties for the three days numbering little more than a dozen. The 20th Battalion on the night of the 1st of April, relieved the Civil Service Rifles, who moved into billets in Senlis, and after two days' rest and a more than welcome bath, the Battalion, now somewhat re-organised, returned to the front line and relieved the 1st Surrey Rifles on the night of the 4th of April. " A " Company held the right, " C " the centre, and a company of the 1st Surrey Rifles. who were attached, held the left. " B " and " D " Companies were in support and Battalion Headquarters was in Bouzincourt. The 9th Royal Fusiliers (12th Division) were on the right of the Civil Service Rifles and the 142nd Brigade on the left.

The few reinforcements who had joined included Major L. L. Pargiter, of the Middlesex Regiment, who came to the Battalion on the 4th of April as second in command.

Such were the dispositions when the battle for Aveluy Wood opened on the morning of the 5th of April.

As usual, the enemy opened with a heavy bombardment on the front line, support trenches, and Bouzincourt, gas shells being freely mixed with the heavier missiles. The bombardment began at 7.0 a.m. and except for three short intervals of about half an hour each, it continued until 4.30 p.m. Throughout the afternoon the bombardment of Bouzincourt was particularly intense. The enemy was excellently supported by his machine guns, which were active all day on the front line and support trenches with both direct and indirect fire.

When the bombardment began the enemy could be seen along the crest opposite the front line in twos and threes (total about 150). These small groups were dispersed by rifle fire, but at about 10.0 a.m. small groups again began to dribble forward over the crest, and these advanced in spite of Lewis gun and rifle fire, by using the cover afforded by huts and sheds, until they reached the trees and broken ground on the outskirts of Aveluy Wood. It is estimated that roughly 300 of the enemy with light machine guns pushed forward in this way. The front line held by the Civil Service Rifles was by this time enfiladed with machine-gun fire and minenwerfers, and under cover of this fire the parties in the broken ground crept forward to within 100 yards of the British front line. These parties showed up several times as if about to rush the position, but whenever they appeared, Lewis gun and rifle fire kept them back, and the intended assault was not delivered.

In the afternoon the enemy was seen to be digging in on the crest from which he had doubled forward earlier in the day, and by 6.0 p.m. this ground was effectually swept by artillery fire, with the result that no further signs of an advance were seen at that point.

By nightfull the enemy appeared to give up the attempt, at all events for that day, and the situation became considerably quieter. "D" Company now relieved the attached Company of the 1st Surrey Rifles in the front line, and this latter Company moved into support. The casualties in the Civil Service Rifles numbered fifty (all ranks), including Colonel Segrave, who was slightly gassed, and who was sent to the transport lines for a well-earned rest, Major Pargiter taking command of the Battalion.

The 6th of April was a day of alarms, but although small parties of the enemy were detected in the early morning moving forward under cover of the mist, there was no real infantry engagement. The snipers were busy on both sides and those of the Civil Service Rifles got many targets, and one of the enemy was captured after being wounded.

Intermittent bombardments were the feature of the day, but the battle died down for good after 10.0 p.m. with the Germans really well held, and with this night came to an end the fighting in the great Retreat on this front, and the Bosche thereafter did not gain any ground at all.

After holding the line for one more day, which was fairly quiet, the Battalion was relieved on the night of the 7th of April by the 17th and 21st Battalions, and marched to billets in Senlis. It was not yet known that the Division was about to move back to a training area, but the rumour soon began to get round to that effect, and the prospect of a real rest acted as a splendid tonic to the weary survivors of the darkest days in the history of the Division. They had been dark days, indeed, but those who came through could look back on them with satisfaction in the knowledge that their Battalion had played its part nobly during a period when a trip to Germany—or elsewhere—had often seemed to be the most probable end to their career in France.

This story of the movements of the 1st Civil Service Rifles during the Retreat is based on the official narrative written by Battalion Headquarters, but it should be borne in mind that the fighting during the last days of March was of so extraordinary a character that the description here given will fall very far short of the affair as it appeared to many of the members of the Battalion. Only those who took part in it will be able to realise the difficulty of describing a series of actions in which the Battalion was split up into several different bodies, each fighting battles of their own, with little or no knowledge of the whereabouts of their comrades. If this feature of the fighting is considered, it will help to explain why so many of the casualties were reported as " wounded and missing " or " missing, believed killed " without any definite information as to the place where they occurred.

The casualties among officers, warrant officers and N.C.O.'s were very heavy, but these serve to emphasise the splendid spirit of the men. Nothing could illustrate their excellent discipline, determination and fighting qualities more forcibly than that assembly at Bazentin le Petit on the night of the 24th of March. In spite of being cut off from their comrades these several small parties had carried on the fight for more than twenty-four hours —often without even a Lance-corporal in charge—and the simple statement that " 10.0 p.m. saw the Battalion reforming at Bazentin le Petit " is in reality a record of the finest achievement of the men of the 1st Civil Service Rifles during the war.

A good many of the N.C.O.'s and men were decorated for their work during the Retreat, but every one of those 230 all ranks who refused to be beaten on the 23rd and 24th of March, 1918, is deserving of the highest praise. It would have been some small recognition of their great gallantry and devotion to duty if the names of these men could have been inscribed on a special Roll of Honour.

CHAPTER XXI

MONTHS OF " WIND UP "

ONE night in Senlis was followed by a night in Hedauville, and then on the 9th of April, after a march to Acheux, the Battalion was conveyed by buses to the back area. The bus journey was pleasant enough at first, but on arriving at Beauval, where the troops were to have been billeted, it was found that all the accommodation had been allotted to other troops.

The bus column halted in the main road outside the village where a draft of 600 other ranks was waiting to join the Battalion. The draft had been waiting by the roadside since noon, and the men had had both dinner and tea in the same spot. But soon after dark the draft received orders to march to the next village, Gezaincourt, the Battalion continuing the journey by bus. The speed of the buses can best be judged by the fact that the draft arrived at Gezaincourt—about three and a half miles away—more than an hour in front of the Battalion.

The next day at Gezaincourt was spent in re-organising Companies and sorting out the huge draft, which was found to contain parties from practically every Battalion of the London Regiment except the Artists and the Scottish. The Civil Service Riflemen were now in a minority in their own Regiment.

The journey was continued on the 11th of April, when the Battalion marched to Domart en Ponthieu, a delightful village, where all ranks would have been happy to remain for the rest of the war. But it was not to be, for the troops were on the move again early next day, and after a fifteen miles' march the training area was reached, and the Civil Service Rifles were billeted in the village of Canchy, close to the historic forest of Crecy. The village was also occupied by Divisional Headquarters, and the billets allotted to the Battalion were consequently poor, everything worth having being appropriated for the use of Divisional Headquarters.

The usual training programme was carried out and drafts continued to arrive until the Battalion grew to an unwieldy size, being over 1,300 strong. But although numerically it was stronger than it had ever been, the vast majority of the men were very raw—recruits who had been hurried out during the panic caused by the Retreat. It was soon found that the Civil Service Rifles had received more than their share of these men, and 250 of them were accordingly sent to the 142nd Brigade.

The only breaks in the routine of training were trips to Abbeville, football matches, and a half-hearted sort of Sports Meeting.

The Divisional Commander visited the Brigade at a Brigade parade at Forest l'Abbaye, on the 18th of April, when he complimented the Brigade on its work during recent operations, and hinted darkly at further " dirty work " in store in the near future.

The concluding sporting event at Canchy was a football match against the Divisional Train, the holders of the Divisional Company, who were well beaten by four goals to nil. While the match was in progress orders were received for the Transport to move early the next day, Sunday, the 28th of April, and for the Battalion to move by bus on Monday morning.

Although the programme of training had been arranged for another week, the sudden orders to move occasioned little surprise, for it was quite a common thing for a " training holiday " to be cut short, and the Transport Section accordingly moved to St. Quen without any fuss.

On the last afternoon at Canchy the *entente cordiale* between the Civil Service Rifles and the villagers was strengthened by a tea-party which Colonel Segrave gave to the village children. To entertain them were engaged the Divisional Cinema, the String Trio and Private Saipe. The latter's conjuring brought down the house, and was so popular that the conjurer, on taking his evening stroll later on, was mobbed by the villagers, who insisted on his giving them a " second house " in the open air.

The bus journey to Contay was uneventful, and on leaving the buses, the Battalion, just over 700 strong, marched to billets in Warloy. A battle surplus of eight officers and 240 other ranks had been left behind at a Divisional Reinforcement Camp at Estrées les Crecy.

The German advance had been held up in the neighbourhood of Albert, and for some weeks now no move had been made on either side, though farther north the allied lines in the Ypres and Armentieres districts had been pushed back considerably. It was not, therefore, surprising when the 21st Australian Battalion was relieved on the night of the 1st of May outside the Albert-Amiens Road that orders were issued to all units to make every possible preparation to meet an enemy attack, which, to use the official language, " is likely to develop on our front in the near future."

During this tour of the trenches the patrols of " B," " C," and " D " Companies, who were the three front line Companies, all reported that at 2.0 a.m. on the morning of the 4th of May, a noise resembling that of steam tractors was heard coming from the vicinity of the railway south of the Albert Road. As a result, the R.A.F. carried out a special reconnaissance at dawn and found four enemy tanks hiding near the railway. These were bombed, two being totally destroyed and the others disabled. The Brigadier General specially commended the Civil Service Rifles on the good work done by the patrols.

The discovery of the tanks, however, only served to increase the warnings of a coming attack, and an otherwise uneventful spell in the mud and water was frequently disturbed by such orders from Division as " See that all men have a hot meal immediately : Attack probable this morning."

On the night of the 6th of May a somewhat complicated relief, owing to a reshuffle of Brigades on the Corps front, brought to an end a surprisingly peaceful stay in the front line. It did not, however, bring much comfort to the troops.

The Battalion was to move back to support trenches in the neighbourhood of Millencourt and Henencourt, but the Companies had the greatest difficulty in identifying their positions, as they turned out to be mere scratches in the ground. The night was black and the rain poured in torrents throughout. The relief was accordingly exceptionally slow and day was breaking ere the support positions were reached.

The Officer Commanding " A " Company found in Millencourt some unoccupied cellars with plenty of straw, and decided to stow his men away there and risk the consequences. " B " and " C " Companies found ruined houses in Henencourt, and " D " moved into a barn in the yard of the château at Henencourt, which had been Third Corps Headquarters during the Somme battle of 1916. Battalion Headquarters was at the Grand Caporal estaminet — a " house " that had been a favourite resort of the men of the Civil Service Rifles during the rest after High Wood in 1916. But how the village had changed since those days ! In 1916 Henencourt had been a tolerably clean inhabited village, but now all was desolation, every house was in ruins, and there was not a civilian to be found anywhere.

By night the Companies occupied their battle positions and tried to dig trenches there, and by day they kept under cover in their billets. A search was made for bath tubs, and a bath-house was started in the Château yard, and apart from occasional shelling of Millencourt and Henencourt, a fairly comfortable time was spent in these villages.

The next visit to the front line was to relieve the 17th London Regiment astride the Millencourt-Albert Road, a mile or so

N

east of the village of Millencourt. The trenches here were new, and so exposed that no cooking could be done there. All food was cooked at the Quartermaster's stores at Warloy and brought up at night, when the troops had their only hot meal of the day. The tea was sent up in petrol cans enclosed in packs stuffed with hay—a method which had been adopted by members of the Transport Section some months previously for keeping tea hot on a long march.

Digging new trenches and wiring were the nightly tasks of all Companies during five uneventful days in this sector, and on relief by the 6th London Regiment—now in the 58th Divison —the Battalion moved back to billets in Warloy, and on the following day the Division moved into Corps Reserve.

The period in Corps Reserve had generally been spent in tolerably comfortable billets in inhabited villages some distance from the firing line, but on this occasion the Division was kept close up, owing to the possibility of an enemy attack, and it fell to the lot of the 140th Brigade to occupy small woods in the neighbourhood of Warloy and Bazieux. The accommodation was distinctly poor, the men having to sleep under bivouac sheets—or trench shelters as they were called officially.

Colonel Segrave accordingly indulged in a little billeting on his own account and fixed his battalion up in comfortable billets in Warloy, observing at the same time that as they were nearer to the front line they were tactically in a better position to meet an emergency. A wordy warfare with the Divisional Staff ensued, and for a few days the Civil Service Rifles hung on to their billets, although the Colonel had been withdrawn to command the 141st Brigade. But soon a move had to be made to the bivouacs in the Bois La Haut, north of Bazieux, where the days were spent by the troops in digging cable trenches near Henencourt Wood, and the nights were often spent in alarms and standing to.

Indeed, a more restless period in Corps Reserve had never been known. All officers were taken to reconnoitre positions of assembly for counter-attack, and to each battalion in the Brigade was allotted a definite objective. It was announced that the attack would be launched on the 20th, and the officers were taken through a kind of rehearsal of their counter-attack.

Nightly bombing raids by enemy aeroplanes added to the discomfort, and on the night of the 18th of May an intense bombardment was heard. Later, an alarm was sounded in an adjacent wood, and the Battalion stood to arms at 2.0 a.m. and remained so for about an hour. Thereafter the troops were made to stand to arms each morning at an hour before dawn as in the trenches, and the cooks had to " keep up steam " in readiness to serve a hot meal at once in the event of an enemy attack on the Corps front. Happily nothing so unpleasant as an attack developed, but the camp was shelled on the morning of the 22nd, with the result that the Transport Section lost an old and tried friend in Corporal Banks, who had been with them continuously since mobilisation. It was cruel luck that he should be killed while in Corps Reserve, after surviving such ordeals as the Somme, Ypres Salient, Bourlon Wood and the Retreat. Two horses were also killed and two others wounded.

The Division moved out of Corps Reserve on the 24th of May, and after a whole day spent in cable burying in the pouring rain, the Civil Service Rifles relieved the 7th East Surrey Regiment in quarries near the Franvillers-Albert road. Here the troops bivouacked amongst guns and howitzers of all calibres; in some cases the men slept, or rather spent the night, under the muzzles of the guns. The only good thing the Battalion got out of this relief was a draft of 10 N.C.O.'s, who had been wounded on the Somme in 1916, and on their return to France had been drafted to the East Surrey Regiment. By a strange coincidence they rejoined the Civil Service Rifles almost on the very ground where they had been trained for the Somme battle, for the Bois Robert, where many of the rehearsals for High Wood took place, was within a hundred yards or so of the bivouacs.

A short stay amid the guns was followed by a move to comfortable but shell-riddled billets in Baizieux—a village somewhat changed since the previous Christmas, when it was occupied by Divisional Headquarters.

The 4th Battalion Royal Welsh Fusiliers was relieved in the Lavieville defences on the 26th of May, and here the Battalion spent four days in support trenches, during the whole of which time all Companies were at work with the Royal Engineers on cable burying. At the end of May 1918, the Civil Service Rifles occupied a field surrounded by new and shallow trenches just north of the Franvillers-Berhencourt road, and about half a mile west of Franvillers itself. These trenches were the rear defences of the Lahoussoye system, but the men occupied tents and bivouacs outside the trenches.

There followed five uneventful days in the front line opposite the village of Dernancourt, and on relief by the 17th Battalion on the night of the 6th of June, support trenches astride the Albert-Amiens road were occupied for three days. The Battalion then relieved the 1st Surrey Rifles in the front line on the immediate left of the sector held previously. This particular area was held by the Brigade for nearly three weeks, the Battalion changing round every four or five days. Nothing worthy of note happened until, on the 19th of June, the Division was relieved by the 58th Division, the 6th London Regiment taking over from the Civil Service Rifles, who had a long march back to the village of Berhencourt, which was reached at about 5 a.m. After a few hours' rest the march was continued to Molliens au Bois, where a tented camp in a sea of mud was taken over from the Queen Victoria Rifles. Here the Regimental Brass Band, which had been entertaining the Commander-in-Chief at General Headquarters for the past six weeks, rejoined, together with the battle surplus and a draft of reinforcements from the Divisional Reinforcement Camp.

CHAPTER XXII

INTENSIVE TRAINING

FORTUNATELY only one day was spent at Molliens au Bois, and on the 21st of June a bus ride took the Civil Service Rifles through Amiens and then round the country for a few hours, and back to Ferrieres, a little village about four miles from Amiens. The Battalion then marched to Guignemicourt, a village without any water supply, a real old-fashioned out-of-the-way country place, which seemed miles away from the war. The big château occupied by Battalion Headquarters was the property of a French " nouveau riche," who, according to the natives, had made his fortune out of beer. He had fled hurriedly during the German advance, leaving all his furniture behind him, but no trace could be found of the commodity which was alleged to have earned him his francs.

A quaint feature of the village life was the town crier with his drum, who took up his stand in front of the sentry outside Battalion Headquarters and made such announcements as the fixed price of coal, flour, etc., for the ensuing month. His services were utilised by the Civil Service Rifles at the end of their stay to announce to the villagers that any claims against the Battalion must be lodged at the orderly room before the Battalion left the village.

To the members of the Civil Service Rifles who were at Guignemicourt, however, the name does not revive memories of an old-world village or of a quaint town crier. The memory that is inseparable from this village is one of eternal parades. There were not only parades for work, but also parades for play, the Battalion, after spending the morning hard at work on the drill ground, being marched to the football field every afternoon to take part in compulsory football. And for officers the day's work was carried on after lights out ; for many were the hours spent in conferences at Battalion Headquarters long after the men were " between the sheets " in their billets.

The compulsory football took the form of six-a-side games, the sides being chosen in alphabetical order throughout each platoon or specialist section. Every able-bodied officer, warrant officer, N.C.O., or man, had to play, and the games were on the knock-out

principle.   Only four games could be played at a time, and
those who were not playing had to look on, but, as the weather
was beautifully fine, the troops soon tumbled to the idea of bringing their writing-pads, with the result that when the Corps
Commander and many of the gilded staff drove up to the ground
on the afternoon of the 25th of June they found a few men playing
football and the majority of the Battalion squatting on the grass
writing letters.   The final was won by a team from " B "
Company.

After the football competition, Major L. L. Pargiter, who was
in command of the Battalion during the absence on leave of
Colonel Segrave, introduced the game of puttocks—a game
which " caught on " at once with the Battalion.   Major Pargiter
was an enthusiast for sport as well as for work, and he combined
the two on the miniature range, where shooting took place every
evening, the prizes taking the form of 10 centimes for every
bull's-eye scored.   This was apparently too easy a method of
making money, for on some evenings nobody put in an appearance
except the Officer Commanding Range and the marker.

The eternal parades naturally provoked a certain amount of
grousing, but none the less the Battalion had reached a very high
standard of efficiency, when Colonel Segrave returned on the
2nd of July, after a month's absence.

On the next day a Divisional water carnival was held at
Picquigny, where R.Q.M.S. Hart improved on his previous
year's success by taking the first two places in the odd craft
race.   He had trained on the horse pond in the village and his
craft finished so far in front of the rest of the competitors that
many of the spectators were unaware that he was in the race
at all.

The Battalion won the Divisional water polo championship
with the following team : Colour-Sergeant W. S. Watts, Corporal
O. S. Wraight, and Corporal T. Byron of " B " Company,
Lance-Corporal H. G. Terry of " A " Company, and Privates
T. N. Smale, " B " Company, S. Paisley and R. Bull, Transport
Section.   Other members of the Battalion who distinguished
themselves were Privates E. Manfield, who was third in the back
stroke race, and Privates F. J. Garnham, " B " Company, and
P. A. Pooley, " D " Company, who with Corporal Wraight and
Private Bull gained for the Civil Service Rifles third place in
the Divisional Relay Race.   Altogether it was a good day for
the Civil Service Rifles.

On the following day Major General Gorringe presented
ribbons to those in the Battalion who had been awarded decorations for their work during the Retreat.

A Memorial Service to Civil Servants who had fallen in the
war was held in the Château grounds on the 11th of July, at the

same hour as the service in Westminster Abbey for the same purpose was being held.

Tho only other incidents worthy of note during the last week at Guignemicourt were the Battalion Sports Meeting, at which " D " Company won far more points than any other Company, and the visit of a photographer from the French Flying Corps. Every Company and Specialist Section and almost every platoon was photographed, as also were the Battalion football team and many of the horses.

The Battalion returned to Warloy on the 12th of July and relieved the First Surrey Rifles in support positions on the Senlis-Henencourt Road on the 15th.

On the 18th of July the welcome news was received of a successful French counter-attack on a large scale in the Soissons region. The news was cheering to all ranks, but no one even suspected that this was the beginning of the end, and that in four months' time the Armistice would be signed.

On the 20th of July the 17th Battalion was relieved by the Civil Service Rifles in front line trenches due east of Millencourt, and a company of American Infantry of the 131st Regiment, 33rd U.S.A. Division, became attached for instruction in trench warfare. The American troops were of fine physique and were very keen, but what seemed to appeal to them most was the excellent cooking of the Civil Service Rifles cooks. Many of them declared that although they were living in trenches they had not been fed so well since they left home.

Each of the four Companies of the 131st Regiment (1st Battalion) spent twenty-four hours under instruction with the Civil Service Rifles, and on the 24th of July, the whole of the American Battalion became attached to the 140th Brigade and relieved the Civil Service Rifles who moved back to Contay. Colonel Segrave and his Adjutant, four Company Commanders and some senior N.C.O.'s remained with the U.S.A. troops until the following day, when all returned to Contay except the Commanding Officer and Adjutant, who were attached to the American Battalion for a further period of two days. In the meantime the four Company Quartermaster Sergeants were attached to the American Quartermaster to assist him in rationing his Battalion while it was in the front line.

After five days at Contay the Civil Service Rifles relieved the 17th Battalion in support to the front line recently held, where they were relieved on the 30th of July by the 19th Battalion, and moved back to the positions on the Senlis-Henencourt Road, now occupied by the forward Battalion of the Brigade in Divisional Reserve.

The month of August, 1918, was certainly an eventful one, for it brought with it a general advance on the whole of the Corps front.

There was little in the early days of the month to suggest the startling changes that were to come over the military situation in the immediate vicinity of the 47th Divisional front, though as time went on, the news of advances in various parts of the allied line revived an enthusiasm that had perhaps been on the wane since the beginning of the year.

There was as yet no talk of a coming attack by the 140th Brigade, and on the night of the 5th of August, after spending two days in Warloy, the Civil Service Rifles relieved the 24th Battalion on the right of the Divisional front, just outside Albert on the Amiens Road. But although there had been no special preparation for an attack, it was thought quite likely that one might soon be made, as the enemy had withdrawn his line from the position round Albert, and even from the town itself it was believed.

" B " Company occupied parts of the two old German front lines, and had sentry groups also along the west side of the railway embankment overlooking the River Ancre. It appeared to be quite true that the Germans had withdrawn, for no trace of one was seen on the Battalion front.

On the 6th of August news was received that Colonel Segrave, who was at the time Acting Brigade Commander, had been promoted to the rank of Brigadier General, and he left forthwith to command the 152nd Brigade in the 51st Division, and the Civil Service Rifles had to part for good with one who had been to them something far more than a Commanding Officer.

Although Colonel Segrave's promotion had been more or less expected for some time, he received very short notice to depart, and was not even given an opportunity to say good-bye. It is difficult to say whether he or the Battalion felt the parting more keenly, for he was loved by those whom he commanded as much as he loved them—which is saying a great deal.

No story of the 1st Civil Service Rifles can be complete without an appreciation of one who is regarded by all who served under him as the finest Commanding Officer the Regiment ever had. His gallantry in the field has already been referred to, and it was fortunate for the Battalion that all its big defensive battles were fought during the year in which Colonel Segrave commanded, for it was in such battles, rather than in attacks which had been rehearsed in every detail, that able leadership meant so much. Both at Bourlon Wood and in the Retreat the Civil Service Rifles owed a great deal to the guiding hand of their Commanding Officer.

But it was not only owing to his ability as a leader, nor to his exceptional bravery under fire, that his presence gave such confidence to the troops. They always knew that in Colonel Segrave they had a Commanding Officer who devoted himself wholeheartedly to the welfare of the Civil Service Rifles. He was a red-hot enthusiast for the Regiment, and would tolerate nothing that was, in his opinion, likely to bring it into disrepute. A tireless worker himself, he would have no idlers among his officers, N.C.O.'s or men.

These are but a few of the qualities in Colonel Segrave which cause men to speak with genuine pride of the fact that they served under him. Outstanding among his characteristics was his pure unselfishness. All that he did was done for his Regiment. He sought no personal glorification. He indeed " did good by stealth and blushed to find it fame." But the splendid work he did for the Civil Service Rifles during the hardest year of the war can never be forgotten by those who had the good fortune to serve under Colonel Segrave.

CHAPTER XXIII

THE GREAT ADVANCE

A SENSATIONAL change came over the military situation on the Divisional front during August, 1918. When the month opened, the front line Brigades were still holding the trenches outside Albert, and were kept in a state of readiness to meet a German attack. It soon became evident, however, that there would be no German attack from that quarter, for it became known on the 3rd of August that the Germans had withdrawn from Albert and the positions around that town, and by the end of the month the troops of the 47th Division, instead of being on the defensive, were in pursuit of a broken enemy several miles east of Albert, and open warfare prevailed once more.

When Colonel Segrave left it was not known who was to be his successor, but in the meantime Major G. G. Bates, M.C., acted as Commanding Officer.

The first indication of the coming advance was a big attack launched by the Allies at 4.0 a.m. on the 8th of August. The Civil Service Rifles were at that time holding front line trenches just outside Albert, on the north side of the Albert-Amiens road. No attack was launched in that area, but there was increased artillery activity throughout the day. On the following day an attack was delivered by the 58th Division immediately south of the 47th Division and an Australian Division further south. Their objectives were the villages of Ville sur Ancre, Dernancourt, Morlancourt, and the German positions in the vicinity. In spite of a ground mist, which made it difficult to follow the operations, the attack was a big success. The Civil Service Rifles were not affected, though the Battalion scouts were sent as spectators to a point of vantage to watch for any developments likely to affect the front held by the 47th Division. It was a curious sight to see a small crowd on a slope on the left flank of the attack, watching the fight at fairly close quarters, like a crowd at a football match.

About this time enemy aeroplanes were active at night, bombing transport lines and billets at Warloy, and the Civil Service Rifles lost their Acting Quartermaster, Second Lieutenant A. L. Mills, and their Assistant Adjutant, Second Lieutenant

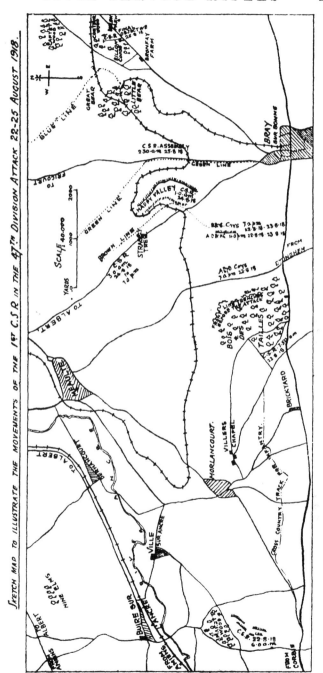

SKETCH MAP TO ILLUSTRATE THE MOVEMENTS OF THE 1ST C.S.R. IN THE 47TH DIVISION ATTACK 22-25 AUGUST 1918.

P. J. Spencer, both of whom were bombed in their billet, which was completely destroyed, the officers being dangerously wounded.

On the 13th of August, after a short stay in support in Baizieux, the Division moved south of the Albert Road and relieved the 58th Division in the neighbourhood of Bray. The Civil Service Rifles relieved the Queen Victoria Rifles in the forward position of the support Brigade. The trenches occupied were the old British and German front lines west of Morlancourt. The Transport Section and Quartermaster's stores moved to the village of Bonnay, which was visited nightly by enemy bombing planes.

On the night of the 16th of August the Battalion moved up to the front line and relieved the 22nd London Regiment on the right of the Divisional front in the Bois des Tailles, just north of the village of Bray.

The Bois des Tailles had doubtless been a very pretty wood in peace time, but it was now strewn with the debris remaining after the German occupation. It had afforded good natural cover for German guns, and in the valley which ran through the middle of the wood were some rather palatial dug-outs. The German guns were still in position, though the emplacements had been destroyed and the ammunition was scattered about the ground. Throughout its occupation by the Civil Service Rifles, the Bois des Tailles was subjected to a steady bombardment, gas shells being used freely every night. The aforesaid valley became saturated with gas and the dug-outs were rendered uninhabitable. Casualties were pretty heavy, and the five days spent in what became known among the troops as "*toute de suite* wood" were distinctly unpleasant.

At midnight on the 20th of August the 20th London Regiment took over the positions in the Bois des Tailles, and the Civil Service Rifles moved back to support positions in a valley near Marett Wood, close to Mericourt L'Abbé. Here the new Commanding Officer, Lieut.-Colonel R. C. Feilding, D.S.O., Coldstream Guards, took over the command of the Battalion.

Colonel Feilding had not had time to get to know his troops before he was leading them in battle, for after one day's rest in support positions, the 140th Brigade moved up on the 22nd of August and was the Reserve Brigade in a big attack launched that morning by the 47th Division, in conjunction with the 12th Division on the left, and an Australian Division on the right.

The programme for the 47th Division was that the 141st Brigade holding the front line was to move forward at zero, and capture and consolidate the first objective, known for this battle as the Brown Line, running parallel with the Bray-Albert road and about 500 yards east of it. The 142nd Brigade was to pass through the 141st Brigade ten minutes after zero, and capture and consolidate the second objective (known as the Green Line.) Corps cavalry and twelve whippet tanks were then to pass through the 141st and 142nd Brigades, and capture the Blue Line (a line of defences from Fricourt to the woods known as Great and Little Bear), the 140th Brigade remaining in Divisional Reserve, ready to move forward and consolidate the Blue Line when captured.

Soon after 6.0 a.m. on the 22nd of August, the Civil Service Rifles marched forward from the positions near Marett Wood, and by 7.50 a.m. the Battalion was in position at the rendezvous —the sunken road running north and south along the western edge of the Bois des Tailles. Here a squadron of cavalry, about 80 strong, was waiting its turn to go forward, and just before 8.0 a.m. this squadron advanced to the attack, accompanied by tanks, but both tanks and cavalry came dribbling back about an hour later, having met with serious opposition.

The Companies of the Civil Service Rifles were now disposed in the fields on either side of the road, awaiting orders. There followed a long interval without any news, and throughout the whole morning nothing definite was heard as to how the attack had developed. Late in the afternoon, however, orders were received as to the part to be played by the Civil Service Rifles in an attack to be delivered by the 140th Brigade the following morning upon the Blue Line. Colonel Feilding had only just explained matters to Company Commanders, when the order was cancelled owing to the withdrawal of the 142nd Brigade from the Green Line, under pressure from the enemy, and the reoccupation by the latter of the Happy Valley (a valley just to the east of the Bray–Albert road, and about a mile north-north-west of Bray).

A gap existed between the right of the 141st Brigade and the left of the Australians, and the Civil Service Rifles were ordered at 7.0 p.m. to fill the gap. Colonel Feilding sent two of his Companies to the front line to dig themselves in along a bank where the gap existed, and two Companies to be in support along the Etineham–Méaulte road, just in front of the old front line in the Bois des Tailles. He established his Headquarters temporarily in the old front line north-east of the Bois des Tailles.

Darkness was falling as the Companies went to take up these positions, and when Colonel Feilding arrived with his Headquarters Company in the old front line in the Bois des Tailles he found the Headquarters of the 141st Brigade close by. He went into these Headquarters to see what further information he could gather, and learnt that the enemy was breaking through, and was believed to be coming on in large numbers. The trench, he was told, should be put in a state of defence, and every rifle would be needed. Headquarters Company was thereupon ordered to line the trench and each man had to make himself a good fire position. Officers' servants and signallers, who had not used their rifles since the Retreat, had visions of a repetition of the Bourlon Wood incident, and every man got to work with his entrenching tool, and made every preparation for the coming fight. Colonel Feilding pushed off into the darkness ahead to find out how much truth there was in the story of the counter-attack. He found all quiet in the front line, which was nearly two miles ahead, and he decided to take his Headquarters Company and two support Companies to the foot of a bank close to the front line. These positions were occupied throughout the next day, when there was considerable shelling from the enemy.

Early on the morning of the 24th of August, an attack was delivered on the Green Line and the Happy Valley. The 140th Brigade was on the left and the 175th Brigade (58th Division) on the right. The Civil Service Rifles were to move through the Happy Valley behind a Battalion of the 175th Brigade, and deal with the enemy in the many dug-outs in the valley. After clearing the valley they were to take up positions just north of Bray and on the east side of the Bray–Méaulte road, in support to the 17th and 21st Battalions, who were to be by that time in the Green Line.

The attack began at 1.0 a.m., and by 2.0 a.m. large parties of German prisoners began to arrive at Battalion Headquarters. The operation had been entirely successful, the Civil Service Rifles having captured 300 prisoners in Happy Valley, as well as a considerable number of machine guns and some trench mortars.

After spending the whole day under heavy shell fire in the positions near the Bray Road, the Battalion moved through the Happy Valley again at night and assembled for a further attack, which was to commence at 2.30 a.m. on the 25th.

For this attack the 140th Brigade was in front, with the 175th Brigade on its right. The Civil Service Rifles were on the right of the 140th Brigade, and the centre of the Battalion's assembly position was an old German prisoners-of-war cage on the Bray–Fricourt Road. It was dark when the men reached the assembly position, and the country was quite strange to all the attacking forces, none of whom had even so much as seen it by daylight. The objective was just over 2,500 yards beyond the assembly position, and was a line of old German trenches on the western edge of Billon Copse, about two miles south of Mametz. In spite of the strange surroundings, total darkness, and the fact that no reconnaissance had been made, the attack went well, and the objective was reached with very few casualties—not more than thirty-five all ranks. The opposition was slight, but a thick fog which settled down before daylight made it very difficult to find even so prominent a landmark as Bronfay Farm, which was about the southern boundary of the Civil Service Rifles' objective. The result was that when Colonel Feilding reached the front line soon after 4.30 a.m., he found that the troops were a few hundred yards short of the real objective. However, he was able to guide them to the so-called old German trench, which " A " and " C " Companies manned as front line Companies, " B " and " D " remaining in the railway loop behind in support.

So ended the first stage of the part played by the Civil Service Rifles in the final advance of the Allies. It had been a long drawn out battle, and the troops had had little or no rest since leaving the trenches near Marrett Wood on the morning of the 22nd of August. The fighting, however, had not been severe, and the total casualties during the few days were only sixty all ranks, of whom only nine were killed.

The men were, therefore, in very good spirits when they marched back, on the 26th of August, to the trenches near Marrett Wood, taking with them one captured minenwerfer, four heavy and ten light enemy machine guns.

There followed the usual visits from the Brigade Commander and Divisional Commander, both of whom congratulated the Battalion on its work during the past few days. They added, however, the news that the advance would be resumed very soon. Major General Gorringe explained that there would be no more coming back to rest while the Division was taking part in this advance. In future the transport lines would move up to the Battalion after a battle, as the general scheme would be that Brigades would be continually passing through each other, and so the front line area of to-day would become the support or reserve position to-morrow.

On the 29th of August the Civil Service Rifles marched to huts in an old French brickfield about a mile north of Maricourt, and close to Montauban. Battalion Headquarters was at Carnoy Craters on the Carnoy–Montauban Road. These craters were a relic of the Somme battle of 1916, when the attack often opened with the blowing of a few mines. The Germans had only recently left this district, and a sharp look-out had to be kept for " booby traps."

The 47th Division continued the advance on the 30th of August, the 142nd Brigade being in front, the 141st in support, and the 140th Brigade in reserve. The Civil Service Rifles moved off from the Brickfields soon after 7.0 a.m., and after a short cross country scramble, halted in Maurepas Ravine about midday. Cookers and limbers followed the Battalion, and soon after halting, the troops received a pleasant surprise in the shape of hot dinner. A draft of two officers and 100 other ranks, who had been following the Battalion for some days, managed to catch it up in Maurepas Ravine during the afternoon of the 30th of August. It was quite a novelty for a draft to join during battle.

The Battalion bivouacked in Maurepas Ravine, and spent the whole of the next day there, but on the morning of the 1st September there began what proved to be the last battle in which the Civil Service Rifles were to take an active part. It was a battle worthy of the occasion, and during the six days while it lasted, the men lived up to the very best traditions of the Regiment. There were very few indeed among them who had embarked with the Battalion in 1915, or even of those who had fought on the Somme in 1916, but the spirit was still there, and the achievements of the 1st Civil Service Rifles in this great battle are worthy of a detailed description. The following account of the operation is founded upon the official report written by Colonel Feilding when the action was over. The narrative can best be followed by reference to the map on page 211.

On the 1st September the 140th Brigade, in conjunction with the 141st Brigade on the right, and the 18th Division (55th Brigade) on the left, was to advance and capture Rancourt and the line of trench following the south-west edge of St. Pierre Vaast Wood. The 1st Surrey Rifles were on the right, the Civil Service on the left, and the Poplar and Stepneys were to follow up and " mop up " Rancourt and the trenches around that village.

The assembly position for the Civil Service was a line about three quarters of a mile south-south-west of Rancourt, between the road leading from Rancourt to Le Forest and the road from Rancourt to Marrieres Wood. Battalion Headquarters was at the cross roads about half a mile east-north-east of Le Forest, with advanced Headquarters in a shell hole near the assembly position.

A certain amount of shelling was encountered on the way up to the assembly position, and the Battalion lost, among others, Sergeant Moore, signals sergeant, one of the few remaining " 17th of March men," who had been present with the Civil Service Rifles throughout their stay in France.

The assembly position was reached at 5.0 a.m., and zero was at 5.30 a.m.

Some anxiety was felt when, at three minutes before zero, the 1st Surrey Rifles had not arrived, but thanks to Second Lieutenant Gray, the Civil Service Intelligence Officer, touch was established before zero

After a five minutes' "crash" by the artillery, "C" and "D" Companies moved forward behind a creeping barrage to take the final objective, followed by "A" and "B" Companies, who were to be in support in trenches running north and south, quarter of a mile east of Rancourt.

The attack was completely successful, prisoners beginning to come down within ten minutes of zero.

Lieutenant E. R. Lascelles, commanding "C" Company, was killed early in the advance, but otherwise the losses were slight, and by 7.30 a.m. all objectives had been reached, and were being consolidated. Touch was obtained with the East Surreys (55th Brigade) on the left, but there was a gap on the right, the 1st Surrey Rifles having been held up.

During the process of consolidation "B" and "D" Companies were shelled heavily from a German Field Gun Battery which remained in action in the open, firing over open sights from about 1,000 yards' range.

An attempt by the enemy to rush through the gap on the right was prevented by Lewis gun and rifle fire from developing, and this brought to a close a good day's work in which the Civil Service Rifles had taken 150–200 prisoners and ten machine guns.

The battle, however, was by no means over, and at 11.30 p.m. the Battalion was relieved by the London Irish and marched to an assembly position on the Rancourt-Peronne road, just S.W. of Bouchavesnes and 300 yards north of the old quarry there, in readiness for a further attack the next morning. Arrived at this assembly position, the Company cooks again earned the gratitude of their comrades by producing an excellent hot meal.

The operation of the 1st of September had been simple and straightforward, and had been carried out without a hitch, but a much more complicated attack took place on the 2nd.

The plan was that the 74th Division should attack from trenches immediately south of Moislains Wood and, after capturing and mopping up Moislains, should take the village of Nurlu. The 140th Brigade was to follow them closely, the Civil Service on the left, the Poplar and Stepneys on the right, and the East Surreys in support. After crossing the Canal du Nord east of Moislains, the 140th Brigade was to wheel left, forming a defensive flank on the high ground to the north of Monastir trench, where they were to join up with the 142nd Brigade, who were to capture this trench. The order from left to right on the defensive flank was First Surreys, Civil Service, Poplar and Stepneys. The 140th Brigade was to follow the 229th, who would also prolong the defensive flank, facing north as far as Nurlu.

The Battalion was in position at 3.0 a.m. and zero was at
5.30 a.m., but, in order to get well up behind the 229th
Brigade " A " and " B " Companies led off at 5.0 a.m. with
" C " and " D " in support and Headquarters bringing up the
rear.

The 140th Brigade was to pass Moislains on the south, and
the formation of the defensive flank therefore presupposed the
capture by the 74th Division of that village.

From the outset the Brigade came under heavy shell and
machine gun fire, and as it moved down the slopes to the south
west of Moislains, under still heavier machine-gun fire directed
from the village and from both flanks.

The casualties caused by this fire were enormous, amounting
to more than half the strength of the Battalion, but the men
went forward without any hesitation, and, as Colonel Feilding
said afterwards, as though they were beating up partridges.
The behaviour of the Civil Service under this sweeping fire
was commented on by the Commanding Officers of other units
present, who said they had never seen anything like it. The
determination of all ranks was ultimately rewarded when
they succeeded in establishing themselves in Moislains trench,
with details of the First Surreys on the left, the Poplar and
Stepneys on the right, and an officer and about a dozen other
ranks of the North Devon Yeomanry.

The garrison of Moislains trench now had to fight hard to hold
the position, for the enemy were occupying the same trench to
the left and Quarry trench in the left rear, while they could
clearly be seen moving in Moislains a quarter of a mile in front,
and assembling in the village and around the huts immediately
south of it.

Simultaneous counter-attacks were, in fact, developed on the
left rear and on the right front, while the enemy at the same
time attempted to bomb up the trench on the left.

Both parapet and parados were manned, and the attacks
across the open were beaten off, but the bombing attacks
continued all day, and, owing to scarcity of bombs, were with
difficulty held up.

It was at once obvious that there were no British troops in
front of the 140th Brigade, though elements of the 74th Division
could be seen in the distance on the right, on a level with
Moislains trench. In the face of the very heavy flank and
frontal machine-gun fire, of the heavy casualties incurred
and of the fact that one flank at least was " in the
air," it did not seem practicable to Colonel Feilding or to
Colonel Dawes, commanding the First Surreys, for their
Battalions to assume the rôle allotted to the 74th Division, and
to attempt, without a barrage, to capture the village, which,

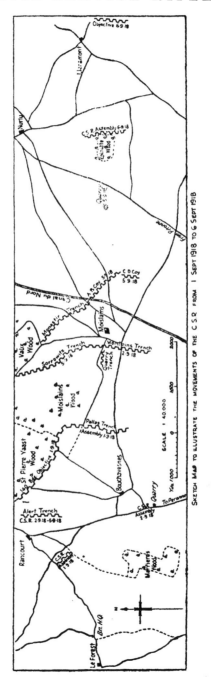

SKETCH MAP TO ILLUSTRATE THE MOVEMENTS OF THE C.S.R. FROM 1 SEPT 1918 TO 6 SEPT 1918

as a result of the failure, or absence, of that Division, was still strongly held by the enemy.

A small local attack by about two Companies was actually delivered by the 74th Division on the right, but, though it made some little progress, and at one point crossed the Canal, it hardly did more than establish the right flank of the 140th Brigade. With this exception, there was no indication of any attack having been delivered by the 74th Division in the vicinity of Moislains. A German Field Gun Battery was, in fact, in action for some four hours in the open, immediately south of the village, and less than 1000 yards east of the Canal, firing over open sights on to the part of Moislains trench occupied by the 140th Brigade.

Colonel Feilding was able to confirm the foregoing account by a very careful examination of the battle-field made afterwards. He saw no British dead either in Moislains or between Moislains trench and the village. The only dead in the vicinity of Moislains trench were those of the 140th Brigade and of Germans killed in the counter-attack previously referred to. Twenty-five men of the Civil Service were found and buried in an hour in this area alone, and others of the Brigade were still lying there.

To quote from Colonel Feilding's report :

" The only dead of the 74th Division whom I personally saw in the section of ground with which my Battalion was concerned were lying about 300 yards from our starting point—the Rancourt-Peronne road. Since these dead were not there when we originally advanced, I can only come to the conclusion, which is shared by all who were with me on the battlefield during the action and after, that here, at least, the 140th Brigade, instead of being in support, found itself with its flanks unsecured, and with the barrage so far ahead as to be useless, carrying out the main attack on a strong enemy position, and that the 74th Division, so far from being in front of us, was behind us."

The position in Moislains trench was held until 10.30 p.m. on the 2nd of September, when the Brigade Commander withdrew the troops, and the survivors of the Civil Service Rifles marched back about three miles and rested in trenches just east of Rancourt.

The Battalion rested here for two days, but even then the fighting was not over, and, reorganised owing to heavy losses on a two Company basis each with two platoons, the Civil Service Rifles took part in another fight on the 5th of September. At 5.30 a.m. on that day, the 141st Brigade passed through the 142nd, and was followed by the 140th at 8.0 a.m., the Poplar and Stepneys in front with the Civil Service and one Company of the First Surreys attached in support.

The Civil Service assembled in Pallas trench, south-west of Moislains Wood, and at noon the two Companies had moved forward and occupied Sorrowitz trench (a continuation of Moislains trench, north-west of Moislains) with Battalion Headquarters and the attached Company of the First Surreys in the sunken road 300 yards behind. Half an hour later, " A-B " Company under Lieutenant R. Upton, crossed the Canal and occupied a position facing north-east on the Canal bank in a continuation of Monastir trench about a quarter of a mile north-east of Moislains. At the same time " C-D " Company, under Captain L. D. Eccles, crossed the canal and occupied a trench further south, parallel with the canal and facing east, formed a defensive flank. The remaining Company was kept in reserve in and around Sorrowitz trench.

At 7.0 p.m., considerable opposition having been met with from the enemy, an organised attack was made on the Peronne-Nurlu road by the Poplar and Stepneys in conjunction with the 141st Brigade and the 12th Division on the left. The right was protected by Captain Eccles' Company and the operation was entirely successful.

At 6.0 a.m. on the 6th of September the advance was resumed. The 19th and 20th Battalions (141st Brigade) moved across the Peronne-Nurlu road, and at 8.0 a.m. the London-Irish and the Civil Service, who had formed up behind in conjunction with the 12th Division on the left and the 74th Division on the right, advanced on a position running north and south, just south of the village of Lieramont.

The Civil Service reached the objective about noon and the men came under heavy machine gun fire from the left, where the London-Irish had not yet arrived. In addition, rapid fire from enemy field artillery raked the men as they appeared over the crest in front of the final objective. Colonel Feilding accordingly took his men back to the reverse slope, where they immediately turned and dug in.

This position turned out to be the " farthest east " of the Civil Service in the advance on this part of the Allied front, for during the night of the 6th–7th September the Battalion was relieved by the Queen Victoria Rifles (58th Division) and moved back to bivouacs in a valley about a mile east of Moislains, close to the position occupied by Captain Eccles' Company on the afternoon of the 5th of September.

The fighting, so far as the Civil Service Rifles were concerned, had come to an end for a time, and the short rest in this valley near Moislains enabled a thorough search to be made of the scene of the heavy casualties on the 2nd of September. The bodies of all the killed of the Civil Service in that battle were buried before the troops left. There was also an opportunity

to count the cost, and it was found that the casualties suffered
during the first six days of September numbered 12 officers
and 317 other ranks, out of a total trench strength of less than
500 all ranks.

It has already been mentioned that Colonel Feilding had not
had time to get to know his men before he was leading them in
battle, but what he saw of them in the battles of August and
September filled him with genuine admiration for and pride in
the men whom he commanded and he at once became fired with
the enthusiasm of his two predecessors. The troops, on their
part, were not slow to see that the Regiment had been fortunate
in gaining a worthy successor to Colonel Segrave for in these
final battles Colonel Feilding's energy knew no bounds. He
was constantly faced with unexpected developments but he
was never at a loss as to how to deal with them. From start to
finish he was " here, there and everywhere " moving about
among the Companies seeing things for himself. What struck
the troops most forcibly perhaps was his coolness, for although
on the 2nd of September particularly, he was faced with
difficulties sufficient to put the best soldier " off his game " he
was perfectly calm and unruffled throughout.

CHAPTER XXIV

BACK TO THE COAL-FIELDS

IT is a far cry from the battle-field to the coal-field, but after the events narrated in the last chapter, the 47th Division returned to the area which it occupied during its first few days in France.

On the 7th of September the Civil Service Rifles went by bus from the vicinity of Moislains to billets at Heilly, and after two nights in that once delightful village, entrained in the afternoon of the 9th for Chocques. The train journey took just over 12 hours, and it was consequently in the small hours of the 10th of September when the Battalion reached its billets in Chocques. Two days later, the 140th Brigade marched to the Auchel area, where it remained until the 27th of September.

Auchel is not by any means a pleasant village, but after the Somme battlefield any place was welcome, and the three weeks spent here were very enjoyable, concert parties and football matches being the great attraction. The chief excitement at this time, however, was the prospect of a trip to Italy. Definite orders had been received for the 47th Division to be transferred to the Italian front, and more than once during the stay at Auchel the Civil Service Rifles actually received entraining orders. The last entrainment order was for the 26th, but, like the others, it was cancelled, and on the 27th of September the Brigade marched to the St. Pol area, the Civil Service Rifles being allotted some very poor accommodation in Foufflin-Ricametz.

On the 2nd of October the Division was transferred to the 5th Army. The Civil Service Rifles moved by train from St. Pol to Merville and marched thence to Lestrem, which was reached at 4.30 a.m. on the 3rd of October. There the men rested in tents for a few hours and in the afternoon the march was continued to Fauquissart, where the night was spent in dug-outs.

On the following day the 47th Division began an advance on to the general line Beaucamps-Radinghem, with the ultimate object of taking Lille. The Civil Service Rifles occupied reserve trenches at Le Maisnil, the advance being carried out by the 141st and 142nd Brigades.

It was no doubt in order to avoid unnecessary casualties, and also to avoid doing any further damage to the town, that the taking of Lille was a slow process. There was no determined attack made on it directly, but one by one the various strategical and tactical positions were captured, and the Germans were forced to clear out eventually on the 17th of October. The capture was a somewhat tame affair, and the first intimation that the British troops had was when a few civilians timidly came out and announced that the Germans had gone. For some days afterwards pickets were posted at all the entrances to Lille and only a privileged few were able to enter the town.

The early part of October was uneventful for the Civil Service Rifles. It was certainly a change to get back once more to trench warfare, but it was only for a day or two, and after the short stay at Le Maisnil, a few days were spent in reserve near Fromelles and on the 14th of October the Battalion marched to Estaires, thence on the 15th to St. Venant, thence to Norrent Fontes, where the Battalion trained for ten days.

Arrangements had now been made for a triumphal march of British troops through Lille and the Civil Service Rifles entrained at Berguette on the 26th of October, and after a journey across the devastated area which had been No Man's Land for more than three years, detrained at Perenchies and marched to Lomme, a suburb of Lille, which was reached at about 7.0 p.m.

The march from the railway station to the factory in Lomme, where the Battalion was billeted, was a memorable one. On approaching the suburb the regimental band struck up the Marseillaise and kept it up throughout the march. The inhabitants—old men, women and children—threw up their windows or lined up on the roadside to sing the words they had not forgotten during the four years of German rule. The kiddies ran by the side of the troops and insisted on shaking hands. The welcome indeed was so spontaneous that it was more impressive than the ceremonial affair two days later.

It was appropriate that the 47th Division should have been selected for the triumphal march through Lille, as it had spent more time in the front line around this town than had any other Division. Further, it claimed to have been the senior division in France at the taking of Lille.

For this, " L'Entrée Solennelle des troupes Britanniques," as it was advertised in the town, which took place on the 28th of October, " C " Company was detailed to form part of a cordon round the Grand Place, and the remainder of the Battalion took part in the long procession through the gaily decorated streets between the cheering crowds of the recently liberated populace.

The Battalion proceeded to Hellemes, a suburb on the eastern side of Lille, and were again billeted in a factory, where German field-post letters were strewn about the floor and orders to troops still posted on the walls. In the afternoon nearly every one enjoyed the interest of a visit to the town, where famine prices prevailed. In several shop windows the following placard printed in red, white and blue had been placed :

" HONOUR AND GLORY TO THE 47TH DIVISION.
OUR ·DELIVERERS."

" LILLE, le 17 Octobre, 1918."

The enterprising Canteen Manager of the Civil Service Rifles sought out the publisher of this poster and secured a batch of posters for sale as souvenirs in the Regimental Canteen. One of them has been framed and now hangs on a wall of the dining room in the Civil Service Rifles' Club.

CHAPTER XXV

THE ARMISTICE

ALTHOUGH the inhabitants of Lille considered the war to be over—as it undoubtedly was so far as they were concerned—the guns could still be heard out on the Tournai road, and on the 30th of October the 47th Division left Lille and continued the pursuit of the enemy. The Civil Service Rifles marched along the Tournai road and spent the night at Chereng, continuing the march next day to Froyennes, a suburb of Tournai, where they relieved the 2/4th South Lancashire Regiment in the front line under conditions which have surely never existed before in any part of the front line in any war.

Froyennes is a suburb of convents and magnificent châteaux. One of the latter had been the Headquarters of Prince Rupprecht of Bavaria when he commanded a German Army Corps. It now became the Headquarters of a half of " A " Company of the Civil Service Rifles.

There were no trenches in the front line at Froyennes, the sentry posts being either in the front room of a house, the back garden or a street corner. In one street the Germans occupied houses on one side, and the Civil Service Rifles the houses opposite.

The suburb was pretty freely shelled, mostly with gas shells, but the houses for the most part were not very badly damaged. In a good many of them and in most of the convents the civilians had remained. They had been allowed to do so because it was thought at first that the advance would soon carry the front line beyond Froyennes.

The advance, however, was held up for some days along this line, which followed the general line of the River Scheldt hereabouts. The Scheldt ran through Tournai and outside the eastern and northern borders of Froyennes.

Tournai was still occupied by Germans at this time, and, as at Lille, the capture of the town was a somewhat slow process.

The situation in Froyennes remained unchanged for some few days, the posts, as has been stated, being mostly in houses by daytime. By night, further posts were held alongside the roads.

The Company Headquarters were all either in châteaux or convents. "A" Company Headquarters was in the Chateau Beauregard, the residence of the Comtesse Thérèse de Germiny, who, although her house had been knocked about by a shell which came through her drawing room wall, remained in residence. The Countess was the "Lady Bountiful" of the village, she having taken under her wing all the poor and homeless who cared to accept her hospitality. To these she gave not only a home, but also refuge from shell fire in her cellars.

The Countess spoke excellent English, and by the kindly interest she took in the comfort of the troops occupying her château, she became quite a favourite of the men of "A" Company.

The "B" Company Headquarters was in a convent for the aged and infirm. In this building were nuns, many of whom had been bedridden for years before the war began. These invalids had all been moved down into a cellar, which the troops endeavoured to make gas proof.

The front line posts were held by "A" "B" and "C" Companies, "D" being in reserve. Roughly speaking, "A" Company was responsible for the east of the village, "B" the south, and "C" the north.

"C" Company's front, in fact, was right outside the town, the posts being between the river and the main road running from Tournai to Courtrai, though by day the men were withdrawn to houses. This front was much wider than that allotted to the other two Companies and it was more in the open. The Company Headquarters was in a convent at the western edge of the suburb. Civilians shared the accommodation with the troops, and it is said that the children played in No Man's Land by day.

Between the posts along the road and the River Scheldt was a wide marsh, and it was the duty of patrols at night to make their way across the marsh and creep along the river bank.

"C" Company had further excitement on the night of the 3rd of November when the Royal Engineers tried to bridge the Scheldt, which at this point is quite a narrow stream. Two platoons, acting as covering party, got into position on the river bank without any difficulty, but as soon as the work began, an enemy machine gun across the river opened fire. The bridging operations were shut down for the night, and the troops were lucky to get away without casualties.

"D" Company occupied a large building, a convent which had been deserted, near the "C" Company Headquarters. The men had had many a worse billet, even when out of the line.

The shelling became more frequent as time went on, and

casualties occurred to several civilians. On the 3rd of November the civilians were ordered to evacuate Froyennes. Hitherto they had simply been advised to go, and told that transport would be lent to them to help them remove their belongings. But it now became necessary to compel them to go, and on the night of the 3rd a fleet of motor ambulances and other transport took them all to a place of safety in Lille. It was a pathetic sight to see the poor old creatures from " B " Company's convent being loaded into ambulances, for they had accepted the situation in the cellar so calmly and philosophically, and they were now loath to leave what had been their home for so many years. It was almost a self-supporting convent, for in the gardens vegetables of all kinds were grown. Many fowls and rabbits were also kept, and the Mother Superior on her departure presented these to " B " Company. Roast fowl in the front line was a luxury which surprised the oldest soldier in the Company.

It should not be thought, however, that life at Froyennes was free from the horrors of war for, the Civil Service Rifles lost one killed and ten wounded in the five days spent there. After the assurance from the people of Lille that the war was over, this was regarded as a heavy casualty list. Of these casualties, Private G. A. Watson, " B " Company, who was killed on the 2nd of November, proved to be the last man of the 1st Civil Service Rifles who was killed in action.

The Battalion was relieved on the 4th of November, and marched to reserve billets in the village of Cornet, just off the main road, and half-way between Tournai and Lille.

Froyennes had been described as a village of convents and châteaux. Cornet can only be described as a village of hovels and mud, but the squalor of this wretched place was forgotten in the excitement caused by the news that the war was now " all over bar shouting," and that the signing of the terms of the Armistice was expected daily.

The Bulgars, the Austrians and the Turks had already accepted terms, but these had caused no excitement. The only terms that mattered to the troops in France were those to be imposed on the Bosches. A big sweepstake was organised in the Battalion at Cornet on the hour at which the Armistice terms to Germany would be signed. But before the prize was won the military situation in the immediate vicinity had undergone a change, and the Civil Service Rifles were pursuing the enemy in open warfare once more.

News was received on the 9th of November that the Scheldt had been crossed and the Germans had left Tournai. The Battalion immediately left Cornet and moved to Froyennes, Companies occupying their old billets. Pursuit of the enemy was slow owing to the fact that the pontoon bridge constructed by the Royal Engineers at Froyennes was the only passage across the river for the whole Division. The arrangement was for the two Infantry Brigades holding the front line to advance simultaneously, with the Reserve Brigade following close up. The 140th Brigade on the right accordingly advanced on Melles, a village about six miles north-east of Tournai on the main road to Ath. The Civil Service Rifles, being the Reserve Battalion, did not move beyond Froyennes on the first day of the advance, but on the 10th of November the Battalion crossed the river and joined in the hunt. Although the advance was continued well beyond Melles the Germans had retreated so quickly that they were not seen even by the advanced guard, and the 140th Brigade halted for the night in the villages around Montroeul Au Bois, the Civil Service Rifles being billeted in the little hamlet of Barberie. The natives gave the troops a warm welcome, for it was only on the previous night that they had been compelled to shelter the retreating Bosches.

It was now decided that each Brigade in turn should furnish the advanced guard for the advance of the Division, and the 140th Brigade was detailed to act in that capacity on the morrow. The Civil Service Rifles would be the vanguard, and the details were explained to Company Commanders late on the night of the 10th. The Battalion scouts, on bicycles, were to move off at 6.45 a.m. and keep in touch with the cavalry screen furnished by the 19th Hussars. The Companies were to move off at 7.30 a.m. and the duty of the Battalion was to advance on the general line of the river Dendre and seize the bridges over the Dendre canal on the outskirts of Ath, not far from Brussels.

This would have given the Battalion its first experience of vanguards in real war, and the troops were eagerly anticipating a visit to Brussels during the next few days. These hopes, however, were never fulfilled, for at 2.30 a.m. on the 11th of November, the news reached the Battalion that the orders for the advance were cancelled. No explanation was given, and a rumour that the war was over was strengthened by an order received later in the morning for the Battalion to march back to Tournai.

The rumour was discredited when the Battalion got on the main road to Tournai and met a whole Division going in the opposite direction, but when a low-flying aeroplane appeared, gaily decorated with coloured ribbons and making a terrible noise with its Klaxon horn, there could be little doubt that the Armistice terms had been signed. This was confirmed by a passing officer in a motor-car, and the news was conveyed to the troops by the Regimental Band, who, by a happy inspiration of Sergeant Blackmore, the Bandmaster, struck up an air which had been popular throughout the British Army during the past four years :

> " When this ruddy war is over
> Oh, how happy I shall be."

It should be placed on record that this was the only intimation of the armistice which reached the Battalion beyond announcements in the Press. The Civil Service Rifles received no official news that an armistice had been granted, although a telephone message from Brigade on the night of the 12th of November gave particulars of the various armaments, etc., which were to be surrendered.

Tournai was reached in the afternoon of the 11th of November, and the men were once more accommodated in a convent, where the nuns came out in a body and expressed their gratitude to the British troops.

So the Civil Service Rifles saw the end of the Great War, and a tamer fini;h it is impossible to imagine. There were many whose ambition it had been to be in the front line on the last day of the war, and many were the conjectures as to what it would be like, but none ever guessed that it would fizzle out in such a miserable and uninteresting fashion. To be left to read of it in the newspapers was about the feeblest finish that could have happened, and while there were jubilations in London and elsewhere on armistice night, there was absolutely nothing in the area occupied by the 140th Infantry Brigade in the nature of a celebration of so great a victory. The district was very gloomy, and its name, La Tombe, appeared a very appropriate one.

Things looked up somewhat on the following evening, when a Battalion concert was held in the Convent, to which the civilians were invited. They did not understand a word of the concert, but they applauded everything vigorously, and at the close, when the chairs were cleared away, the natives went fairly mad with joy at an impromptu dance.

CHAPTER XXVI

HOME

LITTLE remains to be said of the history of the 1st Civil Service Rifles in France, but before the story is closed mention should be made of a few incidents which stand out in the last few months before demobilisation was complete.

After the concert at Tournai the Battalion once more marched out along the road to Brussels, but this time the route was along the lower road, and the troops were employed for a time in repairing the railway at Leuze. They were billeted in the little village of Pipaix, where they made great friends with the villagers and were very happy. It was hoped that even yet they would get to Germany, but a bitter disappointment was in store, for it was decreed that the 47th Division should end its career in France in the same district where it started, and in less than a week the Civil Service Rifles left Pipaix for Willems, a village between Tournai and Lille, where a week was spent before starting the trek across the devastated area to the mud and squalor of the coal-fields around Auchel.

It should perhaps be mentioned that to Sergeant Haycock, the Battalion Pioneer Sergeant, fell the distinction of being the first member of the Battalion to be demobilised. He left Willems for that purpose on the 23rd of November, 1918.

The journey to the coal-fields began on the 26th of November, and, after a night in the suburbs of Lille, the interest of the trek, especially to " the 17th of March man " consisted in a last glimpse at the ruins of La Bassée and the Double Crassier, dominating the village and battle-field of Loos, and, later, the brick-fields at Cuinchy he had fired at so zealously nearly four years ago. The night of the 27th of November was spent at Bethune, within a stone's throw of the Girl's School where the Battalion had been quartered on its first visit to the line. Suppers were obtained at small cafés in the suburbs, but those who looked for the gay patisseries they once knew now found the site of the old town, including the picturesque church, belfry and Hôtel du Nord, a desolate waste of charred bricks ! The next day a war-worn and weary Battalion reversed the march described at the beginning of Chapter II, the journey

223

being extended some two kilometres beyond Cauchy-a-la-Tour to Ferfay.

In spite of Ferfay having been a Corps Headquarters, the accommodation at first was poor, but the troops soon settled down, and, making the most of the wretched conditions, contrived to have a jolly good time during their last days in France.

A number of N.C.O.'s and men distinguished themselves as educational instructors at the classes which were held daily, and Sergeant Blackmore's " Sunday League Concerts " became quite a popular weekly function.

A good deal of football was played, and the Battalion got together excellent teams, both Rugby and Association.

The Association match against the 2nd Battalion Civil Service Rifles, who were beaten by four goals to three, on the 14th of December, was the event of the season. The crowd was a record one and included about 100 members of the 2nd Battalion who were billeted about twelve miles away. In the evening a concert was held in the theatre, the programme being provided by talent from both Battalions.

After a really merry Christmas the Battalion began to melt away. Demobilisation began in earnest with the New Year, and parties of twenty-five or thirty left for England almost daily. Large crowds assembled outside the Battalion Headquarters to give the lucky ones a rousing send-off, and the procession through the village was headed by the Regimental Band, until the day came when the Band played itself out of the village and left for home.

Before that day came, however, the Band had supplied the orchestra for a highly successful revue, " Pack up," which was played in the theatre by a company of officers, N.C.O.'s and men of the Civil Service Rifles trained by Corporal Bailey of " B " Company. The " book " was written by Major D. Young, M.C., second in command of the Battalion, the music was " put together " by Second-Lieutenant P. H. Small, and the play was produced by Corporal Bailey. R.Q.M.S. Hart excelled himself with the wonderful stage effects which he devised.

Of the actors special mention should be made of Private Perrin, Captain " Florrie " Ford, and the two " girls," Lance-Corporal Harnett and Lance-Corporal Flight, and Sergeant Taylor. But the whole Company is to be congratulated on the best show ever given by a Battalion concert party. The production got such an enthusiastic reception that it was given at Auchel and other places for the benefit of other units.

Although demobilisation began just before New Year, it was not until the 10th of May, 1919, that the last remnants, the " Cadre," consisting of about thirty all ranks, reached England.

It should perhaps be mentioned that there was not a single

officer, N.C.O. or man outside the Quartermaster's staff and transport section who served with the Battalion continuously throughout its stay in France.

Included in the Cadre was Sergeant Teasdale, a member of the Regiment for nearly twenty years. For more than nineteen of his twenty years he had been a humble private, and as a raconteur at Regimental concerts he never had an equal. He had been in France with the 1st Civil Service Rifles as a member of the Quartermaster's staff ever since the Battalion landed in 1915. It is said that he accepted his third stripe owing to the keen demand for his stories in the Sergeants' Mess.

The two war trophies that had been preserved by the Civil Service Rifles and brought home also deserve special mention.

One generally expects a war trophy to be some instrument of war, but the Civil Service Rifles war trophies were an instrument of music. viz., a piano, and a presidential chair.

The piano was captured at Nurlu during the heavy fighting on the Somme in the first days of September, 1918, and the Regiment is chiefly indebted to Major Young for this uncommon trophy. It is also through the ingenuity of the same officer that the Regiment was represented in the salving of H.M.S. *Vindictive* at Ostend, whence came the "presidential chair," for it was through his efforts that two pioneers of the Civil Service Rifles found their way to Ostend in 1918, and worked on the salved ship, producing out of a piece of teak taken from the decks, a handsome chair on which the Regimental crest is carved. Thus it transpired that whereas their keenest rivals in the London Regiment are said to have sunk the *Emden*, the 1st Civil Service Rifles can claim to have salved the *Vindictive*.

The home-coming of the Cadre was an even more dismal experience than the celebration of the Armistice, for the party was taken stealthily to Felixstowe of all places, and from there the members drifted away one by one until all that remained were Colonel Feilding and Colour-Sergeant Chubb, the Orderly Room clerk. These were then permitted to return to Somerset House.

But although the Battalion had, as it were, been scattered to the four winds, the spirit of comradeship, which had been so characteristic of the Regiment in war, still prevailed in peacetime.

Already, before demobilisation was nearly completed, a meeting of members of the Regiment had been held at Somerset House, and it had been resolved to proceed forthwith to found a Club as a memorial to those of the Regiment who had lost their lives in the war, and as a place of reunion for those who survive. A temporary home was found at Somerset House, where the School of Arms was converted into a lounge, and on the 28th of April, 1920, the Club was opened by Major-General G. D. Jeffreys, G.-O.-C. London District, who congratulated the Civil Service Rifles on being the first Territorial unit to form such a club, which forges a link between the old generation and the new in the Regiment, and where, for many years to come, the new members of the Regiment will be able to meet those who, in the Great War of 1914–1918, helped to make history for the Civil Service Rifles.

2nd Battalion, Civil Service Rifles

By Major A. C. H. Benké.*

PREFACE

This brief story of the 2/15th Battalion, London Regiment, is written, not as a specimen of literary art, but merely as a record of the work of the Battalion during the War of 1914–1918.

It is compiled from rough notes in my pocket diary, and probably some of the events in the experience of others have been overlooked, and to these I offer my apologies.

I have to thank Lieutenants J. L. Hutchinson, M.C., and T. H. E. Clark for their kindness and assistance in furnishing the notes for the greater part of Chapters IX and XI, especially the accounts of the Capture of Jerusalem, the Turkish Counter-Attack at Tel el Ful, and the journey to Es Salt. In these actions both these officers served with distinction.

I have also taken the liberty to include extracts from a Brief History of the 30th Division in France, in writing up the last three chapters of this book.

A. C. H. BENKÉ.

---

* Major Benké, D.S.O., M.C., acting Lieut.-Colonel, 1919, till demobilised. —EDITOR.

CHAPTER XXVII

FORMATION—TRAINING—IRISH REBELLION, 1916—AND DEPARTURE FOR FRANCE, JUNE, 1916

During the early days of August, 1914, the Headquarters of the Civil Service Rifles at Somerset House was besieged by crowds of younger Civil Servants ; either wishing to re-enlist in their old Battalion, or to start their military career in the Civil Service Rifles, which had been mobilised for Active Service. Many of them were able to gain an entrance into the 1st Battalion, but others were disappointed. From the latter the nucleus of a second line unit was formed, and eventually the War Office authorised the existence of a new Battalion, the 2/15th Battalion, County of London Regiment.

The feeling of a separate existence brought with it great enthusiasm, and although arms, equipment and stores were slow in coming, every one worked hard to make an efficient unit. Training was carried out in the London parks, and each morning the semi-equipped army of recruits marched out of Somerset House for the day's work. Indeed, so slow was the equipping of the Battalion that many of the keener members wondered whether they would be " too late for the war."

However, before very long the new unit, under the command of Lieutenant-Colonel R. G. Hayes, T.D., left London for Dorking. This was, indeed, a pleasant change from the Metropolis, where friends constantly asked the budding rifleman, " Why aren't you at the front ? "

Training was pursued with more realism in the new area ; organisation improved, and the novelty of " billets " was still prevalent. A word of appreciation for the kindness of the people of Dorking might well be included in this book. They did all they could to make the new soldiers comfortable.

Route marches among the beautiful Surrey Hills and sham fights over the surrounding country-side soon brought the physique of the men to a high standard, and the rigors of a cold, wet winter were easily borne. Leith Hill, the pleasure ground of many a week-end in previous years, became the training ground of England's new armies. True, the pack and the rifle made the climbing stiffer, but keenness and enthusiasm to get out to fight the Bosche helped one to forget the additional fatigue.

Early in the spring of 1915, drafts were furnished for the completion of the 1st Battalion at Watford, which had then been ordered to France. This depleted the ranks of the younger unit, but recruits arrived from Somerset House, where a third line depot had been established, and the 2nd Battalion soon recovered its numbers, and shortly afterwards followed in the footsteps of the 1st Battalion which had then left for the front.

The move of the 2nd Battalion from Dorking was the first real move as a unit, and was creditably done. How many hours of worry and labour it involved does not concern us here, but what a contrast to the 2nd Battalion of two years later, which moved its home complete within a couple of hours after the receipt of orders ; every one working with the precision of an automatic machine.

Following so closely on the heels of our 1st Battalion at Watford, added to the welcome of the people of Hertfordshire. The impression left by the parent Battalion was exceedingly fine, and the Watford folk looked upon the 2nd Battalion as part of a regiment they loved ; in fact, they felt a part ownership in the Civil Service Rifles, and continued to thrust upon us all those wonderful kindnesses they had so recently bestowed upon the 1st Battalion. Houses were thrown open for entertainment, baths and meals ; and there was no difficulty in billeting ; every one was welcomed into the household. It must be remembered that at this time the billeting of troops in private houses was new to the people of Britain. In some parts it was a matter for misgivings and suspicions. In Watford, however, the whole town opened their hearts to welcome the Battalion, and, in fairness to the troops, it must be recorded that they lived up to that splendid standard expected of them as soldiers and gentlemen.

The stay at Watford was indeed a happy one, and training was carried out in the local parks at Cassiobury and Munden. Each day areas for manœuvres were allotted to the various Battalions of the Brigade, now known as the 2/4th London Infantry Brigade, comprising the second line units of the Kensingtons, London Scottish, Civil Service and Queen's Westminsters.

Musketry was done at Chalk Hill ranges, a few miles from St. Albans, and by the summer the Battalion was an efficient unit. The earlier heart-burnings of the " fire-eaters " that they would be " too late " were dispersed ; the war on the continent had developed into a far greater conflict than many had ever imagined.

In June, 1915, the Battalion, now under the command of Lieutenant-Colonel E. F. Strange, trekked to Saffron Walden, and encamped in Audley End Park. It was a lovely English summer, and all will remember the glorious golden carpet of buttercups in the camp ; undoubtedly one of the prettiest camps in England. Being under canvas was a new experience for many, but the Battalion soon settled down to its new life away from the home comforts of Watford.

Here the summer of 1915 was passed. Training on similar lines to that at Watford was continued. Classes were instituted for specialists. Day after day the same routine was pursued, until rumours furnished the only excitement ; and such rumours too ! Was the Battalion to be kept in England on Home Service ? Had the War Office forgotten its existence ? Was not the Battalion good enough ? Was it to be a draft-finding unit ? etc., etc.—such were the questions that resulted from these rumours.

Then came the furnishing of a draft of about 100 strong to the 1st Battalion in France, and this in the minds of many sealed the fate of the Battalion. Never would the 2nd Battalion take its place as a fighting unit in the Great War.

However the horizon brightened, and all those men who had only volunteered for home service were ordered to be transferred to the 3rd line unit. It is not for anyone to comment upon the actions of others ; circumstances alter cases, and during the war to act up to the dictates of one's own conscience was the duty of all. Nevertheless, the departure of the home service contingent was a matter of great relief to the 2nd Battalion. True, many good friends were lost, and many who had striven hard for the efficiency and well-being of the Battalion had to bid farewell ; but for those who remained there was that resuscitated feeling that the 2nd Battalion would some day take its proper place in the fight on the continent.

Fresh drafts were received, and a large training company was established where men qualified as trained soldiers and then passed into their respective companies. New N.C.O.'s had to be found, and special classes of instruction were organised, and again the Battalion felt itself to be an independent unit, every one earnest for foreign service.

This history of the Battalion's doings at Saffron Walden must contain a reference to the two treks, the one to Furneaux Pelham and the other to Braintree and Stebbing. It was during these two expeditions that the 2/15th had their first real taste of campaigning ; a day's marching, an outpost or an attack, then a night in the open, which was the nearest approach to the actual war obtainable in England. From a military point of view the success of these operations was, of course, doubtful ; every one had different views, but as a well-known Brigadier always said to the 1st Battalion at the end of a day's operations,

"Shot and shell would tell." However, there can be no doubt that they proved conclusively that the spirit of the Battalion was right, and that all the inconveniences of treks were taken, by all, as part of the game.

By this time winter was approaching, and the canvas camp at Saffron Walden was becoming a rather cheerless place on wet days. On the 26th October, 1915, the Battalion proceeded by road to billets at Bishop Stortford. The whole of the Brigade was billeted in the area, and memories of the happy days at Watford sprung up. The billets were good, and the local people made the Battalion welcome. It is true many billets were crowded, but the size of the town would not admit of so large a concentration as the Brigade, less the Kensingtons who were billeted in a village a few miles south. The stay, however, was not to be a long one, for no sooner had the central cook-houses, miniature range, etc., been thoroughly established, than orders for a move to Ware were received.

On the 29th of November the Battalion packed up, and after a long march of about sixteen miles arrived at Ware. An earnest welcome was given by the townspeople, and the prospect of Christmas in Ware caused every one to keep a bright look-out for any good things Ware might produce. The officers of the Battalion formed a regimental mess in a large, roomy house at the top of the hill overlooking the town, where most of the officers were billeted. In the same building an excellent dining-room, a smoke-room and a card-room had been arranged, all of which proved to be great boons, more especially as the attractions of Ware in the way of evening entertainments were few.

The local drill hall was taken over as a central place for battalion messing, each company marching from its own area for meals. At Christmas time this hall was used for concerts, and a splendid Battalion dinner was held on Christmas Day. Some of the less fortunate members were, however, detailed at that time for aeroplane guards in the surrounding villages. Ware was on the outer defences of London against air raids, and pickets were arranged in the Ware district, armed with mysterious rockets for the purpose of representing anti-aircraft batteries. However, on no occasion was it necessary to use these alarming fireworks, and in spite of being on duty, these outlying posts are believed to have spent a very jovial Christmas. Leave was freely given, and the proximity of Ware to London was a great advantage, as was proved within a very short time ; for on the 22nd January, 1916, the Battalion entrained during the night for Salisbury Plain.

Late in the afternoon of the 23rd, Warminster was reached, and after a march of about four or five miles a city of comfortable looking huts appeared. Their apparent comfort, however, quickly disappeared when the mud of Longbridge Deverill came into evidence. The interior of the huts so recently vacated by a division which had left for France, was little better than the filth outside. However, the Battalion was now becoming accustomed to this kind of thing, and soon settled down. Improvements were made in the camp, and competition between the various units of the Division for the smartest camp was soon astir. The whole Division (now known as the 60th (London) Division) was concentrated between Longbridge Deverill and Sutton Veny. The divisional R.E., A.S.C., R.A.M.C., and R.F.A. appeared in reality, and it was obvious to all that the Battalion was at last part of a real fighting division destined at some time or other to go abroad.

Everything was advancing at a pace, and stores and material were brought up to War Establishment. Training and musketry was being completed, the Regular Army Course having been fired on the local range. Manœuvres by the whole Division became daily routine, and inspections were frequent. Hopes ran high for an early departure for France, when suddenly, on the 28th April, 1916, the Battalion was ordered to proceed to Ireland with the rest of our Brigade.

Political events in Dublin had developed into war during Eastertide, every one was full of the possibility of Dublin ; others said that France was the real destination, and the orders for Ireland were mere camouflage to deceive the Hun ; while others, less optimistic, imagined a permanent exile in Ireland for the duration of the war.

However, all rumours were soon dispelled during the night of the 29th April, and the Battalion entrained at Warminster bound for Neyland near Pembroke Dock.

The following day was Sunday, and the Battalion spent a beautiful summer day on the grassy slopes facing the sea, awaiting embarkation to an unknown port, while the officers were kindly entertained by the Officers' Mess of the 4th Welsh Regiment, which was stationed a few miles inland. Late in the evening a large quantity of rations was issued, and the prospect of a long sea journey arose in the minds of most of us. The night, however, was without alarms, and not until the following morning did the Battalion embark. Part of the unit, together with the transport section, sailed on the *Archangel,* and the remainder on board the *Rathmore ;* both transports leaving the harbour early in the evening.

Here was real adventure at last, sailing to an unknown destination through seas frequented by enemy submarines. At daybreak the coast of Ireland was sighted, and at 4.30 a.m. we were alongside the quays of Queenstown. The disembarkation was without incident beyond the warning that we were now in

" enemy " country. We proceeded straightway through the town to Belvelly Camp on Fota Island. No demonstration was made by the Irish people, and no one could understand why they should be regarded with suspicion. Smiles greeted the troops, and the unfortunate Battalion Signalling Officer, who was leading the Battalion on the march, was severely reprimanded by his superior for talking to some charming Irish damsels. The B.S.O. excused himself on the grounds that he was asking the way ; a reply which brought forth a still further admonition for " enquiring of the enemy." The new camp on Fota Island was situated in a beautiful Irish park, the property of Lord Ballymore, and for the next few days the Battalion was engaged on ordinary field training and not a bloodthirsty battle as many had anticipated.

The weather turned wet, and this fact alone appears to be a sufficient reason for the " Staff " to order a move with its consequent discomfort. On the 6th May the Battalion left the camp at Belvelly and proceeded to Ballincorrig via Cork. The march was performed in the rain, though while actually passing through the City of Cork the weather became kinder, and the streets were lined with the citizens, none of whom appeared to be really warlike. The real sensation, however, was an officer of the Munsters who passed the Battalion. He wore a steel helmet, which at that time was unique and rarely seen in the United Kingdom, and the atmosphere of real war conjured up by that single steel helmet somewhat counteracted the peacefulness of Cork. Leaving the town was to leave the finer weather ; for the rest of the journey the downpour was terrific, and when the Battalion reached Ballincorrig no one was sorry. The Battalion was housed in the local cavalry barracks, and every one will remember the splendid comradeship of the artillerymen stationed there, who did all they could to attend to the needs of the soaked Battalion. The riding school was full of tired Londoners, but how they welcomed those steaming " dixies " of tea prepared by the barracks cooks. Tiredness soon disappeared, and fraternising was the " order of the night " ; officers to the officers' mess, sergeants to the sergeants' mess, and men to the canteen. The horrors of the day's march of 16 miles in the rain were forgotten, and a pleasant evening was spent. A word of thanks is also due to those artillerymen who so kindly took over the Battalion transport on arrival and groomed and fed the horses. Here, indeed, was the brotherly spirit, which existed so strongly in the British Tommy, illustrated.

The next morning the Battalion was astir early, the march was resumed, our destination being Coachford. The journey was shorter, about 12 miles, and the Battalion marched through

some of the most beautiful Irish scenery, small villages like
Dripsey on the route, with its tiny hovels sheltering animals
and fowls in the living rooms, gave us an insight into Irish village
life. Coachford, a sleepy little Irish village, was reached in the
evening, and tents, which had been conveyed in advance by
motor lorries, were soon erected on the local recreation ground,
and the Battalion nestled down for the night. The next day
the march was continued as far as Macroom, the day was fine
and the march fairly short. Early in the afternoon the town
of Macroom was reached, and the population turned out to
welcome the Battalion. The camping ground was situated on
the river banks in the grounds of the ancient castle of Macroom.
By evening time the Battalion had settled down and every one
hoped for a long stay in this glorious spot. The following day
was market day in Macroom, and the town was crowded with
people from the surrounding villages and farms ; officers and men
were allowed in the town, a happy release after the restrictions
in existence since our arrival in Ireland. Shops were besieged
and luxuries were purchased to supplement the rations of
" active service." Talking of purchases, most members of the
Battalion will remember the famous small goat bought by an
officer, which although an affectionate animal, became a nuisance
by thrusting its vocal efforts upon that tent in any battalion
camp which should be approached with bated breath, a salute
and the word " Sir."

Mystery surrounded the first armed party of about 100 strong
which left the camp that night under the guidance of the Royal
Irish Constabulary. However, the following morning all was
common knowledge ; a few Irishmen had been arrested, while
the farm in which they lived had been surrounded by the troops
to prevent escape. These were the " rebels " which the Battalion
had set out to quell.

The stay at Macroom only lasted a few days, and the Battalion
continued its march inland under the command of Major A. A.
Oliver ; our Commanding Officer Lieutenant-Colonel Strange
having been sent to hospital seriously ill. Only a privileged few
knew the day's destination, but towards dusk the Battalion
halted near Mill Street and turned off the main road into a field
where tea was soon prepared by the company cooks. No
tents on motor lorries were to be seen ; a drizzle set in, and
every one wondered whether it would mean a night in the wet
with only waterproof sheets, which had already done great
service throughout the day. Several hours passed, no orders
were forthcoming, and every one became pessimistic. Finally,
however, an entraining officer was appointed with the usual
complement of N.C.O.'s and this ended all discussion. The
Battalion was to move off by train. The geography of Ireland

had been forgotten since school days and the names of likely places were confined to the Limerick and Dublin areas ; however, about midnight the Battalion marched to the station at Mill Street, entrained rapidly and steamed out into the gloom of a wet, misty Irish fog. Tired by the day's march of 16 miles over the moorlands of the Bochragh Mountains every one slept, and no one troubled about our destination. Great was the surprise, however, the next morning to wake and find that the train had pulled up on Rosslare Pier. France was in every one's mouth, and then the memory of the Quartermaster Stores and rear details at Warminster dispelled such ideas. The day was spent on the stone pier of the harbour and eventually at 7 p.m. the Battalion set sail on the *Connaught*, reaching Fishguard after a pleasant crossing of four hours' duration. Little did one think that within a few weeks the same troopship would convey the Battalion to France. Within an hour of reaching Fishguard the Battalion was entrained and started for Warminster, which was reached about 7 a.m. on the 13th May, 1916. After a short march we arrived back at our old camp at Longbridge Deverill. The visit to Ireland soon appeared like a dream, so sudden and so short had it been. The value of the " Irish stunt," as it was commonly called, cannot be discounted, even if actual warfare had not been encountered. The Battalion had learnt to entrain and detrain ; embark and disembark ; and move its home day by day and in general to become a mobile unit. The experience was invaluable.

Back in Warminster the old question cropped up : " When is the Battalion going to France ? " The slightest alteration in the daily routine was regarded by the numerous Sherlock Holmes in the Battalion as distinct clues pointing to an early departure for the front. However, signs soon became very real when additional Lewis guns, field dressings, active service pay books, and identity discs, were issued, and soon the Battalion was complete in regard to stores. A final medical examination was held and innoculation and vaccination were soon in full swing. Embarkation leave was granted and one whole day was spent before the camera ; photographs of companies, sections and specialists were taken. Every one was hopeful.

On the 31st May, 1916, the whole division was inspected by H.M. The King, and it was a splendid sight to see the troops in review order on the slopes of the Wiltshire Downs. The 60th Division was fit and ready for the front ; and on the 21st June, 1916, the final orders were received and the following morning the Battalion, under the Command of Lieutenant-Colonel C. de Putron, entrained at Warminster for Southampton. Many of the townsfolk turned out in the early morning and gave us a hearty send-off.

The following was the list of Officers and Warrant Officers, etc. who left for France :—

Commanding Officer	-	- Lieutenant-Colonel C. de Putron.
Second in Command	-	- Major A. A. Oliver.
Adjutant -	-	- Captain A. W. Gaze.
Medical Officer	-	- Captain F. J. Leech, R.A.M.C.
Quarter Master	-	- Lieutenant A. A. Joslin.
Transport Officer	-	- Second-Lieutenant F. T. Bailey.
Lewis Gun Officer	-	- Lieutenant W. S. H. Smith.
Signalling Officer	-	- Lieutenant P. W. Thorogood.

" A " Company : Captain F. F. Tarver, Lieutenants C. H. Rimington and H. F. Rust, Lieutenant B. Peatfield, and Second-Lieutenant L. H. Hart. Company Sergeant Major H. A. Syrad and Company Quartermaster Sergeant J. C. Sale.

" B " Company : Captain C. A. Bailey, Captain A. C. H. Benké, Lieutenant J. H. Randolph, and Second-Lieutenants A. V. James, S. C. Bennett and H. J. Spencer. Company Sergeant Major H. T. Bassett and Company Quartermaster Sergeant W. D. Shanahan.

" C " Company : Major H. F. M. Warne, Captain K. A. Wills, Second-Lieutenants F. J. Smith, E. E. Andrews, F. E. Gearing, and F. W. Westmore. Company Sergeant Major J. S Oldcorn and Company Quartermaster Sergeant A. J. Rodd.

" D " Company : Captain F. R. Radice, Captain K. W. M. Pickthorn, and Second-Lieutenants F. W. Lewis, C. M. Kilner, G. E. Thompson and K. A. Higgs. Company Sergeant Major H. W. Lovelock and Company Quartermaster Sergeant F. King.

Regimental Sergeant Major A. H. Freemantle (Scots Guards).

Regimental Quartermaster Sergeant A. C. Gibson.

CHAPTER XXVIII

THE journey to France was without incident ; the train from
Salisbury Plain arrived at Southampton Docks about midday
on the 22nd of June, 1916, and after a few hours on the quayside
the Battalion embarked on board H.M. Transport *Connaught*,
the boat which only a few weeks before had brought us over
from Ireland. Complimentary messages from the Embarkation
Staff on the excellent and business-like behaviour of the Battalion pleased us. At about 10 p.m. we set sail, and the calm
sea made the journey comparatively comfortable. True, it was
crowded on board, but not to that extent that it reminded one
of the proverbial " sardines in a box." During the morning of
the 23rd of June the Battalion set foot on the Continent at Havre.
Great excitement prevailed ; the novelty of France, the quaint
French poilus in their blue service kit ; everything, in fact,
seemed to belong to that world of dreams that had for so long
evaded us ; while a group of German prisoners of war on the
quayside added spice to our first taste of foreign service. Rain
set in, however, and made the short march to the rest camp
distinctly unpleasant.

Leave was granted to limited numbers, who immediately
availed themselves of the " good things " in the town, and
incidentally the opportunity of airing their French, much of
which was of the " primer " lesson book type, and was neither
greatly appreciated nor understood by the townspeople, who
replied in good English. But the French people are so polite
that one is encouraged to persevere.

The Battalion retired to their tents for the night, but an
early réveillé at 2.30 a.m. reminded every one that they were
now on " Active Service," and soon the whole camp was astir
preparing to move. After a wait of many hours the Battalion
left (less "B" Company, which moved later in the day) for the
station, and were entrained in the famous "8 Chevaux, 40

Hommes " wagons of which we had heard so much. Any discomfort in travelling in these trucks was recompensed by the novelty of our new surroundings. The French people by this time had become serious over the war, and the route was not lined by cheering crowds as had been the case in the earlier days of the war ; though the French children on the route still made frequent requests for bully beef, biscuits and cigarettes, in their best " Engleesh." The journey terminated on the 25th in the St. Pol area, and the Battalion soon marched to its billets in the villages of Penin, Averdoight, and Roellecourt. These were the first billets in France, but every one managed to settle down comfortably whether in a cottage or in a barn. The local " vins rouges et blancs " were sampled, and the 2/15th Londons appreciated the mystic word " estaminet " for the first time. At times the rumble of heavy artillery could be heard in the distance, and this brought home to us the fact that we were nearing the firing line. Orders were received the following day to move forward to Maroeuil, a few miles north of Arras. The Battalion formed up on the high road from Penin, and started off gaily enough on a glorious summer evening. An advanced aerodrome was passed on the way, and the planes in the air, and the observation balloons in the distance, helped to make the first part of the marching interesting. Gradually the night clouds gathered, and a heavy downpour of rain rather " spoilt things." French " pavé " roads which up to this time had been traversed unnoticed, became torture to tired feet, and troops billeted on the line of march were envied ; however, the Battalion plodded along, and by 11 p.m. reached the battered town of Maroeuil, where a few civilians still remained. Not realising that the town was close to the firing line, and under the direct observation of the German lines, the Battalion freely used its hurricane lamps which reflected their rays on the ruined walls of the buildings, and there can be no doubt that the salvos of shells that greeted us on our arrival had been " asked for."

Only two men were wounded slightly ; not forgetting " A " Company's cooker, which received a direct hit. However, these incidents were quite sufficient to make us realise the unpleasantness of war. Billets were soon found under the able guidance of the " Scotties " of the 51st Division, who apparently knew all the cellars in the town. The Battalion, after having a hot meal, went to bed feeling tired, but many spent a restless night wondering when the next strafe was due. The night was, however, quiet, and the next day, the 27th of June, was spent in finding our way around the town, and investigating the few estaminets which remained open, where we were regaled with the horrible details of war by the men of the 51st Division of

Scottish Territorials who were then holding that part of the front line. The following morning the Battalion moved a few miles farther north under the cover of the valley behind the town as far as Bray, which nestled behind the ridge of Mont St. Eloy, and was out of observation by the Bosche. The Battalion was housed in large Army huts, similar to those we had left on Salisbury Plain. Every one was relieved to get away from the dingy cellars of Maroeuil, our unpleasant reception having given most of us a bad taste of the village and its cellars. On the 29th of June, the Battalion left Bray via Maroeuil for the firing line, and by means of deep communication trenches, which had been dug for a distance of four to five miles from the front line system as far back as Maroeuil, the relief was carried out by day. This was a great advantage to the new Battalion as it became accustomed to that weird feeling of being in a trench, before the night fell and obliterated all.

The surrounding country was covered with red poppies, and the setting sun shone gloriously on this carpet of colour. On the way ruined farms were seen at points of vantage, and near the main road from Arras to Souchez, with its avenue of trees destroyed by shell fire, we passed the famous Maison Blanche, a deep dug-out, large enough to hold a battalion. In nearly every depression in the ground were cleverly camouflaged battery positions, the sight of which encouraged us in our new venture. After a long march through communication trenches the reserve line of the Elbe shelters in a sunken road was reached, and companies were distributed in the support and reserve areas for the night. Seven days after leaving England the Battalion was in the firing line. During the night of the 29th of June, the Bosche raided the trenches of the " Black Watch " in the front line, and many of the Battalion who got mixed up in the " Box " barrage will never forget the terrific local bombardment which lasted for some twenty minutes. The Battalion was fortunate and sustained no loss, but the " Black Watch " unfortunately lost about ten men killed and missing, while others were wounded. For the next few days the Battalion was held in support and reserve, and tours of duty in the front line were made by officers and N.C.O's., under the instruction of the " Black Watch." Dug-out life was studied, and every one became acquainted with the new routine. The Battalion soon acquired the attitude of the " man in the line," and very many thanks are due to those battalions of the Scottish Division which so kindly assisted us to pick up the threads of trench life. On the 2nd of July, 1916, the Battalion took over the front line, and became responsible for that part just north of Roclincourt, and in front of Neuville St. Vaast. The weather was unkind, rain made the trenches extremely unpleasant, and together with the constant salvos of enemy trench mortars known as " Grey Pigeons," " Lead Pencils," " Oilcans," and so on, according to their various shapes and sizes, those first few nights in the line proved rather trying to the Battalion of novices. Casualties were few, and the men soon learnt the " unhealthy " spots in the line, and avoided them whenever possible. This section of the front which was adjacent to the " Labyrinth " had been held by the French during the earlier stages of the war, and sad and gruesome relics of the heavy fighting by our gallant Allies were numerous in the trenches. The Battalion set to work, and did a great deal to improve them, though our work was constantly being destroyed by the intermittent bombardment of the enemy's trench mortars and minenwerfers. Wiring along the front was improved, and patrols were sent out each night into " No Man's Land," although the proximity of the Bosche did not allow much latitude in this respect. At this time the great Somme Offensive had commenced, and the heavy artillery fire farther south could be distinctly heard ; and although the 2/15th Londons had not participated in the actual fight, there was a great consolation in the fact that the Battalion was at last holding part of the line, thereby releasing more seasoned troops for the offensive and at the same time preparing themselves for their turn when it should come.

The insertion of a sketch of this sector might prove interesting at this point, for it was here that the Battalion was destined to spend its stay in France.

The front held by the 179th Brigade was from the Stone Communication Trench on the north to the Victoire Communication Trench on the south, about 2,500 yards in all. Two battalions held the front lines, a third battalion forming the supports and reserves, while the fourth battalion of the Brigade was out at rest at Bray. The 2/15th always occupied the right sub-sector of the Brigade front being relieved by the 2/14th (London Scottish) ; while the 2/13th and the 2/16th Battalions shared the responsibility of the left sub-sector.

The right sub-sector in which the Battalion was located ran from the Vissec Communication Trench to the Victoire, on the right flank.

This sub-sector was again divided into three company fronts as follows :—

(1) Vissec C.T. to Bentata C.T.
(2) Biras Sap to Point ' D.'
(3) Point ' D ' to Bonnell Avenue at Point ' A.'

The front line proper ran along the Doublement, MacIntyre Street, across Argyle Street to Bonnell Avenue. The support line ran parallel to the front line at distances varying from

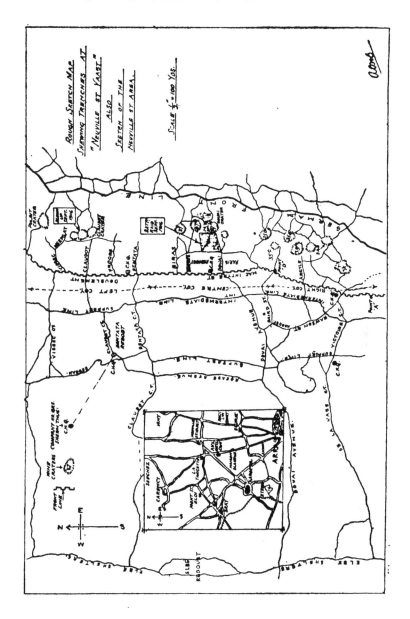

70 yards to 150 yards at the different places, while between the front line and the support line an intermediate line, chiefly occupied by machine guns and trench mortars, had been constructed. Forward of the front line an observation line had been dug, and in the centre of the Battalion front a strong redoubt known as the Paris Redoubt had been constructed. From the front line system connection with the rear was maintained by four arterial communication trenches, the Vissec, Claudot, Douai, and de la Vase. Many minor trenches made the whole system a perfect maze, and many disused trenches added to the difficulties of the network.

Three companies of the Battalion held the front line while the fourth company was in support on the right flank ; the left flank support being furnished by the third battalion in the Brigade. While holding the line, Battalion Headquarters were situated in the Elbe Shelters, but when the line was handed over, and the Battalion had become support or third battalion of the Brigade, Battalion Headquarters transferred their activities to Maison Blanche.

On the 5th of July the Battalion were taken out of the line for a " rest," but the word proved a misnomer. The Battalion was taken back as far as the Aux Rietz Cave in rear of Neuville St. Vaast and La Targette. Three companies were located in the cave, while " A " Company were billeted in dug-outs near La Targette. In the front line the Battalion had the good fortune to be housed in excellent dug-outs bequeathed to us by the French, but in no place on the whole British front could have been more secure from air-raids and shell fire than the Aux Rietz Cave.

Down wooden steps for over a hundred feet the weary infantrymen stumbled, and finally a wonderful underground world presented itself. A large cave capable of holding a thousand men, with hundreds of small candles lighting its sombre darkness, was the new home of the Battalion. Down here cook-houses were established, and all were able to roam about free from bombs, shells and bullets. A hot meal was soon prepared, and the weary Tommies soon fell asleep, in spite of the great heat and oppressive " fugginess " of their underground dwelling. The Battalion had not, however, escaped all the horrors of war, for the orderly sergeants of companies soon appeared and detailed numerous working parties, which were sent up the line that same evening to furnish Royal Engineer mining fatigues. Within a few hours most of the Battalion was retracing its steps through miles of trenches, knee deep in mud and water, to the front line, and after about six or eight hours strenuous work lifting and carrying heavy sandbags full of clay, they returned to the cave at Aux Rietz. A few hours' respite was granted, and then the working parties were again paraded for another tour of duty with the Royal Engineer sappers. In fact, for several days it was a constant procession day and night of weary working parties leaving and returning to the cave. No one grumbled at the actual work with the Royal Engineers, but the long journey to and from the line provided sufficient for a " grouse " ; every one longed for the front line again. The desire was quickly granted, and the Battalion were soon back in the trenches, and not until the 4th of August was it relieved. During this long stay in the line the Battalion became " old soldiers.'. The cook-houses in the Elbe Shelter were thoroughly organised, and provided a hot meal each day to the men and a cup of hot cocoa each morning at " stand down." The daily post and canteen stores came up with the rations each night, having been brought as far as Battalion Headquarters by the transport and Quarter-master's staff ; from which point company ration parties carried them to the front line. Specialists such as signallers, snipers, and bombers, overcame the various difficulties of their work. Every man learnt the way round his own particular sector ; names of trenches, saps and craters became familiar, in fact the whole place became " a home from home." Friends were made with the artillery forward observation officers and men, and the tunnellers on our front became companions in distress. A great deal of mining was carried on in this part of the British front, and our tunnellers were extremely busy combating the activities of the Bosche, and many restless nights were spent wondering whether the constant tapping underground was that of friend or foe.

Casualties were fortunately not very heavy, although one recollects with sadness such incidents as the dug-out in Argyle Street being blown in, burying Sergeant Wigney and his gallant fellows, but on the whole the Battalion had been lucky.

On the 4th of August the Battalion was relieved and marched back to Bray, this time for a real rest. The Quartermaster's staff had prepared a hot meal, and after this repast was finished every one settled down for a well-earned rest away from the continual noise of the front line. The next few days were spent in cleaning up, replacing damaged equipment and boots, writing letters (not forgetting the censoring) and attending sundry parades. Dinners and suppers of varying degree were held either in the huts or in the local estaminets, and every one appreciated the restful green fields and shady trees near Bray, which had not been destroyed by the ravages of war. Entertainment was provided at Acq by the Divisional concert party, and our own Battalion concert party, " The Plumes " of Warminster days was resuscitated in an endeavour to add to the gaiety of life. On the 9th of August His Majesty the King visited the observation posts at Mont St. Eloy near by, and many of the Battalion were privileged to line the route and cheer His Majesty who was accompanied by His Royal Highness the Prince of Wales (our Honorary Colonel) and the Commander-in-Chief, Sir Douglas Haig.

On the 12th of August, after a week's rest, the Battalion again proceeded to the line, and the old life amid the constant " strafes " of the Hun was resumed. Reliefs between companies were carried out with precision, and various fatigue parties, sap guards, gas guards, patrols and wiring parties kept every one busy. Parties of officers and N.C.O.'s. spent a few days with the artillery batteries for the purpose of instruction. Nothing of importance, however, marked this tour in the line, and on the 1st September the Battalion was relieved and marched back to the huts at Bray.

On the 6th of September, we were again ordered up to the trenches. This tour of duty was to be one of importance. A mysterious section of two officers and twenty men were left behind to train for a raid on the Hun lines. The party was under the command of Lieutenant B. Peatfield, with Second Lieutenant G. E. Thompson as his second in command. The raid was of considerable importance as information of the exact disposition of the enemy was urgently required at General Headquarters in order to ascertain which German Divisions had been withdrawn from the heavy fighting on the Somme. The raiding party were trained over a facsimile of the actual ground over which they were to raid which had been dug near Divisional Headquarters. When the party arrived at the trenches on the 10th of September, excitement in the Battalion ran high. The raiders, all of whom were volunteers, were located in a small dug-out in the Paris Redoubt, and made preparations for the show. Unfortunately Private Rule, " B " Company, one of the party, was killed by a trench mortar shell that afternoon, but undaunted the remainder looked forward to the adventure. The raid was to be launched from the Paris Redoubt on the night of the 11th September, and was to be supported by covering fire from our trench mortars and machine guns while the artillery assisted the operation with a heavy local " box " barrage. Early in the evening all the officers concerned in the raid gathered together at Battalion Headquarters in the Elbe, and final instructions were issued, and watches were synchronised. Just as this party came out of the dug-out a salvo of shells arrived and caused great consternation, but no casualties occurred. That evening all sap guards were strengthened, and in the middle of the night every one " stood to," when suddenly the barrage from our lines burst forth with a terrific crash, and the raiding party with its blackened faces sallied forth. No one but those who actually took part in the raid can describe the inferno which reigned for the next few minutes. The Hun soon sent up his S.O.S. signals and retaliatory fire opened up, but most of this fell in the " D " Company area on the left flank of the operation, where two lamps had been specially erected to mislead the enemy as to the actual part of the line from which the raid had started. Shortly afterwards the success of the raid was wired to all companies, and a sense of relief overwhelmed the Battalion. Apparently our fellows had followed closely to the creeping barrage of our trench mortars and had entered the Hun trench, killing or wounding the occupants, and bringing back a few prisoners. Luckily none of our men were killed although wounds were numerous among the raiders, and unfortunately Private J. F. Small of "B" Company succumbed later to his severe injuries. Both officers had been badly wounded but stuck to their job, and inspired the men by their example. Second Lieutenant G. E. Thompson, together with Private A. Small, returning to the Hun trench to rescue the latter's brother who was found to be missing at the first roll call.

Valuable information had been obtained, and only the death of Private J. F. Small, who had been so gallantly rescued, marred the operation. Credit must be given to the artillery, machine gunners, and trench mortar batteries who so ably assisted in making the raid a success.

The raid placed the Battalion on a high footing, and great credit is due to all concerned.

On the 25th of September, the Battalion was relieved, and although nothing of importance happened after the raid, for many nights afterwards we expected a return visit from the enemy.

The return to Bray was accompanied by the usual luxuries of baths at Maroeuil, the concerts at Acq, and the refreshments of the local estaminets. On the 26th, ribbons were presented by the Divisional General to those members of the raiding party who had escaped unwounded ; while on the following day the Corps Commander, Lieutenant-General Sir Charles Fergusson, K.C.B., inspected the Battalion. A few days afterwards, on the 30th September, orders to return to the line were received, and the march was accomplished without loss, although the enemy artillery was active on the roads leading up to the trenches. Nearing the line a great activity on the part of the enemy machine gunners and snipers was noticed, and it was learnt that during the night the Germans had exploded two large mines on our front near the Claudot Sap. The London Scottish were holding that sector of the line that night, and it is to their great credit that the Hun made no inroads on our front. How great a fight they had made was best judged from the heavy casualties they had sustained. "D" Company of the 2/15th relieved this part of the front, and by dint of hard digging under considerable fire soon consolidated the new craters, and linked them up by saps with the observation line. Days of comparative quiet ensued, although at this time the enemy commenced to use large trench mortar shells standing some thirty-six inches high, with a diameter of ten or twelve inches. As a retaliation for this unwelcome increase in the size of missiles a deep emplacement was made in rear of "D" company's sector in the Bessan Redoubt, and in it was placed a very heavy type of British Trench Mortar, having a projectile of similar proportions to those introduced by the Bosche. This shell was nicknamed the "Flying Pig," and to fire it was only an experiment, so all the men in the trenches in advance of the emplacement were temporarily withdrawn lest the shell should accidentally fall short. The test was successful, and large craters about ten feet deep, and twenty yards wide were made in the Hun lines. However, the experiment was not taken by the Hun in the right spirit, and retaliation on his part for the next few days was very brisk. A strafe of shells from guns and minenwerfers of all calibres was poured on to the unoffending infantrymen's heads. Dug-outs were blown up, but the resultant casualties were small. "D" Company's headquarters dug-out was destroyed, and the signallers were entombed, but several hours work got them out, and they were rescued little the worse for their experience.

After these few days of continual bombardment a sigh of relief was breathed when the Canadian Division much depleted in numbers through heavy fighting on the Somme, marched up to take over the trenches at Neuville St. Vaast, and the Battalion left this sector for the last time.

Rumours of transferring our activities to the Somme were soon afoot, and after a few days rest at Bray, the Battalion made tracks for the Abbeville area via Hermaville, Frevent, Auxi-le-Château, and Beauvoir Rivière. Each night billets were arranged in the villages en route, and pleasant evenings in the local estaminets were spent after the day's march. The weather was only moderate but the Battalion was well seasoned by now, and cared little for the discomfort of the trek after its long stay in the trenches. The Battalion finally halted at Francière a few kilometres south of Abbeville, and leave to England was granted to a privileged few. Preparations for a journey to the East were made, and these soon dispelled all rumours of fighting on the Somme.

On the morning of the 15th of November, the Battalion marched to Longpres and entrained on the familiar " 8 Chevaux et 40 Hommes " troop train bound for Marseilles, leaving Longpres at 4.0 p.m. The journey to the south of France was most enjoyable, and the route taken was via Montreau, Dijon, Macon, Pierre Latte to Marseilles. At each of these places a halt was made when rations for the next stage of the journey were drawn, and hot tea prepared by permanent staffs stationed on the route was issued. Although halts sometimes were made in the middle of the night, most men were lured from their uncomfortable beds in spite of the cold nights to drink the hot tea.

The weather though cold was bright, and while daylight lasted everyone drank in the beauty of the French scenery, especially while passing along the valley of the Rhone, with its wonderful river scenes and terraced vineyards, which clothed the rugged slopes of the valley. Marseilles was reached on the 17th of November, after a journey of just over two days, and the Battalion marched to the Rest Camp on the western outskirts of the city. Here it poured constantly, and the whole camp was a veritable quagmire ; fortunately the stay was a short one, for on the 19th November, 1916, half the Battalion marched to the Docks, and boarded the *Transylvania*, one of the large Transatlantic liners, at 11.0 a.m., bound for Salonica, while the other half followed in the *Megantic*, a week later.

CHAPTER XXIX

THE VOYAGE TO SALONICA—MALTA—SALONICA, 30TH NOVEMBER, 1916—JOURNEY TO KATERINA—OUTPOSTS AT STIPI.

H.M. TROOPSHIP *Transylvania*, which was unfortunately sunk by torpedo a few weeks later, set sail from Marseilles at midnight on the 19th November. A rough sea was encountered, and it was afterwards learnt that a tidal wave had swept over the harbour that night, destroying a great amount of shipping. The next day all was calm, and the officers and men of the Battalion became accustomed to their new surroundings, and acquainted with the interior of this huge vessel. Boat drill was the novelty, but even this soon became a " bore," and after the first few parades everybody looked upon the compulsory life-belt attached to one's body as a millstone, rather than the reverse. On the 20th, the islands of Corsica and Sardinia were passed about 4 p.m., and on the following day the vessel steamed along the north coast of Africa. During these days the ·calm Mediterranean lulled all into a sense of peace and security, and only when the three blasts of the ship's syren disturbed the quietness and everyone bustled to their boat stations did one realise the possibility of enemy submarines spoiling the trip. It is said that R.S.M. Freemantle gained a handsome monetary reward for spotting a submarine, but the fact that only the R.S.M. saw it causes doubts in many minds. Regardless of any submarine reported to have been seen by the R.S.M., the *Transylvania* was ordered by its escort of torpedo boat destroyers to put into St. Paul's Bay, Malta, on the morning of the 22nd November, and about midday on the 24th, the liner proceeded into the harbour of Valetta. This harbour is one of the most wonderful in the world, and has a very narrow, heavily fortified entrance leading from the outer bay to the inner harbour, which was full of shipping, while men-o'-war of all classes were constantly passing in and out. The town itself is on the high ground around, and was glistening white under the hot sun of the Mediterranean, which poured down its rays from a cloudless blue sky. During the night of the 24th, a slight mishap occurred to the *Transylvania* and she broke from her moorings, but the Battalion slept on under the protection of the submarine-forbidden harbour, unaware of any possible disaster. It was not until the 27th that the word to proceed was given by the Naval authorities, and a few days' stay at Valetta had been thoroughly enjoyed by those members of the Battalion (officers and N.C.O.'s only, I am afraid), who were permitted ashore. A route march through the town had been arranged for the troops, but unfortunately this had to be cancelled on the receipt of orders to sail.

The journey was continued from Malta without event, and on the 29th November we passed the islands of the Greek Archipelago, the names of which were always in dispute and finally were dubbed with nicknames such as Enos, Kolynos, Thermos, Chaos, and so on. When nearing Salonica several hospital ships, which had been ruthlessly torpedoed, were just visible above the water where they had been beached. The next day, the 30th, the harbour of Salonica was reached, and the Battalion disembarked on the quay during the morning. From the harbour the town of Salonica looked very fine, and extends from the green slopes of the hills on the east along a flat stretch of some five miles to the low dismal country at the foot of the Greek mountains. The town is dotted with mosques and oriental churches, and the famous White Tower on the promenade forms a striking contrast to the low shops and hotels which line the harbour front. However, all this apparent beauty was soon dispelled, and the mud and smell of even the main thoroughfares was simply indescribable. On the quayside hundreds of troops, French, Serbians, Russians and Greeks, were shouting and making the harbour a babel of foreign tongues. The route taken by the Battalion lay through the western end of the town, and the curious shops with their gaily-dressed, though ragged, merchants caused much comment among the troops. Slow, lumbering oxen wagons formed the local method of transport, and these, intermixed with the heavy army motor lorries, caused considerable congestion. After the jumble of traffic through streets a foot deep in mud and filth, the Battalion was relieved to strike the main high road for Dudular. All along this road were signs of military activity ; ordnance stores, A.S.C. dumps, motor lorry parks, and ammunition depots lined the route, and a few miles from the town the Battalion passed two extensive canvas general hospitals. Through this military city, which had sprung up with mushroom-like growth during the war, a railway had been built, and it struck one as being extremely humorous to see a green engine with L.S.W.R. in golden letters on its side puffing along under the control of the R.E. drivers. What visions of Waterloo and leave trains ! This line was continued as far as Monastir, and troop trains of French and Serbians constantly passed up and down. The camp was finally reached after a march of about eight miles, and was situated on barren, desolate ground, which extended from a chain of hills to the marshes along the Salonica–Monastir Road. On this plain the whole Division was concentrated under a huge canvas camp. The ground was rough, uneven, stony and cut by numerous "nullahs." Every one pitched his tent wherever the geographical and geological conditions permitted, and it is regretted that the beautiful straight lines of tents that distinguished our camp at Saffron Walden were no longer to be seen. Natives wandered around the camp and were promptly dubbed "hoojahs," a word which was attached to all things Greek for want of a better descriptive word. These natives presumably desired to sell their fruits and wares, but judging by their mixed uniform of khaki and native garb it was doubtful whether "scroungeing" was not their real intention. On the few more level spots that were available football commenced, and for the first few days life was enjoyable. Letters were again allowed, and in spite of drills and parades it was a most restful time by day. Night time, however, was disturbed by the inroads upon the tired flesh of the troops by numerous "minor horrors of war," which had been encouraged to life by the blankets and conditions generally on board the transport ship. Changes of underclothes were issued and washing in the muddy streams somewhat arrested the unpleasantness. This period was a particularly busy one for the Quartermaster's Stores, and stores and equipment peculiar to the East were issued, among which were bivouac sheets. Each man having been presented, gratis by the thoughtful authorities, with a small khaki canvas sheet about a yard square, together with a pole 2 feet 6 inches long, two tent pegs and a piece of stout cord, bivouac parades were instituted. The erection of a bivouac was not an easy matter on such stony ground, and even when erected (sometimes by the aid of bayonets and entrenching tools, the use of which was soon forbidden) the open end provided little comfort from the cold winds which blew from the hills at night. To add to this discomfort, heavy torrential rains poured down on the 8th December, and bivouacs fell down on their occupants during the night with alarming rapidity, even the bell tents which remained were rooted from their moorings, and an unpleasant night was spent. The ground soon became a quagmire, and in the nullahs streams of brown, muddy water rushed along. The colour of the water used for cooking and making tea was of the same delightful solidity, and there was little difference between the tea before and after brewing. However, the weather improved slightly, and the next item of interest was the arrival of over 100 mules for the transport section, "straight from the nest" as it were, and with no decorous idea of military discipline.

The Quartermaster's Stores was full of pack saddlery absolutely new, slippery and unpliable, and the following day " Bill Bailey's Circus " was in full swing. The transport section, under Second Lieutenant F. T. Bailey, was supplemented by fatigue parties from the Battalion, until each mule had nearly a dozen attendants, all of whom were absolutely necessary. The mules were then dressed in their new kit by the untiring energies of the transport section and their co-opted fatigues and paraded for the Commanding Officer's inspection. This, however, did not last for many minutes ; objections were raised, not forgetting the hind legs, by the four-footed members of the transport, and " saddles reversed " was soon performed. It was infectious, and half the animals soon left the arena with kits incomplete, or at least in quite the wrong places on their bodies. Finally the parade, or rather what was left, was dismissed, and then followed the counting of the mules, several of which had escaped. This, however, did not disturb the Transport Officer, he calmly remarking, " They will turn up at feeding time." The next morning a recount was made, and apparently the mules had decided with which Regiment in the Brigade they would be billeted. Exchanges were made and, needless to say, the receiver was never the chooser. On the following day, after another wet night when the mule lines had become a horrible mixture of muddy transport men, mules and saddlery, the Battalion, complete with transport, was ordered to parade for a route march, apparently not so much for the benefit of the troops, but as a test for the endurance of "Bill Bailey's Circus." The mules were " dressed up " and the saddles loaded with panniers, etc., and after a considerable delay the Battalion started along the road. A few paces was sufficient to bring about a debacle in the column ; packs slipped, and the men were detailed to fall out and reload the mules. Every yard of the route was strewn with loads of all descriptions, many of which had, no doubt, been unevenly weighted. The plain was dotted with muleteers chasing after mutinous mules which had dispensed with their encumbrances and taken flight. How many mules finished the march is not recorded, but sufficient to say the march proved amusing if nothing else. The next few days were spent in scraping mud and salving blankets, waterproof sheets, equipment and saddlery, which had been mislaid in the mud that followed the heavy rain each night. On the Sunday, 10th December, a Brigade route march was ordered, and we were inspected by our new Brigadier, General F. M. Edwards, C.M.G., who had taken the place of Brigadier-General Baird, who had remained in France.

The same afternoon secret orders were received, and by midnight the Battalion, less its transport, was marching to Salonica

Docks.   After a few hours' wait on the quayside, the Battalion embarked on board H.M. torpedo boat destroyer *Mosquito*, and set sail for somewhere in Greece.   Accommodation was very limited, and the black smoke from the funnels of the boat soon covered every one with soot.   The officers and crew of the destroyer did all in their power to secure the maximum amount of comfort for the troops, and the whole of the Battalion officers were given an excellent breakfast in the small ward room. During the afternoon the Greek coast was approached, and in the distance we could see the snow clad peaks of the Olympus group.   The destroyer anchored a few hundred yards from land, and parties of the Battalion were sent ashore in the small boats. Great credit is due to the Naval folk for their handling of these boats, and, with the exception of a few hasty members who jumped ashore out of the boats too soon, no mishap occurred, and with a cheer from both arms of the Service the destroyer left for sea.   The Battalion lined up on the beach at a place called Scala Vromeris.   The weather was glorious and the wet clothes of the unfortunates were soon dried.   Small fires were made on the beach and a frugal meal was partaken.   Scala Vromeris consisted of a few wooden huts, and apparently was the " port," or rather the landing place, of the town of Katerina, which lay a few miles inland.   Only a few Greeks were in occupation, and a large party of Maltese, working under some French soldiers, were housed in the small huts.   Orders were received to march inland, leaving a rear party of about 50 men to await the arrival of stores from Salonica.   The march was along a genuine " Greek " road, the chief constituents of which were mud, holes, ruts and large stones, but the route was without steep gradients, and the town of Katerina was reached early in the evening.   This was a typical Grecian country town, and the natives thronged the streets half in fear and half in jubilation on the arrival of the troops.   On the further side of the town was a large Turkish barracks, and here the Battalion was billeted.   Men soon made purchases at the shops of very inferior tasteless cigarettes, but nuts and fruit were of excellent quality, though the prices were somewhat exorbitant.   A party of officers found their way into a " café," but when one realises that the plates were returned three times to the washer-up before they could be accepted for eating purposes, the quality of this " café " can be better appreciated.   Like the rest of the town and its people it was extremely filthy.

The next day was spent in cleaning up the barracks, which afterwards reached a state of comparative comfort in spite of the broken windows and damaged floors.   The day was peaceful enough, but when the day's rations of bully beef and biscuits had been eaten every one wondered where the next meal was coming from. Neither the stores from Scala Vromeris nor the Battalion transport had yet arrived. The town itself had been practically exhausted of its eatables, and finally the question was settled by means of " local purchase." A flock of sheep was bought by the Brigade, and mutton was issued to the men, but even fresh killed mutton stewed in mess-tins does not make a very substantial day's feed for hungry troops. The Battalion, however, managed to " scrounge," and a few additions were obtained privately from a French Quartermaster's stores located in one part of the barracks, and these helped to eke out the meagre rations. It was a couple of days afterwards before the Battalion transport, which had taken an overland route from Salonica, arrived, and stores also arrived from the shore, though in the meantime it had been necessary to eat our " iron rations." Both the transport and the stores' escort had their special adventures.

At Salonica the Battalion stores had been loaded on flat lighters, which had proceeded to Scala Vromeris in tow of tugs. Heavy seas were encountered and many of the lighters broke loose and some drifted back to Salonica, while others, with half their cargo washed overboard, fought their way to Scala Vromeris. Those that landed back at Salonica proceeded under better conditions a day or so later, and on arrival were soon unloaded by the fatigue party we had left on the sea-shore. Much, however, was lost at sea, including officers' valises, mess boxes, cooks' gear, spare saddlery, Lewis gun panniers, ammunition, blankets, etc., but what remained was carted from the shore to Katerina by the aid of local ox-waggons, which lumbered along at a snail's pace.

The Battalion transport, which had travelled overland from Dudular Camp near Salonica, left there the same evening as the Battalion, and had been brigaded with the transport of the other units in the 179th Brigade, and had been escorted on the route by mounted troops. The journey was not a happy one, and they had only moved at night for purposes of secrecy. This fact alone made travelling difficult, but the wet weather multiplied their troubles threefold. The roads were heavy and badly made, mere tracks across waste land, and maps were indistinct and even incorrect. Many of these tracks were built up above the level of the surrounding country, and so heavy were the floods that the water covered these roadways, and frequently pairs of mules were struggling in the water at the roadside sometimes five feet deep. When the catastrophes happened there was nothing to be done but to cut off the load and give it a watery grave ; no attempt to salve them was possible or even desirable in the darkness. On one of these occasions, when mules and muleteer were thrown into the deeper water, an artillery officer, at great personal risk, dived in and saved the mule driver's life, and Private Phillips, of our own transport section, was highly commended for his assistance, while the officer later received the Silver Medal of the Royal Humane Society for saving life. However, all is well that ends well, and the various parties of the Battalion which had set out from Salonica by different routes reunited at Katerina, but as a result of their respective adventures huge deficiency lists were prepared. For the next week the whole Battalion was employed on road making, and other Battalions assisted the R.E. parties to repair the embankment of the coastal railway from Salonica to Lharrisa, which had been washed away in many places. It was not long afterwards that the deserted railway station we had passed on the way from the coast became a centre of activity. Ration trains arrived daily from Salonica, and a large dump of stores and ammunition was formed at Katerina Station. The Army Service Corps and Royal Engineers did great work, and soon rations, letters, and stores appeared with unfailing regularity from the Base. The Brigade soon established itself comfortably at Katerina, and even the local residents appreciated the situation and replenished their stores with foodstuffs, wines and cigarettes.

A word must also be said in praise of the N.C.O.'s and men of the French contingent in this area. They did all they could to welcome the Britishers, and dinner parties were held nightly in the Turkish barracks in our honour, probably to the detriment of the French ration supply, but that was beside the point ; "a short life and a gay one" was their motto. After dinner, songs in English and French were sung, toasts were drunk and friendships made. These convivial evenings will live long in the minds of those who participated.

On the 20th December, 1916, the Battalion marched out to Stipi, a few miles south of Katerina, to take over an outpost line which had been held by the Queen's Westminsters since our arrival in this part of Greece. The march was over rough country, and the additional kit in the shape of bivouac sheets, waterproofs, blankets, winter clothing and cardigans, extra bandoliers of ammunition fairly broke the backs of the men.

"A," "C" and "D" Companies relieved the outpost line, and "B" Company, with Headquarters, Transport, and Quartermaster's Stores were kept in reserve. The outpost line was along the low ridge of hills which ran from Stipi to Kundariotisa, and strict orders were issued that no movement on the skyline should be made by day. Bivouac camps were therefore erected on the reverse or northern slopes which ran down to the grassy valley of the River Mavourneri. From the southern slopes of this ridge the panorama was wonderful, a flat stretch of country for some twenty miles could be seen in the direction of Lharrisa, so that observation from the defences was perfect. On the further side of the plain rose the gigantic chain of snow-capped peaks, of which Mount Olympus formed a massive centrepiece. This mountain wall cut off the Katerina area from the rest of Southern Greece. Only by way of the narrow seashore plain and through the famous Petras Pass on the west of Katerina could the south be reached. At this time the attitude of Greece towards the Allies was questionable, and the position taken up by the Brigade was to secure the base at Salonica from any attack that might have been made from the south.

The Battalion employed itself now in commencing to dig a defensive line on the southern slopes of the ridge, and trench-digging in this part of the world was extremely laborious, as the ground was practically solid rock.

Barbed wire was not obtainable, and for the purpose of obstacles thick zarebas of short, stiff, prickly thorn bushes which covered the hill-side were used for entanglements. In our spare time football was played, and platoon and company competitions were soon in full swing. A splendid flat field had been cleared near the river bank, and was the scene of many exciting struggles. Christmas was approaching, and funds were collected for additional luxuries. The canteen opened by Brigade at Katerina was insufficient to supply the extra needs for the festive season, and Lieutenant Andrew and an able assistant were sent to Salonica by rail, where a Base Canteen was successfully attacked, and on Christmas Eve large supplies of Christmas goods arrived ; not so much in quantity as we should have liked, but considering the difficulties of transport, Lieutenant Andrew was to be congratulated. Chicken and eggs were purchased from the local villages of Stipi and Kundariotisa, and altogether a happy Christmas was spent in the bivouacs. Christmas decorations were numerous and consisted chiefly of grey-back shirts and underclothing which had become unpleasant to wear and decked the surrounding thorn bushes.

The festival of Christmas was celebrated by the local residents, and I had the pleasure of accompanying the Commanding Officer to the village of Stipi, where the chief man of the village bade us enter his house. Here we were ushered into the best room and seated on mats on the floor while the daughters of the house, in gay dresses, waited upon us, bringing in coffee, aniseed liqueur and apple jelly as refreshments. Conversation was carried on through the medium of the heir to the house, who had picked up a smattering of French in Salonica, where he was employed.

For the men sing-songs were arranged and sports were held, but the festivities of Christmas soon ceased, and the work on the trenches was resumed. New Year celebrations were limited to an excellent concert given in the Turkish barracks at Katerina by the French soldiers, and those who were privileged to attend thoroughly enjoyed their efforts.

The weather continued fairly fine, though spells of heavy rain, and sometimes snow, fell, making life in small canvas " bivvies " rather miserable. The Battalion remained on this outpost line for just over six weeks, during which time a strong defensive line facing Lharrisa had been built, and this was continued to the coast on the left flank by a series of strong points built and manned by the Westminsters. Road making and bridge building were carried on by the reserve Company, and I am sure the local Greeks must have appreciated our efforts, which resulted in the many military roads connecting Katerina with the surrounding villages. Occasionally field days were held by the Brigade, the rendezvous always being the Tumulus, which was an ever-present landmark for miles around our position. Kit inspections were frequent, and the losses of equipment, etc., resulting from our journey from Salonica led to lengthy sittings of a Board of Enquiry, and consequently many entries were made in pay books for loss of kit. In our spare time we played football after the day's work, and keen competitions between platoons and companies resulted. Matches were arranged with the other Regiments in the Brigade, in which the Civil Service came through with considerable credit. For the benefit of officers a riding class, under the Medical Officer, Dr. J. W. Leech (John Willie to all his friends) was instituted, and the quality of riding in the Battalion greatly improved. While referring to John Willie's equestrian ability, one must not overlook his medical skill. His sick parade each morning was divided into two classes ; one from the Battalion and the other from the local villages, which brought their sick for attention. Frequently the Doctor was called out to a village to attend an invalid, and among the natives his skill was considered wonderful ; not that I infer the Battalion did not appreciate his efforts, for his droll manner and Irish humour were characteristics we all loved, and his attention to all ranks was without fault. The only difference was that the natives presented him with fowls, fruit and small gifts, whereas the unfortunate recipient of a No. 9 offered his thanks in words alone. When a man was beyond the curative powers of a No. 9 or its brother pills he was transferred to the Field Ambulance, which had been established at Katerina. The country around was rough, and was only traversed by mule tracks, so that it was impossible to bring motor ambulances up as far as the Regimental Aid Post. The lying cases were, therefore, taken to hospital by means of a strange vehicle drawn by a mule. This vehicle simply consisted of two long poles some twenty feet in length which were attached to the mule after the manner of shafts, while the ends dragged

on the ground behind the mule. These two poles were secured
to each other in rear of the mule, and the stretcher was fixed
resting between the poles, so that the patient's head was higher
than his feet. Whether this was a comfortable means of transit
must be left to the judgment of the victims, but undoubtedly
it was the most suitable means in those parts.

No mention hitherto has been made of " Peter," who was
appointed Battalion interpreter. He was an undersized Greek,
who loved the Regiment, and no doubt worked very hard in the
" Grecian way," and although no one understood his parleys
with the local natives when we wished to dig up their land for
trenches, it is believed that he coerced them by the authority
given to him by the wearing of the Prince of Wales's feather in
his cap. He loved the Battalion better than his countrymen.

About the middle of February the Battalion left the outpost
line at Stipi, and two Companies, " A " and " B " proceeded to
Katerina barracks together with Headquarters Company.
Transport, and Quartermaster's Stores. The other two Companies, under the command of Major A. A. Oliver, moved to
Kolukuri, a few miles west of Katerina, and erected their bivouacs
in Shrine Woods. Here a flank defensive line was held by night
posts. From the 15th of February until the 28th the Battalion
remained in these stations, and the only excitement which broke
the monotony of the life was the visit of a strange aeroplane,
which flew over the square at Katerina barracks. No one
understood its mission and gazed at it curiously, for underneath
its wings were two large blue crosses and not the black Maltese
cross used on German aeroplanes. After it had taken note of
everything it flew away ; no one fired at it, and no one to this
day knows the meaning of this " mystery " plane. Orders from
Brigade to fire at it came later on, but by that time the plane
was well out of the range of our field guns.

On the 28th of February the Battalion concentrated on the
main road near Kolukuri on the way to the Petras Pass and
proceeded up towards the Pass, where a strong defensive position
had been held since our arrival in December by the London
Scottish. The Battalion halted at Kalivia Miljas for the night,
and the most unpleasant night it proved to be with the heavy
rains. The following day orders were received to return to
Katerina, and the Battalion marched back again as far as the
banks of the River Mavourneri, just outside the town. In flood
time the river is over a mile in width, but at other times it
dwindles down to a fast stream only 40 to 50 feet wide. It
was on the rough, dry sandy bed of the river that the whole
Brigade was encamped, and here preparations for a long trek
were made. The weather was fine, but the strong winds that
blew and raised sandstorms made it an unpleasant resting place,

R

and no one regretted the order to move, which was received on the 9th of March.

Before ending this chapter on our stay in Macedonia, the following letter, written from Greece, might prove interesting :—

" Macedonia is a lovely country, and the lack of reading matter a considerable hardship. It is a land of bare treeless valleys, strongly reminiscent of the Veldt and high snow-clad spurs of the Balkans. Of the people, the less said perhaps the better. St. Paul in old time was of the opinion that the Thessalonians were ' lewd persons of the baser sort,' or words to that effect, and my experience is that they have not improved by keeping in the interim. A motley mixture of Turks and Bulgars with a smattering of Greeks, they are undoubtedly picturesque in garb, more undoubtedly filthy in person and habits, and most undoubtedly the finest collection of thieves, brigands and cut-throats that could be brought together. When the brigandage business is slack, as at present, they apparently fill in their spare time as herdsmen and shepherds. We are employing considerable numbers in road making and the other day I heard the following : A party of Greeks came along towards our transport, and one bright youth on sighting them lifted up his voice to his chum, ' Look out, Jack !   Here comes Ali Baba and his forty —— thieves.'

" The days are hot and the nights bitterly cold, while at times a terrifically strong and piercing wind, called the Vardar blast, blows from the Balkans. Taken altogether the majority of us heartily wish ourselves back in France."

CHAPTER XXX

On the 10th of March, 1917, reveille was at an early hour, and by eight o'clock in the morning the 179th Brigade had formed up in column of route together with the Artillery, Royal Engineers, Machine Gun Corps, and Army Service Corps detachments which had joined it since its arrival at Katerina in December, 1916. The whole town turned out to bid us farewell, and the local band played appropriate music in the market place. Flags decked the low-built houses of the town, and the people of Katerina were sorry to lose the Brigade which, during its short stay, poured thousands of " drachmas" into the town coffers, turning indolence and poverty into business and wealth. The French Commandant also did honour to the British troops and furnished a strong guard of honour, which gallantly stood at the " Present " while the Brigade passed by. The first day of the march was to a place called Tuzla, near the coast some ten miles north of Katerina, and although ten miles on a good English road is a small journey, the badly cut-up roads of Greece and the heavy kit the men were carrying made the journey appear to be twice its actual distance. Mules were loaded to their fullest capacity, and many loads slipped off, causing disorganisation on the march. Eventually, after about five hours' marching, the Brigade reached the night's bivouac area, where a terrific cold wind was blowing from the sea. However, " bivvies " were erected and a meal prepared, and every one retired for the night, wondering what the next day would bring.

Every one was astir early the following morning, and after an early breakfast the camp was packed up. Then the real fun of the day commenced ; this was the loading of the mules. Although I have not yet described this performance in detail it might interest those who did not actually participate in the trek. Loads were arranged and specially lashed with strong ropes. The great art was to prepare loads in pairs, each of which was of equal weight. Of course, with such articles as blankets, Lewis gun panniers, ammunition boxes, where an equal number solved the difficulty it was an easy matter ; but when it came to the question of cooks' gear, pioneer tools, officers' valises, and so on, it developed into a matter of either exceeding great skill or pure luck. Having thus made up two loads of equal weight and examined the mule's girth, the muleteer would stand at the animal's head and say nice things to it with a view of taking its attention from the loads. Two men would then stand on either flank of the beast and lift the loads, with the intention of hooking them on to the saddle by the rings attached to the lashing ropes. The loading on both sides had to be performed simultaneously, or otherwise the weight on one side only simply twisted the saddle under the mule, annoying the animal to such an extent that it would immediately kick out and break loose, dashing about with the load under its stomach. Such escapades on the part of the mules were all too frequent ; the mules hated the loads, and to add to the difficulties of the performance commenced to dance a " tango " on the feet of the unfortunate fatigue men trying to persuade it to carry a couple of heavy side loads. Towards the end of this trek, however, the men became aware of this side-stepping by the mules, and eventually experts in each Company developed, and the balancing of the loads, the synchronisation of the hooking-on process, became matters of skill as the result of sad experience.

From Tuzla the line of march was to Livanovan, and as a contrast to the very cold wind of the previous day the sun poured down, and the journey of twelve miles was over the same badly-made roads, while steep gradients were also encountered. On the 12th of March the Brigade proceeded to Gida, a further distance of twelve miles. On arrival a flat piece of ground was found for the camp. On the march each man carried a few pieces of stick or wood from ration boxes, and at the end of the day's march a supply of wood for fires was immediately ready on arrival in camp. During this trek great credit was due to the cooks, both in the companies and the officers' messes, for the splendid way in which they immediately set to and prepared meals for their expectant clients at the end of the day's march. I know that at Gida, Evison (" D " Company's mess cook) and his batman pals had so trained themselves that on the arrival of their Company Officers from the men's lines, after seeing the mules unloaded and the men settled down, a splendid meal of fried eggs and bacon, biscuits and butter, tea, and Welsh rarebit was spread on the mess table-cloth. (" D " Company always boasted of this cloth, regardless of its doubtful snowy whiteness at times.

The next day, the 13th of March, was very trying owing to the great heat and the distance covered, just over 20 miles. A midday halt was made on that part of the road where the transport section had had such a disastrous time on their journey from Salonica in December, and the mule drivers regaled every one with the horrible details of their experiences. The roads were being improved near the town of Topscin by parties of Bulgar prisoners under French guards. As the column approached Topscin village the sounds of music greeted it. The town was in the hands of the French, and their band had turned out to welcome us. The " Marseillaise " and " God Save the King " were rendered alternately while the whole Brigade marched by.

Just after leaving Topscin we crossed the Vardar River, and a couple of miles beyond, the new camping ground was reached ; but the rain which had then set in made the arrival miserable. It was then 6.0 p.m. and every one was dead-beat, but an issue of rum livened us up a little.

The following morning bivouacs were struck and the march resumed as far as Amantovo, a distance of 14 miles, and it was during this march that the first man of the Battalion fell out, and only the excessive heat caused him to faint, showing how splendidly he had stuck to it. The camp at Amantovo was on soft, grassy ground, and the pegs of our bivouacs were driven in with ease, a change after the stony nature of our previous camping grounds. The last part of the day's march had been over grassy downs, and the beautiful weather made it enjoyable. To add to the happiness, however, there was a surprise in store ; a ration of oranges was issued that night. The next day's march was to be performed in two parts. The start was made about 8.0 a.m., and the route lay through pleasant valleys and over undulating grassland. A few miles from Amantovo the Battalion marched past the Commander-in-Chief of our forces in Salonica, General Sir G. F. Milne, K.C.B., and his staff. The General was greatly impressed with the fitness of the Battalion. About midday a halt was called and cooking commenced. Plenty of water, duly chlorinated, of course, was drawn from the local streams. In the afternoon small card parties were made up in the Battalion, others slept, while others read novels ; each man in some sections carried a small sevenpenny novel, and by exchanging there was plenty to read. Just ahead of the Battalion was a tumulus, and from this point it was said that the " line " could be seen, but of course it was forbidden ground. The progress of the Battalion having been thus barred, we settled down to a very pleasant, restful afternoon in the warm sunshine, little dreaming of the eccentricities of the Macedonian springtime.

At twilight the order was given to move off, and with darkness came rain, and such cold rain, too ! The wind sprang up and the first few miles were spoilt by " concertina work " by the column, a most dreaded thing for infantrymen with a heavy kit. However, after the first halt the movement of the column settled down and became more tolerable ; but accidents to the mules soon disorganised the column again and connection in the dark became difficult. The Battalion floundered on through mud and slush over what must have been ploughed land, I think. Mules now began to fall out with unfailing regularity and men were constantly detailed from the ranks to reload them, and a very straggling column resulted. No one seemed to be certain of the way over this strange country in the pitch darkness. No one appeared to have a watch, either, for no halts were called ; certainly the ground was too thick in wet mud for halting purposes, but after three hours marching over such ground in pouring rain all infantrymen felt the strain. Onwards the Battalion struggled, mile after mile, through this awful morass of mud and the pelting rain. Every one longed for a halt, but this was not to be ; not until the Battalion arrived on the outskirts of Karasuli did that precious whistle break the silence. Then every one just sat down in the middle of the road. The men had marched for six hours without a halt or even taking off their packs. Remarkable to relate, the number of men who fell out was practically nil ; there were no estaminets here, and to fall out would mean a lonely night in the desolate wilds of northern Greece ; and this was an unpleasant prospect. At Karasuli a fairly long halt was made and spirits revived, but being under enemy observation no smoking was allowed ; this was the last straw, and the Hun and his Allies had curses heaped upon their heads that night, if ever. Rumour that the final halt was only a few hundred yards ahead helped to improve matters, but even this flicker of hope was damped by the heavy rain that constantly poured down. The whistle sounded again, and off the Battalion moved, though no one knows the route taken to this day. Brigade staff certainly did its utmost to sort out the mixed column of men, mules and transport of all regiments.

The country here was broken by deep gullies or " nullahs " along which the water rushed in torrents. For over an hour the Battalion staggered along over the broken ground, one moment stumbling down a steep rugged bank of a nullah, the next crawling on hands and knees up the slippery bank opposite, and frequently wading nearly waist deep in water. About 1.0 a.m. the Battalion halted. Rain had fallen for hours and the ground was churned up into a quagmire, but a halt, even in these surroundings, was welcome. Men threw off their packs and, in spite of their weariness and exhaustion, it was to be admired that all the mules, which had also struggled through this terrible journey, were immediately unloaded. Kits, rifles and mule loads had been thrown on the ground by the overwrought men, and some just lay down from sheer fatigue ; others stood in the bitter cold and awaited the dawn. Some of the more energetic dared to put up their bivouacs, but soon gave up the idea of sleeping owing to the terrific cold wind that blew. Those who were able to move were issued with rum, but I am afraid that owing to the difficulties of the situation and the fact that many men had fallen into a delirious sleep it was unequally divided, and in the darkness it was difficult to discern whether a staggering man was the outcome of too much marching or too much rum. Towards dawn the downpour ceased a little, but the shivering troops, mud from head to foot, still stood in the withering clutches of the Vardar blast, and one man remarked, looking at the surrounding swamp, " Guess I'm standing in the Blasted Vardar, too ! " Gradually daylight appeared, and what a scene—drenched men, cold, miserable, hungry and tired. The sick parade was extremely large that morning. Many had become so exhausted that they had laid down in the wet mud during the night and the next morning were, of course, physical wrecks ; others had reached a state of delirium and wandered about bereft of their senses, and mention has already been made of the third group, the men who had " really " got the rum. The balance of the Battalion simply felt done up. However, all those who had not been sent to the field hospitals at Karasuli set to work and dragged from beneath the mud, rifles, equipment, bivouac sheets and remnants of the mules' loads, and sorted them into dumps. The sun shone and life appeared possible, even if not desirable, in this wilderness of mud. About midday the Quartermaster's Stores sent fatigue parties to an A.S.C. depôt a mile or so away, and fresh meat and rations were issued. Small fires were soon started and the old " gyppa " was on the boil. Every one looked forward to a nice hot meal, when orders for an immediate move were received. One can pass over this scene without expressing the views of the troops ; it can well be imagined how pleasing it was to see the half-cooked " gyppa " poured away into the mud, as the cooks' gear had to be packed on the mules at once.

Soon afterwards the clank of the entrenching-tool handle against the rifle butt and the rattle of the water bottle and other impedimenta associated with troops on the march was heard. The Battalion moved off with Platoons at intervals of 100 yards. The road from Karasuli was in good condition and had dried up under the warmth of the sun and the constant wind, but a mile or so from the camping ground to that main road was covered with deep nullahs and ravines. As we passed over it we wondered how the Battalion had ever marched over such ground the previous night. Once on the main road a decent step was taken and the troops felt the benefit of a good road, and made headway. However, the wind renewed its violence of tne previous evening and blew into the face of the Battalion so that the benefit of the better road was soon nullified by the Vardar Blast. Clothing was still saturated with the rain of the night before, and the cold wind simply pierced us to the bones. Snow fell and added to the misery of things and soon the country-side was white; to say nothing of the Father Christmas-like appearance of the troops. When darkness came things really became difficult and the march developed into a hopeless plodding along, fighting against a biting cold head wind the whole while. For the first nine miles the route was along the main road, and the mules retained their loads with comparative ease, and not like the previous day's march when they slipped and fell over on the treacherous muddy tracks.

So extreme was the cold that after each ten minutes halt it was with difficulty that men rose from the ground; most of them were frozen stiff. About 10.0 p.m. the head of the column was seen crossing the rough ground on the left of the main road. Hopes were raised, and if even a bivouac in the snow was an unpleasant prospect, the ending of the march was some consolation. Visions of a new camp were becoming plain, but when the Battalion followed this column across the rough ground for over an hour hopes were shattered.

From the roadway onwards men of all regiments in the Brigade lined the route; floundering over the rough ground after a stiff march had proved too much for even some of the stalwarts who had braved the night at Karasuli. Transport limbers and mules blocked the way, either stuck in the small nullahs that crossed the route or else the animals had become too exhausted to move. In fact, it was not an uncommon sight to see dead mules on the ground, having succumbed to the extreme cold, and when mules " gave up the ghost " it can be well judged how the men suffered. No one had any fear of being lost this night should he fall out ; the route was well marked by deserted limbers, dead mules and fallen loads. About midnight the journey ended and the Brigade halted near the deserted farm buildings which were occupied by the Headquarters of the Brigade in the line. When the signal to halt was given every one just sat down exhausted, but the lesson of the previous night had been learnt, and little sleep was attempted. Small fires were lighted and mess tins were brought out and tea was made. " Scroungeing" parties went round and "won" blankets, tarpaulins, etc., from wherever possible, regardless of the Battalion or Company to which they belonged. Some officers, by dint of hard work, had even erected a bell tent, having a limber pole for its support. Whose tent and whose pole were never questioned. The night thus passed fairly quickly and every one made the best of a bad job. The snow had ceased, and it was, therefore, an improvement on the downpour twenty-four hours previously. As soon as daylight came every one was astir with the exception of the favoured few who had confiscated a pile of officers' valises and rigged up a temporary shanty. However, their rest was soon disturbed and orders were given to " fall in." The day was brighter and this cheered us a little. The Battalion soon marched off and soon sites were allotted to Companies in the deep nullahs or ravines about 500 yards from the deserted farm buildings. In the warmth of the sun, the sheltered positions in the ravines soon made us forget the discomfort of the night. The debris of the previous night was collected and every one enjoyed a hot meal which the cooks soon prepared. The afternoon was spent in rest and sleep.

However, war is war, and there is no rest for the wicked. The writer, together with another officer and some N.C.O.'s from each Company, were detailed to go up to the line for reconnaissance purposes that very afternoon. But even the darkest cloud has its silver lining, and after a trudge of four miles the party which had come over the skyline in twos and threes were welcomed by the Headquarters of the London Irish (2/18th London Regiment), and were soon detailed to Companies for the night. It was the 17th of March, and the London Irishmen who had been settled in the part of the line for some weeks celebrated their patron Saint's day in the proper style, and the requisite canteen stores and drinks had been acquired. No one could have been more hospitable, and the wretched advance party which had left Kolonova that afternoon felt that the war was not so bad as it might have been. Perhaps it would not be out of place to mention here that one of the toasts drunk in the Company dug-out where the writer was so kindly entertained was " To our 1st Battalions, the 1st Civil Service Rifles and the 1st London Irish Rifles." These Battalions were serving in France with the 47th Division and had curiously left England on St. Patrick's Day in 1915. The 17th of March is " The day " in the history of our 1st Battalion, but it has its place in the history of the 2nd Battalion. It was the end of what is popularly known as the " Karasuli Trek."

During the past week the Battalion had marched from Katerina, near Mount Olympus, to Kolonova, on the Doiran Front ; a distance of about 100 miles had been covered in seven days. The march was over rough country the whole way. Extremes of weather had been encountered during these few days ; from the hottest of Mediterranean suns at Livanovan to the wettest of oriental rains at Karasuli, and to the bleakest of blizzards and snowstorms that the Balkan Heights at Kolonova can produce. The man who was able to stick to his guns throughout this trek can well boast, and only the terrible experiences of the last two nights of the journey deprived many of the same boast.

CHAPTER XXXI

ON THE DOIRAN–VARDAR FRONT—THE ADVANCE

A SHORT description of the situation on the Doiran–Vardar sector of the Salonica Front will no doubt assist the reader to better realise the type of operations peculiar to this theatre of war. A few miles west of Lake Doiran was a mountainous ridge running north and south, about five or six miles long, known as " P " Ridge. This chain consisted of a series of five distinct peaks, the southern one, " Pip 5," being about 800 feet high, while the remaining four progressively increased in altitude until " Pip 1 " at the northern end reached the height of about 1,700 feet (or 535 metres); this was the famous " 535 " which dominated the country for many miles around, in fact on a clear day the peak could be distinctly seen from the hills at Dudular near Salonica, some 60 miles away. The Bulgar held practically all this ridge of the " Pips " except at the lowest part at the south, where the British had gained a footing. The Bulgar was strongly entrenched on all the slopes of the ridge, and each peak was an almost impregnable fortress in itself.

From the northern end the enemy lines ran due west along a mountainous chain some 1,000 to 1,200 feet high through the town of Devedzili, thence south of Paljorca to Pobreg. Just east of Pobreg the line ran due south for some six miles along another ridge of hills about 600 to 700 feet high which terminated at the " Nose," a fortified stronghold on the borders of Serbia and Greece. From the " Nose " the enemy trenches were situated on the hills just north of Macukova, finally having the right flank on the banks of the Vardar at a point some four miles from the " Nose."

The British line ran from the southern extremity of the " P " ridge in a south-westerly direction to the village of Bekerli, from which point it ran practically due west to the Vardar, where our lines were only about 1½ miles from the enemy trenches. The whole of the British line was on the low hills just north of the Cidemli Dere, a valley through which a small stream of about 20 feet in width bubbled along.

South of this stream the reserve British positions were situated on the chain of the Kolonovan Heights (500 feet) which ran along

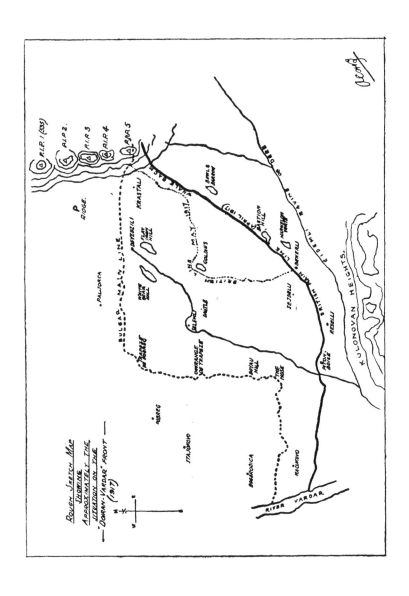

ROUGH SKETCH MAP
SHOWING
APPROXIMATELY THE
SITUATION ON THE
"DOIRAN-VARDAR" FRONT
(1917)

north of Ardzan, Smol and Karasuli. It will therefore be seen that only on our flanks were we in close touch with the enemy ; on the left flank near the Vardar for about four miles east of the river banks as far as Reselli opposite the " Nose " where the enemy line turned north, and on the right flank at the foot of the " P " ridge at its southern extremities south of the village of Krastali. Even at these points the lines were at least a mile apart. The remainder of " No Man's Land " consisted of a plain through which the ravine of the Selemli Dere formed a definite line between the opposing parties. From this ravine the ground was fairly flat for about 500 yards on each bank, but it soon developed into a land of hillocks some hundred feet above the level of the Selemli Dere plain, forming the foot-hills up to the higher ground held by the two armies. In this part of " No Man's Land " were dotted the deserted villages of Dautli, Selemli and Sejdelli. The enemy had taken up a strong defensive line on the high ground which overlooked the whole of the lesser hills on the southern side of the Selemli plain, and his observation on our movements was therefore good. Any movement by day on our part was restricted, and from the commanding position of " P " ridge he could practically look into our trenches which had been constructed on the for-ward slopes of the small hills north of the Kolonovan Heights. In daytime these trenches were therefore only held by a sentry group, while the remainder of the garrison retired to the small bivouac camps which had been dug in on the reverse slopes.

By reference to the sketch map at the commencement of this chapter it will be seen that no further advance on our part was possible beyond the Bekerli Village Line, for from " Pip 1 " the Bulgars could enfilade any camps that were pushed forward. Not until the whole of the " Pip " ridge was gained could any advance on the Vardar section be made.

The British Army had therefore to sit content on the line of low hills, each of which was made into a strong point held by a garrision at night and a sentry group by day. The whole front was strongly wired and the ground or dip between these hills held by a Lewis gun post, or sometimes a Vickers machine-gun section. The wire had been cunningly arranged so that all these re-entrants formed " culs de sac " into which heavy machine-gun fire could be poured by the defenders.

During daytime no one disputed " No Man's Land," but at night time strong patrols were sent out by both sides to obtain the mastery, and prevent raids or surprise attacks on the de-fensive lines that were held. Across the centre of " No Man's Land " was a line of large white stone pillars at regular intervals, representing the frontier between Greece and Serbia ; an interesting fact, though, of course, having no bearing on the actual operations in this part of the world.

The British transport lines and ration dumps were behind the cover of the Kolonovan Heights which ran parallel with the main Karasuli–Kilindir Road which made communication along the rear of our positions comparatively easy. From the transport up to the line the journey was done at night time, except in the case of individual runners, or perhaps two or three men in a party, but so keen was the observation of the Bulgar that even these small parties attracted the unpleasant attention of a " pip-squeak " gun which had the tracks over the ridge " taped " to a nicety.

On the 19th of March, 1917, the Battalion marched up to the line from its bivouacs at Kolonova and took over from the 2/18th London Regiment (London Irish). All reliefs were carried out by night and under cover of darkness the Battalion left its sheltered camp, by Platoons at intervals. Every one had been ordered to maintain silence and no smoking was allowed. All the average man knew was the fact that somewhere over the ridge at Kolonova was the line, how far or how near he was never told, and the order for strict silence on the march led him to believe that the enemy was fairly close to hand, although in point of fact the Bulgar was comfortably settled in the dugouts of his mountain stronghold at least five miles ahead. Knowing this fact the following incident on the march will be appreciated. A nervous private recently joined approached his Platoon Commander with a whisper, " Don't you think that officer on horseback ought to cover his luminous wrist watch ? " True, Major Oliver was in charge of the Battalion canteen, and probably had first choice of the luminous Ingersolls that occasionally came our way, but even the most luminous are not guaranteed to dazzle the eyes at a distance of five miles. However, such was the keenness of this rifleman to save his platoon from a strafe by the enemy artillery.

For a whole month the Battalion held the line from Waggon Hill, just east of Reselli village, to the village of Bekerli. On our left was a battalion of the 180th Infantry Brigade, while our neighbour on the right was the Queen's Westminster Rifles of our own Brigade. The Battalion front consisted of Waggon Hill, which overlooked the Selemli Plain and the village of Sejdelli in front, while the ground on the left flank was low and formed a branch of the Selemli Ravine, and made a dangerous entrance to the rear of our positions just opposite the " Nose." " D " Company occupied this hill, with " B " Company in immediate support in the valley of the Cidemli Dere. The right of the Battalion front was on the high ground near the ruined village of Bekerli, and formed the angle from which the

British line ran north-east through Bastion Hill, Bowls Barrow, Whaleback, Horse Shoe Hill to the foot of " Pip 5 " on the " P " ridge. " A " Company was responsible for the Bekerli defences, with " C " Company in immediate reserve, while Battalion Headquarters were farther back at Bekerli Ford, on the Cidemli Dere. As previously stated, movement was restricted during the daytime, which was spent in sleep, writing letters and card playing, leavened, of course, by fatigues and working parties for the improvements of dug-outs and similar work which could be undertaken by day under cover of the hills. No movement was allowed beyond an occasional runner to the support Companies or Battalion Headquarters. At night time, however, work commenced. The trenches were strongly garrisoned, and sentry groups were posted along the wire, while still farther out in " No Man's Land," about 500 yards from the wire, standing patrols of an N.C.O. and 20 men were posted in order to prevent the enemy from approaching our lines in force.

The support companies furnished large carrying parties to bring up rations, letters and the *Balkan News*, a newspaper specially printed in Salonica for British troops ; all of which arrived from the Quartermaster's stores at Kulonova, about one hour after dark. They also provided working parties to improve the trenches, which for the most part had been blasted from solid rock. Communication trenches were also made up to the forward companies, care being taken to conceal them in the numerous shallow dips in the ground as any sign of digging was sure to be strafed the next day. All earth had to be removed, as the smallest heap of soil above the level of the ground was looked upon by the Bulgar as the commencement of a new gun emplacement and consequently bombarbed. There is no doubt that the Bulgar took every advantage of his higher position, and his observers were very keen, and this together with the wonderful accuracy of his guns made us very careful to conceal all signs of digging.

The support companies also furnished an officer's patrol each night of about 24 men strong. These fighting patrols had orders to approach the enemy's wire on the other side of the plain. How different from the patrols of three or four men on the Neuville St. Vaast front in France, where movement was very restricted. On the Doiran front it became a nocturnal route march. A few points were sent ahead and the main body followed *en bloc*. Although instructions were issued to reach the enemy's wire it was rarely accomplished ; Bulgar patrols were always wandering about on the plain at night. In the area allotted to our Battalion for patrol work were the two villages of Dautli and Selemli, which were much nearer to the enemy's advanced posts than our own. To reach these villages and search them was about the limit of our adventures. The Bulgars were far too strong at this point, for here the Selemli Dere could be crossed by tracks which the enemy jealously guarded. Fortunately, though shots were sometimes exchanged no serious fighting occurred to the 2/15th London patrols. On the return journey towards daylight it was considered part of the scheme to halt at the village of Sejdelli, near our lines, and break down the woodwork in the houses already damaged by shell fire and bring doorposts, window frames and so on back into our lines for the cooks' fire. It was most amusing to hear the patrols heralding their safe return by loudly hammering on the woodwork of Sejdelli. Never a Bulgar fell into the hands of our patrols, but they always returned with plenty of wood.

Although in daytime it was not advisable to wander across " No Man's Land," on one occasion our Intelligence Officer, Lieutenant Andrew, and his batman, Private Joines, spent a day searching the village of Dautli. They walked to the village during the night and hid themselves at dawn in an empty house to watch the movements of the enemy near the fords across the Selemli Dere near by. Great was their surprise, however, when a party of eight Bulgars appeared from the other side of the village carrying some rabbits and hares. Discretion was the better part of valour and Andrew and his batman decided to keep quiet. After a few exciting minutes and by quietly sneaking around the houses they were able to evade the enemy shooting party, and spent the rest of the day quietly enough locating and sketching the enemy forward posts. They returned to our lines in the evening.

Life under these conditions was very pleasant and the Battalion thoroughly enjoyed its stay in this part of the line. The only interruption beyond the casual shelling of our trenches and camps was the occasional visit of a flight of enemy aeroplanes which crossed over and dropped small bombs near our bivouacs. Usually they passed right over and made targets of the horse lines and dumps in rear of the Kolonovan Heights, and only when they were driven off by our anti-aircraft guns did they attempt to expend their efforts on our small hillside camps. Aerial activity on this front was very persistent, and practically every day our bombing planes sailed over and bombed the railways and dumps behind the Bulgar lines.

Occasionally a fight in the air took place, but the commoner sight was the repeated attacks of the enemy airmen on our observation balloon at Kolonova. On one or two occasions it was brought down in flames, but more often the attacker was driven off by our anti-aircraft guns, and on one occasion a direct hit by an " Archie " shell brought down the offending airman. The plane fell in flames near our battalion transport lines, and curiously when the wreck reached the ground the machine gun was still spitting out bullets and a few men of a neighbouring regiment were wounded by them.

The enemy infantry troubled us very little, and only an occasional cross fire between patrols made us aware of their presence, and fortunately they made no endeavours to reach the Battalion front ; although at Bowls Barrow, a few hundred yards on our right, they made a determined raid on the 1st of April on a British post and inflicted casualties.

About the middle of April, however, our artillery became extremely active, and on the 20th the " Nose " and " P " ridge were heavily bombarded. This was the opening of an offensive on our part which was undertaken with a view of capturing the whole of " P " ridge. The bombardment was continued for three whole days with the intention of cutting the fields of wire which protected the Bulgar positions and to destroy his forward entrenchments. On the 23rd of April the volume of artillery increased considerably and continued until the night of the 24th, when the 2/20th Battalion of the London Regiment raided the stronghold of the " Nose." Under cover of this heavy bombardment the Blackheath Battalion approached the enemy wire, and although our artillery had damaged it considerably, it still formed a great obstacle to the raiders. Heavy machine-gun fire was encountered, and the front slopes of the " Nose " were heavily barraged by the enemy, who also used strong searchlights from the crest of the " Nose " which swept the forward part of the position. Only a few gallant fellows ever reached the Bulgar trenches and the casualties were very heavy. For several nights afterwards search parties were out bringing in wounded. For the actual raid there was little direct success, but it served its purpose and acted as feint attack which drew a great deal of the enemy's artillery fire, and thereby assisted the main attack which commenced that same night on the " P " ridge. This was successful, and Pip 4 and Pip 5 were captured after heavy fighting. The Battalion actually took no part in this general offensive, and fortunately the enemy's artillery was so deeply engaged in combating the two serious attacks on their lines at the " Nose " and on " P " ridge that most of us were able to look from our trenches and watch the pyrotechnic display on either side. There can be no doubt that the British suffered heavy casualties in the minor attacks and counter-attacks which followed this initial success on the " P " ridge, but any attack on such strongholds as the " Pips " must of necessity be at great expense. The battle raged for about four days, but gradually subsided, and on the 27th of April the Battalion was taken out of the line and marched back to Tetre Verte, just over the ridge of the Kolonovan Heights, " D " Company remaining

S

at Mektoub in immediate reserve to the London Scottish, who
were holding the line east of Bekerli. Of all the camps in the
Salonican area Mektoub was undoubtedly the safest, as it lay
behind the cover of the hill, and consisted of tiers of dug-outs
built into the very steep side of the hill. While out of the line the
Battalion found fatigues even harder than in the line, for as far
back as Tetre Verte one could wander about unobserved by the
enemy, and, therefore, people who were seen very little in the
front line were now very much in evidence.

On the eighth of May the line from the village of Krastali to
Waggon Hill was slightly advanced in order to straighten the
line which had been pushed forward by the partial success of
the forward movement on the " P " ridge. Of course, this
operation amounted to " peaceful penetration," and no attack
was necessary. The actual advance was made by the London
Scottish and the Westminsters on that part of the line north-east
of the Bekerli village, and was of course continued towards
Krastali by the division on their right. Only " D " Company
from Mektoub was engaged in this operation, having been
brought up in support of the London Scottish as far as Piton 5,
in rear of Middle Hill, and not to be mistaken for Pip 5 on
the " P " ridge. On the 179th Brigade front the movement was
performed without obstruction by the enemy, though further
north-west near the village of Krastali strong opposition was
met by the Division advancing from the Whaleback, and heavy
artillery support had to be given to assist this section of the
advance. Unfortunately one of the supporting batteries was
firing from the dip in rear of Piton 5 and inflicted several
casualties on " D " Company owing to their shells bursting at
the muzzle of the guns. Lieutenant Miles and Private Cutchee
were badly wounded, while Lieutenant F. W. Lewis and
Lieutenant Martin received minor wounds and remained on
duty.

The original line ran from Bekerli village north-west along
the forward slopes of Mamelon Vert, Bastion hill, Piton 6,
Hill 275, Scratchbury Hill, Bowls Barrow, along Whaleback to
Horse Shoe Hill, but after the advance the new line ran through
Pitons 1, 2, 3 and 4, Basin Hill, Single Tree Hill, Tomato hill
over Krastali Nullah forward of Whale Back, and on the Pip
ridge. After the night's operation on the 8th, " D " Company
returned to Mektoub under the cover of a heavy fog, the rest of
the Battalion having remained at Tetre Verte during the advance.

The next night, the 9th of May, " D " Company left Mektoub
as local reserve for the Westminsters, who pushed forward on to
Goldies hill, thus forming a salient in our new line between Basin
Hill and Tomato hill. The taking of Goldies by the Westminsters was resented by the Bulgar, who made a strong attack

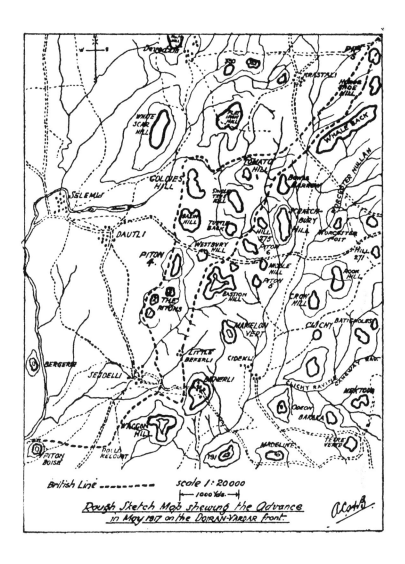

Rough Sketch Map shewing the advance in May 1917 on the Doiran-Vardar front.

British Line --------- scale 1:20000

|— 1000 Yds. —|

on the position with the assistance of a heavy artillery preparation. However, the Queen's Westminsters held on and drove
off the attack after heavy local fighting. On the 10th the
Battalion moved from Tetre Verte and took over the new line
from the London Scottish and also Goldies from the Westminsters.

The advance was comparatively a bloodless victory as far
as the 179th Brigade was concerned, nevertheless it was of great
importance on our front. From the new line the Selemli–
Dautli plain was now under our direct observation from Pitons
3 and 4, Basin Hill, Goldies, and these hills therefore became
positions from which an attack on the Selemli Fords could be
attempted. Furthermore, it denied the Bulgar of the freedom
of manœuvre over the captured part of " No Man's Land," while
facing north from Goldies and Tomato Hill we were in closer
touch with the enemy's advanced posts near Devedzili on the
slopes of White Scar and Flat Iron Hills. It had been impossible
for the British forces to push forward before as we had only
captured Pips 4 and 5 on the " P " ridge a few days previously.
The capture of these two pips enabled our men to occupy more
advanced positions without being under the direct observation
of the Bulgar. The enemy resented very much the aggression
on our part, and constantly shelled the newly-taken hills.

For the first fortnight of this period in the line the Battalion
was employed in consolidating the new positions, and on the
forward slopes of Tomato Hill, Single Tree Hill and Goldies,
trenches were dug and each night miles of barbed-wire entanglements were erected. All this work was carried out under
the protection of strong fighting patrols which took up their
positions on the ravine in front of Flat Iron Hill. In day time
the hills were left in charge of a single sentry group and one
signaller, while the remainder of the garrison retired for the day
into the small nullahs on the rear of each hill ready to counter-
attack should a message be received from the sentry group.
Throughout the day the enemy ranged in the new-cut trenches,
and with the exception of an unfortunate shell which wounded
Lieutenant Hounsell, our forward groups had a charmed life.
Only a minimum force was left behind the hills during the day ;
the remainder of [the men returned to the old camps on Hill 275
and Piton 6. At night time, however, when large working
parties were engaged in consolidating the positions, the enemy's
artillery became very active and many casualties resulted.

However, the hill which received the greatest strafe at nights
was Goldies ; the occupation of this point annoyed the Bulgar
very much. The hill consisted of three distinct peaks one in
front of the other, and were known as Goldies I, II, and III.
Trenches were sited on II and III, while on Goldies I a strong

patrol went out each night. For the first week of our occupation the hill was constantly shelled, and no less than ten distinct batteries showered their offerings on our heads. Fire came from White Scar direction in the north, from Pip 1 and 2 on the right, and from the Ouvrage de Trapeze on the left. In time we became acquainted with the direction of each battery and special sentries were posted who shouted " No. 6," and then all the men on Goldies II bobbed down to the shelter in the shallow trenches, the occupants of Goldies III taking no notice ; but when the sentry shouted, " No. 4 battery " it was the men on Goldies III who bobbed down while No. II men carried on with their work as though nothing had happened. Throughout the night the hill received a constant bombardment, and in one hour alone 600 shells fell near Goldies II and III.

Like the garrisons of the other hills the night garrison on Goldies retired for the day to the nullah in rear of the hill, leaving a small sentry group on Goldies II and III. The only approach to the top of Goldies from our lines was up a small ravine, and the Bulgars were apparently aware of its existence, the place was shelled both day and night, and was christened Pip Squeak Alley. At night, large working parties were sent up from the support battalion of the Brigade and dug a communication trench up the rear of the hill, and also one connecting Goldies II and III, but considerable casualties were incurred while the work was in progress.

The patrol on Goldies I pushed out scouts at night to the ravine in front, and one night a patrol, under Lieutenant Lewis, met a strong force of 20 Bulgars and a short sharp fight ensued. Our losses were only slight, chiefly wounds from bombs, but several Bulgars were killed, Lieutenant Lewis gallantly rushing the post and shooting two of the enemy with his revolver. The next night it was decided to raid the post with artillery support, but the patrol found that the Bulgar had fled. A special watch on this ravine was therefore kept, and Lieutenant Andrew and his batman Joines (" D " Company) spent the next day hidden in the bushes at the foot of Goldies I. A strong post of Bulgars came up to the ravine at daylight and settled themselves comfortably in the ravine, unaware of the watching couple. After a time a Bulgar N.C.O. wandered away from his comrades and approached the hiding place of Andrew and his batman, which was only 25 yards from the enemy. Suddenly the Bulgar's attention was attracted by a walking stick on the ground which had been left by Andrew just before dawn when they took cover in the bushes. The Bulgar picked it up and examined his souvenir, but before he had taken full details of his find Lieutenant Andrew and Private Joines rushed at him and captured him. Whether the other Bulgars near by were struck motionless or whether the N.C.O. was particularly unpopular it is not known, but in broad daylight and in full view of the enemy Andrew and his batman chased their prisoner towards our lines and soon got under the cover of the hill. No attempt was made to follow them, and the Bulgar N.C.O. was soon on his way to Brigade Headquarters. It was an amusing adventure, but the brilliant daring of our two representatives cannot be over-estimated. Surprise had beaten numbers.

The Battalion held these new positions until the end of May when the whole Brigade was taken out of the line and concentrated at Dache near Kolonova. Rumours floated around that Pip 3 on the " P " ridge was to be our objective, but on the 5th of June orders were received to march back as far as Hadji Junas, about 10 miles behind the line. The march was carried out on the night of the 5th of June, and rain poured down making the route over the soft marshy ground near Lake Ardzan slippery and treacherous. The Battalion remained here for three days in hot weather and had an enjoyable rest.

On the 8th of June the march was continued south via Janis and Kukus as far as Sargol. By this time it was apparent that Salonica was to be our destination, and on the 11th of June we arrived at Uchanter, not far from Dudular, our first camp in Salonica, having stayed one day at Nares and another day at Ambarkoy on the route. This trek from the line was much pleasanter than the trek to the line in the previous March. Marching was done at night under the silvery rays of a bright moon, each night's journey being about 15 miles. The weather was now becoming hot and marching at night was far more enjoyable than toiling along under the hot rays of the mid-day sun ; after leaving Hadji Junas the roads were good, and I think the march was enjoyed by most of us ; even the company mules behaved themselves and gave a minimum of trouble.

For the rest of the week the Battalion, in company with the remainder of the 60th Division, spent its time doing what the authorities were pleased to call " intensive training," which meant field work from morn to night. During the night of the 19th of June the Battalion packed up its home and marched to the docks at Salonica. Great secrecy was made of the destination, and even the Commanding Officer and his staff who went down to the ship earlier in the evening were not allowed to return to the camp in case the news leaked out. On the morning of the 20th of June the Battalion boarded the *Abbasieh*, and learning that the boat was one of the Khedival Line, Egypt was soon on every lip. The sea journey was pleasant, and on the 22nd of June, while at sea, dinners celebrating the anniversary of our departure from England, twelve months previously, were held in all parts of the ship.

CHAPTER XXXII

ALEXANDRIA, 23RD JUNE, 1917—ISMAILIA—BELAH—DESERT
TRAINING—GAMBLI AND TEL EL FARA—EL SHAULTH—PREPARA-
TIONS FOR THE PALESTINE OFFENSIVE

ALEXANDRIA was reached on the midnight of the 22nd June,
1917, and every one was pleased to get rid of the ever-present
encumbrance on board troopships—the life belt, which brought
back memories of the *Transylvania*. What a glorious sunrise we
witnessed, the harbour with its white buildings gave us a feeling
that we had at last again reached civilisation after our sojourn
in the wilds of Macedonia. Disappointment, however, was keen
when no leave ashore was granted, and only a few officers on duty
were allowed on the Docks. Lieutenant Lewis and the writer
however, under the pretext of purchasing food for the officers'
messes, spent a pleasant afternoon in the town and honoured
" Groppi's Tea Shop " with our presence, only to return to the
boat to find a train alongside with half of the battalion already
entrained. Early in the evening the Battalion started on its
journey to Ismailia on the Suez Canal. Every one enjoyed the
scenery of the Nile Delta while daylight lasted, and the beauty
of the Egyptian sunset appealed to all. Descriptions of Egypt
are to be found in many books, and I need hardly spend any
time in this short history to describe it, sufficient to say that the
Battalion thoroughly enjoyed the train journey and the excitement of being in a strange land made us forget the war.

Just after midnight the train pulled up at Ismailia and the
desert was struck for the first time. The moon was bright,
making night like day, and under the leadership of camp guides
the Battalion marched through the heavy sand for about a mile
or so and were soon allotted their lines in a huge base camp.
Tea, as usual, was soon made and partaken of. Every one
then retired to their tents and soon fell asleep ; here was a
land, at last, where blankets were not absolutely essential.
However, dawn is early in these latitudes, and the sun shone
down with considerable fierceness from about 5 a.m. The
oppressive heat of the tents soon woke every one, to say nothing
of the heavy hum of the aeroplanes from the local aerodrome,
which flew so low that they missed the tent tops by a few feet,

much to the dismay of the occupants. Flying cannot be carried out with such security in the heat of the day in Egypt, owing to the numerous air pockets, and during our stay at Ismailia reveille each morning was heralded by the heavy drone of these planes.

Ismailia, a small town on the Suez Canal, has a considerable French population, connected with the canal company. The town is very clean, even in the native quarters, while palm groves and tropical gardens furnish a relieving contrast to the surrounding desert of yellow sand. During the war it became the Base of the Australian Imperial Forces and also contained a large British Ordnance Depot. The main railway line from Port Said to Suez passed through the town, and on the east lay the large lakes of Timsah which form part of the Suez Canal. Leave passes into the town were granted, and this freedom was greatly appreciated by the men ; for since the days of Katerina we had not even been encamped near a village. Officers were invited as honorary members of the French Club which provided excellent luncheons and dinners at a reasonable cost. The place was crowded each evening and jolly times were spent there. Leave as far as Cairo and Alexandria was granted, and parties left daily for three days in one of these cities. A certain amount of training was carried out in the early morning and in the evening. The men in their pith helmets and " shorts " soon became acclimatised and accustomed to the terrific heat of the sun. Bathing parades in the lakes were held daily, and on the whole our stay at Ismailia was most enjoyable. At the end of July the Battalion moved by road as far as Kantara.

It was only a few days after our arrival at Ismailia that the Transport Section, minus horses, limbers, mules, etc., joined us from Salonica. They had left on board the *Cestrian*, and while at sea had been torpedoed and landed on the island of Mudros.

The following eye-witness story by the Transport Officer, Lieutenant T. W. Pearson, gives a short description of the sinking of the *Cestrian* :—

" The Battalion and part of the transport personnel sailed for Egypt a few days before the main body of the transport. The remainder of the transport received orders to load and embark on the *Cestrian*, on the 23rd of June, 1917. In addition to ourselves, with our limbers and animals, the Sherwood Rangers Yeomanry and a Divisional S.A.A. column sailed on the boat ; in all about 980 men and 960 animals.

" While we were loading, a German plane came over, but it flew at such a height that no one took much notice of it, but afterwards we thought it may have had something to do with the loss of the *Cestrian*.

" The Staff Veterinary Officers commented very favourably on the condition of our animals.

" We eventually sailed about 9.0 p.m. in the evening, under glorious conditions ; all the men and animals having comfortable berths. We were escorted by two destroyers, and these sailed on either side. We were about 12 or 13 hours out of Salonica early on Sunday morning, the 24th June, having just been dismissed from boat drill, and all was peaceful and the water as smooth as a billiard table, when suddenly the boat gave a terrible lurch ; the water around was churned up and shot to a great height on the starboard side. We had been torpedoed right amidship and the torpedo had struck the boilers, and soon every one was drenched with the sooty water which had been forced out of the funnels, and a funny looking lot we were.

" Part of the torpedo was forced on the upper deck. It was a terrible shock to all, as there was no warning whatever, but no one lost his head, every one went quietly to his respective boat station, without any panic. One of the life-boats allotted to us was broken up by the explosion, and, as an example of the coolness of our men, one of the fellows calmly produced a pocket camera and took snapshots of the damage.

" Nobody was allowed to go down below to the animals, though we could hear them screaming. If the incident had occurred about half an hour later we should have been below at stables and probably there would have been many more casualties. Fortunately, the casualties were confined to the ship's crew below. I heard that one had been killed and several seriously wounded and scalded.

" Within a few seconds, one of the destroyers was alongside and commenced transferring the men from the wreck aboard her by means of ropes and rope ladders, and while this was taking place she was firing at 1,000 yards range at the periscope of the Hun, and is believed to have made a hit. The second destroyer was circling around at full speed to keep the submarine from reappearing. Many of the men jumped overboard on the port side, but all were saved by the second escort. The wireless was soon busy, and in a very short time help came from all directions. The *Cestrian* did not sink at once, but was towed to within a few miles of land when she suddenly went down with all animals on board. It is thought that she would have been towed in safely except for the fact that so many port-holes had been left open.

" The men were landed at Mudros, which was one of the islands used as a base depot during the Dardanelles campaign. We were a queer-looking crowd when we landed ; some with nothing on their feet ; others just in shirts and trousers ; I don't think anyone was fully dressed. The staff on the island were wonderfully kind, and did all that was possible to make us comfortable. Within half an hour of landing at Mudros, all were billeted and were comfortably housed. The A.S.C. officials were very prominent and had rations out to the men in a very short time. During our stay here, the Y.M.C.A. deserves great praise, they got all manner of things for the men free of charge, and organised concerts. They did so well that I believe many of the men wrote home to their parents to send a subscription to the Y.M.C.A. We were on the island for just a week when we were picked up by a boat from

Salonica proceeding with troops of our own Brigade (London Scottish) for Egypt. We arrived in Alexandria minus our transport. I regret to say that the Battalion never had such good animals again all the time in the Palestine campaign as those which we had lost on the *Cestrian*. On arrival in Egypt the Battalion had to have the ' cast offs ' from the other Battalions in the Division who were reducing their strength, and, naturally, they handed to us all their ' duds,' and you never saw such ' clothes racks ' as they were. How the transport ever kept up with the Battalion on trek in Palestine I don't know. As time went on, however, we were able to make exchanges with the Remount Department and got rid of some of our worst.''

To return to the doings of the Battalion in Egypt. Their stay at Kantara, which had by this time developed into an immense base for the Egyptian Expeditionary Force, was only for a day, and they were soon on the train bound for the Palestine Front. This desert railway across the Sinai Peninsula for over a distance of 150 miles was one of the finest engineering feats of the war. Early in the war the British garrison had jealously guarded Egypt by means of outposts along the Suez Canal, and frequent raids on this defensive line were made by the Turks. It was, therefore, decided to push the line right out into the desert, and under the pressure of the Australian Mounted units, the Desert Mounted Corps and certain Infantry Divisions, the Turk was forced north, and when the Battalion joined the E.E.F. the firing line was just south of Gaza and running inland to Sheik Nuran on the south-east, generally speaking along the line of the Wadi Ghuzze. The whole of this advance from the Canal to Gaza had been made over the trackless waste of the Sinai Peninsula desert. In order to provide rations, stores and ammunition to the advancing troops a railway was laid by the Royal Engineers, ably assisted by working parties of the Egyptian Labour Corps of natives. The railway was kept up to the advancing troops at each step forward, and in order to provide water a pipe line ran at the side of the railway. Dumps and depots were made at intervals. At El Arish numerous sidings were built and stores and water were accumulated, and the small oasis of palm groves became a busy advanced base. From this point the line was pushed forward through Rafa, and when the Battalion arrived in Egypt the railhead was at Belah a few miles south of Gaza ; where there were large dumps and also two extensive stationary hospitals. On arrival at Belah the Battalion detrained and marched through loose sand, ankle deep, and great was the relief when it pitched its bivouac near the seashore ; the pleasure of sea bathing was shortlived, for in a few days, on the 29th July, 1917, the Battalion marched inland to join the Desert Corps. It was here at Belah that a new method of transport was introduced in the shape of the Camel

Transport Corps. That fascinating quadruped, the camel, was substituted for the mule, although a few mule-drawn vehicles still remained for general purposes. At Belah there were extensive camel lines ; each camel company, which consisted of 600 camels, having its own area. Ropes were staked across the width of these lines at regular intervals and to these ropes the camels were tethered a few yards apart. Each pair of camels had an Egyptian attendant, who was dressed in a long butcher-blue smock with the letters C.T.C. in red on the chest. These natives took great pride in their lines and kept them particularly clean, while the saddles were neatly arranged just in rear of the camels.

The saddle fitted over the hump of the camel, and at each side near the top of the saddle were fixed two stout bars of wood, about ten inches longer than the saddles, on to which the loads were hooked in rope nets. Water was carried in " fanatis " or copper tanks, which rested on the sides of the saddle. A certain number of men were detailed as camel guides from each company and section in the Battalion.

On leaving Belah, on the evening of the 29th July, the Battalion struck inland in a south-easterly direction along rough-made tracks, but the sand was loose and made the going very heavy. Although it was evening time the heat was terrific, and soon the perspiration was rolling down every one's face and the dust raised by the column soon formed into mud on the face and hands. Every one was choked with dust and eyes and nostrils became extremely painful. No one felt like singing, and even talking was rewarded with a mouthful of sand, one and all just blindly followed on through the cloud of dust raised by the four in front, which could only just be discerned. Water was limited, and it was practically forbidden to drink it ; only a mouth wash or gargle could be indulged in. After struggling for about nine or ten miles in this unpleasant fashion the whole column was relieved to move off the tracks and settle down for a rest. With no movement the dust clouds disappeared, and in the wondrous beauty of the moonlight of a warm Egyptian night bivouacs were soon erected, but water was too scarce to make tea, and doubts arose as to when the next issue would arrive. Nevertheless, tiredness overcame the Battalion, and it was soon asleep. The next morning the sun poured down, but the arrival of the water camels cheered us and the routine of desert life, which was to be our existence for some time to come, had begun. After a day's rest, which included the kicking about of a football by some of the more energetic, the Battalion moved off again in the evening, about 4 p.m., and plodded its weary way past Sheik Nuran to Gamli on the Wadi Ghuzze. This was a repetition of the previous night's march in every detail, except that the ending was not a simple right wheel on to the level desert, but as a special treat a descent of the steep cliffs of the wadi banks had to be negotiated. This descent was difficult with such appendages as company mules, camels and transport, and was followed by a mile over the stony bed of the wadi. About midnight the Battalion halted and settled for the night under the steep banks of the wadi. The next day the companies went out to take over the line on the Gambli defences. Reliefs were carried out by day and companies simply marched over the desert in mass, a most amusing performance after the communication trenches in France and the careful night reliefs on the Salonica Front. At this point of the line the Turks were at least 20 miles away, and, therefore, precautions from shelling were not necessary. This, indeed, was a pleasant part to hold and keep. Strong points well wired around were held, these being about 150 yards apart. The right flank of our line curled back so that it actually faced away from the Turk. The front was protected by night by cavalry patrols of Australian Light Horse, while to the east the Desert Camel Corps was operating as a mobile flank guard. Bivouacs were arranged in the small wadis or fissures in the ground and, of course, movement was not restricted. To those who were not privileged to see this part of the war it would be humorous to think of the sentry by day standing in the trench shewing well above the parapet under the protection of a huge umbrella-like shade which could be seen for miles around. Although the war in this theatre lacked shot and shell it had other horrors in the shape of oppressive heat, limited supplies of water, sandstorms, and numerous flies. In addition to the ever-present insect life associated with active service and the trenches, there were centipedes, scorpions, tarantula spiders and small snakes, which invaded our blankets. Chameleons were also plentiful and were kept as pets, though we never committed the atrocity attributed to a man in a Scottish Division on the Palestine Front who placed a pet chameleon on his tartan kilt and wondered why the poor little beggar suddenly died.

An average day in these parts was as follows : Early morning company drill in front of the wire, breakfast, and then utter collapse and seeking of shade until about 4 p.m. The only joy of the hot day was the arrival of the camels with water, and even this water was strongly chlorinated. Water was drawn from the Wadi Ghuzze where, by digging down for a few feet, pools of water were frequently found. During the day every one lay down and put pieces of muslin over their faces, hands and exposed knee caps, so that the flies should not be too irritating. Each afternoon a hot wind, called the " Khamsin," blew regularly and brought with it a sandstorm. Drifting sand found its way into every nook and cranny ; the food was soon covered and things were generally unpleasant while the storm lasted. It was during one of these afternoons that a private remarked: " They call this a land of milk and honey, eh ! One tin between 20 men and not a b——bee to be seen." However, about 4 p.m. each day the atmosphere cooled a little ; letter writing (not to forget the inevitable censoring), card playing and dinner were the next items on the programme, only to be marred by the company drill and exercises that followed.

At night-time sentry groups were posted by each platoon in its own strong point, and visiting patrols wandered between the posts throughout the night. It was a short night and no aerial torpedoes or other types of frightfulness disturbed the tour of duty. Each evening about 5 p.m. large bodies of Australian Cavalry went out to the front, sometimes accompanied by 'Armoured Cars, and took up an outpost line some five or six miles ahead of the defensive line. But even with this cavalry screen it was possible for a strong raiding party of Turks to attack one of our posts. In fact, only a short time before our arrival, our predecessors had been surprised one morning by a heavy bombardment with field guns, which some adventurous Turks had brought up under cover of darkness.

The Battalion, however, remained in undisputed possession of this part of the line until the 12th August, when it was relieved by the 2/13th Londons (Kensingtons) and retired to Tel el Fara, renowned as being a camping ground of Richard Cœur-de-Lion and his Crusaders. Tel el Fara was a high cliff jutting out into the Wadi Ghuzze and could be seen for many miles around and was used as an observation post. It was the local landmark for all who were lost on the desert. It is an easy matter to be lost on the desert, as each square mile is identical with its neighbours, and only a feature like Tel el Fara helped the wanderer.

The rest of the month was spent in training and lectures, when the heat permitted, and was only varied by an occasional route march in the early morning, not a pleasant outing. The tracks were not watered by the local borough council and chewing grit was the only occupation of the silent troops ; talking and singing was impossible, and this denial always added to the monotony of the march. Practice attacks were also carried out against imaginary enemies.

By the beginning of September the Battalion had moved to El Shaulth, near Shiek Nuran, and remained there to prepare for the offensive which was to be made in Palestine. The men had become accustomed to the heat and no longer was it necessary to reserve parades until evening time. All day and every day training was carried out with vigour, until Brigade operations in the way of advanced guards, attacks and long night marches became frequent. A rifle range was built and field firing was done. It may be interesting to mention that some of our tactical schemes were carried out some six or seven miles in front of the wire of the defences. On one occasion the Brigade set out on a long night march by the assistance of many luminous compasses and numerous pacers, the objective being a lone tree standing in the open desert some ten miles away from our camps. The march was made and by all the careful calculations we arrived at our destination about two hours before dawn. A halt was called, but no trace of the lone tree could be found, and after an energetic search by mounted officers and a consequent " pow-wow " the verdict, " Lost," was given, and there was nothing to do but to wait till dawn. When the sun rose it transpired that we were in the correct spot, but during the night some Australian Troop, which had run short of wood, had cut down the tree which had stood alone in the desert on the previous day, and to all appearances had stood since the days of the Flood, only to be felled by the hand of a " Dinkum." The opinion of the Brigade staff who had arranged this pleasant little outing is not recorded, but it is thought was not complimentary to our friends from the Antipodes.

Plans for the great attack were being drawn up about this time, and officers made reconnaissances towards the Turkish lines. These outings were no small undertakings. A party of officers and grooms would leave El Shaulth about 5 a.m. in the morning and ride over the desert to the more rugged and undulating country to the south of Beersheba, and then spend some hours in the heat of the day in scouting over the hills on foot to become acquainted with the ground, and at the same time doing their best to evade the Turkish patrols which frequented the hills. The party would then rendezvous at a given time in the early evening and start on the homeward journey. A halt would be called about ten miles from the Turkish lines, at which point it was considered safe to disregard the Turk. Here, under the glorious moonlight, a picnic would be held and the adventures of the day would be recounted, and after a smoke the journey would be resumed, camp being reached by about 2 a.m. the next morning. From the Turkish lines to the Wadi Ghuzze landmarks were definite enough, but on the other side of the wadi there was nothing but sand for miles. Everyone knew the most direct route to the camp, and, of course, this was the beginning of an argument which often ended in parties of officers going off in different directions. At different times during the night these parties struck the camp ; some had taken the direct route, some had been misled by lights in other camps ; others found that some camp which had existed when they went out had moved during the day, and so on.

However, on return to camp there was always a hot meal ready, prepared by our faithful batmen, who waited up for us. A word here perhaps would not be out of place in praise of the batmen of the Battalion. Veritable " scroungers," they always thought of their officers, and nothing was too hot or too heavy, not even the Company Commander's valise. At the end of each day's trek or manœuvre they forgot their own fatigue and prepared meals for the mess, the variety of which was confined to the army rations and the ever-present issue of sand.

The only excitement of the war at El Shaulth was the daily visit of two enemy aeroplanes to our camps and a few days' operations at Hiseia, on the Wadi Ghuzze, where we tackled the banks of the wadi instead of trenches dug in the flat sand, and where we had already exhausted the possibility of taking cover on such ground during the attack.

Besides the shortage of water, fuel was also very limited, and Egypt was practically denuded of trees to provide fuel for the E.E.F. One Company cook, however, had different views as to the origin of his firewood, and after vainly endeavouring to chop a hard piece of olive wood which had been issued to him, paused, and with much emphasis consigned the trunk to a far hotter fire than his own, remarking what he required was " wood and not Adam's petrified doorposts."

So far I have only spoken on the warlike side of our stay at El Shaulth, but among the pleasanter things of life was the leave to Cairo or Alexandria which had been granted. With what joy those few miles over the desert to Shiek Nuran were traversed, followed by a scramble for the leave train and then a long train journey on the Desert Railway to Kantara, which took about twelve hours. At Kantara a rush was made for the Divisional Rest Camp, a wash and shave and breakfast and a dash for the first available train on the Egyptian State Railways and then a comfortable journey to Cairo or Alexandria. I need hardly describe either of these cities, for as holiday resorts they hold a world-wide reputation. The return to the line about nine days later was never so pleasant. The heat became oppressive again, the meal at the rest camp at Kantara was adversely criticised, and the desert train journey was monotonous in the extreme. However, on rejoining the Battalion, tales of the Continental, Shepheards, the Pyramids, the Sphinx, the Barrage and so forth were told, while the fellows from Alexandria talked of nothing but the Majestic, the Regina Palace, the Races, Bathing, and Groppi's.

By the middle of October the serious side of the campaign in Palestine had commenced, and most people had had their leave in Egypt. Leave was stopped and football and sports in the evenings, and an occasional Divisional concert party were our only entertainments. The post was regular and parcels were received, although occasionally a foot-note in Battalion orders to the effect that the mails from the United Kingdom on certain dates had been lost at sea through enemy action made us depressed. Canteen stores were plentiful, as we were near the railhead at Shiek Nuran, but they soon became less in quantity as the ration trains were then being employed for war material for the coming advance. Towards the end of October the attack on Beersheba was a popular topic, and the hard training was not to be in vain. The Battalion was fit and strong, although malaria and fever had claimed their victims, and a fair number were sent down to Base Hospitals. However, the Battalion was ready and willing to show the Turks the way to the north.

While at El Shaulth several changes took place in the higher command. Major-General J. S. Shea, C.M.G., had taken over the Division from Major-General E. S. Bulfin, C.B., who had been promoted to the command of the 20th Corps, while Lieut.-Colonel C. de Putron left us to go to the School of Instruction at Zeitoun, near Cairo, his place being filled by Lieut.-Colonel T. E. Bisdee (Duke of Cornwall's L.I.). Colonel Bisdee was intensely popular with all ranks from the first day of joining the Battalion, and in the short time he commanded us before Beersheba he worked wonders. The Company Commanders at this time were Captains C. H. Rimington, F. W. Lewis, K. A.Wills, and A. C. H. Benké.

CHAPTER XXXIII

BEERSHEBA, 1917 (21ST OF OCTOBER TO 4TH OF NOVEMBER)—
WADI WELFARE

THE left flank of the Turkish line, which ran south-eastward from Gaza, formed a stronghold around the south-eastern outskirts of Beersheba. In the main scheme of the advance in Palestine the 60th Division was detailed to attack and take those trenches covering the Khalasa Road which ran from Beersheba on the south-west of the town. On the right of the Division were the 21st Corps cavalry regiment (1/2nd County of London Yeomanry) and they were ordered to make an enveloping movement simultaneously with the main attack on the Beersheba defences. From the desert line held by the Battalion near the Wadi Ghuzze at Gambli a long approach march was necessary. On the 21st of October, 1917, the Battalion moved from the Wadi Ghuzze, near Gambli, where the 179th Brigade had been concentrated. The march was not a difficult one, as the track lay over country of a more solid surface than the desert we had just left, but some sympathy must be given to " D " Company of the Battalion, who had marched some additional eight miles at midday across the desert from Divisional Head Quarters at Shellal, where they had represented the Battalion at a Divisional Church Parade in the morning and had been on parade since the early hours of dawn.

In the cool of the evening the column started out full of glee, knowing that at last a march was to be undertaken without that horrible feeling that the further one went from camp the further one would have to retrace one's steps. The weather was fine and the journey was along the high ground overlooking the Wadi Shanag, a continuation of the Wadi Ghuzze, past the peak of Goz Mabrouk and across the Shanag at Bir Esani to the high ground that lay between the fork of the function of the Wadis Imalaga and Esani, just south of Rashid Bek. About midnight the column halted, and the Battalion took up an outpost line reaching from Rashid Bek, a desolate, empty eastern house standing some 690 feet above sea-level, to the north bank of the Wadi Imalaga. The remainder of the Brigade extended the line to the north as far as the Karm–Beersheba Road. The line was taken up on the 22nd of October, and the Battalion remained here until the 28th of October. During the week forward reconnaissance work was done, and, under cover of the outpost, stores and guns were brought up by means of tractors, while large columns of camels and small white donkeys brought up ammunition, etc. A large dump of foodstuffs and stores was formed near the Khalasa–Esani road, and it was amusing to think that this dump was some few hundred yards in advance of the outpost line, although in front of the dump there was a cavalry screen of Australian mounted troops. Even if the Turk had attacked in force the outpost line would have proved a strong defence, though perhaps the dump and its camel lines would have been sacrificed. Strict orders were given to the officers in the line that no one was allowed through the line without strict scrutiny, as small bodies of nomadic Arabs acting as spies were always wandering about this neighbourhood. One evening a horseman approached one of our posts and was promptly halted. He was challenged. He argued in his Australian twang that he was friendly, but the officer was adamant and ordered him to advance for further investigation, to which he replied, " Do I look like a —— spy with these 400 —— camels ? " and lo ! from the darkness in front loomed a silent column of camels which had lost their way when returning from the dump and had not used the recognised gap in the line further to our right flank.

During this week every one wrote letters as it was a doubtful thing when the post would next be sent, once the advance had commenced. Every one rested and no movement by day was encouraged. Such relaxation came as a welcome change after the weeks of hard gruelling, and, to quote the words of our Commander-in-Chief, Field-Marshal Sir Edmund Allenby, on the occasion of his admission to the Freedom of the City of London, when he referred to the 60th Division :—

" Before it attacked Beersheba it was exercising so hard to keep fit that the G.O.C. ordered his men to eat and drink more and not work so hard."

Not only for purposes of rest, however, was this stay made at Bir Esani. We had left our old line with its water supply many miles away, and it was necessary for the R.E.'s to develop and exploit wells that existed at Abu Ghalyun under the cover of the mounted patrols out to our front.

Our own part of the line was held by " C " and " D " Companies, with " A " and " B " in support. Fortunately the Turk did not trouble us, although a short distance further north a skirmish took place between the 74th Division and the Turk near the Karm–Beersheba road. The enemy was driven off with loss and gave no further trouble. On Sunday evening, the

28th of October, the march was resumed as far as Abu Ghalyun, which lay some seven or eight miles south-west of the Beersheba defences. The march was only a matter of a few miles and was along the level though stony bed of the Wadi Imalaga. The Battalion halted but bivouacs were not erected, and the very minimum of movement was made. It was a glorious day, and final preparations for the attack were made; aeroplane maps were studied and final orders were issued. The Commanding Officer told the Company Commanders, and through the usual channels the real facts of the case were put before the private soldier. Arrangements for transport and water were made, but the great event was the issue of a small bottle of tea and rum to each man. Rum was not a regular issue in this hot climate, but by this time (October) the nights were becoming colder and the light kit worn by the men required something more than keenness to get at the Turk to cheer the dawn, hence the rum and tea. No sign of the enemy was seen this day except two Turkish aeroplanes flying at a great height over the concentration of troops from Karm to Abu Ghalyun, but British air scouts were soon after them and by great skill drove them down. Later, when the plates in their cameras where developed at Cairo, a complete set of photographs showing the concentration of troops was obtained. Had these planes succeeded in reaching their lines our reception at Beersheba might have been even warmer.

On the evening of the 30th, before leaving Abu Ghalyun, the Commanding Officer, Lieut.-Colonel Bisdee addressed the Battalion and in a few words told us what he expected of us. The result was never in doubt, and the regiment rose as one man and cheered him. It is safe to say that at no time previously was the morale of the Battalion so high, and the morrow augured badly for " Jacko," as the Turk was called. It was our first time " over the top," as a Battalion, and every man from the Colonel down to the latest-joined private determined to prove that the 2nd Battalion of the Civil Service Rifles was worthy in every way to uphold the traditions of the Regiment, which had been so gloriously upheld in France by the 1st Battalion. The 60th Division had had a great deal of hard work and a rough time with no prospect of glory, but that night it was to start a career of much glory equal to that of any Division in the War.

The first stage of the march towards Beersheba that night was as far as Wadi Mirtaba, where the R.E.'s had developed an efficient water supply a little more than two miles from the Turkish positions. Here the whole of the wheel transport was parked under the cover of the steep banks of the wadi, and the infantry shed their packs and resumed the march in fighting kit.

From this point we were only accompanied by camels carrying ammunition and medical and signal stores. A section of the Machine Gun Corps was attached to the Battalion here, for the actual attack.

From this point the Khalasa Road ran direct to Beersheba and formed a splendid guiding line through the wadis and hills on either side. From aeroplane maps sketches of the wadis had been reproduced, and each wadi had been allotted a familiar name ; the local Arabic names were far too difficult to memorise. Such names as Service, Scottish, Kensington, Westminster, St. Pancras and Blackheath were given ; while each Battalion had named the wadis in their own particular sector by popular names ; some of our nicknames were Strand, Dorking, Watford, Walden and Ware Wadis.

About 3,000 yards from the Wadi Mirtaba the Khalasa Road was joined by the Wadi Halgon, and from this point right up to the Turkish trenches they intertwined so much that one could hardly tell whether one was walking on the road or in the wadi ; from this fact the quality of the " road " can be best judged.

At night-time the Turks sent out patrols to the hills in advance of the trenches, and from these patrols resistance soon came in the shape of rifle fire, and after sharp skirmishes they were driven back to their lines. The only casualty on our side was a camel belonging to " C " Company. Later machine-gun fire down the road became heavy and the Companies soon got off the road into their prearranged wadis, where protection was good. It might be mentioned here that the wadis in this part were not deep ravines some sixty feet deep, like the Wadis Ghuzze, Imalaga and Mirtaba, which we had passed, but were simply small valleys between the hills, where a dried watercourse was termed a " wadi " after the larger variety further south.

The advanced guard was carried out by " D " Company, with orders to reach Poplar Wadi, about 500 yards from the enemy trenches, and to form a defensive line on the ridges on the further side of the Wadi ; this was carried out without loss, and strong forward positions were taken up in advance of Poplar Wadi on both sides of the Khalasa Road. Patrols went forward nearly to the enemy lines and were able to ascertain that there were no wire entanglements in front of the enemy position. This information was invaluable to the artillery, as many rounds of ammunition were saved, instead of bombarding imaginary wire. From aeroplane map photographs, definite lines of white spots could be detected in front of the line of trenches, but that night it was proved that they were merely white stones cunningly arranged by the Turk. Throughout the night Turkish machine-

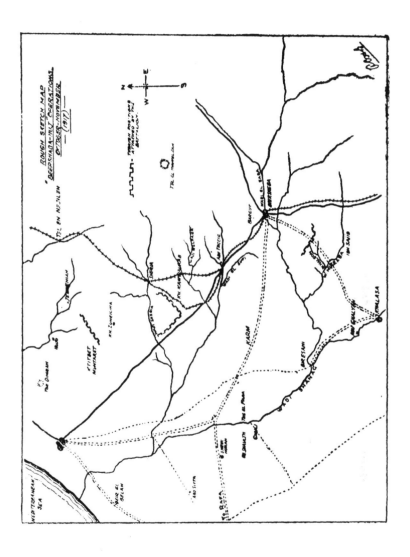

gun fire was intermittent and spattered the whole front with bullets. When dawn broke, any advance up the Wadi Halgon was impossible, as it was raked by the fire of two machine guns. Runners kept clear of the road and made their way to the forward companies by rushing over each ridge into the wadi in front. One runner, however, unaware of the dangers of the Wadi Halgon, calmly strolled along in the early morning and of course, drew violent fire both from machine guns and rifles on to his tracks, and after a certain amount of dancing about he fell down. Every one thought he had been hit, but Captain Wills, regardless of his personal safety, dashed from the cover of the Wadi and ran out to the man. This again was the cause of a further hail of bullets, and Wills fell down near the man. Thinking that both of them were dead the Turks ceased fire, but a moment or two later Captain Wills got up and made a successful dash for safety in the wadi, and although the Turks reopened their fire they did not hit Wills, who was no worse for his adventures. The man, inspired by Wills, got up a few minutes later, and also made a dash for our wadi, through a hail of bullets. Now comes the amusing side of the incident. The breathless runner handed us a note, and when it was opened the following words were exposed : " What time shall the platoon drink its rum and tea ? ——, Lieutenant, Officer Commanding —— Platoon, ' C ' Company." Needless to say no reply was sent to this request.

So much for the events of the night and early morning in the Wadi Halgon.

In the general scheme it was arranged that the 181st Brigade on the left of the 179th Brigade, should attack and capture the strongly fortified hill known as " Hill 1,070," which towered up in advance of the general line of the Beersheba defences. Not until this hill was captured was the main attack to be made.

As soon after dawn as light permitted, the operation of wire-cutting on the enemy's advanced works on Hill 1,070 was commenced by the Artillery and was continued, with short checks owing to dust clouds, until 8.30 a.m., when the 181st Brigade moved to the attack, which was undertaken by the 2/22nd and 2/24th Battalions, London Regiment, under cover of an intense barrage and overhead machine-gun fire.

At 8.42 a.m. the positions were entered and captured, the Artillery lifting on to the reverse slopes.

During this phase the 179th Brigade, led by the 2/14th and 2/15th Battalions were gradually moving forward for the attack on the main positions in conjunction with the 181st Brigade. At 10 a.m. the latter had reorganised and were reported ready for the next phase, which was preceded by wire-cutting on the part of the Artillery. This having been completed by 11 a.m., orders were received from the 20th Corps for the assault to take place in conjunction with the 74th Division on the left at 12.15 p.m. By 12.45 p.m. the whole of the enemy main positions were in our hands, and our left artillery group were left free to assist the attack of the 74th Division, who were slightly checked on our left.

While the operations against Hill 1,070 were proceeding the Battalion formed up under cover for their attack, and orders had been previously issued to " D " Company in the advanced positions that should the Turk leave his trenches on our direct front, as the result of the attack on Hill 1,070, he was to be pursued with fire. Odd men had been seen to retire, and the message came through that the Turks were retiring, and " D " Company lined their ridge and poured fire into the enemy trenches. However, the message of the Turks' retirement which came from a rear observation post was not quite correct, and was far too sanguine. The retirement was not so whole-sale as had been anticipated, and the Turk returned strong retaliatory fire. " D " Company stuck to their positions, and although suffering heavy casualties, continued to fire at the Turks in the trenches. While this battle of cross fire was pro-ceeding orders for the general advance were given, and, under the covering fire of the advanced company, the attacking Companies " B " and " C," with " A " Company in immediate support, rushed the enemy's line. In spite of heavy opposition no one hesitated, and the attackers assaulted and captured the trenches, killing the occupants and pursuing with fire those who had retired. The Turks fired until the very last moment, and when our fellows were within bayoneting distance held up their hands and cried " Kamerad " or " Arab." They were poorly clad, and apparently the sprinkling of German N.C.O.'s had kept up their morale until the sight of our bayonets. By 12.45 p.m. the position was in our hands, and a line some 800 yards beyond the trenches was immediately consolidated. Patrols pushed forward, but little was seen of the Turk ; only small groups could be seen in the distance running away as fast as their legs could take them.

In clearing the trenches to our right flank, Private E. J. Cook, " C " Company, the last unwounded member of his Lewis gun team, greatly distinguished himself. Crawling out of the trench he engaged a German-manned machine gun point-blank, and although the Lewis gun was hit and he was twice severely wounded, he continued to serve his gun until the enemy gun was knocked out, whereupon it was promptly captured by a bombing party.

The cavalry who had worked around the flank from the east of Beersheba occupied the town that evening, and the Reserve

Battalions of the 6oth Division were sent forward to cover our front.

The conclusion of the day's planned operations was marked by the concentration of the attacking Brigades in the captured positions, with outposts pushed out on the high ground over-looking Beersheba. The 2/13th (Kensingtons) which had been detailed for this duty in our Brigade succeeded in capturing two 77mm. guns which had been causing us casualties earlier in the day.

To return to the actual attack by the Civil Service Rifles, the whole operation had been a great success, and in spite of considerable casualties the losses could not be considered too heavy. " D " Company, the advanced Company, had suffered most while giving support to the attacking Companies. " C " Company had the next highest total, as it was their misfortune to advance over the machine-gun swept valley of the Wadi Halgon. The casualties in " B " Company were much lighter, as they were able to use the cover of the small branch nullahs in their advance. " A " Company had very few casualties, but this does not reflect that they did not do their share ; it was their fortune. The whole Battalion had at last been able to display its fighting qualities in a real attack. The Battalion's captures included three officers and over 50 men, while more than sixty dead Turks were buried by us afterwards in their old trenches.

An amusing incident of the final scene of the attack was when the stentorian voice of one of the sergeants of " C " Company was heard during the lull in the rifle fire, shouting, " All officers and sergeants "—an order which had palled on our ears at the close of the numerous practice attacks during our training on the desert.

The evening was quiet enough and the Battalion was not worried by Turkish artillery fire, and it was only an hour after the success of the attack was known, when the Battalion transport under Lieutenant Pearson and the water camels under Lieutenant Gearing arrived from their hiding-place in the Wadi Mirtaba, where we had left them the previous evening. Souvenir-hunting in the Turkish lines was our evening pastime ; but not until search parties had found and collected all the killed and wounded and every man was accounted for.

The night was cold, but men availed themselves of the protec-tion of the trenches, and some of the more fortunate succeeded in obtaining captured tents and bivouac sheets ; but these were unpleasant dwellings and smelt horribly. With the dead Turks lying around, the whole place was no health resort. The Turk was a filthy fellow, as his trenches showed, and the whole area was infested with flies. The next day the dead Turks were collected and buried in their trenches. The British guns had fired with great accuracy into the trenches, and in one instance had knocked out a machine gun and its team of eight men.

On the 1st of November the infantry were employed in clearing the battlefield while the 519 Field Company, R.E., entered the town of Beersheba soon after dawn for the purpose of water development.

The captures by the 60th Division included two 77 mm. guns, many machine guns, 15 officers and 193 other ranks unwounded, and 5 officers and 85 other ranks wounded.

On the morning of the 3rd of November the Battalion moved to the valley on the south-eastern outskirts of the town. The whole valley was crowded with British troops and transport. Beersheba as a town appeared to be of little value, but its importance as a stronghold on the flank of the Turkish line was considerable. Water was obtained from the wells which had been quickly repaired by the R.E.; the Turk having blown up the winding gear before he left. In the town, prisoner of war compounds were established, while a still larger compound for the natives and Arabs of the surrounding district was made in the valley outside the town.

The soil of the valley where there is some moisture is exceedingly rich and is rudely cultivated by the natives, and in the tracks around Beersheba the Bedouin find ample pasturage for their flocks and herds which in the evening assemble around the wells as they did 3,000 years ago. The desert of Beersheba is very beautiful in spring and early summer when the surface is carpeted with herbage and flowers; but later in the year it is parched and desolate in the extreme, not a tree breaking the monotony of the landscape or the rays of the sun. It was in the latter state when we arrived.

On the evening of the 3rd of November the Battalion moved again to Bargut, some two miles or more north of the town of Beersheba, but were not privileged to pass through the town; passing it on its western outskirts. At Bargut a bivouac camp was erected, and the Quartermaster's Stores and transport sections moved with us. Officers were allowed the benefit of their valises which had been reduced to 25 lb. in weight, and blankets were issued to the men.

Meals were soon prepared, and a day of complete rest away from the filth of the Turkish trenches was thoroughly enjoyed by all.

At this time it had become apparent to the Higher Command that the enemy had been able to anticipate our threat of enveloping his left flank, by a concentration of his reserves on the high ground in the neighbourhood of Khuweilfeh. The Corps Commander therefore decided to throw our whole weight upon the centre of the Turkish defences represented by the Kauwukah system and a series of works extending some 5,000 yards to the east, and at the same time occupying the enemy's left flank by the employment of the 53rd Division and mounted troops at Khuweilfeh.

Accordingly the 60th Division moved over in the direction of Kauwukah on the 4th of November, the Battalion moving to Wadi Welfare, a distance of 7 or 8 miles as the crow flies. This was a most trying march over sandy desert and the sand was not of that " golden " type which one associates with the east when reading books, but was of a dirty black variety, and our memories went back to that first dusty march from Belah to Abu Sitta some months previously. Every one was covered with black dust, and eyes and nostrils became unbearable. Water was limited and the day's supply had not been received before starting. The water camels had returned to Beersheba, but here the supply was insufficient, and they were re-directed to Abu Irgeig, which was about 7 miles in the direction of Gaza, and in quite a different direction to that taken by the Brigade.

The ground over which we travelled was extremely hilly, and the Battalion constantly descended into deep wadis and ascended over the steep ridges for practically the whole of the last four miles. It was getting dark, and the difficulties were tremendous, and credit is due to those responsible that the various battalions of the Division ever found their allotted areas, most of which were in the beds of deep wadis. The Battalion halted about 10.0 p.m., and an outpost line covering the Divisional front was taken up by the 181st Brigade. No water, however, was obtainable. All we knew was that the camels had gone back as far as Beersheba, and knowing the difficulties of the march that we had encountered, the possibility of the camels arriving that night appeared remote. However, shortly after midnight a small voice was heard on the surrounding heights, " Who is down there ? " " 2/15th," we shouted. " Thank God," uttered the small voice, " How the devil do you get down there ? " No one could say how we had got down into this basin-like dip, in the darkness it appeared to be surrounded by steep cliffs. The small voice was heard no more, but an hour afterwards the swishing of the water in the " Fanatis " was heard approaching along a branch wadi, and Lieutenant Gearing appeared, followed by his convoy of water camels and their weary leaders. How this officer performed the journey that night from Bargut to Beersheba and thence to Abu Irgeig—where water was drawn—and eventually across the wilderness to the Battalion, which was concealed in one of the many holes in the ground, is beyond imagination. The water camels, with their officer and his Company guides had dragged over a distance of at least 15 miles in the dark. Even Gearing himself cannot explain ; in fact, he never attempted, and " Sparrow," as our tiny water officer was called, simply grinned and felt pleased. There were heroes in the battle of Beersheba, but no one was so deservedly popular as Gearing that night. He had done great things through sheer grit, where thousands would have failed (and not without reason). Great was the relief on the arrival of the water camels, and then our minds turned to the transport and Quartermaster's stores with its precious rations which had not yet arrived. However, ere long the voice of Lieutenant Pearson (not a small one this time) was heard, and we knew that the "gods" were with us. The route taken by the Battalion had been impossible for wheeled transport, and it had been diverted some four miles back on to a different track. Even this second route was extremely difficult, but the transport section " stuck to their guns," and after a somewhat lengthy and tedious journey had struck the Battalion. It was simply a matter of " striking," too. Maps were indistinct, and in the darkness every wadi is a replica of its neighbour ; signposts were badly needed in these parts. However, daylight came, and this put a better complexion on the state of affairs.

Officers were called to Headquarters and given details of our next attack which was to be against the centre of the Turkish line in Palestine, at a place called Kauwukah. The rest of the day was spent in reconnaissance of the ground. Landmarks were few, but all hoped for the best, and compass bearings were taken. Final preparations were made in the evening and rations were issued. Water again presented a difficulty, as the wells at Abu Irgeig had run dry, but it was hoped that the R.E. would open up a new source during the night.

CHAPTER XXXIV

KAUWUKAH AND RUSHDI SYSTEMS—ATTACK—SHERIA—MUNTARET —HUJ—NEJILEH—AND TO GAZA VIA SHERIA

THE position to be attacked was on the high ground at Khirbit Kauwukah, just north of the Beersheeba–Gaza Railway and south of Sheria. This was an extensive stretch of trenches about four miles long, which faced south-west from near Samarra Bridge to Abu Heirira on the Wadi Sheria. The left of this trench system was swung round forming a strong defensive flank facing south-east, and it was against this flank that the 60th Division was to make its attack. In front of our objectives stretched an open plain for over a mile and, of course, formed an excellent field of fire for the defenders.

The general plan of attack consisted of an enfilade assault from the east to be started by the 74th Division on our right attacking and rolling up the enemy's works east of the actual Kauwukah System, followed by our own Division which was to operate against the main defences with one Brigade of the 10th Division on our left ; each Division being echeloned back from the right.

Careful arrangements were necessary with regard to the timing of the advance of each Division in order to safeguard the possibility of the troops of the 60th and 10th Divisions being enfiladed from the enemy's works to be attacked by the 74th Division before the latter had accounted for them.

By the flanking attack it was hoped that the 10th Division on our left would reach the Abu Heirira Redoubt, a strongly-fortified mound on the edge of the Wadi Sheria. In the 179th Brigade the Westminsters and Kensingtons were to form the attacking Battalions and the Civil Service were to be in support ; the Brigade Reserve being the London Scottish. A second Brigade of the Division, the 180th Brigade with the London Irish (21/8th) and the St. Pancras (2/19th) Battalions as attacking Battalions were to push forward on our right. The 181st Brigade, of Hill 1,070 fame, being the Divisional Reserve. After the first lines of the enemy's works had been captured, it was intended that the 2/15th and the 2/19th Battalions should continue the advance and take the rest of the Kauwukah

System in enfilade as far as the Rushdi System which adjoined just on the banks of the Wadi Sheria ; while the Battalions of the 10th Division on our left should concentrate their energies on the strong redoubt at Abu Heirira, and thus complete the capture of the Turkish positions from the east as far as the Wadi Sheria.

During the night of the 5/6th of November, 1917, the Battalion moved from the Wadi Welfare to its position of assembly preparatory to the opening of the action by the 74th Division on our right at 5.0 a.m. The position of assembly was some two miles south-east of the left flank of the Kauwukah System, and under cover of the undulating ground we waited for the result of the 74th Divisional attack. One thing which worried us, however, was the fact that our water supply had not yet reached us ; the camels which had left for Abu Irgeig on the previous evening had not been heard of since. Just as every one gave up hope Gearing and his camels appeared over the crest in front. Here was another adventure of our camel officer. Finding no water at Abu Irgeig, and learning that some was obtainable nearer Beersheba, Gearing trudged back, got the water, and then made a " bee-line " for the Kauwukah System along the Beersheba-Gaza Railway line. True, the route was well defined on the map, but when one thinks of the journey back towards Beersheba from Abu Irgeig wells is a matter of about eight miles, and after that a night march of ten miles towards Kauwukah on the return, it was a grand performance and an exhibition of determination for which Gearing deserved praise. He had apparently arrived at the position of assembly just previous to the Battalion, and seeing no Battalion he had pushed on towards the Turks, and when dawn came, seeing nothing in front of him, decided to return, and luckily met us at the appointed place. Water was quickly issued, and every one was relieved for at least 24 hours.

Being in reserve is always a weary job and always one of anxiety ; if all goes well in front it is easy ; but should things go all wrong it is horrible. During the early morning the 74th Division had gained their objectives, and by 8.0 a.m. it was decided to commence operations on our Divisional front. An artillery bombardment of the Turkish trenches was commenced, and the Battalions deployed for the attack. However, from observation it was seen that much of the strong barbed-wire entanglements in front of the Turkish lines was still uncut, and it was decided that two batteries of R.F.A. should go forward and cut the wire at point blank range. By this time the Westminsters on our direct front had advanced to the ridge overlooking the plain in front of the enemy's trenches, and were suffering many casualties. Suddenly, in rear of our Battalion large clouds of dust were seen, and from these clouds came galloping two batteries of artillery. On they galloped through the extended lines of the Battalion which lay in support near the railway bridge at Samarra, and over the ridge in front until they gained the open plain. Here they unlimbered their guns and opened a rapid rate of fire on the Turkish lines. The battery horses at once returned back over the ridge for cover from the heavy shower of shrapnel which was coming from the enemy gunners. The teams returned at the gallop, but many horses were riderless and teams were often dragging one of their number either dead or wounded. In front of the ridge, in full view of the enemy, the two batteries continued to pour fire on the Turkish entanglements. They were paying for their gallantry, and many wounded artillery officers and men crawled back over the ridge to receive medical attention at the advanced dressing station that had been erected at Samarra Bridge, under cover of the embankment. Only a few men finally remained with the guns, and under the command of a corporal—who afterwards received the D.C.M.—they continued to successfully carry out the cutting of the wire. The whole incident was an inspiration to the infantry, and the gallantry of our brothers in the gunners encouraged us in our attack, which commenced to push forward about midday. The Battalion followed closely on the heels of the Westminsters, with " D " Company leading. Extended order with lines about 70 yards intervals in depth was the formation adopted. Once over the ridge the Battalion came under heavy machine-gun fire and also a shrapnel barrage. But just ahead we could see the Westminsters pushing on towards the trench line which was strongly garrisoned, and with a final rush at 1.0 p.m. they captured their objective. The Battalions on their flanks had also succeeded, and the first lines were won. Without a moment's delay we, together with the 2/19th on our right, pursued the enemy and captured many lines of trenches without a great deal of opposition. Occasionally a machine-gun would hold us up for a few minutes, but it was soon out-flanked and the line advanced again. All resistance was broken down and the garrisons killed or put to flight. Not until the whole of the Kauwukah and Rushdi systems were in British hands did the Battalion halt, and then finally took up a position overlooking the Wadi Sheria about 2.0 p.m. in the afternoon.

A defensive line in the vacated trenches was made, and in the distance across the valley of the wadi columns of Turks with their transport could be seen hurrying to get out of range of our artillery fire. The whole attack had been successful and our casualties were comparatively light. Great losses had been inflicted on the enemy, and many prisoners were captured. The comparative lightness of our casualties was probably largely due to wide extensions and also to the élan displayed by all ranks who, once they got in close touch with the enemy, pursued him relentlessly, giving him no time to develop counter-attacks or occupy a fresh line of resistance.

The flanking attack of the 60th Division had swept forward over the trenches and the 10th Division on our left altered their direction slightly and concentrated on the Heirira Redoubt, which consisted of a large mound literally honeycombed with trenches and machine-gun emplacements. On the Battalion front things soon quieted down, but on the right flank of the Division the Turk had concentrated and was strongly resisting the British advance towards Sheria Railway Station.

At 3.30 p.m. on the 6th of November orders were received from the XXth Corps to establish a strong bridgehead across the Wadi Sheria in order to secure the water supply ; the 10th Division being ordered to relieve the 60th Division in the captured works.

Accordingly the 180th and 181st Brigades were ordered to advance and form a bridgehead north of Sheria in order to attain that object, and were supported by the Divisional artillery, the 179th Brigade remaining in Divisional Reserve. The 74th Division were ordered to operate on our right, with their left resting on Khirbit Barrata. At 5.30 p.m. one Company from the 180th Brigade had captured Sheria Railway Station, securing some prisoners and two machine-guns, while two Battalions from each Brigade prepared to cross the Wadi Sheria and occupy Tel el Sheria, the high ground north of the town.

Before evacuating Sheria Station, however, the enemy had succeeded in firing a large ammunition dump south of the station which commenced to explode just previous to the launching of the attack. The conflagration raged for some hours, and so illuminated the country in the vicinity that further progress was rendered temporarily impossible. Nevertheless, the ground over which the attack was to be made was carefully reconnoitred, and at 3.30 a.m. on the 7th the attack was launched by the 2/17th and 2/20th Battalions of the 180th Brigade west of the Railway, and the 181st Brigade was represented by the 2/22nd and 2/23rd Battalions east of the railway.

The enemy offered a determined resistance, but by 4.30 a.m. our objectives were gained. During this part of the day's operations our captures included 4 field guns, 4 machine-guns and over 150 prisoners. The Turks were disinclined to accept their defeat without further efforts, and at 9.25 a.m. developed a strong counter attack against the line now held by the 180th Brigade, but this was effectively broken up by concentrated machine-gun, Lewis gun and rifle fire, assisted by the supporting artillery, with great loss to the enemy.

During the foregoing operations the 2/15th Battalion in common with the remainder of the 179th Brigade had handed over their captures in the Kauwukah and Rushdi systems to the 10th Division and were brought back a few miles and remained for the night of the 6/7th of November in reserve near Sammara Bridge. Little rest, however, was possible, as the weather was extremely cold. The next morning was spent in reorganising after the previous day's attack, and in the early afternoon we were ordered to move to the Wadi Sheria.

About 4 p.m. on the 7th the Battalion, with the London Scottish on its left, moved forward from a ridge on the eastern side of the valley of the Wadi, " B " Company under Captain Lewis leading. While moving across the open we were heavily shelled. After crossing the Wadi, however, the advance was pressed, and after considerable opposition and stubborn fighting the enemy was driven back and we established an outpost line on the high ground west of the Wadi. During this advance " B " Company, as advance guard, had engaged a considerable force of Turks, but led by the personal dash of their Company Commander, they pushed forward and inflicted severe losses on the enemy. The Battalion soon followed up and passed over a large Turkish camp where " B " Company had captured an anti-aircraft gun, and the night was spent in digging in. Patrols pushed forward, but no sign of the Turk was found. Taking up this line ended the second phase of our operations in Palestine. Beersheba and Sheria had fallen under the pressure of the 60th Division. The following summary from Divisional Headquarters on the attacks on Kauwukah and Sheria defences will no doubt be interesting.

" The total prisoners at the end of this stage amounted to 31 officers and 521 men. During the whole of the day the Division was engaged in severe local fighting, while at times the hostile shell fire, especially in the afternoon, was particularly troublesome, the Turkish command obviously realising the importance of denying us access to the water supply in the Wadi Sheria. It afterwards transpired from prisoners' statements that picked troops had been hastily formed into composite units and entrusted with the defence of the position. The large number of enemy regiments represented among the prisoners lent colour to these assertions, the opposing commanders doubtless fully realising the vital importance of delaying our advance at this point in order subsequently to secure the exposed flank of the retreating Gaza garrison."

On the following morning, the 8th of November, the situation had sufficiently cleared for an advance to be made upon Huj, a few miles north-east of Gaza, where it was thought there would be an efficient water supply. Transport and water camels had joined the Battalion, and we were complete to move off about 7 a.m. Cavalry patrols were sent forward to gain touch with the enemy, who was retiring with all speed. The ground was undulating grassland with an occasional outcrop of sandy desert, and movement was fairly easy. The 179th Brigade formed the advance guard of the Division, having the 2/15th Civil Service and 2/14th London Scottish as its leading Battalions and covering a wide front. Instructions were issued to advance towards the high ground near Khirbit Muntaret, which was known to be occupied by the enemy. For several hours under glorious weather conditions the Brigade pushed forward across the undulating country and found no signs of the enemy except his numerous dumps which he had left hurriedly behind him. About 10 a.m. cavalry patrols brought in information to the effect that the enemy was strongly entrenched on the high ground on the north of the village of Muntaret, and the Battalion was deployed for attack. There was a considerable force of Turks near Muntaret and they were well supported by artillery. The Battalion, having " C " Company under Captain Wills for their advanced guard, opened out into irregular artillery formation or, in other words, " blobs " of Platoons at 150 yards interval. The approach to Muntaret was over an open stretch of country, and while going over the ground the Battalion came under very heavy artillery fire, and suffered considerable casualties. " C " Company soon opened out into extended order and advanced to the bottom of Muntaret Hill which was steep and, except for a small ravine a few feet deep, offered little cover. In spite of the machine-gun and rifle fire from the trenches, " C " Company crept up the hill for the final assault, and within a few hundred yards of the enemy the men took off their packs and prepared for their final charge. Led by Captain Wills, they captured the position (thus forestalling the cavalry, whose objective it had been), while the London Scottish on their left made a flank attack on the position at the same time. The rest of the Battalion soon followed on to the ridge, having also dumped their packs at the foot of the hill. However, the Turkish artillery continued to heavily bombard the captured position, and it was necessary to dig in and consolidate. Further advance was impossible across the plain west of Muntaret, and any attempt to cross the plain would mean considerable casualties from shell fire. The G.-O.-C. Division, Major-General Shea, came up and ordered the Worcester and Warwick Yeomanry to charge the Turkish batteries which were holding up our advance. None of us had had the fortune to see the Balaclava Charge in the Crimean War, but it was our privilege to see a similar type of gallantry,

U

and I insert here an account from a newspaper cutting of the charge.

" On November the 8th the Londoners while occupying a ridge less than two miles from the enemy lines, came under extremely heavy gun fire. Meanwhile the Yeomanry had come up. The Londoners' commander, who had seen the whole enemy's position and their guns, ordered the Yeomanry to charge them. There were 10 troops of Worcester and Warwick Yeomanry, commanded by a Colonel, Master of Hounds.

" He and his men swept over the ridge in successive lines about 2,000 yards from the enemy, raced down the slope across the flat, partly obscured by a mound in front. Over this rise the yeomen spurred their chargers, took the final rise at a terrific pace, the ranks somewhat thinned by gun, machine-gun and rifle fire, which the enemy switched off the Londoners soon after trails of dust told of advancing cavalry.

" The cavalry's target was not so much the infantry as the guns. Giving full-throated cheers they went straight for the field and heavy pieces. There were 12 guns in action against these valiant boys from the Shires—nine German-made field guns and three 5·9 howitzers. The field guns banged as fast as the Austrian and German gun crews could load them, but every enemy artillery man was sabred by his piece. The Londoners heard the fire of all the guns stop dead almost at the same moment."

After witnessing this magnificent feat of arms and benefiting by the resulting " cease fire " from the Turkish guns, a hasty meal was taken and a short halt was made. Later on in the afternoon under the protection of the London Scottish as advanced guard, the Brigade pushed forward in the direction of Huj. The 2/14th breasted the high ground at Tor Dimrah, near Huj, about 4.50 p.m. in the evening of the 8th of November, and were soon followed by the rest of the Brigade. It will thus be seen that between 3 a.m. on the 6th of November and 4.50 p.m. on the 8th, the Division marched 23½ miles, in the course of which advance the Kauwukah and Rushdi systems of defensive works were captured, the bridgehead at Sheria stormed, a deter-mined counter attack repulsed, and the Turkish rearguard driven from Muntaret to beyond Huj, entailing attacks upon three defensive positions on the way.

The total captures by the Division in the whole operations amounted to 12 guns, 26 machine-guns, 51 officers and 907 other ranks.

The following newspaper extract, I think, might be included here without any shadow of a boast, and summarises our doings from the commencement of the Palestine campaign.

" The achievements of the London Territorials, who had the hardest part to do in the thrust from our right flank, will rank in the deeds of the war. A distinguished officer of my acquaintance, who has seen nearly three years of war in France and watched every movement of the London County Territorials here, told me that he could not speak of these warriors without a lump rising in his throat. This is his considered judgment :—

" ' These Cockneys are the best men in the world. Their spirits are simply wonderful. I don't think any division ever went into a big show with higher morale. After three years of war it was refreshing to hear the men's earnestly expressed desire to get into action again. These grand fellows went forward with the full bloom upon them. There never was any hesitation. Their discipline was absolutely perfect, and their physique, and courage alike magnificent. Their valour was beyond words. The Cockney makes the perfect soldier.' "

In eight days the men marched 66 miles and fought a number of hot actions. The march may not seem long, but Palestine is not Salisbury Plain.

On reaching Tor Dimrah near Huj on the evening of the 8th of November, the Battalion was bivouacked on the grassy slopes and waited for water and rations to be brought up from Sheria. During the evening a large British bombing squadron of some 30 planes flew over our heads and no doubt dropped their missiles with great effect on the columns of retreating Turks fleeing northwards.

Late at night water and rations arrived and these, together with cigarettes made from dried tea leaves, helped every one to retire for the night satisfied with the day's work.

For the next two days we remained here and the Battalion was reorganised ; transport came up from Sheria and fatigue parties were sent back to Muntaret for the packs which we had dumped just before the attack ; while others had been left as far back as Sheria by " C " Company who it will be remembered started off from the Sheria Wadi as an advance guard. Unfortunately the water supply at Huj was not so promising as expected and the damage done to the wells by the retreating Turk did not help matters. Horses and mules were sent out in all directions without finding a sufficient supply and lack of water became so acute that the Artillery men near by sacrificed their own limited supply for their horses. The difficulty of our own transport is best described by the following letter from Lieutenant Pearson, our transport officer at the time :

" On one occasion we left the lines at 5.30 a.m. with the animals to go about 10 miles for water, and had to be back ready to move off at 2.30 p.m. When we arrived at the given place there were several thousands of Australian Cavalry horses, artillery horses, and several infantry units, animals with only one 30-foot long portable trough. The Australians' horses had not had any water for over 36 hours, so you can imagine there was no system or order, the horses could not be held back. We had to return without

watering, and arrived back at 2 p.m. In the meantime, the Battalion
had received further orders to the effect that they would not move
until next day. After feeding the animals, and after the men had
had a snack, we were told there was a well near at hand. We
went in search and found it was about 60 feet deep and had to pull
up a bucketful at a time by means of a long rope ; anyway, we
arrived back at 1.30 a.m. The men and animals only having had
one meal at midday between 5.30 a.m. and 1.30 a.m. the next day.
We moved off at 8.30 a.m. the same morning."

The foregoing incident actually occurred while we were at
Tor Dimrah on November 9th, 1917.

From the heights at Tor Dimrah the result of our recent
fighting could be well appreciated. A few miles to the south-
west could be seen the town of Gaza, the scene of heavy fighting
some months previously, while to the west stretched the coastal
plain which ran up country as far as Jaffa. Frontal attacks
on Gaza had proved unsuccessful earlier in the year, and therefore General Allenby decided to attack from a flank. The line
of attack commenced at Beersheba and was made in a north-
westerly direction, rolling up the Turkish line from the east,
and hoping at the same time to reach the north of Gaza in time
to cut off the garrison. While this flank movement was in
progress local frontal raids on Gaza were made under heavy
artillery bombardments from both land and sea. However,
the Turkish leaders were able to thwart the full intention of
the scheme and by their strong resistance, by powerful flank
guards at Kauwukah, Sheria and Muntaret, were enabled to
give time for their troops at Gaza to retire north with minimum
losses. However, as soon as the Gaza front gave way, the
XXIst Corps under our old Divisional Commander, General E. S.
Bulfin, relentlessly pursued the Turks as far as Jaffa.

Except for the 53rd Division, our own Corps, the XXth, was
withdrawn from the pursuit and, in order to assist the advance,
much of our corps transport was lent to the XXIst Corps. The
53rd Division just mentioned had been kept at Khuweilfeh
just north of Beersheba since the beginning of the offensive,
and had fought manfully against repeated attacks and thereby
protected the right flank of our advance across Palestine.

On the 11th of November the Battalion moved a few miles
north-east to the Wadi Jemmemiah where the whole of the
surrounding country was covered with well planned trenches
and all the valleys covered with machine-gun emplacements ;
but the numerous ammunition dumps round about signified
how hastily the Turk had withdrawn without making a strong
resistance. Only a day was spent here, and on the 13th we
moved still farther north to Nejilah ; a pleasant spot after the
filth and dust which existed around Jemmeniah. The route

was lined with large collections of war material which had been left by the retreating Turk and everywhere was desolate and uninviting. Not until a mile or so from Nejilah did the scenery improve and then a stretch of undulating grassland presented itself; a restful change for our tired eyes after a lengthy stay on the glaring yellow desert. A few flocks of sheep strayed over the pastureland and the quaintly dressed shepherds, at last, presented to us a fair representation of Biblical Palestine as we had imagined it in our youth. This was the first clean, healthy spot, free from sand and the filth which the Turks always left behind them, we had struck since our arrival at Belah.

For three days the Battalion remained here on these grassy hill-sides overlooking a wide plain of pasture land to the north. Just near the camping ground a stream of crystal clear water flowed and bathing parades were again indulged in. To give the Britisher his due, he does love cleanliness and even through the recent advance most of the men had used a portion of their limited ration for purposes of shaving, although a proper wash was out of the question. No parades were ordered and a restful time was spent at Nejilah. However, difficulties arose with regard to supplies ; much of our corps transport having been lent to the other corps pursuing the enemy. Consequently the Battalion was ordered to return to Sheria.

As I have already said the Turk revelled in filth and pollution, and no better illustration could be seen than the Sheria area where he had apparently had a large base camp since the early days of the war. For miles around Sheria the place literally stank and flies were present in their millions. The ground was strewn with dead Turks, camels, horses and mules, and the presence of these carcasses did not improve the polluted atmosphere. However, the desert was expansive and camps were arranged as far from this debris as possible.

While we had been fighting during the past few weeks miracles had been performed by the A.S.C. and R.E. The former corps had worked well and supply dumps had been advanced with rapidity ; camel and horse transport working in conjunction with the railways in the captured area. The latter corps had repaired the Turkish railways and used the captured rolling stock to good purpose ; other sections of R.E.'s had exploited the wells and obtained good supplies of water in the Wadi Sheria.

November the 17th, just after the arrival in the Sheria area, was known as " Parcel Day ": it was the first post since our departure from our desert line on the Wadi Ghuzze. Not only letters arrived but huge bags of parcels ; nearly every man received a parcel. The owners of many, however, were not to be found ; some had given their lives for their country while others had been sent to base hospitals either wounded or sick. But each platoon or mess made short work of these and divided the spoil ; it was an unwritten law and not stealing. Luxuries were plentiful and hundreds of tea parties and dinner parties were held that evening. Every unit, however, has its " grousers," not that they mean any harm, but it is their privilege as British Tommies. They could not legitimately grouse this night with all the good things around so they turned their morbid thoughts to treks and predicted a move on the morrow, when every one would be laden with luxuries. Their prophecies came true and the following morning camp was struck and the Battalion marched towards Gaza as far as Muntaret. On the 19th of November the march was resumed to the outskirts of the town of Gaza. The day's march was not a great distance but the downpour of heavy rain in the evening drenched all. This was the commencement of the rainy season in Palestine.

CHAPTER XXXV

THE MARCH FROM GAZA UP COUNTRY—ENAB—THE CAPTURE
OF JERUSALEM—TEL-EL-FUL—BIREH.

AT Gaza the Battalion bivouacked just to the north of the town.
" Town " was perhaps a complimentary term for Gaza at that
time, for it was in a deplorable state. The proud town of the
Philistines and the scene of Samson's deathly triumph had been
most thoroughly treated to every type of missile known to the
British forces, from rifle bullet to the 12-inch naval projectile,
and there was ample evidence of the efficacy of that treatment.
Scarcely a whole wall remained, big gun emplacements built
of concrete and iron rails, though skilfully hidden, had been
utterly destroyed and most of the trenches flattened out. Before these had stood formidable obstacles in the shape of cactus
hedges, which had proved themselves more efficient than any
barbed wire, but what remained of these was liberally sprinkled
with shrapnel holes. In short, Gaza had been made as unhealthy
as it was possible for us to have made it, and at last the Turk
had been made to quit, though not without a struggle.

Through the centre of the town a clearing had been made and
the broad-gauge railway was being rapidly advanced. The
methods of the R.E. railway construction companies are well
worth a short description. They were the essence of efficiency.
First the R.E. officer with a few satellites carrying the necessary
instruments would prospect and decide the direction of the
line, and he was quickly followed by a large gang of the Egyptian
Labour Corps who, armed with a tool similar to an adze, but
without that instrument's sharp edge, and a bag similar to a
carpenter's, would immediately set to work to clear the ground
and make the necessary cutting or embankment. The sight
of some hundreds of these natives swarming over the position
was exactly like an overturned ant-hill. Every one seemed
to run in different directions, and to the uninitiated confusion
appeared to reign supreme, but the work was completed at a
pace which would have made a " ca'canny " trade union
delegate weep with anguish. When the necessary alteration
to the landscape had been effected more labourers would appear,
each carrying a huge railway sleeper which was dumped roughly

in position, later to be arranged properly and levelled by soldier platelayers. This work was no sooner completed than lengths of rail were dumped upon and quickly secured to the sleepers by means of fish-spikes. The rails were then trimmed, levelled and bolted together and very shortly afterwards were being used by the construction train, which with its supply of material, could thus closely follow the quickly moving construction gangs. The " permanent " way thus made could not, it is true, attempt to rival that to which we were accustomed, but an adequate supply of transport was absolutely necessary for the success of the E.E.F. at that time, and in those days no branch of the Services worked more quickly or efficiently than the railway construction companies to maintain the supply line.

After a short rest at Gaza we commenced our march north-wards on the 19th of November, 1917. Our actual destination was unknown, but the " lying jade " had been busy and the magical word " Jerusalem " was ever on her lips. Private soldiers or humble subalterns do not presume to understand the ways of an Army Commander. They have, in the famous game of war, not even the status of a pawn, but nevertheless are for ever weighing the pros and cons of each and every move-ment they are required to make and thus if anyone had, but two short months ago, been rash enough to suggest that Beer-sheba was the opening move of a game that was to end in the capture of the Holy City, they would have suggested that the unfortunate one had been disobeying divisional orders and by not wearing his helmet had caught a touch of the sun. But the situation had rapidly changed since the dreary days of the Gambli defences, and Jerusalem was in fact well within our reach. True it was that our grip had not been closed upon it, but the days of the Turk in the home of Christianity were for ever numbered.

Rain had fallen heavily for a short time during our stay at Gaza and though its advent had been a welcome change we later had cause to regret the hot sunny days of the Sinai Desert. The flat coastal plain which runs north from Gaza has been cultivated land ever since Biblical times, and is the most fertile spot in the whole of Palestine, and in consequence the most thickly populated, though the total number in the whole land, apart from the cities such as Gaza, Jaffa, Ludd and Jerusalem, would disgrace a small English county. A plentiful crop of barley which had been grown had been recently cut ; indeed rumour had it that a famous " Scotch " whisky firm had nearly failed owing to the lack of supplies from Palestine ! The course of our march was set through fields of stubble. When it was hot and dry, there arose stifling clouds of dust, and when wet the sticky nature of the ground could even bring a "caterpillar tractor" to a standstill. The change, however, from endless sand was at first welcome and we found great delight in passing through the native villages. These were amazing collections of mud huts, windows were unknown and of sanitary arrangements there were none ; yet the inhabitants though inexpressibly dirty seemed quite happy and contented with their lot. When opportunity arose we supplemented our meagre rations by purchasing eggs, figs, nuts and oranges. The last named were most welcome. We had seen no vegetables for months and the supply of fruit undoubtedly did much to dispel the ill effects of this enforced denial of " greens." The number to be obtained for one Egyptian piastre (2½d. English) varied, but the native drove a hard bargain if you failed to obtain at least six magnificent Jaffa oranges for that small sum. Many indeed did show in their dealings with us characteristics of the descendants of the twelve tribes with which we are all familiar, but at least one of them met his match. One famous youth, noticing that a coloured Egyptian bank note had a remarkable purchasing power, was smitten with a brilliant idea. Hurriedly quitting the village market place he produced a gaudy label from a tin of jam and succeeding in persuading a hoary-headed old extortioner to part with the whole of his stock of oranges on the understanding that the aforesaid label was worth untold gold. That youth of course had no right to be a private soldier " foot-slogging " through the Holy Land ; he had missed his vocation which, was that of a company promoter in the aeroplane or munition line at home. So many oranges were eaten on that march that, later on, drafts marching up from Gaza were known to have followed this trail of orange peel and found their way across Palestine to Jerusalem.

Marching is a thirsty business in any country and when for the most part the march is made enveloped in clouds of dust, it becomes even a still thirstier business. We had had long training in that fine art of marching from dawn to dusk without having recourse to the water-bottle, and that training stood us in good stead in those November days. The supply of water was an ever-present anxiety with the higher command, and in spite of the exploration of wells by the Royal Engineers, we were only allowed the meagre amount of one water-bottle full per man per diem, and this had to be carefully husbanded if the owner desired to partake of tea ration at the end of the day. He who could not produce a mugful of water could not draw a mugful of tea, and this was strictly adhered to.

It was our great good fortune during the whole campaign never to miss our daily supply of water, and for that great credit is due to Lieutenant Gearing, who was in charge of the water camels. He had an uncanny knack of finding his way to us over trackless unknown country, and wherever we bivouacked for the night he was sure to arrive very shortly afterwards with his precious convoy of water camels. His trials cannot here be recorded and their recital on paper would never convey an adequate impression of his difficulties, and yet no one in the Battalion ever did better work. Such deeds are not rewarded with decorations, but perhaps this tardy recognition of his work will in some way convey to him our appreciation of his excellent work.

Water was not the only difficulty. Rations were very short. We had been for weeks on what the A.S.C. called "mobile" rations, which was the official name for four biscuits, one tin of bully beef and a small ration of tea and sugar for each man every twenty-four hours. This was occasionally supplemented by jam, but even then it was a wearisome diet. "Smokes" became very scarce and the old substitute of dried tea-leaves was often in use. Fuel was conspicuous by its absence, as also were mails.

However we did not grumble too much when we realised the difficulties of transport. The railway embankment built over the Wadi Ghuzze had been twice swept away by floods and all rations, etc., had to be brought by motor lorry from Gaza, and as there were no roads it was a trying experience for the A.S.C., particularly as two of the Motor Transport companies had been but recently formed and rushed up from the Base and immediately given the task of supplying a rapidly moving Division over 50–60 miles of trackless country.

In spite of all we pushed on through Beit Hanun, Deir Siniid, Mejdel, Mesmeyiah, and Junction Station until about the 24th of November when at Latrun we set foot on the first metalled road we had seen since leaving Kantara. Latrun is about midway between Jaffa and Jerusalem and a few miles to the north-east the road enters the Judean Hills at Bab-el-Wad, and after negotiating two ranges of hills approximately 2,500 feet high it reaches Jerusalem which is set at the top of a third and higher cluster of hills.

The effect of marching on a hard road after months of sand and soft soil was soon felt and our feet and footwear quickly began to show signs of wear. Boots, the leather of which had perished through exposure and lack of grease, were soon worn through and even the oldest and best of soldiers suffered from sore feet. The road itself though labelled "metalled" was not in good condition. The Turk was ever notorious for the bad state in which he kept his communications and this one was no exception to the rule. It had not been repaired since the visit of the Kaiser many years before, and the defects were soon aggravated by the passage of much transport. It was an

ROAD TO JERUSALEM NEAR BAB-EL-WAD.

JEBEL KURUNTUL (Mount of Temptation) AND JERICHO.
Occupied by London Troops February 2nd, 1918.   The traditional scene of
Christ's Temptation.

To face page 314.

exhausting climb and it lasted for a long time. The road was bounded on the one side for the most part by a precipice and on the other by the steep hillside, except for a few places where it ran through deep cuttings, and one could speculate on the chances of success of any troops attempting to force such a road against the opposition of a few well-armed British troops and the result of the speculations was distinctly unfavourable to the attackers. Yet the Turk had been hurried from hill to hill with little loss to our troops. As we toiled upwards we momentarily expected to get our first view of the Holy City. We knew definitely by that time that such was our objective and with the words of Holy Writ in our minds—" a city that is set on a hill cannot be hid," we eagerly awaited the vision. That moment was however denied us for many a day, and it is a matter of conjuncture whether in any of our minds we felt satisfied when that view was obtained. It is rather ironical, but nevertheless a fact, that the first portion of Jerusalem we saw was of German origin—the tall tower of the Kaiser's palace on the Mount of Olives.

We eventually reached the crest of the first range of hills at Enab, and descending into the valley on the opposite side we entered an area which in comparison with the deadly wastes left miles behind seemed like paradise. The hill sides were pleasantly wooded, the road was good, fuel and water were in abundance and a little monastery was discovered to possess a stock of most excellent wine made from the fruit of the vines for the cultivation of which the hillsides were terraced. We remained near Enab for some days and enjoyed life. One company was unlucky and was sent up to relieve a post of the 75th Division which had been sorely tried in holding what they had gallantly won but the remainder of the Battalion enjoyed a well earned rest. The troops were in great need of it, but the animals were in a much worse condition. Owing to the difficulties of maintaining supplies the transport animals had for nearly a month been on half rations and had done a tremendous amount of very hard work. They were tired and worn and in fact were so hungry that the steady diminution of the size of the tail boards of the limber and the amount of leather harness eaten by the animals caused the transport officer (Lieutenant Pearson) many anxious moments.

The remaining brigades of the Division moved up behind us and the Division took over the right of the line from Soba through Kushil, Nebi Samwil to Beit Izza. Nebi Samwil, so called by the reason of its being the traditional burying place of Samuel, was a distinct thorn in the side of the Turks. This high hill overlooked Jersualem and threatened the road to the north from that city and our presence there was much resented by the Turks. They made strenuous endeavours to recapture the hill but all their efforts failed. When the 180th Brigade took over the hill there was on the top of it a splendid mosque with a graceful minaret. But Boche gunners with the Turk were no better in their respect for things religious than their brethren in France and it was not long before the minaret and mosque were utterly destroyed by a concentrated bombardment of heavy metal.

The final preparations for the attack on Jerusalem having been completed, the 74th Division which had by this time come up in rear took over Nebi Samwil from the 180th Brigade and we concentrated near Soba. The 179th Brigade were to attack the left of the Turkish position near Ain Karim, and if possible effect a junction with the 53rd Division, which was struggling up the Hebron road. The 180th Brigade were to attack up the main Jaffa-Jerusalem road through Kolonieh and Lifta while the 181st Brigade were in reserve.

On the night 7/8th December we advanced from Soba, crossed the Wadi Surar and at 3.30 a.m. on the 8th of December the Brigade attacked the high ground overlooking the Wadi Surar and south of Ain Karim and were speedily successful. This operation was a difficult one and its success was essential to the main operation. The whole brigade with mountain batteries descended the precipitous hillside in single file. It was a wretched night with no glimmer of moonlight to assist us and the rain fell heavily. The whole route was fraught with much danger to life and limb, but was negociated without a casualty. The main attack was delivered by the other regiments in the Brigade but we were called upon to assist. " C " Company who had taken the Jura Heights and were subjected to three determined counter attacks, the last two of which " C " Company helped to break up, were sent to the help of the Kensingtons.

Meanwhile Captain Leech, our medical officer, hearing that our sister Battalion had sustained over a hundred casualties, came up under heavy fire from two machine guns which were still holding out in a building of Ain Karim in our rear. He and our stretcher bearers, particularly Privates Davey and Eels, rendered most gallant service to our own and the Kensington wounded for which, and for their timely assistance, " C " Company earned the grateful thanks of that regiment's C.O. By 4.0 a.m. all objectives had been gained and one hour later the main attack up the Lifta road commenced. Much stubborn resistance was met with, as the Turk was well dug in and the progress of the attack was retarded by the fact that our help was not forthcoming as had been expected. This was not our fault. We had hoped to effect a junction with the 53rd Division, and then advance together, but the 53rd were by then many miles away fighting hard to come to our assistance. The resistance they met with delayed them and we in consequence were subjected to much hostile artillery fire from our right flank and unable to push forward. The weather was very bad, a high and bitterly cold wind and torrential rains made conditions extremely uncomfortable. We were clad only in tropical kit, had been exposed to the elements on hills nearly 3,000 feet high for over twenty-four hours and were by no means in a happy frame of mind. The Turk was also making himself extremely objectionable and we were supplied with many gifts in the shape of shells. Our opinions of Jerusalem at that time are not fit to be recorded here, and they did not change for many a long day. Near Lifta the Turk was making strenuous efforts to keep us out, but by 3.30 p.m. he was dislodged by a gallant bayonet attack, and Lifta was occupied at dusk. We pushed on to the outskirts of Jerusalem and remained in battle outposts.

That night pandemonium reigned in the Holy City. The Turk was evacuating as quickly as possible, so quickly that when a patrol of the 180th Brigade advanced from Lifta in the early morning of the 9th of December it was met by the " Mayor " who proffered the surrender of the city. Major-General Shea was instructed to accept it and did so at 1.0 p.m., and Jerusalem passed for ever out of the dominion of the Turks.

We were billeted that night in an empty school in a garden named " Abraham's Vineyard," and next day moving out to the north took up an outpost line at Shafat on the Jerusalem-Nablous (Shechem) road where we remained till the 15th of December when we returned to billets in Jerusalem, in the school in " Abraham's Vineyard." Jerusalem was the first town worthy of the name that we had seen since leaving Ismailia and to many the prospects held out when viewed from afar off was not fulfilled on closer inspection. The weather was cold and wet, but we made light of such minor discomforts, being so overcome with the novelty of being in Jerusalem. The idea seemed so fantastic. This ancient city which for centuries had been a bone of contention between East and West was at last in Christian hands and withal in the hands of the London Division ! True it is that our Welsh friends of the 53rd Division had lent a very helping hand by struggling up the Hebron road, but nevertheless it was to the London Division that credit was due for the releasing of this home of Christianity from the hands of its enemies. Yet withal it was difficult to arouse any real sentiment concerning this famous city. It was inexpressibly dirty, the people comprised all the nations and races known in Biblical times and since, and they like the city were very dirty. Of sanitation there appeared to be no sign and outside the Jaffa Gate the main water cistern, which from its accumulation of rain-water provided drink for the greater part of the city, had to all appearances not been cleansed since the time of Herod. The railway station, a comparatively modern addition, was in a state of chaos, although perhaps the R.F.C. were to blame for that. The fine ancient wall which, with the Temple site—and the water cisterns—was one of the only original things left from Biblical times, had been cut into at the request of the Kaiser and a hideous clock tower crowned with a large clock by " Dents " had been built in the gap made. Appallingly dirty fellows in charge of a few decrepit animals attached to a kind of cab stood near the clock tower plying for hire, but their condition was such that it needed no General Routine Order to forbid us to use them. Of the Holy Places within the city we were allowed only a view from the outside until some months later, but we studiously traversed the whole city armed with the Padre as guide and a Bible as guide-book. We visited the Temple site, the Church of the Holy Sepulchre, David's Tower, and traversed the so-called Via Dolorosa complete with its sites of the supposed halts of Christ during His journey with the Cross. The pool of Siloam was an offensively smelling puddle of dirty water, whilst the Brook Kidron was a mere trickle. Indeed, the whole aspect of the city dispelled in the minds of most of us that vision we had often had in our youth and had forgotten of Jerusalem the Golden. Whatever faith we had in the genuineness of the Holy Places was sorely tested and it was not long before we came to the conclusion that one either had to view every-thing through rosy-tinted spectacles and believe all that was said, or be convinced that most of it was sham and accordingly see the castles built up in our boyhood rudely shattered by a simple historical fact. Nevertheless Jerusalem possessed a great attraction for us. Outside the old city had grown up a comparatively new town with many modern buildings, and to the north was a genuine church of England—St. George's Cathedral.

The shops began to display their goods openly for the first time for three years, and the natives offered fruit—figs, oranges, nuts, etc.—for sale in the market places. And indeed it was an event of some importance to be able to walk the streets of the famous city Jerusalem and feel that one was really a Crusader, a descendant of those hardy people who 800 years ago had borne the heat and the burden of the day clad not in khaki drill, but in armour. The amount of correspondence which was handed over to the Army Postal Service was enormous—

and written let it be noted for the main part on German paper by German pencils—and in many a home in England to-day is treasured a Divisional Christmas Card for 1917 sent from Jerusalem. We had ideas of being able to spend our Christmas in the city, but that was not to be, and on Christmas Eve, 1917, we relieved the 180th Brigade in the line Beit Hannina—Tel-el-Ful astride the Nablous road. The weather became very bad and the climatic conditions were by no means pleasant. The line was held on the west by the Kensingtons in front of Hannain, and on the east by the Westminsters in front of Tel-el-Ful, and we were in support. Bivouacs had just been erected and we were settling down for a wet cold night when the Colonel sent for Company Commanders.

Headquarters was situated in an old tomb cut in the solid rock and entering we saw the C.O. seated at the head of a roughly made table and near him his senior officers. When we had all arrived he said " Just listen while I read out the Brigadier's Christmas greetings."

" . . . it is expected that the enemy will attack at dawn on Christmas morning."

It was an awkward moment, but the Colonel at once relieved the temporary gloom which had settled on us during the reading of the message by adding at the end " and England expects that every one will give the Turk a hearty Christmas greeting."

Dispositions were soon made. " A " Company moved out in support of the Kensingtons at Beit Hannina and " D " Company to the Westminsters, who were holding the line at Tel-el-Ful. The Companies were very weak and " D " Company was reinforced by No. 11 Platoon of " C " Company, the remainder of the Battalion moving to a hill behind Tel-el-Ful. It was midnight before the move was complete and nothing remained but to wait for dawn. It was a most appalling night ; a high wind and torrential rain make life very unpleasant when one is in bivouacs on top of a hill 3,000 feet high. Our bivouacs were flooded and we were soaked to the skin, but it was realised if the Turk attacked under such conditions he would be a hardier man than we expected. Christmas morning broke and the grey light from the east disclosed one of the most dismal pictures dawn could ever disclose. Jerusalem almost hidden in driving rain on Christmas morning ! As we expected, the attack did not take. place, though we could not but realise the irony of our dear friends at home hurrying off to church to sing " Christians awake, salute the happy morn," when the dear ones for whom they prayed had just spent the most miserable night of their existence in waiting for a dawn which in no circumstances could have been called happy. The rain continued all Christmas Day until the morning of the 26th when the sun came out and cheered us. That the attack was imminent we all knew, but the sun revived our spirits and by midday we were willing to tackle all the Turks in Asia. We had suffered several casualties from exposure, but a supply of whale oil for the feet did much to check wholesale sickness. Information came through that the attack really would take place on the 27th, and a few minutes after midnight of the 26/27th, the Turks pushed in an advanced post in front of Tel-el-Ful. The first main attack came about one hour later, supported by heavy artillery fire on the Westminsters' position in front of Tel-el-Ful. Shortly afterwards the Kensingtons were also heavily attacked to the west of that hill. The Turk had been reinforced by new troops from the Caucasus and was making a desperate effort to retake Jerusalem, so the brunt of this attack fell on our positions which covered the main road, and only road from the north. Two platoons of " D " Company were soon sent up under Lieutenant T. H. E. Clark to reinforce the left Company of the Westminsters and the struggle was intense. Eight attacks in all were made on the position in front of Tel-el-Ful, and in the heaviest just before dawn the Turks succeeded in effecting a footing in the main positions. The situation was grave and Colonel Gordon Clarke of the Westminsters thereupon ordered the officer in charge of " D " Company (Lieutenant Hutchison) to take the remainder of his Company and eject the Turk with the bayonet. This counter attack made by No. 16 Platoon, " D " Company, and No. 11 Platoon, " C," under Lieutenant R. H. Harris, M.C. ("Bulldog" Harris of the 1st Battalion), under the command of the O.C. "D " Company, in spite of severe shell fire, ejected the Turk from the main position, though not without sustaining severe losses. Lieutenant Harris, with a party of seven or eight men, became detached and was surrounded. They fought to the last and Harris, accounting for at least three of the enemy himself with the bayonet, was killed. All the remainder of his party were either killed or were wounded and taken prisoners. These were the only prisoners we lost in Palestine, but their loss was due solely to the vigour with which they pushed home their attack. The remainder of the Company lost heavily and had when they took over the line from which they had ejected the Turk but 50 per cent. of their original strength. Junction was made with Lieutenant Clark and the line was reorganised and held throughout the remainder of the day in spite of repeated attacks which were supported by heavy artillery shelling. The following letter received by our C.O. a few days later gives an appreciation of the value of the work done ;

Photo by Turner & Drinkwater, Hull.

2nd Lieut. R. H. HARRIS, M.C.
Killed in Action, Palestine, 1917.

To face page 320.

CIVIL SERVICE RIFLES 321

"Head Quarters, 60th Division,
"31st December, 1917.
"MY DEAR BISDEE,

"I visited the post held by the platoons of your Battalion in front of Tel-el-Ful. The number of dead, their attitude, their closeness to the parapet, the bomb and shell holes, are all witnesses to the grim struggle of your splendid men. They must have inflicted not less than 300 casualties in all. The fact that they maintained their line intact against heavy odds and a brave and determined enemy is an incident of which your Battalion may well be proud.

"I should much like to know who commanded the platoons and how many casualties they had.

"Accept my warmest congratulations on their courage and determination.

"Yours sincerely,
"(Signed), A. C. TEMPERLEY, Lieutenant Colonel,
"General Staff, 60th Division."

On the left in front of Beit Hannina, "A" Company did no less glorious work. After being in the line in the early morning they were withdrawn until about midday when the Turk made his final onslaught on our line. He pressed his attack right up to the stone breastworks which had been erected, and fought with determination. As on the right in the early morning, the situation was critical and "A" Company were called up to assist. In company with the Kensingtons they counter-attacked with the bayonet, and forced the enemy back. In this action, Lieutenant R. W. G. Andrews greatly distinguished himself.

A story of the 27th December would be very incomplete without mention of the gallantry of the other ranks, and particularly the stretcher bearers. These latter went out time after time under heavy rifle and machine-gun fire to bring in wounded comrades. Private Martin, "D" Company, went out with a fellow stretcher-bearer, Ridley, some forty or fifty yards from cover, and placed a wounded man on a stretcher. Whilst doing this Ridley was shot through the head, Martin thereupon, in spite of the fact that he was much the smaller of the two men, got his pal on his back, and commenced to carry him in. He stopped exhausted half-way, and after a brief rest shouldered his burden again, and got him under cover only to find that he was dead. Quite undismayed he again went out with another man, and succeeded in bringing in the first man safely. All this was done under aimed rifle and machine-gun fire. Martin afterwards was awarded the Military Medal although recommended for the V.C. When told of his reward a few days later all he said was "What about Ridley, sir, I did no more than he did," and that epitomises the self-sacrificing spirit of the stretcher-bearers. (Martin was killed in France some

x

months later while gallantly attending the wounded under heavy fire.)

" A " and " D " Companies were withdrawn from the line on the evening of the 27th December, and joining up with the remainder of the Battalion followed up the Turkish retirement northward next day, which resulted from the crushing blow by the 10th and 74th Divisions on the Turks' right flank.

The importance of the operations near Jerusalem at Christmas, 1917, were never properly realised at home. They were the result of the one really determined counter attack that the Turk made during the whole of the Palestine campaign. Jerusalem, and the crumpling of our right flank was his objective, and to attain it he brought down several new divisions from the Caucasus, but the result to him was not a victory but a real defeat, crushing casualties, and an immediate loss of many more miles of country.

Referring to our subsequent advance, Mr. W. T. Massey, the official Press correspondent at General Headquarters said in his dispatch, dated 31st December, 1917 :

" The rapid advance in most difficult country is due to the overwhelming defeat of the Turkish attempt to retake Jerusalem on December 27th, when, after resisting desperate attacks, the British delivered a masterly counter-stroke, causing the Turks, who had suffered tremendous losses, to yield almost impregnable positions and fall back along the Shechem (Nablous) Road, leaving in our firm possession points of great strategical importance."

General Allenby in his dispatch referring to the same operations says :

" The heaviest fighting took place to the east of Jerusalem— Nablous Road. Repeated attacks were made against Tel-el-Ful, a conspicuous hill from which Jerusalem and the intervening ground can be overlooked. The attacks were made by picked troops and pressed with great determination. At only one point did the enemy succeed in reaching the main line of defence, but he was driven out at once by the local reserves "—

and later referring to the western side of the road where " A " Company were engaged, he says :

" At 12.15 p.m. the enemy launched an unexpected attack of great strength against the whole front, in places he reached our main line of defence, but these successes were short lived, for, in each case, local counter-attacks carried out immediately were successful in restoring the line."

After the defeat of the Turk the Division pursued him, and a couple of days later were successful in capturing the heights at Bireh about ten miles north of Jerusalem. While passing through Ram Allah on the way to Bireh, some of the men we had lost when fighting at Tel-el-Ful were found wounded, having been left behind by the Turks.

CHAPTER XXXVI

THE capture of the Bireh Heights, and driving the Turk towards Nablous, completed the capture of Jerusalem, as far as attacks from the north of the city were concerned, but on the east and south-east there was still danger. On the 1st January, 1918, after a night in Jerusalem, the Battalion was ordered to take up an outpost line to the south-east of the town from Sur Bahir just off the Bethlehem Road, running in a north-easterly direction via Khirbit Jubb er Rumm to Abu Dis, just outside Bethany. The line, therefore, formed a defence about three or four miles from the city. Sur Bahir was held by " D " Company, Khirbit Jubb er Rumm by " C " Company, while " A " and " B " were at Abu Dis. The day was fine when the Battalion marched out of the town during the morning, but before proper communication could be established along the line, a heavy rain fell, and the whole countryside was enveloped in a thick mist. Each company, therefore, had to form its own strong points, and wait for dawn on the following day. In the darkness and mist it was impossible to move over the rough hilly country, and patrol work was limited to a couple of hundred yards. However, the next morning in brilliant sunshine patrols were pushed out, but no sign of the Turk was to be seen. Communication with the flank companies was obtained, and rations and water supplies were sent out to each of the companies in the line. Every one looked forward to a quiet tour of outpost duty. " D " Company, however, received orders to push out as far as the monastery at Ibn Obeid on the Wadi en Naar, which in Biblical times was known as the Brook Kidron, and was three miles south-east of Sur Bahir. The new line, therefore, ran from north to south, from Abu Dis to Ibn Obeid, passing through Jubb er Rumm. The country over which the line ran was composed of stony hills with deep wadis in the valleys, sometimes 500 feet below the summit of the surrounding hills. The monastery at Ibn Obeid which was the southern terminus of the line stood on the top of the cliffs of the Wadi en Naar which descended steeply for some 800 feet to the bed of the Wadi.
The monastery had been the scene of some heavy fighting a

few weeks previous to our arrival, in which a battalion of the Middlesex Regiment had fought with distinction, and had driven off repeated attacks of the Turks. When " D " Company, however, came upon the scene everything was peaceful. Only a few monks lived in the monastery, and they were soon packed off to Jerusalem, in case they acted as enemy spies. On the 10th January, the whole Battalion was relieved by the 2/13th Battalion (Kensingtons) on this outpost line, and moved to Bethany.

At Bethany three companies were billeted in the local school and a monastery near by, while " A " Company took up an outpost position at Sniper's Post, overlooking the Jericho road, about a mile or so ahead of the Battalion. Here we reorganised our specialist sections which had suffered heavy losses in the fighting around Jerusalem during the latter part of December. A new draft had just arrived from England, and they were initiated into the art of warfare in the East by constant training over the local hills. The remainder of the Battalion was employed on " road making," or perhaps I should say making cart tracks through the wadis near Abu Dis, and occasionally a strong force of about 200 men would reconnoitre the ground in front of the Turkish positions along the Jericho road ; especially towards the Arak Ibrahim Caves, some four miles away, where the Turk had a considerable garrison.

On the 20th " D " Company relieved " A " Company at Sniper's Post, but except for the occasional noise of two captured field guns at Bethany which were used against the Turks at Arak Ibrahim Caves, there was no sound of war. Six days later the Battalion moved back to Jerusalem and billeted in some empty schools in the German part of the city, while many of the officers were placed in private houses. The journey was full of interest, and the Mount of Olives, the Garden of Gethsemane, St. Stephen's Gate, were passed among other famous sights. On the way we met a Jewish funeral ; we thought that the Macedonian method of carrying the coffin lid in front of the procession, with the body exposed to the eyes of the curious, as being a crude method, but this funeral was even more gruesome. The party rushed along the road at a great pace, and the corpse wrapped in a blanket was merely suspended by cord at the head and foot to a long pole, which was carried on the shoulders of two men, while the body limply swung from side to side as they hurried along.

During this stay in the city of Jerusalem, parties under the expert guidance of our Padre (Rev. G. C. Cavalier) were allowed to visit the Holy Places in the town. I need hardly recite the wonders of the Holy City as many guide-books will do so far better. As far as the Battalion was concerned we enjoyed the privilege of seeing these ancient Biblical landmarks. Souvenir hunting in the shops and the purchasing of food stuffs (chiefly fruit and bread, which was of a greenish hue when cut, and of the consistency of gluten) formed the chief amusement during the day. At night time, however, the two Divisional concert parties, the " Barnstormers " and " Roosters," both of which had made great " hits " in Cairo and Alexandria, were in full swing at their respective temporary theatres, and provided us with splendid recreation.

Major Grissel from the 74th Division took over command of the Battalion on the 28th January, our own Commanding Officer, Lieutenant-Colonel Bisdee, having been granted leave to the United Kingdom.

Danger, however, soon occurred from the epidemics of disease and fever in the city, and the Battalion was moved out of the town to tents and bivouacs on the slopes of the Mount of Olives ; Headquarters being in a sheik's house near by. The camping site was just off the Nablous Road, overlooking the Garden of Gethsemane, and was on dry, dusty terraces of barren land which in a few days became a wretched quagmire. Heavy torrents of rain continually poured down for four days and four nights without a break, and every one was swamped out and miserable. Refuge each night was taken in the Divisional theatres, and large parties would march across the city in the pouring rain simply for the comfortable shelter of the " theatre." When the weather had cleared a little the Battalion was employed on road-making, and one day an exhibition of " sangar " building was given by a company of Indian troops who were past-masters in hill-fighting.

It was, however, unhealthy to live in the mud of the camp, and the Battalion was moved up to Sir John Grey Hill's house at the top of the hill. It was a large desolate mansion, overlooking the valley of the Jericho Road, while in the far distance the Moab Mountains could be seen. A short stay of two days here and the Battalion was moved to bivouacs in the wadis of the Abu Hindi Wadi on the 13th of February, where preparations were made for an attack eastwards over the hills towards the Jericho Plain.

The Turkish line east of Jerusalem consisted of a line of entrenched strongholds on the hills some eight miles from the city. The southern extremity of the line rested on Muntar, a high hill just east of Ibn Obeid Monastery, and came north via Jebel Ektief, Talat ed Dumm, across the Jericho Road to the Arak Ibrahim Caves, and thence over Ras el Tawil to the deep ravine of the Wadi Um Farrar.

The British line ran practically parallel to this line, a few miles nearer the city, with Ibn Obeid forming the right or south flank,

and ran north via Jubb er Rumm, Abu Dis, Sniper's Post, on to
the Jericho Road, and thence north over Suffra to Mukmas.

The intention of the attack was to drive the Turk from the
high ground on the west of the Jordan Plain, and thereby render
the Holy City immune from attack from the east.   The advance
was to be made in three distinct phases as follows :
    " (1) The capture of Muntar, Arak Ibrahim Caves and Ras el
Tawil.
    " (2) The capture of Jebel Ektief and Talat ed Dumm.
    " (3) To advance to the steep cliffs overlooking the Jericho or
Jordan Valley."

The three Brigades of the 60th Division were holding the line
in this sector, and the objectives were allotted as follows :
    " (a) 181st Brigade, Ras el Tawil.
    " (b) 180th Brigade, Arak Ibrahim Caves and Talet ed Dumm.
    " (c) 179th Brigade, Muntar and Jebel Ektief.

In the 179th Brigade, the 2/14th Battalion (London Scottish)
were given the hill of Muntar as their objective, and they concentrated in the depths of the Wadi en Naar near Ibn Obeid.
During the night of the 19th of February the companies deployed and crept up the hill-side under cover of darkness.   At
dawn the trenches were heavily bombarded, and the attack was
pushed home under the artillery support.   The hill was captured, and fortunately the strength and resistance of the enemy
had been over-estimated, with the result that the Scottish
casualties were small.   The same morning, the 180th Brigade
were successful and captured the caves at Arak Ibrahim in the
centre of the Turkish line with comparatively few casualties.
Further north, however, the 181st Brigade had met with strong
opposition at Ras el Tawil, and after several hours of heavy
fighting gained possession of the hill and put to flight a strong
force of Turks.   Casualties, however, on both sides were fairly
heavy.

The first phase of the advance had proved successful, and the
battalions detailed for the second day's move were able to push
forward and prepare for the assaults on Jebel Ektief and Talat
ed Dumm.   Like the first day's operations the second day's
attacks resulted in the objectives being taken, although the
fighting was more strenuous as the objectives were surrounded
by more difficult country, which provided the defenders with
better cover.   The Turk, finding himself overwhelmed and
outmanœuvred, retired over the hills to the Jordan Valley,
covering his withdrawal with machine-gun rear-guards so that
the third day's work came under the heading of " peaceful
penetration."   Thus the 60th Division was master of the Jordan
Valley from the commanding heights on the west of the plain,

and the possibility of an attack on Jerusalem from the east had disappeared.

To return to the particular part in these operations performed by the 2/15th Battalion it will be remembered that they were in bivouacs in the Wadi Hindi on the 13th February.

For the few days previous to the commencement of the advance we were occupied in road-making in the wadi beds to assist the bringing forward of guns, ambulances and transport for the attack. Reconnaisances were also made towards the front, and on one of these "stunts" our Brigade Major, Captain Sherston, was seriously wounded in the leg.

On the early morning of the 19th of February we were awakened by the artillery fire from Abu Dis, where our heavies were assisting the attack of the London Scottish on Muntar. A few hours later we learnt of the success, and realised it was now our turn. During the morning the Battalion gradually moved along the valley of the Wadi Hindi under cover of the surrounding heights, "D" Company forming the advance guard. After advancing some three miles the Battalion was halted as further advance was impossible by day. Under the cover of an outpost line the Battalion rested until darkness came, thus making further progress possible. During the afternoon patrols were sent out and reconnaissance towards Jebel Ektief was made, and resulted in a sharp skirmish with the Turkish advanced posts, but no casualties occurred to our party, although several Turks were seen to be carried away on stretchers.

About 6 p.m. the order was given to advance to the attack, and three platoons of "D" Company were ordered to "make good" the high ground west of the deep ravine in front of Jebel Ektief while a fourth platoon under Sergeant Cross moved along the wadi bed to a point where the deep wadi in front of Jebel Ektief branched off to the left. When these platoons had pushed ahead sufficiently the remainder of the Battalion marched along the wadi in order to reach the line of deployment before daybreak.

Probably of all the country over which the Battalion had passed throughout its stay in both Salonika and Palestine none could compare with the deep ravines and precipitous cliffs over which the advanced guard had to pass, and if this statement is accepted, there is no need for further comment on the difficulty of the advance. To move forward a matter of three miles occupied a full six hours of hard climbing over ridges and difficult descents down precipices. The night was exceedingly dark, and great credit is due to Lieutenants Clark and Neall, platoon commanders in "D" Company, for maintaining their direction and reaching their objective ; the men behaved splendidly and struggled along through this wretched patch of the Holy Land.

Fortunately no opposition in strength was met except an occasional volley of fire from the Turkish advanced posts, but they soon retired to their main position on Jebel Ektief. Great caution, however, was necessary as large bodies of the enemy had been seen that afternoon leaving Jebel Ektief, and advancing towards our lines. When, however, the advanced guard had reached the limit of their advance, the Battalion pushed along the bed of the stony wadi, and were supposed to halt at the junction of the wadi in front of Jebel Ektief and the main wadi, where they hoped to turn the corner into their place of deployment. However, the noise had apparently disturbed the Turk, and he constantly poured machine-gun fire on to this junction corner. It was therefore found necessary to find another way into the Jebel Ektief Wadi, and the only way was to climb the steep, precipice-like sides of the main wadi on to the high ground held by " D " Company. This was accomplished, but how, no one can tell ; when the Battalion with its Lewis guns, regimental aid post, and signalling mules reached the crest, dawn was appearing in the east. It was decided, therefore, to make a hurried descent into the Jebel Ektief Wadi in spite of the casual fire from the enemy's snipers and machine guns. Luckily the going down into the second wadi was easier and more speedily accomplished than the climb from the first wadi, and just as daylight arrived the tail of the Battalion disappeared into the bed of Jebel Ektief Wadi, out of sight of the Turks. Once in the bottom of the wadi the companies sorted themselves out and prepared for the actual assault, " A " and " B " being the attacking companies, " C " in support, and " D " in reserve. It had been arranged that the 2/13th (Kensingtons) were to assault the position on our left, having approached the wadi at Jebel Ektief by a night march on a parallel route to the one we had taken. Unfortunately, the ground over which the Kensingtons had to pass had proved too difficult, and when daylight came they found themselves perched on a precipice unable to cross the deep ravine before them.

At seven o'clock on the morning of the 20th February, the artillery opened up a heavy bombardment on the hill. The advance up the hillside described officially as " trickling forward " should have taken place under this barrage, while the assault was timed for eight o'clock when the barrage was to lift.

Unfortunately little or no progress could be made owing to the fact that the heavies were shelling the " bench mark " some 1,000 yards behind the enemy's forward lines thereby leaving the enemy's machine guns undisturbed, while at the same time other machine guns on our left raked us, those, in fact, which should have been concentrating their attention on our brother battalion, the Kensingtons, who had been so unfortunate in their advance march.

At eight o'clock, when we should have assaulted, the attack was therefore hung up for a while. An hour later a Forward Observation Officer having come up, a second barrage was fired for fifteen minutes concentrating accurately on the forward Turkish trenches.

At the same time " C " Company was taken from support, and by means of quick concealed movement succeeded in moving to our left flank, thereby taking up the position and rôle in the action which should have been the Kensingtons'.

" C " Company was able to make some ground and also was able to give great assistance to " A " and " B " Companies by bringing enfilade fire to bear on the snipers and machine guns that were holding them up.

As this second barrage lifted, the Battalion assaulted the steep hill and in spite of heavy frontal fire were successful in capturing the first line. By this time the two companies of the Queen's Westminsters had come up on to our left, and under the gallant leadership of Captain Flower silenced the machine guns which had enfiladed our attack. When the first ridge was gained it was found that a valley beyond led to the second ridge, and here the Turks were again strongly resisting. After a breather, however, the " Charge " was given, and the men, led by Captain Wills and Company Sergeant Major Oldcorn of " C " Company, rushed over the valley and gained the second ridge only to find a still further ridge strongly held. Machine-gun fire from the flank was still causing considerable casualties to us, but after a breather, the Battalion assaulted the third ridge, and thus completed the capture of Jebel Ektief. The Turks fled down the precipitous slopes, into the Jordan Valley, and could be seen collecting in small groups as though preparing for a counter-attack. The Battalion's casualties in this action numbered about one hundred.

Further north of Jebel Ektief, the London Irish of the 180th Brigade had succeeded in capturing Talat ed Dumm after heavy fighting. The Turk, however, still had isolated machine guns on the hills between the recently captured positions of Jebel Ektief and Talat ed Dumm, and these poured a persistent fire into our flank. In the late afternoon the Kensingtons came up on our left, and soon cleared the ground of these irritating machine guns, and by the evening everything was quiet except for an occasional shell from a Turkish battery which could be seen some couple of miles away across the Jordan Plain, well out of the range of our guns. Just before dark we had a splendid view of the Jericho Plain.

No other valley in the world presents such extraordinary

physical features, none other has been the subject of such various theories as to its origin and character. From our position on the eastern edge of Jebel Ektief, the ground sloped steeply for about 2,000 feet to the flat plain below, which stretched for over twenty miles to the foot-hills of the Moab Mountains. Winding through the plain the river Jordan could be seen in places where its steep banks were broken by small branch ravines ; while to the south the dismal flat water of the Dead Sea was visible. The only town on this extensive plain was Jericho, and as the light failed it appeared as a dead city of mud huts.

The following morning, the 21st February, the London Scottish were moved on to the plain as far as the white ruins of Neba Musa, and Australian cavalry patrolled the Jericho area. The Turk had crossed the Jordan, and all was quiet. About midday, however, four enemy planes flew over our positions, and but for a remarkable cloud which suddenly enveloped the hill, would no doubt have poured bullets into our bivouacs. When the cloud lifted they were nowhere to be seen. For two days the Battalion remained on the heights of Jebel Ektief, and although free from fighting it was a most strenuous business carrying rations and water from the Quartermaster's Stores and Transport which were now in the Jebel Ektief Wadi, from which the attack had started, some 600 or 700 feet below the summit of the hill.

On the 23rd February, the Battalion was ordered to move as far back as Jerusalem.

CHAPTER XXXVII

ON the 23rd of February the Battalion left Jebel Ektief, and after some discussion in the wadi near the transport lines, some companies chose the route via the Wadi Hindi, Abu Dis and Bethany, while others struck across country over a distinct track, supposed to be the remains of a pilgrims' road to the Jordan, and thence along the main Jerusalem–Jericho Road, via Bethany. Which was the better route has not been decided, sufficient to say that the troops hated both. Rain poured down when we were half-way to Jerusalem, and when Sir John Grey Hills' house was reached late at night no one had the heart to argue as to the better way from Jebel Ektief. On the following day (Sunday) we availed ourselves of the rest. In the evening many attended Divine Service in the huge chapel of the German Emperor's Palace, near to the Mount of Olives. It is a huge structure, and a wonderful view of the surrounding country could be obtained from the tower. It was used as a Corps Headquarters during the operations around Jerusalem ; not quite the purpose for which the Kaiser had intended it. The chapel was wonderfully decorated inside, but the two things which struck one as being odd, and even profane, were the panelling of the altar, which was decorated by the crests of each of the Kaiser's sons ; and the ceiling, which was divided into two parts ; one containing a beautiful painting of the Son of God, while the other contained, equally well painted, a picture of the Kaiser and his wife sitting on their thrones !

On the 25th of February the Battalion moved from Jerusalem, further north to Mukmas ; the route was along the Nablous Road as far as Er Ram, a distance of about five miles, and here we struck off the main road eastwards over the roughly made military roads as far as Jeba. Here the route became more difficult and was across rough mountain paths making it necessary at times for the Battalion to march in single file. The transport could not travel the whole route, and was halted near Mukmas, from which point camels and mules carried stores and rations. The Battalion halted on the hills near Umm et Talah, and outposts facing the Jericho plain were taken up by " D " Company.

The distance as the crow flies from Jebel Ektief to Umm et Talah was about five miles, but the country was of such a nature that the only route between these points entailed a long march through Jerusalem, a distance of nearly twenty miles. Just in front of the outpost position was Jebel Kuruntul, reputed to be the Mount of Temptation. For nearly a month of delightful weather all was peaceful on our immediate front. Occasionally patrols pushed out to the front and explored the deep ravines leading on to the Jericho Plain, but only once were we fired on by the Turks, and then from a considerable range, probably 1,000 yards. Acting on the principle, however, that the Devil finds work for idle hands to do, that wonderful pastime for tired troops was revived, namely road-making, and large fatigue parties were so employed. It had been a source of great interest to some of us that nowhere behind the Turkish lines, away from the four main roads which run north to Nablous, south to Bethlehem, east to Jericho, and west to Jaffa from the city of Jerusalem, could any trace be found of ways of communication, except an occasional mule track; whereas, behind our own lines, a network of specially constructed tracks was always to be found. It was a mystery to us how the Turks ever moved their guns, men and supplies in sufficient quantity to even replace normal daily wastage, but the fact that after the repulse of the counter attack on Jerusalem in December, 1917, a Turkish Quartermaster surrendered to one of our posts because he, a Quartermaster, could not get sufficient food, may indicate that they suffered from shortages through lack of roads and means of communication.

We had often gazed at dawn on the gorgeous sunrise over the Mountains of Moab, and seen the dull silver of the Dead Sea turned to burnished gold; we had also seen that white streak across the dark plain of Jericho which denoted the presence of that wonderful stream, the Jordan, but the thought that the words of the old song "One more ribber to cross" would ever come literally true never entered our heads. If it did we gave it no serious thought. We had heard of the Jordan Valley and its appalling heat in summer (for had not the Turk left in Jericho a note to the effect that they would return in the autumn to bury us), and also were familiar with the expression "go to Jericho," so, indeed, had no wish to spend any time there. If the shades of the hereafter are hotter than the scene of Joshua's miracle they can have no terrors for the 60th London Division. "Brass hats," however, have ever since their creation been seers of visions and dreamers of dreams, but their decision to give us an Easter holiday in Moab could only have been the result of a nightmare.

Accordingly, the 21st March, 1918, saw the 60th Division concentrated with the Anzac Mounted Division in the Jordan

Valley, ready to carry out a raid on a scale unheard of in the annals of the war: that is, penetrating over thirty miles into enemy territory of the wildest nature, with the destruction of the Hedjaz Railway at Annam as the objective. The Civil Service Rifles crossed the river on the afternoon of the 23rd of March by a pontoon bridge at Makhadet Hajlah, which had been gallantly constructed under fire by the Engineers, and moved up the left bank of the river, passing on our way the Commander-in-Chief, General Allenby, and the Duke of Connaught, who was on a tour of inspection well within range of the Turkish field artillery. Our object to the north was to rout out a nest of machine guns which was delaying the crossing at the El Ghoranyieh Ford some five miles to the north, but to our delight this particular body had realised the threat to their rear, and had "impshied."

We bivouacked for the night in the Wadi Nimrin, near Umm Enkhala, and at 5.0 a.m. the next day moved out in support of the London Scottish and the Queen's Westminsters, who attacked the hill of El Haud which, held in force by the Turk, barred the second means of approach to Es Salt—that by way of the Wadi Arsinyet.

A Boche "pip squeak" battery, which endeavoured to hinder us, drew the attention upon itself of one of our own 4·5 howitzer batteries, and speedily ceased fire. We were not called upon to assist, and were fortunate to witness a most successful attack in open order against an extended position. The sight of lines of London infantry advancing calmly under a heavy enemy field and machine-gun fire, and also of the final assault with the bayonet was one to be remembered and treasured. El Haud was taken with little loss to our forces, and we moved up to the foot-hills and bivouacked in the Wadi Arsinyet, near El Haud.

The river Jordan at Makhadet Hajlah is 1,200 feet below sea level, and El Haud is 846 feet above, and the weather changed, becoming steadily worse. The night was wet and bitterly cold, and we were not sorry to start at 7.0 a.m. the next day on our advance up the Arsinyet track to Es Salt (Ramoth Gilead).

In heavy rain up a most slippery, muddy, and stony track, we toiled upwards and upwards as advanced guard to the Brigade, which, with a Regiment of Australian Light Horse and Mountain Battery, was soon strung out in single file. Communication was maintained with the 181st Brigade on the main Es Salt Road by means of a portable wireless installation, carried by the Light Horse. After a most exhausting climb of nearly 3,000 feet, we arrived on the outskirts of Es Salt about 1.0 p.m., thoroughly fatigued and soaked to the skin. The weather was bitterly cold, and it was felt all the more, for in a little over twenty-four hours we had moved from the tropical heat of the Jordan Valley up some 4,800 feet to the climatic conditions in winter of the top of a mountain higher than Snowdon. The Turk had retired hurriedly, and offered little opposition, and further progress being impossible owing to our exhausted state we bivouacked—and slept in inches of mud. The night was disturbed by much rifle fire from Es Salt, and at dawn on the 26th, No. 16 Platoon was detailed to reconnoitre the town. Under Lieutenant Andrew, who was acting as O.C. Company, they entered the town to find no trace of the Turk, and to receive a tumultuous welcome from the population who, during the night, had kept up a " feu de joie " from their house-tops, which noise we had interpreted as hostile rifle fire. We were the first British infantry to enter Es Salt, for it was not until some hours later that the 181st Brigade, which had been moving up the main road from Shunet Nimrin, arrived in the town. Supplies were lacking owing to the great difficulty of getting the camels up the slippery mountain track, and an officer was detailed to proceed to the 181st Brigade and bring back some water camels—water being the pressing need.

The remainder of the Division moved up the Annam road, and the defence of Es Salt was left to the Civil Service Rifles. The same evening the Battalion moved out to the north-east of the town to Keh Huda (3,597 feet), and took up a position covering the route from the north to Es Salt.

News came through of a possible attack by some 2,000 Circassian cavalry, and arrangements were at once made for their proper reception. Time available was short, but by toiling all night under the protection of standing patrols of the Australian Light Horse, dawn on the Maundy Thursday saw the 2/15th snugly settled ready behind stone sangars. Firing started with the first light of dawn and continued throughout the day, but no serious attack was attempted by the Turk.

At dawn on Good Friday, under cover of a thick mist, the Turks attacked with bombs a post in the centre of the Battalion. An energetic reply with Mills hand and rifle grenades, and a burst of fire from a machine gun resulted in their speedy repulse. The mist suddenly lifted, and opposite a neighbouring post was discovered a Turkish captain and his batman, with their kit complete. He was brought in and it transpired that he had set out with 200 men to assault the hill under cover of the mist, but his left flank got too far forward and pressed the attack before the remainder were ready, and they in consequence— like the burglar who heard the noise overhead—thought all was lost and fled, leaving their officer stranded on the hillside. In his pocket was found a small diagram which showed the relative positions of all our Lewis and machine guns, and this caused no little searching in the mind, for we had, as we thought,

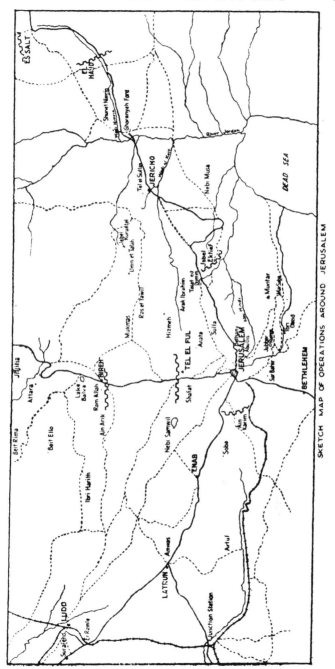

SKETCH MAP OF OPERATIONS AROUND JERUSALEM

camouflaged them successfully. However, even if he, the captain, knew, his snipers apparently did not, for, though throughout the week-end we were continually sniped, one of our Lewis guns, though continually in action, had not a shot fired at it.

There were constant alarms, and on the night of the 30th/31st March " D " Company repulsed four separate determined attacks on their position, with no loss to themselves. On the right and left " A " and " B " Companies were troubled slightly, but the brunt of the defence of Es Salt fell on the centre of the line.

The situation was nevertheless serious, and the 2/14th and 2/16th Battalions were brought back to Es Salt.

The Battalion was relieved on the night of the 31st of March, and at dawn moved down to the south side of Es Salt. The Divisional withdrawal from Annam, the assault on which place had not been entirely successful, was now in full swing, and the majority of the Armenian population of Es Salt, terrified at the prospect of the return of the terrible Turk, was hastily evacuating the town. The road, which had been churned up by men, horses, guns, and wheeled transport, was inches deep in liquid mud, and was packed with refugees. Old men and boys, women and children of all ages, with their household goods in large bundles on their backs, staggered along obsessed with great fear. Their flight was terrible, and not a few of us hurriedly realised that it is not only troops who suffer in war time. We could give little assistance ; our own baggage wagons were already over-burdened and our own loads were heavy, but we did what we could.

At 8.0 a.m. on the 1st of April (Easter Monday), after standing in full marching order in the mud for a solid hour, we started our retirement, and though hindered and hampered by the crowd of refugees which surged and swayed either side of us, we marched steadily until 5.0 a.m. next day, when we emerged from the hills at Shunet Nimrin, and bivouacked for a few hours, after which we continued and, crossing the Jordan River by the Ghoraniyeh Ford, we arrived at a position in the Wadi Nuemiah about 3 p.m., having covered a distance of about thirty miles since 8.0 p.m. the previous night.

Every one was footsore, dirty, unshaven, with seven days' growth of beard, and thoroughly tired, but we soon settled down to our first proper night's rest for nine days, during which time we had experienced almost the extremes of heat and cold, and had marched about seventy miles through some of the most atrocious country our army has ever operated in. The other Brigades had fared even worse than we had, but the whole Division had covered itself with honour, and had no reason to be dispirited at the apparent failure of its novel enterprise. Gains in warfare are not measured by territory alone, and the influence of this raid—indeed it was almost a campaign—had a far reaching effect on the strategy of the Palestine campaign.

We were happy, on our return to the Jordan Valley, to welcome back from leave in England our Commanding Officer, Lieut.-Colonel Bisdee, and the Battalion, though it had worked well under its temporary Commander, was delighted to see its Commanding Officer back once again, and it speaks much for the spirit of comradeship of the Regiment that no one was perhaps more pleased to be with us again than Colonel Bisdee himself.

After a day's rest in the valley, we moved once again up towards Jerusalem, and halted at Talat ed Dumm for twenty-four hours. At Talat ed Dumm there is a wayside house reputed to be the Good Samaritan Inn of Biblical times. After this short rest we again pushed up the old Jericho road, which we had come to know almost as well as the Strand. On arriving at Jerusalem we were again billeted on the Mount of Olives. The road from Jericho goes through particularly desolate and wild country, and no doubt in years to come, many a Civil Service Rifleman, when questioned by his offspring concerning the man who fell among thieves, will truthfully say, "If you had seen the road you would not be surprised."

It was not a habit in those days to keep us idle, and we were soon moved on up the Jerusalem–Nablous road via Bireh and Ram allah to the Wadi el Jib, where we temporarily relieved the 10th (Irish) Division. The Battalion was in reserve, and bivouacked on a terraced hillside which was covered with fig trees and vines. It was very hot, and we were glad to resume our summer kit. The camping ground was one of the most pleasant we had experienced in Palestine, and we made the most of it. There were flowers and plants in great profusion, and botanists amongst us spent hours collecting specimens ; one of them, a botanist by profession, collected a hundred or so specimens which he had never seen before, and which he could not name.

Of actual war we saw but little, occasional bombing raids were made by enemy planes, but our chief enemy was just behind us—a gunner officer in charge of an 18-pounder battery, whose idea of humour was to give an order for ten rounds gun fire regularly each night at varying times between midnight and 4.0 a.m. Our considered opinion of this gentleman cannot be published here.

A week later we moved back as far as Attara, where we gave a most sincere and regretful God speed to our Colonel, who left us to take command of the 2/13th Battalion London Regiment. Colonel Bisdee had joined us at El Shaulth in September, 1917,

Y

and no Commanding Officer was ever so popular, both with his officers and men.   He had instilled into the Regiment a magnificent spirit, and it is no idle boast to say that the Regiment would have gone into action anywhere and under any circumstances with Colonel Bisdee, with no misgivings and fully aware that, whatever happened, he would be their leader.

Photo by Searle, S.W.

LT.-COL. T. E. BISDEE, D.S.O., M.C. (D.C.L.I.)
Commanded 2nd Battalion, 9th October, 1917, to May, 1918.

To face page 338.

CHAPTER XXXVIII

ON the 23rd of April, 1918, the Battalion marched south from Attara and encamped for the night just north of Ram Allah, near Lake Ballua. The march was carried out during the evening, and the bright weather made it enjoyable. On the two following days the journey was continued towards Jerusalem, and on the night of the 25th we halted at Shafat, a few miles north of the city. Rumours of another " stunt " across the Jordan were then confirmed, and on the night of the 27th the Battalion marched down the Jericho road once more to Talat ed Dumm, arriving there about 11.0 p.m., where the concentration of transport foreboded another operation on a large scale. The following evening the Battalion moved to the Jordan Valley, and crossed over the river at Ghoraniyeh Ford, which was then held by Indian troops. Although it was only April the heat in the valley was terrific during the day, and white troops would, no doubt, have suffered considerable losses from disease had they been stationed there for any considerable length of time. The next day was spent amid the thick brushwood on the plain, and every available piece of shade was used, but even under this protection the damp heat was nigh unbearable, and only a minimum of clothing in the shape of drill shorts were worn by most. There was a large concentration of troops in the area, and preparations were made for an attack on the foot-hills of the Moab Mountains.

On the 30th the attack was launched by the 179th Brigade, the Westminsters on the left and the London Scottish on the right, while the 180th Brigade was operating farther south. Under a heavy artillery bombardment the troops advanced from their positions of deployment, which they had taken up during the night. They attacked the first ridge and, after heavy fighting, obtained a footing. Many prisoners were captured and casualties were inflicted on the enemy. The 2/15th were held in reserve at Ghoraniyeh Ford, and when a crowd of over 200 prisoners appeared we felt that the operation was so successful that we should not be needed ; it transpired afterwards, however, that these Turks were not captured in the actual assault, but had been detailed to reconnoitre our concentration on the plain, and while coming over had walked into the London Scottish, who were pushing forward for the attack. They made no resistance, and were soon sent to the rear as prisoners.

After the first ridge had been taken it was found that the whole position was strongly held by the Turk, and that further advance over deep ravines swept by machine guns would be very difficult. Repeated attempts were made to push forward, but only heavy casualties resulted. The actual objective of the 179th Brigade was a steep hill called El Haud, which lay some six miles east of the Jordan, and formed part of a continuous line of steep, rocky hills that bordered the Jericho Plain on the east.

On the night of the 30th April the London Scottish had only been able to gain the first ridge of El Haud after heavy fighting, and during the following day held on to the captured ground with the idea of pressing forward the attack at dawn next morning. In order to support this second effort " A " and " B " Companies of the 2/15th pushed forward to the foot of El Haud, to act as local supports. The second attack on the 1st of May was also unsuccessful, not only at this one particular spot but along the whole Divisional front. Heavy machine-gun fire swept each ridge, both from the front and the flanks, so cunningly had the Turk arranged his emplacements. Throughout the day desultory fighting took place and small local attacks were made, but no general advance could be accomplished. During the evening of the 1st of May " C " and " D " Companies were brought up from the Wadi Nimrin, where they had been moved the previous night, and during the night of the 1st the Battalion relieved the London Scottish on El Haud. Orders were received on the same night to attack at dawn. This meant a busy night in reconnoitring. " A " and " B " Companies were detailed for the attack, with " C " Company in support, and just before dawn they deployed for the attack on the right flank of the hill, from which point it appeared the approach to the summit was easiest. " D " Company remained in possession of the captured ridge.

The attack was launched forward with great spirit and dash, but was met with the same murderous fire that had swept down the London Scottish in their attempts, and the 2/15th could only push forward a little way, gaining some 500 yards and a small hill, thus forming for themselves an unpleasant little salient into the enemy's lines. Even then casualties were fairly heavy, and the work of carrying back the wounded was made more hazardous by the Turk, who fired on every stretcher with his machine guns throughout the day. Captain Peatfield, " A " Company, was reported missing, but late at night he returned under cover of darkness, having lain out all day in the sun, a few yards from a Turkish machine gun, apparently dead.

At dusk the wounded were collected, and "A" and "B" were withdrawn, "C" Company staying on the captured ground and hastily organising it for defence by building sangars.

During the afternoon two platoons of "D" Company, under Lieutenant K. P. Neall, had attempted to push forward from the main ridge, but the progress was soon arrested by heavy machine-gun fire, and this proved conclusively that frontal attacks were impossible. From the result of this local attack it was learnt that between ourselves and the Turk was a deep ravine with precipitous banks. The night of the 3rd of May was fairly quiet except for the intermittent machine-gun and rifle fire from both sides. On the following morning, however, the Turk made a determined counter attack on our immediate right, against the London Irish of the 180th Brigade. Curiously, just before this counter attack took place, four enemy planes flew over our lines and poured machine-gun fire down at us. They did little actual damage, and one of them was brought down by our Lewis-gun fire. Every one was on the alert for a repetition of the aeroplane attack and sought cover behind the numerous boulders on the hill. However, the planes sailed out of sight behind the summit of El Haud, and just as every one thought of coming from their cover a sentry group in front of the Battalion on our right shouted "they're coming over," at which every one near by took immediate cover, but were soon surprised to find that no aeroplanes appeared but that a force of Turks about 250 strong rushed their position and drove them off. The Turkish "coup," however, was short lived, and an immediate counter attack by the "Irish" sent them hurrying back to their lines with loss. However, the incident was disastrous to that Company of the 2/15th which was holding the little salient which had been gained during the morning attack of the previous day, as the Turk was able to pour machine-gun fire into the rear of "C" Company, causing casualties. The gallant action of Private Freer, a signaller, in remaining at his telephone though severely wounded and under close-range rifle fire, materially assisted the "Irish" to regain their position, for Captain Wills, of "C" Company, was thus able to send back information which led to the "Irish" receiving adequate support from our machine guns and eighteen pounders.

Later in the day the enemy aeroplanes returned, but this time devoted their attentions to the transport lines and A.S.C. dumps near Ghoraniyeh Ford. For the rest of the day the infantry could make no progress, and spent their time watching the artillery bombardment of those places where machine guns had been located. The Turk was clever in concealing his emplacements, and it was only in the evening when a slight breeze sprang up were we able to detect one that had been firing at us throughout the whole day. This machine gun was in a cave in the hill side, and the entrance to the cave had been cleverly camouflaged with a blanket of the same colour as the surrounding rocks, and not until the breeze caused the blanket to move was it realised that the fire had been coming from an apparently solid rock. However, attentions were soon upon this spot, and one of our machine guns poured heavy fire into the cave, tearing the blanket in shreds, and no doubt killing the enemy gunners.

On the evening of the 4th May orders were received that the whole of the British Force would be withdrawn to the Ghoraniyeh Bridgehead as the Turks had sent a considerable force down the Jordan Valley from the north, and which had been driven back by our cavalry that afternoon. However it was realised that should this attack by the Turk succeed ι,ιr left flank and our line of retreat would both be seriously threatened. In the Battalion arrangements were made for " D " Company to be left as a rear-guard, holding the hill of El Haud until the rest of the Battalion had got a good start across the plain. " D " Company kept up an occasional Lewis gun and rifle fire for nearly an hour and then left the hill to the mercy of the Turks. Every one was relieved to reach the wire entanglements of the Ghoraniyeh defences the gaps in which were guarded by Indian cavalry. The amusing part, however, was that when the Battalion returned to its bivouac area of a few days previous they found " D " Company there first. Apparently being a smaller force they were more mobile and certainly they knew the shortest cut home. Once inside the wire a few hours' rest was granted, and at 3 a.m. the withdrawal was resumed as far as Tel el Sultan, a ruined village near Jericho. We arrived at our bivouac area early in the morning, and in the glorious warmth of the day every one enjoyed a thorough rest after the unsatisfactory hard fighting of the past few days. Before leaving the subject of El Haud a word of praise is due to the Divisional R.A.M.C. for the splendid manner in which they evacuated the wounded during the fighting, and had erected a large field hospital tent well within range of shell fire under the slopes of El Haud.

On the 6th of May the Battalion had the surprise of its life, when orders were received to pack up and move to Jericho, where motor lorries were to take us as far back as Jerusalem. Never in its existence had the Battalion partaken of such luxury, but it is regretted that we all thought that this kindness to tired troops was to move them to another part of the front where they were needed in a hurry.

In the late hours of the afternoon the Battalion boarded the lorries and the convoy started its journey to Jerusalem, along the new Jericho road, which is a masterpiece in mountain roads, and was built under German influence. About half-way home we met several regiments of Indian cavalry proceeding in the direction of the Jordan Valley, where they were to hold the line during the summer months. Many of them wore the Mons Star ribbon, and apparently had seen fighting in France. After passing these troops rain commenced to fall and those who had greedily sought the seats beside the driver paid the penalty and were soon drenched through. The lorries pulled up just north of Jersualem on the Nablous road, from which point each load of men marched independently to the camping ground near Shafat, which we had occupied only a week previously. The writer was detailed to supervise the unloading of the Battalion, and when they had finally " debussed " he made his way to Shafat probably about 45 minutes after the first party of the 2/15th had left their lorry. In spite of the rain and the muddy ground bivouacs had been erected and each one had a small candle burning inside. To see the camp from the roadway it would have appeared to a casual observer that it had been in existence for several weeks, so expert had the Battalion become in erecting its temporary home. Finding his bivouac the writer was soon presented with a plate of bread, bully beef, pickles, cheese and a mug of tea by his batman.

On the 7th, the G.O.C. Division inspected the Battalion and complimented it on the splendid way in which it had stuck to its unsuccessful work in the recent visit across the Jordan.

The following day the Battalion moved north a few miles as far as Ram Allah ; the march was not long, the road was fair, and the weather was glorious, and by 2 p.m. the Battalion had settled down in its new area, and dinners were being cooked. I have already referred to the speed with which the Battalion made themselves at home on the night we arrived at Shafat, but as a further illustration the following true story may be given. On this day's march we were followed by the London Scottish, who were in turn followed by an officer of our own Battalion and a draft fresh from England who were on their way to join us. Having missed the Battalion as it left Shafat this new officer attempted to catch us up. We arrived at our bivouac area and moved off the road to allow the Scottish to pass to their camp which was farther north. We immediately put up our bivouacs and commenced cooking. The new officer and his men followed the Scottish for some two miles only to find that the encampment he had passed some 25 minutes before was really that of his own Battalion. It was hard to make him realise that we were only just ahead of the Scottish on the march and turning off the road had immediately set to and erected our camp.

Here news of a long rest reached us, and we were told that after the next day's march to Ain Arik we should have a complete rest. On the way to Ain Arik we were inspected by the Commander-in-Chief, General Allenby, and on the afternoon of the 9th arrived at our new camp. The camp was situated on the rocky slopes of a deep wadi ; little ledges were however found for " bivvies," and each company made itself at home in its particular area. The slopes were covered with many small trees, and it was undoubtedly one of the prettiest spots in Palestine that we had visited. Here the Battalion remained for 10 days, and everything was done to make the rest enjoyable. At the top of the wadi near the main roadway a few level places were found and football competitions, both inter-Battalion and inter-company were arranged. A Brigade Sports Committee was set up and a varied programme of games, sports and transport competitions was arranged. The final placings were as follows : 2/15th Battalion, 10 points ; 2/14th Battalion, 10 points ; 2/16th Battalion, 3 points ; and 2/13th Battalion, 3 points. Great credit was due to the excellent turn out of our transport section, and also our Lewis gunners in their particular competitions. In the Brigade football final the London Scottish beat the Queen's Westminsters after a hard game. The Divisional Concert Party arrived and gave nightly performances in a large marquee. In the Battalion itself company concerts were held, a piano being hired all the way from Jerusalem through the personal efforts of Lieutenant Phelps. The whist drive held by " B " Company must also be included in the " mention in dispatches." Shooting competitions were held at a small range built at the bed of the wadi, and Battalion sports, limited to the three-legged, sack, egg and spoon type of race, were held on the flat bed of the wadi and proved a huge success. There was no suitable ground for sprinting, and even the course for the comic races had to be cleared of large stones by a voluntary fatigue party. One competition of the afternoon which deserves special mention was a " beauty competition for the best dressed lady." The originality of the aspirants was marvellous, and real harem dresses with the aid of bacon wrappings, etc., were among the prize winners. Canteen stores were plentiful and " dinner " parties were given throughout the camp each night. A real happy time was spent here and the Battalion was loath to leave Ain Arik when orders were issued on the night of the 19th May.

The Battalion procceeded next morning to Beit Ello by a circuitous route around the many hills in that part of Palestine. A pleasant camping ground was found, and after a night's rest we proceeded the next morning to Beit Rima, which was near the centre of the British line in Palestine which then extended from Jaffa, on the west, to a point just south of Nablous on the east. Here the proximity of the enemy's observation posts necessitated us to place our bivouacs under the numerous olive

trees on the terraces round the village. For the next week or
so the Battalion rested by day and each night large working
parties sallied forth north of the village of Beit Rima to dig a
system of trenches for the defence of the hill.

Rumours of France commenced to float about, and these
rumours soon developed into fact. On the 29th of May, 1918,
the Battalion, together with the London Scottish and Queen's
Westminsters of the same Brigade, bade farewell to the 60th
Division.

In France, heavy fighting and the stupendous thrust by the
Germans in the spring of 1918, necessitated that seasoned troops
from the East should proceed to the Western Front. Certain
Battalions of the 60th Division were therefore withdrawn from
the Palestine Front leaving on an average one white Battalion
in each Brigade, and filling up their vacancies with Indian troops.

Leaving Beit Rima the Battalion trekked to the Jaffa area
via Ibn Harith, Amwas, near Latrun, to Surafend, near Ludd,
which had then become the British railhead for the western
flank of the British line in Palestine. The marches were carried
out by night as the summer heat became too trying for any
movement by day. The nights were warm and glorious, a bright
moon shone throughout the march, the roads were in good
condition, and every one enjoyed the journey. Only one night
was spent at Surafend, and in the afternoon of the 2nd of June
the Battalion marched to Ludd Station and travelled throughout
the night, reaching Kantara by 5 a.m. on the 3rd. A short
march to the rest camp brought the journey to an end, and here
we were met by the advance party under Lieutenant Neall,
who allotted us to our proper lines in the camp.

At Kantara we were fortunate to be given a part of the Divisional Rest Camp and were not bothered to erect tents as was
the lot of other battalions in the Division. The camp kitchens,
canteens and mess tents were at our disposal, and this saved a
great deal of work and organisation. Immediately on our
arrival large parties were granted leave to Cairo and Alexandria,
and except for morning parades and ordinary camp duties
those who remained took every advantage of the benefits of life
in a base camp. The local cinema huts, concert party marquees
and canteens were packed each night, and every day bathing
parades in the Suez Canal were held. The weather was extremely
hot and the bathing parades were a great boon. Preparations
were also made for an early departure to France.

On the evening of the 15th of June, 1918, the Battalion
paraded and marched to Kantara Station and entrained
for Alexandria, which place was reached by 5 a.m. the following
morning. The train ran alongside our transport, the *Indarra*.
As soon as the train stopped on the quayside we were busy

transferring our stores, and for a couple of hours fatigue parties were constantly up and down the gangways. When this work was completed the Battalion paraded alongside the boat and then marched up the gangway, leaving their pith helmets in heaps on the dock side ; it was a pathetic farewell to Egypt, where we had thoroughly enjoyed ourselves.

The *Indarra* remained alongside for the day, but no leave ashore was granted, and the time was spent in allotting boat stations and issuing life-belts. The following morning we moved to the middle of the harbour, and during the day bathing from the side of the boat was permitted, and although a certain amount of flotsam floated around the ship the warm sea water was most delightful. Non-swimmers were advised to put on their life-belts in order to gain confidence in case the journey was ill-fated, and in many cases the men proved to themselves the efficiency of the belts in actual water. Practice alarms for boat stations added to the " pleasure " of the day. About mid-day the *Indarra* was joined by four other transports, namely, the *Kaiser-:-Hind*, *Malwa*, *Caledonia* and *Canberra*. This convoy left the harbour in the evening in single file and was escorted by armed trawlers and some naval vessels ; to one of which was attached a captive balloon for purposes of detecting submarines which frequented the area around the entrance to Alexandria Harbour. Several aeroplanes also flew over the convoy, and not until we were some 50 miles out to sea did our aerial escort leave us, when we were handed over to the care of ten Japanese destroyers and then the trawlers from Alexandria returned.

By the time the Alexandrian escort had left us the transports had lined up abreast of each other with a distance of roughly 500 yards between each boat, and this formation was retained throughout the voyage, the ten Japanese destroyers forming advanced, rear, and flank guards.

The journey across the Mediterranean was without incident, and the coast of Italy came into view early on the morning of the 21st of June, and the convoy steamed towards Taranto Harbour. When the boats arrived within the wide bay just outside the entrance to the inner harbour every one was relieved, but excite-ment was intense when the guns of the escort opened rapid fire on our left. Immediately the Japanese flag was run up the mast of each of the destroyers and frantic signals were sent from the Commander's boat, which was ahead of the flotilla. Three of the destroyers rushed at full speed to a spot about two miles to the left of the convoy and immediately commenced to drop depth-charges, the explosions of which shook the sides of the *Indarra* even at that distance. Torpedoes, however, had already been fired by the enemy submarine, which had apparently been lying in wait in the harbour only a couple of miles from an Italian Naval Base. One of these torpedoes came at a terrific speed, leaving a white wake in its trail, and passed in rear of the *Malwa* on our left, and only missed the bows of our own boat by a few yards. The second torpedo passed about 200 yards ahead of the convoy. The course of the transports was immediately altered and with a zig-zag route the boats hurried to their berths just outside the narrow entrance of the inner harbour ; while the Japanese destroyers continued to drop depth-charges around the suspected position of the German submarine. No official result was published, but it was reported in Taranto that the submarine was sunk by the explosion of the depth-charges.

The following day the *Indarra* moved through the narrow channel into the inner harbour. So narrow is this entrance that the sides of our troopship only missed the high walls on both sides by a matter of five or six yards. In the inner harbour were battleships of all sizes belonging to the Italian Navy, and one marvelled how our allies could allow enemy submarines to lie in wait just outside without any interference, for on our arrival not a sign of an Italian warship was seen in the outer harbour. In the peacefulness of the still waters of the inner harbour, which was several square miles in area, we remained until the early hours of the following morning, and just after dawn the Battalion disembarked by means of lighters which carried us to the temporary pier erected on the shallow beach near the British Base Camp.

It was the 23rd of June, 1918. Just a year previously we had landed in Egypt, and two years practically to the day since we had left England for France. Once again our feet were on the continent of Europe and we felt we had left the East for good. We looked forward with no little anxiety to our coming return to France, though many maintained that we were bound for the Italian Trentino Front, and arriving at Taranto and not Marseilles lent colour to this possibility.

CHAPTER XXXIX

JOURNEY THROUGH ITALY AND FRANCE—RECONSTRUCTION—
MOULLE—ST. SYLVESTER CAPPEL—MONT ROUGE—LOCRE—
DRANOUTRE—MONT VIDAGNE.

ON arrival at the pier at Taranto beach a short march brought us to our lines in the Base Camp. Only one day was spent here, and the following evening we entrained for France. During the day canteen stores were bought for the journey from the large Expeditionary Force Canteen, but no leave into the town was granted. Orders were issued for entraining that evening, and an amusing paragraph appeared to the effect that troops were requested not to refer to our gallant Allies, the Italians, as " Italianoes," " Ice-creamoes," " Chip Potatoes," etc. The route by train was along the east coast of Italy, and the train left the camp siding about 8 p.m. on the evening of the 24th June, 1918.

The first part of the journey was practically along the seashore and there was nothing of special note about the scenery. Halts were made at Bari, Foggia, Termoli and Castellammare, which town was reached about 1 p.m. on the 25th. By the following midday we had reached Rimini, having passed through Ancona and Pesaro en route. As far as Rimini the scenery had not been above the average of the coastal scenery of Kent or Sussex, but shortly after leaving the town the railroad branched inland towards Faenza ; and on this part of the journey the scenery was beautiful, the countryside being rich with summer flowers of bright colours, while the perfect blue of the sky overhead added to the richness of the colour scheme. Faenza was reached by 4 p.m. on the 25th June, and a long halt was made in a siding and men were permitted to leave the train and stretch their legs a little. Hitherto the halts had been short and just long enough to permit the issue of hot tea which had been prepared at wayside cookhouses previous to our arrival. At Faenza the long halt of several hours permitted officers to visit the town, where a decent meal was procured at one of the hotels. Time also enabled many of us to purchase and send home as souvenirs, pieces of artistic pottery for which the town is noted. Early in the evening the journey was resumed, and our next halt was made in

348

the large station of Bologna, just after 8 p.m., when we caught a passing glimpse of the quaint Cathedral and University in the town. The people on the station cheered us as the train pulled up ; a decided change from the apathetic gaze which had been our greeting from the southern Italians. While standing in the station a long ambulance train full of wounded Italian troops drew up alongside our train and fraternising between the two armies commenced, cigarettes and souvenirs were exchanged, and when the hospital train moved out we gave a hearty cheer to our wounded allies. A short time afterwards our train steamed out of Bologna, and by dawn the following morning we were passing through the glorious mountain scenery of Northern Italy. The train wended its way along deep valleys and pierced through the long tunnels which are numerous in the Apennines. The route taken was through Novi Liguire, Ronco to Sampier-darina, just west of Genoa ; the railway skirting the city at this part of the journey. During the afternoon of the 27th we halted at Savona where an enthusiastic crowd gathered and cheered us ; no doubt thinking that the Battalion was part of the British Forces which had so materially assisted the Italians in their recent victories on the Trentino Front. We did not disillusion these kind people and accepted their flowers, fruits and, cigarettes. From Savona the journey was continued along the sea shore, and we enjoyed the beauty of the calm, blue, sunlit Mediterranean on our left, and on the other hand the steep cliffs covered with bright flowers and dotted here and there with pretty little towns and beautiful gardens. At 11 p.m. that night the train pulled up at Ventimiglia, the frontier station where certain international formalities were gone through by the railway officials. However, such things did not worry us, and we spent the halt in the railway refreshment cafés and buffets. Unfortunately, the beauties of the Mentone–Cannes Riviera were passed at night-time and the only excitement of the night was the gamble in most carriages while we were passing Monte Carlo. Early on the morning of the 28th June we reached the outskirts of Marseilles. The railway ran along the north-eastern side of the town on high ground, and a splendid view of the harbour and city was obtained. From this point the route went northwards via Miramas, Avignon, where we crossed the Rhone to Le Tiel, which town we reached at 10.30 p.m. that night, and obtained an excellent meal at the railway buffet. The rest of the beauty of the Rhone Valley, which many of us had enjoyed some eighteen months previously, was lost in the darkness. Lyons was passed early the next morning, but it was sufficiently light to obtain a splendid view of the city and its bridges, which had been denied us in the outward journey to the East. After passing through St. Germains au Mont D'or the railway branched off to the west and a long halt was made at Paray–le–Monial, giving us the opportunity of exploring the quaint provincial French town for about an hour, when the journey was again resumed. During the night we passed through Moulins, Nevers, and Gien, and on this part of the trip we passed a train containing the London Scottish which had been delayed owing to a fire breaking out in one of the trucks. During the morning of the 30th June we arrived near Versailles about 10 a.m., at which point the network of railways is extremely intricate and hopes of passing through Paris were high at one moment when we appeared to be travelling towards the capital, only to be dashed to the ground the next when the train shot over the points in quite a different direction. Over this network of railway lines outside Versailles the train halted, shunted, went forward, moved backwards until we became quite bewildered as to the real direction of Paris, but when we eventually passed through the station of Poissy it was settled once and for all that we were not going near Paris. The day was beautifully warm and every one was getting tired of this long train journey with its constant jolting, when the train pulled up miles from nowhere. Every one descended from the train to the fields alongside and enjoyed a " leg stretch." The signal was against us, and in spite of the frantic whistle of the engine it did not fall. None of the railway officials could account for the stoppage, so we enjoyed the freedom of the fields for about two hours. Eventually, however, the shrill whistle of the engine warned us that the journey was to be continued, and as the train slowly moved, every one made a dash for their truck. Every one was present except two officers, and we all worried about their apparent predicament or even perhaps their desertion. However, about a mile further up the line the train pulled up and the two truants appeared. Apparently they had gone off to a village further up the line in search of luxuries in the shape of eggs, butter, fruit, etc., and before leaving had made a compact with the driver (no doubt with the aid of a few francs) to wait for them at a given point if the train was permitted to pass the signal. After this incident the train crawled along until the town of Gisors was reached, and here the explanation of our delay was apparent. The train in front of ours, carrying French troops and transport, had run into a stationary engine in the station, and as the result of the collision, several carriages had been smashed up and the engine derailed, causing casualties among both troops and horses. After some delay, which allowed us to visit the cafés in the town near the station, we proceeded on our journey, and early on the 1st of July we passed through Etaples, where the large British Cemetery brought back to us the real horrors of war after a pleasant journey across the Mediterranean and the long and interesting train ride through Italy and France. From Etaples the journey to Boulogne was through a particularly dull piece of country, and consisted of a continuous line of dumps, hospitals, camps, hutments, ordnance depots, etc.

About midday on the 1st of July, 1918, the Battalion detrained at Audricques, a large Royal Engineer locomotive repair depot. The scenery at this place was not particularly pleasing ; all railheads are surrounded by the same old ration and ammunition dumps, but the W.A.A.C.'s, whom we had never seen before, brightened our lives at that particular moment It must be remembered that we had not seen a real fresh-complexioned English girl for over two years. Not that I am belittling the beauty of their French sisters or even the particular charms of the girls of Italy, Macedonia, Egypt and Palestine, but to us there were none to touch the homely loveliness of the British girl.

Orders were soon issued by the new Divisional Staff which had met us on our arrival, and we proceeded to billets at Moulle, not an excessive distance, it is true, neither were the roads dusty and rough like the tracks we had traversed out East, but after a week in the train it was a trying march.

Here we were informed that we were to form part of the 30th Division which had been recently reconstructed and was under the command of Major-General W. de Williams, C.M.G., D.S.O., and with the London Scottish and the Queen's Westminsters we were to form the 90th Infantry Brigade under Brigadier-General G. A. Stevens, D.S.O.

The other two brigades in the Division were the 21st Brigade, consisting of the 1/6th Cheshire Regiment, 2/23rd London Regiment and the 7th Royal Irish Regiment, and the 89th Brigade, containing the 2nd Battalion South Lancashire Regiment, 7/8th Royal Inniskilling Fusiliers and the 2/17th London Regiment.

The following extract from a brief history of the 30th Division gives an idea of the state of affairs on our joining the Division :—

" The various units of the Division were collected together at the beginning of July, occupying an area around Cassel, where Divisional Headquarters were. But the Division was hardly ready to go into the line without some training and preparation. This was particularly the case since there were indications that the enemy was going to attack again on the Kemmel–Hazebrouck Front. The French troops holding the line between Kemmel and the Mont des Cats had been relieved by British troops at the beginning of the month, and the defensive systems still required a good deal of attention, so that during the month of July the Division was busy enough. The various battalions within the three Brigades of the Division had to get to know each other. The various arms of the Division had to learn to work together for defence and offence, the

Palestine Battalions had to accustom themselves to the warfare of 1918, which had changed since their departure for Salonica in 1916. While the whole Division had to prepare for, and practise its rôle as Reserve Division to the 10th Corps with a series of counter-attack programmes in the event of an enemy attack taking place. This involved careful organisation and co-ordination of each arm for the various situations that might arise, from the piercing of the line by Mont Rouge, to a thrust on the south-western slopes of the Mont des Cats.''

From the 2nd of July to the 7th the Battalion was comfortably billeted at Moulle and carried out intensive field training in the neighbourhood. Our Battalion organisation was soon revised and completed, and the Battalion was initiated into the revised methods of warfare in France in 1918. Leave was granted to the United Kingdom in limited numbers, it being in most cases the first home leave for two years.

On the 7th of July the Battalion marched to La Nieppe, between St. Omer and Cassel, and stayed there for the night. The next morning the march was resumed as far as Eecke, where the Battalion was billeted in a couple of large farms between the villages of St. Sylvester Cappel and Eecke. The Battalion, in common with the remainder of the Division, became responsible for the defence of the reserve line at Coq de Paille, south-west of Mont des Cats. Each day reconnaissances of the various routes from our billets to the position, and also a complete study of the system itself, was made by officers and N.C.O.'s. On several occasions the Battalion marched up at night and manned the trenches for practice purposes, while schemes for counter attacks from the trenches were worked out and practised. During the day field training was carried out with vigour, while on those evenings when we were not detailed to march up to the Coq de Paille defences for the night, Company concerts, assisted by our own drum and fife band, which had again been organised, were held. Except for the night time, when the enemy persisted in shelling a dump of artillery ammunition near our farms, our stay at Eecke was quite enjoyable. Leave was still granted, and parties continued to leave each day for the United Kingdom.

On the 13th of July we were inspected by General Plumer, the Army Commander, who complimented us on our turn out— The usual " splendid lot of men " business which we all know.

German attacks on our front were threatened to take place on the 18th of July in the region of Mont Rouge, and the Battalion was accordingly ordered to move up through Boeschepe and was held in reserve for the night in the rear of Mont Rouge, with orders to occupy and defend the line of reserve trenches covering Berthen should the attack develop. However, beyond the usual artillery fire the night was quiet, and we returned just after daybreak to our billets near Eecke. Training was continued for another week, and on the 25th the Battalion moved up to the line near Mont Rouge and relieved the 17th Royal Scots in the support trenches on the Locre sector. Nothing of special interest occurred beyond the usual unpleasantness of trench warfare. Movement by day was practically impossible owing to the German observation from Mont Kemmel, on our left front. For five days we remained in this sector of the line, and were relieved on the night of the 30th by the 2/14th London (Scottish) and marched back towards Boeschepe. We had suffered a few casualties from shelling, but it was great experience for the officers and men who had joined the Battalion since its departure from the French front in 1916. Those of us who remembered the old line at Neuville St. Vaast were struck by the absence of those splendid dug-outs which we had occupied during our first visit to France. On the 3rd of August the Battalion moved back as far as St. Sylvester Cappel and enjoyed a week's rest.

At the end of the week the Battalion moved to the line and took over the Locrehof sub-sector as supports, and were moved up seven days later to the front line trenches, relieving the London Scottish. Only two days were spent in the front line, when we were relieved by the Queen's Westminster Rifles and returned from the line to Moth Farm, which lay midway between Boeschepe and Godewaersvelde, and while in rest here it was arranged that our Division should attack the Dranoutre Ridge. We overlooked the German lines throughout their length from the Mont Noir–Mont Rouge Ridge, but the Bosche had the advantage in the possession of the Dranoutre Ridge, a long spur running down from Mont Rouge through Locre, with Dranoutre at its tip, which high ground represented, after successive ebbings and flowings, the mark of the Hun tide of advance there. This ridge, looking down as it did into our front trenches, made approach by day almost impossible ; and it set bounds to movement, cooking and life there generally, which only those who had to live there could properly appreciate. The 35th Division, whom we had relieved, had long ago made up their minds to take the ridge, but wet weather set in and their patrols reported the going across " No Man's Land " impossible ; it was therefore left for us to accomplish.

The attack was fixed for the night of the 21st/22nd of August. It entailed an advance of some 300 yards over swampy ground, pocked with shell-holes, the crossing of the River Douvre here a small stream, the ascent up through the straggling Wakefield and Mowbray Woods to the crest, where stood two strongly

Z

fortified posts—the old farms of Romp and Locrehot—a total advance of about 1,000 yards. The going was really difficult in the last part, where to the usual tangle of rough grass, shell-holes new and old, odds and ends of trenches and dug-outs was added the presence of trees and some undergrowth, the navigation of which even in daylight and without an enemy or the impedimenta of attack requires a certain care.

The London Scottish represented the 90th Brigade in this show, and that the attack was carried out with courage and great credit is due to the 2/14th Londons, who showed that the Palestine troops were equal to any demands that the Western Front might make upon them.

During the night following the attack the Civil Service Rifles relieved the Scottish in the captured line, which merely consisted of odd shell holes, and there withstood a determined counter-attack delivered by storm troops. Under continual heavy artillery, trench mortar, and machine-gun fire, we helped to consolidate the new front line. Fighting patrols were pushed forward and great courage was displayed by members of the 2/15th, particularly Sergeant P. J. Kelly's patrol, " C " Company, at Locrehof Farm, and by Lieutenant H. J. Mallett's patrol, " D " Company.

Wakefield Wood, which was on our front, was heavily shelled with gas shells, but this did not deter the Battalion, and on the 24th of August we drove off a determined counter-attack by the Boche. Local fighting continued until the 26th ; but the consolidation of the line progressed, when the Battalion was withdrawn and retired to the comparative security of the dug-outs on Mont Rouge, and on the following day returned to our old billet at Moth Farm for a couple of nights, when a return to Mont Rouge was made.

On the 1st of September the enemy withdrew from Mont Kemmel, and the British line was immediately pushed forward as far as Daylight Corner, and close to Wulverghem. On the night of the 3rd–4th of September we relieved the London Scottish near Wulverghem, which was merely indicated by a notice board with " This is Wulverghem," and a few chipped and broken tombstones which marked the site of the church. Our orders were to carry on the same policy of advancing as far as possible without a full-dress attack. But we were now up against the outposts of the enemy's main line of resistance ; he held the high ground, and furthermore the ground was of the worst possible type for advance under fire. Hardly a yard of it but had been wired at some time in one direction or another. In fact, it looked exactly as if the wire had taken root and spread like brambles. What was not wire was shell-holes or old trenches full, or perhaps only half full, of water. Any advance

at all was creditable. There was, too, from this time a noticeable increase in artillery fire of all calibres, with a fair amount
of gas from our line back beyond Daylight Corner to beyond
Kemmel. Wulverghem and Daylight Corner succeeded Locre
and Canada Corner as targets, with Kemmel as a substitute
for the Mont Rouge Hills. Thus, though the left company of
the 2/15th Londons managed on the 4th to advance their right
about 200 yards and establish new posts east of Wulverghem,
efforts during the night of the 4th–5th yielded little in the way
of progress, but more in the way of heroism when Private Cleaver
stayed by his wounded comrade in " No Man's Land " until
they were found two or three days later. But even as this bald
outline suggests, there was plenty of work and opportunity for
both leadership and initiative, whether on the part of the Company
Commander, e.g., Captain Andrew, whose bold reconnaissances
were of as great value to his Company as to the Battalion,
or on the part of the Platoon Commanders—Sergeant E. G.
Ward, " B " Company, who held on all day in an isolated
position far ahead of the general line, or Private Shepherd,
" D " Company, who specially distinguished himself by keeping up communication under fire between his own platoon,
which was isolated in front, and his Company. On the
night of the 5th–6th we were relieved by the Queen's
Westminsters and marched back to Donegal Farm, at the foot
of Mont Kemmel, leaving the 2/16th to carry on our work of
" peaceful penetration." After a couple of days' stay here we
marched back as far as Mont Vidagne, where our rest consisted
of furnishing strong working parties for road making and clearing
up the area near Westoutre. The Battalion transport and
Quartermaster's Stores moved up from Nonne Bosch, near
Godewaersvelde, which had been their home since the beginning
of August, to a place just west of Westoutre. Not only had this
rear headquarters provided us with rations and letters regularly
while we were in the line, but they had prepared for us a concert
party, a revival of the original " Plumes," who had worked hard
and got together an excellent programme under the able leadership of Lieutenant K. P. Neall, our assistant Quartermaster.
A full-dress rehearsal was given in a marquee on the 14th of
September on the rear slopes of Mont Vidagne. Other units of
the Brigade were invited and gave the party a great reception.
One must remember that although the party did not reach the
excellence of a London theatre, or even the " Barnstormers "
(one of our Egyptian Divisional concert parties), it was composed
of men of the transport and Quartermaster's staff who came up
the line each night with rations and shared with the Battalion
the unpleasantness of enemy artillery fire and aerial bombing
raids. It was not a party of selected entertainers who retired

from the fray for the sole purpose of becoming efficient music-hall artists.

On the 16th the Battalion was moved to Mont Noir and Major Benké assumed command.* Working parties still continued to work in the Westoutre area, while parties of officers were detailed to make a thorough reconnaissance of the line just beyond Wulverghem and facing Messines Ridge, with a view of relieving the 6th Cheshire Regiment. However, this work was in vain, orders for the relief were cancelled, and we were ordered to move farther south and occupy the support area on the Neuve Eglise Sector, taking over from the Royal Inniskilling Fusiliers.

On the 19th of September the Battalion marched from Mont Vidagne over the captured area as far as Bailleul, which town was now completely devastated, and then turning east arrived at Neuve Eglise about midnight. The relief was carried out successfully, although everyone was tired after their march of some ten or eleven miles.

*Lt.-Col. Gaze proceeding on leave.

CHAPTER XL

In the Neuve Eglise area the Companies were spread over a considerable area, the whole of which was under the direct observation from the German lines on Messines Ridge. "A" Company was in immediate support to the London Scottish, who were in the line on Hill 63, north of Ploegsteert Wood, while the remaining three Companies were dotted along the defensive line of trenches just east of the village of Neuve Eglise. The Battalion was under orders to garrison this reserve line should the Bosche make an attack on our immediate front. Movement, of course, during daylight was restricted, and at the slightest sign of smoke the enemy would deluge the area with shells, and during one of these strafes "B" Company had to move its home further back, but not without suffering a few casualties. "A" and "C" Company were also unfortunate one night while furnishing working parties in the line, and several of their men were killed and wounded during an enemy bombardment of Hill 63. On the whole, however, a quiet time was spent in this area, and the Battalion was ordered up the line on the 26th of September. We relieved the 6/7th Inniskillings and took over the line in front of Messines town from the right of the main road from Wulverghem to Messines. Headquarters was situated near South Midland Farm, "A" Company were in the front line on the sector adjoining the road, and "C" Company on their right, having Stinking Farm as their right flank. "B" Company provided supports to both front Companies, while "D" Company were held in reserve behind South Midland Farm. The intention was that within a few days the Battalion, in conjunction with other units, should attack and capture Messines Ridge, so that the first days in the line were spent in reconnoitring our front, from which it was learnt that the enemy had a plentiful supply of machine guns. At night-time we were also busy in bringing up and distributing stores which are peculiar to an organised attack, such as red lights, Verey pistols and so forth. To recapture the ridge was less an operation by itself than an operation supplementary to a much larger attack further north.

The 2/16th Queen's Westminsters were on our right and the 2/17th Londons on our left. The main road from Wulverghem to Messines formed the general line of the direction of our attack. On the Divisional front the first objectives were some enemy strong points close to our front line, and directly in front of our Battalion were three such strongholds, viz., Big Bull Cottage, Boyles Farm and Rome Alley. The attack was timed for dawn on the 28th, and at 5.30 a.m. our artillery opened up their bombardment on our front. It was not a creeping barrage, which had by that time become fairly perfect, but was rather a treatment of carefully-selected places and areas to cover the advance of our Companies on their allotted strong points to be attacked. Both our attacking Companies got well off the mark under this artillery preparation and possessed themselves of their objectives, the greatest resistance coming from Big Bull Cottage, where most of the occupants were killed, and before 7 a.m. the Battalion had claimed seventeen prisoners and nine machine guns. The Battalion on our left were also successful in capturing Mortar Farm and Ontario Farm. This clearing of the way for the advance to the Messines Ridge, though perhaps more an affair of fighting patrols than a staged attack, called for a good deal of initiative on the part of Company, Platoon and Subordinate Commanders in rushing and getting around machine guns when even the mere covering of the ground alone presented considerable difficulties. All the enemy strong points to be attacked had the armaments of machine guns, Captain Peatfield's Company, " A," our left attacking Company, accounting for six, Second-Lieutenant Pittam leading the platoon that captured them. Lance-Sergeant P. Mason, of " A " Company, mopped up a post of four with no little dash and skill, helped by the daring reconnaissances of the previous night, in which Private J. Volke had a notable share.

" C " Company (Captain F. H. Du Heaume) had also pushed forward and captured a network of trenches known as Rome Alley, driving off the garrison and killing a few of the enemy, while their patrols afterwards pushed towards Gabion Farm, which was strongly held by the enemy. Against this strong point " C " Company had to form a defensive flank, as the 2/16th Battalion had not advanced in the first stage of the day's operations. No determined counter-attack was made on our front, although the enemy was active with his snipers and machine guns.

" B " Company moved forward during the attack from their position in support and occupied our original front line, while " D " Company was brought up to occupy the support line vacated by " B " Company.

The new front was then held pending the result of the greater attack taking place further north, while on our right the 2/16th Battalion (Queen's Westminsters) assisted during the afternoon on the left flank of the attack of the 31st Division through Ploegsteert Wood, which met with considerable resistance, and the Westminsters suffered considerable casualties. The actual attack took place about 3 p.m. in the afternoon of the 28th, and turned out to be no easy task. The element of surprise which had assisted us was of course entirely lacking, and the progress of the troops on our right was attended with difficulties, and the Bosche made a determined stand, but under pressure gradually gave way.

By this time the success of the operations further north had begun to tell and, pressed on his right flank as well as in front, the enemy began to withdraw over the ridge in the late afternoon. His passage over the ridge, which of course was visible, was hastened by our artillery and machine-gun fire, which the sight of the enemy on the run in broad daylight naturally provoked. More than that, the Division could now, while still preserving the role of flanking the attack further north, push on to the ridge. Orders were accordingly issued for further patrols to advance over the ridge in the evening and secure a line east of Messines itself, curving back on the right to keep in touch with the troops there. This implied following the dip into the hollow of the Steenbecque River and its steepish rise to the top of the ridge, the whole way a pitted and torn desolation of the familiar type. Progress in the dark—it was pitch dark that night—was necessarily slow over such ground.

During the late afternoon and the evening our advance companies pushed forward, meeting small resistance from the enemy's rearguards. " A " Company on the left were able to push forward past Hospice Mill and actually entered the ruined village of Messines before midnight. The advance of " C " Company was necessarily slower as the troops on our right were held up, and it became necessary for us to form a defensive flank. Unfortunately, it was found inadvisable to hold the village of Messines, as the Battalion on our left had also met some strong resistance, and the salient which we formed became particularly unpleasant and it was ordered that we should withdraw from the village itself and occupy Hospice Mill, on the western outskirts, where " B " Company had pushed out in support of " A " Company during the advance to the village. In view of the advance being continued the following day, it was decided that " D " Company should relieve " A " Company in the front line, and " B " Company should continue as supports and " A " and " C " Companies be held in Battalion reserve. Great credit is due to all concerned for the excellent manner in which this reorganisation was carried out on such a dark night and over strange country covered with shell-holes, trenches and with entanglements. The first day's work had been very successful.

Our casualties were comparatively small when one realises the advance we had made, and most of them were the result of heavy artillery fire which had continued all day on our old front line, and, curious as it may seem, Headquarters suffered most, one unlucky shell killing nine and wounding five others seriously. Amongst those killed by this shell was our R.S.M. H. W. Lovelock, well known to both the 1st and 2nd Battalions.

By daylight on the 29th, however, the ridge was ours for the taking, and in the heavy mist at dawn parties of the Battalion pushed forward and by seven o'clock were in the village and over the ridge. Messines, with its memories of four years' fighting, passed into British hands again, and this time for good. There was, indeed, little else than memories, save the jagged cairn which had been the church, the ruined houses which had been made into concrete blockhouses, some of them left intact, or nearly so, and a few broken tombstones on the site of the cemetery. The Messines Ridge in the chill of a misty, late September morning, when you have been fighting since dawn the day before, and do not know where in the mist the enemy is hidden, provides neither time nor the place for philosophising. The ridge, from being an objective, became merely a road to the valley of the Lys. Somewhere there, as not infrequently in the history of Flanders, we might expect a stand to be made. The task of the Division was to see that it was made as far east of the ridge as possible—at any rate, as far as the line of the Ypres–Comines Canal, so well known and so little loved in the Salient farther north.

In order to carry out this idea the Battalion was ordered to push forward at dawn and advance as far as Houthem, and if possible make for the line of the Canal, a distance of over three miles. Except for constant artillery fire the first mile of the advance on our actual front was carried out with few losses to ourselves. However, we soon came under the direct observation of the captive balloons behind the German lines, and his artillery fire became heavier and well directed.

As no other British troops were to be seen over the ridge it was decided to halt about 2.0 p.m., and while waiting for further developments we had the pleasure of seeing one of our airmen bring down two of the enemy balloons in flames. They were immediately replaced by another balloon, but its life was short and the airman returned and downed it. An enemy plane, flying low, came over our position, but luckily no artillery fire resulted.

Just after 2.0 p.m. we saw a British skirmishing line advance on our left, and patrols soon got in touch, to find that it was the

2nd Battalion of the South Lancashires, of the 89th Brigade, who had pushed through the 2/17th Londons and taken up the pursuit. After consultation between the two Battalion commanders it was decided to push on together towards Houthem Church, as the 2nd South Lancashires were in touch with a Battalion of the 41st Division on their left. On our right matters were not so clear, and the heavy machine-gun fire confirmed our idea that the Boche was making a stand. The first part of our advance from Messines was over ground which had been in our hands the previous winter, while the latter half was enemy territory and unknown to us. The "going" down the slope was easier than on the west side of the ridge, though still a desolation of rank grass and old shell-holes. Houses, of course, there were none. Remnants of trenches and wire entanglements still served to remind us of the former British front line area. The only solid things were the pill-boxes left vacant, and in many cases intact, by the retreating enemy. By our rapid advance we were able to materially assist the advance of the 41st Division on our left by outflanking the enemy machine-gunners.

On our right the advance had been taken up by the London Scottish, and during the night of the 29th of September they entered Warneton.

After we had linked up with the South Lancashires we were able to push forward without meeting much opposition, and lost only a few men wounded. When darkness came we had reached the Ypres–Comines Canal, and took up a defensive line near the Canal near Houthem, turning our right flank to face south, as we had not at that time obtained touch with our troops on the right. We used the numerous pill-boxes as rain began to fall, and except for intermittent artillery fire and an occasional burst of machine-gun fire which caused us a few casualties, the night was quiet. Signal communication by lamp was obtained with Brigade Headquarters on Messines Ridge. By dawn on the 30th of September our right flank was secured by the Queen's Westminsters who arrived during the night, and the Brigade formed the extreme right of the great advance which was proceeding successfully from the banks of the Lys to the north. The River Lys forming a protection to the retiring enemy made it necessary for a great deal of preliminary work to be done before any advance in that direction could be undertaken.

Next day brought no further advance on our front, the 30th Division was flanking an attack rather than making one, and so regulated its movements to those of the forces on the left where the line went away north-east towards Gheluwe and onwards. We were free to close up the tail of the Division behind Messines Ridge, to improve shelter where there was none— which was practically everywhere—to clear roads, and to count the spoil. The number of prisoners taken was small, but if there is a peculiar pleasure in capturing guns which have shelled you for days and nights together, that pleasure was ours, for the Division took four 8-inch howitzers, three 5·9-inch howitzers, one 5·9-inch gun, three 4·2-inch howitzers and a similar number of guns, and 24 field guns. Any one who cared might possess himself of a trench-mortar or a machine-gun with sufficient ammunition for a month's fighting. The whole battlefield was, in fact, strewn with material from trench boards to 15-inch " duds "—relics of the British bombardment the previous year. The only road for transport and guns was the Wulverghem–Messines road. A very large crater completely demolishing it had been blown just east of the Steenbecque, where the road ran over an embankment. The enemy had also placed 36 tank mines across the road. These were all removed and the crater bridged to take lorry traffic by midday on the 29th of September. On the morning of the 30th the Divisional front, which had been gradually lessened in width by the advance from the north of the 41st Division and on the south by the 31st Division, was handed over to the reserve Brigade (the 21st Brigade) and the Battalion was withdrawn and marched back to Messines Ridge, and occupied old Hun dug-outs and pill-boxes near Blauen Mullen, where Colonel Gaze rejoined from leave. Our rest, however, was soon disturbed, and the area was heavily shelled, causing casualties, especially among the men of " B " Company, and after a short and unpleasant stay on this part of the ridge the Battalion moved to Oosttaverne Wood, a little farther north. The march proved exciting, as a Boche plane came over our lines and cleverly set fire to five of our observation balloons in such quick fashion that no less than ten airmen were parachuting to earth at the same time.

Oosttaverne Wood proved a very desolate spot, and it was with great difficulty that the Battalion obtained sufficient cover from the cold weather. Most of the dug-outs and pill-boxes in this devastated wood were under water. However, being free from enemy observation and the consequent artillery fire made up a great deal for the discomfort. A few days later the Battalion went farther back towards Wytschaete, where a fairly clean area was found and better accommodation was discovered. It was a restful time and some of the more energetic members of the Battalion journeyed to Ypres to see the " sights." Lieutenant-Colonel A. W. Gaze, M.C., left the Battalion for a Senior Officers' Course at Camberley, and the command of the Battalion was given to Lieutenant-Colonel A. C. H. Benké, M.C.

CHAPTER XLI

ON the 11th of October, 1918, the Battalion left their camp
near Wytschaete and marched to take over the line at America
Corner, about 1½ miles north of Wervicq. This relief entailed
a long march of about 12 miles. The first part was done during
the morning, when a halt was made under the cover of a small
ridge about a mile west of Houthem. The weather was fine
and the enemy artillery did not bother us on this part of the
journey. On the way we passed two derelict British Tanks,
relics of our advance in 1917. From the halt advance parties
of an officer and a few N.C.O.'s from each Company went forward, but it was not until dusk that the Battalion was able to
continue their march over the canal bridge at Houthem and
thence via Tenbrilen. The roads were difficult, and as the
country had been in enemy hands many new tracks and roads
had been made, and, together with the darkness and the inevitable
rain which accompanies most marches, attacks and reliefs, the
latter part of the journey became very trying. The advance
parties who left earlier in the day came under very heavy
artillery fire near their destination, and were met by large parties
of British troops who had been " gassed "—an unpleasant omen.
The whole area near America Corner was soaked with gas, and
the place was littered with dead horses. The Headquarters
of the Battalion we were to relieve had been reduced to the
Commanding Officer, who lay on the floor of the dug-out blinded
by the gas, while practically all the remainder of Headquarters
Company had suffered from the gas shells and had been evacuated.
The R.A.M.C. men, who were busy in this gas-stricken zone,
which was still being shelled when the advance parties of our
Battalion arrived, deserved the highest praise for their devotion
to duty. Here, indeed, was a pleasant outlook, and before
the Battalion had arrived some of our own advance party had
suffered and had to be evacuated, including Acting R.S.M. Dyer,

who, unfortunately, was killed later on in the day, an enemy shell landing right on the ambulance car in which he was travelling some six miles farther back. In the evening heavy rain fell, and the Battalion struggled in the dark along the shelled roads which were now covered in thick mud. About 11 p.m. the Battalion arrived at America Corner, and fortunately at that time when the shelling had diminished, only to learn that the Battalions in the line on both flanks were just about to raid the Boche lines. Before the Companies could form up under their guides, a heavy artillery duel opened up, and, of course, every one took immediate cover wherever possible. Luckily only a few minor casualties resulted, and the relief was continued. The Battalion, however, had practically no time to learn anything of their new surroundings before daybreak, as the enemy continued to shell the area throughout the night. When dawn came it was found that we were under observation from the Boche trenches, and that Battalion Headquarters was only a matter of 250 yards from the front enemy trenches, and overlooked by Wervicq Church, where the enemy had an Observation Post. Not that there is anything particularly daring about this fact, but Battalion Headquarters is always the centre of attraction for thousands of runners from rear authorities, asking for the quantity of jam, etc., when the real thing to be considered is the enemy artillery and the preparation for the coming attack. Besides, constant callers always make a place conspicuous, even if that place is in a quiet suburban street, and with the perfect observation of the enemy we had no desire to become conspicuous. Throughout the day the enemy continued to shell the area, devoting much of his " gaseous " attentions on America Corner. Two days were given to us to acquaint ourselves with this sector, and as no movement was possible by day it meant a great deal of night work and practically no rest.

The night before the attack rations were brought up on pack mules by our Quartermaster, Captain Joslin, and his assistant, Lieutenant Wright. Both these officers found great difficulty in persuading the mules to come up with the rations, and the prospect of being heavily shelled on the return journey while in charge of these stupid animals was not encouraging for them. However, they were soon relieved ; an orderly put his head into the pill-box entrance and gravely informed them that a shell had just arrived and disposed of their four-footed friends. Wright had a leave warrant for England on the morrow in his pocket, yet he came up to this inferno just to wish us " Cheerio and Good Luck," although his attendance was not officially necessary.

The attack was ordered for dawn on the 14th of October,

and the artillery opened up a most terrific barrage at 5.30 a.m., and after a four minute bombardment of the enemy front lines the attack was launched under the same heavy volume of artillery fire which gradually crept forward. " Jumping-off " lines had been laid out the previous night, and from these the Battalion advanced close on the creeping barrage in which a great number of smoke shells were used. Within 30 minutes of the commencement of the attack, German prisoners poured into our lines ; apparently under this fierce artillery fire they had made very little resistance in the front line. No less than 313 prisoners, including 9 officers, passed through our Battalion Headquarters within a half-hour.

The 2/14th attacked on our left and with us were successful in reaching the first objectives near the railway line from Wervicq to Menin.

Some individual cases of gallantry reported were : Sergeant B. Coultard, " B " Company, who, with his Platoon, did yeoman work, and rounded up 45 of the enemy ; Corporal C. D. Lodge, " C " Company, with his men cleared the wire defences of a strong point and carried it ; Private Oakes, " D " Company, single-handed rushed an enemy pill-box, put 14 of the enemy out of action, with rifle and bombs and then took 10 prisoners. Lance-Corporal J. Barnsfather, " B " Company, and Corporal W. J. Mash, " D " Company, were not far behind in their performances.

All along the line the first rush had succeeded, and under cover of a barrage from our artillery the Battalion halted and consolidated in preparation for a counter-attack. While the attack was proceeding all occupied areas behind the Boche lines were bombarded with a great number of gas shells. Although the resistance from the Boche troops was small, their artillery was not slow in replying to our fire, and a heavy bombardment of the British lines was soon in full swing.

The next step was to exploit this initial success and to push on up to and, if possible, across, the River Lys, whilst the enemy was still disorganised and his guns on the move. On the right this involved the clearing of Wervicq, in whose narrow streets and half broken-down houses there were still a good many machine-guns and snipers. By this time the mist and smoke had gone, and the advance was entirely uncovered in any way, for there was practically no ground cover here. Patrols pushed out towards the Lys as soon as the first objective was gained were held up by machine-gun fire, and, in part, by the old wire that still remained.

From the newly-captured position the ground on our direct front sloped gradually to the River Lys, and it was devoid of all cover in daylight it was impossible to push forward without incurring unnecessary casualties. In the dusk, however, patrols pushed out and found that the enemy had retired to the farther bank of the river, but had destroyed all the bridges by fire. About midnight, however, "A" Company, under Captain Du Heaume, were able to make a crossing by a bridge which had not been quite destroyed, just to the right of our direct front, and afterwards he was able to take his Company along the farther bank and form a bridgehead near Bousbecque. Under cover of this bridgehead the Sappers, under Major Atkinson, R.E., placed a pontoon bridge across the river, though during the whole of its construction the work was hindered by artillery and machine-gun fire. Just after dawn the remainder of the Battalion crossed the river and occupied Bousbecque, a village which had been badly damaged by our artillery.

We cleared the village and in the early morning were able to form a defensive line on the far outskirts. It was, however, impossible for us to push on any farther, as we were held up on our direct front by a heavily-wired line of trenches known as the Linselles Switch. Furthermore, on our right the situation was not quite clear and heavy fighting was in progress, while the London Scottish on our left were unable to effect a crossing of the Lys owing to the flat nature of the ground to their front, which was swept by machine-gun fire from the high factories on the farther bank nearer Menin. Later in the day, however, the 14th Division had forced a crossing near Wervicq, and were able to push up on our right, and on this flank the enemy gradually withdrew. During the afternoon the London Scottish came over to their right and crossed our pontoon bridge and came into Bousbecque. By this time the enemy had left the Linselles Switch under our pressure, and we were able to occupy the high ground east of the village of Bousbecque from Mont D'Halluin to Roncq. The line was continued on our right by the 31st Division which had then pushed through the 14th Division, while on our left the 2/16th Londons (Queen's Westminsters) continued the line north-east as far as Reckem, having experienced some hard fighting in crossing the Lys just south of Menin by means of rafts made from old doors, duck-boards, etc. In the evening the London Scottish moved from Bousbecque to Roncq for the night, when they were ordered to continue the pursuit next morning after their night's rest.

During the night of the 17th of October the Battalion held the Mont D'Halluin—Roncq outpost line, but as the Boche was retreating fast and was not expected to make a real stand until he reached the River Scheldt, the night was peaceful, and the civilians in the neighbourhood gave our men a hearty welcome. In the farm occupied by Battalion Headquarters the Hun had left his playing cards on the table in the middle of a game, while at the piano were fragments of German songs.

The next morning the London Scottish continued the pursuit on the Brigade front, while the 2/15th and 2/16th followed in their wake in column of route, as far as Kruistraat. Not until passing this village did the 2/14th meet any opposition, but on the ridge a couple of miles beyond were many well-placed and concealed enemy machine-guns which arrested their progress. According to plan the Scottish were to have passed over this ridge that day, but in view of this enemy rear-guard were unable to do so. In spite of this temporary hold-up, however, our own Battalion was ordered to billet in farms practically in the firing line. Remarkable as it may seem, the London Scottish support Company was actually behind our Battalion Headquarters, where we were enjoying a nice hot meal, and slept in comfortable beds.

During the night while we slept, however, the 2/14th pushed over the ridge, and the next day we resumed our march forward. Except for the visit of a Boche plane which flew over our column and was brought down by Lewis gun fire, the journey to Aelbeke was without incident. That night we were in comfortable billets in private houses and farms near the town which had been untouched by the ravages of war. The stationmaster where the writer was billeted produced an English Grammar which he had studied for this " day " when British troops should arrive, and consequently spent the evening in questioning us in his laboured English.

On the following days the advance was continued by the 2/14th and 2/16th Battalions, and except for a slight check at Rollinghem, where the enemy had two field guns firing from the market place, little opposition was met. On the 20th these advance Battalions had reached the high ground at St. Genois overlooking the Scheldt, the patrols of the London Scottish actually reaching the banks of the river that night. However, the enemy resistance showed signs of increase, and heavy artillery fire from the farther banks of the river informed us that the Boche was making a stand here. On the same night the Battalion moved forward towards Petit Tourcoing, and were billeted in the farm-houses just behind the St. Genois Ridge.

The advance being held up by the German defences on the east bank of the Scheldt, the Brigade was withdrawn from the line and remained in billets in the Petit Tourcoing area until the end of the month. As much rest as possible was given to the troops, and in the fine autumn weather sports and football were indulged in. The countryside had not been destroyed by war, and looked very clean and beautiful after the desolation of the Messines area, where the ebb and flow of the fighting had destroyed nature for miles around. During our stay here the 30th Divisional Concert Party ("The Optimists") gave us an excellent evening's entertainment in one of the large barns, and except for a few practice attacks over the open we had a restful time. The appearance of home-made rafts on a local pond at the end of the month, however, made us think seriously of watery graves in the Scheldt.

On the 1st of November we were ordered to take over the line at Avelghem on the Scheldt, and after a trying march we relieved a Battalion of the King's Royal Rifles. Although our approach march was disturbed by enemy shelling we suffered no casualties. Avelghem itself was on the banks of the Scheldt and was overlooked by the Mont D'Enclus (150 feet) on the farther bank. Previous to our recent advance the town had been a peaceful market town, but now it was battered to the ground by the German artillery, and the last few civilians were leaving in haste when we arrived. The line held by the Battalion was on the bank of the river in front of the town and extended north as far as Rugge, where a bridgehead on the farther bank had been established.

The care of the bridgehead was entrusted to " B " Company, under Captain Lewis, while the remaining Companies occupied cellars in the town and in the farm-houses near by. Our days were spent underground, as the Boche had complete observation of our lines, but at night our transport brought up rations, and we prepared ourselves for the next day under the ground. Each morning just before dawn the enemy barraged our position with a heavy artillery " strafe "—no doubt anticipating a further attack from us.

On Sunday, the 3rd of November, the Boche concentrated his attentions on Avelghem Church, and in about six hours of constant shelling reduced a most beautiful building into absolute ruin. The following day the Battalion was relieved, and returned as far as Knocke, about four miles farther back. After a night's rest here a further move was expected and in the evening orders were actually received from Brigade. Billeting parties left for the new area and commenced their work. The Battalion soon followed, accompanied by the inevitable rain, only to be turned back on reaching the new area to find that the change had been cancelled. When we returned to our former homes we found another unit occupying the best places, and it was with difficulty that we found accommodation. However, this crowding only lasted for one night, and the next morning we moved still farther back, a distance of about six miles, just to the north of Belleghem.

On the 9th of November the enemy evacuated Mont D'Enclus, and the next day we were brought forward towards the Scheldt as

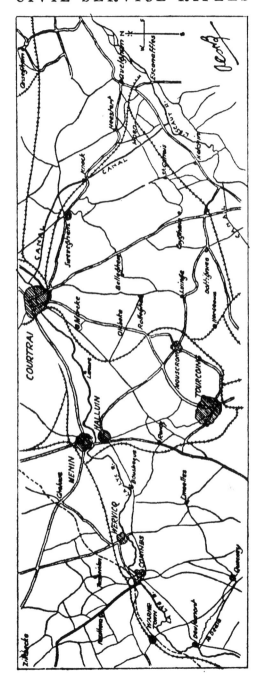

far as Heerstert, just west of Avelghem. On arriving in the village
we found it full of troops and heard rumours that British cavalry
had passed through earlier in the day. At the same time, however,
a German Taube was hovering overhead, and we anticipated a
bombing raid that night. We realised that the Boche had
retired so far that his artillery was unlikely to trouble us, but
we hated this inquisitive 'plane circling overhead.

That night rumours of an Armistice became prevalent. Every
one turned out of his billet and, led by our Drum and Fife Band,
we paraded up and down the main street of the village. In
the midst of this excitement, however, news came from Brigade
that no official news had been received confirming the rumoured
cessation of hostilities, and this so depressed us that we gradually
faded away one by one to our billets. The next morning ordinary
routine was pursued, and no one dared to utter the word " armistice " without receiving disparaging remarks from his hearers.

About 9.0 a.m., however, the official telegram came through
and the rumour of the previous night was confirmed. All the
excitement of an armistice, however, had been squashed the
previous night ; the sting had gone. During the afternoon
a thanksgiving service was held in the local church. The
Battalion remained at Heerstert until the 15th November, and
many took advantage of the opportunity of visiting the enemy
defences on the banks of the Scheldt under more peaceful conditions than anticipated. A couple of large fatigue parties
were furnished for work at Escanaffles on the east of the river,
but difficulty arose with regard to the supply of rations, etc.,
and the Battalion was withdrawn and marched back to the
St. Annes Area, south of Courtrai, which had now become an
important railhead.

The rest here was much appreciated, and beyond the passing
of military transport there were no signs of war. Parades were
held in the morning, but the remainder of the day was devoted
to games, chiefly football. Passes to Courtrai were freely
granted.

A ceremonial parade for the presentation of medal ribbons
was held on the 26th of November on the local aerodrome,
and beyond the preparation for this parade little demand was
made on the energy of the troops.

On the 30th of November orders were received to move back
still further to the St. Omer area, and this necessitated a five
days' trek. The first day's halt was made at Linselles, where
we saw the terrible effect of the British artillery fire during the
attack over the River Lys in October, and also the wanton
destruction of the Hun hordes, who had deliberately broken
furniture and mirrors, and had slashed the covering from up-
holstered furniture. The night's billets were very uncomfortable,

but as it was for one night only no one troubled. The next day we proceeded to Verlighem, and here we were quartered in an extensive hut encampment which the Germans had cleverly concealed from aerial observation, in a thick wood. A comfortable night was spent here in the bunks so recently vacated by our enemies. All along the route to this point were signs of the hurried retreat of the Boche, and we wondered why he had left such strongly-defended points with so little real resistance. In places the wire entanglements were 30 yards in depth, through which no troops could advance without a terrible massacre. The third day's journey took us to Armentieres, and it was appalling to see this great town practically razed to the ground. Undoubtedly the retiring Hun had blown up many of the fine buildings and churches by mines, and except for a few French troops wandering about the ruins, there was no sign of human habitation. The day's march ended at Sailly-sur-la-Lys, and here in absolute desolation the cover of dug-outs and tumble-down buildings, the Battalion rested for the night. Opposite Battalion Headquarters on the main road was a huge German cemetery containing no less than nine thousand numbered graves ; a grim relic of the heavy fighting in this area in March, 1918, the dates on the crosses being evidence of the period. Many French peasants were wandering aimlessly over the fields, looking for their lost treasures, and it was pathetic to see them building temporary homes with the old material, such as ammunition boxes, corrugated iron, biscuit tins, and so forth, which littered the old battlefield. The following morning the march was continued through Estaires and Merville, and the same devastation greeted us all round. It was not until evening time, when approaching St. Venant, that we met occupied farms where the occupants carried out their daily toil regardless of the adjoining desolation. A short journey on the 4th of December just south of the Nieppe Forest brought us to our destination at Boesinghem, a few miles north-east of Aire, when Lieutenant-Colonel Gaze rejoined from England, and again took over the command. Billets were soon arranged, and improved on our acquaintance—combined with hard work and cleaning, which did a great deal towards this improvement. Arrangements were immediately made for Christmas time, and when the 25th of December arrived everything was carried out with great success, although doubts were entertained until the very last minute as to whether the goods would arrive in time. At Boesinghem touch with our 1st Battalion in the Lillers area was obtained, and inter-Battalion football matches were arranged.

From this time the Battalion commenced to fade away. The fighting over, demobilisation set in, and every day some familiar faces left the Battalion to re-enter civil life. Early in January the Battalion moved to Etaples, where, after a stay of about nine days, they entrained for the Dunkirk area and encamped at Mardyck. In February the Battalion, much depleted in strength, developed into a " General Purposes " Battalion, and carried out Base duties. In the following month they were relieved of these duties, and moved to Pont de Petite Synthe, only to be moved again by train to the Etaples area, first staying at Dannes and then at St. Cecile Plage.

From here " C " and " D " Companies were detailed for duty at a Prisoner of War Camp near Boulogne.

In May a further move was made towards Abbeville, and a new home was found in the Ciquier Area. Demobilisation increased at a great pace, and by September only 155 other ranks remained. Canteen stores were sold to another regiment, and without canteen stores no regiment can exist.

3rd Battalion Civil Service Rifles

BY MAJOR H. DUNCAN LEWIS

THE 3rd, subsequently the Reserve, Battalion, was raised in May, 1915, for the purpose of furnishing drafts to the 1st and 2nd Battalions. Lieutenant-Colonel R. C. Hayes, T.D., relinquishing the command of the 2nd Battalion, was appointed Commanding Officer, and retained the position until he was disabled by an unfortunate accident during a Madsen gun demonstration on the miniature rifle range at Wimbledon in May, 1918. He was succeeded by Lieutenant-Colonel C. M. Mackenzie, D.S.O., who commanded the 2nd Battalion of the Kensingtons in France and Palestine. Lieutenant-Colonel Mackenzie remained with the Battalion until it was broken up shortly after the Armistice, when he was appointed Commandant of the Demobilisation Camp at Wimbledon.

The men were at first billeted at their homes and assembled daily at Somerset House for preliminary organisation, drill and route marching.

Richmond Park.

After a short period the Battalion went into camp at Richmond Park with other third-line units of the 1st and 2nd London T.F. Divisions, under Brigadier-General C. S. O. Monck. Living together in camp made it possible to commence instilling into the men that sense of military discipline which is the first qualification of a soldier, and progress in this direction soon became apparent. At first the training was necessarily on somewhat elementary lines owing to various causes, such as the want of experienced officers and N.C.O.'s, lack of arms and equipment, etc., but in the course of time, as these disabilities became gradually less and the syllabus of training more systematised, there followed marked improvement.

An early difficulty felt by the Commanding Officer was in regard to senior officers. A number of smart and promising junior officers had been posted to the Battalion, many of whom later on served with distinction at the Front, both in France and Palestine, but at the time they were new to military duties. This difficulty was met to a great extent by the transfer, first, of

Major G. W. Turk from the 101st Provisional Battalion, and shortly afterwards, of Major H. D. Lewis from the 2nd Battalion. In August, 1915, when the latter officer was transferred, the organisation of the Battalion consisted of two companies of six strong platoons each.

Captain C. J. Bowen was gazetted as Adjutant, which post he held until August, 1917, when he was seconded for service in East Africa. He was succeeded in turn by Captains R. F. Guyton, W. L. C. Rathbone, M.C., A.M., and F. C. Olliff. The important post of Quartermaster was filled by the appointment of Captain W. G. Hodge, late Quartermaster-Sergeant of the 2nd Battalion, and, except for a period of ten months, when he exchanged duties with Captain A. Toomey, of the 1st Battalion, he remained with the Battalion until the end. It is difficult to overestimate his services : his untiring zeal and efficiency, combined with firmness and tact, have given him a place in the front rank of those officers who have served the Regiment in a similar capacity. He was ably assisted by Regimental Quarter-master-Sergeant J. S. McIntyre, until the latter went overseas early in 1918.

The Battalion was very fortunate in its Medical Officer, Captain F. M. Hughes. He endeared himself to all ranks by his kindly interest in, and attention to, all his patients, and when he left for France the whole Battalion turned out to give him a send off. Every one learnt with gratification that he was the recipient later of the Legion of Honour for gallant conduct.

Sergeant-Major G. Weaver was appointed Regimental Sergeant-Major, and was succeeded in 1917 by Sergeant-Major B. J. Jolliffe, from the 1st Battalion.

Barnes.

The Battalion remained under canvas in Richmond Park until the 20th November—the last few weeks under trying conditions of cold and wet—and was then transferred to billets in Barnes. Here training was continued for six weeks under the disadvantages consequent upon the separation of the men at the close of each day's work.

Hazeley Down.

Early in January, 1916, the Battalion was moved to Hazeley Down, 3½ miles to the south of Winchester, where a camp of considerable size was formed, consisting mainly of third-line units of the 2nd London T.F. Divisions, including at first the Kensingtons and the Queen's Westminsters and later, when these two Battalions left, the London Scottish—the three other Battalions of the 4th Reserve London Brigade.

The camp was situated in an ideal position on the southern slope of one of the many downs in the neighbourhood : with stretches of well-wooded country, intersected by good roads, it formed altogether a most suitable region for military training. There was a range close by, at Chilcomb ; there were trenches on Fawley Down, about a mile away, and at the camp there was plenty of space for digging, and bombing, and assault courses, as well as a good miniature range.

For two years—the greater part of its life—the Battalion made its home at this camp, and from here draft after draft was sent out, mainly to the 1st, partly to the 2nd Battalion, and occasionally to other units at the respective Fronts.   The drafts had been trained, thanks very largely to the efforts of the disabled officers and N.C.O.'s from Overseas, as far as possible in the limited time at disposal.

When leave was given at the beginning of 1917 to enrol boys of 18, the strength of the Battalion mounted rapidly, and for some months stood at a total of about 2,400.   These lads were of an excellent type, and as it was possible to give them a much longer training than the other recruits, they became quite good soldiers and many of them proved suitable for, and were given, commissions.   Under the special recruiting system, admirably worked by Lieutenant C. E. Doubleday, Officer Commanding Depot, the ranks of the Battalion were reinforced by much the same class of man as joined the Regiment in pre-war days.   When that system ceased, in 1918, the Battalion had to accept whatever men were sent to it by the Recruiting Officer, but particular pains were taken, and with great success, to imbue them with a sense of the best traditions of the Regiment.   Indeed, throughout its career, whether on or off duty, both in billets and in camp, the conduct of the Battalion was worthy of the regimental badge.

While at Hazeley the Battalion was organised in six companies as follows :—

" A." Major G. W. Turk.
" B." Major H. D. Lewis.
" C " and " D." Various officers, mostly from Overseas, amongst others : Majors F. M. Warne and E. W. Neales, Captains A. C. Bull, L. D. Eccles, D. H. Miall, W. L. C. Rathbone, M.C., A.M.
" E." Captain G. H. Stone.
" F." (Men from Overseas.)   Various officers from Overseas.

Attached to " B " Company were Machine Gun and Signalling Detachments under the command of Lieutenants A. E. Smith and O. H. Mattison, respectively.

The gradually increasing number of experienced officers and N.C.O.'s returning from Overseas, either from partial disablement or for periods of rest, rendered most valuable service by furnishing the Battalion with instructors in all branches of training. Exceptionally good was the work of the Musketry Staff, in charge, successively, of Captain H. A. Berry, Lieutenants J. A. G. Falkner and C. S. McKay ; and of the Physical Exercises Staff, under Captain H. G. Edney.

As regards messing, the men were well looked after, as was always the case in the regiment, which has been particularly fortunate in its Quartermasters. The food was good and varied, and the arrangements generally were on several occasions the subject of most favourable comment on the part of Inspecting Officers. Sergeant T. V. Weaver rendered valuable service with this work.

The Regimental Institute, which had been started in Richmond Park, with Major H. D. Lewis as P.R.I., was much developed at Hazeley and, as there were plenty of funds forthcoming from the rebate on the canteen money, everything was done to make the Institute attractive. The G.O.C. Southern District, on the occasion of a visit to it in 1917, said that it was one of the best he had seen in the command. Liberal grants were made for the purpose of adding to the men's comfort and towards meeting the expenditure on games and sports.

Shortly before leaving Richmond permission had been given to form a band, subject to the proviso that fit men were not withheld from draft, and while at Barnes and during the first year at Hazeley the Battalion possessed a really good Brass Band ; but as the men composing it were gradually dispersed, its place was taken by quite a fair drum and fife band.

Close touch was kept with the 1st Battalion in France, and while at Hazeley visits which were much appreciated in the Battalion were paid by Lieutenant-Colonel W. H. E. Segrave, D.S.O., and by the late Major F. W. Parish, D.S.O., M.C., both of whom had endeared themselves to the Regiment.

Wimbledon.

On Saturday, December 22nd, 1917, the Battalion said goodbye to Hazeley Down, and entrained for Wimbledon, where it went into camp with the third-line units of the Queen's Westminsters and the 17th London, and where it remained until disbanded at the end of 1918.

Here the work of training was carried on as earnestly as at Hazeley, varied with occasional air-raid alarms, culminating in that of Whit-Sunday.

In May, 1918, occurred the serious accident to Colonel Hayes, which caused his retirement from the command, and about the same time another change also took place. Brigadier-General H. P. Burn, C.M.G., D.S.O., of the Gordon Highlanders, from the famous 51st Highland Division, succeeded Brigadier-General C. S. O. Monck in command of the Brigade.

In October, Major H. D. Lewis was appointed Officer Commanding Depot, and was followed in the command of " B " Company by Lieutenant L. C. Morris, M.C., a young officer, who distinguished himself while in command of a Company of the 1st Battalion in the fighting at Bourlon Wood.

Shortly after the Armistice the Battalion was broken up, most of the men not due for demobilisation being transferred to the 6th London Regiment at Blackdown, and the officers to the 9th London, also in the Aldershot Command.

The number of recruits that passed through the 3rd Battalion was approximately 6,000.

Regimental Aid Fund.

In July, 1916, Sir John Lithiby, a former member of the Regiment, inaugurated a Fund with the object of providing comforts for the men at the front, food and other necessaries for the prisoners of war, and temporary help, where needed, for the widows and dependents of men killed.

An influential Committee, representative of almost all the Government Departments, was formed ; with an Executive Committee, consisting of past and present Officers of the Regiment, with Sir H. J. Gibson, K.C.B., as Chairman, and Sir John Lithiby as Honorary Secretary.

The appeal for subscriptions met with a ready response. £2,850 was received for the general objects of the Fund, chiefly from the Public Offices and the Officers and men of the Regiment ; while a further £5,000 was subscribed for the prisoners of war, by the Regiment, the Public Departments, the Central Prisoners of War Committee, and the relatives and friends of the men themselves.

The comforts most appreciated by the Battalions overseas seemed to be luxuries wherewith to supplement the ordinary rations, and consignments of various kinds were, from time to time, sent out from home both to France and Palestine. In addition, the Commanding Officers were supplied with funds to use at their discretion in brightening the sombre monotony of trench life whenever opportunity offered.

The appeals from widows and dependents were fewer than had been expected, but many necessitous cases were helped in a quiet and unobtrusive way.

The chief activities of the Fund were connected with the care of the prisoners of war, of whom there were about 210 at the date of the Armistice, scattered throughout the various prison camps in Germany and Palestine. Each man was provided at intervals with a complete outfit of clothing, and three food parcels with bread, tobacco and cigarettes were sent to him every fortnight. This work was carried out at the Depot under the direction of the Officer Commanding, Captain C. E. Doubleday. Most of the parcels reached their destination safely, and the men, on their return after the Armistice, expressed great appreciation of what had been done for them. Only a few, happily, had to complain of exceptionally harsh treatment at the hands of their German captors.

In accordance with its rules the Aid Fund was closed early in 1921, and the General Committee, with the approval of the Charity Commissioners, disposed of the unexpended balance of £1,929, by presenting £1,500 to the Old Comrades' Association, and the remainder to the Officer Commanding the Regiment to be applied to the erection of a Memorial to the officers and men who had fallen during the War.

C. DOUBLEDAY,

CHAPTER XLIII

THE RECONSTITUTED BATTALION

THE first step towards securing the future of the Battalion may be said to have been taken when friends of the Regiment in 1918 approached authority with a view to the Prince of Wales assuming the Honorary Colonelcy, so long held by his grandfather, but it had been considered advisable to wait the termination of hostilities. In 1919, however, a letter was received from the Controller to his Royal Highness, stating that the Prince of Wales would accept the position. The appointment which followed in due course was received with unbounded delight in the Regiment.

Many months of delay on the part of the Army Council in forming their post-war policy in regard to the Territorial Force had a most deleterious effect, and thus when the task of reconstituting the Regiment was commenced many difficulties were experienced, the bands of comradeship had loosened, and there was a marked disinclination among the greater part of those who had worn khaki for so long in war to put it on again in peace, whilst the absence of a " young entry " into H.M. Civil Service destroyed our main source of recruits.

The command of the Regiment was offered to Major Viscount Bury, M.C., Special Reserve Scots Guards, who accepted and was appointed Lieutenant-Colonel in February, 1920. He was thus the third of his name to have the honour of commanding the Regiment. A letter was received on behalf of Lord Grenfell, Colonel of the King's Royal Rifle Corps, pointing out that during the war the Civil Service Rifles, among other battalions, had been affiliated by Army Council instructions to the regiment of which he was Chief, and requesting that the feeling of the Regiment as to the continuance of the connection should be made known to him in reply. Answer was accordingly made that though the Regiment highly appreciated the honour of having been linked to the tradition of so distinguished a Corps, yet they now felt that they would like to stand on the merits of their war record rather than to shelter under the magnificent reputation in the making of which they had not taken part. It was added that the Regiment had for years carried out line drill and had only for a short period drilled as riflemen.

The Commanding Officer was fortunate in securing as Adjutant, Captain (Brevet Major) W. H. Ramsbotham of the West Yorkshire Regiment (Prince of Wales's Own). He also applied successfully to the Coldstream Guards for a Regimental Sergeant-Major in the person of C.S.M. Stevens, D.C.M., and later, through the instrumentality of General Jeffreys, two Sergeant Instructors were obtained from the same regiment. Captain A. A. Joslin was appointed Quartermaster, a position he held in the Second Battalion throughout the war. Captain A. E. Evans, R.A.M.C., who had served in that capacity with the 1st Battalion in France, was appointed Medical Officer. The following Officers and N.C.O.'s were appointed to the various companies :—

" A " Company.—Major H. F. M. Warne, Captain G. E. Thompson, D.S.O., Lieutenant F. W. Hounsell, C.S.M. Hyder, C.Q.M.S. Lewis, M.M.

" B " Company.—Captain R. J. S. Gold, Captain P. Davenport, M.C., Lieutenants S. A. Seys, M.C., J. L. Hutchison, M.C., C.S.M. Torbell, C.Q.M.S. F. Trout.

" C " Company.—Captain L. D. Eccles, Captain H. M. Blomfield, (from 5th Buffs), Lieutenant P. E. Beddow, Second-Lieutenant J. S. Oldcorn, D.C.M., C.Q.M.S. Ibbett, M.M., and Sergeant (A/C.S.M.) A. C. Ridlington, M.C.

" D " Company.—Captain T. N. Sharratt, Lieutenant W. D. Hooper, Lieutenant P. H. Hall, C.S.M. Callingham, C.Q.M.S. Sale.

Recruiting started slowly and by midsummer some eighty members had joined, to which number was added the Band of twenty-four members, under Band-Sergeant H. W. Blackmore. The Band had all served in this capacity on the Western Front with the 1st Battalion.

It was felt that there was no better way of influencing recruiting than by reviving the Annual Midsummer Camp. This battalion, alone of the 2nd London Division, was fortunate in obtaining leave for this, and a contingent of the Regiment, under command of Major Warne, spent a happy fortnight at St. Martin's Plain, Shorncliffe. R.S.M. Stevens at this camp earned the commendation of the G.O.C. London District, General Jeffreys, for the remarkable progress made by recruits under his zealous teaching.

After camp recruiting began to quicken in pace. The Sergeants' Mess was re-established. The custom of holding two yearly dinners of the Officers' Mess had been revived, and the first of these was held in November. Among the guests was

the newly-appointed Commander of the 4th (Grey) London
Infantry Brigade, Colonel F. G. Lewis. Subsequently, H.R.H.
the Prince of Wales was approached and he honoured the Regi-
ment by attending the Mess Dinner held in the Alexandra Room
of the Trocadero on the 4th April, 1921. There were also present
Sir Warren Fisher, K.C.B. (Secretary to Treasury) ; Sir Henry
Gibson (Auditor-General) ; Major-General Jeffreys (G.O.C.
London District) ; Sir Neville Smyth, V.C. (G.O.C. 47th (2nd
London) Division) ; Colonel F. G. Lewis, Holland Martin, Esq.,
C.B.E. (Chairman County of London Territorial Force Associa-
tion) ; and many old commanding officers of the Regiment,
including Colonel A. M. Renny, Lieutenant-Colonel Segrave,
Lieutenant-Colonel R. Fielding, Lieutenant-Colonel W. F. K.
Newson, Lieutenant-Colonel A. W. Gaze, Colonel R. G. Hayes,
T.D., Major A. C. H. Benké, Sir John Lithiby and Sir Charles
Walker, K.C.B.

A third dinner, held in November, 1921, at the Civil Service
Rifles' Club, was honoured by the attendance of Lieutenant-
General Sir Francis Lloyd, G.C.V.O., who in an admirable
speech gave encouragement to those who are working hard for
the continued existence and future of their Regiment.

During the time which had elapsed since the Armistice, the
activities of the Regiment had been kept well in the public
view. The Regiment had taken part in the processional march
of the London troops in 1919, when the representatives of the
1st and 2nd Battalions were led respectively by Lieutenant-
Colonel Feilding and Lieutenant-Colonel Gaze ; at the unveiling
by the Duke of York of the memorial to London troops erected
in front of the Royal Exchange, and on the occasion of the
presentation of colours to battalions of the 56th Division at
the Horse Guards' Parade by H.R.H. Princess Mary it had
helped, in company with other troops of the 47th Division, to
line the parade ground. The Regiment also sent detachments
to the unveiling of the memorial to King Edward VII, and also
to the unveiling of the memorial to those men of the Post
Office (many of whom served in the Regiment) who fell in the
late war.

At Easter, 1921, the pre-war custom of a visit to the Guards
Depot at Caterham was revived, and over 100 other ranks received
the traditional hospitality and welcome from all ranks of the
Depot. This was a great success and had much influence on
recruiting. After this camp great efforts were made by members
of the Regiment, and the effects were just beginning to be
shown, when an event disastrous to the Regiment, as far as
recruiting was concerned, occurred. For the month previous to
April, 1921, recruits had been coming in at the rate of twelve to
fifteen per week, and had that rate of increase been maintained

a satisfactory increase of strength would have been seen by
midsummer. In April, 1921, the Defence Force was formed.
Members of H.M. Civil Service were forbidden to join. The
Headquarters Staff were taken away and Headquarters given
up to a force which had nothing in common with the Regiment.
With the exception of shooting, all its activities were suspended.
For over three months this state of affairs continued and had a
blighting effect on the regimental prosperity. The other regiments of the Division on the disbandment of the Defence Force
secured a large number of recruits from those who had served in
the Defence Unit bearing their names, whilst the Civil Service
Rifles, through no fault of their own, lost not only those who
would have joined had not the Defence Force been formed, but
received merely a few individuals as recruits from among all
those who had enlisted in the Defence Force. In spite of these
difficulties the task was resumed. The Regimental Shooting
Programme, seriously curtailed, was carried out, while in July,
1921, at the first post-war camp of the Grey Brigade at Shorncliffe, over 200 other ranks attended. The Regiment there
maintained its reputation for efficiency, and the Battalion
signallers under Sergeant Maddocks earned commendation by
the Inspecting Officer of being the best trained signallers in the
Division, whilst the band by their excellent performances on the
Leas at Folkestone and in Camp brought themselves into deserved
prominence.

In the world of sport the Battalion team reached the semi-final
of the Divisional Football Championship, whilst the Civil Service
Rifles Harriers gained second place in the Cross Country
Championship. The season's shooting at Bisley was crowned
by winning the Middlesex Cup on 10th September, 1921 ; this
cup conferring the primacy for the year on the Regimental team
over those from all Territorial units in the six Home Counties.
Relative to the winning of this Trophy a letter was received from
the Secretary to the Prince of Wales expressing his Royal
Highness's pleasure. Accompanying the letter was a large
signed photograph of H.R.H., which, sent as it was on the eve
of the departure of H.R.H. on his visit to India gave to all ranks
highest gratification as evidence of the support and interest felt
for his own Civil Service Rifles by the Prince of Wales.

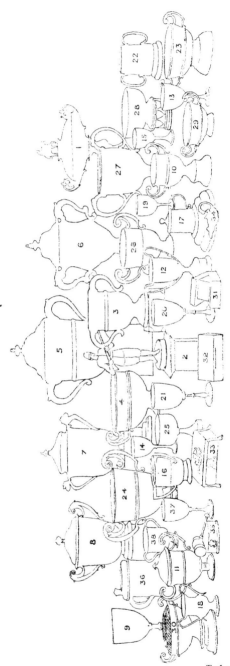

To face appendix I.

APPENDIX I

REGIMENTAL PLATE

Serial No.	Regimental Plate.	Battalion or Company Cup.	Year Given.	By Whom.	What Purpose.
1	Prince of Wales Cup	Battalion Cup.	1863	H.R.H. Albert Edward Prince of Wales	Best Shot.
2	Lord Bury Cup (Replica of Rifleman)	,,	1862	The Viscount Bury (First Commanding Officer.	Best Shooting Company.
3	Lord Albemarle Cup	,,	1896	Lord Albemarle (Eighth Earl)	Company General Efficiency.
4	Lord Arran Bowl	,,	1908	Lt.-Colonel Earl of Arran	Shooting.
5	*Daily Telegraph* Cup (1902)	,,	1902	Proprietors, *Daily Telegraph*	All troops in London District.
6	,, ,, ,, (1903)	,,	1903		
7	,, ,, ,, (1904)	,,	1904		
8	,, ,, ,, (1905)	,,	1905		
9	Harris Inter-Company Cup	,,	1899	Private L. Harcourt Smith (Harris)	Tug-of-War.
10	Sway Ambulance Cup	,,	1905	Inhabitants of Sway	Inter-Battalion Competition in 23rd Field Army Brigade.
11	Royal Military Tournament Tug-of-War Cup	,,	1901, 1902, 1903	Royal Military Tournament.	Won outright in 1903.

APPENDIX I—continued.

REGIMENTAL PLATE—continued.

SERIAL No.	REGIMENTAL PLATE.	BATTALION OR COMPANY CUP.	YEAR GIVEN.	BY WHOM.	WHAT PURPOSE.
12	Wolsley Cup	"I" (Cyclists) Coy.	1904	Proprietors, *Daily Telegraph*	Competition in Southern District.
13	Audit Challenge Cup	"A" (Audit) Coy.	1873	—	Inter-Company Shoot.
14	Battalion Match Challenge Cup.	Battalion Cup.	1894	Battalion	Shooting.
15	Lombard Cup	"A" (Audit) Coy.	1876	Mrs. Lombard	Drill.
16	Jeston Bowl	"A" (Audit) Coy.	1884	Captain Jeston	Shooting.
17	Trendall Cup (gilt, 1918)	"H" (Admiralty) Coy.	1907	Captain Trendall	Shooting.
18	Challenge Cup	"A" (Audit) Coy.	1912	Edmund Yates	Sectional Efficiency.
19	Edmund Yates Cup	Post Office Companies	1871	Battalion	Shooting.
20	Battalion Challenge Cup No. 8	"C" Coy. (Post Office)	1883		Shooting (Inter-Company).
21	Battalion Challenge Cup No. 14	"D" (Inland Revenue) Coy.	1894	Battalion	Shooting (Inter-Company).
22	Laboratory Cup	"E" (Inland Revenue) Coy.	1895	Government Laboratory.	Marching and Shooting (Inter-Section).
23	Old Members' Bowl	"F" (Inland Revenue) Coy.	1902	Old Members of "E" Company.	Most Efficient Member.
24	Du Cros	"H" (Admiralty) Coy.	1898	Harvey Du Cros	Shooting.
25	Marriott Cup	"I1" (Admiralty) Coy.	1909	Corporal Norman J. Marriott.	Shooting.

APPENDIX I—continued.

REGIMENTAL PLATE—continued.

SERIAL No.	REGIMENTAL PLATE.	BATTALION OR COMPANY CUP.	YEAR GIVEN.	BY WHOM.	WHAT PURPOSE.
26	Acland Cup	"I" (Cyclists) Coy.	1905	Lieutenant F. D. Acland (afterwards Under-Secretary of State for War).	Sectional Efficiency.
27	McKay Challenge Cup ..	"H" (Admiralty) Coy.	1885	McKay	Shooting.
28	Austen Chamberlain Bowl ..	"H" (Admiralty) Coy.	1900	The Right Honourable Austen Chamberlain.	Shooting.
29	Lamb Bowl	Sergeants' Mess.	1902	Major and Adjutant G. Lamb.	/
30	Old Boys' Bowl	"B" (Savings Bank) Coy.	1909	Past and Honorary Members.	Team Competitions.
31	Campbell Snuff Box in Case	"A" (Audit) Coy.	1862	J. D. Campbell.	
32	Woods Cigarette Box ..	"A" (Audit) Coy,	1892	Captain R. Lennox Woods.	
33	Dickson Cigarette Box (wood)	Battalion Cup.	1910	Surgeon-Major T. H. Dickson.	Officers' Mess.
34	Baillie Hamilton Spirit Lamp	"A" (Audit) Coy.	1870	J. B. Baillie Hamilton.	
35	Eccles Hammer and Stand ..	"A" (Audit) Coy.	1888	Major Dorset Eccles.	
36	Middlesex Cup (for the year 1921/2).	Challenge Trophy.	1860	London and Middlesex Rifle Association.	Inter-Battalion Team Shoot.
37	Hayes Cup	3rd Battalion.	—	Brevet-Colonel R. G. Hayes.	
38	Plain two-handled Silver Cup	No details.	No details.		

2 B

APPENDIX II

STAFF.

Commanding Officers.

Colonel William Coutts, Viscount Bury,
K.C.M.G., V.D., A.D.C. .. .. .. 1860—1890.
Colonel Richard Mills, C.B., V.D. .. .. 1890—1892.
Colonel Arnold Alan, Viscount Bury
(became 8th Earl of Albemarle in 1894) 1892—1901.*
Lieutenant-Colonel H. B. H. Tytheridge,
V.D. .. .. 1900—1904.
Lieutenant-Colonel The Earl of Arran, K.P. 1904—1908.
Lieutenant-Colonel The Hon. C. S. H.-D.-
Willoughby .. .. 1908—1912.
Lieutenant-Colonel R. G. Hayes, T.D. .. 1912—1914.

* In command of Infantry C.I.V., South Africa, 1900.

THE GREAT WAR.

1/15 Bn. London Regiment.

Lieutenant-Colonel The Earl
of Arran .. .. .. October, 1914—November, 1914.
Colonel A. M. Renny .. November, 1914—July, 1915.
Lieutenant-Colonel H. V.
Warrender, D.S.O. .. July, 1915—November, 1916.
Major (acting Lieutenant-
Colonel) W. F. K. Newson December, 1916—January, 1917.
Captain (acting Lieutenant-
Colonel) H. Marshall, M.C. February, 1917—July, 1917.
Lieutenant-Colonel F. W.
Parish, D.S.O., M.C. .. July, 1917—September, 1917.
Lieutenant-Colonel W. H. E.
Segrave, D.S.O. .. .. September, 1917—August, 1918.
Lieutenant-Colonel R. C.
Feilding, D.S.O. .. .. August, 1918—March, 1919.

2/15 Bn. London Regiment.

Colonel R. G. Hayes, T.D. ..	October, 1914—May, 1915.
Lieutenant-Colonel E. F. Strange, C.B.E.	May, 1915—May, 1916.
Lieutenant-Colonel C. de Putron	May, 1916—October, 1917.
Captain (acting Lieutenant-Colonel) T. E. Bisdee, D.S.O., M.C.	October, 1917—May, 1918.
Lieutenant-Colonel A. W. Gaze, M.C.	May, 1918—1919.
Major (acting Lieutenant-Colonel) A. C. H. Benké ..	——, 1919—April, 1919.

3/15 Bn. London Regiment.

Colonel R. G. Hayes, T.D. ..	May, 1915—July, 1918.
Lieutenant-Colonel C. M. Mackenzie, D.S.O. ..	August, 1918—March, 1919.

AFTER THE WAR.

Lieutenant-Colonel Walter, Viscount Bury, M.C.	February, 1920—December, 1921.

Adjutants.

Captain W. Ennis	1860—1862.
Captain A. W. Adair	1862—1863.
Major G. C. S. Lombard	1864—1886.
Major A. G. S. Beadnell	1886—1891.
Captain N. A. D. Barton	1891—1896.
Captain G. Lamb	1896—1902.
Captain B. J. Majendie	1902—1905.
Captain E. F. Ward	1905—1907.
Captain H. T. Manley	1907—1909.
Captain C. Fitzclarence	1909—1913.
Captain W. F. Parish	1913—Aug, 1914.

THE GREAT WAR.

1/15 Bn. London Regiment.

Captain F. W. Parish ..	August, 1914—October, 1915.
Captain J. C. D. Carlisle, D.S.O., M.C.	October, 1915—January, 1916.
Lieutenant A. M. Lester ..	January, 1916—March, 1916.
Captain W. E. Ind, M.C. ..	March, 1916—June, 1917.
Captain P. Davenport, M.C.	June, 1917—April, 1919.

2/15 Bn. London Regiment.

Captain A. W. Gaze, M.C. ..	October, 1914—March, 1918.
Captain S. C. Hall	March, 1918—March, 1919.

3/15 Bn. London Regiment.

Captain C. J. Bowen	May, 1915—November, 1917.
Captain F. C. Oliff	November, 1917—December, 1918.

AFTER THE WAR.

Captain and Brevet Major W. H. Ramsbotham ..	May, 1920—December, 1921.

Regimental Sergeant-Majors.

R.S.M. G. Stevens	1860—1868.
R.S.M. P. Kenny (11th Regiment)	1868—1886.
R.S.M. T. Winscombe (Grenadier Guards)..	1886—1896.
R.S.M. W. Wilson (Grenadier Guards) ..	1896—1905.
R.S.M. J. Pride (Grenadier Guards) ..	1905—1907.
R.S.M. A. Toomey (Scots Guards)	1907—1914

THE WAR.

1/15th Battalion London Regiment.

R.S.M. A. Toomey	August, 1914—August, 1915.
A./R.S.M. B. J. Jolliffe ..	August, 1915—December, 1915.
A./R.S.M. R. H. Haylett ..	January, 1916—March, 1916.
R.S.M. W. Richards.. ..	March, 1916—February, 1918.
A./R.S.M. W. F. Torbell ..	May, 1918—December, 1918.

2/15th Battalion London Regiment.

R.S.M. A. Freemantle ..	April, 1915—October, 1917.
R.S.M. H. W. Lovelock ..	October, 1917—September, 1918.
A./R.S.M. R. Dyer	September, 1918—October, 1918.
R.S.M. D. C. L. Edwards, D.C.M.	October, 1918—December, 1918.

3/15th Battalion London Regiment.

R.S.M. G. Weaver	April, 1915—August, 1917.
R.S.M. B. J. Jolliffe ..	September, 1917—April, 1919.

After the War.

R.S.M. F. Stevens (Coldstream Gds.)	May, 1920—November, 1921.

APPENDIX III
MEMBERS WHO SERVED IN SOUTH AFRICAN WAR.
Imperial Yeomanry.

Trooper G. H. Addison.
Trooper C. S. Anderton.
*Sergeant E. Baldrey.
Corporal W. Bartholomew.
Trooper F. R. Bell.
Corporal J. Bird.
Trooper E. Bryant.
Lieutenant A. C. Carey.
Lieutenant R. W. Cousins.
Trooper K. V. Cowie.
Trooper N. B. Cowie.
Trooper W. R. Cunningham.
Trooper R. H. Dailley.
*Trooper W. P. Dean.
Lieutenant D. Dewar.
Lieutenant T. C. Fryer.
*Sergeant H. S. Greensill.
*Trooper D. Jervis.
Sergeant S. Lloyd-Jones.
Trooper R. McGregor.
Lieutenant R. G. S. Miller.
Quartermaster-Sergeant T. Moran.
Trooper C. Morgan.
Lieutenant F. G. Morley.

Trooper V. H. Morshead.
Trooper D. J. Mosses.
Lance-Corporal R. B. Newson.
Trooper W. S. Nunn.
Trooper S. M. Page.
Trooper W. H. Parker.
Trooper F. M. J. Ross.
Trooper J. A. Rowan.
Trooper E. A. Rutherford.
Trooper R. O. Sage.
Trooper C. E. Savage.
Staff-Sergeant S. H. Schneider.
Trooper E. G. Seymour.
Corporal E. A. Streatfield.
Trooper P. A. Stuchbury.
Trooper H. C. Sword.
Trooper E. C. Todd.
Lieutenant A. E. Trembath.
Trooper E. H. Turff.
Corporal A. H. Walker.
Corporal A. P. Ward.
Sergeant W. W. Watson.
Trooper H. Whitaker.
Sergeant-Major J. A. Williams.

*Trooper F. W. Young.
* Died in the War.

C.I.V.

Lieutenant-Colonel A. A. C. Earl
of Albemarle.
Sergeant F. G. Ager.
Sergeant H. J. Allen.
Private C. O. Boot.
Private T. P. Brett.
Private S. W. Briggs.
Private R. H. Buckland.
Driver R. Burgess.
Private E. D. L. Churton.
Corporal A. S. Collard.
Private G. L. Crampton.
Private E. C. Crick.
Private F. R. Cripps.
Private R. A. Daws.
Private A. J. Firth.
Private H. Fisher.
Private L. Franzmann.
Private J. E. Gerahty.
Private A. W. Gough.
Private G. C. Grimsdale.
Private A. G. M. N. Harper.

Corporal A. E. Harris.
Private W. B. Hart.
Private W. Hatchard.
Private R. H. Haylett.
Private F. Henderson.
Private W. Hildred.
Driver R. H. Hutchinson.
Private B. J. Jolliffe.
Bombardier H. S. Law.
Private D. M. M. Kenzie.
Private H. H. Mears.
Private A. D. Mellish.
Private E. J. Miller.
Private S. Moore.
Private W. F. K. Newson.
Sergeant A. A. Oliver.
Private H. N. Page.
Lance-Corporal G. E. Pitcairn.
Private J. W. Reading.
Bugler W. Reed.
Private E. F. Rolls.
Private J. A. Ross.

C.I.V.—continued.

Private R. J. Sparks.
Private H. A. D. Stephens.
Private H. C. Tebbutt.
Private F. R. Thomas.

Private F. T. F. Watts.
Private F. W. Wheeler.
Lance-Corporal W. E. Wood.
Corporal J. L. Worsfold.

Royal Irish Rifles.

Private E. A. O. Barnes.
Private A. A. W. Buckstone.
Private E. V. Chubb.

Private S. Harper.
Private E. W. H. Harrald.
Private L. H. H. King.

South African Constabulary.

Private G. B. Anderson.
Private D. W. Prout.

Private R. A. Kelly.

Royal Engineers.

Sapper H. A. Mann.
Lance-Corporal J. H. Reeves.

Lieutenant P. Warren.
Lieutenant W. J. Woolley.

Army Service Corps.

Private H. T. Bassett.

Special Service.

G. R. H. Nicholls.

Field Hospital.

Corporal T. L. Adamson.
Private M. Cunningham.
Private A. W. Haigh.

Private E. B. Luck.
Staff-Sergeant J. E. Newell.
Corporal H. C. Robson.

APPENDIX IV

SCHOOL OF ARMS.

Royal Military Tournament Challenge Cup Winners.

1901 Second-Lieutenant T. P. Hobbins (Foils).
1902 Lieutenant T. P. Hobbins (Sabres).
1907 Major F. J. Brett (Bayonets).
1909 Captain W. T. Kirkby (Foils).

1898 Physical Drill with Arms.
1900 Physical Drill with Arms.
1900 Bayonet Exercise.

1901 Tug-of-War (110 stone).
1903 Tug-of-War (110 stone).
1904 Tug-of-War (110 stone).

1906 Officers' Bayonet Fighting Team.

Royal Military Tournament (Army and Navy Championship Medals).

1907 Lance-Corporal A. P. Chalke, 3rd (Bayonets).
1908 Sergeant A. P. Chalke, 2nd (Bayonets).
1908 Private W. W. Marsh, 3rd (Sabres).

Royal Military Tournament Silver Medallists.

1895 Corporal C. W. Whitehurst (Bayonets).
1896 Sergeant C. W. Whitehurst (Bayonet and Lance).
1897 Sergeant C. W. Whitehurst (Sabres).
1897 Private T. P. Hobbins (Bayonets).
1897 Private T. P. Hobbins (Bayonet and Sword).
1898 Private T. P. Hobbins (Bayonets).
1899 Lance-Corporal T. P. Hobbins (Foils).
1899 Lance-Corporal T. P. Hobbins (Sabres).

1899 Lance-Corporal T. P. Hobbins (Bayonet and Sword).
1900 Corporal T. P. Hobbins (Foils).
1900 Corporal T. P. Hobbins (Sabres).
1900 Corporal T. P. Hobbins (Bayonets).
1900 Sergeant A. D. Bell (Bayonet and Lance).
1902 Sergeant A. D. Bell (Sabres).
1903 Private W. W. Marsh (Sabres).
1903 Private W. W. Marsh (Bayonet and Sword).
1905 Private A. W. Horley (Foils).
1905 Lance-Corporal A. P. Chalke (Bayonets).
1906 Private W. W. Marsh (Foils).
1907 Ambulance-Sergeant F. C. Reynolds (Foils).
1907 Lance-Corporal A. P. Chalke (Sabres).
1908 Private C. L. Harley (Foils).
1909 Private J. F. McLaughlin (Foils).
1909 Lance-Sergeant E. A. Lippold (Bayonets).

Amateur Championships.

1899 Lance-Corporal T. P. Hobbins (Sabres).
1900 Corporal T. P. Hobbins (Foils).
1901 Second-Lieutenant T. P. Hobbins (Sabres).
1902 Lieutenant T. P. Hobbins (Sabres).
1908 Private W. W. Marsh (Sabres).
1909 Private W. W. Marsh (Sabres).

See p. 396 for Appendix V

APPENDIX VI
CASUALTY LIST.

K. in A. = Killed in Action. D. of W. = Died of Wounds. D. P. = Missing; Death Presumed. Illness = Died of Illness. As P. of W. = Died Prisoner of War.

Month	Line	1915					1916					1917					1918					1919					Totals
		K. in A.	D. of W.	D. P.	Illness	As P. of W.	K. in A.	D. of W.	D. P.	Illness	As P. of W.	K. in A.	D. of W.	D. P.	Illness	As P. of W.	K. in A.	D. of W.	D. P.	Illness	As P. of W.	K. in A.	D. of W.	D. P.	Illness	As P. of W.	
JANUARY	1st Line						4	4				6	2															16
	2nd Line																											2
	Attached to other Units																											
FEBRUARY	1st Line				1		2	5				3	2		1									3				17
	2nd Line											2	1		9		19	3		1							26
	Attached to other Units																	1										1
MARCH	1st Line							1				2	1				20	2	1		2			8				37
	2nd Line																1	1		3						4		9
	Attached to other Units																8	2										10
APRIL	1st Line	1	1		1		1					17	5		1		13	1										41
	2nd Line																			1								1
	Attached to other Units																4	4										8
MAY	1st Line	19	7	18			23	8	10	1		4	1				2	1			1							95
	2nd Line											4	3				3			1						5		16
	Attached to other Units									1								1										5
JUNE	1st Line	1					6	3				38	7	14			2	2	1									75
	2nd Line											1	1	1						1								4
	Attached to other Units											13	1				1											15

		C1	C2	C3	C4	C5	C6	C7	C8	C9	C10	C11	C12	C13	C14	C15	C16	C17	C18	C19	C20	Total
JULY	1st Line		4				3	3	1	18	5											34
	2nd Line						7	3			3	1			1							13
	Attached to other Units										3											3
AUGUST	1st Line	1				1	1	1		7	2	3			15	15	1					45
	2nd Line					4	4	3							11							18
	Attached to other Units				1					8	2	1			7	4	1					23
SEPTEMBER	1st Line	14	1	21		129	4			7	3	4			27	18						229
	2nd Line					5	4				5	1			23							33
	Attached to other Units									4	5				6	1						17
OCTOBER	1st Line	6	3			62	28	39		4	1	1				1		7				144
	2nd Line					9				15					5	6						43
	Attached to other Units									4		2			6	1	1					14
NOVEMBER	1st Line	11	2			12	2			32	13	4		2				1				78
	2nd Line									2	7											10
	Attached to other Units									9	3	3										15
DECEMBER	1st Line	15		3		4	1	2		16	19	17		1								82
	2nd Line									24	5	1	16*	1								47
	Attached to other Units																					1
TOTALS		69	22	21	2	272	70	72	2	244	93	53	19	4	174	67	3	16	3	12	9	1,227

* Drowned on H.M.T. *Aragon*.

Transfers to other units (including re-enlistments into Regular Army) - 4,088

Transfers to the 15th Battalion London Regiment - 261

Commissions granted from ranks of the 15th Battalion London Regiment - 967

Total Mobilized on 5th August, 1914 - 869

Total Enlisted since 5th August, 1914 (direct into the Regiment) - 8,588

Total served overseas (including those subsequently transferred to other units and those transferred to the Regiment) - 7,002

Total served at home (including those subsequently transferred to other units, and those transferred to the Regiment) - 2,716

Prisoners of War—(1) Germany - 213

(2) Turkey - 4

APPENDIX V

A Statement of the strength of the Corps at the end of each year from 1860 to 1914.

Year.	A Co.	B Co.	C Co.	D Co.	E Co.	F Co.	G Co.	H Co.	I Co.	K Co.	Band.	Staff.	Total.
1860	81	133		102		153		64	—	—	—	—	533
1861	72	117		102		138		62	—	—	—	—	491
1862	72	99		88		125		56	—	—	—	—	440
1863	79	102		89		118		65	—	—	—	11	464
1864	60	149		81		83		73	—	—	—	10	456
1865	61	165		95		82		67	—	—	—	9	479
1866	51	70	77	66	61	—	73	63	—	140	20	12	633
1867	49	71	73	52	55	—	61	67	—	149	23	11	611
1868	55	59	64	48	60	—	61	63	—	105	20	10	545
1869	63	44	47	38	53	—	59	57	—	106	21	10	498
1870	59	35	41	32	54	—	60	54	—	115	24	14	488
1871	59	36	45	40	65	—	61	56	—	112	24	15	513
1872	51	31	39	67	63	—	42	51	—	99	24	14	481
1873	46	31	52	81	57	—	40	41	—	85	24	13	470
1874	68	29	56	78	55	—	40	42	—	72	27	13	480
1875	71	28	57	70	62	—	37	51	—	83	25	10	494
1876	68	22	50	56	50	—	44	52	—	81	28	10	461
1877	75	28	53	54	55	—	48	44	—	110	15	13	495
1878	66	32	55	54	60	—	39	43	—	101	23	12	485
1879	56	29	52	53	57	—	60	40	—	100	21	13	481
1880	62	20	47	50	41	—	71	40	—	97	21	12	461
1881	57	19	62	48	50	—	100	45	—	100	24	13	518
1882	55	15	78	51	53	—	108	46	—	100	22	14	542
1883	55	12	105	60	79	—	105	44	—	111	27	12	610
1884	50	5	121	60	74	—	91	37	—	107	27	11	583
1885	55	—	122	64	79	—	89	39	—	106	26	12	592
1886	56	—	127	69	79	—	86	53	—	99	23	10	602
1887	53	—	112	53	61	—	78	52	—	87	34	11	541
1888	50	—	115	49	50	—	64	49	—	64	30	11	482
1889	51	—	107	45	45	—	48	44	—	65	35	11	451
1890	66	—	94	51	59	—	53	34	—	71	36	11	475
1891	70	—	102	56	75	—	52	39	—	77	39	11	521
1892	82	110		64	88	—	64	48	—	80	40	10	586
1893	86	42	130	65	92	—	77	55	—	88		11	646
1894	108	63	87	67	94	—	90	65	—	88	36	11	709
1895	110	80	90	90	97	—	99	80	—	79	40	11	776
1896	114	82	99	102	112	—	107	79	—	62	42	10	809
1897	101	84	103	100	106	—	94	74	—	60	60	11	793
1898	84	86	97	92	101	—	86	63	—	60	67	11	747
1899	82	98	106	85	106	—	83	66	—	63	69	11	769
1900	81	90	115	95	119	55	104	93	40	56	68	10	926
1901	73	96	120	97	119	63	99	102	57	58	62	10	956
1902	60	79	114	90	96	61	90	79	59	36	61	10	835
1903	53	72	99	83	77	61	89	78	63	33 K. 34 Cadets	60	10	812
1904	45	68	96	77	71	50	79	61	76	36	58	12	729
1905	47	65	99	69	79	50	77	58	70	47	69	12	742
1906	57	82	95	73	75	69	76	56	63	57	68	12	774
1907	57	88	92	70	73	80	69	64	64	57	69	12	795
1908	—	—	—	—	—	—	—	—	—	—	—	—	—
1909	116	93	136	87	81	87	98	85	—	—	21	10	814
1910	124	91	116	93	79	85	108	75	—	—	27	11	809
1911	124	84	107	93	79	81	112	77	—	—	26	7	790
1912	126	83	93	84	67	73	108	66	—	—	25	3	728
1913	129	100	105	87	72	72	104	81	—	—	19	4	773

" KEY."

List of Companies, showing Departments and Offices from which they recruited.

" A " Company	Bank of England. Metropolitan Water Board. Inland Revenue.	" F " Company	L.C.C. Insurance Offices.
" B " Company	Post Office Savings Bank.	" G " Company	Whitehall.
" C " Company	General Post Office.	" H " Company	Admiralty.
" D " Company	Inland Revenue.	" I " Company	Cyclist Company.
" E " Company	Customs. Inland Revenue.	" K " Company	Bank of England (before it was amalgamated with " A " Company).

APPENDIX VII

DECORATIONS AND AWARDS: OFFICERS.

Distinguished Service Order.

RANK.	NAME.	BAR.
Major - -	Benké, A. C. H. - -	
Major - -	Carlisle, J. C. D. -	
Lieut.-Colonel -	Segrave, W. H. E. -	Bar to D.S.O.
"	"	2nd Bar to D.S.O.
Capt. - -	Kemble, H. H. - -	
Capt. - -	Thompson, G. E. -	
Lieut.-Colonel -	Warrender, H. V. -	

Military Cross.

RANK.	NAME.	BAR.
Major - -	Andrew, R. B. W. G. -	Bar to M.C.
Capt. - -	Balfour, F. D. - -	
Capt. - -	Barnes, B. - -	
2nd-Lieut. -	Barnett, C. E. - -	
Capt. - -	Bates, G. G. - -	
Major - -	Benké, A. C. H. - -	
2nd-Lieut. -	Booth, T. J. - -	
Lieut. - -	Burtt, L. B. - -	
Major - -	Carlisle, J. C. D. -	
Major - -	Coles, E. A. - -	
Lieut. - -	Crofts, S. W. F. - -	

DECORATIONS AND AWARDS: OFFICERS—continued.

Military Cross—continued.

RANK.	NAME.	BAR.
Capt. - -	Davenport, P. - -	
Capt. - -	Fallon, P. - - -	
2nd-Lieut. -	Foot, W. V. - -	
Lieut. - -	Fraser, J. A. T. -	
Lieut.-Colonel -	Gaze, A. W. - -	
Lieut. - -	Goldsworthy, R. O. W.	
Capt. - -	Gozney, C. M., R.A.M.C.	M.C. and Bar.
2nd-Lieut. -	Gray, F. - - -	
Lieut. - -	Hoste, W. E. - -	
Lieut. - -	Hutchison, J. L. -	
Capt. - -	Ind, W. E. - -	
Leut. - -	Ivey, W. L. - -	
Capt. - -	Kemble, H. H. - -	
Lieut. - -	Lewis, F. W. - -	
Lieut. - -	Knox, A., R.A.M.C. (attached)	
Capt. - -	Martin, G. B. - -	
Capt. - -	McSweeny, D. L. -	
Capt. - -	Middleton, R. - -	
2nd-Lieut. -	Moore, R. V. - -	
Lieut. - -	Morris, L. C. - -	
Lieut. - -	Osborne, F. - -	
Capt. - -	Peatfield, B. - -	Bar to M.C.
2nd-Lieut. -	Pittam, A. P. - -	
Capt. - -	Rathbone, W. L. C. -	
Capt. - -	Roeber, W. C. - -	
2nd-Lieut. -	Samuel, T. A. J. -	
2nd-Lieut. -	Sanger, A. W. - -	
Lieut. - -	Seys, S. A. - -	
Lieut. - -	Smither, S. T. - -	M.C. and Bar.
Lieut. - -	Whitting, A. - -	
Capt. - -	Wills, A. K.- - -	
2nd-Lieut. -	Wilson, A. - - -	

Other Decorations.

RANK.	NAME.	DECORATION.
Capt. - -	Burnett, L. T. - -	O.B.E.
Lieut.-Col. -	De Putron, C. - -	Legion of Honour. Croix De Guerre.
„	„	
Capt. - -	Gold, R. J. S. - -	Order Du Merite Chevalier.
2nd-Lieut. -	Mallet, H. J. - -	Croix De Guerre.
Capt. - -	Matthews, C. N. -	M.B.E.
Capt. - -	Rathbone, W. L. C. -	Albert Medal (2nd Class).
Capt. - -	Roeber, W. C. - -	O.B.E., St. Stanislas with Swords, 2nd Class, St. Anne with Swords, 3rd Class,
2nd-Lieut. -	Settle, H. D. - -	Belgian Croix De Guerre.
Major - -	Stokes, G. E. - -	O.B.E. (Mil. Div.)
Capt. - -	Thorogood, P. W. -	O.B.E.

Mentioned in Despatches.

RANK.	NAME.	TIMES MENTIONED IN DESPATCHES.
Lieut. - -	Andrew, R. B. W. G.	
Capt. - -	Barnes, B. - - -	Three times.
Capt. - -	Bowen, C. J. - -	
Capt. - -	Branthwaite, R. W., R.A.M.C.	

Mentioned in Despatches—continued.

RANK.	NAME.	TIMES MENTIONED IN DESPATCHES.
Lieut. - -	Brasher, W. H. - -	
Lieut. - -	Burtt, L. B. - -	Three times.
Major - -	Carlisle, J. C. D. -	Three times.
Lieut. - -	Chalmers, R. - -	
Lieut. - -	Clark, T. H. E. - -	
Lieut. - -	Craig, W. H. - -	Twice.
Capt. - -	Crofts, H. M. - -	
Capt. - -	Coles, E. A. - -	
Capt. - -	Davenport, P. - -	Three times.
Capt. - -	Dobrantz, A. G. -	
Lieut. - ·	Du Heaume, F. H. -	
2nd-Lieut, -	Fallon, P. - -	
Lieut.-Col. -	Gaze, A. W. - -	Twice.
Capt. - -	Gold, R. J. S. - -	Twice.
2nd-Lieut. -	Hale, G. L. - -	
Capt. - -	Hall, S. C. - -	
Colonel - -	Hayes, R. G. - -	
Capt. - -	Ind, W. E. - -	Twice.
Capt. and Qmr.	Joslin, A. A. - -	
Capt. - -	Kemble, H. H. -	Twice.
Capt. - -	Lewis, H. T. - -	Twice.
Capt. - -	McSweeny, D. L. -	Twice.
Lieut. - -	Morrow, A. - -	
Major - -	Oliver, A. A. - -	Twice.
Capt. - -	Olliff, F. C. - -	
Lieut. - -	Pearson, T. W. - -	
2nd-Lieut. -	Pickhard, L. W. -	
Lieut.-Col. -	Segrave, W. H. E. -	Twice.
Lieut. - -	Seys, S. A. - -	
Lieut. - -	Smith, F. J. - -	
Major - -	Stokes, G. E. - -	Twice.
Lieut.-Col. -	Strange, E. F. - -	
Capt. - -	Thompson, G. E. -	
Capt. - -	Thorogood, P. W. -	
Capt. and Qmr.	Toomey, A. - -	Three times.
Lieut.-Col. -	Warrender, H. S. -	Four times.
Capt. - -	Wills, K. A. - -	

DECORATIONS AND AWARDS: OTHER RANKS.

Military Cross.

RANK.	NAME.	RANK.	NAME.
C.S.M. -	Brett, T. P.	C.S.M. -	Harris, R. H.

Distinguished Conduct Medal.

RANK.	NAME.	RANK.	NAME.
Cpl. -	Amsden, C. S.	Sgt. - -	Lawrence, S.
C.S.M. -	Bailey, W.	Pte. - -	Leigh, A. B.
L.-Cpl. -	Barnfather, J. D.	C.S.M. -	Levey, O. S. H.
Sgt. - -	Bowman, H. E.	C.S.M. -	Lord, F.
Pte. -	Branton, W. H.	R.S.M. -	Lovelock, H. W.
C.S.M. -	Burden, R. H.	Cpl. - -	Mackenzie, A. D.
Sgt. - -	Carroll, P. J.	L./Sgt. -	Mason, P.
Pte. - -	Castell, E. C.	Sgt. - -	Moore, W. H.
Sgt. - -	Christey, F.	L.-Cpl. -	Mills, S.W.
Sgt. - -	Cook, E.	Sgt. - -	Neil, J. J.
Pte. - -	Cook, E. J.	Sgt. - -	Nottingham,E.B .
L.-Cpl. -	Coney, H. R. H.	C.S.M. -	Oldcorn, J.
Sgt. - -	Coulthard, R.	Cpl. A./Sgt.	Pritchard, W. C.
C.Q.M.S. -	Crick, E. C.	Sgt. - -	Riddle, H. B.
L.-Cpl. -	Douglas, W. M.	C.S.M. -	Robertson, F. C.
Sgt. - -	Eager, G. L.	C.S.M. -	Salmon, H.
Sgt. - -	Edwards, B. C. H.	L.-Cpl. -	Seeley, G. J.
C.S.M. -	Eggleston, T. H.	Sgt. - -	Smith, G. B.
A./L.-Cpl.	Foot, G. B.	Sgt. - -	Strong, F. G. L.
Pte. - -	Harris, H.	A./Sgt. -	Sugars, R. C.
R.Q.M.S. -	Hart, W. B.	,,	,, and Bar.
Sgt. - -	Hodges, S. H.	Sgt. - -	Thomas, H. D.
Sgt. - -	Hundleby, H. S.	A./Sgt. -	Tom, G. A.
Pte. -	Hutt, F.	Cpl. A./Sgt.	Tuck, W. G. M.
A./R.S.M. -	Jolliffe, B. J.	Pte. A./L.-	Wakelin, S. J.
Sgt. - -	Jones, T. W.	Sgt.	
C.S.M. -	Kidd, A. T.	Sgt. - -	Williams, F. G.
Sgt. - -	Knapp, E. M.		

2 C

DECORATIONS AND AWARDS: OTHER RANKS—continued.

Military Medal.

RANK.	NAME.	RANK.	NAME.
Pte. A./L. Cpl.	Adlington, S.	Pte. - -	Breckon, H. W.
		Cpl. - -	Bressey, S. H.
Pte. - -	Amey, H. J.	Pte. - -	Brown, F.
Sgt. - -	Andrews, J. G. C.	Sgt. - -	Brown, G. L.
L.-Cpl. -	Angel, R. L.	Sgt. - -	Browning, F. E.
Pte. - -	Armfield, H. L.	Pte. - -	Bullock, C. F.
L.-Cpl. -	Armstrong, L. F.	Pte. - -	Chamberlain, V.
Pte. - -	Armstrong, J. S.		N.
Sgt. - -	Arnold, S.	Pte. - -	Church, T. D.
Pte. - -	Arthur, R. J.	Pte. - -	Cleaver, E. G.
Pte. - -	Ashdown, A. G.	Pte. - -	Connor, E. C. G.
Pte. - -	Auty, H. A.	Sgt. - -	Cox, A. T.
Pte. - -	Axford, E. W.	Sgt. - -	Cronin, J. B.
Pte. - -	Ayling, F. W.	Pte. - -	Crossley, W. G.
Pte. - -	Ayres, A. E.	Pte. - -	Cutting, R.
Sgt. - -	Bachell, G. T.	Pte. - -	Cutts, E. F.
Pte. - -	Baker, K. L.	L.-Cpl. -	Darmody, J. F.
Pte. - -	Ball, J. T.	Pte. - -	Davey, F. R.
L.-Cpl. -	Barnes, R. J.	L.-Cpl. -	Davis, W. E.
,,	,, and Bar.	Pte. - -	Dawson, V. L.
Pte. - -	Baston, E.	L.-Sgt. -	Donald, A. D.
Cpl. - -	Bazley, R. J. B.	Pte. - -	Durrad, W. H.
Pte. - -	Beadle, C. W.	Pte. - -	Edgley, E. E.
Pte. - -	Bell, D. M. P.	Pte. -	Edwards, L. D.
Cpl. - -	Bellingham, F. S.	Pte. - -	Eels, P.
Pte. - -	Benstead, L.	A./Cpl. -	Emler, H. J.
Cpl. - -	Bishop, H. C.	Sgt. - -	Feesey, R. W.
Cpl. - -	Blackaby, E. W.	Pte. - -	Flanagan, L.
Pte. - -	Bott, G. A.	Cpl. - -	Fletcher, S.
Pte. - -	Bowes, G. R.	Pte. - -	Folds, C. E.
Sgt. - -	Bowman, H. E.	Pte. - -	Foster, H.
Pte. - -	Boydell, J.	Sgt. - -	Fowler, G. E.
L.-Cpl. -	Bradford, M. E.	Pte. - -	Freemont, L. T.
Pte. - -	Bradley, A. F.	Pte. - -	Freer, W. B.
Pte. - -	Bradshaw, D. G.	Sgt. - -	Galen, J. J.
Pte. - -	Branch, L. H.	Sgt. - -	Gallant, N. E.

DECORATIONS AND AWARDS: OTHER RANKS—continued.

Military Medal—continued.

RANK.	NAME.	RANK.	NAME.
Sgt. - -	Galloway, J. M.	Pte. - -	Judson, E. F.
Cpl. - -	Garner, W. J.	L.-Sgt. -	Kelley, P. J.
Sgt. - -	Gooding, D.	L.-Sgt. -	Kelly, P. J.
Sgt. - -	Gray, F.	A./Sgt. -	Kelsey, H. G. R.
Cpl. - -	Greig, T. P.	,,	,, and Bar.
Sgt. - -	Hague, P. S.	Pte. - -	Kindell, R.
Pte. - -	Hales, A. C.	Sgt. - -	Knight, N. G.
Sgt. - -	Hall, M. W.	,,	,, and Bar.
Cpl. - -	Hanna, C. H.	Pte. - -	Knott, G. E.
Sgt. - -	Hare, A.W.E.W.	Cpl. - -	Lehan, W. C.
Pte. - -	Harris, W. R.	Sgt. A./	Levey, O. L. H.
Pte. - -	Hatton, G. L.	C.S.M.	
Sgt. - -	Haycock, T. F.	Pte. - -	Lewis, A. J.
A./L.-Cpl.	Hearn, S. W.	C.Q.M.S. -	Lewis, F. A.
Pte. - -	Hicks, H. E.	A./Sgt. -	Lichfield, H.
A./Sgt. -	Hiscocks, P. C,	Pte. - -	Linnell, H. J.
Pte. - -	Hockley, H. J.	Cpl. - -	Lodge, C. D.
Pte. - -	Hogwood, H.	Sgt. - -	Mallett, W.
Pte. - -	Holmes, A.	Sgt. - -	Manthorp, C.
Pte. - -	Holt, T.	Pte. - -	Martin, R.
Pte. - -	Hooart, F. N. G.	Cpl. - -	Mash, W. J. R.
Sgt. - -	Hughes, E. F.	Cpl. - -	Mason, A. J.
,,	,, and Bar.	Pte. - -	Matheson, F. E.
L.-Cpl. -	Hull, B.	Sgt. - -	McKinley, W. R.
L.-Cpl. -	Hutchinson, L. R.	L.-Cpl. -	Milner, M. G.
Sgt. A./	Ibbett, C.	Pte. - -	Milroy, D. J. H.
C.S.M.		Pte. - -	Molony, J. L.
C.Q.M.S. -	Irving, W. J.	Sgt. - -	Moritz, H. C.
A./Cpl. -	Irwin, W. L.	Sgt. - -	Morris, L. G. P.
Pte. - -	Jenkins, J. H.	L.-Cpl. -	Myatt, A. F. W.
Pte. - -	Joines, H. E.	Sgt. - -	Neil, J. J.
,,	,, and Bar.	L.-Cpl. -	Nelson, C. W.
Sgt. - -	Jones, C. F.	Cpl. - -	Newton, N.
Cpl. - -	Jones, T. I.	Pte. - -	Nicholas, R. E.
Sgt. - -	Jones, T. J.	A./Cpl. -	Nicholas, R. E.
		Cpl. - -	Pattison, S.

DECORATIONS AND AWARDS: OTHER RANKS—continued.

Military Medal—continued.

RANK.	NAME.	RANK.	NAME.
Pte. -	Pearce, A. E.	Sgt. -	Steele, H. J.
Pte. -	Pett, E. J.	Pte. -	Strugnall, E.
L.-Sgt.	Pilgrim, K. F.	Pte. -	Surridge, A. J.
Sgt. -	Pinder, H. F.	Sgt. -	Swain, J. H.
L.-Cpl.	Plastow, H. A.	L.-Sgt.	Taylor, A. C.
A./Sgt.	Portch, W. G.	Pte. -	Taylor, J. E.
L.-Sgt.	Rapps, F. T.	L.-Sgt.	Tickle, S. J.
Pte. -	Reed, T.	Sgt. -	Tickle, F.
Pte. -	Reuss, W. H. L.	Cpl. -	Titterell, F. A.
Cpl. -	Ritchings, A. A.	Sgt. -	Treves, H. G.
	W.	C.S.M.	Tubb, H. C.
L.-Cpl.	Roylance, W. G.	C.S.M.	Turner, T. E. F.
Sgt. -	Russell, J.	L. Cpl.	Underwood,E. G.
Cpl. -	Sanderson, W. K.	Cpl. -	Underwood,A. E.
Pte. -	Scott, F.	Pte. -	Vernhan, H. A.
Pte. -	Scott, F. L. G.	Pte. -	Vernon, P. H.
Pte. -	Shephard, W. H.	Cpl. -	Wallace, J. A.
L.-Cpl.	Shirley, R.	Sgt. -	Ward, E. G. C.
,,	,, and Bar.	L.-Cpl.	Wearn, C. E.
Pte. A./Cpl.	Skinner, F. C.	Sgt. -	Webber, A. J.
L.-Cpl.	Small, A.	Cpl. -	White, F. T. G.
Pte. -	Smedley, H. L.	Pte. -	Wighton, W.
Pte. -	Smith, S. A.	Cpl. -	Williams, W. A.
L.-Cpl.	Snelling, W.	Pte. -	Wilson, C. H.
Pte. -	Sparham, A. G.	Sgt. -	Wright, H. F.
Pte. -	Spicer, F.	Pte. -	Wright, W. S.
A./Cpl.	Stanton, W. S.		

DECORATIONS AND AWARDS: OTHER RANKS—continued.

Other Decorations.

RANK.	NAME.	DECORATION.
Pte. - -	Ashdown, A. G. -	Medaille d'Honneur Avec Glaives en Bronze.
Pte. - -	Brotherton, E. A. -	Belgian Croix de Guerre.
Pte. - -	Castell. E. C. - -	Ditto.
Sergt. - -	Cross, C. G. O. - -	Medaille, Barbatie Si Credinta.
L.-Cpl. - -	Fletcher, S. - -	Belgian Croix de Guerre.
Pte. - -	Gunton, B. - -	French Croix de Guerre.
Cpl. - -	Hammer, C. F. -	Ditto, and Decoration Militaire.
Sergt. - -	Manthorp, C. - -	Italian Bronze Medal.
Pte. - -	Mills, S. J. - -	French Croix de Guerre.
Sergt. - -	Nottingham, E. B. -	Italian Bronze Medal and Silver Medal for Mil. Valour.
Pte. - -	Pegler, H. W. - -	Medaille d'Honneur Avec Glaives en Bronze.
Sgt. - -	Riddle, H. B. - -	Silver Medal for Mil. Valour, and Italian Bronze Medal.
Cpl. - -	Ramsay, H. - -	French Croix de Guerre.

Mentioned in Despatches.

RANK.	NAME.	RANK.	NAME.
Pte. - -	Beadle, C. W.	L.-Sgt. -	Hodgson, J.
A./Cpl. -	Bernard, S. A.	A./Sgt. -	Hughes, R. J.
Pte. - -	Boldwater, L. A.	A./L.-Sgt. -	Hughes, E. F.
,,	,, (Twice.)	L.-Cpl. -	Hulford. E.
Pte. - -	Bowes, G. R.	Pte. - -	Hutt, F. G.
C.S.M. -	Bowstead, J. E.	C.Q.M.S.	Ibbett, C.
Pte. - -	Buck, B. R.	Pte. - -	Joines, H. E.
A./Sgt. -	Chapman, H. H.	C.S.M. -	Levey, O. L. H.
L.-Cpl. -	Ching, A. J.	A./Cpl. -	Linnell, H. J.
A./R.Q.M.S.	Collins, J. C.	Sgt. - -	McKimm, T. G.
Sgt. - -	Cooper, P. V.	L.-Cpl. -	Mundy, A. S.
L.-Cpl. -	Coney, H. R. H.	C.S.M. -	Mutlow, L. H.
Sgt. - -	Cottrell, T. A.	Sgt. - -	Newman, B. C.
C.S.M. -	Crick, E. C.	L-Cpl. -	Oliver, G.
Sgt. - -	Cross, C. G. O.	Sgt. - -	Owen, P. S.
Sgt. - -	Davey, S.	Sgt. - -	Parish, H. S.
L.-Cpl. -	Doubleday, R. E.	Pte. - -	Shirvington, T.
A./C.S.M. -	Dyer, B. C.	L.-Cpl. -	Simmons, H.
Pte. - -	Ennis, J.	A./Sgt. -	Tom, G. A.
Pte. - -	Forward, H. A.	A./L.-Sgt.	Tuck, W. G. M.
R.Q.M.S. -	Harman, A. R.	Pte. - -	Walder, W. J.
Sgt. - -	Harriss, F.	L.-Cpl. -	Weedon, G. H.
R.Q.M.S. -	Hart, W. B.	Sgt. - -	Wright, G. B.
	(Twice.)		

Brought to Notice for Gallant and Distinguished Conduct in the Field.

Pte. - -	Gunton, H.	Pte. - -	Perry, S.
L.-Sgt. -	Mason, P.	Pte. - -	Vernon, P. H.
Pte. - -	Pegler, H. W.		

APPENDIX VIII

OFFICERS WHO SERVED IN THE PERIOD 1914-1919.

This list necessarily includes the names of all officers serving with the Regiment, and of those officers who served with the Battalions overseas who joined from other Regiments.

It is feared in some cases the rank shewn will not be correct. Apologies are tendered to whom they are due.

DARKER TYPE REPRESENTS OFFICERS WHO DIED.

RANK.	NAME.	RANK.	NAME.
2nd-Lieut.	**Acworth, G. W.**	Lieut. -	Bambrough, P. B.
2nd-Lieut.	Adamson, T. L.		
Capt. -	Alexander, B.	2nd-Lieut. -	Banister, F. F.
2nd-Lieut.	Alison, D. S.	Lieut. -	Barclay, L.
Major -	Andrew, R. B. W. G.	Capt. -	Barnes, B., M.C.
		2nd-Lieut.	Barnes, F.
Lieut. -	Andrews, E. E.	Lieut. -	Barnes, R. C.
Lieut. -	Appleton, A.	Lieut. -	Barnett, C. E., M.C.
Lieut. -	Arundel, T. H.		
Lieut. -	Atkinson, M. C.	Lieut. -	Barnett, G. P.
2nd-Lieut.	**Attwood, S. A.**	2nd-Lieut.	Barratt, L. L. E.
2nd-Lieut.	**Aylmore, A. G. A.**	2nd-Lieut.	Bashford, W. R.
		2nd-Lieut.	Batchelor, T. C. N.
Capt. -	Bach, H. J. G.	Capt. -	Bates, G. G., M.C.
Capt. -	Bailey, C. A.	2nd-Lieut.	Battock, H. C. T.
Lieut. -	Bailey, D., D.C.M.	Lieut. -	Beddow, P. E.
		Lieut. -	Beecham, E. J.
Lieut. -	Bailey, F. T.	Lieut. -	Beetlestone, H.A.
Qmr. -	Bailey, J. G. M.	Capt. -	Bell, A. D.
Lieut. -	Bailey, W.	Lieut. -	Bell, A. F.
Lieut. -	Baker, A. G.	Major -	Benké, A. C. H., D.S.O., M.C.
Major -	**Balfour, F. D.**		
2nd-Lieut. -	Ballance, L. A.	2nd-Lieut.	Bennett, P. A.

Roll of Officers—continued.

RANK.	NAME.	RANK.	NAME.
Lieut. -	Benton, H. B.	2nd-Lieut.	Campbell, C. W.
Capt. -	Berry, H. A.	Major -	Carlisle, J. C. D.,
Lieut. -	Berry, H. A.		D.S.O., M.C.
Lieut.-Col.	Bisdee, T. E.,	Lieut. -	Castle, D.
	D.S.O., M.C.	Capt. -	Cavalier, Rev.
Lieut. -	Bonner, G. L.		C. J.
2nd-Lieut.	Booth, T. J.	Lieut. -	Chalmers, R.
Capt. -	Bowen, C. J.	2nd-Lieut.	Charter, H. E. J.
2nd-Lieut.	Bowers-Taylor, A.	Lieut. -	Cheeseman, R. C.
2nd-Lieut.	Boyes, J. F.	Major -	Chew, R. C.
Lieut. -	Boyes, W. E.	2nd-Lieut.	Childs, A.
2nd-Lieut.	Boyes, W. E.	2nd-Lieut. -	Chilvers, R. C.
2nd-Lieut.	Bradberry, W. R.	Lieut. -	Chudleigh, R. N.
Surgn.-Capt.	Branthwaite, R.	2nd-Lieut. -	Clark, H. R. E.
	W., R.A.M.C.	2nd-Lieut. -	Clark, S. G.
2nd-Lieut. -	Brantom, W. H.	Lieut. -	Clark, T. H. E.
Lieut. -	Brasher, W.	Lieut. &	Clark, W. H. D.
Major -	Brett, F. J.	Qmr.	
Lieut. -	Briggs, R.	2nd-Lieut.	Clarke, A. E.
Lieut. -	Bright, T. A.	2nd-Lieut.	Clarke, R. F.
Major -	Brightman, J. H.	2nd-Lieut.	Clegg, C. F. G.
2nd-Lieut.	Broad, W. V. M.	2nd-Lieut.	Clifford, G. C.
Lieut. -	Brooks, H. E.	2nd-Lieut.	Coldicott, H. E.
Lieut. -	Brooks, H. E.	Major -	Coles, E. A., M.C.
Lieut. -	Broughton, L. T.	Capt. -	Collins, E. H.
2nd-Lieut.	Broughton, S.	2nd-Lieut.	Collins, F. C.
Lieut. -	Bull, A. C.	2nd-Lieut.	Cooke, R. C.
Lieut. -	Bullin, W.	2nd-Lieut.	Covey, E. J.
2nd-Lieut. -	Bullock, A. M.	2nd-Lieut.	Cox, H. P. F.
Lieut. -	Bulton, O. F.	Lieut. -	Craig, W. H.
Lieut. -	Burch, S. W.	2nd-Lieut.	Cribbett, W. C. G.
2nd-Lieut.	Burchett, W. J.	Capt. -	Crofts, A. W. G.
Lieut. -	Burden, E. O.	Capt. -	Crofts, H. M.
Lieut. -	Burtt, L. B.,	2nd-Lieut.	Cunningham,
	M.C.		H. F.
Lieut. -	Burtt, L. L.		
Lieut. -	Burtt, V. S.	Lieut. -	Dabbs, S. E.
Lieut. -	Byles, E. F.	2nd-Lieut.	Daly, P. A.

Roll of Officers—continued.

RANK.	NAME.	RANK.	NAME.
Capt. -	Davenport, P., M.C.	2nd-Lieut.	Francis, W. J.
Capt. -	**Davies, L.**	Lieut. -	Fraser, J. A. T.
Lieut. -	Davis, A. E.	2nd-Lieut.	French, J. H.
2nd-Lieut.	**Denny, E.**	Capt. -	Galfin, A. C.
Lieut.-Col.	De Putron, C.	2nd-Lieut.	Gallaher, H. E.
Capt. -	Diggins, A.	**2nd-Lieut.**	**Garratt, M. H.**
Major -	Dobrantz, A. G.	Lieut.-Col.	Gaze, A. W., M.C.
Capt. -	Doubleday, C. E.		
2nd-Lieut.	Dredge, P. J.	**Capt.** -	**Gaze, G. A.**
Capt. -	Du Heaume, F. H.	Lieut. -	Gearing, F. E.
		2nd-Lieut.	George, H. W.
Lieut. -	Duncan, A.	Lieut. -	Gillings, V. de F.
		Lieut. -	Girard, R. S.
Capt. -	Easton, F. J.	2nd-Lieut.	Glynn, A. H.
Capt. -	Eccles, L. D.	Lieut. -	Godfrey, H.
2nd-Lieut.	Edmed, W.	2nd-Lieut.	Golby, H. J.
Lieut. -	Edney, H. G.	Capt. -	Gold, R. J. S.
2nd-Lieut.	Ellis, T. H.	Lieut. -	Golding, F. L.
2nd-Lieut.	Emmett, A. H.	2nd-Lieut.	Gordon, F. A.
2nd-Lieut.	Ena, A. S.	Capt. -	Gormanston, The Viscount, J. E. P.
2nd-Lieut.	Enoch, B. J.		
Lieut. -	Etheridge, A. H.		
2nd-Lieut.	Ewen, P.	Lieut. -	Gosney, H. S.
		2nd-Lieut.	**Goswell, O. S.**
2nd-Lieut. -	Falkner, J. A. G.	**2nd-Lieut.**	**Gray, F.**
Lieut. -	Fallon, R., M.C.	Major -	Greswell, T. de la G.
Capt. -	**Farquhar, H. B.**		
Lieut.-Col.	Feilding, R. C., D.S.O.	Capt. -	Grimsdale, G. C.
		2nd-Lieut.	Grove, C. S.
2nd-Lieut.	Fitter, B. A.	2nd-Lieut.	Guy, H. W.
2nd-Lieut.	**Fletcher, E.**	Capt. -	Guyton, R. F.
2nd-Lieut.	Flew, W. L.		
Lieut. -	Foot, W. V., M.C.	2nd-Lieut. -	Habbijam, J. F.
		Lieut. -	Hale, G. L.
Lieut. -	Ford, R. W.	2nd-Lieut. -	Halifax, J. W.
2nd-Lieut.	Forsyth, W. J.	Lieut. -	Hall, P. H.
Lieut. -	Francis, T. B.	Capt. -	Hall, S. C.

Roll of Officers—continued.

RANK.	NAME.	RANK.	NAME.
2nd-Lieut.	Hallas, J. E.	Capt. -	Hughes, R. B.
Lieut. -	Hamill, J. M.	2nd-Lieut.	Hughes, R. C.
Capt. -	Hanks, A. G. T.	Lieut. -	Hutchison, J. L., M.C.
2nd-Lieut.	Harris, R. H., M.C.	Lieut. -	Hutton, P. G.
Lieut. -	Hart, L. H.		
2nd-Lieut.	Harrowing, T. C.	Lieut. -	Illing, R. W.
2nd-Lieut.	Hasleham, G. H.	Capt. -	Ind, W. E., M.C.
2nd-Lieut.	Haslett, S.	Lieut. -	Ivey, W. L., M.C.
Col. - -	Hayes,R. G.,T.D.		
2nd-Lieut.	Hemsley, C. M.		
Lieut. -	Hepworth, E. C.		
Major -	Hide, L.	Lieut. -	Jackson, P. H.
Major -	Higginbottom, H. E.	Capt. -	James, A. V.
		2nd-Lieut.	James, P. A.
Lieut. -	Higgs, K. A.	2nd-Lieut.	Jamieson, C. M.
Lieut. -	Hilder, G. D.	Lieut. -	Jarvis, L. J. W.
Capt. -	Hill, F.	Lieut. -	Jarvis, M. F.
Capt. -	Hill, M. G.	2nd-Lieut. -	Jones, E.
2nd-Lieut.	Hobson, R. L.	Capt. -	Jones, H.
Capt. and Qmr.	Hodge, W. G.	Lieut. -	Jones, P. F.
		Lieut. -	Jones, R. L.
Lieut. -	Hodgson, C. H.	Capt. and Qmr.	Joslin, A. A.
2nd-Lieut.	Hoole, G.		
Lieut. -	Hooper, G. B.		
Lieut. -	Hooper, W. D.		
Lieut. -	Horne, J. C.	Lieut. -	Kapping, C. H. S.
Lieut. -	Hosken, E.	2nd-Lieut.	Kearley, H.
Lieut. -	Hoste, G. M.	Capt. -	Kemble, H. H., D.S.O., M.C.
Lieut. -	Hoste, W. E., M.C.		
		2nd-Lieut.	Kettle, E. W.
Lieut. -	Hounsell, F. W.	Capt. -	Kilmer, C. M.
Capt. -	Houseman, A. W.	Capt. -	Kimber, W. J.
Lieut. -	Houslop,W. A. S.	2nd-Lieut.	King, A. E.
2nd-Lieut.	Howard, W. F.	2nd-Lieut.	King, H.
Lieut. -	Howard-Grafton, G. C.	Capt. -	Kinsman, J. C. P.
		2nd-Lieut.	Kirk, R. L.
Capt. -	Hughes, F. M.	Major -	Kirkby, W. T.

Roll of Officers—continued.

RANK.	NAME.	RANK.	NAME.
Lieut. -	Labhart, C. L.	Capt. -	Mathews, C. N.,
2nd-Lieut.	Lacy, W. B.		M.B.E.
2nd-Lieut.	Lambert, W. B.	Lieut. -	Mattison, O. H.
2nd-Lieut.	Lander, D. L. C.	Lieut. -	Maxwell, E. W.
Lieut. -	Lane, A. D.	Lieut. -	Mellett, G. T.
Lieut. -	Lascelles, E. R.	Lieut. -	Mellis, A. W.
2nd-Lieut.	Leech, F. J. W.	Lieut. -	Mends, E. G.
Capt. -	Leighton, A.	Capt. -	Miall, D. H.
Lieut. -	Lester, A. M.	Lieut. -	Miall, E. J.
Capt. -	Lewis, F. W.,	Capt. -	Middleton, R.,
	M.C.		M.C.
Capt. -	Lewis, H. D.,	Lieut. -	Miles, E. C.
	T.D.	Capt. -	Millar, C. W. A.
Capt. -	Lewis, H. T.	2nd-Lieut.	Miller, R. W.
2nd-Lieut.	Louch, J. D. G.	Lieut. -	Miller, S. L.
2nd-Lieut.	Love, J. B.	Lieut. -	Mills, A. L.
		Lieut. -	Mitchell, G. R.
2nd-Lieut. -	MacDonald, J. S.	2nd-Lieut.	Mitchison, M.
Lieut. -	McDowall, A. C.	Lieut. -	Moore, R. W.
Lieut. -	McKay, C. S.	Lieut. -	Moran, J.
Lieut. -	McKay, H. G.	Lieut. -	Moriarty, D.
Lieut. -	McMahon, J. J.,	Lieut. -	Morris, L. C.,
	D.C.M., M.C.		M.C.
Lieut. -	McMuldroch, R.	Lieut. -	Morrow, A.
Capt. -	McSweeney, D.	Lieut. -	Moss, G. H. C.
	L., M.C.	Lieut. -	Mouland, H. J.
2nd-Lieut.	Mallett, H. J.	2nd-Lieut.	Munn, F. A.
Lieut. -	Malthouse, C.	2nd-Lieut.	Murless, H. R.
2nd-Lieut.	Marchant, C. V.	Lieut. -	Murray, W. J.
Lieut. -	Margrett, G. M.	2nd-Lieut.	Muxworthy, T.
Lieut. -	Markham, L. A.		
Lieut.-Col.	Marshall, H.,	Lieut. -	Nation, F. R.
	M.C.	Capt. -	Neales, E. W.
Lieut. -	Martin, E. J.	Lieut. -	Neall, K. P.
Lieut. -	Martin, F.	Lieut.-Col.	Newson, W. F. K.
Lieut. -	Martin, G. C. Y.	Lieut. -	Newton, C. F.
Lieut. -	Martin, L. S.	2nd-Lieut.	Noel, C. A. B.
Lieut. -	Matheson, H.	Lieut. -	Northam, J. McC.

Roll of Officers—continued.

RANK.	NAME.	RANK.	NAME.
Capt. -	Nutbrown, L. A.	Capt. -	Rathbone, W. L. C., M.C.
2nd-Lieut.	Oldcorn, J. S., D.C.M.	Lieut. -	Ray, G. H.
		Lieut. -	Ray, L. R.
Major -	Oliver, A. A.	Lieut. -	Reeve, J. S.
Capt. -	Oliver, A. D.	Lieut.-Col.	Renny, A. M.
Capt. -	Olliffe, F. C.	Lieut. -	Richardson, F. M.
Lieut. -	Osborne, F., M.C.		
Lieut. -	Osborne, T. L.	Capt. -	Rimington, C. H.
		Capt. -	**Roberts, A.**
		Lieut. -	Roberts, G.
2nd-Lieut.	Page, W. E.	Lieut. -	Roberts, G.
2nd-Lieut.	**Palin, O. E.**	Lieut. -	Robertson, E. J.
Lieut.-Col.	Parish, F. W., D.S.O., M.C.	2nd-Lieut.	Robinson, A. E.
		Capt. -	Roeber, W. C. T., O.B.E., M.C.
Lieut. -	Pearson, T. W.		
Capt. -	Peatfield, B., M.C.	Lieut. -	Rothwell, J.
		Lieut. -	Rushman, G. W.
Lieut. -	Phelps, F. W.	Capt. -	Rust, H. F.
Lieut. -	Pickard, L. W.		
Capt. -	Pickthorn, K. W. M.	2nd-Lieut.	Samuel, T. A. H., M.C.
Lieut. -	Pickup, F.	Lieut. -	Sanger, R. W.
2nd-Lieut.	**Pilcher, A. M.**	Capt. -	Satow, G. L.
Lieut. -	Pilkington, G. V.	Major -	Saunders, A. E., T.D.
Lieut. -	Pittam, A. P., M.C.		
		Lieut. -	Schofield, J. A.
Lieut. -	Plowman, T. R. (Died 1/1/20)	**Lieut. -**	**Scott, B.**
		Lieut. -	Scott, P. E. W.
Lieut. -	Porter, W. W.	Col. -	Segrave, W. H. E., D.S,O.
Lieut. -	**Potts, J. P.**		
Capt. -	Praeger, I. P.	Lieut. -	Sellick, R.
Lieut. -	Prynn, G. W.	Lieut. -	Settle, H. G.
Lieut. -	Pulley, A. S., M.C.	Lieut. -	Seys, S. A., M.C.
		Capt. -	Sharratt, T. H.
		2nd-Lieut.	Shepherd, E. P.
Capt. -	Radice, F. R.	Lieut. -	Silletoe, S. A.
Capt. -	Randolph, J. H.	Capt. -	Simmons, T. H.

Roll of Officers—continued.

RANK.	NAME.	RANK.	NAME.
Lieut. -	Simpson, H. H.	2nd-Lieut.	Thorpe, A. E.
2nd-Lieut.	Small, T. H.	2nd-Lieut.	Thrower, S. W.
2nd-Lieut.	Smart, C.	Lieut. -	Tickle, P. J.,
Lieut. -	Smart, C. A.		M.M.
Lieut. -	Smith, A. E.	Lieut. -	Titcombe, J. J.
Lieut. -	Smith, F. J.	Lieut. -	Titcombe, L. A.,
2nd-Lieut.	Smith, R. F.		D.C.M.
2nd-Lieut.	Smith, S. K.	2nd-Lieut.	Tomkins, C. J. D.
Capt. -	Smith, T. A.	Capt. -	Toomey, A.
Capt. -	Smith, W. S. H.	2nd-Lieut.	Townend,A. C. H.
Lieut. -	Songest, C. B.	2nd-Lieut.	Townsend, E. L.
Lieut. -	Souter, A.	Capt. -	Trembath, A. E.,
Lieut. -	Spencer, H. J.		D.C.M.
Lieut. -	Splatt, H. J.	Capt. -	Trembath, C. H.
Capt. -	Stanton, O. W.	Major -	Trembath, F. F.
2nd-Lieut.	Stevens, G. C. D.	Major -	Turk, G. W.,
2nd-Lieut.	Stevenson, C. S.		T.D.
2nd-Lieut.	Stileman, C. H.	2nd-Lieut.	Tysoe, W. L.
Major -	Stokes, G. E., O.B.E.	Lieut. -	Upton, R.
Capt. -	Stone, G. G. H.		
2nd-Lieut.	Stoneman, W. T.	Lieut. -	Vigar, A. L.
Col. - -	Strange, E. F., C.B.E., T.D.	2nd-Lieut.	Walker, A. W. E.
Lieut. -	Stringer, J. W. T.	Lieut. -	Walker, W. J.
2nd-Lieut.	Sutton, H. J.	Lieut. -	Wallis, J. A. D.
		2nd-Lieut	Ward, E. K.
Capt. -	Tarver, F. F.	2nd-Lieut.	Ware, B. K.
2nd-Lieut.	Tatum, G. E.	Major -	Warne, H. F. M.
Lieut. -	Taylor, A. L.	Lieut.-Col.	Warrender, H. V., D.S.O.
2nd-Lieut.	Taylor, L. H.		
2nd-Lieut.	Taylor, S. A.	Capt. -	Wass, E. J.
2nd-Lieut.	Temple, W.	Lieut. -	Watts, F. W.
2nd-Lieut.	Thompson, F. D.	Lieut. -	Webb, W. P.
Capt. -	Thompson, G. E., D.S.O.	Lieut. -	Wenham, J. K. L.
		Lieut. -	Westmore, F. W.
Capt. -	Thorogood, P. W., O.B.E.	Lieut. -	Wheatley, J. M.
		Lieut. -	Wheeler, E. N.

Roll of Officers—continued.

RANK.	NAME.	RANK.	NAME.
Lieut. -	Wheeler, F. M.	Lieut. -	Wilson, F. R.
Lieut. -	Whitaker, C. R.	2nd-Lieut.	Wiltshire, E. T.
Capt. - -	Whiteley, A.	2nd-Lieut.	Wimpey, A. B.
Lieut. -	Whitting, A.,M.C.	2nd-Licut.	Woods, T.
Lieut. -	Wilcocks, H. F.	Major -	Woolley, E. J.,
Lieut. -	Willi, J.		M.C.
Capt. -	Wills, K. A., M.C.	Lieut. -	Wright, H. R.
2nd-Lieut.	Wilmott, C. A.		
Lieut. -	Wilson, A., M.C.	Major -	Young, D.

LIST OF OFFICERS OF 1ST BATTALION ON LANDING IN FRANCE, MARCH, 1915.

Bt.-Col. A. M. Renny.
Major R. Chew.
Major H. V. Warrender.
Capt. W. F. K. Newson
Capt. H. H. Kemble.
Capt. A. E. Trembath.
Capt. H. M. Crofts.
Capt. R. J. S. Gold.
Capt. G. E. Stokes.
Capt. G. A. Gage.
Capt. H. B. Farquhar.
Lieut. J. C. P. Kinsman.
Lieut. A. Roberts.
Lieut. F. R. Radice.
Lieut. T. H. Sharratt.
Lieut. H. T. Lewis.

Lieut. L. Davies.
Lieut. R. Chalmers.
Lieut. A. C. B. Benkè.
Lieut. J. C. D. Carlisle.
2nd-Lieut. H. J. Sutton.
2nd-Lieut. H. R. E. Clarke.
2nd-Lieut. B. Barnes.
2nd-Lieut. F. C. Olliff.
2nd-Lieut. C. F. B. Stevens.
2nd-Lieut. G. G. Bates.
Capt. and Adj. F. W. Parish.
Hon. Lieut. and Q.M. W. H. D. Clark.
Surg.-Capt. R. W. Branthwaite
Capt. A. G. T. Hanks, R.A.M.C.

APPENDIX IX

Other Ranks who served in the period 1914–1919.

Dark Type REPRESENTS THOSE WHO DIED ON ACTIVE SERVICE.

Alexandra, H. T.
Allen, W. J.
Allen, J.
Adams, J. P.
Anderson, G. F.
Adams, P. E.
Andrews, A. J.
Allinson, J. H. D.
Audre, R. B.
Allen, S. T.
Arthur, E. F.
Alvery, G. C.
Andrews, F. C.
Allen, T. E.
Archer, G.
Adams, A. A.
Armstrong, A. F.
Ashleigh, A.
Almond, P. K.
Askham, W.
Arnold, J. G.
Andrews, W. L.
Avery, S. E.
Armstrong, H. O.
Andrews, G.
Adams, P. E.
Armstrong, J. S.
Armstrong, L. D.
Austen, W. H.
Arthur, J. E.
Allen, R. C. J.
Allen, E.
Allcock, O. P.
Andrews, E. E.
Arundel, T. H.
Asquith, J. R.
Alliston, G. H.
Allen, P. F.

Alexander, F.
Astbury, T. W.
Astle, E.
Avis, A. J.
Arculus, H. J.
Andrews, C. J.
Aylmore, A. G. A.
Allen, H. T.
Attwell, L. W.
Aylmore, G. H. A.
Addison, G. H.
Allen, P. W.
Allen, A. H.
Angel, A. J.
Allen, B. G.
Angel, H. A. E.
Archer, T. H.
Arkcoll, A. G.
Arthur, R. J.
Arnold, N. E.
Armstrong, J. F.
Avison, J. H.
Amos, T. W.
Aitken, R. S.
Ashworth, W. H.
Amphlett, C. E.
Allin, H. E.
Alder, H. F.
Aird, A. P. McG.
Allshorn, F. L.
Andrews, A. C.
Aston, R. F.
Aird, R. J. M.
Acott, L. J.
Andrews, A. J.
Altman, A. G. J.
Ayres, H. S.
Austin, S. A.

Atwell, G. H.
Aish, G.
Adams, G. J.
Allam, G. B.
Ayling, A.
Admans, H.
Atton, H. A.
Ainsworth, D. J.
Archer, T. L. B.
Ainsworth, G. T.
Anderson, D. B.
Anthony, E. V.
Arnold, S.
Acres, C. H.
Avon, E. F.
Adams, G. E. J.
Allison, R.
Archard, J.
Andrews, P. R.
Axford, D. S.
Axford, E. W.
Adlam, T. J.
Atkins, A. N.
Adams, R.
Anthony, G. E.
Achard, C. E.
Ashworth, J. R.
Attwood, S. A.
Anderton, J. A.
Allen, H. E.
Archer, W. E.
Alvery, R. T.
Allen, J. H.
Amsden, C. S.
Anderson, C. N.
Arnold, G.
Addis, F. L.
Allistone, W. C.

415

Avis, W. J.
Applin, G. C.
Archer, J.
Ackworth, G. W.
Amey, H. J.
Archer, H. F.
Archer, S. W.
Atkins, F. M.
Alvey, P. G.
Ayling, F. W.
Anderson, E. S.
Austin, O.
Anyan, W.
Allman, W. P.
Adams, W. M.
Allden, H. W.
Ayre, F. O.
Armstrong, W. N.
Ashton, L. C. B.
Ashdown, A. G.
Altass, P.
Aspland, G. T.
Anderson, S. E.
Allsford, H. E.
Austen, A. J.
Armfield, A. R.
Abbott, J. E.
Allsopp, W. H.
Ailion, E. C.
Archer, C. G.
Armstrong, F. B.
Averre, N.
Andrew. P. H.
Allen, T.
Allen, C. J.
Anderson, H. I. W.
Adams, J.
Anthony, I.
Armfield, H. L.
Arpthorp, E. H.
Ames, A. J.
Andrews, A. A.
Ashby, A. C.
Ainsworth, W.
Austin, T.
Angell, W. J.
Allen, L. E.

Awburn, G. T.
Ashby, A. O.
Adams, R. S.
Arthur, J. C.
Aylmore, F. W.
Auty, H. A.
Aglionby, F. B.
Allen, F. C.
Alabaster, R. W.
Adams, C.
Atkins, E. W.
Armour, W. F.
Acarnley, C. E.
Angel, A. J.
Archer, A. A.
Ansley, H.
Anderson, D.
Allchurch, C. A.
Atkawes, H. L.
Anderson, C.
Aubrey, C.
Ashwell, E. J.
Alston, F.
Apthorpe, F. W.
Allen, L. H.
Askew, T. A.
Anders, L.
Adams, A. T.
Austin, R.
Allen, A. O.
Aldous, A. H.
Allen, J. W.
Atkinson, W. H.
Addington, W. G.
Abbotts, J.
Aston, J. B.
Albutt, G. L.
Adams, C. H.
Adams, F.
Abrahams, L.
Alsop, G. B.
Anderson, C. F.
Allen, F. G.
Ames, R. T.
Archer, N.
Andrews, S. H.
Alldridge, R. H.

Ames, F. E.
Audley, G. E.
Allen, J. W.
Allington, C. W.
Allen, J.
Allen, W. V. M.
Andrews, E. A.
Albin, W. G.
Andrews, H. E.
Anderson, H. J.
Allen, W. J.
Ashforth, E.
Anderson, W. E.
Ablett, A.
Andrews, C. H.
Ainsworth,
    W. St. J.
Archard, E. F.
Allen, G. W. H.
Adams, F.
Amphlett, A. G.
Abel, B. F.
Adcock, C.
Arthur, F.
Alexander, D. F.
Arnold, A. R.
Arnott, R. R.
Abbott, C. I.
Angear, A.
Agar, C. W.
Archard, E. A.
Auvache, J. W.
Ashton, J. J.
Amery, M. F.
Allison, F. B.
Alford, R. S.
Ayliffe, A.
Ashton, A. E.
Ainley, C. E.
Anstey, A. T.
Allen, F. R. L.
Andrews, J. S.
Ayres, A. E.
Allan, R. C.
Andress, A.
Austin, W. H.
Atherton, J.

Ainley, W. W.
Arnold, T. J. B.
Anderson, A.
  (alias Abrahams.)
Austin, E. G.
Abbey, J. G.
Aslett, J.
Adlington, S.
Alldridge, A. W.
Andrews, H.
Ainsworth, S. C.
Arthur, O. T.
Atkinson, S. J.
Agg, T. E.
Allen, S. V.
Adcock, R. E.
Allen, R. N.
Arscott, E. G.
Allistone, W. C.
Allan, C. G.
Alexander, F. F.
Abraham, L. L.
Allcoat, J. W.
Allen, S. E.
Adlam, C. R.
Aspden, H. J.
Addison, F.
Alvery, R. T.
Anderson, F. J.
Ash, A. E.
Andrews, W. H.
Austin, H. L.
Allen, L. F.
Amner, A. W. A.
Ardley, H. R.
Almond, W. W. G.
Allen, S. A. E.
Austin, A.
Abbott, B.
Abbott, M. F.
Amis, R.
Allford, G. J.
Ackland, H. D.
Affleck, W. M. B.
Armour, D. C.
Alabaster, E. W.
Abrahams, E.

Allen, J. W.
Atkin, F. W. A.
Ayres, A. V.
Anderson, C.
Abbott, A.
Aulsford, G.
Ashby, J. S.
Abrams, J.
Ashton, T.
Ayres, W. E.
Allsop, T.
Arnold, W. E.
Appleby, R.
Arundell, T. H.
Allmen, H. M.
Ashley, W.
Ambrose, P.
Angel, R. L.
Ainsworth, L. L.
Andrews, J. L.
Amos, E. V.
Audley, G. E.
B
Berry, H. A.
Brown, B. H.
Bacon, S. V.
Brightman, J. H.
Beadle, H.
Blake, C. S.
Braine, E. A.
Bowen, C. J.
Burbidge, J. W.
Booker, E. W.
Battersby, H.
Bruback, H. A.
Butcher, E.
Betts, F.
Barnes, C. H.
Battrum, E. D.
Bristol, L.
Bilbrough, A. H. B.
Bailey, A. W.
Barrett, H. L.
Bennett, P. J.
Benke, A. C. H.
Bates, G. G.
Batten, K. C.

Baudains, P. G.
Bulgin, A. H.
Batley, A. G.
Barnes, B.
Breen, P. T.
Burgess, T. B.
Bull, A. C.
Barrett, H.
Bishop, C. H.
Borer, F. W. V.
Baxter, H. L.
Baker, E. C.
Boorer, A. F.
Butcher, A.
Burgess, H. W.
Blackaby, N. A.
Brown, F. E.
Barlow, H.
Bullar, A. J.
Bools, R. G.
Belk. S.
Boff, W. C.
Burton, F. R.
Baynes, A. J.
Blake, W. H.
Bird, L. A.
Bowstead, J. E.
Bayliss, J. E.
Blake, W. E.
Bourne, J.
Blake, R. R.
Bressey, S. H.
Berry, H.
Barltrop, E. W.
Butcher, A. S.
Bridge, F. G.
Brace, T. F.
Brookes, A. C.
Brown, W. P.
Bailey, G. S.
Bobringer, F. G.
Banks, H. B.
Barrow, A. M.
Bridge, P.
Bartram, H. F.
Budgen, P. E.
Bosworth, L. F.

2 D

Benke, F. W.
Bell, F. G.
Booty, A.
Brockett, H. E.
Ball, A. A.
Brett, L. M.
Bennett, W. A.
Brown, H.
Burr, J. D.
Bull, F. W.
Bridel, H. S.
Broadbent, S. W.
Bendle, F. J.
Bennett, H. B.
Bryan, S. A.
Blackaby, E. W.
Bennett, H. P.
Byrne, E. J.
Barratt, W. M.
Bowman, H. E.
Bouchley, F. G.
Bull, H. F.
Brooks, J. W.
Byrne, D. M.
Brace, J.
Beadle, C. W.
Bell, J. W.
Bucknill, W. F. C.
Boon, F. M.
Bailey, W.
Bruce, H. S.
Banfield, W.
Brooks, W. A.
Barrett, E. S.
Brinn, A. L.
Bacon, E. A.
Bell, A. W.
Brandis, H. G.
Bates, E. H.
Bussell, H. R.
Betts, S. H.
Boddy, A.
Brierley, W.
Bortles, L.
Barrell, R.
Birt, R. A.
Boxer, H. S.

Beard, B. J. L.
Bassett, E.
Barrett, L. L. E.
Bolingbroke, J. G.
Border, T. A.
Bostock, C. A.
Brock, A. H. J.
Brockway, H. S.
Barnes, H. S.
Bartley, H. N.
Berry, H. H.
Blick, J. F.
Bridge, H. E.
Brown, E. L.
Bendle, H. C.
Burnell, H. F.
Bocquet, W. M.
Bray, A.
Barnes, J. A.
Beazley, R. J. B.
Bell, A. H.
Bilcliffe, B. L.
Bradbury, J. V.
Bull, L.
Baker, G. L.
Bailey, A. G.
Bayliss, P.
Bedford, T. J.
Benison, L. S.
Blanchard, F. G.
Bone, G. J.
Bright, T. L.
Brown, H.
Bunce, J. H.
Bernstein, S. H.
Brookling, H.
Butt, C.
Bigby, R. F. M.
Bennison, J. W. E.
Bonner, C. R.
Bird, J. H. W.
Bonner, P. R.
Brugel, R. C.
Brown, L. J.
Brown, W. S.
Bullock, H. P.
Bazley, G. W.

Boutcher, E.
Baker, G. D.
Bazley, J. J.
Branton, W. H.
Briggs, T.
Brooman, G. L.
Bull, R.
Baillie, J. G.
Barley, H. J.
Bradshaw, C. F.
Brown, J. N.
Brooks, W. F.
Barcham, R. N.
Boulter, A. J.
Bowler, H. E.
Brook, C.
Budd, C. P.
Bastow, E.
Beer, R. G.
Beech, W. E.
Baker, A. A.
Batstone, J. L.
Bernard, S. A.
Berry, B.
Blaber, P.
Bonner, H.
Boyd, W. H.
Brattle, D. B.
Bromiley, B.
Brown, A. W.
Bugler, G. E.
Burleigh, T.
Button, C. F.
Boyes, E.
Belch, H. C.
Brewer, H.
Brown, P. W.
Bedford, C. C.
Bellingham, F. S.
Beaby, L. W.
Beatty, A. H. W.
Blyton, S. A. R.
Barker, C. N.
Bullock, H. H.
Brooks, L.
Bower, C. J.
Batch, H.

Bartram, W.
Boorman, P. L.
Burnett, J. W.
Branson, A. J.
Barlin, G.
Bluemel, F. W.
Barnett, H. E.
Butler, T. C.
Barcham, H. S.
Blurton, G.
Bolton, F. R.
Bolton, P. C.
Brockman, G. R.
Bryer, W. C.
Brilliant, N. M.
Bentley, J. T.
Burgess, G. B.
Bowden, P. E.
Best, E. A.
Brown, J. W.
Baden, L.
Bradley, A. W.
Bolton, A. H.
Barnes, C.
Barnes, G. E.
Born, J.
Black, W. A.
Bowden, C.
Benstead, L.
Brown, E. W.
Bell, D. C.
Bowyer, G. H.
Burtt, J. R.
Barrett, A. H.
Bayley, J. R.
Bonner, A. H.
Boorer, G. S.
Blackmore, F. R.
Baker, A. V.
Ball, J. T.
Bird, H. W. J.
Boxall, E. E.
Batchelor, A. E.
Bush, R. V. A.
Bryant, F.
Backshall, F. J.
Bryant, S. J.

Brock, L.
Brown, E. C.
Blyth, C. R.
Bishop, W. J.
Butcher, L. C.
Batsford, E. W.
Bradford, W.
Brown, G. B.
Butler, C. W.
Bradshaw, D. B.
Braybrooke, F. N.
Byng, R. F.
Burt, A. G. L.
Bishop, S. W.
Brennan, C. J.
Brown, J. W.
Ball, H.
Brown, F.
Baker, T. W.
Bassett, C. E.
Benham, J. C.
Bowers, F. M.
Burningham, L. A.
Brown, E. P.
Bell, A. F.
Babington, H. W.
Buxton, E. A.
Bone, F.
Burgess, F. G.
Bathurst, W.
Bentley, E. C.
Barham, W. S.
Barlex, M.
Bell, A. C. F.
Burgess, H. A.
Butcher, S. H.
Byne, G. C.
Billinghurst, J. H.
Bolding, A. S.
Bachell, T. T.
Baker, A. J.
Baker, E. H.
Bassett, G. A.
Beckett, P. W.
Bradfield, W. A.
Brightwell, J. H.
Brockwell, A. A. T.

Ball, H. F.
Biggs, E. S.
Blackwell, H. J.
Brown, H. J.
Berkshire, W. G.
Baker, S. H.
Barnes, L. F.
Brooks, L. G.
Brewer, J. O.
Barnes, R. J.
Beer, B. C.
Bennett, W.
Bickmore, P.
Bonfield, S. M. C.
Borland, R.
Borrie, C. E.
Bowman, V. A.
Brown, A. V.
Burwood, W. R.
Bell, F. D. L.
Braithwaite, F. L.
Bray, L. L.
Beecham, E. J.
Berry, G. F.
Bennett, F. E.
Brown, S. A.
Boss, W. R.
Bowen, W. A.
Browning, F. E.
Bedford, H. G.
Bassham, C. D.
Brewer, W. J.
Burden, J. E.
Burroughs, C. H.
Bartlett, C. F.
Brown, F. G.
Bennett, F. M.
Biddle, J. L. P.
Bower, T. H.
Brooker, B.
Burr, W.
Bradford, M. E.
Brookhouse, W.
Baxter, W. C.
Bush, E. A.
Browne, A. L.
Beer, C. M.

Banyard, H. W.
Baker, A. K.
Beagent, S. H.
Bridges, A. W.
Banyard, P. C.
Bouckley, J. A.
Browne, H. O.
Bourne, C. A.
Boseley, H. W. D.
Brown, A.
Bigg, J. B.
Barrow, A. W.
Bailey, C. F.
Barlow, R.
Ballam, F. G.
Bright, T.
Brooks, E. T.
Bailey, A.
Bishop, W. E.
Burns, E.
Butcher, C. G.
Barber, H. L.
Bruce, A. V.
Bush, L. E.
Brown, J.
Bradley, H. P.
Breary, C.
Bruns, A. G. V.
Benjamin, J. R.
Brookes, H.
Bosworth, H. V.
Burke, M. L.
Bourner, H. G.
Burdock, C. N.
Bovington, W. J.
Burdock, H.
Bright, G. W.
Brooks, E. A.
Breed, R.
Billingham, F. A.
Beaney, E. W.
Blanks, J. W.
Bacon, P. E.
Barton, H.
Bettison, C. F.
Bazil, W.
Brakespear, E. H.

Brighton, S.
Broomfield, R. A.
Bull, G. F.
Bareham, S. V. F.
Baxter, L. F.
Brant, F. T.
Bryant, H.
Bennett, L. J.
Barton, E. C.
Bates, T. B.
Bridges, W. H.
Brooker, H. G.
Bullemore, H.
Bryant, D. E.
Baizley, J. M.
Bolton, F. W.
Bargery, H. W.
Briggs, H.
Baker, W. J.
Brown, F. J.
Bush, E. L.
Baker, A. D.
Baldwin, W. E.
Ballands, J. H.
Bines, F.
Black, T. G.
Bowers, A. S.
Braithwaite, P.H.
Brockway, W. H.
Browning, S. L.
Burn, P. D.
Banfield, A. H.
Blackmore, A. W.
Barnett, W. J.
Bannister, F. F.
Benwell, W. L.
Beer, G. L.
Blanchard,
              A. C. D.
Bonnett, E. J.
Budd, R. L.
Backhauser, H. F.
Batson, F. J.
Bothamley, P.
Badcock, H. C.
Bowerman, C. E.
Bullock, C. F.

Bass, R. J. V.
Bear, C. A.
Baker, F.
Bolger, W. J.
Burdett, W. C.
Brown, T. P.
Belville, F. A.
Baird, G.
Baird, J.
Burgis, E.
Butler, J. F.
Bell, H. S.
Benton, H. B.
Bilby, W. H.
Beard, W. H. G.
Byford, A. H.
Barnicott, R. S.
Brown, A. S.
Bolland, S. P.
Bascomb,
          R. Mc. K.
Batchelor,R. O. F.
Breckon, H. W.
Brown, A. L.
Birdsall, H. W.
Buser, R. L.
Baldwin, E.
Bynoe, C. C.
Brown, R.
Beddis, F. J.
Brown, R. A.
Barker, H. A.
Brownbridge,
              H. E.
Booth, A.
Brown, F. J.
Bell, W. G.
Buckley, J.
Butcher, A.
Briggs, R. Mc.C.
Baylis, H.
Barker, G.
Byatt, G. W.
Bourne, W. H.
Bastable, W.
Byfield, J.
Bond, F.

Bransgrove, C. W.
Bayliss, T. A.
Barratt, J.
Bolton, S.
Bruce, J.
Bailett, E. M.
Buston, J. J.
Buck, H. S.
Baker, F. C.
Bullock, A. M.
Belcher, F. C. L.
Bradbury, A. T.
Bussy, P. M.
Bamforth, T. S.
Barrett, A.
Blair, W.
Bryant, A.
Burt, L. G.
Bainbrigge, H.
Boyes, A. J.
Browne, W. G. H.
Bradshaw, A.
Balser, J. F.
Butcher, F. H.
Barrow, R.
Box, T. R.
Brackell, H. S.
Burridge, G. T. J.
Bambrick, W.
Bryett, E. H.
Birkin, H.
Best, C.
Brock, W. C.
Beyer, T. E.
Breckhill, J.
Blackeboy, C. F.
Bloy, A.
Burroughs, W. T.
Baker, F. L.
Burrell, J. H.
Burton, W. T.
Betteridge, E. L.
Blackhall, A. H.
Brydon, W.
Bell, R. D.
Brant, W.
Boydell, J.

Burt, W. H.
Beverley, A. G. B.
Bailey, C. E.
Blackmore, G. H.
Baker, H.
Barnes, T. P.
Byford, G. W.
Burton, A. J.
Boreham, W. J.
Barnes, H. B.
Burleigh, W. F.
Barnard, A. H. B.
Braithwaite, E. C.
Burgess, A. J.
Blee, P. G.
Bigden, J. E.
Brodbeck, E. C.
Burne, O. O. C.
Barber, F.
Billings, W. A.
Buck, W. I.
Beckwith, E. R.
Barry, T.
Baker, C. R. T.
Back, A. A.
Burrowes, R. H.
Brookes, P. D.
Benstead, A. R.
Boughton, E. G.
Barrett, F.
Bishop, W. T.
Beharrell, R. C.
Barrett, E.
Byatt, C. R.
Brown, A.
Banks, E. J.
Bailey, J. B.
Beadle, A. J.
Bates, G. A.
Blacklee, J. H.
Brooks, C. E.
Bennett, J. R.
Berry, P. H.
Brotherston, G. J.
Brooker, H. E.
Banyard, L. A.
Barnfather, J. D.

Benford, W. D.
Beck, R. F.
Baxter, F. C.
Brangwin, L. U. I
Blanchard, F. O.
Barron, W.
Bartlett, A. P.
Batstone, T. W.
Beard, E. J.
Berry, W.
Bewers, T. R.
Bolton, F. V.
Bolton, G. A.
Bristow, J. W.
Brown, L.
Brown, A. G.
Browning, J.
Bunnell, S. A.
Brent, W. H. S.
Bullen, G. J.
Beer, A. G.
Bell, E. G.
Baskerville, W. I
Buckland, F. B.
Boulton, A. J.
Beetleston, H. A.
Brown, A. H.
Brown, W. B.
Balshaw, C. A.
Bugden, W.
Brammall, S. G.
Boyes, W. E.
Boatswain, A.
Barker, G. R.
Botting, M.
Bartell, H. C.
Byron, T. H.
Brunskill, W.
Barrett, B. A.
Bryard, B. V.
Bartlett, A.
Bishop, A. A. B.
Borden, A. G.
Burton, S. G.
Busby, T. W.
Blanks, C. G.
Beaton, L.

Burgess, C. L. E.
Barnes, F. V.
Brown, F. J.
Butler, W. H.
Boden, E.
Branch, L. H.
Barrell, A. S.
Bolton, R. E.
Baldock, J. W. R.
Beck, D. R.
Brown, R. A.
Bracking, E. F.
Bass, T.
Babington, G. W.
Baldwin, W. J.
Bennett, J. C.
Bott, H. E.
Berg, L. W.
Byrne, P.
Blyth, R. C.
Berg, J. S.
Bird, C. J.
Back, B. R.
Boeck, E. F.
Barnett, A.
Bredon, W. V.
Brittain, R. J.
Beatley, J.
Brockett, A. J.
Baker, H. D.
Buss, H. S.
Bullock, E. J.
Benstead, C. H.
Bennett, J. K.
Brisley, E. C. E.
Bell, H. J.
Bennett, A.
Bishop, B.
Brough, R. F. W.
Burroughs, W. A.
Brickwood, E. W.
Burnell, H. F.
Burge, A. B.
Buger, J. E.
Bridge, H.
Burgess, A. A.
Barnett, G.

Ballantine, J.
Beckett, P.
Burgess, A. E.
Brooks, H. W.
Britton, J. F.
Barrell, W. G.
Bland, H. C.
Baines, S. V.
Bishop, W. H.
Barrell, H. J.
Berry, A. O.
Birnbaum, M.
Barnett, J. L.
Bowes, G. R
Brotherton, E. A.
Bourne, H. R.
Brooks, H. E.
Baldwin, S. F.
Bird, W. A.
Barraclough, M. S.
Blackmore, C. H.
Bowyer, A. W. C.
Bolton, H.
Britt, E. J. R.
Beasley, W.
Blanchard, E. G.
Bellamy, H. S.
Barnett, J. T. R.
Beadles, A. W.
Bland, R. B.
Bees, W. E.
Bell, W.
Barnes, M.
Baker, H. T.
Butler, J.
Burden, W. F.
Bates, A.
Burton, H.
Butler, F. H.
Bates, V. W.
Bennett, I.
Binks, J. R.
Bradfield, L. F.
Bowing, S. H.
Beauchamp, H. R.
Bastian, L.
Brimacombe, R. M.

Bowkett, H. G.
Bickford, T.
Buss, T.
Brown, T.
Brown, J.
Bantim, A. C.
Bridge, E. W.
Bailey, D. W.
Bailey, J. C.
Bowler, H. J.
Bruce, T. A.
Brewster, C. C.
Broom, R. J. W.
Beverstock, F.
Beard, E. G.
Brinton, H. W.
Bennett, P.
Beacham, R. C.
Bryant, L. A.
Barber, C. P.
Butler, S. E.
Bolton, C.
Blatch, E. J.
Barton, P. T.
Barnard, J. T.
Brooks, H. L.
Byles, E. F.
Bailey, J. R.
Blackburn, A.
Bruty, S. D.
Bevis, C. C.
Benison, A. E. A.
Butcher, A.
Beecroft, T. W. H.
Brightman, A. J.
Blackwell, S. G.
Byatt, J. D.
Blake, W. J. H.
Bell, J. J.
Burton, S.
Brennand, A. E.
Bromell, W. H.
Bunn, H.
Bonner, F.
Brock, H. W.
Baldry, S. F. T.
Brewer, W. E.

Bryce, S. G.
Bennett, T. R.
Baines, A. R.
Bracey, B.
Branninger, E. F.
Blackburn, E. E.
     J.
Bellamy, R. T.
Bennoson, H. P.
Barkus, W. T.
Bennett, K. E.
Blamire, H.
Bremner, A.
Bussell, G. R.
Bennett, W. A.
Bradbury, A. M.
Bonner, G. L.
Bull, S. J.
Buggey, A. E.
Barnes, F. S.
Blunsun, E.
Braham, W.
Bartram, C.
Burnett, B. R.
Brunning, E. S.
Berry, G. E.
Brand, A. J.
Bellingham, W. J.
Bishop, H. J.
Bowen, J. G.
Barber, G. P.
Bell, D. Mc.
Beale, A. G.
Brown, F.
Baine, A. E.
Burford, G. G.
Bascombe, R. J.
Buckley, H.
Burn, G. P.
Brackell, H.
Bushnell, S. V.
Britain, C. T.
Barrie, V. P.
Bates, J. N.
Brain, D. O.
Bradley, R. H.
Britton, D. L.

Brothwood,
    W. C. V.
Blunt, R. H.
Bowden, H. R.
Brock, E. R.
Bernstein, B.
Brazier, A. G.
Bowditch, H. F. H.
Belcher, F. W.
Bateman, O.
Bence, H. O.
Bennington, L.
Burr, F.
Brill, P. E.
Bosworth, A. E.
Bowring, H. P.
Bell, E. W.
Bell, A.
Bell, C. W.
Buchan, G. B.
Barrow, V. F.
Baker, L. M.
Balmer, G. A. R.
Brown, E. A.
Blaxland, E. P.
Bird, G. E.
Barnfather, F.
Bradshaw, E. B.
Bentham, R. L.
Brown, L. C.
Blunt, F. V.
Bowen, R. G.
Brunskill, M. E.
Batchelor, W. G.
Barnett, C. E.
Barlow, R.
Bailett, E. M.
Bell, F. C.
Barnett, G. P.
Boulden, E.
Baker, K. L.
Bennett, E. R.
Beaumont, J. W.
Buckley, R. S.
Bernstein, S.
Boldison, G. Y.
Beall, G. E.

Bartlett, G.
Baker, F. C.
Banks, W. E.
Bird, C. D.
Burnip, C. W.
Barton, C. H.
Brookes, F. L.
Bonshor, H.
Barry, W.
Brady, A. S.
Brown, R. J.
Brewer, F.
Burrows, T. R.
Bamford, H.
Brown, T. E.
Beaney, W. J.
Boniface, R. D.
Bott, H. N.
Barratt, J. E.
Baldwin, H.
Beak, E.
Brown, J. E.
Bull, A. J.
Branthwaite, J.
Burney, O. R.
Bullocke, C. R.
Bennett, C. G.
Beavan, C. S.
Billingham, E. H.
Billing, F. J.
Beckley, E. R.
Byrne, R.
Baigent, F. W.
Brockington, F.
Brook, A. E.
Beckett, J.
Biggs, E. N.
Billett, C. G.
Bembridge, R. H.
Baughan, E. A.
Bennett, W. G.
Box, H. T.
Barenty, J. L.
Brookman, W. H.
Brown, H. W.
Bidgood, S.
Bell, E. L.

Brown, S. W.
Buckley, T.
Bayne, E. S.
Burton, W. H.
Brown, A. A.
Baynes, J. E. L.
Best, S. G.
Baldwin, A. F.
Bates, L. S.
Brown, F. E.
Barker, J. G.
Blake, L. S.
Burgess, F. S.
Blythe, T. L.
Baker, W. T.
Basson, K.
Beach, W. C.
Baalam, T. H.
Bush, J. A. W.
Burroughs, E. H.
Banks, S. A.
Blunt, J. E.
Beach, S.
Bates, W.
Bambrough, A. V.
Booth, H. S.
Baker, B.
Barnard, C. H.
Buck, A. I.
Bennett, H. D.
Botting, R. A.
Brown, T.
Butler, A. E.
Birch, A. E. S.
Bartholomew,
                D. A.
Brodie, A. W.
Blackford, F. S. P.
Barker, W. S.
Bandy, E. C.
Beddall, T. R.
Bennett, J. R.
Bunce, O. E.
Beesley, A.
Baskett, E. W.
Bedford, C. A.
Blee, D.

Bull, A. J.
Bulgin, A. H.
Border, H.
Bish, W.
Baker, E. M.
Backshall, G. T.
Bilby, F. J.
Brownbridge, R.
Baker, A. J.
Barton, F. R.
Beesley, C. W.
Berkin, W. W.
Boston, A.
Brandon, E. W.
Buzzo, C. H.
Baptie, W.
Beadle, R. S.
Brewster, W. P.
Brown, H. T.
Bull, C. R.
Burford, G. C.
Burnett, A.
Brown, S.
Balkwill, J. H.
Bellingher, J.
Bridgland, T. E.
Bumpstead, A. E.
Busby, A. A.
Brown, W. A. R.
Bailey, W.
Barnes, A. J.
Bartram, F. H.
Bonham, J. A.
Blake, W. G. A.
Brown, E. J.
Bailey, W. H.
Bassett, A. A.
Biggs, F. J.
Bowyer, R. B.
Brookson, E. A.W.
Busby, G. B.
Best, F. H.
Barford, C. R. G.
Bartlett, C. R. W.
Burnett, C. J.
Barker, A. A.
Bunker, E. St. C.

Brock, R. M.
Broad, D.
Brain, W.
Brown, J. H.
Burton, J. C.
Bowring, A.
Bridger, J. H.
Bennett, M. G.
Baker, W. F.
Beddo, B.
Boomer, F.
Brake, F. D.
Barraclough, T.
Bennett, I. R.
Blythe, K. J. R.
Bull, T. W.
Blackmore, C. H.
Blick, W. T.
Bloodworth, P. J.
Burlow, F. G.
Buckle, R. W.
Barber, T. J.
Bennett, H. J.
Bence, W. H.
Bird, C. W.
Baxter, H.
Baker, R. J.
Ball, F. G. W.
Birch, W. A.
Barwell, J.
Bonas, H. J.
Bywater, S.
Baverstock, J.
Bonney, J. A.
Barber, T. S.
Broomhead, R.
Boyl, G. F.
Butland, W. G. R.
Bayliss, E.
Butler, A. E. F.
Bailey, A.
Bourton, F. H.
Beach, W.
Boyce, J.
Boyce, J. W.
Beeny, W. C. G.
Baverstock, H.

Bloomfield, H.
Broad, W. H.
Berrington, W. A.
Biscoe, J.
Bartlett, E. A.
Branch, W.
Barber, W. H.
Bott, G. A.
Buckingham,
      R. W. P.
Burrowes, W. O. B.
Benjamin, J.
Bennett, C. L.
Bradley, A. F.
Brown, H. H.
Boorman, S. C. M.
Burman, A. R.
Budd, H. G.
Burton, W.
Balls, G. H.
Bishop, B. A.
Bond, W. G. S.
Benson, F. W.
Benstead, A. J.
Bartram, T. G. C.
Bearsley, H. E.
Brown, J. G.
Barratt, H. H.
Bevan, W. S.
Beard, P. L.
Boon, B. H.
Brooks, T. G.
Byford, T. W.
Bish, W.
Burford, F. W.
Bartlett, G. A.
Berry, E.
Bookless, A. W.
Barrett, R. H.
Brooks, T. E.
Burns, T. E.
Beckingham, E. L.
Buick, W.
Baker, D.
Brewster, T. G.
Baron, J.
Brown, E. W. A.

Bush, H. A.
Barringer, A. G.
Bonner, G. R.
Brandon, E.
Brillard, W. D.
Brook, A. E.
Binstead, V. H.
Butler, E. R.
Baker, M. J.
Balm, S. G.
Brockman, J.
Bristow, F. W.
Bave, A. J.
Brown, J. W.
Barker, A. A.
Brown, S. H.
Burton, J. W.
Baxter, B. C.
Bray, C. C.
Bew, F. J.
Billinghurst,
      R. H. S.
Brock, W. A.
Bowen, T. E.
Bacon, A. G.
Bradbury, W.
Bray, J. A. W.
Burnett, W.
Benest, F. A.
Bennett, R. A.
Bennett, R. A.
Baker, W. M.
Burns, H.
Bartling, G. W. H.
Boome, G. P. B.
Barron, W. A.
Beadle, A. J.
Baker, H. T. G.
Beere, J. H.
Brown, F. J.
Battman, A. E.
Blackwell, F. A.
Bramley, A.
Bullchambers,
      A. H.
Butler, M.
Black, J. A.

Bishop, E.
Bradley, R. V.
      C
Church, T. O.
Champness, A.
Clifford, W. H.
Callie, G.
Cox, A. R. H.
Chick, T. P.
Crane, W. F.
Croal, B. V.
Cave, A. J.
Cork, F. T.
Charles, M. E.
Carbery, H. T.
Chick, E. R.
Cook, A. J.
Cheale, H. J.
Carr, L. O.
Cottrell, T. A.
Crews, E. K.
Caiger, P. T.
Cuthbert, R. P.
Chater, J. T.
Cave, R. G.
Clark, T. H. E.
Cornwell, P. D.
Carpenter, H. F.
Cory, C. H.
Cheale, A. W.
Coker, F. G.
Callagham, J. F.
Clark, F. A.
Cronin, J. F.
Carlile, R. W.
Cartman, J. V.
Crawley, C. W.
Chapman, L. J.
Curtis, A. H.
Chinn, C. G.
Cook, R. A.
Carson, W. A.
Cogman, W. E.
Cansdale, C.
Clinkscales, A. B.
Clive, W. G.
Creswell, A. T.

Coleman, B. C.
Carlisle, P.
Chapman, B. M.
Callinson, H. J.
Collerette, F.
Cullington, M. W.
Cartnell, T.
Clapp, M. F.
Clark, D.
Clulow, F. R.
Churchill, H. B.
Coster, G. H.
Crockett, E. G.
Clarke, J. E.
Chapman, D. P.
Collins, A. T.
Clark, A. W. H.
Childs, C. L.
Criswick, W. G.
Clarke, H.
Covey, C. E. H.
Carpenter, J. E.
Christie, J. G. D.
Clark, R. E.
Carpenter, A. J.
Cherry, A. D.
Cottam, C. J.
Clarke, W. D.
Clay, R. H.
Carroll, F.
Chatterton, W. O.
Craig, W. H.
Cook, C.
Cramp, J.
Church, R. H.
Cousal, W.
Cheesman, R. C.
Creber, W. M.
Cook, D. W.
Cook, E. J.
Collyer, L. F.
Comber, J.
Colven, W. A.
Cooke, H. A.
Cobb, T. G. H.
Chalmers, R.
Collingburn, J.

Curtis, B. L.
Curtis, A.
Clarke, J. F.
Connold, E.
Cox, R. W. T.
Collison, T. A.
Clements, S. L.
Catchpole, T. P.
Croydon, F. E.
Christy, F.
Cowell, W. E.
Carey, H. E.
Colson, F. J.
Cox, S. W. C.
Chalmers, J. C.
Cahill, A. E.
Covey, W. S. J.
Coles, D. J. R.
Colsey, G. R.
Clarke, R. F.
Cain, W. F.
Calcutt, J. S.
Chudney, G. A.
Clarke, W. R.
Clift, W. R.
Cope, P. R.
Copeland, G.
Curd, C. W.
Carrdus, T. L. V.
Chadfield, J. M.
Christie, W.
Crawshaw, N. E.
Crosbie, R. P.
Coniam, G.
Cronin, J. M.
Cudmore, A. W.
Charlton, G. H.
Clayton, L. J.
Cook, A. G.
Copin, F. C.
Coward, F. A.
Crombie, A. D.
Cruiks, W.
Currie, J. A.
Clarke, R. H.
Clemans, H. C.
Coleman, P. V.

Cooke, E.
Cooper, P. V.
Coulson, J. A.
Clark, G. D.
Cornwell, A. G.
Cartwright, L. J.
Champeny, C. B.
Chapman, A.
Coe, H. F. J.
Crombie, C. H.
Croydon, A. D.
Chalke, J. E.
Cousens, L. F.
Carter, A. H.
Cossins, W. J.
Coward, D. C.
Carroll, H. E.
Chapman, S.
Collins, J. E.
Cox, R. E.
Cooper, F.
Coates, J. C.
Clarke, W.
Cecil, H. W.
Clarke, F. A.
Clarke, R.
Carroll, P. J.
Curtis, H. S.
Connor, E. C. G.
Crooks, W. E.
Connolly, W. P.
Carr, D.
Chibbett, L. J. S.
Childs, D. R.
Clarkson, E. A.
Cook, C. J.
Cook, W. L. G.
Clarke, A. E.
Cox, C.
Cooley, C. B.
Cockley, C. A.
Crane, H. H.
Cross, C. G. O.
Cullingford, L. S.
Charge, R. O.
Claridge, C. M.
Cockram, A. F.

Crocombe, S.
Crawfurd, A. J.
Curtis, W. S.
Charlton, W. C.
Colverd, T. H.
Cooper, H. G.
Chisholm, K. D.
Cooper, C. E.
Chapman, H. H.
Clark, J. P.
Calthrop, J. L.
Caswell, G. E.
Crossley, W. G.
Coakeley, N. F.
Compton, F. C. H.
Crabb, P. R. L.
Couldrey, S. D.
Chapman, F. M.
Critchinson, C. F.
Cassidy, J. J. F.
Cornell, W.
Church, S. R.
Ching, A. J.
Curry, H. J. R.
Coxon, F. W.
Coombs, A. A.
Costen, W. H.
Carmen, H. M.
Codd, A. E.
Carter, C. H.
Cade, F. G.
Coleman, A. W.
Clark, E. J. A.
Coulthard, R.
Colson, H.
Castell, E. C.
Coakeley, B. A.
Costa, R.
Crowe, F. A.
Cook, W.
Coughty, F. W.
Croker, L. H.
Copeland, F.
Chalk, A.
Cock, E.
Cole, G. H.
Clarke, H. J.

Curtis, J. T.
Clarke, W. G.
Cooper, A.
Christey, W. T.
Cox, H. T.
Chadwick, R. F.
Chambers, W. A.
Cutts, E. T.
Carter, A. J. E.
Capell, R. W. H.
Copp, F. A.
Ching, H. J.
Curry, H. J. R.
Collister, D. W.
Carpenter, A.
Carpenter, G. D.
Cast, C. E.
Cole, G. E.
Coster, J. A.
Crabb, S. J.
Crosby, H. C.
Cherry, K. C.
Cleary, M.
Couchman, J. A.
Carey, A. E.
Combe, H. R.
Cook, A. W.
Coit, E. C. D.
Critchley, G.
Cossins, A. L.
Cook, E. K.
Counsell, F. E.
Cubitt, D. F.
Churchill, E.
Cutmore, H.
Calder, W. O.
Callender, R. T.
Chambers, F. R.
Cooper, W. A.
Coppack, F. V.
Carpenter, A.
Clancy, A.
Clifton, E. J.
Cobbledick, T.
Corne, A. C.
Crampton, W.
Carter, H. E.

Clarke, O.
Cox, J. J.
Cronin, J. P.
Care, J. S.
Clarke, A.
Clements, E. F.
Cowling, C. F.
Carter, S.
Chadler, E. R.
Chapman, H. E.
Clement, H. C.
Cordy, P. J.
Clayton, P. H.
Craven, J. E.
Counter, F. G.
Cooks, A. V.
Copsey, F. M.
Capleton, A.
Chance, J. J.
Callop, L.
Curtis, A. C.
Chalker, W. T. S.
Carrick, M. W.
Campbell, J. E. S.
Cubison, E. M.
Carey, S.
Cross, T.
Carter, A. J.
Couch, H. C.
Carter, L. F.
Carrington, J. H.
Curtis, H. J.
Campbell, H. J.
Currie, A. H. C.
Cooper, G. H.
Collar, F. F.
Carnaghan, J.
Couchman, A. G.
Child, H.
Chave, R. G.
Comber, W.
Crawford, C.
Collings, F. C.
Clark, H. W.
Chamberlain,
          V. W.
Collins, J.

Curd, R.
Cole, H. C.
Cooley, J. W.
Cracknell, E. E.
Cracknell, H. P.
Cracknell, W. H.
Clayton, L. W.
Carrott, L. H. G.
Clark, C.
Chatburn, R. W.
Colbert, F. G.
Cossins, E. H.
Condell, F.
Cruise, L. R.
Champress, A. W.
Chambers, H. G.
Chapman, F.
Cooper, F.
Cook, J. E.
Cozens, J. G. C.
Cranfield, A. C.
Crayford, J. W.
Cross, H. A.
Colgate, A. W.
Cole, A.
Chenery, E. C.
Cawley, F. E. J.
Corish, P. J.
Cruwys, E. E.
Collip, E. G.
Cutting, R. A.
Champion, W. G.
Clare, F.
Chesterfield, D.
Clark, R. M.
Cleaver, T. G.
Cornell, J. E.
Cooper, G.
Cawley, A. V.
Capon, C.
Claridge, H. C.
Cook, B.
Cooper, F.
Cox. W. M.
Cassidy, P. J.
Caswell, L. C.
Clarke, E.

Clifton, C. L.
Cobbett, A. H.
Croll, J. C.
Crowhurst, C. S.
Clifton, C. W. H.
Collyer, L. F.
Casey, G.
Chubb, L.
Collins, H. A.
Cowherd, S. C.
Connett, H.
Cornelius, C. L.
Cornell, T. W. B.
Collings, J. H.
Cothall, V. W.
Costerton, F. R.
Chapman, P. W.
Chaplin, S.M.
Clark, W. R.
Conzina, A.
Copestake, V. H.
Cawdell, S. S.
Cunnane, M.
Caldicott, B. S.
Cansdale, T. D.
Collings, R. H. H.
Clare, A. L.
Carter, P. A.
Cattermole, W. R.
Cleeland, J.
Challis, F. H.
Collins, P. W.
Corbin, G. S.
Clemmit, W. B.
Corps, R. W.
Camrass, E.
Cunningham,A.R.
Croall, W. A.
Chambers, F. A.
Chandler, A. E.
Curtis, E. E.
Cornish, A. W.
Cronin, G. P.
Cutting, R.
Carter-Brown,
            E. A. R.
Clift, T. V.

Coote, P. C.
Clark, W. E. L.
Cormack, J. S.
Clarke, H. G.
Chudleigh, R. M.
Cox, E. J.
Clover, R. V.
Carter, A. R.
Cox, H.
Chandler, P.
Cox, J. H.
Claydon, T. A.
Cooper, G.
Carby, B. H. C.
Capon, R. W.
Cowan, J.
Cutchee, R.
Cutchee, H. D.
Cook, H. A.
Caldicott, W. L.
Carter, R.
Common, G. C.
Chapman, J. P. C.
Cook, J.
Callingham, M. T.
Cobb, A. L.
Cockroft, J. W.
Cooper, O. W.
Christeson, H. G.
Cowherd, T. B.
Cookman, O. L.
Calder, E. P.
Collins, A.
Charter, P. W.
Cony, J. D.
Clarke, P. E.
Clay, G. W.
Cooke, A. D.
Churchill, H.
Cleaver, V. T.
Cresswell, W. W.
Cullingford, C. P.
Clemence, J. A.
Cannon, L. F.
Campbell, C. D.
Cannell, E. W.
Chauffourier, W.

Cheeseman, L.
Cochran, A. K.
Cox, D. G. S.
Cockrem, W. J. C.
Clarke, S. C.
Chitty, A. G.
Cook, E. E.
Cheadle, D. W.
Chilton, J.
Collins, A. E.
Curtis, A. R.
Chandler, P S.
Cutts, F.
Coombs, A. W.
Courtney, H.
Corbet, A.
Chapman, F. E.
Carlile, C. D.
Crane, H. J.
Cohen, R. W.
Conridge, A.
Cook, W. F.
Cox, F.
Clark, E. C. B.
Clapton, S. A.
Cook, W. J.
Chessall, A. R. H.
Campany, V. F.
Cox, H. P. F.
Christey, A.
Coates, J. B.
Cartwright, H.
Colverd, S. O.
Clarke, C. F. B.
Cracknell, E. L.
Cross, W. A.
Cook, C. H.
Crosby, J.
Cole, H. S.
Cutmore, R.
Collins, G. S.
Cross, J. C.
Chambers, H.
Cleaver, E. C.
Chambers, A. W.
Chinery, L. E.
Culling, H. R.

Cooper, W.
Crosby, R. H.
Cull, W. S.
Crow, F. H.
Carter, F.
Copeman, W.
Corrie, F. D.
Cooling, F.
Crampton, A. W.
Cronin, J. B.
Clements, P. C.
Clarke, F.
Collett, W.
Cripps, F.
Cummings, W. G.
Cowan, H. F. H.
Carter, J.
Carter, W. T.
Clarke, A. G.
Cudmore, H. V.
Collins, A. E.
Coombs, E. G.
Cooper, A. W.
Cooper, E. F.
Cowley, F,
Cooper, E. C.
Congdon, R. B.
Clark, R. C.
Cartwright,
    A. W. J.
Cohen, A.
Chase, P.
Cook, F. S.
Cook, W. J.
Curt, H.
Cole, V.
Colton, F. W.
Carr, T. F. W.
Catchpole, G. W.
Chamberlain,
    J. R. W.
Cowling, E. J.
Carey, A. E.
Croxford, G. E. H.
Coleman, W. H. C.
Carter, W. S.
Claxton, W. H.

Coleman, W. G.
Cleaver, A. E.
Cozens, F. H.
Clanfield, H.
Cook, A. J.
Culham, A. A.
Clark, E. M.
Critchfield, W.
Cording, S. G.
Collins, L. S.
Cooke, E. E.
Cox, A. T.
Costella, A.
Catellino, M. J. V.
Coxall, D.
Cairns, B.
Court, G.
Cole, J. L.
Campin, W. C.
Cartwright, R. S.
Copping, W. F.
Cooke, J. G.
Cannar, R.
Chalmers, J. R.
Cantelo, J. W.
Clark, F. G. H.
Craske, R. L.
Cox, L. M.
Clipstein, H. H.
Childs, E. W.
Crosby, E. A.
Clarke, T. D.
Came, A.
Cullingford, G. F.
Collins, A. C.
Curram, E. J.
Colyer, W. E. F.
Clay, J. W. L.
Chipperfield, G. J.
Calvesbert, J. A.
Collings, J.
Clarke, L.
Cocoran, E.
Carter, A. R.
Cayless, R. W.
Cowburn, J.
Chambers, C. E.

Cross, W. D.
Case, R. H. W.
Crouch, G.
Cohen, L.
Carpenter, W.
Carroll, G. G.
Cordery, T.
Coster, F.
Cooper, A. J.
Cooter, V. C.
Clayton, J.
Candlish, A.
Couchman, A.
Clayton, H.
Cousins, H. W.
Cooling, H. F.
Cooper, E.
Coomber, F. C.
Cheek, R. S. K.
Chapman, C. G.
Conder, F. A.
Chamberlain,
          W. H.
Chapman, R. W.
Clarke, F. L.
Crook, J. B.
Carline, F. G.
Chaplin, C. H.
Clark, E. S.
Chapman, T.
Couridge, A. G.
Costa, A.
Cook, G. F.
Collier, J. J.
Congdon, J. C.
Cornell, E. G.
Charnock, F. B.
Clipstone, E.
Clayton, H.
Crew, M.
Chalker, E. G.
Cowling, A.
Clayton, W. J.
Claridge, R. A. A.
Cook, R. C.
Chapman, G. F.
Currie, K. M.

Currie, A. E.
Cove, W. J.
Curtis, B.
Cuttell, R. A.
Croyden, C. H. J.
Caweth, S. H.
Carpenter, E. E.
Cowden, P. A.
Cantelo, H. R.
Cousins, E. E.
Cozens, E. R.
Cheer, A.
Cox, F. E.
Capel, G. H.
Campbell, M.
Cowley, E. W.
Cusden, G. H.
Coote, H. H.
Cherrie, L. W.
Curran, W. J.
Cobbett, C. J.   .
Clarke, H. W.
Cope, L. F.
Chamberlain,
          G. D.
Cornelius, A. E.
Channon, P.
Cookson, W. C.
Coulthard, J.
Cator, B.
Cooper, G.
Colyer, S. H.
Chase, W. P.
Culling, H. A.
Cook, F. S.
Cusden, L.
Clulow, E.
Cruickshank, W.
Chapman, W. H.
Coates, G. F.
Cocks, R. B.
Collingwood,
          C. H. M.
Courage, J. R.
Calvert, M.O.
Camp, W. R.
Chapman, W. W.

Corney, J.
Currier, S. W.
Commens, W. H.
Costa, J.
Chittock, C. H.
Clowes, H.
Casson, H.
Cumberbirch, J.
Chirney, L. E.
Campin, E. J.
Clapham, J.
Cocks, L. H.
Crane, W. S. G.
Collins, D. R.
Couzens, F. W.
Cornford, C. F.
Cunningham,
          R. H.
Colebrook, G.
Clayton, H. H.
Capewell, H.
Chidgey, A. H.
Cox, F. J.
Champ, W. H.
Copeland, R. T.
Cartwright, A.
Chapman, F. R.
Cameron, W.
Clay, H. S.
Collingburn, J.
Crompton, D. R.
Costley, G. R.
Chadd, G. T.
Chambers, W. H.
Collins, R. P.
Cusdin, H. R.
Clayton, F.
Coates, H.
Clarke, R.
Coleman, E. A.
Chapman, C. A.
Coldicott, B. S.
Cook, F. T.
Cornish, H. P.
Cox, T.
Clark, H.
Chandler, A. E.

Cleary, J. P.
Curram, J. T.
Clarke, S. A.
Cain, W. E.
Chance, J. A.
Corble, H. F.
Carter, S. T.
Cooke, A. J.
Colvin, L. T.
Cook, D. H.
Cormack, W. H.
Cook, H. F.
Cane, M. H.
Cuthbert, L. A.
Comber, J. S. W.
Chapman, E. W.
Cubitt, H. A. H.
Court, W. D.
Carter, A. F.
Case, C. H.
Christie, G. S.
Custerson, E.
Coleman, L. S.
Cattell, W. F.
Collin, W. R.
Cansick, C. W.
Cashen, J. J.
Church, T. L.
Crudge, P. J.
Craven, H.
Caulder, H. J.
Cohen, I. W.
Church, D. H.
C h a d n e y, H.
T. H.
Clay, A. A.
Church, L. E.
Clarke, W. G. F.
Constable, A. M.
Collings, W.
Chilton, P. J.
Cox, J. C. W.
Capel, J. E.
Chapman, R. A.
Chorley, W. S.
Clarke, F. C.
Crouch, A. E.

Campbell, C. W. V.
Corey, F.
Carpenter, W. T.
Collier, C. K. S.
Castigon, D. W.
Coleman, H.
Chapman, G.
Cherrington, A.
Collyer, A. E.
Craven, R.
Crawley, A. E.
Crisford, W. S.
Cambray, J. F. H.
Christie, G. R. R.
Cornish, W. J.
Courcha, W.
Calf, P. W.
Carpenter, J. L.
Chesters, C. F.
Crookall, H.
Curman, D. A. A.
Came, F. J.
Clifford, A.
Clouting, F. E.
Coulter, B.
Croydon, E. C.
Creedy, H. J.
Cox, H. W.
Crookes, W. G.
Cooper, A.
Child, H. C.
Clarke, E. G.
Cameron, C. J.
Crawford, A.
Cozier, H. D.
Chalmers, D.
Clark, H. E.
Chambers, J. E.
Cook, G.
Coles, W. V.
Cobham, G. E.
Cox, E. E.
Clarke, A. G. C.
Cox, R. G.
Clisby, C. F.
Carter, G. E.
Crabtree, L.

Cross, V.
Coe, W. B.
Carlton, R. P.
Chapman, F. W.
Chadwick, C.
Cockett, B. G. R.
Cutts, E. G.
Collier, J. E.
Carley, J. T.
Cook, J.
Crews, H. E.
Carr, A. C.
Catherick, W.
Clark, W. T.
Coles, G.
Costick, A. E.
Cowderoy, T. C.
Cowley, E. W.
Cheevley, E. W.
Cumming, W.
Clarke, J.
Chadwick, L. W.
Conisbee, J.
Chadley, J. H.
Ciani, A.
Cook, W. E.
Crosby, G. H.
Cutter, J. E.
Cockburn, T. B.
Clarke, E. V. H.
Cave, P. S.
Cutcher, T.
Connolly, P.
Cooper, T. J.
Cullimore, T. H.
Coker, E. F.
Cavo, H. J.
Carr, T.
Chalmers, A. P.
Childs, G. W. C.
Churchard, P. W.
Cross, T. H.
Conyard, S. W. H.
Cepley, H.
Cheeseman, T. W.
Cole, W. R.
Cross, T. F.

Carter, F. C.
Cleary, T. M. A.
Crooks, L. R. A.
Chipling, J. M. D.
Crome, G. A.
Carr, M. R.
Coombs, G. A.
Curran, J. S.
Calestrerne, H.
Cottee, L. E.
Cousens, L. F.
Clarke, H. E.
Claridge, G. F.
Clark, H.
Crawley, C. G. G.
Colson, H. A.
Cuming, L. C.
D
Davenport, P.
Doubleday, C. E.
Dye, W. A.
Dodge, T. W. M.
Darby, J. F.
Davison, W. R.
Dobrantz, A. G.
Dolbear, F. H.
Dealler, F. E.
Davies, W. L.
Dawe, T. G.
Dicks, J.
Dibben, R. H.
Davis, L. S.
Dines, P. J. F.
Dartnell, A. G.
Dawe, F. W. H.
Damer, F. A.
Douglas, L. S.
Davison, E.
Denber, A. J. C.
Davidson, A. S.
Dodds, A.
Davy, C. H.
Dodd, E. E.
Dunne, M.
Dodge, A. A.
Davies, L.
Davis, A. H.

Dowton, F. H.
Day, T. W.
Druett, L. H.
Diplock, A. B.
Darnton, F. H.
Dabbs, S. E.
Dorken, H. G.
Dornan, A. B.
Diggins, H.
Dodds, M. W.
Downie, H. F.
Dawe, A. S.
Dree, W. H. S.
Dellow, F. E.
Durrant, W. J.
Deubert, H. A.
Dunning, C.
Dyer, F. L.
Davis, A. J. E.
Davies, O. M.
Denham, S. T.
Dunkling,
T. W. E.
Dary, H. S.
Derwent, A. H.
Doherty, J. W.
**Drinkwater,
C. E. H.**
Drury, A. L.
Dunkley, H. L.
Dance, F. J.
Dickson, E. W. A.
Donan, P. V.
Dunkley, R. W.
Dyer, P. R.
Davis, S. C.
De-Courcy, H. B.
Denby, A. H.
Denby, H. S.
Dickson, J. R.
Drayson, J. D.
Dunn, P. G.
Durrant, G. D.
Durrant, R. G.
Davis, W. G.
Diesch, R.
Dobson, H.

Dodd, F. J.
Davis, A. G.
Defries, A. E. V.
Davis, W.
Day, C. R.
Domeney, W. H.
Duck, S.
Dutton, P. J.
Davies, M.
Downes, B.
Drew, F. J.
Dennett, G. A.
Davies, A. R.
Driver, G. L.
Davison, A. B. C.
Damant, P. J.
Davis, F. G.
Dalby, E. J.
Darlison, E.
Daniell, H. G.
Davie, A. J.
Davies, B. R.
Dawson, V. L.
Dearlove, L. B.
Demment, M. W.
Dixon, W.
Dodd, G. S.
Davies, T. H.
Daniels, W. H.
Davis, H. C.
Deamond, J.
Dodwell, S. S.
Dean, E.
Drane, J. C.
Dobbie, A. F.
Driver, B. W.
Dickinson, J. R.
Davey, S.
Daley, P. A.
Dicker, W.
Downey, S. W.
Davies, R. B.
Downing, R. G.
Dod, K. L.
Davidson, J. A.
Dyer, B. C.
Denton, G. F.

Davey, F. R.
Denning, T. W.
Drake, A. C.
Davis, H.
Daniels, J. H.
Dafforn, B. J.
Davidson, G.
Dunscombe, H. W.
Dawson, W. A.
Dawkins, D. K.
Da Costa, E. V.
Davison, W. H.
Dawkins, C.
Dean, S.
Dye, J. D.
Dabbs, H.
Douglas, G.
Dale, A.
Davidson, A. C.
Dennison, A.
Dickson, W.
Denington, A. S.
Duggan, A. J. F.
Doughty, M. F.
Dowsett, F. W.
Deller, R. T.
Dewhurst, R.
Dore, F. A.
Davies, E. W.
Davey, A. J.
Dredge, H.
Dacey, J.
Daley, C.
Day, L.
DeWardt, F.
Dugard, E. S.
Dunn, L. H. S.
Davidson, T. A.
Dale, A.
Dawkins, H. A.
Donald, A. J.
Dowdell, H. B.
Duncan, W.
Davis, E. F.
Dicker, W. R.
Dance, W. R.
Derrett, F.

Doggett, A. C.
Dale, W. G.
Dyke, A. B.
Drew, C. W. A.
Daley, R.
Down, R. E. V.
Dicks, S. H.
Deane, F. L.
Doody, H. W.
Doughton, W. C.
Darwall, R.
Deeves, S.
Davies, S. J. R.
Dear, H. F.
Dibble, L. F.
Dickinson, C. C.
Dobson, A. R.
Day, S. F.
Dancer, T. S.
Dormer, R.
Dockett, C. J. F.
Drew, B. L. N.
Dutton, R.
Davies, B.
Dormann, J. A.
Davies, J. E.
Dickinson, W. E.
Dear, E.
Dowden, W. L.
Day, T. L.
Drury, S. J.
Davey, F. W. G.
Deem, H. T. S.
Dale, Y. F. W.
Dwyer, J.
Douglas, W. M.
Dobbs, F. W.
Davies, G.
Drucker, E.
Deeks, C. K.
Darlow, J. W. E.
Dove, W. A.
Deeves, T.
Digby, P. B.
Davis, L. A.
Dyer, W. E.
Davies, W. S.

Donan, E. B.
Day, E. W.
Davis, W. E.
Drane, S. C.
Dancyger, M.
Dengate, S.
Darmody, J. F.
Dark, V.
Diss, H. R. G.
Davies, A. O.
Davies, H. N.
Doubleday, R. E.
Davis, P. E.
Davis, G. W.
Dunkley, E. L.
Davies, D. G.
Davey, E. B.
Dillow, H. E.
Dodge, F. J.
Davies, W. G.
Devine, L.
Dawes, J. A.
Davies, J. D.
Dunster, A. L.
De-Bourcier, H. L.
Dawes, A. H.
Diprose, J. L.
Dring, G.
Dongworth, W. H.
Davies, F. R.
Dibley, J. J.
Donnelley, W. L.
Dawn, H. G.
Davis, H. G.
Darbourne, F. P.
Davies, W. N.
Dilrew, F.
Dummer, J. M.
Dawson, G. C.
Dilley, P. D.
Davies, W. A. J.
Denchars, H. J.
Denby, J.
Dewhurst, R. S.
Druitt, N. V.
Dowler, H.
Deane, G. L.

2 E

Doughty, J.
Deasy, T.
Davis, C. A.
Doughty, H. G.
Dutchett, W. R.
Durbridge, J. T. P.
Dales, N. L.
Dixon, J. W. S.
Downie, W.
Dredge, A. E.
Davies, J.
Dewdney, F.
Donall, A. D.
Dunford, A.
Dawson, W. V.
Dunn, R. V.
Durrant, R. A.
Dewar, A. W. D.
Duke, D. D.
Derbyshire, G. B.
Davy, A. G.
Down, P. G.
Davies, H. H.
Dale, W. T.
Day, F. H.
Dell, A.
Daniel, H.
Dormer, H. J.
Dobbs, D. O.
Darvill, F. D.
Dickens, J.
Diamond, R. McG.
Dallas, D. N.
Downes, D. W.
Doubleday, C. W.
Dyer, H.
Duffield, H. A.
Davis, J.
Dann, P.
Dopson, A. C.
Deavin, H. C.
Dantzig, D.
Davis, H. C.
Durham, C. W.
Davies, E. L.
Dickson, R.
Dresser, T. K.

Davis, A.
Dudman, L.
Drury, C. E.
Deeley, F.
Durrant, R. G.
Driver, R. J.
Dale, W. E.
Day, G. S.
Davis, J. F.
Davies, D. L.
Dolder, A. A.
Dyson, S. G.
Dickens, H. T.
Dorn, E. H.
Dorman, P. M.
Davison, R. W.
Dunn, A. J.
Doble, H. G.
Dorey, S.
Dykes, H. J.
Doidge, W. J.
Dilloway, C. A.
Dove, J. A.
Dean, W. A.
Dyer, C. H.
Dawson, F. W.
De-Wael, W. R.
Davison, H. J.
Davies, E. G.
Dadd, L. S.
Dyke, R.
Davis, H. A.
Davies, L.
Day, G.
Deane, A. C.
Donkin, C. W.
Doswell, J. A. H.
Denton, H. C.
Dyer, F. E.
Davies, R.
Du Fen, J. P.
Dickins, G. J.
Doggett, R. G. E.
Day, W. F.
Davies, H. J.
Day, G. W.
Dawes, E.

Dawson, H.
Davies, P. H.
Davis, F. E.
Davis, E. N.
Duce, O. A.
Dunn, F.
Druce, H. A.
Deas, R. J.
Duncan, S. B.
Davies, W. H.
Duffell, S. G.
Dixon, G. E.
Duck, C J.
Drummond, D.
Davis, C. F.
Dell, J. E. W.
Dellow, E. F. P.
Dewing, C. J.
Davies, J. E.
Davey, T. F.
Duncan, A.
Davies, H. F.
Dixon, W. D.
Dunn, T. L.
Durrant, T. W.
Durrad, W. H.
Donaldson, T.
Dudley, A. F.
Drake, A. S.
Dell, W. R.
Dearlove, F. G.
Dowlen, G. W.
Dimelow, S. J.
Dwyer, C. J.
Dawson, F.
Davies, C. S.
Davies, F. G.
Drury, V. J.
Darley, T. W. E.
Dawkes, W. H.
Dukes, H.
Dash, W. C.
Dorn, C. J.
Davies, H. W. G.
Day, A. T.
Dyke, J. W.
Dabis, E.

Davies, J. M.
Daldry, S. G.
Davie, H. J.
Davy, P. R.
Davey, P. W.
Drummond, J.
Dawson, V. L.
Deacon, A. C.
Davis, F. W.
Dean, H. L.
Dodgson, F.
Dulin, G. R.
Davies, T.
Durrant, H. W.
Drury, F. H.
Dans, G. G.
Dant, S. H.
Dickinson, A.
Durban, P. A.
Day, C. A.
Dixon, H. E.
Denham, T. E.
Douglas, A. T.
Day, A.
Dennis, S. W.
Davies, F. W.
Dean, A. E.
Daniels, F. J.
Denyer, H. J.
Davies, J. H.
Davies, H. L.
Dickens, F. C.
Dishman, S. K.
Dunton, F. E. W.
Dalby, C. T.
Davies, G. A.
Dyke, F. W.
Drew, A. E.
Doke, E. F.
Down, K. A.
Deaves, A.
D'Eye, E. A.
Donovan, D.
Draper, O. H.
Daniell, E.
Doggett, D. C.
Dunkley, E. T.

Davies, W. H.
Dunnage, F. E.
Dallard, E.
Davies, W.
Draper, A. H.
Day, W.
Deigan, R.
Desmond, T. D.
Duggan, W.
Dickens, C. W.
Dawson, W. O.
Douard, E. L.
Dudman, J. A.
Daw, W. J. E.
Davis, C. T. W.
Donoghue, W. H.
Dorey, W. J.
Dyos, A. J.
Doan, J.
Daivell, A.
Duncan, D. C.
Danson, J. N.
Draper, C. J.
Davies, W.
Dumpleton, E.
Darnell, A.
Dobson, W.
Darby, J. W.
Daynes, G. C.
Dixon, A. J. D.
Dalton, S. H.
Dixon, J.
Driskell, F. G.
Dounes, G. F.
Dennis, H.
Dyer, L.
Daniels, H.

E

Evans, T. H.
Evans, W. K.
Evans, J. S.
Ellingham, V. E.
Eaton, R. M.
Eakin, H. S. C.
Ennis, W. E.
Elkin, P. H.
Evans, F. J.

Everson, W. J.
Evans, E. A.
Ellis, W. M.
Everitt, W. G.
Everitt, W. W.
East, A. A.
Edwards, J. H. L.
Evans, D. F.
Eagle, W. E.
Emerson, H. D.
Evans, D. W.
Evans, W. G.
Ellsley, C. W.
Edgill, H. D.
Ewings, H.
Empson, C. W.
East, B. M.
Edney, H. E.
Edzley, E. E.
Edwards, L. M.
Elwell, C. M.
Elliott, G. H.
Evans, A. B.
Evans, E. J.
Evison, H.
Elkington, R. H. H.
Endacott, A. D.
Evans, R. B.
Edwards, H.
Emery, G. R.
Esden, H. A.
Everett, G. J.
Emler, H. J.
Eastop, F. A.
Edwards, L.
Ellor, H. E.
Elledge, W.
Ellor, J. F.
Eels, P.
Evershed, G. D.
Eagle, N.
Etheridge, E. A.
Ellingham, C.
Edwards, J.
Ellis, E.
Eve, R. M.
Evans, J. L.

Etheridge, J. E. E.
Eaton, C. T.
Earl, G. A.
Essery, E. C.
Evison, E. R.
Evans, E. G.
Eagles, L. G.
Ellicott, B. W.
Edge, H.
Ellerington, H.
Evans, W.
Eccles, L. D.
Eccleston, J.
Evans, T. E.
Elliston, A. J.
Eades, C. E.
Elliott, P. J.
Ellis, G. W.
East, A.
Ennis, J.
Everett, L. A.
Evans, P. G.
Ellis, J. G.
Earl, P. A.
Ellwood, W. E.
Edmonds, H. P.
Elliott, G.
Ellis, F.
Edge, H. W.
Evans, M. J.
Ellwood, H.
Edmonds, M. W.
Eads, J. R.
Ellum, S.
Edwards, J. H.
Ellingham, E. G.
Enright, A. W.
Edwards, B. C. L.
Eisele, G. S.
Edser, S. C.
English, C.
Every, W.
Edwards, L. P.
Ewell, H. L.
Edwards, T. E.
England, W. H.
Elkin, J. T.

Eggers, C. W.
Ellis, A.
Ellis, S. E. R.
Edey, E. G.
Evison, C. H.
Everad, D.
Everatt, W.
Easter, R.
Ellis, F. E.
Ediss, A. C.
Earl, C.
Empson, H. C.
Evans, J. L.
Edmonds, J.
Eickhoff, J. A.
Evans, E.
Ellis, E. D.
Evans, F.
Ensor, W. A.
Ede, E. E.
Elkington, C. J.
Embery, S. W.
Eaton, C. F.
Ellis, J. C.
Edwards, R. F. C
Evans, A. D.
Emery, R. W. J.
Ennor, E. M.
Elvis, A. H.
Elliott, E. A.
Edwards, H. J.
Everitt, B.
Ecroyd, W. C.
Emary, W.
Edwards, T. B.
Emery, A. T.
Edwards, W. H.
Edwards, W. N.
Ellwood, C.
Edmonds, A. E.
Emery, R.
Ellis, A. E.
Ellis, G. B.
Ellery, J. W.
Evans, F. T.
Ebden, W.
Eyears, W. J.

Edgington, A.
Eagle, C. W.
Ellingham, F. H.
Ellis, A.
Ellis, A. J.
Evans, D.
Evans, I. J.
Edmondson, H. C
Evans, D.
Evans, F. S.
Ellis, L. F.
Emmett, H. J. L.
English, P. W.
Ewins, T.
Ellery, J. J.
Edwards, W.
Ellis, H. E.
Evans, I. J.
Eames, W. H.
Edwards, A. C.
Eades, F. E. A.
Emery, E. G.
Eley, J. R. S.
Evan, S. E.
Ellis, B. L.
Emery, C. H.
Evans, B.
Emm, L. H.
Elliott, S. C.
Eaton, J. W.
Edwards, E.
Ednie, D.
Edgerton, A. W.
Entwistle, F.
Ember, E. W.
Evans, W. P.
Enock, E. J.
Elliston, G. E.
Ellis, J.
Ewbank, R. M. G.
Edwards, L.
Evans, F. S.
Evans, C. H.
Ellingham, G. H.
Evans, A. W.
Eager, H. H. P.
Evans, R. J.

Edwards, J. E.
Edwards, F. J.
Eversfield, A. D.
Edwards, H. C.
Evans, W. H.
Evans, E. J.
English, W. K.
Elliott, E. F.
Elliott, L. P.
Elsdon, H. C.
Edwards, J. H.
Eddicott, G.
Edwards, H. A.
Eckitt, R. C.
Elvy, A.
Evans, H. E.
Eason, W. H.
Edwards, G. F.
Edmonds, J. H.
Ewing, G. P.
Elliott, A. S.
Ede, F. J.
Ely, W.
Eyre, J.
Efford, F. S.
Evans, S.
Edwards, W. D.
Eels, J.
Eldridge, C.
Ellicott, W. J.
English, W. F.
Ellison, H.
Emery, C.
Ensoll, H.
Eyles, W. R.
Elgar, S. C.
Eeles, H.
Edwards, G.
Eeles, F. C.
Emmerson, G. F
Evans, J.
Etheridge, E. J.
Eden, T. C.
Edwards, W. H.
Eaton, W. E.
England, E.
Exell, A. S.

Elliott, S. T. G.
Eland, G.
Evans, G.
Eager, G. L.
F
Flanagan, F. J.
Fletcher, O. C.
Fryer, C. W.
Fowler, J. G.
Fitzgerald, J. H.
Foster, H. J. B.
Foucard, N. A.
French, E. J.
French, R. H.
Fell, D.
Farrar, G. R.
Fussell, B.
Figgins, A. P.
Forster, F. D.
Feeley, J.
Franklin, R. H.
Foster, H.
Foster, R. S.
Falkingham, J. H.
Fudge, S.
Facon, W. S.
Fearon, C. J.
Farmer, E.
Fabb, A. G.
Fenton, G. W.
Fields, E. C.
Fergusson, W. G.
Fowler, G. E.
Fryer, C. W.
Fall, P. J.
Fereday, E. B.
Ficken, G. J.
Fitzgerald, J. H.
Fuller, W. E.
Fenton, W. H.
Flynn, B. C.
Fabian, C. B.
Faulkner, L.
Fearne, H. J.
Fletcher, E.
Fennell, L. J.
Fenton, C. L.

Fereday, L. H.
Firkins, H. P.
Ford, C.
Foster, H. K.
Frost, E. C.
Fraser, J. A.
Foreman, E. K.
Fright, S.
Fearnley, C.
Fowler, G. E.
Foot, G. B.
Freshwater, H. W.
Forward, H. A.
Funston, H. E.
Field, L. F.
Foster, E. J.
Foster, A. D.
Fowler, W. S.
Fairbairn, G.
Fewings, J. H.
Flynn, F. B.
Forrest, W. W.
Flook, T. E.
Fabb, B.
Fraser, W. S.
Flanagan, L.
Ffoulkes, W. H.
Flood, W. W. G.
Frampton, C.
Fear, W.
Fenson, E. H.
Franks, S. T.
Freeman, H.
Field, J. W.
Farindon, R.
Fisenden, C. H.
Featherstone,
        F. W.
Ferrier, W. J.
Findlow, A.
Ferry, F. N.
Farebrother, S. N.
Fogg, S. H.
Freeman, G.
Fuller, A. F.
Fisher, W. C. J.
French, E. J.

French, H. T.
Finlayson, W. J.
Folds, C. E.
Foster, H. L.
Field, H. H. W.
Finch, F. N.
French, W. H.
Farman, S. L.
Faulkner, A. L.
Fox, D.
Florant, A. C.
Figgins, H. F.
Funston, L. W.
Farley, W. E.
Fowler, S. D.
French, H. J.
Franklin, G. F.
Forth, H.
Finnis, S.
Faulkner, H. H.
Fifield, H.
Finigan, A. L.
Ferris, A. C.
Fear, W.
Facey, W. H.
Fowler, P. G. E.
Freemont, L. T.
Fisher, A.
Fitzsimmons,
        G. W.
Flatman, F. C.
Foster, S. W.
Freeston, G. B.
Fareweather, A. C.
Fuller, H. S.
Flewry, G. J.
Fea, C. A.
Fish, A. R.
Field, R.
Field, T.
Fisher, H. C.
Fothergill, W. H.
Fisher, A. S.
Fry, J. F. B.
Funnell, E. J.
Fisk, F. A.
Fish, F. H.

Farden, F. D.
Flight, E. H.
Franklin, F. H.
Fautley, C. C. T.
Franklin, C. L.
Freer, W. B.
Fenning, A. E.
Faulkner, F.
F i n d l e y ,   G.
        E. W.
Forster, H. W.
Fletcher, H. J.
Farrow, H. J.
Foster, B.
Fletcher, S.
Fossey, H. E.
Fox, F. W.
Fitchett, S.
Felton, C. A.
Freeman, L. G.
Fowlie, W.
Freemantle, G. S.
Fincham, D. I.
French, E. J.
Frencham, S.
Fitt, W.
Ford, W. O.
Fullagar, C. H.
Forth, H. T.
Fenn, G.
Fennell, H.
Ferris, H. W.
Frost, F.
Field, W. J.
Foster, T. G.
Francis, G. W. B.
Finch, E. L.
Fentum, L. C.
Fitz, L. R.
Flanagan, R. C.
Farran, F. C.
Farrow, A.
French, J. H.
Fose, A. T.
Fenner, H. H.
Ford, F. E.
Fletcher, T. R.

Farrar, H.
Forder, G. L. N.
Faulkner, C. J.
Friston, E. C.
Fitzgerald, M. G.
Ford, R. A.
Floyd, A. H.
Flowerday, A. J.
Frost, C. R. E.
Foot, W. V.
Foot, T. E. R.
Farrow, A.
Farrier, J. J.
Fairweather, P.
Foster, W. M.
Fox, R. W.
Ferris, R. M.
Frith, F.
Friend, F. G.
Fowler, H. W.
Francis, A. E.
Franklin, W. H.
Fenn, W. T.
Foulger, T. R.
Fairservice, H. R.
Fogg, G. B.
Ferguson, A. J.
Folkard, P. G.
Franklin, N. E.
Faithfull, F. C.
Foot, W. E.
Faulkner, L. A.
Fifield, T.
Freezer, T. R.
Firth, C. J.
Flight, G. H. B.
Fuller, D.
Firmage, F. G.
Fowle, F.
Francis, H. E.
Fitt, G. W.
Finch, J. H.
Fowke, L. F.
Farrier, G. T.
Fry, W. C.
Fleming, W. A.
Freeman, H.

Findlay, J. A.
Fookes, E. H.
Fergusson, M. C.
Feist, R. J.
Fickling, B.
Forrest, J. H.
Fayers, G. C.
Farris, C. T.
Fowler, R. T.
Fulker, B.
Foy, C. P.
Finch, W. E.
Farris, R. H.
Francis, W. J.
Fawcett, J. Y.
Fisher, H. H.
Farquharson, I.
Fletcher, E.
Fairweather, L.
Ford, E. W.
Fyfe, J. C.
Fairclough, H. T.
Feldmar, L. T.
Forrest, W. S.
Fletcher, E. S.
Filer, A. J.
Fowles, E. G.
Farrar, A. T.
Foulds, J. R.
Fisher, W. L.
Fisher, W. H.
Fenwick, F. W.
Franklin, V. F.
Freeman, H.
Fry, A. E.
Flanagan, W. F.
Fletcher, J.
Foster, E. H.
Foskett, F. C.
Fenwick, N.
Fordham, E. R.
Farley, E. A. C.
Fish, J. T.
Flew, W. L.
Farbon, C. R.
Fitz-Rayne, W. A.
Freer, F.

Fraser, G. H.
Fricker, L. J.
French, P. H.
Ford, H. W.
Fenton, C. L.
French, P. H.
Fellows, W. E.
Fisk, A. G.
Foster, J.
Field, H. E.
Field, J. W.
Free, A. N.
Flood, H. F.
Fillmore, C. S.
Forster, J. P.
Fairminer, J. L.
Fereday, A. H.
Farrell, W. M.
Friend, R. D.
Fillmore, V. G.
Fletcher, J.
Ferrier, F. J.
Fitzgerald, E.
Fenwick, J.
Flaherty, N.
Ford, A. F.
Furness, G.
Fricker, B. J.
Fullerton, L.
Faulkner. R,
Finlayson, W.
Farley, E. R.
Fox, B. R. V.
Farrand, H.
Ford, G. R.
Fox, W. H.
Fox, H. W.
Franklin, H. J.
Fry, J. H.
Faultless, R. H.
Forsgate, R. J.
Friedlander, J.
Fenn, H. L.
Fraser, J. A.
Fincham, H. A.
Furlong, A. J.
Farnden, F.

Farrow, H. J. G.
Favell, W. F. J.
Ford, H. G.
Field, F.
Fathers, F. J.
Ford, F. L.
Floyd, A. H.
Feest, E. P.
Fredman, A.
Forrest, H. A.
Fairhurst, A.
Falcus, J.
Falla, A. W.
Folgate, W. C.
Farrow, S. G.
Field, G.
Fell, G.
Fairbrother, J. W.
Finch, A. E.
Fowler, J.
Furssedonn, C. E.
Forman, F.
Frost, H. A.
Fleming, W. A.

G

Green, A. E.
Graham, E.
Gardner, W. B.
Gray, F.
Graham, J.
Goodman, G.
Goldston, R. G.
Green, S. A.
Greenwood, W. H.
Godby, A. G.
Gurney, F. A.
Gay, F. W.
Greenless, H.
Goulding, L. J. B.
Gosney, H. S.
Gershon, L.
Green, T. F.
Gattie, B. B.
Green, S. W.
Guiton, M. J.
Grimer, A. T.

Gellatley, S. H.
Gadsby, C. G.
Galloway, J. M.
Grapes, G.
Greenfield, A.
Griffiths, W. R.
Gulliford, F. G.
Gillman, A. C.
Gurnell, J. K.
Goodman, E. G.
Goss, E. O.
Gordon, A. A. Mc.
Grammel, W.
Gordon, H. E.
Glass, W. F.
Gurney, F. S.
George, A. J.
Gordon, H. R.
Glen, D. C.
Graham, R. M.
Greensmith,
      L. C. G.
Gibbons, A. F.
Grover, W. G.
Gulby, H. F.
Gray, C. G.
Graham, J. A. L.
Griffiths, L. W.
Goord, F. G.
Green, G. F.
Gold, H. D.
Gold, R. C.
Garton, R. W.
Glass, S.
Gill, T. M.
Goodwin, L. F.
Grant, L. D.
Garratt, W. B.
Goodman,
      W. A. H.
Gray, P.
Gilbert, R. A.
Gell, J. B.
Goodwin, W. R.
Gray, E. O.
Green, C.
Gurney, J.

Gammidge, L. N.
Garrett, G. D.
Gefford, R.
Gordon, J.
Gower, E. G.
Green, R. G.
Grugeon, A. S.
Gray, F.
Goldwater, L. A.
Gregory, T. E. G.
Gobey, H.
Gregory, E. W.
Green, C. R.
Godfrey, A. E.
Grosvenor, V. W.
Gamage, E. F.
Gabriel, J.
Garland, J. V.
Garthwaite, J. K.
Gibbs, C. H.
Gill, W. J.
Goldstein, B.
Greig, T. P.
Gooding, D.
Guilford, P. G.
Garner, W. J.
Gray, A. L.
Gray, L. G.
Green, G. G.
Gardiner, J. T.
Geary, A. J. C.
Grimble, A.
Gibbs, L. W.
Glennon, F. H.
Grimmer, R.
Geary, E. C.
Graham, F. W. F.
Gunton, B.
Gale, E. C.
Gilbert, E. A.
Garland, H. W.
Gardner, R.
Gibbons, H. V.
Green, W. H.
Gingell, H. S.
Gibbs, W. G.
Griffiths, R. H.

Garratt, T. W.
Gruselle, H. E. J.
Glover, H. N.
Gibbard, W.
Grimsey, P. G.
Godwin, F. W.
Greenwood, A. E.
Gander, R. H.
Gilles, F. H.
Green, C. E. H.
Green, F. G.
Gillman, H. E. V.
Grey, A. L.
Grater, S. J.
Galloway, C. J.
Gravell, S. G.
Green, A. P.
Grooshky, S.
Gallagher, J.
Grantham, G. H.
Gadd, J. D.
Goodwin, A. S.
Gray, W. C. R.
Garrett, F. W.
Goldstein, A.
Graham, J.
Griffiths, J. H.
Goldsmith, G. H.
Gay, A. H.
Gordan, F. A.
Gozzett, F. C.
Gonnaway, P. A.
Givan, V.
Graham, P.
Griffiths, F. L.
Gash, N.
Griffiths, H. J.
Glover, G.
Gilchrist, S.
Gould, P. C.
Graham, S.
Gowen, H. S.
Grevatt, G. W. H.
Gluyas, B.
Goatley, W. E.
Grimsley, H. E.
Green, S. A.

Germaine, C. J.
Glithero, C. W.
Glithero, T. A.
Galen, J. J.
Griffiths, J. L.
Gwyer, F. C.
Goodfellow,
      H. C. L.
Gray, A. E.
Golding, H.
Grist, W. E.
Gibbons, C. C.
Geeves, S. L.
Gilders, L. F.
Giles, G. E.
Glover, H. G.
Griffiths, T. C.
Goodleman, S. H.
Gerrard, H. C.
Gibbs, A. E.
Gott, S. E.
Green, A. S.
Goss, H.
Gibson, J.
Genlloud, F. D.
Goodwin, S. W.
Goodwin, W. J.
Galway, G. L.
Grey, G. R.
Gurney, G. C.
Gillett, W. A.
Gill, G. H.
Game, T. G. A.
Griffiths, T. L.
Goodman, J. H.
Grayson, H. J.
Godfrey, F.
      A. J.
Godfrey, H.
Guest, W. J.
Gould, G. F.
Garnham, F.
Grantham,
      F. E. D.
Giggall, E.
Gunning, C.
Goulding, A. E.

Gibson, C. F. O.
Garside, F.
Greenoak, E.
Goodliffe, R. A.
Gillings, W. H.
Garland, B.
Gibbon, E. N.
Goodwin, F.
Grafton, C. B.
Gibson, A. H.
Green, A. E.
Gildersleve, A. E.
Grant, F.
Gumbrell, G. J.
Goode, A. J.
Greenwood, L. R.
Goodyear, F. G.
Godfrey, W. F.
Gilbert, A. G.
Geddes, E. H.
Garnett, J. H.
Gayland, P. H.
Gilbert, R. P.
Gibbs, E. W. H.
Green, H. T. E.
Gethin, T.
Grundy, J. A.
Griffiths, E. T.
Gibson, E. A.
Garrett, R. A.
Gatenby, G. F.
Gough, A.
Gerrish, C.
Grainger, A. A.
Geddes, D. J. M.
George, H. W.
Griffiths, R. S.
Glasscock, J. A.
Gosling, H. C.
Gush, L. J.
Garwood, E. H.
Gason, C. J.
Grist, H.
Groom, W. H.
Grylls, C. W.
Gardner, A.
Gruchy, C. R.

Goss, J. H.
Gilbert, A. H.
Grace, G. K.
Graves, P.
Gould, J.
Graves, T. W.
Green, T. A.
Gilbert, W. G.
Guivor, W.
Grout, T. B.
Groves, L.
Geater, D.
Garrett, P. H.
Gaw, W. G.
Geddes, M. F.
Golding, F.
Green, C. C. B.
Guyton, R. F.
Gilles, F. H.
Goff, P. A.
Goddard, W. F.
Gibbon, J.
Griffiths, G. T.
Griffiths, E.
Gibbs, S. J.
Gibson, H. S.
Glass, F. G.
Graham, A. J.
Gould, R. H.
Gogay, A.
Gardiner, L. L.
Gale, F. C.
Gould, W.
Griffin, G. W.
Guildford, G. T.
Green, G. S.
Garrick, E.
Gaiser, J. E.
Gilbert, F. W.
Gay, G. A.
Goodman, C. C.
Grady, A. H.
Gurr, J. H.
Gates, W. H.
Gates, A. W.
Gregory, C. S.
Grout, F.

Galbalby, J.
Golden, W. P.
Grove, G. F.
Gordon, J. H.
Gibbs, H.
Green, A. S.
Gowen, F.
Gardner, E. J. O.
Greenwood, W.
Gale, R. T.
Gwinnell, E. A.
Gunton, R.
Goldman, H. A.
Gray, C. T.
Green, J. M.
Garman, F.
Gunyan, A. C.
Golden, E. J. D.
Glover, F.
Grant, G. H. St. J.
Greenhalgh, S.
Godber, J. W.
Gard, F. C.
Gammon, A.
Gardiner, C. F. G.
Gover, T. H.
Grant, S.
Graham, W. F.
Grant, J. A. W.
Goodson, W. E.
Gibson, R. M.
Griffiths, L. H. W.
Gubbins, R. P.
Grist, A. V. M.
Gover, T. J.
Grace, F.
Grimwade, B. S.
Gold. R. F. S.
Green, N. H.
Geaves, C. W.
Gascoigne, G. W.
Gore, W. J.
Gates, H. R.
Godwin, H. L. A.
Graham, E. R.
Greenbury, H. E.
Goswell, O. O.

Girling, J.
Grieve, I. J.
Golden, E. T.
Gunn, J. W.
Gardiner, A. J.
Gill, W.
Goodway, C. A.
Greaves, C.
Gee, J. C. B.
Girdler, W. C.
Ginger, W. E.
Griffin, O. J.
Gardner, J. C. B.
Greener, J.
Godfrey, L. C.
Greer, C. J.
Gilder, A. C.
Groutage, J. H.
Gilkes, A. A.
Gordon, W.
Gore, H.
Gaylor, E. A.
Greener, L. E.
Gillwir, A. W.
Gale, F. A.
Gledhill, E.
Gray, L. S.
Gallon, E.
Guest, J. C.
Gilberthorpe, F.
Groves, H.
Golightly, L. G.
Gates, G.
Gleave, W. V.
Grant, G.
Griffiths, J. R.
Gardner, G. A.
Gray, C. W.
Grady, W. J.
Galliford, H. J. T.
Gardner, J.
Grierson, J.
Ganby, J. L.
Gruzeiler, P.
Green, C. H. R.
Galpin, R. G. E.
Griffin, G. A. J.

Guard, F. B.
Griggs, W. L.
Gooding, H. H.
Goldbourne, A. R.
Gillett, E. L. P.
Gibbs, C. E.
Galpin, L. P.
Goldberg, M.
Green, S. J.
Goodman, A. S.
Grove, F. W.
Gibson, W.
Granville, G. H.
Goadby, H. C.
Goode, A.
Gough, C. T.
Groves, L. G. W.
Gardner, R. J.
Green, L. J.
Grover, H. J.
Godby, W. A.
Gadsdon, L. J.
Graddage, J. A. R.
Griffiths, F.
Gomm, A. H.
Green, W. B.
Goff, W. T.
Germain, C. G.
Gowlett, G. H.
Griffiths, L. E.
Gallehawk, C.
Godbolt, P. J.
Gadd, W. A.
Goodey, E. F.
Price, F. G.
Grover, A.
Gibson, L.
Goss, R. C.
Gowland, J. H.
Gray, T.
Gowan, P. H.
Greenhill, E. R.
Griffiths, A.
Griffiths, J.
Guymer, G.
Garrett, A.
Groves, T. R.

Greenwood, D. W.
Gosnold, W. F.
Gunn, H.
Grace, A. L.
Gower, A. E.
Gifford, L. H.
Grimshaw, R.
Gillett, A.
Gosling, G. J.
Goding, F. G. E.
Gourlay, J.
Gilbert, A. E.
Gummery, J. W.
Godsell, W. H.
Greaves, E.
Gilkes, H. W.
Grayson, W.
Green, J. L.
Green, T.
Gubbins, W. G.
Goodman, S. A.
Goldfinch, A.
Gifford,:H.
Garnham, E. J.
Goodman, E. E.
Gurney, E. P.
Garrett, E. A.
Gunyon, C. C.
Gale, D. W.
Godwin, F. H.
Gower, J. W.
Goldsmith, P. L.
Gardner, A. G.
Green, J. M.
Goldwater, L. A.
Gaylard, B.
Gibson, C. M.
Griffiths, E. P.
Grist, F. C.
Grylls, C. W.
Goodyear, W. J.
Groves, H. J.
Graves, C. W.
Gamble, R. B.
Goodale, H. M.
Gillbanks, J. B.
Gillett, J. N.

Greenslade, S.
Gardner, W.
Garner, J. L.
Gibbons, E. T.
Gilby, S. A.
Glenister, F. A.

H

Hodgson, A. W.
Hale, W. L.
Hall, W. J.
Hicks, E. J.
Howett, F.
Hodge, W. G.
Hart, C. J.
Hiley, F. C. W.
Henderson, W. W.
Haatson, J. R.
Harris, A. P.
Harmer, A. A. D.
Harris, F. V.
Hall, J. R.
Holland, A. E.
Hughes, C. H.
Hards, C. R.
Holmes, G. C.
Horn, A. C.
Hedderley, R. F.
Hayes, C. W.
Harper, R. J.
Hammond, A.
Henson, H. H.
Hill, C.
Hearn, T.
Hollies, H. J.
Huckle, F. R.
Highbett, H. A. Á.
Hellier, H. R.
Harris, A. P.
Hargrave, W. B.
Hunt, P. G.
Hiscox, T. A.
Hume, C. W.
Hart, W. S.
Halcrow, J. W.
Huthwaite, A.
Harris, J. T.

Hartill, H. W.
Hilton, C.
Hall, L. G.
Howell, T. W.
Howell, R. O.
Huckle, H. G.
Hills, J. W.
Hant, R. A.
Harrington, W.
Hull, B.
Houslop, A. S.
Houseman, A. W.
Hall, C.
Hingston, S. F. T.
Hammond, H. T.
Howell, A. E.
Hetherington, R.
Hall, P. H.
Holmes, A.
Houlshan, B. F.
Hanscombe, J. E.
Hicks, A. H.
Hamill, C. H.
Hartley, C. H.
Hellastern, A. W.
Hambling, E. J.
Hill, W. D.
Holton, C. H. E.
Hogwood, G. H.
Hawdy, G. W.
Hammond, W. C.
Hooper, E. H.
Haycock, S. F.
Harrison, H.
Hucker, T. K.
Holt, A. R.
Holt, F.
Hitchcock, S. T.
Higgs, A.
Hennessey, C. R.
Harris, J. H.
Hinchey, A. E.
Hull, H. M.
Hanes, V. G.
Henry, C. G.
Harper, C. H.
Hall, W. E.

Hyman, I.
Hawkins, H. C.
Hutchinson, A.
Hiscocks, P. C.
Hurley, J.
Harding, W. J.
Howard, W. F.
Harmon, F. A.
Horth, H. R.
Holmes, G. C.
Hare, A. D. W.
Harris, W. H.
Hider, A. L. G.
Hyam, G.
Hone, J. H.
Hyder, C.
Harrington, H. E.
Hunt, H. T.
Hill, S. H.
Hopps, F. L.
Hare, A.
Hart, C. J. W.
Hall, S.
Holmes, J.
Hall, L.
Hooling, S. T.
Hoste, W. E.
Harle, W.
Horsley, W.
Haylett, R. H.
Hart, W. B.
Hall, C. H.
Head, R. I.
Hill, W. L.
Hirst, C. C.
Hollidge, F. G.
Haycroft, L. C.
Hobson, H.
Hawkins, A. H.
Hayward, A. R. C.
Hine, W. H.
Hanna, J. H.
Herbert, R. C.
Harrison, S.
Hart, C. B.
Hoskins, H. W.
Hudson, F. R.

Hall, F. H.
Hall, H. W.
Hall, L. P.
Hall, W. T.
Hankins, F. H.
Harrison, F.
Hartley, H. R.
Hayward, F.
Henson, A. D.
Hilder, F. C.
Hobart, G. S.
Honour, A. F.
Hooker, P.
Horne, H. G.
Hunt, J. C.
Hyde, J. H. S.
Hunt, P.
Howard Grafton,
L. N.
Hansford, G. R.
Hargrave, S. G.
Harland, C. H.
Harris, C. G.
Harris, E. S.
Hart, H.
Hatch, A. A.
Hayman, F. S.
Head, H. A.
Herring, W.
Hind, M. J.
Hobbs, J. M.
Hooper, J. P. L.
Hull, C. A.
Harman, A. R.
Hull, C. B.
Hanna, C. H.
Hart, D. E.
Hollobone,
H. E. W.
Hulford, E.
Harper, W. J.
Harris, G.
Hart, J. W.
Howard, R. G.
Haynes, C. S.
Hebbert, E. N.
Hudson, L. S.

Harlow, R. E.
Howard, F. R.
Hatfield, H. E.
Heal, L. R.
Hendley, P. G.
Hotson, A. C.
Hughes, E. F.
Haughton,
T. G. L.
Hundleby, H. S.
Hallier, H.
Harris, D. W.
Hawkins, H. I.
Hawley, F. W.
Harris, C. H.
Haynes, H. V.
Heath, L. E.
Harling, F. W.
Henshall, D. E.
Herring, S. V.
Huggons, A. F.
Hyman, J.
Hurrell, J. R.
Hale, G. L.
Heywood, S. W.
Hodges, N. H.
Howlett, J. H.
Howlett, F. G.
Hollington, C. W.
Hill, F.
Harris, R. J.
Hammer, C. F.
Harrison, N. V.
Hennings, L. B.
Hearne, H.
Henderson, W.
Hall, M. W.
Harris, F.
Hall, A. E.
Humpherson,
C. E.
Hunter, F. H.
Hill, M. M.
Hussey, M. R.
Hodges, S. H.
Haycraft, H. C.
Henry, J. W.

Harnot, F. H.
Henry, J. A.
Hollis, F.
Hall, G.
Humphreys, F. A.
Hodges, A. E.
Harding, A. E.
Hogg, L. A.
Hunt, E. J.
Harrison, A. E.
Hawkes, R. W.
Hobson, H. L.
Haines, L.
Hay, H. F.
Howard, W. G.
Hitch, H. H.
Hall, E. A.
Harris, A. V.
Hughes, E. G.
Hillman, J. W. H.
Hillman, H. J.
Hackman, A. L.
Humphreys, W. A.
Hines, T. H.
Holland, H. C.
Hughes, A. W.
Hayden, B. R.
Howard, S. F.
Hertz, A.
Halstead, H. L.
Hughes, S. G.
Humphreys, W.
Harling, A. T.
Hollands, E. A.
Hopkins, S. H.
Holmes, G. E.
Hobday, C. F.
Harris, T. W.
Harverson, C.
Harris, S.
Hodgkinson, E. D.
Hattersley, A. E.
Hayden, A. J.
Horrex, A.
Hoskins, A. D.
Harvey, H. R.

Hooper, J. J.
Hooper, H. H.
Holder, G.
Hunter, P.
Hutt, F. G.
Henderson, R. E.
Halsey, H.
Hunt, W. V.
Hodgson, E. C.
Howson, J.
Hards, W. G.
Hay, E.
Himley, A. R.
Hall, E.
Hardy, E. S.
Harrison, A. G. R.
Hockley, H. J.
Howard, J. E.
Hooker, C. S.
Hitch, F. A.
Houslop, S. S.
Harrington, B. L.
Harris, W. T.
Holland, H.
Horan, H. L.
Hornegold, F. G.
Hubbard, F. A.
How, W. R.
Haines, J. W.
Harris, H. E.
Hicks, H. E.
Humphreys, G. W.
Hales, A. W. F.
Harvey, E. W.
Head, A. E.
Huggins, F. H. G.
Howard, H. A.
Harrison, G. H.
Hague, P. S.
Heath, A. G.
Heath, A. R.
Humphries, E. A.
Harley, A. C.
Hodges, L. J.
Hopkins, V.
Hudson, A. D.

Harris, E. J.
Hurst, J.
Hart, A. S.
Hollis, L. A.
Harris, M.
Harris, S. J.
Hunter, W. A.
Hancock, H. A.
Harper, W. G.
Herbert, J. D.
Harris, E.
Hatten, E. W.
Hayes, W.
Hindes, L. R.
Hourihane, P. J.
Haslam, W.
Hoskin, H. J.
Hill, C. W. D.
Heading, P. J.
Hall, F. W.
Hayer, J. J.
Hooley, R.
Hurrell, S. F.
Harman, W. H.
Hunt, T. W.
Hosking, A. E. V.
Hughes, W. J.
Hatcher, W.
Horwood, V. W.
Hall, F. J.
Harris, T. W.
Hawker, A. G.
Henshaw, W.
Hunt, A. F.
Hayden, D. E.
Howlett, B.
Hogbin, C. W.
Holman, E. V.
Hartley, E.
Hay, W. L.
Henrich, A. S.
Hodges, A. J. C.
Humphries, J. M. S.
Haynes, F. J.
Hall, A. B.
Hales, A. C.

Hinrich, E.
Habbyjam, J. F.
Harman, L.
Harris, A. L.
Hart, E. J.
Hatcher, F. G.
Hill, A. F.
Hughes, R. J.
Humphrey, F. G.
Hollows, F. B.
Hardy, G. F.
Hillier, R.
Holmes, F.
Hartley, W. N.
Harries, W.
Holland, J.
Harmer, G. B.
Haines, A. S.
Hinn, C. E.
Hiscox, W. V. C.
Holliday, C. J.
Haworth, H. S.
Hammett, K.
Hosegood, S. P.
Hill, W. F.
Hyde, A. V.
Harman, A.
Huthwaite, C. H.
Hollobone, A. J.
Hood, R. S.
Harvey, N.
Harris, J. E.
Holt, A. G.
Hughes, G. T.
Hall, E. E.
Hudson, L. S. T.
Humphreys, W. H.
Hall, O. A.
Hatch, J. S.
Hillmann, A. G.
Hollox, C. H.
Hutchison, J. L.
Hall, W. M.
Hoehn, G. C.
Howie, J. P.
Hutchison, L. R.
Halcrow, H. E.

Heggadon, C.
Harvey, F.
Harris, W. S.
Hill, G. A. S.
Hale, A. G. W.
Harris, H. C.
Hill, E. N. V.
Hawkins, H.
Hicks, J. A.
Hickman, T. F.
Hardcastle, R. C.
Hunter, R.
Hartford, E. F.
Holmes, G. E.
Healy, J. W.
Humphreys, E. W.
Hall, H. J.
Hatton, W. D.
Hitchcock, R.
Hanson, F. W. H.
Hownam, W. E.
Hooler, W. T.
Hillier, J. S.
Holbrook, F. R.
Holmes, H. C.
Humphreys, H. G.
Harrison, L.
Hitchener, E. B.
Harries, G. R.
Holland, P. M.
Horton, R.
Heath, B. A.
Hall, T. H.
Higgins, J. W.
Hill, R.
Hussey, F. C.
Hall, E. J. T.
Hawkins, F. M.
Hawley, R. W.
Harrison, A.
Howson, H. C. O.
Huleatt, R. Q.
Harrison, D. W.
Hart, E.
Harris, L.
Howell, S. J.
Hollidge, A. S.

Heelis, W.
Heinrich, E.
Hudson, F. H.
Holmes, W. E.
Hill, H. F.
Howes, C. C.
Hyrdon, A.
Higgins, F.
Holdway, E. W.
Holthusen, H. S.
Hansford, F. A.
Heard, L. V.
Hopkins, H. E.
Hart, E. J.
Harvey, S. B. W.
Hooper, G. B.
Hunt, A. L.
Howell, G. T.
Holt, L.
Hopkins, A. A.
Holding, E. J.
Heyes, J. P.
Hart, W. I.
Haddock, W. F.
Henshaw, G. W.
Horn, W.
Hill, R. E. G.
Horsley, J. C.
Horsley, S.
Hindmarsh, G. B.
Hewlett, A. M.
Hopkins, F. P. V.
Hyne, L. J.
Hills, L. N.
Honney, E. A.
Halls, S. M.
Hayward, H.
Haddock, N. R.
Hotten, W. G. E.
Hewson, E.
Hagger, H. W.
Hookham, J. E.
Hunt, G.
Harvey, R. W.
Henton, W. H.
Hawkins, J. H.
Hutchison, A. J.

Hallas, J. E.
Hunt, J. F.
Hustwait, J. W.
Hedge, F. J.
Hammond, A. M.
Houston, J. Mc M.
Harris, E.
Hart, C. J.
Hamilton, C. J. H.
Heslop, W.
Hart, H.
Harpum, G.
Healey, D.
Hughes, C. W.
Harrison, F.
Hopkins, E. B.
Hutton, G.
Hearne, F.
Hempell, H. L.
Head, A. H.
Haywood, W.
Howell, W. H.
Hollidge, W. E.
Hall, A. J.
Howell, F.
Harper, J.
Hughes, C. A. H.
Hall, G. L.
Holmes, E. S.
Huckle, W. G.
Handel, S.
Hasler, H.
Hunt, P. F.
Hornell, R.
Harding, H. G.
Horwick, S. A. J.
Hambley, R.
Hodgkinson, S. T.
Hedge, A. G.
Haines, C. F.
Haine, A. J.
Hearne, H. D. A.
Hargrave, L.
Hearn, S. W.
Harrison, F.
Harman, A. W.
Horwood, A. G.

Harman, F. G.
Hopkins, R. G.
Head, E. T. C.
Halls, H. F. E.
Hawkins, W. B.
Hails, W. G.
Hunt, C. E.
Hulley, J.
Howse, A. V.
Hesse, H. H.
Humphries, H. G.
Higham, W. E.
Hayne, L. C. G.
Head, G. S.
Height, F.
Hurle, I.
Herrick, P. E.
Humphrys, W.
Hills, J. W.
Hailes, F. U.
Hutchinson, A. E.
Hunter, F. H.
Harrison, P.
Hyde, E. F.
Hillman, F. J.
Hall, R. E.
Hastie, T. A.
Hill, C. E.
Hook, W. B.
Howe, E. J.
Hutchins, S. F.
Horsman, J. T.
Hargrave, J. A.
Hewett, H. J.
Haworth, C. B.
Hibbert, C.
Howard, R.
Harris, H. G.
Howard, J. C.
Heath, C. W.
Harding, F.
Hayward, E. J.
Harrison, W. R.
Hunsworth, F. S.
Honychurch, C. R.
Honychurch, P. G.
Hurly, H. T.

Heath, F. J.
Hanna, W. J.
Hindle, L. M.
Hawtin, J. S.
Hawkins, P. G.
Horlock, E. G.
Hull, C. D.
Holmes, J.
Horner, L.
Halle, N. W.
Hymers, C.
Hughes, G. E.
Harvey, C. W.
Hyde, L. L.
Hudson, T. A. F.
Hughes, H.
Hughes, R. C.
Harness, W.
Hislop, F. W.
Hughes, W. W.
Hatch, W.
Hall, F. H.
Harvey, W. W.
Howfield, G. B.
Hooper, T.
Howson, F. F.
Hurst, A.
Hutchings, B. T.
Hennessey, P.
Harris, S. R.
Hawkins, C. C.
Holly, P. J.
Hawker, L. A.
Hammett, W.
Hayward, V.
Hill, J.
Hawkins, W. R.
Hicks, A. E.
Halton, G. L.
Houslop, L. W. G.
Hay, A. T.
Hodge, A.
Howard, R. F.
Humphreys, A.
Harrison, G. A.
Hilder, G. D.
Howgill, F. J.

Huddlestone, D.
Hanes, L. W.
Hill, L. G.
Howes, A. J. E.
Hoskins, H. O.
Hook, W. E.
Hodges, F. G.
Hewlett, L. H.
Hudson, H.
Hale, D. J.
Hyam, E. P.
Hawkins, A. W.
Hodgetts, C. W.
Hogben, S.
Hill, M. G.
Horsewood, F.
Hawkins, C. H.
Hann, C. A. C.
Haynes, A. E.
Hutchings, D. A.
Hutchinson, W. R.
Hodge, J. C.
Hosegood, J. M.
Hill, H. R.
Halsey, R. H.
Harris, C. F.
Hawkes, R. H.
Hancock, R.
Hunt, C. G.
Harragan, A. C.
Heeler, F.
Hake, H. E. J.
Hatten, J. T.
Hardy, A.
Harding, G.
Harvey, E. S.
Hart, E. J.
Haynes, H. E.
Holland, C. F. R.
Higman, N.
Hill, E. A.
Hoskin, A. S.
Holt, L. A.
Haywood, H. P.
Henderson, N.
Heather, G. F.
Heygate, F. C.

Houghton,
       A. L. N. D.
Huntsman, J. E.
Hall, H. J. C.
Howard, J. W.
Harfield, H. A. L.
Hunter, W. J.
Hale, H. C.
Hague, G. W.
Hunter, J. E.
Hopewell, P.
Hewitt, S. D. A.
Hardy, R. G.
Hutchins, W. C.
Hyde, H. C.
Horne, E. W.
Hargraves, J. H.
Howard, W. C.
Hurle, J.
Holland, T. W.
Howes, L. H.
Hooper, L. F.
Hennell, A. L.
Heathcote, A. V.
Hartley, W. F.
Hewer, J.
Hughes, W. D.
Holmes, G. C.
Henshall, H. D.
Hussey, E. F. W.
Harries, H. A.
Harnett, S. P.
Harris, J. L.
Hammond, C. L.
Hawkins, W. P.
Hart, G. P.
Hall, P. E. W.
Ham, N. E.
Higginson, E.
Hardy, E. W.
Harper, J.
Hoare, G. E.
Hanlon, S. J.
Hecker, W. R.
Harman, G.
Hughes, F. P.
Harkness, A. C.

Hutcherson, C. W.
Hand, W. R.
Humm, C.
Haywood, S. T.
Hodgkinson, W. E.
Hewitt, W. A.
Haskell, W. L.
Hiscocks, W. J.
Holland, R. H.
Harvey, E. W.
Hooker, J. K.
Hadland, F. N.
Hampson, S. R.
Hall, S. E.
Hams, F. W.
Hawbrook, H.
Haynes, A. R.
Harding, W. G.
Harris, G. T.
Hoodless, W. F. H.
Hayter, P. H. C.
Hewens, R. C.
Harnden, T. E. B.
Hole, C.
Hickson, T. H.
Healing, W. R.
Harvey, S. B.
Hadley, C. V. D.
Helstrip, G.
Hull, A. G.
Havard, J. H.
Harper, W.
Harvey, B. J.
Henwood, W. J. D.
Heald, J. L.
Houghton, P. M.
Hayton, J.
Hammond, D. R.
Hanby, J. W.
Hollingsworth, H.
Hallett, S. J.
Hammersley, S.
Haywood, F.
Hitchin, F.
Hoare, R. P.
Hooper, C. T.
Haycock, J. H.

CIVIL SERVICE RIFLES 449

Henry, J.
Hollands, C. A.
Harrison, C. A.
Hopkins, P.
Houlberg, E. J.
Heath, W.
Hainsworth, W.
Harbarow, E. E. S.
Heather, C. J.
Hore, S. F.
Hewlett, A.
Howes, J.
Haddock, K. E. V.
Halls, F. T.
Hack, P. E.
Hey, F.
Hazell, T. R. W.
Heath, F. C.
Hines, H.
Huxtable, J.
Harvey, G.
Horn, C.
Hansard, N.
Halliday, C. D.
Hyde, G. E.
Howell, L. P.
Holden, R. S.
Holland, R. H.
Hammon, W. E.
Hames, G. R. H.
Holliday, B.
Harvey, C.
Harris, S. D.
Heath, S. J.
Hazlewood, H. W.
Heavens, G. T.
Humphries, F.
Honeywell, G. T.
Hall, W. C.
Hamill, W.
Hobbs, G. F.
Harrison, H. W.
Hollands, T. A. G.
Harris, T. F.
Holtham, A. W. D.
Hill, R. P.
Holbrook, H. C.

Hutchinson, T.
Hillier, S. B.
Hotson, W. J.
Harley, T.
Hooten, J. S.
Henken, G. F.
Hollingworth, C. F.
Holloway, D.
Hooker, R.
Hovell, C. A.
Harrington, N. F.
Harris, A. W. M.
Hughes, C. P.
Harris, T.
Hollingdale, C. H.
Herbert, R.
Hall Haynes, T. E.
Hall, W. C.
Hart, G. E.
Higgins, F. E. J.
Haigh, H. S.
Hicks, E. J.
Handyside, J.
Henott, C.
Holbrook, M.
Heath, E.
Hotten, J. W.
Hover, J. H. E.
Hemsley, J. A.
Hawkins, H. R.
Humphrey, L. E.
Hall, E. J.
Hayes, D. J.
Holland, A. J.
Hynds, F. C.
Harvey, H. F.
Holland, R. W.
Haines, A.
Holme, A.
Horwood, H.
Hook, S. A.
Hollett, N. P.
Harcourt, C. W.
Hyland, C.
Hope, P. O.
Hayes, T. J.
Hull, J.

Heffer, G.
Hedges, H. A.
Heath, F.
Helliwell, H.
Hammond, C. G.
Hazell, N.
Hinds, E. P.
Hutchinson, W.
Hilder, E. C. R.
Hall, N. G.
Hale, G.
Hale, J.
Hall, F. S.
Hawkins, A. R.
Hutchins, J. W.
Hanson, A. W.
Hope, G.
Hobbs, J. E.
Hemsley, G. R.
Harris, W. A.
Horne, E. A.
Hockridge, W. G.
Howlett, W. W.
Hudson, D. A.
Harriss, A. R.
Hall, S. F.
Hawkins, W. J.
Hollander, S.
Hunt, E.
Hotston, T.
Horner, J.
Howard, C. F.
Hall, G.
Hake, C. W.
Hart, W. D.
Harvest, S. E.
Halford, H. J.
Hart, E.
Head, W.
Holman, E. W.
Hurst, R. H. C.
Hyde, P.
I
Ives, H. J. M.
Isaac, G. W.
Irving, W. J.
Illing, R. W.

2 F

Ind, W. E.
Ives, A. J.
Irwin, A. G.
Irwin, J. W. E.
Ibbett, C.
Igglesden, G. F.
Innocent, E. P.
Ingram, F. R.
Ive, G. F.
Idle, G. S.
Ingram H. D.
Ivey, W. L.
Ivamy, E.
Ingram, A.
Isaacson, H. A. S.
Ince, S. M.
Ironside, W.
Inskip, D. C.
Ireland, D. J.
Ingram, F. E.
Ingram, A. G. W.
Illing, A. C.
Irons, E. W.
Ireland, W. B.
Ince, N. M.
Ingram, C. E.
Irwin, W. E.
Irwin, G.
Isaacs, J.
Ison, L. J.
Ison, W.
Ireland, W. G.
Ingham, H.
Inkpen, J.
Innes, G. D.
Ing, T. W.
Izzett, C. E. C.
Illing, R. G.
Illing, R. W.
Innes, A.
Ingram, G.
Illingworth, H. W.
Ilett, F.
Ingram, H.
Ingles, F.
Inglefield, A. E.
Irwin, W. L.

Irish, —
Inwood, —
Ingram, —
Imray, —
Ingham, —
Ivey, —
Izzard, —
Innell, E. H.
Iveson, D. G.
Isted, A. J.
Irvine, G.
Isaac, L. F.
Indge, C. J.
Ibett, C. H.
Izzard, A.
Isaac, W. C.
Iddon, R.
Imber, A. E.
Ingram, C. J.
Imray, T.
Izzard, W.

J
Jessop, W. J.
Julian, N. M.
James, A. L.
Jeans, G. H.
Jamison, E. H.
Jacobs, D.
Jesty, E. T.
Jones, C.
Jones, W. E.
Jay, H. J. S.
Jackson, W. E.
Jeffree, J. S.
Jestin, **M.**
Johnson, A. S.
Johnson, A. R.
Jones, T. F.
Jones, A. H.
Jackson, F.
Jukes, S. E.
Jackson, J.
Jones, A.
Johnson, J. A.
Jacobs, A. E. A.
Jarvis, A. W.
James, P. E.

Jackson, H. G.
Jenkins, A. D.
Jamison, C. M.
Jiles, L. J.
Jarvis, A. O.
Jones, W. I.
Jesson, A.
Jeffs, I. S.
Jewell, W. E.
Joseph, C. L.
Jarvis, E. E.
Jarvis, E. F.
Jones, J. H.
Jones, C. H.
Jones, D. E. C.
Jarvis, B. H.
Joffe, M.
Jones, T. I.
Jones, W. M.
Jennings, G.
Jacobs, B. O.
James, A. R.
James, S. D.
Jenkins, A. G.
Jobling, S. F.
Jones, H. H.
Jolley, W. H.
Jackson, J. S.
Jobling, R.
Jamison, D.
Jacobs, H. E.
James, W. A.
Johnstone, C. P.
Joffe, J.
James, E. F.
Jones, G. E.
Jiles, P.
James, A. V.
Jones, R. A.
Jamison, E. W.
Jagger, F. A.
Johnstone, A. E.
James, L. H.
Jones, P.
Jones, C. F.
Jabelman, A. H.
Jeffries, W. J.

Jones, R. W.
Jeffery, C.
Jones, C. R.
Johnson, J. H.
Jones, R. T.
Jacques,
    C. G. R. H.
Jordan, G.
Jones, J. L.
Jennings, S. G.
Jones, W. E.
Jones, T. W.
Jefford, G. R.
Johnson, H. L.
Jones, W. J. H.
Jolly, H. C.
Jobson, C. T.
Jones, J. W. T.
Jackson, V. A.
Jones, F. V.
Jones, H. C.
Jordan, C. J.
Johnson, F. G.
Jacomb, A. J.
Jeffery, S. J.
Jefferies, L. C. A.
Jowett, A.
Johnson, P. C.
Jack, G.
James, A. E.
Johnson, H. L. C.
Joyce, C. H.
Jardine, R. C.
Johnson, W.
Jackson, H. M.
Jones, C. T.
Jeffcoate, E. P.
Jackson, B. H.
Johns, W.
Jones, B.
Jones, W. T.
Johnston, T.
Jones, H.
Jenkin, C. P.
Johnson, G. A.
Jeans, G. W.
Jenner, A. E.

Johnson, R. F.
Jeffrey, F. S.
James, W. G.
Janes, R. A.
James, H. P.
Jepson, C. W.
Jones, E.
Jeapes, C. J.
Jefferys, A.
Jackson, A. F.
Jolly, H. F.
James, T. A.
Jenkins, O. G.
Jenkins, J. H.
Johnson, S. T.
Jackson, G. S.
Jarvis, H.
Johnson, F. T.
Jeeves, W. G.
Jarratt, R. C.
Joines, H. E.
Juniper, C. C.
Jeffreys, A. W.
Josling, W.
Jones, E. J.
Jenner, J. O. F.
Johnstone, T.
Jennings, H.
Johnson, W. C.
Jacobs, N.
Johnson, O. C.
Jeffs, A. M.
Johnson, J. W. J.
Johnson, G. W.
Judson, E. F.
Jenkins, G. W.
Johnson, F.
Jenkerson, L. J.
Julier, E. S.
Jeffery, J.
Johnston, J. W.
Jefferiss, T. P.
Jerram, T. W.
Jeffery, W. E.
Jarvis, P. H.
Jotham, H. J.
Johnson, F.

Joslin, L. M.
Johnson, J.
Jenkins, J. A.
Johnson, P.
Jackson, A. E.
Joines, A.
Jenkins, W. J.
Jenkins, F. E.
Jones, E. H.
Jenkins, R.
Jaques, C. W.
Joines, W. A.
Jeffery, A. G.
Jones, J. P.
Jones, G. B.
Johnson, H. J.
Johnson, A. T.
Johns, P. L.
Jones, S. H.
Jefferson, H. D.
Jones, E. G.
James, A. J.
James, S.
Jennett, V. D.
Jones, V. G.
Jackson, W. M.
Jones, F. L.
Jones, T. W.
Jennings, F.
Jenkins, G. A.
James, D. M.
Jones, A. P.
Johnston, A. A.
Johnson, H. J.
Jeal, W. F.
Jennings, G. R.
Jones, H. M.
Johnson, E. E.
Jenkins, J. M.
Jory, W.
Johnstone, W.
Judge, T. C.
Jackson, W. C. D.
Josland, S. C.
Jefferies, W. E.
Jacobs, T. C. H.
Jones, J. O. C.

Johnston, **W. H.**
Jennings, A. R.
Jenkins, J. W.
John, C. C.
Jewitt, S. H.
Jehn, E. H.
Jacob, W. L.
Johns, A.
Jones, W. T.
Jenvey, S. H.
Jarvis, W. G.
Jewitt, H.
Joyner, R.
James, G. W. V.
Jones, J. T.
Jordon, L.
Jasper, S. R.
Johnson, F. J.
Jones, G. F.
Jarman, J. S.
Jackson, H.
Jacob, A. P.
Jones, T.
Jones, H. R.
Joel, H. E. O.
Josephson, A.
Jones, T. R.
James, M. B.
Jones, C.
Jenner, H. J.
Jolly, H. H.
Johnson, T. H.
Jones, W.
Judd, J. S. T.
Jeansonane, Y. R.
Johnson, E. S.
Jones, E. R.
Jeffs, A. E.
Joyce, E. J.
Johnston, W.
Jones, A. H.
Jones, G. A.
Jones, F.
Jackson, W. T. N.
Jefferson, F. C.
James, S. L.
Johnson, T. C. M.

Jones, J. M.
Johns, L. S.
Jones, G. S.
Jones, A. B.
Johnson, E. N.
Jepps, W.
Jackson, J. H.
Johnson, A.
James, A. J.
Jowitt, J.
Jones, E. H.
Jakes, F.
Johnson, E. A.
Jones, G.
Jolly, H. A.
Jesty, H. V.
Junkison, A. C.
Johnson, D.
Jarvis, S, D,
K
Kemp, W.
Kennedy, C. W.
King, T.
Kinsman, J. C. P.
Kent, H. T.
Knapp, E.
Kemp, E. W.
King, F.
Kelley, R. W.
Knopff, W. H.
Knight, G. V.
Kelsey, H. J. R.
Kelby, P. J.
Kerr, P. W.
Kay, M. K.
Kidd, A. T.
Kent, D. B.
Killip, J.
Knell, E. W. H.
Keogh, J.
Keen, T.
Kesby, B. A. N.
Kyle, J. A.
Keeler, G.
Kettle, E. W.
King, P. R.
Keena, J. H.

Kilby, A. H.
Kirby, E. O.
Keeley, H.
Kemp, A. A.
Kidd, S. J.
Kitching, E.
Kirby, W.
Kerslake, S. S.
Kent, W. B.
King, L. J.
Kootz, C.
King, E.
Knapp, E. J.
Kenchington,
    G. W. A.
Kingston, H. J.
Kemp, O. G.
Kinnison, J. S.
Kemp, G. W.
Kenchington, D. S.
Kershaw, L. F. R.
Kingham, F. A.
Kerswell, E.
Kirkpatrick, H. J.
Kernot, F. A. W.
Knapp, F. G.
Kilduff, W.
Kennedy, K.
Kindell, R. H.
Knight, N. G.
Knight, L. T.
Kitch, H. M.
Kirby, A.
Kerr, A. M.
King, W. T.
Keen, P. S.
King, H.
Knapp, A. H.
Knott, L.
Knight, H. A. W.
Knowles, V. O.
Knight, S. T.
Kilby, C. C.
Kent, H. C.
Kempton, T, D,
Kirkness, J.
Kershaw, G.

King, E. T. R.
Knight, E. C.
Knight, G. L.
Knight, L. R.
Kelland, P. G.
Knight, P.
King, A. J. B.
Knight, E. J.
King, F.
Kinman, J. B.
Kendall, A.
Kierman, J. F.
Kirkness, C.
Kelly, J.
Kirk, R.
Kite, F.
Knight, S. J.
Kersey, S. F.
Kilby, J.
Kers, E. R.
Knight, H. S.
Kew, H. S.
Knight, S. H.
Kearns, G.
Knowles, J. C.
Kidner, H. J.
Kettle, L. L.
Kerrod, A.
Kerr, W. T.
Kingsbury,
      I. J. F.
Kenny, J.
Knapp, E. M.
Kinnock, H. B.
Kidner, G. M.
Kitteridge, H. H.
Kenny, A.
Key, L. H.
Keane, H. C.
Kitchen, J. W.
Kennedy, W. J.
Keg, E. L.
Kelso, J.
Kenchington, H.
Keel, W. J.
Knott, G. E.
Kay, J.

Kallenback, F. E.
Kemp, E.
Katon, J. D.
King, N.
Knight, H.
Kingston, W. H.
Kinnersley, T. C.
Killick, J. C. T.
Krent, A.
Kenning, J. H.
King, S. W.
Kent, A. H.
Kilroy, F. G.
Knight, F. W.
Kemble, F. T.
Kelland, E. J.
Kirkland, F. H.
Kent, H. J.
Kinsville, C. V.
Knowlden, A. G.
Kellett, W. A.
Kendall, L. R. E.
Kelley, E. J. M.
Knight, A. C.
Kynaston, A. M.
Keightley, W; D.
Kesby, H. H.
Knight, C. F.
Kennedy, G. A.
Keetch, H.
King, W. H.
Kerry, J. H.
Keay, J.
Kelly, E. G.
Kershaw, W. E.
Kay, J. B.
Keen, F. H.
Kerr, A. M.
Krushaar, L. G.
Kibble, W. T.
Kersley, W. H.
Kirby, L. J.
Kemp, G.
King, W. G. E.
Keen, F. J.
Kennett, W. F.
Kirkley, T.

Knight, R.
King, S. H.
Kilburn, H. B.
Keep, F. A. O.
Kenworthy, F. B.
Kewley, C. H.
Kerridge, H.
Knivett, C. T.
King, E.
Knights, E. W.
Kennedey, L. A.
Knight, L. R. C.
Kynaston, J. W.
Kemp, F.
Knapp, L. A.
Kately, G. H.
K e n t i s h , W.
      E. J.
King, L.
King, L. M.
Kingston, H. J.
Knight, M. R.
Kew, A. J.
King, H. F.
Kebble, F. W.
Kirby, S.
Kitchen, A.
Kennedy, H. D.
King, H. F.
Kingswell, A. J.
Kingseller, D. J.
King, C. R.
Kilbey, A. D.
Kennett, E. C.
King, A. C.
Kent, A. J.
Kibble, C. G. W.
Kemp, F.
Kersley, L. F.
Knight, C. H. A.
Keen, O.
King, B.
Kendall, A. J.
King, S. H.
Kirby, A.
Keen, V. C. R.
Keith, H. G.

L

Le-Messurier, C. C.
Lintott, J. W.
Ludball, W. A.
Langton, J. A. T.
Lewis, H. P.
Lovett, G.
Lambert, W. B.
Lyon, S. T.
Lighton, F. O.
Lane, A. W.
Lee, J. M.
Law, W. F.
Lippold, S. A.
Lord, F.
Ling, F. W.
Lubbock, L. F.
Latter, E. A.
Lewis, F. W.
Little, W. H.
Liles, J. H.
Lockley, N. C.
Lowe, W. G. S.
Lewis, H. T.
Lidiard, H. M.
Lilley, H.
Lilley, H. G.
Lynden, A. H.
Lawson, R. J.
Lester, A. R.
Lucas, F. J.
Lane, W. A.
Little, E.
Lewis, C. H.
Lack, H. W.
Lovell, H. F.
Lowton, H. L.
Leeming, C. C.
Langton, J. A. F.
Lewis, H. W.
Legg, E. E.
Lawson, H. J.
Leggett, J. G.
Liddiatt, P. H.
Lovelock, H. W.
Lee, E. H.
Lewis, L. C.

Lake, E. R.
Lindsay, J. E.
Lloyd, F. S.
Laver, A. W.
Leask, N. B. S.
Leppard, H. C.
Levey, O. L. H.
Llewellyn, R. C.
Lloyd, F. H.
Loxdale, E.
Lane, C. H.
Lawman, E. J.
Leech, E. J.
Lindley, E. W.
Lake, A.
Lyon, E. A.
Little, W. E.
Ley, A. V.
Lyons, E. H.
Lake, F. J.
Loynes, J. W.
Lewis, H. A. C.
Lisle, W. S.
Letheren, R. C.
Luttman, F. E.
Leeming, R.
Lalhart, C. L.
Latchford, P. F.
Legg, A. E. J.
Lloyd, A.
Littledale, J. W. F.
Lawrence, S.
Lennard, P. C.
Louch, L. A.
Louch, J. G.
Luty, F.
Lotty, W. C.
Losman, D.
Light, F. E.
Lennell, H. J.
Lethebe, W.
Levy, D.
Lewis, A.
Lewis, F.
Langford, S. H.
Lumer, J.
Lockyer, W. G.

Lenton, J.
Lawrence, F. W.
Laurence, H.
Lane, E.
Lewis, E. O.
Lodge, C. D.
Legg, W. A.
Lovett, W.
Lugg, C. C.
Long, L.
Lock, J.
Lister, M.
Lindop, N.
Larkin, A.
Lambeth, F.
Lilley, W. A.
Locke, W. E.
Litchfield, H.
Langley, G. F.
Laurence, W.
Lowden, F. N.
Lindridge, P. H.
Lloyd, F. W.
Lawrence, H. W.
Lee, R. P.
Lawrence, A. H.
Lambert, A. J.
Lehan, W. C.
Leicester, W.
Levine, J.
Lucraft, E. H.
Leggatt, G. J.
Lennard, B. R.
Lines, P.
Lawrence, B. C. W.
Lawson, G. J.
Lovett, F. J. W.
Lynch, D.
Leopold, W. E.
Lewis, G. O.
Lamprell, H.
Leckie, J. F.
Lawrence, H.
Lewis, A.
Lyons, E. A.
Lane, J. R.
Layton, B.

Levell, E.
Lanning, S. P.
Luxton, E.
Llewellin, C. A.
Lister, A. E.
Leopold, A. A.
Laughton, C.
Lee, L. H.
Le Cheminant,
A. H.
Lee, H. S.
Leopold, A. V.
Looker, E. G.
Lewis, J. S.
Locke, J.
Lovett, E. A.
Liggi, A. S.
Lewis, E. O.
Larne, A. J.
Larne, C. F.
Lambert, E.
Lansley, A. E.
Landymore, E. R.
Landymore, P. V.
Lamb, C. E.
Lee, H. P.
Lee, P. R.
Lugg, H. D.
Leonard, E. G.
Lewis, R.
Long, A. G.
Last, E. F.
Lamerton,
L. C. M.
Lacy, W. B.
Lacy, E. A.
Larkin, R. S.
Luff, R.
Linfield, A. F.
Lennell, E.
Langdon, G. T.
Lyons, J. A.
Leach, C. C.
Lickess, H.
Lancaster, W. T.
Lambden, W. H.
Long, A. J.

Lewis, G. S.
Liptrot, R. W.
Linsdell, N.
Langford, L. E.
Leech, C. H.
Lawrence, R. A.
Lovegrove,
W. T. F.
Lilley, J. L.
Lockwood, B.
Letch, A. W.
Little, A. S.
Luckhurst, C.
Lord, W.
Lown, L. C.
Levesly, G.
Lines, K.
Levens, C. A.
Landymore, L. L.
Lewis, L. V.
Lamb, G. W.
Long, A. E.
Lloyd, L.
Lenzbury, A.
Lorely, J. R.
Lazonby, J. C.
Leech, C. H.
Lambert, P. G.
Lancashire, J. B.
Lockyer, F. J.
Leach, P. C.
Lewis, F.
Lardner, H. F.
Leach, E. A.
Launden, P. C.
Larren, W. J.
Leigh, G.
Longstaff, P. E.
Leigh, A. B.
Lucas, Y.
Lane, F.
Littleboy, J. W.
Leask, A. M. S.
Lowes, A. W.
Liddiatt, P. H.
Lloyd, H.
Larkin, M. J.

Liversidge, E.
Lovegrove,
A. S. L.
Loader, A. V.
Lee, J. A. T.
Lucas, E.
Lyon, A. E.
Lawson, H.
Larkman, W.
Lewis, A.
Leech, J. H. L.
Linton, J.
Lovejoy, P. T.
Lucas, J. B.
Lane, F. G.
Lloyd, H.
Lawrence, A. E.
Lister, H. E.
Lennon, F.
Lilley, P. C.
Levitt, G.
Lock, A. F.
Llewellyn, E.
Llaman, I.
Lennor, F. C.
Lotter, J. W.
Lucking, H. C.
Leach, R.
Lawes, A. A.
Lincoln, J. T.
Lane, A. L.
Lomas, F. W.
Lawrence, B. M.
Langley, E.
Ludbrook, J.
Lewis, E. R.
Lott, H. I.
Lambert, F. T.
Lovelace, E. F.
Lee, M. H.
Lloyd, G. S.
Lander, J. W.
Law, H.
Louis, P.
Law, A. H.
Lond, G. E.
Lumby, H.

Le Vierge, J.
Leggatt, E. F.
Laidler, A. L.
Lane, H. E.
Landeg, J. W.
Linney, J. J.
Lowe, H. S.
Lewis, D. W.
Loughlin, W.
Lee, B. I.
Lenton, R. W. A.
Livesey, J. C.
Lohmann, R. C.
Leach, J. A.
Long, J. H.
Loader, H. W.
Leeks, A. L. L.
Lever, F.
Lyons, M. L.
Leverett, A.
Lambert, G. D.
Lissenden, G. S.
Leach, L. C.
Lockhart, W.
Le-Hurcey, E. R.
Luck, B. N.
Lambert, J.
Longhorn, W. J.
Lane, E. E.
Lysaght, D. J.
Leech, S. P. L.
Leck, A. W.
Leask, L.
Leach, G.
Lamb, A. W. J.
Lewis, T.
Lewis, C. R.
Lumbard, T. L.
Long, W. M.
Lawrence, J. W.
Linnington, O. W.
Longfield, S. P.
Lewis, E. J.
Love, T. E.
Lyle, J. W.
La Roche, W. J.
Little, W. J.

Lea, A. W. C.
Longworth, J. T.
Lister, A. H.
Langridge, F. J.
Lloyd, P. H. R.
Lewis, D.
Lewis, J. R.
Lock, A. W.
Lewis, A. H. C.
Lloyd, S. D.
Longland, F. H.
Lovell, H. C.
Lewis, F. S.
Lewis, A. J.
Lonsdale, H. G.
Lowe, C. L.
Lucas, C. E.
Lush, A.
Lord, A.
Lawson, W. A. D.
Lindsay, A. J.
Lawrance, H.
Lingham, M. F.
Lea, J. B. D.
Lowry, W.
Lupton, C. A.
Lee, C. J.
Lonnon, W. J.
Lilley, H. G.
Larne, A. J.
Lazarus, J. A.
Lee, G. B.
Lane, A. E.
Larking, S. M.
Loveday, P. W.
Lalouette, J. V.
Layton, W.
Longstaffe, P. W.
Lorman, W. H.
Lindblom, A. F.
Leaver, F. R.
Lowery, G. T.
Lewis, J. H.
Lightfoot, E. L.
Luck, H. R.
Lewis, C. G. T.
Lawrence, A. E.

Linton, S. H. C.
Leech, A. H.
Lazarus, L.
Lloyd, H. J.
Loeber, H. C.
Lawman, F. T.
Little, P. A. J.
Lakin, C. J.
Livermore, A. W.
Leggatt, G. E.
Littleboy, E. J.
Ling, C. R.
Lord, E.
Lingard, R.
Longbottom, G. H.
Lawrence, C. W.
Leech, L. W.
Loring, A. C. J.
Lowe, E. V. O.
Ling, C. H.
Lobb, W. W.
Lawrence, G. F.
Leslie, F. M.
Livesey, R.
Lawrence, E. J.
Law, E. R.
Lawton, E.
Lee, A.
London, A. E.
Lilley, W. B.
Laycock, T.
Lloyd, H. E.
Longman, E. H.
Lynch, O.
Lansdown, H. F.
Lea, G.
Logsdail, F. H.
Langley, S. H.
Lewis, F.
Lings, G. A.
Linge, H. W.
Lowe, J. J.
Leigh, F.
Lingley, H. J.
Lawrence, S. J.
Langton, H. I.
Leyden, D. C.

Laver, A. H.
Longmuir, J.
Low, W. E.
Lotty, W. C.
Lewis, P. J.
Linsell, H.
M
Miller, H. C.
Magee, W.
McKimm, T. G.
McSweeney, D. L.
Mitchell, G. J.
Majer, W. G.
Milward, S. R.
Martin, A. S.
Marriott, W. S. M.
Marson, A. E.
Marshall, E. J.
McMillan, R. A.
Mills, H. A.
Maddox, E. H.
Marchant, E. A.
Martin, P. W.
Martin, R.
May, G. C.
Middleton, C. G.
Mugford, H.
Moody, A. A.
Munden, J. A.
Masterman, A. F.
Miller, H.
Magenty, E. R.
Marshall, J. M.
Maton, W. T.
Matzinger, E. A.
Molony, J. L.
Morton, C.
Maclean, D. A.
Maddox, T. G.
Madell, P. A. L.
Mansbridge, E. W.
Mason, P. C.
Matthews, R. P.
Metson, G. F.
Miller, G. T.
Morrow, B. A.
Moss, W.

Moxon, S. H.
Mycroft, F. S.
Meden, Hvd.
Meden, Rvd.
Miles, H. T.
Moore, A.
Miller, W. J.
Moore, A. J.
Mutlow, L. H.
Matthews, F. G.
Miller, P.
Morgan, F. F.
Mallett, H. J.
Mallett, S. H.
Martin, N. F.
Moody, R. E.
McConchie, J. A.
Morant, C.
Moss, T. P.
Milward, S. L.
Mindel, G. H.
Michie, A.
Millwood, W. H.
Matthews, P. T.
Mitchell, L. C.
Molyneux, E. J.
Molyneux, C. H.
Maidiarmid, S. J.
Macauley, D.
Martin, S. S.
McWhirter, A. V.
Malin, H. S.
Moore, H.
Marsden, C.
May, A. F.
Mills, C. C.
Mooney, E.
Moritz, H. C.
Mason, A. J.
Morant, L. H.
Mullins, H. S. A.
Miles, E. C.
McFarlane, D.
Moore, L.
Morgan, G. L.
Mouatt, S. R.
Machan, G. W.

Mansell, G.
Marshall, E. E.
Mallett, W.
Morcombe, P. R.
Myland, A. L.
Manly, J. A.
Molyneux, W.
Macbeth, J.
Mickleburgh, C. A.
Mount, J. B.
Miller, H. H.
McKay, L. N.
McCathie, T. E. G.
Mutch, H. G.
McDermott, A.
McAuley, F. J.
Martin, W. J.
McGauran, H. C.
Murray, H.
McDonnell, H.
Moore, A.
Morgan, E. J.
Metcalf, C. J.
Martin, T.
Marshall, F. M.
Middleton, E. F.
Martin, E. J.
Morgan, W.
Moss, A. G.
Martin, W. S.
Mannering, L. F.
Miller, W. J.
Manfield, R. J.
Millbourne, V. E.
Myall, E. A.
Meadowcroft, L. V
Mansbridge, E. W.
Miles, H. T.
Meadowcroft, J. L.
Mills, G. W. C.
Moore, S. R.
Murphy, W.
Moore, W. H.
Merrick, B. R.
MacGillwray, S.
Mathie, P. D.
Morgan, W. K.

Mitchell, C. C.
Mitchell, W. B.
Millage, L. J.
Morris, L. G. P.
Moore, C. H.
Moore, F. T.
Murphy, M. E.
May, W. J.
Moore, C.
Moss, G. H. C.
Marlow, W.
McKimm, D. S. A.
May, A. E.
Munden, C. A.
Manfield, E. C.
Mash, W. J. R.
Morgan, W. J.
Murray, W.
March, J. E.
Murray, D. A.
McCullagh, V. J.
Medrow, W. A.
McKay, C. S.
Manthorp, C.
Mahoney, S.
Morice, L. O.
Major, O. J.
Mayo, H.
Mayhew, H.
McCandlish, W. E.
Madden, E. W.
Miller, W. J.
Moss, G. E.
Munsey, T. F.
Male, C. E.
Mehl, J. S. D. E. N.
Mares, A. R.
Maddocks, F.
Maddocks, R.
Morriss, L. A. G.
Moynihan, M. J.
Marks, A. H.
Marsh, A. E.
Marlow, H.
Muchmore, A.
Milner, M. J.
Moxham, A. T.

McAdam, C. H.
May, J. A. E.
McMillan, Q. C.
Marriott, C. J.
Mitchell, V. J.
Martin, J.
Moore, E.
Meredith, E. S.
Mackenzie, A. D.
Mitchell, G. V. S.
Mills, S. M.
Moss, C. F.
McNicol, J. C.
Morgan, F. C.
MacGillivray, C.
Marchant, G. S.
Murdock, A. J.
Matthews, C. N.
McGrath, J. W.
Marshall, H.
McMuldroch, R.
McMillan, W.
Malthouse, I.
Medway, P. B.
McLachlan, R. E.
Marshall, G. Y.
Morton, E. R.
Marsh, J. H.
Mulhern, J.
McInnes, A. E. G.
Mansfield, G.
Manning, C.
Menhennitt, R. V.
Myles, A. J. G.
Morrison, H. S.
Moore, W. G. E.
Matthews, C. F.
Marsh, F. H.
Mason, F. H.
Mills, R. E.
Mansell, A.
Mullinger, P. E.
Merrett, A. E.
Milan, C. C.
Martin, F.
Mason, J. G. J.
Marsh, W. B.

Myerscough, L.
Merrick, W. R. P.
Mumford, R. W.
McCaffry, R. W.
Marchant, T. H.
Marychurch,
        E. W. A.
Mellis, A. W.
Munro, G.
Munn, F. A.
Mould, O.
Moran, J. W.
Martin, F. A.
Maynard, G. E.
McLeod, J. N.
Mallett, A. E.
Moyle, J. N. McF.
Modrach, W. F.
Martin, W. E.
Mitchell, A. C. F.
McIntosh, C. C.
Messenger, W. F.
Moring, A. F.
Magrath, J. G.
Milroy, D. H. J.
Marriott, C. J.
Mitchell, W. J. D.
Martin, R. E.
Munn, J. H.
Mitchell, F.
Marshall, G. V.
Morrice, A. E.
Moss, C. E.
May, A. V.
Manhood, A. J.
Morris, L. C.
Moore, C. A. G.
McCullagh, A. T.
Mason, H. F.
Milton, J.
Merifield, W. J.
Medway, C. E.
Mumford, G. W.
Murray, C. E.
Mitchell, F. C.
McAdoo, T. J.
Males, H. J.

Martin, G. H.
Mann, W. A.
Mackintosh, S. J.
Martin, W. H.
Moyes, G. A.
Marston, E.
Miller, G.
Munish, W.
Macnicol, D.
Mason, P. G.
Mann, W. J.
Murray, H. F.
Manners, A. E.
Mill, F. C.
Mouson, H. E.
McNamara, E. C.
McLeod, H.
Moody, G.
Murrell, F. W. S.
Mercer, K.
Morris, E.
Moss, G. T.
May, P.
Meason, F. A.
Millwood, F.
Minter, R. L.
Morris, E.
Muir, A.
Morton, W. H.
McGrath, J. W.
Martin, W. R.
Masson, L. F.
Maskell, S. V.
Marsh, E. J. W.
Miell, H. S.
Maxall, W. H.
Maxwell, J. R.
Milam, H.
Moore, C.
Maynard, J. J.
Moore, E. F. S.
Moss, H. G.
Marley, T. J.
Miller, R. P.
Micklem, A. J.
Mould, W. E.
Mould, H. E.

Milton, B.
Morton, R. N.
Minihane, J. W.
McNally, J. B. J.
Mellows, H. J.
Morgan, F. T.
Manners, F. J.
Marhoff, F. H.
Marshall, T. L.
Morris, J.
Masterton, J.
Mundy, P. D.
Mason, W. B.
Mann, W. J.
Morris, H. B.
Morris, E. R.
McCarthy, D.
Morris, R. A.
Matthews, E. C. R.
Mitchell, S. J.
Michaels, J. M.
Malton, R. H.
Milborrow, C. D.
Moate, W. H.
Meredith, H. B.
Middleton, H. A.
Munday, H. S. S.
Miller, H. F. A.
Mardell, G. E.
March, A.
Marriott, E. P.
Marlow, G.
Morton, J. H.
Marsh, J. W.
Marks, R.
Mansfield, R.
Myatt, A. F. W.
Mills, H. G.
Miles, D. F.
Marshall, A. J.
Miles, E. C.
Manning, E. H.
Mink, R. H.
Maunder, S. V.
Maloney, W. W.
Marshall-King, A.
Mitchell, F. C. H.

Miles, H. O.
Martin, H. D.
Morgan, I. M.
Marshall, H. G.
Manford, R. F.
Morris, A. S.
Miller, J.
Munns, G. A.
Moore, R.
McPherson, H. F.
Morell, I.
Mills, W. E.
Miggleton, L. W.
Miller, A. J.
Millbourn, C. J.
Martin, B.
Mallett, W. J.
Murray, T. E.
Mills, H. G.
Mitchell, J.
Marsh, A.
Monro, D.
Massie, A. J.
Middleton, H. J.
Morgan, D. B.
Martin, J. E. F.
Moore, H. W.
Mercer, W. J.
Martin, H.
Marchant, S. S.
Morey, H.
Mitchell, G. J.
Maxwell, J.
MacGeagh, J. Y.
Moss, F. J.
Miller, F.
Miles, H.
Marjoram, J. A.
Martin, O. E.
Mayne, E. I.
Membury, B. J.
Meyer, A. H.
Murray, J.
Marsh, T. V.
Mayer, L.
Martin, W. J.
Miles, H. W.

Mortyn, A.
Marriage, J. D.
Moutrie, L.
Mills, R. W.
Muir, H.
Mann, H. V.
Mason, J. W.
Meade, F.
Major, J.
Mogan, J.
Morrris, E. F.
Murkett, W.
Mills, R. A.
Margetti, C. P.
Manfield, J. H.
Mason, F. R.
Mills, A. L.
Mason, W. H.
Middleham, A.
Marchese, E.
Miles, W. G.
Musk, C. W.
Manners, W.
Meager, J.
Mason, I.
Mason, H. P.
Monk, H. J.
Mason, B. G.
Meakin, A. G.
Medland, A. S.
Moore, L. G.
Morris, P. J.
Moss, E.
Maher, W.
Mutton, J. W. H.
Melsom, K. L.
Miles, W. H.
Mayhew, W. H.
Marsh, W. A.
Morris, J. F.
Mead, F. E.
Miller, F.
McKimm, T. G.
McClellan, W.
Mason, A. E.
Morelli, E.
Mather, J. H.

Metcalfe, E.
McGreevy, J.
Metherell, L. A.
Murrell, M. J.
Moseley, H. F.
Monk, W. W.
Munday, A. S.
Munro, C. A.
Morgan, C. L.
McDowall, A. C.
Morgan, G.
McFadden, R. E.
Morris, A. C.
Mack, W. J.
Milward, J. J. W.
Matthews, A.
Mills, W.
Miller, A. G.
Mills, S. J.
Matthews, W. E.
Major, T.
Martin, W. E.
Mitchell, J. H.
Moore, F. W.
Morley, J.
Mills, A. W.
Maundrell, T. J.
Maxwell, J. E. H.
Monckton, R.
Morgan, I. C.
Mead, F. G.
Markham, F.
Moyle, W. E. C.
Marshall, F. H.
McKinley, C.
McInery, M. P.
Marshall, H. L.
Meldrum, J. W.
Muncastor, W. M.
Moore, H. S.
Mann, E.
Moyce, L. J.
Masters, E. H.
Musk, V. F.
Manwaring, A. H.
Marley, J. O.
Munday, H.

Meatyard, F. R.
Martin, F.
Morteo, R. J. P.
Martin, C.
Munday, E. T.
May, G. W.
McGinn, W.
Moss, F. W.
May, E. C.
Mumford, W. V.
Moulder, H. A. E.
Myatt, A. S.
Minton, F. S.
Madyon, C. F.
Musk, S. E.
Morley, E. G.
Mabb, W. J.
Mison, H. F.
Marshall, H. P.
Moxham, A. J.
Mass, G. F.
Morgan, H. C.
Maidwell, G. H.
Marshall, T.
Maybee, H. J.
Medowell, A. E. W.
Mills, F. H.
Maugham, F. C.
Morris, S. O.
Matthews, S. F.
Morton, F. E.
Mather, S. J.
McGhee, J. W.
Martin, W. A.
McKinstrey, G.
Mitchell, F. J.
Manwood, V. E. A.
McLaren, E. R.
Marchant, C. G.
Masterton, W.
McKay, H. G.
Masters, P. E.
Matthews, D. E.
Mellish, F. W.
Mackie, D. J.
Morris, H.
Minshull, C. F.

Mountford,
　　　J. E. L.
Merry, J.
May, H. C.
Marshall, J. T.
Mason, T.
Mahony, P. J.
Martin, G.
Merricks, C. G.
Mills, C.
Mirrow, G. H.
Motts, C, H.
Morris, J.
McKinnon, J.
Mummery, F. J.
Masten, J.
McKinnon, J. F.
Macken, S. J.
Milne, D. F.
Mellor, A.
Morgan, C. L.
Macmillan, G. C.
Marsh, R.
Moyse, C. D.
Millington, J.
Milton, H. W.
McCulloch,
　　　G. McN.
Mann, F. G.
Mew, E. H.
Miles, A. F. J.
Macdonald, D. G.
McGrath, J. C.
Mitchell, R. A.
Mason, W. C.
Macken, F. C.
McCraith, L. N.
Morgan, S.
Murray, E. W.
Martin, S.
Maybank, D. R.
Matthews, C. V.
Morris, G. F.
Milton, C. H.
Maynard, L. A.
Mist, G. J.
Moore, R. D.

Martin, F. J.
Marchese, E.
Maunder, G. S.
Milborne, A. R.
Morris, J. H.
Morgan, R.
Marchant, H. T.
Milner, J. C.
Meams, W. E.
Martin, B. G.
Marshall, L.
Marshall, R. H.
Milnes, G. A. F. C.
Matthews, L. G. A
Moody, G. S.
Machin, L.
Markey, S. L.
Moore, A.
Mullins, D. C.
Mason, E. G.
Morton, L.
McWilham,
　　　W. D. N.
McArdell, J. H.
McDonald, G. P.
Meloy, F. L.
Miller, C. H. M.
Mennie, J.
Mills, T. G. P.
Mason, G. F.
Mason, S. H.
Moreton, H. B.
Macrae, A. C.
Monteath, R. B.
Matheson, F. E.
Mead, A. J.
Matthews, C.
Mills, E.
Moulding, T. G. R.
Mason, C. C. W.
Millward, W.
Miller, R. B.
Morris, R. C.
Martin, A. H.
Mabey, R. V.
Mills, G. J.
Matchin, A. W.

McNulty, J.
McDuell, J.
Morgan, H. W.
Mancey, G. O. J.
Madden, J.
McIntyre, G. W.
Maher, H.
Manners, G. D.
Moore, E. F. S.
McDermott, C. C.
Molyneux, M. W.
Maidment, W. C.
Morgan, A. E.
Morgan, W. J.
Matthews, W. E.
Morley, N.
Marsham, W. F.
Miller, W. H.
McFarlarlane, F.
Moore, H. L.
Mothersill, J.
McAdam, R. I.
Morton, E. G. T.
Morton, F. J.
McRorkell, K.
Melville, E. W.
Miller, E. G.
Marshall,
　　　J. A. H. G.
Marsh, L. T.
Male, A. E.
Milnes, H. L.
Marks, L.
Mills, E. F. G.
Middleton, F.
Maryon, H. A.
Meacham, C. G.
Manders, C. J.
Martin, E. A.
Maynard, J. H.
Mitchell, T. H.
Mockford, J. B.
Mason, T. G.
Milne, W.
Mason, J.
MacNicol, A.
Martin, J.

Moss, H. V.
Muller, G. O.
Moyse, S. W.
Moseley, G. E. L.
McVeigh, F.
Monksfield, H. R.
Muddle, C.
Mogridge, A. E.
Meale, H.
Morton-Sale, P. A.
McCool, J.
Morton, J. J.
Moye, F. W.
Morton, H.
Metcalfe, H.
Marshall, A.
McInnes, J.
Meadows, O.
Murton, J.
McCarthy, R.
Matthews, C. A.
Mytton, E. P.
Mason, T. H.
Moore, R. C. H.
Morris, P.
Mann, F. E.
Moore, G. W.
Mayhew, G. F.
Miriam, L.
Mair, F. C.
Mayes, A. J.
Marriott, R. S.
Mendham, G. W.
Macdougall, R. D.
Martin, A. E.
Moore, W.
McCarthy, W.
Morris, J.
Marchant, E. J.
Marshall, J. S.
Milam, A. E. E.
Marsh, R. H.
Mascall, W. H.
N
Naylor, A. J.
Naish, E.
Nicol, R. R.

Nichols, H. W. S.
Nobbs, A. B.
Newman, B. C.
Newling, C. H. Q.
Nichols, F. B.
Nicholas, R. E.
Newman, G. H.
Nicholls, W.
Norris, A. H.
Newson, R. B.
Narraway, S. D. J.
Nichols, S. C.
Nowell, S. A. G.
Newsam, E. S.
Nottingham, E. B.
Nichols, R. W.
Norris, H.
Norman, S. J.
Northam, S.
Nuthall, W. W.
Nawton, F. C.
Newman, H. W.
Norris, W. E.
Nelson, A. H.
Newman, C. J.
Noel, C. A.
Nash, F. H.
Norton, R. D.
Nicholson, A. F.
Nattriss, H. A.
Newman, N. W.
Neill, G. J.
Neall, R. P.
Nash, H. M.
Nixon, F. H.
Nelson, G. W.
Newman, P. J.
Nightingale, W. F.
Nicholas, J. H.
Neave, L. R.
Norman, F. L.
Neagle, J.
Newman, S. R.
Neate, F. C.
Norman, H. M.
Norton, W. N.
Nash, H. T.

Nethersole, J. M.
Neale, A. S. R.
Nicholls, F. J. C.
Nunn, C. F.
Norman, S. J.
Nave, H. J.
Noble, E. E.
Neill, J. J.
Nash, I. J.
Nicholls, H. W.
Nalson, A.
Neale, H.
Newman, W. W.
Nicholson, W. D.
Nicholass, E. W.
Nutton, H. E.
Newey, H.
Norris, W. T.
Newell, F.
Nixon, J. H.
Nicholls, R. W.
Needham, S. G.
Nye, P. T. C.
Nicholass, J. H.
Nicholson, T. L. E.
Newson, J. J.
Noyce, W. J.
Norris, E.
Nicoll, W. M.
Nathan, N.
Norgrove, J. W.
Nicholls, P. E.
Norman, W. H.
Newbury, W. S.
Neil, A. Mc
Norton, G.
Newton, W. H.
Newman, C. J. B.
Nelson, H. M.
Nixon, C. H.
Newton, C. D.
Newman, W. N.
Nicholas, R. B.
Needham, C. W.
Nalty, F. J.
Norwood, J. F.
Nutt, E. V.

Nurse, J. A.
Neill, P.
Newton, N.
Norris, H. E.
Newton, F.
Newell, A.
Nash, F. W.
Newman, B. C.
Nurse, F. R.
Newlin, H. W.
Newlin, T. E.
Narraday, E. C.
Norton, H. A.
Newman, C. V.
Norton, G.
Newland, H. G.
North, H.
Newlove, C.
Newby, G. F.
Nash, A. F.
Neale, E.
Nichols, A. H.
North, W. H.
Nesbitt, J. C.
Nott, H. R.
Nutting, E. W.
Nelson, F. K.
Newling, A. H.
Neale, A. T.
Nisbet, T. Y.
Nelson, F. W.
Newton, D.
Neave, L. J.
Nockles, W. E.
Neave, J. S.
Nicholas, J. O.
Nunian, W.
Nash, F. G.
Naylor, V. J. R.
Norris, C. H.
Newton, R.
Neves, W. H.
Neale, G. H.
Newton, H. R.
Nuttall, G. C.
Neal, R. T.
Nixon, J.

Norris, J. H.
Nidd, E. H. C.
Nankivell, H. G.
Newman, W. E.
Noise, H. W.
Newland, F. W.
Nathan, P. O.
Neate, A. J.
Neave, W. C.
Nimmo, J.
Nunn, W. V.
Neason, H. A.
Newton, H.
Newton, A. J.
Newstead, J. H.
Nicholls, W. S.
Noble, E. E.
Newman, D. R.
Nicholson, J. G.
Nash, F. R.
Newland, G.
Newman, A. J.
Nevell, L. W.
Northfield, F.
North, J. F.
Newns, E. L. B.
Nobbs, A. C. W.
Nimmo, F. T.
Nesbit, A. W.
Newnham, F. R. C.
Nicholas, W. E. C.
Needham, D. J.
Nelson, G.
Neale, W. L.
Nash, F. G.
Neville, G. E.
Norris, L. A.
Newling, E. F.
Nottage, A.
Nicholls, R. W.
Norwell, T. S.
North, H.
Newnham, H. W.
Newman, W. G.
Newman, L. W. G.
Nevill, E. A.
New, S.

Nash, H. E.
Norris, F. A.
Nunn, F. G.
Nicholls, F. G.
Norman, E. W.

O

Owen, P. S.
Owen, R. C.
O'Neill, J. E.
Oldcorn, H. F.
Orrett, J. S.
Ostler, W. E.
Oldham, W.
Osborn, C. E.
Oldcorn, J. S.
O'Callaghan, D. J.
Oliver, G.
Oldham, H.
Oatway, L. E.
O'Neill, R.
Old, H.
Ogg, G. A.
Othick, N.
Overton, H. A.
Olliff, F. C.
Offwood, H.
Orwin, F. R.
Oakley, G. McD.
O'Reilly, F. J.
O'Halloran, M. A.
Oborn, V. H.
O'Neill, W. J.
Oulds, S. W.
Orr, J. G.
Ogilvie, C. W.
Overall, F. W.
Ormsby, F. A.
Owen, W. C.
O'Callaghan, W.
Oldham, H.
O'Connor, J.
Overbury, C. A.
Organ, W. E.
Oldfield, F. J.
O'Halloran, T. J.
Oesterman, S.
Ottrey, J. A.

Overell, **W. P.**
Orton, C. W.
Oliver, W. E.
Owen, A. T.
Olding, W. G.
Oliver, A. C.
O'Reilly, R, J.
Overall, G. E.
Ogle, E. J.
O'Gorman, O. H.
Osgood, S. L.
Ockenden, H. S.
Orange, R. G.
Oke, W. R.
Olford, F. C.
Osman, G. W.
Osborne, A. E.
Obourne,
        A. R. R. P.
Oliver, A.
Owen, E.
Osborne, A.
Oliver, H. A.
Ottley, W. G.
Osborne, A. W.
Orchard, M.
Ogus, G. H.
Oliver, H.
Oram, R.
O'Grady, A. J.
Overden, H. A.
Osborne, P. R.
Ostler, S. E.
Owen, A. G.
Over, C. W. D.
Olding, F. B.
O'Beirne, J. P.
Ormond, E. F.
O'Flaherty, T.
Overin, R. C.
Owen, G. C.
Osborn, P. A.
Owens, W.
Osborne, F. G.
Osborne, R. H.
O'Shaughnessy,
        T. S.

Offord, F. L. V.
O'Connell, S. J. S.
Oram, J. W.
Owen, L. T.
Oliver, J.
Osborne, E. W.
Oldfield, F, G.
Osborne, G. W.
Oakes, W.
O'Connor, J. M.
Orengo, A. J.
Ovenden, J.
Outram, G. W.
O'Connor, P. A.
Owers, L. F.
Oliver, S. F.
O'Reilly, F. W.
P
Price, C. J.
Pack, A. J.
Pinn, T. S.
Potter, A.
Pritchard, E.
Paterson, H. C. B.
Pickering, J.
Page, C. K.
Prussia, R. C.
Powley, C. E. N.
Perry, H. B.
Phillips, E. E.
Porter, W. J.
Pinchin, W. H.
Proud, H. H.
Plumbley,
        C. F. S.
Penfold, A. G.
Polka, S.
Phillips, R. L.
Pratt, E. C.
Palser, C. J.
Perkins, W. G. A.
Preedy, A. E.
Pratt, J. H.
Pautard, H. P.
Page, H.
Phillips, E. A.
Perks, H. A.

Pearse, E. A.
Pook, W. J.
Pearce, J. S.
Peters, W. C.
Pearce, V. G.
Pulman, R. B.
Perry, E. A.
Paisley, F.
Preston, F. G.
Power, A. G.
Probyn, J.
Phillips, J. E.
Phillips, C. E.
Postle, J. E.
Pattison, S.
Parker, A. E.
Pendry, A. W.
Pitkin, W. S.
Pritchard, G. S.
Payton, C. J.
Page, A.
Pearson, C. E.
Pocock, B. L. E.
Pickering, R. C.
Phillips, R. E.
Pike, H. A.
Payne, V. C. W.
Pearson, T. W.
Pickering, J.
Pfordten, F. von
        der
Price, L. J. J.
Probyn, H. W.
Page, L. A.
Perry, R. A.
Poiter, C. L.
Payne, H. J.
Phillips, W. E.
Porter, A. R.
Phillips, C. V.
Prevost, J. H.
Phillips, F. A.
Parker, C. J.
Pamphilon, R. A.
Pratt, A. E. M.
Portch, W. T.
Pledge, H. W.

Pruden, S. A. H.
Page, D. G.
Pettman, F. L.
Philpott, E. C.
Potter, S. B.
Parker, F. L.
Pickett, G. M.
Pratt, B. A.
Proctor, W. G.
Palmer, R. J.
Patton, H. F.
Payne, F.
Payne, R. A.
Postle, P.
Peel, C. W.
Peacock, E. J.
Powell, A. E.
Parkinson, H. G.
Pendrill, W. G.
Price, H. C.
Phillips, E.
Pounds, H. C. S.
Pennington, E. G.
Porter, F. J.
Park, C. B.
Payne, T.
Page, C. K.
Parish, C. A.
Pratt, F. H.
Parish, H. S.
Pritchard, W. C.
Parr, N. G.
Paton, A.
Pitts, A. W.
Palfreman, A. E.
Percival, B.
Powell, E. C.
Polley, G. E.
Pye, J. W. K.
Porter, A. W.
Plain, F. C.
Plowman, C. W.
Perridge, F.
Platt, A.
Pearson, H. S.
Pearson, R.
Pitt, E.

Pulford, W. E.
Power, G. A. V.
Purper, L. P. V.
Putt, A. E.
Parker, S. V.
Peacock, B. L.
Pullinger, E. L.
Procter, S.
Petty, W.
Powell, F. W.
Pike, C. J.
Platt, F.
Prior, G. W.
Palmer, V. A.
Prior, F. H.
Paulger, L. E.
Powell, S.
Pace, S. R.
Passmore, E.
Pankhurst, A. J.V.
Plastow, H. A.
Palmer, S. E.
Pentecost, H. J.
Prideaux, H. L.
Page, W.
Park, R. T.
Pethurst, C. D.
Pierpoint, G.
Pryor, A. S. A.
Perry, P.
Packham, L. A.
Packham, V. D.
Pearce, S. E.
Prince, W. H.
Peterson, W.
Picton, R. S.
Parker, H. P.
Pullen, A.
Pickin, W. H.
Page, A. E.
Pett, E. J.
Phillips, A. J.
Pickard, G. H.
Pilbrow, J. E.
Pryde, G. B.
Petty, W. E.
Porter, L.

Prophet, C.
Perceval,
  W. V. St. L.
Pickering, E. C.
Page, E. L.
Price, A. J.
Palmer, W. S.
Perry, W. E. N.
Pilgrim, A. J.
Prichard, A. I.
Phillips, E. A.
Parker, A. E.
Pickering, H. W.
Pass, W.
Payter, H. H.
Pearce, H. J.
Pardoe, C. H.
Preece, S.
Praagh, B.
Pashler, P. W.
Playford, E. J.
Page, S. C.
Perry, S.
Pick, B. G.
Pyle, A. F. E.
Page, E. G.
Parker, J. E.
Pain, B. M. F.
Parker, A. W.
Pinder, H. F.
Pile, H. A.
Powell, E.
Powell, J. J.
Parker, F. W.
Parkins, H. A.
Pugsley, C. C.
Palmer, H. W.
Parsons, C. W.
Philips, C. W.
Padgett, G. E.
Preestnall, W.
Parker, B.
Perks, C. T.
Parker, L. S.
Parkes, F.
Parnum, J. H.
Phillips, L. P.

2 G

Phillips, J.
Pepper, C. W.
Parsons, W. H.
Parsonson, J.W. S.
Picking, R. T.
Potts, F.
Palmer, T.
Pates, A.
Pittam, A. P.
Pawson, P.
Parsons, C. J.
Pearson, A. F.
Pennell, F.
Perkins, R. R.
Powell, A. E. J.
Parkin, P. W.
Packett, F. M.
Pink, E. J.
Potter, W. H.
Pomroy, S. L.
Palmer, P. J.
Player, F. W.
Pope, L. F.
Preston, C. E.
Pearcy, A. F.
Pope, H. T.
Powell, W. J.
Penny, H. J.
Price, W. J.
Panting, E. H.
Philpot, H. J.
Parr, A. P.
Pitcher, G. W.
Porter, F. N.
Pook, W.
Parslow, J. W.
Plasom, H. S.
Pitt, E. A.
Payne, C. W. S.
Parrett, A. T.
Pean, P. D. F.
Patrick, M. G.
Preston, H. G.
Peters, W. E.
Pickering, A.
Pollard, W. J.
Pilgrim, K. F.

Palmer, L.
Pledger, N. L.
Prance, W. J. F.
Page, E.
Parr, A. S.
Parker, E. C.
Pickford, S. S.
Pierce, S. J.
Pool, W. E.
Prouting, A. J.
Price, J. C. E.
Powell, F.
Palmer, C. J.
Payne, J. J.
Parmley, B.
Pincham, E. W.
Powell, R.
Pennell, G.
Perkins, C. G. S.
Prudence, W. J.
Pannell, W. G.
Pariente, J.
Pibworth, H. A.
Pike, H. T.
Pratten, T. R.
Pye, C. H.
Pendergast, J. A.
Phillips, F. J.
Potter, E. R.
Parcell, F.
Parrett, H. J.
Pye, C. H.
Peard, H.
Pollard, H. E.
Penton, T. E.
Parfitt, E.
Partridge, B. A.
Pointing, S. J.
Pilkington, G. V.
Penfold, A. H.
Phipps, G. F.
Pailthorpe, D.
Patten, C. C.
Paul, G. E.
Price, H. F.
Pilcher, C. W.
Parr, S.

Preston, C. H.
Payton, C. A.
Pratt, W. C.
Pratt, H. A.
Porritt, J. E.
Parkin, L. C.
Paine, R. C.
Paine, A. S.
Pean, H. D. C.
Pearce, J.
Pope, H. G.
Pratt, R. E.
Prescott, J.
Puxley, R. G.
Payn, E. W.
Parr, S. C. F.
Pugh, E. T.
Pickup, F.
Presswood, F.
Peete, W. J.
Pomroy, A. C.
Poole, J. C.
Plowright, H. C.
Palmer, E. W.
Parkin, W. H.
Papworth, W.
Preece, J. E.
Palmer, F. A.
Purkiss, R.
Parker, L. F.
Pratt, T. E.
Page, R.
Peters, H. R.
Pilcher, A. M.
Picker, H. J.
Pledger, G. E.
Pottle, T. J.
Perry, E. T.
Parsons, A. B.
Payne, H. E.
Pritchard, G. H.
Phasey, A. J. H.
Phillips, C.
Penney, E. J.
Palmer, L. A.
Puddephatt, J. S.
Palmer, J.

Pickford, J.
Pennell, W.
Phillips, O.
Palmer, W. G.
Priest, F. J.
Perry, F. G.
Perry, E.
Parr, C. E.
Prunier, V. A.
Parry, G. A.
Pawsey, R. J.
Parsons, O.
Pocknall, G.
Pearce, A. E.
Pryer, G. A. E.
Parr, W. C.
Pitt, G. E.
Peat, A. G.
Paul, H. B.
Pinchard, A. H. B.
Paley, E. A.
Peake, J.
Parsons, S. W.
Philipowitz, W. C.
Palin, O. E.
Plater, C. H.
Platt, E. J.
Pond, F.
Philpott, G.
Parkinson,
A. R. F.
Pegler, H. W.
Pearce, J. R.
Payne, J. W.
Pankhurst, W.
Purcell, W. F. L.
Peacock, A.
Presland, L. H.
Phillips, D. C. B.
Pratt, H. G.
Pocock, G. W.
Powell, G. L.
Potter, B.
Potter, A.
Powell, F. B.
Perry, F. E.
Pusey, R. E.

Pryke, B.
Pratt, E. C.
Pilgrim, E. V. H.
Price, W. E.
Payne, H.
Purdy, G. H.
Preedy, C. J.
Payne, A. E.
Piggott, E. S.
Pollock, C. S.
Pearce, C. G.
Payne, G. J.
Prideaux, T.
Pope, A. W.
Page, P.
Percival, W. H.
Price, W. J.
Parsons, E. H.
Pannell, C. C.
Parkinson, M.
Pratt, F. G.
Paterson, D.
Phillips, J. A.
Powell, P. L.
Poulter, D. H.
Price, F. G.
Phillips, C.
Panter, F.
Perks, W. E. J.
Peek, A.
Pitt, A. H.
Poulter, L.
Pike, E. E.
Pearce, E.
Plumridge, M. N.
Pearce, C.
Pearson, L. H.
Payne, W.
Parnell, W. T.
Page, W.
Price, F. E.
Petterson, E. J.
Pickford, J. P.
Pannell, J.
Pallister, N. W.
Prosser, J. B.
Phelp, W. E.

Pennyead, H. R.
Peaty, E. G.
Phillips, C. J.
Powell, H. A.
Pooley, R. A.
Pratt, L. C.
Patterson, J.
Prevett, F.
Prince, W. G.
Preece, S. R.
Pepper, R. J.
Pryke, W. R.
Packer, L. J.
Powell, C. J.
Pebody, K.
Parrott, A. W.
Penn, C. C.
Page, H. L.
Parkyn, H. M.
Pearson, H. W.
Perkins, K. S.
Patterson, H.
Please, M.
Pearson, J. H.
Pilkington, O. F.
Pierce, H. E.
Peppard, N. S. F.
Potter, F. E.
Pretty, W. R.
Palmer, C.
Parkin, L. J. L.
Perrin, H.
Press, H. E.
Pollock, J.
Price, H. W. G.
Potter, F.
Parsons, D. P.
Parker, F. H.
Peagam, W. F.
Precious, A. M.
Palmer, A. L.
Peters, W. S.
Proctor, G.
Peake, R. R.
Press, W. C.
Preece, J. E.
Podger, F. H. J.

Peterkin, J. D.
Pearce, H. L.
Phipps, G. E.
Prevot, F. C.
Parker-Ashley,
    A. G. W.
Pearce, S. C.
Potton, S. E.
Packham, W. H.
Patmore, J. A. F.
Phoenix, J. R.
Perry, E. C.
Porter, W. B.
Pausey, F. W.
Price, S. F.
Prada, P. J.
Probyn, W. A. T.
Parker, H. W. J.
Palmer, N. G.
Palfreyman, J.
Padgham, F. W.
Peach, J. H.
Prior, J. R.
Prior, W. P.
Pedgrift, G.
Pope, F. G.
Pope, F. R.
Palmer, W. R. G.
Pepper, E.
Phillips, C. W.
Price, H. S.
Phillips, W. B.
Prisk, S. R.
Philpott, S. E.
Pullen, G. J. J.
Popplesdorff, A.
Price, J. H. M.
Philpot, C. C.
Porter, S. H.
Pearce, J.
Pain, G. P.
Perrett, L. C.
Parker, A. A.
Platts, A.
Pyke, T. L.
Parry, T. E.
Palfrey, P. C.

Powell, F. W.
Pateman, H.
Parker, L. C.
Phillips, A. R.
Palmer, F. G.
Povey, J. W.
Pritchard, B. R.
Pearson, F. C.
Punell, A.
Phillips, L. J.
Pearman, G. R.
Parsons, H. R.
Presland, W. A.
Parsfield, F. S.
Payn, A. W.
Penhallow, C.
Powell, B.
Pentecost, T.
Pearce, C. J.
Pearson, H. E.
Peacock, V. H.
Pike, A. G.
Prall, E. T.
Pettit, R. J.
Preest, J. J.
Page, H. Mc W.
Perry, G. L.
Porter, G. H.
Phelps, W. G.
Prudames, A. E.
Peters, R. E.
Pratt, H. G.
Piper, J. H.
Pope, H. F.
Pascoe, E. J.
Pattman, E.
Pearson, L. F.
Patterson, A. E.
Parker, S.
Parker, H.
Purser, G. H.
Patterson, W. H.
Piddington, A.
Parkinson, C.
Pugh, D.
Potter, T.
Pavie, H.

Porter, H. Mc D.
Peterson, F.
Pigram, F. L.
Page, G. A.
Patten, P. A.
Parker, H. T.
Portnell, C. H.
Pinson, C. H.
Price, H. T.
Polland, F.
Peyton, H. S.
Parkinson, C.
Poole, H.
Presland, J. W.
Powell, B.
Pinhorne, W. F. B.
Porter, J. F.
Putland, R. E.
Pearson, G.
Pottle, H. R.
Page, T. W.
Parker, W. A.
Panter, A. R.
Pick, H. W.
Proctor, F. L.
Parry, R. A.
Panter, A.
Pickering, J. P.
Perry, G. A.
Pankhurst, S. J.
Preston, A. R.
Puckett, C. H.
Pottle, A.
Palmer, T. W. A.
Parker, E.
Petchley, H.
Patrick, F.
Porter, H. E.
Perrin, H.
Pearson, H. W. T.
Poskitt, J. F.
Pither, S. R.
Powell, W.
Parsons, J. A.
Plumridge, A.
Probert, C. H.
Pickett, G.

Plank, C. F.
Pooley, P.
Petford, F. C.
Phillips, A. J.
Payton, E. L.
Paling, T. E.
Parsons, J.

Q

Quinton, C. J.
Quartly, R.
Quick, W. G.
Quinton, R. A.
Quaif, H. A.
Quartermaine, H.
Quarterman, S. T.
Quigley, J.
Quantrill, F. J.
Quiggin, A. H.
Quigley, P. J.
Quinton, B. R. V.

R

Robinson, A.
Rimmington, C. H.
Richardson, E. T.
Robertson, F. C.
Roberts, W. G.
Rolfe, J.
Rich, R.
Roach, M.
Rathbone, L.
Rutledge, J. J.
Roskilly, A.
Rickman, H. E.
Rayner, H. W.
Ruby, A. T.
Rouse, C. V.
Ryan, P.
Ritson, E. H.
Richards, A.
Russell, J.
Randall,
E. F. H. C.
Reardin, L. A.
Radice, F. R.
Reeves, J. W.
Rowles, H. G.
Robson, P. M.

Russell, A. H.
Ramsey, D. E.
Rowe, A. W.
Roberts, J. W.
Rogers, A. B.
Rayner, L. S. P. H.
Rothfield, A.
Roberts, R.
Ribbons, J. E.
Rudkins, S. J.
Riddle, H. B.
Richardson, W. J.
Ruber, E. B.
Randolph, J. H.
Robinson, E.
Royston, H.
Rothman, W.
Reed, G. F.
Royal, A. H. W.
Randle, W. E.
Redgrave, A.
Rich, R. R.
Rudd, R. G.
Regensburg, L. A.
(alias Ray, L. R.)
Robinson, E.
Rapps, F. T.
Ridout, A. E.
Reed, J. H. W.
Richardson, L. J.
Rushman, G. W.
Roberts, H. L.
Reay, C. R.
Richardson, H. H.
Robson, H. S.
Rose, A. G.
Rees, E. D.
Rickard, R. Y.
Ridout, G. S.
Rogers, A. M.
Rose, J. H.
Reader, J.
Riding, E. J.
Richardson, J. E.
Redman, W. T.
Randall, F. H.
Robb, A. J.

Roberts, A.
Roberts, B.
Roddis, H. A.
Rumsey, G. O.
Rayment, F. J. H.
Reed, P. A.
Richardson, H. E.
Robinson, B. H.
Robinson, C. H.
Robinson, F. M.
Rule, A. G.
Roessti, F. J.
Richardson, F. M.
Read, L. J.
Redding, P. J.
Roeber, W. C. T.
Robinson, O. B.
Ritchings,
A. A. W.
Roberts, J. F.
Ramsay, A. A. W.
Reeks, P. E.
Robinson, A. J.
Reddy, V. S. F.
Richardson, G. W.
Reeves, W. J.
Rendell, H. O. W.
Ramsay, R.
Raggett, G. C.
Rotherham, A.
Rogers, J. A.
Reynolds, J. F. G.
Roberts, B. J.
Reader, B. A.
Radcliffe, J. E.
Ridden, B.
Riseborough, C.
Rondeau, G. O. O.
Ralph, J. A. A.
Reeve, E. A.
Richards, H. E.
Riley, J. A.
Robinson, E. J.
Roxbrough, H. R.
Roser, F. C.
Riley, G. F.
Rooth, L. A.

Redman, D. F.
Roffey, W. J.
Randell, H.
Rayner, M. A.
Rice, H. A.
Rowlands, D. D.
Rogers, J. L.
Rowe, H. J. P.
Roylance, W. G.
Reddick, L.
Robbins, W. G.
Rye, F.
Richardson, A. N.
Roberts, J.
Rewcastle, G. B.
Read, H. H.
Roberts, E. E.
Rostron, J.
Russell, E. F. R.
Rodnight, W. B.
Roworth, F. E.
Reid, E. M.
Rees, H. G.
Robins, A. L.
Rossiter, B.
Radford, J. F.
Richards, B.
Robson, R. E.
Rowthorn, S.
Ross, W. N.
Raven, A.
Roden, A. D.
Rowe, G. H.
Roy, A.
Rudiger, C. E.
Rayner, M. L.
Reynolds, E. R. G.
Riches, R.
Roberts, R. P.
Ross, A. A.
Richards, F. H.
Roper, W. A.
Rogers, E. A.
Roberts, D. H.
Rice, P. H.
Radmore, H. E.
Robinson, D.

Richardson, A. W.
Robathan, L.
Reardon, E. L.
Richardson, F. J.
Reeve, S. A.
Reeve, E. L.
Roberts, H.
Read, F. D.
Reich, N. W.
Roberts, J.
Reed, J. R.
Rutter, W. R.
Redhead, St. G.
Reis, V. C.
Rank, S.
Randolph-Brooker
        S. T.
Russell, A. W.
Ricker, C. F.
Rowe, A. H.
Rhodes, P. L.
Ross, J. G.
Richardson, F.
Ransley, H. H.
Russell, P. S.
Royston, T. A.
Ricketts, F. E.
Rowland, A. A.
Rossiter, W. R.
Russell, J. C.
Robinson, A. C.
Ralph, F. G.
Roberts, R. A.
Reeder, J. N.
Ridley, A. L.
Richards, H. R.
Rogers, F. N.
Rogers, P. D.
Ray, J. S.
Ramsden, S.
Roper, B. F. H.
Roberts, D.
Ryan, J. F.
Rolfe, W. W.
Rooke, A. S.
Roope, W. S.
Richardson, F. F.

Rowland, G. W.
Reid, E.
Reid, H. J.
Reid, R. H.
Rose, W. T.
Rowles, J. R.
Rates, H. G. G.
Rigden, S.
Rogers, M. P.
Rowland, R. J.
Reddington, B. J.
Reed, T.
Rocke, H. A.
Raper, W. H.
Richards, N. J. P.
Rogers, A. H.
Rogers, A. B.
Roberts, C.
Rilstone, R.
Roberts, F. L.
Robinson, B.
Rolfe, H. W.
Russell, W.
Ralph, L. W. H.
Rose, W.
Rabin, H.
Rourke, A. E.
Round, G. A.
Rogers, A. W.
Rawlinson, F.
Rouse, F. H. S.
Ripley, W. W.
Rasberry, J.
Reeves, B. G.
Russell, F.
Richardson, B. E.
Redworth, J.
Rider, E. A.
Reid, E. C.
Reynolds, L.
Robeson, H. S.
Reece, J. W.
Robbins, W.
Ryder, C. A.
Richardson, W. J.
Reeves, H.
Roberts, V. B.

Ridley, J.
Russell, W. A.
Reed, G. C.
Robinson, T. G.
Risby, G.
Ramsay, J. H.
Ravenhill, W. C.
Ruter, L.
Robinson, J. A.
Rayner, F.
Rowbottom, F. J.
Rudland, S.
Rushton, W. N.
Rosser, R. W. R.
Ritchie, T. S.
Riddle, H. E.
Rolfe, R. J. G.
Rogers, H. J.
Ruffell, A. T.
Rees, J. T.
Robinson, G. W.
Rose, L.
Reed, C. W.
Reynolds, G. W.
Ruegg, W. F.
Rhodes, C. T.
Robertson, J.
Reed, A. J.
Richardson, W. H.
Richards, G. H.
Richards, T. D.
Russell, B.
Rodgers, S.
Rickus. L. W. E.
Read, F.
Rosenberg, H.
Rose, N. A.
Richardson, R.
Robinson, H. R.
Roberts, F. C.
Ridgway, R.
Ricketts, E. C.
Reynolds, G. H.
Robinson, R.
Renshaw, A. F.
Reynolds, J. N. K.
Rogers, H.

Robbins, E. W.
Robertson,
       D. E. C.
Rulf, A. B.
Roeper, E. F.
Roberts, H. O.
Reeve, W. E.
Reid, J. B.
Rake, G. P.
Rushman, W. F.
Risby, A. C.
Redman, F. H. R.
Rochester, W.
Rickaby, G.
Rowe, W. J.
Roddick, R. J.
Ritchie, A.
Retallack, E. H. S.
Richardson, J.
Rose, H.
Reeve, J. S.
Raybould, H.
Rainger, P. G. J.
Rook, B. W. L.
Richardson, A. B.
Rogers, A. H.
Ryan, F. G.
Richardson, P.
Robertson, C.
Redcliffe, F. R.
Reekie, W. J.
Rowe, E. G.
Rumbold, D. J.
Robinson, E. W.
Reynolds, C. F.
Richardson, J. O.
Rice, R.
Roper, R. J.
Robson, R. K.
Rhodes, A.
Robinson, H. M.
Richards, E. C.
Ragge, J. Y.
Robinson, H. L.
Ruxton, A. J.
Robinson, N.
Rabbinowicz, E.

Robson, A.
Rees, J. P.
Rooms, A. J.
Robinson, T. W.
Read, L.
Richards, A.
Robins, E. H.
Reeve, E. G.
Rutter, R.
Richards, A.
Reeves, A. J.
Rudge, J. W. J.
Rutland, L. G.
Rich, P. J. N.
Royal, R.
Roberts, A. T.
Read, F. H.
Rowley, E. C.
Robinson, H. R.
Robinson, F. T.
Rowswell, E. V.
Reid, A. J.
Rudkin, C. A.
Ramsay, A. C.
Ralston, G. A.
Randall, G. J.
Reed, L.
Reynolds, S. C.
Reynolds, H. A.
Rushbrook, A.
Russell, P. A.
Rice, C. A.
Rickard, S. H. A.
Robinson, R. C.
Robinson, G. H.
Reeve, A.
Rossiter, A. L.
Robinson, A. V.
Root, A. J.
Richards, C. F.
Rippin, H. G. C.
Ryan, A. H.
Reason, J. W.
Roberts, H. S.
Robertson, J. F.
Reece, S. H.
Russell, H. A.

Rackley, E. J.
Roberts, C. T.
Richards, D. M.
Rogers, R.
Rees, L. W.
Reeves, T. J.
Russell, T.
Rogers, J. F.
Russell, A. W.
Rogers, J. F.
Russell, A. W.
Ray, E. E.
Rudkin, R. J.
Roberts, A.
Rowell, W. A.
Reynolds, A.
Rinett, H. G.
Roddick, J. G. S.
Rogers, E. R.
Raven, S. E.
Reed, G. F.
Read, J. W.
Ratcliffe, J.
Rowland, F. W.
Regan, R. A.
Reynolds, S. W.
Robey, A. J.
Robson, R. Y.
Reeves, J.
Reis, C. A.
Robinson, C. F.
Robinson, E. L.
Rose, W. J.
Rose, L. F.
Rice, J. J.
Reach, C. T.
Read, H. E.
Ringham, J. W.
Rae, R.
Royce, J.
Roberts, W. G.
Russell, A. J.
Russell, C. F.
Rogers, A. W.
Rush, P. S.
Reuss, W. H.
Redhouse, H. A.

Richards, P. C.
Robertson, A. E. A.
Ransley, E. W.
Roebuck, G.
Rowe, H. M.
Richardson, R. J.
Reeves, J.
Riding, J.
Reed, S. A.
Reed, H.
Rimmer, P.
S
Searle, S. J.
Smith, F. J.
Smith, J.
Snell, W. J.
Swabey, L. A. W.
Simpson, G.
Scar, G. S.
Seys, S. A.
Stratton, C. O.
Smith, F. M.
Stoaker, H.
Stannard, F. W.
Spicer, C. S.
Squire, R. H.
Sharratt, L. H.
Somers, V. H.
Sergent, A. G.
Sarll, A. B. C.
Syme, W.
Smith, H. L.
Shanahan, J. E.
Shanahan, W. D.
Suckling, P. H.
Sheldon, S. W.
Smith, H. S.
Smith, E. S.
Smith, C.
Sale, J. C.
Simpson, G.
Skertchley, M. B.
Stokes, W. J.
Shave, S. O.
Scott, A. E.
Slade, C.

Sayers, C. W.
Slater, W. S.
Syrad, H. A.
Smith, W. J.
Sergeant, H. V.
Schneider, C. M.
Sanderson, W. K.
Shorter, J. F.
Sugars, R. C.
Strong, P. G. L.
Sergeant, C. L.
Sebborn, H. P.
Spencer, W. H. R.
Strafford, L. G.
Shepherd, R. O.
Smith, H. L.
Squires, E. C.
Symons, A.
Sparkes, A. S.
Stangroom, W. H.
Selby, A. C.
Scott, H. J.
Smith, C. G. S.
Smith, C. C. G.
Stafford, H. C.
Starling, S. E. R.
Slade, P. G.
Stebbing, G. B.
Stevenson, W. R.
Snelling, F. W.
Skinner, H. C.
Salkeld, D.
Skillern, W. G.
Stewart, J. C.
Shirer, F. G.
Sartain, A. J.
Stevens, A. E.
Seton, S. J.
Shipton, B. A.
Stewart, E. J.
Skawyer, W. J.
Sharp, P. M.
Shorey, F. K.
Stanbrook, F.
Shearne, F. E. C.
Staines, S.
Smith, W. E.

Spinks, V. A.
Scadeng, W.
Swain, J. H.
Samuels, P. J.
Scott, B. C.
Salter, J. W.
Stone, R. W. S.
Schleffer, H. A.
Sparge, E.
Stone, C. H.
Soal, E. W.
Scott, F. T.
Smith, F. C.
Salmon, H.
Sweet, R. G. I.
Speight, F. O.
Scarth, G. S.
Stratton, F. J.
Scott, E. C. H.
Smith, L. H. G.
Softley, R. W.
Shurley, H. D.
Simpson, J.
Smith, F. C.
Smith, J. D.
Snellgrove, A. E.
Stebbings, J. K.
Strong, L. G.
Shellard, J. G.
Smith, H. J.
Sutcliffe, H. P.
Seville, K. A.
Sheppard, F. C.
Stanley, M. W.
Stenning, C. H.
Sease, G. W.
Sutherland, K. C.
Shackle, E. H.
Shackle, W.
Skinner, F. J.
Smith, F. R.
Stevens, C. G. B.
Stevens, R. H.
Skerrett, H. R.
Scrimshaw, A. L.
Shanks, D. B.
Smith, A.

Smith, F. M.
Shepherd, H. A.
Sidwell, E.
Snawdon, F. W.
Steele, H. J.
Stevens, H. J. V.
Smedley, H. L.
Sharp, A. M.
Sprigge, F. H.
Slee, A. G.
Stratford, A. B.
Scammell, P.
Steane, P. H.
Studd, E. P. H.
Shaw, F. V.
Smith, R. S.
Stranson, W. R.
Stribling, G. H.
Saunders, G.
Step, G. E.
Schutz, W. A.
Sormani, P.
Spencer, H. J.
Stevens, J. P.
Smith, L.
Snelling, F. J.
Spielman, I.
Stamfield, E. C. H.
Seymour. H.
Saunders, J. T.
Sutton, A. F.
Stalley, C. B.
Sheppard, W. H.
Saunders, R. F.
Stanton, W. S.
Shirvington, T.
Short, E. W.
Silverstone, A.
Sirett, E. M.
Sloan, T. W.
Smith, B. L.
Smith, C.
Smith, C. F.
Smith, T. A.
Smith, W.
Stafford, C. F.
Stewart, D. A.

Striking, G.
Stone, W. D.
Sutherland, C.
Slade, H. A.
Small, L. J.
Sacksen, H. M.
Scott, G. A.
Smith, F. C.
Smith, H. F.
Slatter, P.
Souter, H.
Stockman, F. W.
Suhr, V. R. I.
Stimson, C. B.
Sarson, A. C.
Smith, W. H.
Shepherd-Jones,
G. S.
Saqui, H.
Sylvester, F.
Scott, L. J.
Stanhope, H. H. S.
Smith, G. B.
Scott, M. A.
Small, J. F.
Singleton, C.
Smith, S. R.
Scagell, M. V.
Steward, A. P.
Smith, S. A.
Sandford, A. G.
Shiels-Bruce, J. H.
Smith, A. E.
Stephenson, J.
Slack, H. B.
Sawyer, A. E.
Smith, H. D.
Sheldrake, A. H.
Slattery, E. C.
Simmons, H.
Stockwell, C. B.
Salter, H. J.
Sheppard, P. G.
Sundquist, J.
Stevens, W.
Sheppard, V. F.
Samman, A. B.

Smith, J. G.
Smith, H. W.
Smith, G. F. J.
Stanley, G.
Seal, F. A.
Stratton, H. C.
Strickland, T. E.
Steer, H.
Smith, W. T.
Shaddick, H.
Stow, F. W.
Sherlock, E. G.
Smith, G. T.
Scammen, V.
Stadden, F. F.
Seacombe, A. E.
Seacombe, S. J.
Smith, W. H.
Symes, A. R. T.
Skertchley, C.
Smith, S. E.
Seymour, C.
Shipp, S. G.
Stokes, E. C.
Smith, C. F.
Stragnell, E.
Sinfield, R. F.
Stevens, R. A.
Stacey, A. E.
Savell, G. W. H.
Smith, J. F. W.
Such, A.
Sanderson, C. A.
Sinclair, E. H.
Snelling, T. A.
Spurgeon, K. J.
Stockwell, H. S.
Smith, N. G.
Simpson, G. H.
Sawyer, W.
Shepherd, A.
Simmons, H.
Scott, F. W.
Spurge, C. H.
Steele, P. L.
Streeter, G. A.
Sears, H. F.

Simpson, A.
Stevens, J. S. R.
Stoakes, A.
Stodart, F. A. G.
Swiney, L. C.
Sisley, G. O.
Smith, G.
Saban, G. H.
Schank, H.
Soar, F. L.
Salmons, W. T.
Saltmarsh, O. N.
Sherlock, C. A.
Shirley, R.
Stringer, J. W. T.
Summers, J. A.
Shaw, L. F. L.
Smeed, E. J.
Stotesbury, P.
Stent, F. R.
Sharp, W. F.
Spence, J. F.
Simmons, L.
Smith, W. A.
Stemp, A.
Stewart, D.
Simmonds, H. R.
Smith, G.
Scannell, B.
Sanders, A. P.
Silcox, E.
Simms, C. R.
Stacey, E. J.
Simmons, T. H.
Smith, C.
Strong, A.
Stebbings,
H. K. J.
Stenning, A. G.
Shackleford, W. A.
Stevens, A.
Smith, G. H.
Sabey, E. L. S.
Smith, H. A.
Sherman, G. E.
Staples, G. W. M.
Stine, E. W.

Sanderson, C. J.
Seale, C. G.
Stringer, L. J.
Savage, F.
Sherman, F. W. R.
Smith, W. J.
Stacey, F.
Stone, H. R.
Skitter, H. J.
Scott, S.
Sutherland, A. W.
Shanahan, G. B.
Smee, T. F.
Saunders, S. T.
Streker, W. R.
Scruby, A. E.
Snellgrove, A. E.
Stanley, A. E.
Stone, G. A.
Stanfield, G. F.
Small, A.
Senior, R. H.
Shelton, G. F.
Skipper, E.
Stockwell, C. F.
Sympson, F. R.
Summerhayes,
T. E.
Salmond, A.
Sheldrake, P.
Scott, H. M.
Smith, A. R.
Shurrock, A. V.
Sharp, G. B.
Smith, S. W. R.
Spillman, F. W.
Surridge, A. J.
Smithers, W. F.
Sackett, E. L.
Sell, C. W.
Skidmore, H. J.
Sell, F. W.
Sparrow, H. R.
Sharp, N. H.
Stockwell, W. S.
Snell, H. J.
Smart, R. E.

Street, B. O.
Samuels, G. M.
Stevens, W.
Sheppard, R. T.
Sankey, A. L.
Saville, S. W.
Sculpher, J. M.
Selby, W. J. H.
Shears, H.
Smith, G. E.
Strudman, A. V.
Swabey, S. B.
Sutton, J. E.
Stringer, H.
Speakman,
      W. T. J.
Saunders, F. J. R.
Scott, J.
Simpson, W.
Snell, E.
Swinson, G. W.
Small, J. A.
Smith, A. H.
Southwood,
      V. P. E.
Saunders, H.
Stonham, H. W.
Songer, E.
Sullivan, G.
Somerville, W. E.
Skipworth, F. G.
Sparks, A.
Swann, N. L.
Simons, G. D.
Shirley, A. J.
Steed, W. W.
Smith, E. A.
Staines, E. R. A.
Stillman, G. H.
Smith, W. E.
Stark, F. C.
Smith, E. G.
Stephenson, J. H.
Smith, F. W. J.
Spencer, R. E.
Steed, F.
Smith, C.

Sherwood, F. T.
Souter, A.
Steward, J. J.
Spicer, D. P. R.
Swallow, F. B.
Sharpe, J. H.
Sawtell, G. K.
Somper, N. M.
Season, G. R.
Smith, S. J.
Shearmen, C. R.
Soper, W. E.
Sarbutt, B. A. W.
Shirley, E. J.
Struckett, W. C.
Spalding, E. W.
Stokes, L. R.
Seale, B. T.
Smith, W. B.
Spurdens, F. W.
Stebbings,
      F. A. C.
Smith, S. C.
Sutherland,-J.
Schen, R. Z.
Stepto, C. F.
Schwab, A. E.
Sexton, F. J.
Surrey, W.
Slatter, A. C.
Sabourin, J. W. R.
Sutor, F. P.
Scott, E. D.
Smart, R. W.
Sanger, F. W.
Simmons, P.
Salisbury, E. W.
Stevens, J. S.
Sewell, S. F.
Sweet, F. W. C.
Spencer, J. C. M.
Shrimsky, I.
Stevens, W. H. R.
Schineberg, N.
Stansbridge, **A. G.**
Studd, G. D.
Smith, R. W.

Smith, A. W.
Stacey, E. C.
Stafford, J. E.
Snow, B.
Swabey, A. G.
Speed, H.
Snelling, W.
Strachan, K. A.
Spriggs, F. W.
Skinner, C. F.
Shearsky, A. E.
Scheidigger, E. R.
Schooling, G. R.
Speichley, F.
Stannard, A. E.
Smith, C. A.
Smyth, L. J.
Stanley, W. H.
Sanders, A. E.
Smith, J. H.
Shepherd, F. C.
Sullivan, J.
Scrivener, G.
Sainsbury, G. O.
Salisbury, B.
Salisbury, C. G.
Surman, F. G.
Squire, A. H.
Sexton, R.
Sparham, A. G.
Spencer, C. F.
Short, F.
Sandes, I.
Sole, C. G.
Savage, G. C.
Sweet, R. J. G.
Smith, E. J.
Serle, C. W.
Spackman, H. J.
Scott, H.
Scouller, C. J.
Sealey, A. H.
Smith, S. J.
Stroud, C. O.
Spencer, F.
Stokes, C. B.
Smart, C.

Smith, S. G.
Spilman, J. H.
Staples, A. A.
Simpson, W. H.
Stredwick, C. A.
Saddington, H. H.
Sherman, F. A.
Smith, C.
Shennon, J.
Selley, A. C.
Stephens, G.
Strohmenger,
        F. J.
Snell, C. D.
Scotchbrook, E.
Simons, F. T.
Souter, P.
Sharp, H. F.
Stacey, S. A.
Shatwell, W.
Seddon, J. U.
Saipe, L.
Stoneham, C. H.
Spring, W. M.
Spinn, S. G.
Simmonds, P.
Satow, J. L.
Sims, H. J.
Scotchmer, E. F.
Smith, A. R. T.
Sanson, A.
Sharp, H. C.
Suffell, F. J.
Sainty, D.
Smith, C.
Stair, F. H.
Souter, G. B. M.
Stacey, C. B.
Sells, R. W.
Severs, A. R.
Shelley, S. A.
Stott, C. R.
Sopp, H.
Sillitoe, S. A.
Spooner, J. C.
Smith, F. W.
Smith, H. C.

Sharp, T. P.
Smith, H. T.
Skinner, F. C.
Solomon, N.
Seymour, H. A.
Sutherland, J.
Shaw, E. C. H.
Simmond, G. A.
Sirett, M. C.
Staines, W. E.
Smith, C. H. K.
Savage, H. G.
Smith, A.
Stray, P. H. G.
Smith, J.
Scott, J. N.
Short, A. E.
Saunders,
        H. J. H.
Straker, H.
Snell, W. J.
Scott, G. F.
Sanders, E. R.
Stevens, A. G.
Solomon, J. J.
Strike, J. H.
Swaite, H. H.
Salmon, B.
Still, S.
Steel, J.
Slade, A.
Snooker, R. H.
Spicer, F.
Setchfield, H.
Steward, B. J.
Snellgrove, H.
Scott, C.
Stretch, J. H. T.
Sweet, A. E.
Shea, J.
Stimpson, S. A.
Stean, W.
Sayers, J.
Savell, J. W.
Sewell, F. C.
Smart, G. H. R.
Stratford, A.

Smith, H. F.
Steward, J. G.
Seib, P. C.
Sargent, A. W.
Strean, P. C.
Sabin, A. J.
Saunders, A. T.
Simmonds,
        H. F. R.
Spencer, E. S.
Smith, P. C.
Storry, A.
Sturgeon, R. R.
Smith, W. I.
Sewell, R. V.
Shaw, H. W.
Smith, H. B.
Smith, S.
Steer, A. J.
Sinclair, P.
Silk, E. T.
Smith, S. W.
Smart, H. H.
Schroder, P. R.
Sanders, S. A.
Smith, A. F. P.
Smith, F. J. E.
Sorzans, L.
Smith, J. G.
Saberton, B. G.
Stevens, C.
Skilton, C. T.
Scott, W. D.
Swaine, A. V. A.
Smith, R. D.
Stuart, E. C.
Smith, D. H.
Smith, W. E.
Sutton, F.
Swanson, J. S.
Swell, E. C.
Soutter, F. J.
Sherwood, R. S.
Shears, E. W.
Sullivan, J.
Scott, E. A.
Spicer, L. E.

Smyth, R. H.
Smith, G. W.
Sheppard, H. T.
Sewell, E. T.
Stevenson, W. H.
Sutton, H. A.
Steward, G. E.
Stevens, H. R.
Scott, S. F.
Smith, S. J.
Simpson, R.
Sole, C. W.
Shuter, A. A.
Spicer, W. A. R.
Shute, G. A.
Smith, E. C.
Saunders, W. J.
Spencer, E. C.
Smith, H. G.
Smethurst, H.
Simpson, F.
Scotcher, G. O. S.
Scotter, E. V.
Staniland, H. R.
Stuchbery, E. F.
Sendell, A. W.
Sweetenburgh, W. E.
Stearman, H. C.
Stratton, W. T.
Snow, R. P.
Smith, F. E.
Sawyer, L. P.
Scruby, A, E.
Stride, W. E.
Softly, B. S.
Stroud, R. P.
Sax, C. W.
Stewart, C.
Smith, A. V.
Sturman, F.
Savory, C. J.
Schofield, R. F. A;
Shephard, D. A.
Shephard, W. H.
Simmons, W. T.
Stripp, H. F. E.

Stuart, C. A.
Simpson, A.
Seeley, G. J.
Stanley, C. G.
Springham, C. J.
Seamer, A. S.
Swyer, R.
Summers, S. G.
Shales, K. H.
Sells, G. S.
Sims, R. M.
Starkings, P. L.
Smith, G.
Smith, C. G.
Scott, C. R.
Scott, A. E.
Smith, D.
Sharman, V. G.
Sly, F. G. E.
Salmon, C. T.
Stephenson, P. E.
Spence, J. G.
Start, C. A.
Simpson, A. L.
Sanders, W. M.
Sexton, P. C.
Smart, F. P.
Sewell, J.
Stokes, C. J.
Smith, C. W.
Sparshott, H. L.
Sinnott, R. E.
Sheldrake, R. F.
Spandler, T. R.
Smith, W.
Spence, A. M.
Summers, J. N.
Sleep, H.
Stanlake, S. A.
Smeaton, J. P.
Swain, H.
Schofield, J. A.
Stockings, E. C.
Sangway, H. W.
Smith, R. B.
Scott, L.
Sparks, N. I.

Shaw, T.
Stevenson, S.
Sutton, W. G.
Saxelby, F. M.
Snook, G.
Stratt, C. B.
Smeeton, B. R.
Scott, J.
Smethurst, H. C.
Skrimshire, F. A.
Stone, S. A.
Smith, L. J. W.
Saywood, A.
Snow, C. F.
Savage, A. W. H.
Smith, J.
Simms, J. W.
Stevens, S. H.
Sercombe, K. W.
Salisbury, A. G.
Smith, A. G.
Salisbury, A. J.
Smith, F. H.
Stock, W. C.
Salmon, W. J.
Slade, E. J.
Stephenson, A.
Standen, W. G.
Squires, P. A. J.
Skeens, A. V.
Stears, F. D.
Short, F. H.
Sadler, H. H.
Slatter, H.
Shorter, J. F.
Smith, G. E. S.
Stonier, J. L.
Smith, S. F.
Sale, A. A.
Smith, W. L.
Stokes, J. B.
Stone, H. F. W.
Starkey, J. S.
Smith, H. T.
Smethurst, J. H.
Shaw, J.
Sheahan, J. F. R.

Simpkin, A. H.
Saunders, P. A.
Sweet, H. H.
Starling, F. G.
Sabey, E. L. S.
Sherlock, D. J.
Smith, J. C.
Sparks, R. B.
Seldon, M. J.
Symes, V. A. E.
Sugars, R. C.
Swanne, H. A.
Sedgley, W. N.
Silk, H. V.
Savory, A. C.
Saunders, E. C.
Singleton, G. H.
Shaldon, F. W.
Simon, T.
Smith, W. J.
Stapleton, C.
Sledge, F. G. N.
Smith, E. A. W. H.
Shearsmith, E.
Sloan, P.
Sidwick, A. G.
Sparks, C. J.
Stewart, J. O.
Stone, A. G.
Slater, A. J.
Stuart, C. S.
Shearman, R. J.
Spencer, W. J. A.
Smith, A. E.
Stillman, F. G.
Summerfield,
W. W. J.
Spinks, W. W. L.
Sparrow, H. H.
Self, R. H. W.
Smith, A. F.
Sutton, S. R.
Sanders, G. E.
Shanks, J. E.
Shelton, G.
Spiers, W.
Staples, A. H.

Stewart, F. J.
Setterfield, H. E.S.
Smith, E. W.
Smith, W. C. H.
Seymour, A. J.
Simpson, P. S.
Strutt, G. B.
Simpson, F. E. C.
Stockings, J.
Sucker, H. E.
Sangwell, F. C.
Simpson, J. H.
Smith, H.
Stenning, S.
Sennitt, E. W.
Stevens, E. A.
Standivan, E. D.
Stevenson, W. F.
Sandys, T.
Sansum, A. G.
Selwyn, W. H.
Shippey, E.
Skinner, C. G.
Stacey, S. J.
Stokes, E. F.
Solloway, H. E. G.
Starling, W. G.
Sweetingham,
A. H.
Spink, J.
Spooner, H.
Stables, F.
Sheen, P. C.
Shewbridge, J.
Shoobert, G. W.
Smith, A. F.
Shubrook, H. G.
Smith, J. D.
Stump, T. H.
Scott, A. J.
Smith, H.
Stanion, W. J.
Stafford, W. E.
Smedley, W. E.
Sheppard, F. C.
Smith, A. F.
Snow, H. R.

Stringer, C. H.
Strike, F. J.
Shepherd, G.
Smith, S.
Smith, J. W.
Spooner, G.
Sharrod, F.
Summerlin, A.
Spriggs, T.
Stolley, H. C. W.
Smith, J. B.
Smith, J. H.
Suatt, A. R.
Spring, J. T.
Stamper, F. H.
Sales, A. C.
Sanford, W.
Speake, P. W.
Stillwell, T. W.
Sumpter, V. S.
Sampson, C.
Snell, F. J.
Smith, V. B.
Suckling, A. E.
Swatman, R. C.
Sumpter, H.
Start, P. G.
Shanks, D. B.
Smith, S. S.
Simpson, H.
Swain, J.
Smith, W.
Scott, F.
Simpson, A.
Steven, A.
Stewart, E. J.
Smith, H. W.
Simpson, R.
Sharrad, R. A.
Stein, I. A.
Stewart, C. B.
Smith, D. H.
Smith, W.
Sinfield, F. W.
Skinner, A. R. M.
Sykes, F.
Swindells, J.

CIVIL SERVICE RIFLES 479

Stafford, R. A.
Shrubsole, H.
Sutherland, G. W.
Silbold, P. H.
Sica, A.
Simpson, J.
Swan, R. G.
Seabrook, W.
Schwartz, E. J.
Sargant, E.
Shore, S.
Smith, P.
Shepherd, W. J.
Smart, H. E.
Slater, E.
Simmonds, H.
Sharp, H. W.
Shrubb, H. J.
Smith, W.
Sheen, W. J.
Smith, E. W.
Smith, G.
Smith, S. A.
Stansfield, J.
Stockbridge, W.
Smale, J. N.
Seale, A. W. F.
Shead, S. F.
Smith, H.
Snellgrove, C. B.
Stevenson, J. T. B.
Squires, H. T.
Scott, A. J.
Smith, W. G.
Smith, W.
Smith, H. T.
Storey, W. J.
Strangwood, J. W.
Smith, H. J. E.
T
Todd, H. G. W.
Turk, A. S.
Turner, P. W.
Thurston, F. S.
Trinder, G. H.
Templeman, H. V.
Tiplady, F. C.

Turner, J. H.
Trout, F.
Thomas, W. G.
Tolson, R. A.
Tanner, H. J.
Tickle, P. J.
Tinker, J. E. B.
Tomlins, J. E.
Tyrrell, A. J.
Tuffill, H.
Tryance, F. J.
Thomas, J. H.
Turner, W. G.
Taylor, F. E.
Thompson, D.
Tuffill, S.
Tyler, F.
Talbot, B. W.
Tickner, J. C.
Treadwell, A. W. R.
Tuck, W. G. M.
Tacagni, W. J.
Taylor, A. C.
Thorogood, R. W.
Tyson, B. A.
Thomson, G. P.
Tyrrell, H. C.
Treliving, P. T.
Taylor, A. W.
Taplin, W. G.
Tredianick, F. S.
Thompson, R. J.
Tosio, A.
Twentyman, J. J.
Thain, S. G. C.
Thomas, A. G.
Thomas, F. A.
Taylor, C. H.
Trent, H. S.
Tucker, S. C.
Turner, R. A.
Turner, G.
Tristram, E. B.
Tracey, A. J. F.
Tanner, H. J.
Thorburn, I. M.

Thomas, W. G.
Thomas, I. W.
Trembath, C. H.
Thackery, A. A.
Teasdale, E. G.
Thorne, F. O.
Trembath, F. F.
Taylor, H. G. L.
Taylor, J. S.
Tidmarsh, R. D.
Tucker, C. M. A.
Turnbull, J.
Thom, C. W.
Toynton, S.
Theobald, E. M.
Taubman, E. W.
Thirkettle, H. G.
Tristram, F. W.
Taylor, S. C.
Tee, T. J.
Teumer, J.
Thurgood, C. M.
Timber, B. A.
Titherley, A.
Tyler, P. H.
Terry, H. G.
Tardif, V. S. A.
Taylor, S.
Trenaman, S. E.
Tay, E. G.
Thomas, B. L.
Tyler, H. H.
Tipping, F. B.
Tagg, H. J. A.
Turvey, .W H.
Tegetmuir, L.
Thomas, F. W.
Thomson, J. M.
Taylor, J. A.
Topping, N.
Tucker, H. G.
Tarlton, E. H.
Thompson, E. G.
Tait, R. C.
Tate, D. W.
Taylor, P. E.
Thomas, F. R.

Tom, G. A.
Taylor, F. G.
Taylor, B. E.
Turner, J. R.
Tickle, F.
Turner, A. E.
Tong, C. J.
Tyrell, A. J.
Tidbury, J. J.
Twiner, A. S.
Taylor, W. G.
Tennant, H. R.
Tall, C.
Taylor, S. H.
Tarrant, W. L.
Truelove, C. H. A.
Taylor, A. G.
Turner, F.
Taylor, H. G.
Terleski, A. J. S.
Taylor, W. E.
Torckler, W. C.
Treves, H. G.
Tucker, K. D.
Tolley, P. G.
Truelove, F. A.
Todd, **M.** S.
Tannant, G.
Taverner, P. S.
Taylor, W. C.
Thorpe, C. H.
Thompson, H.
Thorpe, A. E.
Thomson, J. R.
Thompson, E. J.
Trenaman, S.
Towers, R. B.
Trimm, J.
Twaits, T.
Troughton, S. H.
Turner, A.
Tippen, C. A.
Thornton, W.
Titcomb, A. T.
Thomas, A. J.
Tarver, L. C.
Thompson, B.

Tanter, F.
Timbrell, W. F.
T r o u n s o n,
    D. J. C.
Tomkins, A. C. B.
Tester, C. J.
Turner, H.
Taylor, F. E.
Tuckett, W. J.
Thomsett, L. L.
Twite, G. J.
Tinham, T. W. G.
Turner, F. G.
Talbot, D.
Taylor, D. M.
Thomas, L. E. O.
Trotman, F. W.
Turville, W. A.
Tress, N. W.
Terry, A.
Thomas, J. G.
Tyndale, W.
Teale, H. C.
Taylor, F. W.
Taylor, S. E.
Thomas, F. A.
Toon, P. W.
Thurlow, S.
Tolhurst, E. H.
Thomas, T.
Thorpe, A. C.
Tomlinson, L.
Tanner, A.
Toynton, H. A.
Turner, H. F.
Tinkler, H. L.
Turland, A.
Thomson, A. J.
Taylor, A. L.
Thomson, J. W.
Tomkins, D. C.
Townsend, J.
Travers, R. J.
Timbs, C. A.
Turner, A. E.
Tatum, G. E.
Thomas, G. E. R.

Tyrell, F. K.
Trotter, D.
Thomas, K. D.
Taylor, G. N.
Talintyre, R. W.
Tadgell, N. R.
Toynton, G. A.
Tobin, H. J.
Taylor, J.
Turner, H. W.
Thatcher, C. A.
Tully, E. R.
T i m p s o n,
    J. H. V.
Tombleson, B.
Tarrant, H. F.
Turnbull, N. G.
Thiall, A.
Turner, J. D.
Taylor, E. C.
Taylor, L. O.
Thorne, R.
Taylor, A. E.
Taylor, A. J.
Thurlow, R. A.
Tilliott, H. L.
Tyler, F. J.
Thomas, W. H.
Trend, J. R.
Trim, S, G.
Taylor, H. N.
Tierney, H. T.
Titherington,
    W. W.
Turner, C. G.
Thompson, A.
Titheradge, H. W.
Talbot, C. H.
Thomas, B.
Trundle, G. W.
Taylor, H. G.
Tierney, P.
Taylor, B.
Turner, S. C.
Thornton, C. E.
Tingay, H. C.
Turner, W. C.

Taperell, V. E.
Thomas, J. E.
Thacker, J. G.
Theobald, C. H.
Tibble, W. S.
Turner, H. S.
Townley, P. R.
Turner, S. B.
Tasker, A.
Thomas, J. P.
Trower, F. W.
Treacher, H.
Thacker, J. D.
Titton, J.
Tozer, A. E.
Taylor, T. W.
Tomes, F. J.
Titterell, F. A.
Tanner, J.
Taylor, L. S.
Turner, J. M.
Twobig, W. W.
Tibbs, W. J.
Thompson, G. A.
Taylor, W.
Tyrie, T. M.
Thompson,
      W. P. G.
Taylor, J. E.
Trigg, F. A.
Toulson, T. J.
Tewson, J. F.
Tatler, C. R.
Thorpe, S. B.
Taylor, L. H.
Townsend, S. J.
Thomas, E.
Taylor, J.
Tibbs, E. E.
Trudgett, J.
Trew, W. E.
Treays, E. A.
Thomas, H. R.
Turner, A.
Turner, A. C.
Turner, B. W.
Tiplady, A. A.

Thorpe, E.
Tull, A. C.
Threader, G. H.
Toy, C. F.
Turner, E. G.
Tattersall, R. C.
Tattersall, P.
Thornton, A.
Turner, R.
Thorpe, S. H.
Thorpe, J. O.
Turton, E.
Turner, H.
Thompson, P. F.
Thomas, F. A.
Thomas, E. J.
Tact, W. S. M.
Turner, E. J.
Tricker, H. A.
Tucker, E.
Taylor, E. T.
Trigg, G. T.
Turner, F. J.
Thompson, W. J.
Tr o u s d a l e,
      A. H. R.
Thomas, W. E. W.
Tarryer, J. G.
Tremey, M.
Teal, A. G.
Teasel, T. R.
Thompson, H. F.
Tomlinson, A.
Tibbles, F. W.
Temple, F. J.
Turk, A. P.
Tate, J. L.
Thomas, A. J.
Taylor, J. H. D.
Thomas, H. H.
Tomsett, P. E.
Taylor, J. A.
Tully, J. B.
Townsend, W. V.
Tautz, H. C.
Tonkyn, F. M.
Tarran, J.

Taylor, C. E.
Turnnidge, G. T.
Tettenbaum, A.
Tanner, M. A.
Thomas, I. R.
Taylor, F.
Taylor, H.
Tidy, A.
Tooley, C. F.
Turner, H. H.
Thompson, A. R.
Taylor, V. C.
Talbot, H. G.
Tate, W.
Taylor, P. P.
Tansley, K. E.
Trotter, J.
Topping, G.
Tonkyn, W. D.
Thompson, F. H.
Telfer, H.
Tootill, J. B.
Timmins, G. F. E.
Talbot, E. S.
Taylor, B.
Tossell, J. W.
Turner, C. E.
Thirtle, J. L.
Thompson, H. P.
Thwaites, R.
Thomas, L. J.
Tucker, A. W.
Teasdale, H.
Taylor, W. C.
Tollyfield, J. W.
Taylor, S. H.
Trebbeck, E. R.
Tustin, G. E.
Thurgood,
      J. W. R.
Turnpenny, L. S.
Turnbull, W. C.
Tanner, B. G.
Turner, H.
Tillson, H. J.
Thompson, H. H.
Tayler, A. H.

2 H

Thompson, J.
Taylor, W.
Townley, P. V.
Thornton, G. S.
Tucker, W. C.
Taylor, P. E.
Tester, F. H.
Thompson, J. A.
Terrett, A.
Thornton, L. S.
Thomas, T.
Thorogood, W. J.
Twitchett, A. R.
Tucker, F. L.
Thomas, J. H.
Thomas, H. W.
Tilley, F. J.
Thomas, A.
Thompson, H.
Tuffs, H. L.
Tapscott, J.
Todd, A. W.
Tilly, J. R.
Twilley, A. G.
Tait, G. J.
Thorn, T. W.
Travell, F. W.
Teahon, E.
Tullett, A. G.
Tyler, W. H. R.
Thomas, W. C.
Titheridge, A. E.
Taylor, W. A. W.
Thomson, H. W.
Tate, W. H.
Taylor, F.
Thrift, H. H.
Tobin, M.
Truslove, A.
Tomlinson, F. W.
Topley, C.
Turnham, B. L.
Tait, S.
Tonge, H.
Tindall, F. C.
Tranter, A. V.
Timben, B. A.

Thompson, C. W.
Thurgood, W. J.
Thaine, F. F.
Thurlow, W. V.
Tizzard, A. J.
Tucker, F. J.
Thompson, A. R.
Turrell, G. L.
Thompson, G. W.
Tolliday, A.
Threadgold, J. G.
Tye, E. C.
Turrell, W.
Tatterton, E.
Todd, H. R.
Tremain, W. C.
Tate, W. H.
Taylor, R.
Turner, N.
Taylor, F. G.
Tribe, J. D.
Titmarsh, G. T.
Turville, R. R.
Trott, O. C.
Tossell, E.
Turnbull, R. A.
Turner, J. H.
Turner, A. S.
Tudball, W. A.

U

Underhill, G.
Ure, J. M.
Usher, C. J.
Underwood, V. J.
Upham, C. D.
Urquhart, J. C.
Underwood, A. E.
Urry, E. C.
Usher, H. B.
Urry, W. E.
Uren, W. F. T.
Upton, J.
Umfreville, W. H.
Underwood, E. G.
Underwood, A.
Upham, G. A.
Underwood, A. T.

Underwood, W. J.
Ubank, T. W. J. F.
Undery, H. E.
Upton, H. G.
Urquhart, J. C.
Upperton, J. G. J.
Utting, R. F.
Upchurch, C. M.
Upham, G. A.

V

Vandepeer, D. E.
Vowles, G.
Vedy, L. G.
Varrall, S. W.
Vickers, W. J.
Van de Ven, L.
Vereker, A. J.
Vernon, P. H.
Vowles, C. H.
Vincent, F. G. V.
Varney, W. V.
Vayro, H.
Ventris, F. W.
Vigurs, A. J.
Vincent, J.
Vinsen, A. G.
Vernham, H. A.
Valda, F.
Vandy, E. J.
Viccars, R. J. W.
Vince, J. C.
Vaughan, A. E.
Vandersluis, W.
Vincent, J. G.
Vinen, G.
Violet, S.
Vales, W. J.
Veysey, J.
Vince, C.
Vanstone, W.
Vorstius, A. G.
Viney, F. W.
Vannozzi, S.
Vickery, G. W.
Voizey, G. A.
Vooght, A. P.
Vinten, J. T.

Vale, G.
Venables, S. W.
Vigurs, A. H. L.
Verrall, L. G.
Vail, F. G.
Verrinder, S. A.
Vernon, E. J.
Vane, J. S.
Vaughan, H. S.
Vanner, A. K.
Verney, G.
Verney, W. A.
Veal, A. E.
Voice, S. J.
Volke, J.
Vaughan, J. W.
Verini, A. L. A.
W
Williams, W. H.
Webber, G. H.
Withers, F. M.
Winter, F. H.
Wood, W. J.
Wass, E. J.
Woodthorpe, H. L.
Wager, H.
Warren, F.
Watkin, A. J.
Walton, A. L.
Whitton, F. W.
Wells, C. E.
Wilson, W. H.
Walker, F. D.
White, A. E. D.
**Westcombe,
G. E. D.**
Willshire, L. A.
Ward, R. S.
Willis, K. M.
Webber, A. J.
Wardley, M. E.
Wallace, J.
Williamson, J.
Ward, P. B.
Wilson, C. E.
Williams, C. A
White, H. E.

Watson, F. E.
Williams, R.
Watson, A. R.
Whiteman, H. R.
Wigney, J.
Wreford, G. M. F.
Wilson, J. R.
Watson, D.
Watkins, H. H.
Wade, W. C.
Wright, G. B.
Warton, H. E. R.
Wilkes, C. E.
Walkiden, A. J.
Ward, W. A.
Walker, T. P.
Wiles, B. C.
Watkins, C. H.
Watts, W. S.
Whitehead, C. J.
Wills, A. E.
Wilson, C. H.
Whitfield, H. B.
Wyld, G.
Wyld, W. F.
Whenman, W. T.
Walker, W. C.
Wheddon, W. H.
Weston, R. C.
Woodford, R. W.
Walker, A.
Williams, L. H. T.
Wright, P.
Winter, L. P.
Wilson, A.
Wilkinson, H. A.
Wales, G.
Webb, W. T.
Williams, D.
Webb, S.
Willis, A. W.
Weeks, E. G.
Walker, W. J. H.
Whitaker, T. J.
Walder, W. J.
Walsh, E. G.
White, C. B.

Walkey, E. D.
Whenman, L. C. G.
Wright, T. S.
Woods, F. G.
Wright, H. F.
Webster, W.
Ward, G. V.
West, S. G.
Wright, H. R.
Wood, E. C.
Wheeler, F. H.
Westrop, S. B.
West, E. C.
West, J. S.
Wheeler, C.
Walker, D. M.
West, C. B.
Woolley, W.
Wellstead, P. T.
Wagstaff, F. H.
Wright, W. S.
White, S. E.
White, P. S.
Williams, P. B.
Watts, P. A.
Webber, H.
Whittington, A. G.
Williams, T.
Webb, H. W.
Williams, F. H.
Whittingham, M.
Wadland, W. R.
Wakelin, S. J.
Wainwright, M.
Walker, H.
Warr, E. C.
Wells, W. L.
Whittington, A .L.
Wiles, J. W.
Winks, H. H.
Wrangham, T. F.
Wallace, C. P.
Williams, J. W.
Williamson, A. C.
Windeler, C. F.
Winfield, R. J.
Winter, R. B.

2 I

Witney, G.
Woodford, R. W.
Wootton, J. L.
Whatmore, D. G.
Watson, W. R.
Wakefield, E. E.
Wolfendon, F.
Walker, C. E.
Wilkins, P. E.
Woodley, L. A.
Watts, F.
Widdicks, F.
Wood, A. R.
Wood, R. J.
Watson, R. A.
Walter, F. G.
White, H. A.
Worthing, L. S.
Walker, T. C.
Whitbourn, E.
Williams, R.
Willis, H.
Wilson, K. J.
Winslow, H. S.
Wolveridge, J. F.
Woodward, F. D.
Wykes, E. A. I.
White, H. G.
Weaver, T. P.
Webb, A. H. W.
Woods, F. N. W.
Watkins, E. G.
Winterton, J. M.
Woolger, T. A.
West, F. J.
Williams, A. F. M.
Williams, H. T. M.
Worrall, G. H.
Warden, C. C.
Wallis, R.
Weldon, F.
Wade, A. G.
Weekes, R. E.
Weshott, W. E.
Wilson, W. H.
Willshire, J.
Wright, C. M.

Walker, W. J. T.
Wood, H.
Waters, B. L.
White, R. W.
Wilson, J. A. P.
Winterton, A. W.
Willerton, D.
Ward, C. L.
Wiggs, W.
Ward, H. B.
Wesson, A.
Wiffen, W. B.
Watson, N. T.
Williams, R. A.
Watson, G. R.
Wimpenny, H. V.
West, E. J.
Wilkins, J. C.
Wheeler, J. F.
Whelton, J. H.
Warren, J. E.
Weeks, P. M.
Wilkinson, E.
Wright, E.
Ward, W. J.
Winstanley, C. L.
West, A.
Wooderson, G. F.
Wood, H. S.
Woodward, J. A.
Williams, J. L.
Whittington, H. C.
Webb, C. A.
Weeks, F.
Walker, C. S.
Williamson, A. W.
Wolstencroft,E. A.
Webb, W. H.
Webber, E.
Watkinson, F. S.
Wallis, S.
Wood, R.
Woodgate, C. G.
Windrum, C. H.
Wren, F.
Watkins, E. F. H.
Woolrych, E. B.

Watts, C.
Webb, J. E.
Webster, A.
Wombell, J. H.
Walters, J. A.
Walmisley, R. B.
Wynne, J. A.
Willis, G. C.
Winkworth, O. S.
Wallis-Smith,
      W. H.
Warrilow, W. J.
Wilson, A.
Windett, C. E.
Woodcock, O. F.
Wareham, A. L.
Wright, A. E.
Walker, G.
Walton, W. C.
Waterworth, T. P.
Watts, F. W.
Weedon, G. H.
Wheatcroft, C. J.
Walsh, S. M. J.
Wade, R.
Wakeford, M. H.
Wareham, A. E.
Warr, W.
White, A. S.
Wilkinson,
      L. W. V.
Williams, W.
Wilson, J. B.
Woods, G.
Wright, W. S.
Wedd, H.
Wills, S. B.
Wakely, G. F.
Wearn, C. E.
West, A. F.
Wicks, B. F.
Webber, F. J.
Wallace, J. C.
Ward, E. H.
Williamson,
      G. H. J.
Watling, S. T.

Wharton, E. H.
Wigley, C. H.
Wright, P. D.
White, W.
White, A. J.
Wilcox, H.
Wintle, A. F.
Wraight, H. C.
Wakely, A. E.
Wraith, W. H.
Wilkes, A.
Wright, O. C.
Wheeler, E. C.
Wartnaby, W.
White, A.
White, H. T.
Williams, G. A.
Williams, N. H.
Wraight, O. S.
Warr, W. F.
Welch, W. J.
Wade, H. F.
Wallis, P. V. J.
White, J.
Walsh, R. W.
Warman, E. J.
Webster, H. S.
Webber, J.
Whitcombe, W. G.
Wire, B.
Wrigglesworth, A. H.
Wells, S. T.
Walker, J.
Wade, A. W.
Wade, A. H.
White, W. F.
Wilks, A. W.
Williams, P. H.
Wright, G. H.
Wadworth, F. T.
Waterlow, A. E.
Wright, W.
Ward, W.
Woodcock, J. H.
Wilson, H. L.
Wilson, A.

Watson, L. J.
Woodham, H. H.
Walker, N. P.
Whiting, H. C.
Wood, A. A.
Woodward, G.
Webbe, C.
Wilson, W. F.
Wilkin, E.
Williams, W. A.
Wainwright, W. E.
White, F. C.
Williams, F. N.
Worthington, H. T. B.
Walker, V. S.
Wyatt, F. S.
Webb, W.
Willoughby, A. J
Winter, W. D.
Wolfe, J. R.
Wolfe, A. B.
Woodham, A. P.
West, A. W.
Winch, F.
Woods, T. F. C.
Willis, G. A.
Whittingham, S. A.
Woodcock, H. G.
Williams, T. R.
Wills, B. J.
Whittingham, A. R.
Wilding, J. C.
Williams, W. F.
White, C. C.
Waldron, F. A.
Webb, A. W.
Wilson, C. R.
Williams, I. H.
Wesson, J. N.
Webb, H. N.
Weller, A. R.
Worland, H. J.
Warren, E. A.
Weir, A.

Willis, W. H.
Whitby, J.
Walker, R. B.
Walcott, L. H.
Whiffin, E.
Wilkie, W. R.
Ward, C. E.
White, C. L.
Watten, C. J.
Wallis, L. J. G.
Willson, H.
Windybank, L. A.
Woodroof, F. J.
Watts, T. E.
Woodward, W. T.
Warren, F. F.
Ware, R. W.
Winson, W.
Wickenden, S. W.
Williams, H. E.
Wise, U. A.
Wilding, A. C.
Welch, R. E.
Whiting, H. J.
Warn, H. D.
White, R. E.
Wills, J. L.
Wright, G. A.
Wootton, H. L. J.
Warren, F. C.
Wills, H. R.
Walton, N. H.
Williams, F. C.
Wallington, H. J.
Webb, P. A.
White, H. S. N.
Wells, F. A.
Wallace, A. F.
Wickham, A. W.
Wood, L. G. N.
Webb, W. H.
Wheeler, P. J.
Wood, W. H.
Wighton, W.
Wilcox, G. W.
Ward, H. E.
Watson, H. R.

Waglyn, O.
Wagland, E. G.
Wickham, T. H.
Webb, F. T.
West, C. E.
Wicks, A. E.
Wright, A. H.
Worsfold, S. G.
Warwick, D.
Windle, J. L.
Waghorn, S. H.
Woodman, W. A.
Wright, G. H.
Webbersley, S.
Westcombe, N. G.
Williams, J.
Waggett, J. G.
Williams, A. J.
Worthington, J. B
Wardale, J. S.
Ward, G. H.
Wright, W. D.
Wallace, R. C.
Whisk, J. S.
Williamson, J. B.
Wharton, E.
Woodfield, W. T.
Williams, W. J.
Wilson, H. J.
Wallis, J. C. T.
Watts, F. D.
Wells, F. S.
Woodley, C. E.
White, H. E.
Webb, L.
Warrington,
          R. C. O.
Wilcoxson, J. K.
Wilkins, H.
Williams, B. C.
Wills, R. T.
Whife, G. S. J.
Windybank, E.
White, B. E.
White, S. V.
Worn, W.
Waterton, D.

Wilkinson, A. E.
Wells, H. G.
Wallpole, S. W. P.
White, W.
White, F. T. G.
Wheeler, H. T.
Wilson, A. J.
Watson, V.
Williams, H. H.
Wood, C. A.
Webster, C. H.
Waterton, W. H.
Windibank, C. W.
Williams, J. J.
Williams, A.
Westwood, S. E.
Winn, J. N.
**Weatherstone,
          G. L.**
Whiteman, E. G.
Webber, H. J.
Weaver, T. F.
Wills, F. J.
Wright, H. J.
Wheatcroft, S.
Watson, W. D.
Worrall, S.
Westbrook, A. P.
Westaway, A. J.
Wright, N. F.
Whitehouse, G. A.
Watkinson, W. E.
Wilkinson, H. T.
Woolgrove, E.
Wall, F.
Woodgate, C.
Wise, R. T.
Whitney, A. J.
Wheeler, J. P.
Webb, T.
Wild, J. F.
Welham, W.
Ward, E.
Woolcock, R. J.
Woolfe, F. G.
Woodson, J. T.
Walker, H. A.

Wyler, J. M.
Wills, R. C.
Weedon, G. C.
White, E. A. O.
Wagstaff, W. M.
Welsford, W. J. N.
Weston, S. C.
Wilson, S. H.
Woodbery, H. G.
Wyatt, R. E. H.
Williams, W. H.
Ward, S.
Ward, G.
Williams, H.
Ward, C.
Worrell, G. F.
Wingfield, H. J.
Webb, J. S.
Whotton, W.
Watson, F.
Warnes, C. J.
Williams, C. J.
Webb, H. F.
Woods, A.
Watson, H.
West, G.
Wood, W. A.
Ward, F. A.
Wright, T. P.
Weare, W. A.
Watson, V. E.
Withers, W. G.
Walters, W. F.
White, H. E.
Warsaw, D.
Warsaw, E.
White, G. P.
Weadon, R. C.
Williams, W. J.
Westley, C. E.
Welch, C. L.
**Wakefield,
          W. J. A. S.**
Wright, S. A.
Waldron, S. C. R.
Ward. H. E.
Woodford, P.

Wade, B.
Woods, W. E.
Warwick, E.
Winder, A. S.
Wilson, H. C.
Wall, J. J. G.
White, T. H.
Williams, C. J.
Watson, J. W.
Waters, W. A.
Watts, C. P.
Wesson, E. H.
Wilkinson, A. W.
Walton, W. L.
Whittle, R. A.
Winchester, C. C.
Wallace, W. C.
Wright, W. S.
Westly, W. C.
Wood, J. G.
Whittaker, A. J.
Westlake, H. J.
Willcocks, P. S.
Watling, B. L.
Whitlock, S.
Whippie, W. E.
Wapshott, F. E.
Webster, W. R.
Wilson, J. G.
Williams, S.
Walker, C. A.
Wiggell, W. F.
Watson, E. A.
Westlake, T. C.
Williams, N. W.
Wareham, F. R.
Wilshere, E. E.
Whitney, W. G.
Ware, F. E.
Witty, H.
Wiggins, H. S.
Withers, I. C.
Walker, F. G. H.
Whichelow, T. L.
Whittingham,
B. V.
Whitaker, C. A.

Williams, G. W.
Webber, F.
Walton, G. S.
Wilkie, R. J.
Wilbraham, B.
Woodward, H.
Walker, W. H.
Woodroffe, F. A.
Wright, A. E.
Ward, C. H.
Williams, H. C.
Walden, S.
Watts, H. W.
Williams, W. P.
Williamson, W.
Wilson, C.
Wigginton, J. P.
Western, G. C.
Ware, T. H. H.
Wingfield,
A. W. G.
White, F. H.
Wingrave, C. G.
White, P. D.
Watkins, G. F.
Watt, W. G. F.
Walden, W. C.
Warwick, J.
Ward, L. W. C.
Wright, A. E.
Walsh, O. H.
Washer, G. H.
Wagg, G. A.
Wheeler, R.
White, F. C.
Williams, J.
Wilson, C. J.
Wilkinson, R.
Walker, T. R.
Watts, A. J.
West, G. W. A.
Wray, C. F.
Wallace, G.
Williamson, G.
Wheeler, C. N.
Williams, H.
Walker, L. W.

Webber, O. G. H.
Wright, C.
Williamson, A. O.
Williams, E. J.
Willmin, B. A.
Waghorne, H.
Wright, G. E.
Willis, S.
Withers, W. G.
West, F. J.
Wright, A. E.
Wilkins, W.
Wardle, A. R.
Wootton, S.
Walton, R. I.
Wells, H.
Webber, A. H. B.
Woodhouse,
H. A. P.
Woodward, A.
Whiddett, A.
Walesby, L. G.
Wigley, W. H.
Williams, W. W.
Whisk, C. K.
Willis, H. R.
Wraight, W. E.
Wells, J. D.
Ware, W. J.
Wills, H. J. S.
Waithman, W. E.
Wollman, M.
Westcott, H.
Webber, G. W.
Wells, S.
Will, A.
Wrigglesworth,
A. H.
Weighill, F.
Wooster, S. J.
Ward, R. B.
Waskett, F. J.
Ward, J. W.
Wootton, W. A.
Wootton, T. W.
Watts, A. J.
Watson, H.

Westhorp, J. W.
White, H. C.
Wakeford, A. C.
White, C. J. R.
Wheeler, F. H.
Webster, L. H.
Wade, J. S.
Wallis, H. V. G.
Welch, A. C.
Woodcock, A. L.
Wills, B.
Woodley, A. F.
Winters, H. W.
Wilson, S. J.
White, R. G.
Williams, G. F.
Wayman, B. J. R.
Whitehouse, J. N.
Whitfield, L.
Walker, G.
Wharton, R. G.
Williamson, C.
Wilkins, H. A.
Wates, S. W.
Wills, S. B.
Wyld, A. N.
Worth, S. J.
Worthington, J.
Williamson, B.
Williams, T.
Waller, F. H.
Woodland, C. G.
Wodehouse, A. E.
Wayland, C. F.
Williams, R. A. V.
Wyatt, J. S.
Walker, G. P.
White, G. B.
Whall, S. E.
Wheeler, J.
Webb, B.
Williams, G. F.
Wagner, L. R.
Waring, J. D.
Wilson, A. A.
Wheeler, W. J.
Woodgate, G. W.

Whitten, A. T.
Williams, B. L.
Webster, J. L.
White, W. J.
West, H. B.
White, A. J.
Walker, F. J.
Walters, C. A.
Westall, E. A.
White, E. H.
Wimbury, E. B.
Wallace, M.
Wood, J. F.
Wall, E. G.
Wallis, W. C.
Walker, V. E.
Woodland, E. D.
Wallin, A.
Wood, W. J.
Woods, S. G.
Wootton, C.
Warner, C. J.
Weller, W.
Ware, H.
Williams, W. V.
Watsham, E. F.
Wilkes, W. J.
Wood, W.
Williams, E.
Webb, O. J.
Waller, V. W. H.
Waymark, B. P.
Watson, H. W.
Webster, J.
Wright, H.
Willcocks, W. R.
Whitehead, C.
Wilson, R. W.
Whitaker, J.
Williamson, E. W.
Watts, H.
Willis, H. J. W.
Wainwright, H. R.
Woolger, R. G. W.
Welfare, E. H.
Watson, D.
Watkins, C. H.

Wilkinson, A. R.
Watson, D.
Wilson, J. H.
Warren, S. V.
Wells, E. A.
Walker, R. A.
Warwick, H. F. G.
Webster,
    F. W. K. G.
Wright, R. W.
Wood, H. A.
Welch, H.
Williams, J. G.
Ward, J. W.
Wilkinson, H. F.
Watkins, C. H.
Wellington, W.
Wright, F.
White, G. R.
Williams, J. T.
Woods, W.
Worley, E. F.
Wright, A.
Wood, F. J.
Webb, C. H.
Winwright, G. F.
Wood, F. S.
Wright, T.
Walton, F. B.
Watson, H.
Woollard, N. H.
Williams, A. J.
Witts, H. Y.
Watson, F.
Woods, W. G.
Wasp, J.
Wheeler, E. B.
Williams, J. R.
Wright, A.
White, W. E.
Wormald, R. G.
Wallis, H. H.
Wentworth, H. A.
Woodfield, F. E.
Wilson, H. M.
Welsford, E. G.
Williams, H. J.

Wilson, L. C.
Wells, R. A. C.
West, S. C.
Wynne, J. D.
Watson, W. N.
Whippy, S.
Wilson, L. G.
Wood, S. A.
Weedon, C. A.
Wagstaff, P. E.
Whitley, A.
Webb, W. R.
Weeden, G. H.
Warren, W. J.
Y
Young, K.
Yeo, E. L.

Yardley, L. A.
Young, F. C.
Young, C.
Young, A. F.
Yates, O. W. P.
Yuille, D. McG.
Young, C. J.
Young, C. W. C.
Young, F. J.
Yates, F. G.
Young, D.
Young, L.
Yates, C. F. D.
Young, K. H.
Young, S. K.
Young, E. W.
Yale, F. H.

Yeo, G.
Young, F. A.
Yeomans, L. A.
Youl, H. J.
Yates, W. J.
Yeo, A. O. S.
Yates, A. E.
Young, J. E.
Yeats, P. H.
York, T. H.
Young, W. J.
Young, J. L.
Yalsley, J.
Young, E. W. B.
Z
Zobel, W. E.
Zeidler, L. A.